Contemporary Missiology

Contemporary Missiology
AN INTRODUCTION

BY J. VERKUYL
translated and edited by Dale Cooper

WILLIAM B. EERDMANS PUBLISHING COMPANY
GRAND RAPIDS, MICHIGAN

Library of Congress Cataloging in Publication Data

Verkuyl, Johannes.
  Contemporary missiology.

  Translation of Inleiding in de nieuwere Zendingswetenschap.
  Includes bibliographies and index.
  1. Missions—Theory. I. Title.
BV2063.V42313 266'.001 78-17585

ISBN 0-8028-0363-6

Translated from the Dutch edition,
Inleiding in de nieuwere Zendingswetenschap,
© Uitgeversmaatschappij J. H. Kok, Kampen, 1975.

Contents

Preface

In 1954 Dr. J. H. Bavinck's monumental book *Introduction to the Science of Missions (Inleiding in de Zendingswetenschap)* was published. I still consider Bavinck and Dr. Hendrik Kraemer as my "gurus." In 1965 after a lengthy term of service in Asia I was given the honor of taking over one of Bavinck's many duties: I became associate professor and later full professor at the Free Reformed University of Amsterdam (in addition to serving as General Secretary of the Netherlands Council of Missions).

The time has come for a new introduction to the science of missions, for gigantic changes have happened since 1954. My predecessor's book reflects the age when missions were still seen as going in one direction only — from the West to the other continents. That time is past; the traffic now proceeds in many directions. We now live in an age of growing mutual assistance as together we fulfill our worldwide task.

Bavinck's book reflects that time when colonialism was coming to an end. Today we live in a world where Asia, Africa, and Latin America have a growing influence in world affairs, and Christians from those continents occupy a very decisive position in ecumenical affairs. It goes without saying that missiology ought to reckon with these changes.

We often hear that theology, properly performed, is a *theologia viatorum*; that is, it serves as fare for pilgrims who are enroute. This is especially true for missiology. Often the comment is made that missiology should prepare for her own funeral. According to many, the aforementioned changes have emptied missiology of any significance. This, however, is completely untrue. Since the "homefront" and base for gospel communication are now *everywhere*, missiologists working closely with the churches must carry on their labor in all six continents with *ecumenical* vision.

In the New Testament, theology arose as missiology, that is, as reflection on the missionary activity in the apostolic era. Witness, for example, the letters of Paul. Today, too, the study of mission must accompany missionary practice in all six continents.

In this book we shall concentrate on Asia, Africa, Latin America, and the Caribbean and Pacific areas. By doing so I do not intend to deny that Europe is an area fit for missionary activity. Indeed it is. In fact, part of my teaching assignment at the university involves the study of gospel communication in Western society, and I hope someday to devote a book to this subject. But this book is concerned especially with the aforementioned parts of the world, which embrace more than two-thirds of the world's population and are ripe for mission.

This book is designed only as an introduction. It goes without saying that there is need for locally written monographs about churches and societies. For this reason I make frequent reference to literature for further study and orientation.

Sections of several chapters from this introductory book have appeared previously in specific periodicals. These publications are noted in the pertinent chapters.

I wish to take this opportunity to thank publicly my friend, Rev. Dale Cooper, whom I learned to know during the period in which he studied missiology in Amsterdam. He translated the Dutch original of this work with great care and precision and also made the revisions necessary for making this handbook suitable for an English-reading public.

I dedicate this book to my wife. Her dedicated and sincere care both for me and for our children made a home which at the same time could also serve as a base of operations for work in those churches and societies in which we were privileged to live and work.

J. VERKUYL

CHAPTER I
Prolegomena

THE TERM "MISSIOLOGY"

The selection of a name for a discipline is not unimportant. It would be wrong to overestimate its importance, but the choice of a name does stand in close connection to what one sees as the most distinctive feature of his field of study.

Through the years a great variety of names for the science of missions has been proposed, and many of these names are in actual use. Gustav Warneck, a pioneer in the science of missions, suggested the term *Missionslehre*, theory of missions, which is still used to describe the course of missiological study at the Free University. Warneck also entitled his three-part book *Missionslehre.*

In his book *The Encyclopedia of Sacred Theology* Abraham Kuyper suggested several names which never caught on. In part 3 of his book, Kuyper proposed the term *prosthetics*, which is borrowed from Acts 2:41, 5:14, and 11:24 and is derived from the Greek verb *prostithestai*, "to add to the community." Kuyper had other terms: *auxanics*, "to multiply and spread out," and *halieutics*, "to fish for men." This last term had already been suggested by J. I. Doedes in his *Encyclopedia of Christian Theology* in 1876. Doedes himself preferred the term *prosthetics* and described missiology as the search for the most productive methods by which to Christianize those areas still unchristian.

This term puts undue limits on our field of study. A discussion of methods is an important part of missiology, but missiology does not end here. Kuyper's term was never used, although it is true that Donald McGavran, one of the most widely known contemporary American missiologists, calls his school the Church Growth School. In fact he limits missiology to researching the growth of churches — *auxanics*, one might say.

At the beginning of the twentieth century the name coined by Robert Speer was used: "missionary principles and practice."

In the Netherlands the phrase most often used is "theology of the apostolate." A. A. van Ruler, J. C. Hoekendijk, E. Jansen Schoonhoven, and J. M. van der Linde use it. Although Hoekendijk's famous dissertation, *Kerk en Volk in de Duitse Zendingswetenschap*, still employs the phrase "science of missions," his later publications also use the phrase "theology of the apostolate." Both H. N. Ridderbos and G. Brillenburg Wurth in the book *De Apostolische Kerk* and H. Bergema in his inaugural address made several objections to the use of this phrase. Their chief objection is that when one uses such terms as "apostolic" and

1

"apostolate," he is emphasizing the content of the apostolic *martyria*, *didachē*, *kerygma* and the authentic authority but not the specific activity of *apostellein*. To a degree I share their objections. In addition, when one employs this term, he completely erases the differences which exist between the disciplines of missiology and evangelism. To be sure, these disciplines impinge upon each other and in the future must increasingly "cross-fertilize" each other; they are not, however, identical. J. Dürr offers similar objections to this term in his article "Kirche, Mission, und Reich Gottes."[1]

In his book *Hope in Action* H. J. Margull opts for the phrase "theology of evangelism." In England the phrase "theology of mission" (or "missions") is being used increasingly. The French speak of *science missionaire* ("missionary science").

Personally, I prefer the internationally accepted term "missiology," which, though it does not differ essentially in meaning from the phrase "theology of the apostolate," does nevertheless make clear to everyone that the focus of interest is not primarily the content of the message but rather is the missionary action of God and the men and women he mandates. Furthermore, I prefer this term because I believe that wherever possible we ought to encourage uniformity in the use of language and terminology. In his handbook on missiology, the Roman Catholic missiologist Ohm quotes one of his colleagues: "Eine einheitliche Terminologie liegt im wohlverstandenen Interesse aller Konfessionen."[2]

Once in a while philological objections are made against the term "missiology." Raoul Allier comments in his article "Missions and the Soul of a People" that by joining two words, one of them from Greek and the other from Latin, one ends up with a linguistic monstrosity.[3] It is comforting, however, to note that such "monsters" occur rather frequently. Think, for example, of the term "sociology" and all the other "-ologies."

The term "missiology" is of rather old vintage. Quite naturally, since the beginning of church history many derivations appeared from the Latin translation of the Greek verb *apostellein: mittere, missio, missiones,* etc. The derivation *missio* only surfaces in the sixteenth century when both the Jesuit and Carmelite orders of monks sent out hundreds of missionaries. The publications of the *Sacra Congregatio de Propaganda Fide* dating from this century also use this term. Ignatius of Loyola and Jacob Loynez consistently employ the term *missio*.

For the sake of clarity and to broaden the uniform use of language, I opt for the term "missiology."

MEANING OF THE TERM

Having chosen this term, I now wish to make a few comments about its content, breadth, and depth. It is not sufficient simply to use words like *missio,* "mis-

---

1. Johannes Dürr, "Kirche, Mission und Reich Gottes," *Evangelische Missions Magazin* 97 (September, 1953): 133–145.
2. T. Ohm, *Machet zu Jüngern alle Völker: Theorie der Mission* (Freiburg im Breisgau: Wewel, 1962), p. 37.
3. Raoul Allier, "Missions and the Soul of a People," *The International Review of Missions* 18 (1929): 282–284.

sions," and "theory of missions." We must develop the theological content of these terms so that we begin to use them with an awareness of their meaning and scope. Of course, my comments are only provisional at this point. A fuller description can come only after I have developed the biblical foundation within systematic missiology.

The world missionary conference held in Willingen, West Germany in 1952 revived a very ancient term which stemmed from the time of the Trinitarian discussions: *missio Dei*. When we look back upon the history and the theology of missions, there is no denying that a great deal of anthropocentric and ecclesiocentric language was used. There was talk about *our* mission, *our* missionary area, *the* missionary center, *the* missionary operation, etc. At Willingen a Copernican revolution happened, at least as regards terminology. In the stage of preparatory reports there was already talk of "God's mission, not ours." One of the core sentences taken from the final report of the 1952 Willingen conference is: "The missionary movement of which we are a part has its source in *the triune God Himself.*" Karl Hartenstein went even further in his report *Mission zwischen Gestern und Morgen* ("Missions between Yesterday and Tomorrow"),[4] and George Vicedom wrote his famous book *Missio Dei* ("The Mission of God") after the Willingen conference.[5] Vicedom's theme is: "He, God, is the acting Subject in mission." God the Father sent the Son, and the Son is both the Sent One and the Sender. Together with the Father the Son sends the Holy Spirit, who in turn sends the church, congregations, apostles, and servants, laying them under obligation in discharging his work. Another emphasis of the Willingen conference and the later Mexico City conference was the relationship between the *missio Dei* and the *missio ecclesiae*. "There is no participation in Christ without participation in his mission."

Men like John Taylor and Johannes Aagaard point out that to be faithful to the Bible one should not refer to the *missio Dei* but to *missiones Dei*. The one mission of the triune God takes shape in the innumerable particular *missiones*: missions to villages and cities, to seafarers and city dwellers, to students and farmers, etc. In addition, the word *missiones* underscores that God involves not only special groups and individuals in his tasks, but that the *missio Dei* also leads to *diakonia*, that is, to participation in development, to sharing in the whole plurality of services which we are called to perform in his name as we carry out the *missio Dei*.

The renowned periodical of the World Council of Churches and its Commission on World Mission and Evangelism was earlier entitled *International Review of Missions*. Its present title is *International Review of Mission*. The change in title resulted from the influence of the phrase *missio Dei*. But the term *missiones* quite properly calls attention to the relationship between *missio* and *missiones*, to the one *missio Dei* and the plurality of *missiones* connected to it.

Later still, the concept *missio hominum* surfaced, which emphasizes that in addition to viewing the strictly ecclesiastical tasks and work in the light of

4. Karl Hartenstein, et al., *Mission zwischen Gestern und Morgen: Vom Gestaltwandel der Weltmission der Christenheit im Licht der Konferenz des Internationalen Missionsrats in Willingen* (Stuttgart: Evangelischer Missionsverlag, 1952).
5. George F. Vicedom, *The Mission of God: An Introduction to the Science of Mission* (St. Louis: Concordia Publishing House, 1965).

Jesus, the Pioneer and Perfecter of the *missio Dei* (cf. Heb. 12:2), we ought to see *all* work done in service to society as inspired, led, and directed by him. Presently missiologists are engaged in a heated discussion of the statement: "God acts in history." How are the events within salvation history and world history related? Obviously they do not coincide precisely. Sins, demons, and the demonic powers are also active in history. History is not merely a record of the unhindered progress of salvation history; there is also the element of the unholy and wicked, against which God acts as both Judge and Liberator. Though this is not yet the place to discuss this issue more deeply, I do wish to indicate at this early point that the discussion about *missio Dei* has focused too little on the question of how God's acts in history can be discerned and how the *missio ecclesiarum* is related to this process of discerning his acts.

Are the "signs of the times" which stand so central in the present discussion nothing more than a pious or sanctimonious explanation of the facts of history? How can we avoid a form of ideologizing the facts, as so often results from such interpretations of contemporary history?

What are the criteria for analyzing and judging the historical processes? Is the primary concern an interpretation of history, or must we give our attention to history because it is the place where we, with our eyes on the Messiah and his kingdom, must discharge our missionary mandate? Jesus Christ is the criterion for God's saving deeds in history. He is the true vine planted in history. In him we see God's intentions for human life in this world. In and through him we come to see what kind of fruits God is concerned with from the harvest field of history.

"God acts in history." Of course, but where? Allow me to make only this preliminary comment: wherever love for God and one's neighbor is blooming, there God is engaged, and the signs of the messianic kingdom become visible. Thus the *missiones ecclesiarum* are connected with the *missio Dei* only when, in union with Christ the true vine and under the guidance of the Holy Spirit, they display the fruits of love for God and neighbor in countless ways.

The phrase *missio hominum* ("missions by men") coined by Gensichen is of course open to misunderstanding. Putting the expressions *missio ecclesiarum* and *missio hominum* next to each other could suggest that the missions of the churches are not human missions and that "church work" is something completely set off from the work of men and women in society. But the intent of the expression is clear. Its purpose is to show that even the nonecclesiastical activity of people in society, as long as it counters any type of evil and is purposefully performed in ways that help and heal, is connected either knowingly or unknowingly with the *missio Dei* in the world.

Kosuke Koyama depicts the distresses in a rural area of one part of Asia. His book, *Waterbuffalo Theology,* describes the evils of leprosy, malaria, ignorance, powerlessness, poverty, etc.[6] He goes on to tell how a variety of organizations are combating these evils. Then he asks, "Who sent those men and women?" The answer follows: "They too are capable of serving the *missio Dei.* God has sent them. In a certain respect they too are 'God's missionaries'."

Such is the meaning of the disputed phrase *missio hominum.* Everything directed toward welfare, liberation, and the unshackling of the fetters of injustice

6. Kosuke Koyama, *Waterbuffalo Theology* (London: SCM Press, 1974).

— in short, everything "salvation-oriented" — has to do with the *missio Dei* and is within the perspective of the messianic kingdom.

Definition of Missiology

Missiology is the study of the salvation activities of the Father, Son, and Holy Spirit throughout the world geared toward bringing the kingdom of God into existence.

Seen in this perspective missiology is the study of the worldwide church's divine mandate to be ready to serve this God who is aiming his saving acts toward this world. In dependence on the Holy Spirit and by word and deed the church is to communicate the total gospel and the total divine law to all mankind.

Missiology's task in every age is to investigate scientifically and critically the presuppositions, motives, structures, methods, patterns of cooperation, and leadership which the churches bring to their mandate. In addition missiology must examine every other type of human activity which combats the various evils to see if it fits the criteria and goals of God's kingdom which has both already come and is yet coming.

Some Clarifying Notes on This Definition

Presently there is a lot of talk about science functioning as a critic of society. This is proper and applies to missiology too. In a "time of testing" like the present, missiology ought to test the practice of world mission, world service, and development projects and programs against the standards of the Bible; she ought to inspect thoroughly those who administrate such programs and to serve them with advice.

Ecclesia reformata semper reformanda ("a Reformed church is continually reforming"); this also holds true for the *missiones ecclesiarum*. The same principle applies to society: *societas semper reformanda*. In his essay "Bringing Our Missionary Methods Under the Word of God," Lesslie Newbigin writes: "The Church must in every generation be ready to bring its tradition afresh under the light of the Word of God."[7] But not only must we examine our methods. The structures of the congregations; the relations between Western churches and those in Asia, Africa, and Latin America; the nature of the *missiones ecclesiae* today; and the plans for future projects must also be put under the examining light of God's Word.

In this definition I have tried to underscore that missiology is a thoroughly theological discipline. The Middle Ages said a discipline qualified as theological when it *Deum docet* ("teaches God"), *a Deo docetur* ("is taught by God"), and *ad Deum ducet* ("will lead one to God"). This definition, which places the concept of *missio Dei* so centrally and grows out of the trinitarian teaching, directs our attention to the God who, in Hoekendijk's words, begins, governs, protects, and completes his mission while enroute to the final revelation of his kingdom.

Today students of this discipline are increasingly being referred to as *missiologists*. Usually these people have logged some time in the area of practical

7. Lesslie Newbigin, "Bringing Our Missionary Methods Under the Word of God," *Occasional Bulletin* 13 (November, 1962): 1–9.

experience and thus can prevent their scholarly work from turning into arid theorizing. A majority of missiologists concurrently serve as advisors to missionary, service, and developmental agencies. We missiologists are called to do our work on the threshold of the third millennium after Christ's birth, amid the giant changes and shifts in the world situation.

I make one final point: missiology may never become a substitute for action and participation. God calls for participants and volunteers in his mission. In part, missiology's goal is to become a "service station" along the way. If study does not lead to participation, whether at home or abroad, missiology has lost her humble calling.

THE PLACE OF MISSIOLOGY IN THE ENCYCLOPEDIA OF THEOLOGY

There was a day when missiology was accorded no place in the encyclopedia of theology. She was not even given standing room. All this happened when theology was done in ecclesiocentric or ethnocentric fashion; rather than the kingdom being in the spotlight, the individual, the nation, or the church received all the attention. By the nineteenth century, however—in K. S. Latourette's words, "The Great Century"—missions had expanded so broadly that the need for the theological study of mission became apparent, and a spot had to be cleared for missiology in the theological encyclopedia. Of course, one must not exaggerate the difficulty missiology had in getting that spot. Father André Seumois allots 500 pages in his *Introduction à la Missiologie* to this issue, and it is hard to escape the feeling that the importance of this matter is slightly overdrawn.[8]

We shall now review suggestions and statements made by various authors on the role of missiology in order to better formulate our own position on this issue.

Schleiermacher on the Place of Missiology

Friedrich Daniel Schleiermacher was the first theologian in the great century of missions who thought about the position of the science of missions within the wider discipline of theology. During his youth he had met the Herrnhutters, and this meeting had left a permanent impression on him.

In the second edition of his *Kürze Darstellung des theologischen Studiums*, Schleiermacher makes room for a couple of sentences on what he calls the "Theorie des Missionswesens."[9] These are included in the section on "Praktische Theologie." Treating the issue of catechesis, Schleiermacher adds that when it is done among the "religious strangers who live in the vicinity or region of a church," a theory about "how to deal with the converts" becomes necessary. In

8. André Seumois, *Introduction à la Missiologie* (Schoneck and Beckenried, Switzerland: Administration de la Nouvelle Revue de Science Missionaire, 1952).

9. Friedrich Schleiermacher, *Kürze Darstellung des theologischen Studiums zum Behuf einleitender Vorlesungen* (Hildesheim: Olms, 1850).

paragraph 298 Schleiermacher comments: "Possibly a theory of missions which for all intents and purposes still does not exist could be added at this point."

Schleiermacher makes a distinction between "continuous missions" (in regions where colonial or geographic relationships exist) and "sporadic missions" (like those of the Moravian Brothers, for example). Yet Schleiermacher did not actually perceive a separate category for missions. His missionary thinking is thoroughly limited by both culture and history.

Schleiermacher's theological weakness is mirrored in his missiology. By identifying truth with man's religious consciousness, by reducing the gospel to contemporary thought forms, and by failing to appreciate the theological categories which cannot be so reduced, Schleiermacher ended up with a contorted view of missions.

Strikingly, yet typically, Schleiermacher treats the subject of missions more broadly in his section on ethics than in his section on practical theology. Writing from the perspective of ethics, he views missions as a cultural responsibility in specific situations where Western culture penetrates non-Western cultural areas. The call to mission, however, is not universal. On page 190 of his *Reden über die Religion* he makes the surprising claim that missions are not to be seen as the call to proclaim and to show salvation to all mankind, but rather the missionary "must always carry his fatherland with its laws and customs along with him and look upon the higher and better things of life wherever he goes."

In Schleiermacher we meet head-on one of the prominent representatives of a romantic cultural-Protestant notion of missions. This is more fully explained in Otto Kübler's book *Mission und Theologie: Eine Untersuchung über den Missionsgedanken in der systematischen Theologie seit Schleiermacher.*[10]

This is not the place to go more deeply into this issue, for our immediate concern is the issue of the place of missiology in the encyclopedia of theology.

Missiology in the Thought of Abraham Kuyper and J. H. Bavinck

Walking in the footprints of Schleiermacher, Abraham Kuyper puts missiology among the practical disciplines or, as he calls them, the diaconological group. Kuyper divides the group into the didactic, presbyterial, diaconal, and laic disciplines. Calling it "prosthetics," Kuyper includes missiology among the didactic disciplines. Kuyper describes the goal of prosthetics as "The study of divinely-ordained and most useful methods of Christianizing those areas and people who are outside of Christ."[11]

J. H. Bavinck also puts missiology among the practical disciplines. In his book *An Introduction to the Science of Missions,* Bavinck argues for missiology to be treated and viewed as independent, though not isolated, from other theological disciplines. This independent entity Bavinck wants to put in the diaconological

10. Otto Kübler, *Mission und Theologie: Eine Untersuchung über den Missionsgedanken in der systematischen Theologie seit Schleiermacher* (Leipzig: T. C. Hinrichs'sche Buchhandlung, 1929).

11. Abraham Kuyper, *Encyclopaedie der heilige Godgeleerdheid,* 3 vols. (Amsterdam: J. A. Wormser, 1894), p. 520.

group. In so doing he makes objection to Kuyper, who put it in the didactic group. He correctly notes that missions involves not only teaching, but also service. (He could have also added the dimension of fellowship.)

Missiology as Part of Church History

In his 1887 discourse *Das Studium der Mission auf der Universität,* Gustav Warneck, author of the first "Missionslehre" in Europe, stated his view of the place of missiology. He argued for incorporating the history of missions within the wider study of church history, the biblical foundation for missions within the biblical disciplines, and the study of missions proper within the framework of practical theology. He thus divided missiology into three separate studies and insisted that church history be one of the three. John Foster of England, C. Mirbt of Germany and K. S. Latourette of the United States argued for including all of missiology within church history. In Sweden this is also the usual practice. In the Netherlands, too, some theological schools incorporate missiology within church history and even set it within the study of twentieth-century church history.

Missiology as Part of Dogmatics

H. Diem argues for putting missiology within the study of systematic theology, or more specifically, in the study of the doctrines of the Trinity and eschatology.[12] The *missio Dei* described in Matthew 28 points toward an eschatological event which happens not outside of history but within the history of missions and drives history on toward its goal and conclusion. Missiology's task is to render an account of the proclamation events which go forward to the end. The message of the triune God, first described and explained in a Greek-Roman atmosphere of religious polytheism and metaphysical monotheism, must now be unfolded by young churches in their own unique theologies against the backdrop of the religious ideas current in their world.

To my knowledge this plea for inserting missiology into systematic theology never received support. In fact, as is obvious from the above, it is difficult to put missiology exclusively into *any* of the general categories. Missiology is involved with all the theological disciplines.

For this reason, more earnest and frequent appeal is recently being heard for making the missionary sciences a separate group complementary to the other disciplines. In a commemorative book honoring Walter Freytag entitled *Basileia,* the Norwegian missiologist O. G. Myklebust wrote the essay "Integration or Independence."[13] He expressly called for independence because whenever missiology is integrated into one or more of the other disciplines, it does not receive its due.

Manfred Linz calls missiology a "complementary science" *(komplementar-Wissenschaft).* He develops this idea more extensively in an

---

12. H. Diem, "Der Ort der Mission in der systematischen Theologie," *Evangelische Missions Magazin* 111 (1967): 29–42.

13. Olav G. Myklebust, "Integration or Independence," in *Basileia: Walter Freytag zum 60. Geburtstag,* ed. J. Hermelink and H. J. Margull (Stuttgart: Evangelische Missionsverlag, 1959).

essay in *Einführung in das Studium der Evangelischen Theologie.*[14]

> The science of mission shall have to become concrete when cultural and geographic boundaries are crossed. For theology, theologians, and the church she points out the distant stranger living among our neighbors and the neighbor living among distant strangers. She takes careful note that salvation [*heil*] is designed for all human beings and that the service of reconciliation may not be restricted to the familiar horizon of our own land and environs. Mission is indivisible and the world is indivisible.

To this truth missiology must forever be pointing; in so doing she plays a crucial, complementary role. The burden of missiology is to answer the question facing the church: does her life conform to her calling to be the "salt of the earth" and "the light of the world?"

Without hesitation I join the ranks of those who describe missiology as a complementary science.

As for the study of evangelism, I believe it clearly and exclusively belongs to the practical disciplines. Disciplines related to evangelism — that is, the other practical studies, exegesis, hermeneutics, church history, apologetics, and systematic theology — are so taught as to take into account only the issues facing Western society. No account is taken of the issues people face in the developing countries. Therefore by holding forth the missionary dimension missiology must round out the other branches of theology and thus render real service in communicating God's law and gospel throughout the world.

THE RELATIONSHIP BETWEEN MISSIOLOGY AND OTHER DISCIPLINES

Theological Disciplines

No extensive explanation is necessary; the relationship is quite obvious. I shall limit myself to a few comments. The relationship between missiology and evangelism is so direct that in some universities one professor teaches both and combines them under the title "Theology of the Apostolate." Evangelism (*evangelistiek*) has to do with the scientific study of communicating Christian faith in Western society, while missiology centers on communicating it in the regions of Asia, Africa, Latin America, and the Caribbean. But these disciplines frequently "cross-fertilize," especially during treatment of topics as urbanization, industrialization, secularization, and methods of gospel communication. It goes without saying that there is also a connection between missiology and the other branches of practical theology.

Biblical studies, especially exegesis and hermeneutics, are crucial not only to a good understanding of the *missio ecclesiae* but also to a correct view of methods of communication. It is important to note that the majority of exegetical studies on the foundation of missions have been written by missiologists themselves. At this point missiology is acting as a complement to the existing disciplines of Old and New Testament exegesis.

14. Manfred Linz, "Missionswissenschaft und Oekumenik," in *Einführung in das Studium der Evangelischen Theologie,* ed. R. Bohren (Munich: Kaiser Verlag, 1964).

Hermeneutics, too, is very important for missiology. The Gospels are in fact life-size photos of how the gospel was presented in a variety of milieus. The New Testament book of Acts presents many models of gospel communication among groups of people such as Jews, sophisticated heathen, devotees of archaic religions, etc. The importance of these hermeneutical models for missiology cannot be easily overestimated.

The branches of *systematic theology,* that is, dogmatics, history of dogma, and apologetics, are valuable for missiology, even as missiology can complement systematic theology. For example, in teaching the history of dogma the controversy with Islam often goes largely unnoticed. Or again, Western apologetics pays almost no attention to developing an apology for the world of Asia and Africa, etc.

Ethics as studied in the West is now dealing with issues from which developing countries can learn and which they can profitably use in the very near future in their own situations. And from her side missiology begs for help from ethics in the ethical issues facing the young churches. At their very core all the issues facing the developing nations are ethical issues.

In the area of *church history,* missiology has much to learn from the history of Western missions. Likewise, there are a variety of reasons why it is preferable to treat the history and historiography of the young churches within the framework of missiology.

Missiology of course stands in close connection to *ecumenics.* Both set their sights on the whole church and the relationship between churches as well as on the whole world to whom the gospel is proclaimed. Practical reasons obviously require that Western ecumenical relationships be studied within the framework of recent Western church history and that growth of Asian, African, and Latin American ecumenical ties be treated by the missiology department. In this manner each department can round out the other.

Finally, missiology and the *science of religion* are so closely connected that one hardly needs to defend keeping them together. Without a phenomenology of and history of the current religions, proper dialogue with and missionary approach to these religions are impossible. But missiology must study not only the encounter with other faiths, but also the encounter with the ideologies. This is a special way in which it can complement other branches of theology. Regrettably, theological faculties usually devote scant attention to the ideologies.

Nontheological Disciplines

There is no sense in parading all the nontheological disciplines before us to view the connection of each one with missiology. I shall indicate only those which have a practical as well as a theoretical tangent to missiology.

The findings of *cultural anthropology* are crucially important for understanding the context of the young churches. The methods and results of *non-Western sociology* are highly important for missiology. Therefore, every doctoral student in missiology is strongly advised to minor in cultural anthropology or non-Western sociology. Sociology of religion and ecclesiastical sociology are likewise of crucial value.

In the realm of economics, missiology takes great interest in the *economics of developing nations*. Doctoral students in missiology frequently minor in this area, too. Since the young churches are going through a phase of developing their political and social awareness, the two disciplines *political science* and *polemology* are also very important. Missiologists and students of the history of the developing nations have a complementary role to play in these areas as well. More and more we are coming to see the close connection between world mission, world service, cooperative ventures in national development, and efforts for justice. By focusing on this connection still another rather neglected truth comes into view: political scientists and polemologists must learn to look beyond the Bosporos and Dardanelles.

So much for our comments. Writings in the field of missiology clearly show that its relationship to other disciplines is not merely theoretical but living and vital.

THE POSITION OF MISSIOLOGY WITHIN THEOLOGICAL EDUCATION

A place in the theological encyclopedia does not necessarily mean that a specific discipline thereby automatically has a spot reserved for it within the theological curricula of faculties, theological colleges, and seminaries. In this section we shall inquire how and where missiology actually achieved its place in the theological curriculum. Not that our present concern is not to delve into the history and content of missiology. A later chapter will provide such a *tour d'horizon*. For the present we aim only to discuss as briefly as possible the role of missiology within theological education. For more information on this topic one can consult the very comprehensive study done by the Norwegian scholar, O. G. Myklebust, *The Study of Missions in Theological Education*.[15]

Early Studies of Missiology

During the latter part of the thirteenth and early part of the fourteenth centuries, Raimon Lull continually urged the Roman Catholic church to establish schools for studying those languages spoken by the peoples to whom the gospel had yet to be proclaimed. His chief interest was Arabic, and in 1276 he personally founded a seminary on Majorca for the study of the "idiomata diversa" of the missionaries. At his urging the Council of Vienne (1311) established chairs for the study of these languages in Rome, Bologna, Paris, Oxford, and Salamanca. Their lifespan was not long.

In 1622 the East India Trading Company requested the theological faculty of Leiden University to sketch a plan for a proposed seminary for pastors who were planning to serve in India and who could thus concurrently work for the

15. Olav G. Myklebust, *The Study of Missions in Theological Education: An Historical Inquiry into the Place of World Evangelization in Western Protestant Ministerial Training with Particular Reference to Alexander Duff's Chair of Evangelistic Theology*, 2 vols. (Oslo: Egede Instituttet: hovedkommisjon Forlaget Land og Kirke, 1955–57).

"conversion of the heathen." Anton Walaeus drew up the requested plan. It showed striking similarities to the design of Roman Catholic seminaries. The demanding proposal called for no less than twenty separate courses, including theology and philosophy interspersed with activities such as prayer, fasting, visitation of the poor, and the practice of piety. All these requirements had to be met before one was sent out. Candidates lived in Walaeus' house. The maximum number of students at any one time was six, and only twelve preachers were trained during the ten-year life of this school.

The East India Company abolished the seminary in 1633 for reasons which are unclear. On the one hand, the results did not seem worth the heavy costs to the company. On the other, the preachers were so well trained that they did not easily fit into the company's plans for them to become its willing and ready instruments. Several pleas to reopen the school were never granted by the company.

A third attempt was A. H. Francke's *Collegium Orientale Theologicum* in Halle founded in 1702. This, along with Leibnitz's *Akademie der Wissenschaften* in Berlin, was a training center for theological candidates to "propagate the faith through knowledge" ("propagatio fidei per scientias"). The impact on missiology and the training of missionaries was very slight, according to Gerhard Rosenkranz.

In 1627 the *Collegium Urbanum de Propaganda Fide* was founded in Rome. It had a profound impact upon the many students who went there for study.

At the Danish-Halle mission, Ziegenbalg, by providing for important work opportunities before sending missionaries out, stimulated not only the practice of but also theoretical reflection upon missionary activity.

The Modern Era: The Official Study of Missiology in Universities, Faculties, and Seminaries

Germany and Scotland

In 1864, *Dr. Karl Graul* (1814–1864), director of the Leipzig Mission, made the initial try at introducing to Europe the scientific study of missions. In that year he delivered a speech which qualified him as a private teacher at Erlangen; in it he made a plea for including missiology in the "universitas litterarum." Among other things, he said: "This discipline must gradually come to the point where she holds her head up high; she has a right to ask for a place in the house of the most royal of all sciences, namely, theology." This was the first knock on the theological faculties' door.

Graul's Elijah-mantle fell on *Dr. C. H. Plath* (1829–1901), inspector of the Berlin and Goss Mission. He lectured in missiology at the famous Humboldt University of Berlin. He taught privately at first (1867) and later became honorary professor, that is, one who is not an official member of the faculty.

The year Plath began as private teacher in Berlin (1867), *Alexander Duff* (1806–1878) assumed his task as missiologist at the New College in Edinburgh by delivering his inaugural address entitled "Evangelistic Theology." Previously Duff had rung up a number of successes by establishing some Christian colleges in India, which today are still providing useful service.

However, his appearance as professor of missiology was not as successful. Duff's biographer, William Paton, whose sobriety matched his enthusiasm in describing Duff, related in his book, *Alexander Duff, Pioneer of Missionary Education* (1923), that in the first winter semester he lectured on "God's Decrees before the Creation" and at the conclusion of the second semester he ended up in the New Testament.[16] After his departure the chair of missiology was eliminated.

Gustav Warneck was born on March 6, 1834 in Naumberg and died on December 26, 1919 in Halle. The first person to receive an official appointment to the chair of missionary science, he was made professor extraordinary at the University of Halle and taught *Missionslehre* from 1896 to 1908. He entitled his inaugural lecture "Mission's Right to Citizenship in the Organism of Theological Science" (1897). He was a real pioneer for missiology and was the driving force behind organizing European missionary conferences.

In 1874 Warneck founded the *Allgemeine Missions Zeitschrift*, which from the very beginning strove not only to include material about existing mission agencies but also to treat the subject of missiology itself. Through this scientific missionary periodical came the push for similar periodicals in Germany, America, the Netherlands, and Scandinavia.

Toward the end of his life Warneck put all of his insights into a three-part book, *Evangelische Missionslehre*, which is subtitled "An attempt at a theory of missions."[17] His insights appeared in a series entitled *Zimmer's Handbibliothek der praktischen Theologie*. In a later review we shall come back to this first draft of a theory of missions.

In 1968 the German Society of Missionary Science (*Deutsche Gesellschaft für Missionswissenschaft*) held its golden anniversary celebration at which Gerhard Rosenkranz honored Warneck as the pioneer in the field of missiology. Regardless of all the criticism which may properly be leveled at Warneck's ideas, including those from Professor Hoekendijk of the Netherlands, no one can discount the pioneer importance of Warneck for the academic study of missions. When the Marburg University decided in 1950 to make missiology a required course for every theological student, this was the crowning success of Warneck's early work. Missiology gradually came to be offered at virtually every German theological school.

Several other names are worthy of mention in this connection. *Julius Richter* (1892–1940) taught missiology in Berlin and gained attention by thirty publications dealing with missionary institutions. *Carl Mirbt* of Gottingen (1860–1929) did much to raise missiology to the "full position of a science," to borrow Gerhard Rosenkranz's phrase. His chief interests were missionary statistics and the relations between missions and the governmental authorities in the colonial era of missions. *H. W. Schomerus* of Halle (1879–1945) specialized in what we today would call the theology of religions.

Dr. Walter Freytag (1899–1959) was the first missiologist at the University of Hamburg. He founded the Missions Academy which is based there. He com-

16. William Paton, *Alexander Duff, Pioneer of Missionary Education* (London: SCM Press, 1923).
17. Gustav Warneck, *Evangelische Missionslehre: Ein Missionstheoretischer Versuch* (Gotha: F. A. Oerthes, 1897–1903).

bined a life of busy service as General Secretary of the German Evangelical
Missionary Council with that of professor at Hamburg, and after the Second
World War became the most prominent representative of German missionary
science. His deep humility coupled with his fine sensitivity to the concerns of the
young churches and his service of reconciliation assisted Freytag in bringing not
only Hamburg but all of German missiology out of the morass of *Volkstum* into
which so many Germans had fallen. Freytag made missiology capable of serving
the ecumenical cause. His place in Hamburg is now occupied by *H. J. Margull*,
author of *Hope in Action*.[18]

In the German universities the chairs of missiology were often held either
by students of the theology of the religions (Horst Bürkle in Munich, Gerhard
Rosenkranz in Tübingen, and E. Damman in Marburg, to name several examples)
or by actual missiologists such as Hans Werner Gensichen of Heidelberg, Peter
Beyerhaus of Tübingen, and the late George Vicedom of Neuendettelsau, author
of *The Mission of God: An Introduction to the Theology of Mission*.

The Netherlands

The Roman Catholic University of Nijmegen became the first Dutch university to
establish a chair of missiology when it appointed *Professor Alphons Mulders* as
lector in 1930 and as full professor in 1936.

The Free Reformed University of Amsterdam was the first Protestant
school to found a chair of missionary science. *J. H. Bavinck* became the first
Dutch Protestant professor of missions and for several years did his teaching at
both the theological school of Kampen and the Free University. Bavinck assumed
his position toward the close of 1939 by delivering an inaugural lecture entitled
"Proclaiming Christ to the Nations." His book *An Introduction to the Science of
Missions* sums up Bavinck's missiological thinking.[19]

On June 23, 1969 an official cooperative venture between the missiology
and ecumenics departments of the various Dutch universities began at Utrecht.
This Inter-university Institute of Missiology and Ecumenics was the brainchild of
J. C. Hoekendijk. His many years as secretary of the Netherlands Missionary
Council impressed him with the fact that there was urgent need for a thorough
examination of the many questions posed by missions and world service. He
found that traditional agencies lacked sufficient time for this study.

Hoekendijk also came to realize that missiology and ecumenics can no
longer be studied separately since they are so closely intertwined. Both of these
disciplines are directed toward the whole church and the whole world. The church
addresses its gospel proclamation to the world, and the mutual relationships the
various churches sustain with each other must be geared to this work. The
decision was made to start a single institute but to maintain two separate departments within it — one for missiology and the other for ecumenics. The institute's
headquarters and ecumenical section are in Utrecht, but the missiology department is at Leiden.

18. Hans Jochen Margull, *Hope in Action* (Philadelphia: Muhlenberg Press, 1962).
19. Johan H. Bavinck, *An Introduction to the Science of Missions* (Nutley, N.J.:
Presbyterian and Reformed Publishing House, 1960).

Space does not permit a review of the status of missiology at other European universities. For further reference see the study of Myklebust mentioned above. We cannot bring this section to a close, however, without making a few comments on missiology as it is carried on in the United States.

The United States

Like Europe, the United States took a long time in putting the study of missions into the curriculum. Toward the close of the nineteenth century the student missionary *élan* was simply overwhelming. The so-called missionary awakening at Mount Hermon, Massachusetts in 1886 gave the impetus for forming the Student Volunteer Movement. The Mount Hermon gathering lasted twenty-six days and was led by *Dwight L. Moody*. Among the two hundred fifty students present there were such slogans as "All should go and go to all" and "The evangelization of the world in this generation." At the close the number of students who had dedicated themselves to missionary service had swelled from twenty-one to one hundred. This group gave birth to the Student Volunteer Movement headed by *Dr. John R. Mott*. The movement's influence widened to a degree hitherto unknown and spilled over into England, Ireland, Switzerland, and the Netherlands.

The Student Volunteer Movement stood in increasing need of worthwhile missiological study material. Atlases, statistics, and books on linguistics, history, and the history of religions appeared. Books such as Robert Speer's *Missionary Principles and Practice* (among others that he wrote), Wells Williams's *Middle Kingdom*, and Arthur Smith's *Chinese Society* also answered this need.

Pressure was gradually increasing for introducing missiology as a subject into the curricula of seminaries and divinity schools. After a couple of faltering tries Union Theological Seminary of New York first gave the science of missions its permanent place in the curriculum. *Daniel J. Fleming*, appointed in 1918, was the first full-time professor. Soon other renowned seminaries like Yale and McCormick also began using part-time personnel to teach this subject.

The Missionary Research Library, with its present headquarters at 3041 Broadway in New York City in the tower of Union Theological Seminary, stimulated the desire for introducing missiology as a university course. Ever since John Mott led a drive for establishing this library, it has become a major resource for missionary studies.

In 1911, Hartford Seminary Foundation established its Kennedy School of Missions, which opened new possibilities for missionary training and emphasized concentrated study of various geographic areas of missionary activity. For example, there were China studies, Africa studies, and Muslim-area studies. Though the seminary no longer offers missionary studies, it is still producing its famous periodical, *Muslim World*.

The drive to increase the number of professorships in missiology came chiefly after the year 1920. The Student Volunteer Movement was gradually disappearing, and this expanded the need for those interested in missions. "It was widely believed that by placing a professor of mission in a seminary the waning tide of missionary interest and zeal might be stemmed." Missions professors were engaged to deliver sermons and speeches to the congregations to recruit missionary personnel.

By about 1940 there were few seminaries which lacked a department of missions, and by 1966 there were at least 100 seminaries offering courses in missions and 132 lecturers teaching them (usually in combination with other courses.)

At university divinity schools several professors raised the level of higher education in missiology. *Kenneth Scott Latourette* of Yale was author of the famous series *History of the Expansion of Christianity*. *R. Pierce Beaver,* once a professor at the University of Chicago Divinity School and a member of the United Church of Christ, ranks as a leading statistician, historian, and library expert. In 1952 Beaver organized the Association of Professors of Missions in North America, which now has about 100 members. In a report given at Selly Oak in 1967 Dr. Beaver noted the dismaying fact that the number of university chairs of missions is declining in the United States. The trend seems to be toward maintaining missiology only in denominational seminaries. He said: "Every university and seminary needs a professor of missions to be a living symbol of the church's worldwide mission and to be the agent who summons students and faculty to engagement in it." If missiology should ever disappear from the American seminary, it would mark a great loss and would result in the strong growth of provincialism and parochialism among both faculty and students. I am happy to note that there are still outstanding professors of missions at a few universities which offer doctoral programs, such as Yale (Charles Forman), Duke (Creighton Lacy), and Southern Methodist (William Richey Hogg).

Complementing but not replacing the study of missiology at the university level are the short, intensive courses of study offered at the Overseas Ministries Study Center in Ventnor, New Jersey. The center also makes a contribution to missiology in its publication, the *Occasional Bulletin of Missionary Research*.

The trend in United States' universities and seminaries is to absorb missiology into the course in ecumenics or history of religions. This is lamentable. As I see it, Beaver is correct when he says that chairs of missiology need a double base. First, they require theologians who see that the task of theology is worldwide and therefore are willing to concede a spot — a spacious spot — to missiology in the curriculum. Second they require missionary and diaconal agencies who, in formulating mission policy and facing administrative questions, look to the missiologists for their input. Beaver prefers to separate the disciplines of missiology and science of religion rather than to combine them as often happened in the past.

An interesting missiological initiative is headed by *Dr. Donald McGavran.* He formed his Institute for the Study of Church Growth as a service for evangelicals. Now located at Fuller Theological Seminary as a graduate school of World Mission, it has come to serve a much broader group. Another important research institute is the Missions Advanced Research and Communication Center (MARC) in Monrovia, California, a division of World Vision International. This center, headed by Edward R. Dayton, uses the most advanced information systems and computer technology for developing an information center on world Christianity. It also publishes the *Mission Handbook* of North American Protestant ministries overseas.

A major development was the founding in 1973 of the American Society of Missiology, which now has over 500 members and publishes a quarterly journal, *Missiology*.

The U. S. Center for World Mission, established in 1976 at Pasadena, California by Ralph D. Winter, coordinates studies and strategies for reaching unreached peoples with the gospel.

CHAPTER II

Protestant Missiology prior to the Nineteenth Century

Every branch of theological science functions within a specific historical matrix. None operates *de novo*. Proper practice of one's theological discipline requires communication with one's "fathers" and contemporaries as well as an openness toward the future. Contact with the past and the present as well as an eye toward the future is necessary. Our attention in this chapter is not on the history of missions or the history of the young churches. We focus rather on the history of the theoretical study of missions and matters related to this study. Any good missiology is also a *missiologia viatorum* ("pilgrim missiology"). We are enroute. The future is open. We cannot be content with repeating the past. Time and again we must confront new situations, new questions, new problems, and new challenges. But to be ready to meet these new issues makes communication with our fathers and our contemporaries vitally necessary.

Two introductory comments are necessary. First, in the following paragraphs we shall restrict ourselves merely to a look at the missiology of churches stemming from the sixteenth-century Protestant Reformation. This is not to underestimate the importance of Roman Catholic missiology. On the contrary, it is so important as to deserve separate treatment in a later chapter. Second, our emphasis is primarily on the *scientific* practice of missiology.

THE SIXTEENTH-CENTURY REFORMERS' VIEWS ON MISSIONS AND MISSIOLOGY

Anyone searching for the heralds of the theoretical study of missions ultimately arrives at the so-called further Reformation; he meets up with the old and new Pietism which both accompanied and stimulated early practical missionary work. Why the Reformers themselves did not encourage the sending out of missionaries or contribute to the theological study of our missionary task has been treated by many authors. The Reformers lived during the era of Columbus and Vasco da Gama, and the great Roman Catholic *Congregatio de Propaganda Fide* was going full steam. Roman Catholics such as Bellarminus, Suarez, Thomas Bozuis, Philippus from Utrecht, and Johannes Bretteius all made their contributions to the study of missiology in that era.

Why, then, did the Reformers scarcely stimulate missionary activity and make no noteworty contribution to missiological study? Gustav Warneck, Kenneth Scott Latourette, and others have exhaustively researched this question. They cite the following reasons:

(1) The Reformers (wrongly) believed that the missionary mandate of Matthew was limited to and fulfilled in the apostolic era. It is incomprehensible that the Reformers and their contemporaries did not relate Jesus' promise in Matthew 28 to be present even to the end of the age to the fulfillment of their missionary task, but it is undeniably true. It took later figures such as Saravia and William Carey to prove the Reformers wrong.

(2) The Reformers were preoccupied with the work at hand — the Reformation in Europe.

(3) The Reformers were enmeshed in a momentous political and military struggle against medieval Roman Catholicism and consequently did not have the material resources necessary for taking on worldwide tasks.

(4) Both Luther and Calvin believed the princes and other public authorities were responsible for maintaining public worship, and therefore both the German Lutherans and the Swiss Calvinists had no direct contacts with non-Christian peoples.

(5) It is possible to defend the thesis, as S. van der Linde did in his book *Zending in Nederland*, that the Reformers did stretch their every nerve for evangelizing, recalling, and re-Christianizing; however, the work of proclaiming the gospel worldwide did not lie within their purview.

(6) The attempts of Walter Holsten and Werner Elert to prove that Luther did have a vision for world mission are somewhat forced. Holsten cites only one passage from Luther in which Luther argues that Christians held as war prisoners by East-European Turks should catechize their captors. It is hard to deduce a whole view of world mission from that single exhortation.

John Yoder, a well-known Mennonite professor from the United States, tried to argue that Mennonites, Hussites, and other Reformation "stepchildren," to use Lindeboom's term, did develop both the theory and practice of mission and the proclamation and planting of churches.

It is going a bit far, however, to claim that missionary activities were carried on among non-Christian peoples; rather, congregations were built up and strengthened in the Scandinavian countries, Poland, Italy, Hungary — that is, all lands within the *Corpus Christianum*. The work was geared toward revival and a recalling of the people to authentic Christianity as these groups defined it. In those circles, too, a rise in the level of missionary consciousness had to wait until a later time and was initiated only with the coming of the so-called further Reformation and Pietism. Then actual Protestant participation in world mission and the theoretical reflection upon this activity really began.

SIXTEENTH- AND SEVENTEENTH-CENTURY DUTCH MISSIONARY PROJECTS

In the above comments we indicated that the impetus for mission and missionary theory began, not with the Reformation, but with the "further Reformation" and the old and new Pietism. Roman Catholic scholars correctly conclude that in the history of missions the first Protestant drafts of a missiology arose in the Netherlands. Dutchmen such as Saravia, Heurnius, Walaeus, Voetius, and Hoornbeeck were "the first Protestants who spoke for a theory and practice of mission among the broader masses," to quote P. M. Galm's book *Das Erwachen des Missionsgedankens im Protestantismus der Niederlande.*[1]

The undisputed cause for this awakening of interest lay in the founding of the East India Trading Company, for when it was established the Dutch churches, acting from motives both pure and impure, felt called to begin missions in such regions as Ceylon, Formosa, Java, and the Moluccan Islands. Such missionary activities commenced in 1598 under the influence of Rev. Petrus Plancius, a theologian, geographer, and organizer of world voyages. His noteworthy mixture of talents, which was not uncommon in those days, stimulated his interest in missions, science, and commerce.

It is not my intention to describe at this point the connection between the East India Company and the churches. Instead, I want to draw attention to the fact that Protestant missionary activities in that era paved the way for missiological thinking. To do this we shall look briefly at the first theologians coming from Reformation churches who made a contribution to missionary thinking.

Hadrianus Saravia (1531–1613)

Hadrianus Saravia was one of the first Protestant theologians who not only engaged in the practical work of missions but also contributed to the development of missiology. Born of a Spanish father and a Flemish mother, Saravia worked as a Reformed (*Gereformeerd*) preacher in the cities of Antwerp, Brugge, and Ghent. After a lengthy break in England which made him sympathetic to the Anglican episcopal system, he came to the Netherlands to begin a five-year stint as professor at Leiden University. Reproached at Leiden for his Anglican tendencies, Saravia returned to England where he wrote *De diversis ministrorum Evangelii gradibus, sicut a Domino fuerunt instituti* ("On the Various Levels of Ministers of the Gospel as They have been Instituted by the Lord"). Written in London in the year 1590, the treatise argues for the office of ecclesiastical bishops who stand in the line of apostolic succession and are given apostolic authority to send out people in missionary service. Theodore Beza opposed this idea by claiming — quite incorrectly — with all the other Reformers that the missionary mandate of Matthew 28 ended with the apostolic age. Yet he conceded that in given circumstances the church may be expanded. Apostolic sanction, however, is unnecessary; for this work every Christian is competent.

Saravia countered with an expanded rebuttal, *Defensio tractationis de diversis Evangelii gradibus* ("Defense of the Treatise on Various Levels of the Gospel"), written in 1594.

The well-known Johann Gerhard also opposed Saravia. Nonetheless Saravia's plea for commitments to missions had considerable influence on men

---

1. P. M. Galm, *Das Erwachen des Missionsgedankens im Protestantismus der Niederlande* (Oberbayern: Missionsverlag Sankt Ottilien, 1915).

such as Justus Heurnius and Gisbertus Voetius, as well as on the Danish-Halle Mission and the English Puritans. Saravia particularly influenced one of the first missionaries to the Indians of New England, John Eliot.

Justus Heurnius (1587–1651)

Heurnius, who combined both medicine and theology in his career, published in Leiden in 1618 a treatise which significantly advanced mission work during the age of the East India Trading Company. Entitled *De legatione Evangelica ad Indos capessendo*, the book is dedicated to Prince Maurits and the Seventeen Gentlemen of the East India Company. Heurnius writes: "We are living between two eventides: Here the Pope is extinguishing the light and yonder in the East is Mohammed. The end is near; the Angel (Revelation 14) is flying through the heavens with the eternal Gospel in his hands." Heurnius sensed the danger involved in pursuing riches and the tendency of colonial powers to exploit. He urged that the present opportunity in Asia be used in service of the gospel.

Chapters one, four, five, and six set forth Heurnius' attempt at a biblical foundation for mission. In chapter three he discusses the methodology of missions, making particular mention of the need for Bible translation and plain biblical preaching. In chapter eight he describes the missionary mandate which comes to all, including seamen, traders, and soldiers.

After a conflict with the East India Company which followed fourteen years of service in India, Heurnius returned to the Netherlands and took a post as preacher in Wijk bij Duurstede. His book is broad in scope and quite likely had some formative influence on William Carey. There is no question that it played a role in bringing the Danish mission into existence.

Gisbertus Voetius (1589–1676)

Voetius was professor at the University of Utrecht and entitled his first lectures on missiology *De plantatoribus ecclesiasticis*. Voetius treated each of the following topics seriatim: the grounds of mission, the vehicles of mission, the object of mission, and the purpose of mission. As Voetius saw it, the first goal of mission is the conversion of the heathen; the second, the planting of churches; and the highest, the glory of God. His other written works, *Selectae disputationes* and *Politica ecclesiastica*, contain lengthy passages on missions. Voetius was an expert on Roman Catholic missionary literature and borrowed heavily from it.

Johannes Hoornbeeck (1617–1666)

Hoornbeeck, a pupil of Voetius in Utrecht and Walaeus in Leiden, was the author of no fewer than four missiological works. Later he began his teaching career at the University of Utrecht and then moved on to Leiden University, where he subsequently died. Two of his books are of special interest: *Summa Controversarium Religionis* (1653) and *De Conversione Indorum et Gentilium* (1665). The first book was written completely by Hoornbeeck, while the arrangement for the second book was done by editor David Stuartus, a Leiden professor. Hoornbeeck wrote the seventy-six page introduction to the second book. Hoornbeeck's assignment in the book, as he gives it, is to describe briefly the heathen history which both the early Christian and present-day missions confronted. He devotes special attention to their religious ideas and is intent on pointing out some lines of approach for converting the heathen.

According to Hoornbeeck, the command to missions comes to us not only from the pages of the Old and New Testaments but also from the example of the Apostles and the best men and women through the ages of Christian history (note that the missionary mandate is not only for the Apostles). The parable of the Good Samaritan also spurs one on to mission work, according to Hoornbeeck; he identifies the Good Samaritan as the Roman Catholics with their zeal for missions while the unfeeling priest and Levite are equated with the Reformation Christians. Indeed, unless we do go out in missionary service, God will send a disaster our way to drive us out.

Hoornbeeck completely agrees with Voetius on the church's obligation to become a sending agency. He even sketches a plan for a Protestant counterpart to the Roman Catholic *Congregatio de Propaganda Fide* whose delegates from all over the world would be in constant contact and would thus support each other. Of course, this would also have advantages for both state and commerce.

Universities must keep theological students informed on missionary matters, establish seminaries, and train missionaries. Governments must support the ministers by means of money and authority, claims Hoornbeeck. As yet this has not happened, he says. Although he would not require it, Hoornbeeck prefers that a preacher who goes to India remain there permanently.

Finally, Hoornbeeck discusses the means and methods for doing mission work. He holds up the example of the Jesuits who master the native languages, preach, catechize, give medical care, etc. He urges the Reformation churches to surpass the Roman Catholics in their zeal for this work. Dr. Galm, the Roman Catholic historian, points out that Roman Catholic mission activity and literature stimulated Hoornbeeck's views in many ways.

All of the early missiological essays reflect a certain embarrassment about the wealth of Roman Catholic mission activity compared with the Protestant in the Reformation era and beyond; the authors try to incite the Reformation churches to engage in missions. Very soon afterwards such initiatives for practical and theoretical thinking about the missionary task begin to emerge from countries such as Germany, England, Scandinavia, and the United States.

It is interesting to discover that Jan Amos Comenius, bishop of the Moravian brothers in the Lowland countries from 1656 to 1670 "came to the conclusion that the whole Church of God is called to become an instrument of his *world mission.*"[2] Only in the later time of von Zinzendorf and the Bohemian Brethren (*Unitas Fratrum*) did these ideas of Comenius become fleshed out and implemented.

2. See the essay by the expert on Comenius, J. M. van der Linde, "Jan Amos Comenius und die Niederländische Missionstheologen seiner Zeit," *Acta Comeniana* 2 (XXVI), 1970.

FRAGMENTS OF MISSIOLOGICAL REFLECTION DURING THE EIGHTEENTH AND NINETEENTH CENTURIES, THE PIONEER PERIOD OF MISSIONS

We now wish to go farther down the historical path of the science of missions which for the Reformation tradition began in the Lowland countries during the sixteenth and seventeenth centuries. The professional study of missiology got its real second start in the days of Gustav Warneck in the nineteenth century. Nonetheless, it would be foolish to claim that not even fragments and "trial runs" come out of the eighteenth and early nineteenth centuries. There *was* some work done in the area of missiological reflection, and it came chiefly from people whose life and work gave the impetus to missionary activities in the eighteenth and nineteenth centuries.

In his dissertation, J. C. Hoekendijk may be correct that the Danish-Halle mission which began in 1706 produced no separate theology; the writings of Philip Jacob Spener (1635–1705), who wrote *Pia Desideria*, and August Herman Francke (1633–1727) do, however, give directions for doing evangelism and building up young churches. Both Ziegenbalg and Plutschau, the first missionaries sent out by the Danish-Halle mission, gave a good account of their missionary views through their writings and extensive correspondence even though they had no developed systematic missiology. Any reputable study of the history of missions pays due regard to these men from the pioneer era. I shall choose only a few examples to prove that even in this early period there were gestures in the direction of theoretical missionary thinking.

Nicolaus Ludwig von Zinzendorf (1700–1760) and his biographer and successor, August Spangenberg, made strong starts in this direction. Though von Zinzendorf's famous book, *Instruktion an alle Heydenboten*, is not yet a full introduction to the science of missions but rather an encouragement to fulfilling the missionary task, these instructions are nevertheless loaded with missiological insights. In his book *The Meaning of Ecumenical*, W. A. Visser 't Hooft is absolutely correct in claiming von Zinzendorf was the first man to so join missions with ecumenical work that the one became unthinkable without the other. It is also worth recalling that Karl Barth in his book *Protestant Theology in the Nineteenth Century* classifies von Zinzendorf as the deepest christological theologian of his century.

For my second illustration I refer to William Carey, Baptist shoemaker and lay preacher, who later blossomed into becoming the founder of the more recent missionary movement. He contributed to the theoretical study of missions in numerous ways. Carey's missionary principles are found chiefly in two writings: *An Enquiry into the Obligations of Christians to Use Means for the Conversion of the Heathen* (1792), and *The Form of Agreement Respecting the Great Principles Upon Which the Brethren of the Mission at Serampore Think It Their Duty to Act in the Work of Instructing the Heathen* (1805). Carey viewed neither of these books as scientific treatises but wrote them only to encourage tackling the work of missions and to give practical instruction. Both of these writings and the practical work which they sparked gained for Carey the title "Father of Modern Missions." J. S. Dennis was right when he wrote: "Carey's *Enquiry* marks a distinct point of departure in the history of Christianity. It laid the foundation of missions in accurate information, careful consideration and wise use of means, as well as in the obligation of Christian duty."

One of Carey's most important contributions is his extensive refutation in section one of the *Enquiry* of the thesis defended by the Reformers "that the missionary commission (Matt. 28:16–20) was sufficiently put into execution by what the apostles and others have done. It is thus that multitudes sit at ease and give themselves no concern about the far greater part of their fellow-sinners, who to this day are left in ignorance and idolatry."

A second important contribution of Carey is his basing the call to do mission work, not in the lost condition of sinners or in pity for them, but in obedience to the Lord's command. Moreover, he provides a compact history of missions and records the latest geographic discoveries with extreme accuracy. Then Carey follows with a consideration of the tools, means, and goals of mission work. The whole book bespeaks an involvement with the issues of that day. For example, he was completely engaged in the war against slavery and did not dodge the fight against the basic structures of colonialism. It is little wonder that not only Carey the man but also Carey's missionary principles gained attention and became the object of wide study.

Carey also proposed the convening of world missionary conferences. He hoped to hold the first in the year 1810, a hope which was realized exactly one hundred years later in the conference at Edinburgh. Another of his fundamental ventures was Serampore College, established to train Indian preachers and to study thoroughly the religious and cultural context in which they worked. Thus the foundations were laid for an indigenous ministry and a *theologia in loco*.

My third illustration of early theoretical missionary thinking is found in the works of Jonathan Edwards (1703–1758), the Calvinistic revivalist American preacher and theologian who played a leading role in the Great Awakening. According to church historians, the missionary ideas he developed in one of his writings had heavy influence during the whole of the nineteenth century. They expanded the thinking of many and inspired many to missionary service. It is entitled *A Humble Attempt to Promote Explicit Agreement and Visible Union Among God's People in Extraordinary Prayer for the Revival of Religion and the Advancement of Christ's Kingdom on Earth, Pursuant to Scripture Promises and Prophecies Concerning the Last Time* (1847). Today this treatise would be put into the category of "promotional literature," but in that time its function was similar in many respects to missiological treatises today which assist those keenly interested in missions.

Edwards' ideas classified him as a representative of the "New England theology." He emphasized love as the motive for missions and the kingdom of God as the goal. These ideas come through not only in the above-mentioned book but also in *God's Chief End in Creation* and other books. He himself set the pace in mission work not only by his evangelism activity among his own people but also by his work among the Indians.

So much for the illustrations. A brief journey through the history of missions in the eighteenth and nineteenth centuries will disclose a theoretical study of missions at many points. The writings of men like Robert Moffatt

(1795–1883), David Livingstone (1813–1873), Alexander Duff (1806–1878), John Nevius from Korea, Hudson Taylor, Gottlieb Pfander, and a host of others include both general and specialized studies in the history of missions and contain the building blocks for a full missiology. However, in my judgment it is preferable to study these men and their work in a course on the history of missions rather than in missiology since their chief concern was the practice rather than the theoretical study of missions. Nonetheless their ideas often sprouted deeper roots than those of official missiologists.

BIBLIOGRAPHY

Holsten, W. "Reformation und Mission." *Archiv für Reformationsgeschichte* 44 (1953): 1 ff.

Latourette, K. S. *Three Centuries of Advance: A.D. 1500–1800.* Vol. 2 of *A History of the Expansion of Christianity,* 7 vols. New York: Harper, 1944–45.

Littell, F. H. "Protestantism and the Greater Commission." *Southwestern Journal of Theology* 2 (October, 1959): 26–43.

Schaufele, W. *Das missionarische Bewusstsein und Wirken der Täufer; Dargestellt nach oberdeutschen Quellen.* Neukirchen-Vluyn: Neukirchener Verlag, 1966.

Warneck, G. *Abriss einer Geschichte der Protestantischen Missionen von der Reformation bis auf die Gegenwart, mit einem Anhang über die Katholischen Missionen.* Berlin: Verlag von Martin Warneck, 1913.

Wiswedel, W. "Die alten Täufergemeinden und ihr missionarisches Wirken." *Archiv für Reformationsgeschichte* 40 (1943): 183–200.

Yoder, J. H. "Reformation and Mission." *Occasional Bulletin* No. 6 (June, 1971).

CHAPTER III

The History of Missiology during the Nineteenth and Twentieth Centuries

For convenience' sake we shall organize our discussion of nineteenth- and twentieth-century missiology geographically, discussing Germany, England, the United States, etc. successively. Although of course there are few disciplines which show fewer limitations by geographic boundaries than missiology, it is nonetheless true that through the years missiology has acquired unique characteristics in each land. Dividing the discussion geographically therefore is not without rhyme or reason. What follows is by no means an effort to be exhaustive, for this would make the study unwieldy. This is merely an overview.

GERMAN MISSIOLOGY

In Germany the nineteenth century was the century of missions. Following Halle and Herrnhut (the latter founded by Zinzendorf), which had already begun, the nineteenth century saw the rise of transconfessional, independent missionary societies in Basel, Barmen, Hamburg-Bremen, and Berlin. Then, especially after 1848, came the Lutheran missionary societies (Dresden-Leipzig, Hermannsburg, Neuendettelsau, Beklum) whose purpose was to transport the Lutheran confession from Germany to the mission field.

In a two-part study, *Mission, Konfession, Kirche*, published in 1967, Johannes Aagaard, the Dane from Aarhus, describes the changing relationships and mutual tensions between the Lutheran church and these mission societies through the years.[1] The book is subtitled "The problematic of integration in the nineteenth century in Germany."

In our short review of the German contribution to the development of missiology, we shall select only a few leading figures and publications for consideration. We begin with Gustav Warneck.

The Missionary Ideas of Gustav Warneck

We already referred to Warneck's pioneer work in acquiring for missiology a place in theological education. We now wish to comment briefly on the content of his

---

1. Johannes Aagaard, *Mission, Konfession, Kirche: Die Problematik ihrer Integration im 19. Jahrhundert in Deutschland*, 2 vols. (Lund: Gleerup, 1967).

missiological work. His publications include: *Pauli Bekehrung, eine Apologie des Christentums* (Gütersloh: Bertelsmann, 1870), *Das Studium der Mission auf der Universität* (Gütersloh: Bertelsmann, 1877), *Moderne Mission und Kultur* (1879), *Die gegenseitigen Beziehungen zwischen der modernen Mission und Kultur, Abriss einer Geschichte der protestantischen Missionen* (1882–1910), *Welche Pflichten legen uns unsere Kolonien auf?* (1885), and *Evangelische Missionslehre* (Gotha: F. A. Oerthes, 1897–1903).

We shall restrict ourselves to a brief consideration of some of Warneck's ideas as they are found in his *opus magnum, his Evangelische Missionslehre.* Because this is a trail-blazing effort in systematic missiology, we choose to give it a slightly fuller treatment in this overview.

Part I. In this section we find Warneck's attempt to arrive at a foundation for mission. From the perspective of dogmatics, Warneck sees a need for missions since Christendom is "the complete and final revelation of God . . . [and] the absolute religion." While other religions may have "hints of truth and intimations of salvation" (*Heilsanweisungen*), Christianity alone possesses the full truth and salvation. For Jesus, the Christ who became man, is a "universal person with the blood of universal salvation (*Heilsuniversalismus*) coursing through his veins, so to speak." "Being sinful and therefore in need of salvation and yet redeemable because human nature bears a divine likeness," all of humanity depends on him for that life-giving stream which flows from him and penetrates the whole. "As the herald of this message of salvation, mission is the naturally necessary consequence of the absolute character of Christianity." Justification by faith in Christ and in his return brings redemption. "Redemption is God's gracious gift providing points of contact to a man fallen in sin until such time as a stubborn rejection of this gift becomes apparent."

But Warneck claimed that ethics, too, provides a foundation for the missionary enterprise. The cardinal virtues of faith, hope, and love provide missionaries with power, while the commandments "are in accord with human temperament not only, but also [comprise] man's universal ethical ideal."

Warneck follows this section with still another basis for mission — the biblical-theological basis. As he develops what he calls "the Biblical faith of the old school," he attacks men like Weisz and other representatives of modern theology. He delves deeply into the Old and New Testaments, especially into the "Mission theology of Paul." The book of Ephesians receives special attention, for it depicts the genuine character of the church as "a new social structure transcending all natural human ties and possessing a universal character."

Then Warneck arrives at his ecclesiastical foundation for mission. "Only the Christian religion has a church, [and] to her belongs the inherent task of world mission." The church is "the institute of healing [*Heilsanstalt*] for all humanity." But ". . . she must engage in mission for her own sake [as well]. From it she exists; if she were to give it up, she would be cutting off her very own lifeline." Through missionaries and the churches which they establish, the "Christianizing of nations" takes place. Noting how modern culture has penetrated so far and wide, Warneck claims that mission work can serve as an "act of atonement" and therefore is both "honorable and a moral obligation."

The fifth basis which Warneck develops is ethnologic. He talks of the "distinct personality" of each and every human being which must be regarded as inviolable. Missionaries must erect bridges which reach the cultural and religious heritage of the people to whom they go. "However otherwise misguided a prayer may be, one can still hear the faint strains of Our Father in it."

Finally, Warneck develops an historical basis for mission.

Part II. In this section Warneck discusses the various agencies of mission. He takes up such diverse organizational matters as the place of independent missionary societies, the role of the missionary, missionary support, marriage, etc. He also devotes a section to what he calls "supporting agencies" (*missionarische Hilfskräfte)* and includes under this rubric — as was customary for that time — the role of medical missionaries. He also places female evangelists in this category.

Part III. In part III Warneck describes the missionary areas of the world in all their geographic and religious diversity. He has an interesting section on how to select a mission field and indicates a degree of support for the new "comity agreements"—something quite progressive for his day.

Warneck then goes on to describe the mandate to mission, the heart of which he sees as "the Christianizing of peoples" (*Volkschristianisierung).* True to German missiology of that time, he urges missionaries to "take due note of national customs and national attitudes" and reflects a paternalistic attitude to what he calls the "natives."

In a speech celebrating the golden anniversary of the *Deutsche Gesellschaft für Missionswissenschaft,* Gerhard Rosenkranz noted that Warneck's work was marked at many points by the temper of his time. "Such standard words of his time as nature, spirit, life, organism, universalism and education permeate this work." His work thoroughly mixed biblical theology with natural theology, kingdom proclamation with national consciousness, man's blood relationship to his fellow man with his divine relationship to God, mission with national indoctrination, an emphasis on individual conversion with Christianization of entire peoples, and the concept of a church among the people with a people's church (*Volkskirche).*

According to Rosenkranz, Warneck's *Missionslehre* combined a Biblicist orthodoxy with pietistic devotion and a romanticism reminiscent of Herder and Schleiermacher. His real and lasting contribution to missiology is that he, like the pathfinders Graul and Plath, tried to aid missionaries in achieving a "theoretical and comprehensive treatment" of the work in which they were involved. The tone of his introduction is modest: "Someone has to be first in daring to undertake this bold venture, and since I am the one, I hope it may be said of me: *in magnis voluisse satis est.* Others who follow me will then improve on my work."

Although German missiology has taken a new turn since the Second World War, for many years prior to that Warneck's *Missionslehre* was the standard work for both the theory and practice of German missions.

Karl Hartenstein (1894–1952)

Karl Hartenstein was one of Germany's most prominent missiologists in the prewar era. A native of Württemberg in southern Germany, he was director of the

Basel Mission until 1939. During the war he returned to his native town to lead the Wurttemberg church and to speak on behalf of the Basel Mission throughout southern Germany.

Hartenstein was strongly influenced by Karl Barth's theology and was one of the first missiologists to set forth the implications of Barth for missions. One of his chief concerns was to purify Christian motives for mission. In important books such as *Zur Neubesinnung über das Wesen der Mission* and *Die Mission als theologisches Problem*, he developed one of his favorite themes: the importance of eschatology as a missionary motive. The essence of the church, according to Hartenstein, "is participation in God's plan of restoration and participation in his mission for the salvation of the world. The Church exists through her mission. Mission is the original and essential duty of the Church, her only reason for existing."

Working together, both Hartenstein and Walter Freytag performed yeoman service in attempting to restore ecumenical relations after the war. In his book *Mission zwischen Gestern und Morgen* he reported on the International Missionary Council's Willingen conference held in 1952, which did much to restore those relations.

Walter Freytag (1899–1959)

One of Germany's most profound and influential missiologists was Walter Freytag, whose origins lay in the Herrnhut community and whose diverse study in Hamburg accurately reflected the diversity of his interests during his career. While at Hamburg, Freytag studied such subjects as pedagogy, psychology, and Chinese religious history. During his term as secretary and later as director of the Deutsch-Evangelische Missionshilfe, he wrote two books: *Allgemeine Missionsnachrichten* and *Das Wort in der Welt*.

After the war had ended, Freytag guided the German missions through the delicate stage of resuming their work. Appointed chairman of the German Missionary Council in 1946, Freytag gained universal respect and international acclaim for his leadership during this tense time. He also participated actively in the work of the International Missionary Council. During his career as a missiologist, Freytag made a series of three extended study trips throughout Asia, each time making an indelible impression on those whom he met by his ability to identify with their joys and cares and to advise them after listening keenly to their pleas. But in addition to all this, Freytag both founded and became a professor at the Missionsakademie affiliated with the University of Hamburg.

In this short review of Freytag's life, I want to mention at least one famous book of his, *Die junge Christenheit im Umbruch des Ostens,* written in — note well the year! — 1938 just after he returned from one of his trips. In addition to the early books of John Taylor, this one book set the stage for a new approach to the historiography of young churches. Note the question Freytag poses: "The question is whether in the end the man of the East will have lost himself, whether he will be hopelessly subservient to the spirit of the West or whether he will emerge from the encounter a new man, who has found the way to a peculiar creature, reshaping of his life, as a nation and as a person." Freytag probes deeply into the issue of what Western influence is doing to the world of Asia in general and to the young Christian churches there in particular.

After the war, Freytag made countless speeches and wrote countless articles treating a whole range of missiological issues. Following his death his students incorporated a number of them into a two-volume set, *Reden und Aufsätze,* which was published in 1961. The broad range of topics makes it completely impossible to review these books here, but I do recommend them to anyone preparing himself for missionary service. They are a veritable showcase for the contemporary issues in mission.

On Freytag's sixtieth birthday an international company of his friends and colleagues honored him by publishing an especially interesting symposium of studies entitled *Basileia.* The book was edited by J. Hermelink and P. Beyerhaus, and though Freytag lived long enough to see it published and have it presented to him, he died shortly thereafter enroute to a speaking engagement.

Walter Holsten

Walter Holsten is professor of religion and mission at the University of Mainz. His most important book, *Das Kerygma und der Mensch: Einführung in die Religions- und Missionswissenschaft,* was published in 1953 and calls for a new understanding of the Bible and the Reformation which will radically affect what we understand by the term "mission."[2] He determines "to free missiology from the onus of her past and set her on a new foundation."

What is Holsten's "new foundation"? In his own words, it is "the kerygma of the New Testament, the message of the God who has acted decisively in Christ and whose actions demand response." Kerygma and man are the two foci of Holsten's theology, but Holsten reveals his Lutheran confessional past when he first reduces the whole kerygma to the matter of the sinner's justification and then proceeds to construct both his science of religion and his missiology on this narrow base and to fill them with anthropological and existentialist content.

After having erected the superstructures on this new base, Holsten proceeds to draw out the consequences of what he has done. In the field of the science of religion, he makes a fundamental distinction between the Christian (*evangelische*) science of religion, which interprets the various religions in existentialist fashion from the perspective of the kerygma, and the non-Christian science of religion, which does not.

According to Holsten, man must come to see that he exists only in relation to God; being human, he exists *coram Deo.* But Wilhelm Andersen accused Holsten of thereby making the task of mission too narrow. The Bible reveals that as Christ sees him, man is more than a mere being who exists in the present as both condemned and justified: he is a being with both a past and a future.

When Holsten goes on to apply his missiology, one can also see him squeezing everything into his tight *justificatio fidei* scheme. He has room neither for creation nor for re-creation in his view. Wilhelm Andersen was right when he

---

2. Walter Holsten, *Das Kerygma und der Mensch:. Einführung in die Religions- und Missionswissenschaft* (Munich: Kaiser Verlag, 1953).

observed: "A genuine kerygmatic foundation does not force individual declarations into some rigid scheme but allows room for their fulness and depth to come through."

Wilhelm Andersen

Wilhelm Andersen, whose name must not be confused with that of the American missiologist G. H. Anderson, began his teaching career at the Breklum Mission, continued it at the Prediger-Seminar in Schleswig-Holstein sponsored by the Evangelical Lutheran Church in Germany, and then moved on to occupy the chair of systematic theology at the Augustana Hochschule in Neuendettelsau.

Andersen wrote two important pieces, both of which reflect specific recent trends in missiology. For many years missiology has often displayed rather anthropocentric, ecclesiocentric, and cultural biases. But under the influence of individuals such as Lesslie Newbigin and George Vicedom and with the special impetus provided by the Willingen conference in 1952, missiology has now taken a more trinitarian and theocentric turn. In this connection, Andersen published an intriguing research pamphlet under the auspices of the International Missionary Council in 1955 entitled *Towards a Theology of Mission*.[3] The focal points of his missiology are creation, redemption, and reconciliation. When he wrote his pamphlet, Andersen was picking up some of the themes which were contained in the statement issued by the Willingen conference. In part the statement reads: "Mission has its source in the Triune God. Out of the depth of his love to us, the Father has sent forth his own beloved Son to reconcile all things to himself, that we and all men might through the Spirit be made one in Him with the Father in that perfect love which is the very nature of God."[4]

In the symposium edited by Gerald Anderson, *The Theology of Mission*, Wilhelm Andersen contributed an essay which developed his ideas further. Entitled "Further toward a Theology of Mission," the essay treats the questions which the author's previous work had left unanswered: How are creation and reconciliation related? What is the connection between salvation history *(Heilsgeschichte)* and world history *(Weltgeschichte)*? Is Hoekendijk correct in viewing the church merely as an instrument of the *missio Dei*, or are there two distinct functions for the church to fulfill: sending and gathering?

Though Andersen's work often reflects his lack of practical missionary experience by remaining too much on the level of the theoretical, he does make a valuable contribution to strict theological reflection.

Hans Jochen Margull

Since 1960 H. J. Margull has been connected with the missiology department at the University of Hamburg and heads the Institute of Missionary Science there.

3. Wilhelm Andersen, *Towards a Theology of Mission: A Study of the Encounter between the Missionary Enterprise and the Church in Its Theology* (London: SCM Press, 1955).

4. "The Missionary Calling of the Church," a statement by the Willingen conference of the International Missionary Council, held July 5–17, 1952, in Willingen, Germany, *International Review of Missions* 41 (1952): 562.

He acquired great international experience in the vital issues of missions when he served the World Council's Division of World Mission and Evangelism as secretary for evangelism. He is still a member of the administration. Though Margull, like Andersen, lacks practical experience in missions, he did in part fill the gap by serving for several years as a teacher in Japan.

Margull is best known for his work in trying to view both evangelism and mission as constituent elements of one larger whole. Both are, as it were, concentric circles around the Apostle of our confession — Jesus Christ himself. Given this perspective, Margull seeks for cross-fertilization between the two wherever possible.

In my judgment Margull errs in reserving the term "evangelization" only for work done in the West and using the term "mission" to apply to work done only in non-Western countries. Such a clean division is impossible, for in some non-Western developing countries there are areas where churches already exist and yet where evangelism needs doing in the local environs of those churches. On the other hand, some areas in the West have wandered so far from Christianity that Christians find themselves in the midst of a full-scale mission situation.

Margull's *opus magnum, Hope in Action*, reflects some of the discussion carried on at the Evanston assembly of the World Council of Churches. In addition, during his term as secretary in Geneva, Margull headed a group studying the missionary structures of the congregation and edited its published report: *Mission als Strukturprinzip* (Part I) and *Die Welt im Wandel* (Part II).

Margull is one of those postwar German theologians who have broken through their past confessional and geographic provincialism and now participate fully in ecumenical discussion and development.

Manfred Linz

Manfred Linz formerly served as an assistant at the University of Hamburg's Seminary of Missionary Science, but now works for North German Radio. In 1964 he published his doctoral dissertation, which he had begun under Walter Freytag, entitled *Anwalt der Welt*.[5] The book surveys the history of twentieth-century missionary preaching up to the Second World War. By carefully examining the sermons preached on the well-known biblical missionary passages, Linz attempted to distill and extract the several motives for mission prevalent during the period. He went on in his last chapter to sketch his own theology of mission.

It is most instructive and revealing to see what preachers have actually done with texts like Matthew 28:18-20, Isaiah 2:2-5, Isaiah 60:1-6, Mark 13:10, Matthew 24:14, etc. For example, Linz has discovered that preachers often use the *locus classicus* of missions, Matthew 28:18-20, without even mentioning mission or the world within which mission takes place. Or else the preachers so accent the matter of obedience to Christ's missionary command that they ignore what Linz thinks is the real point of the passage, the transfer of sovereign authority to Jesus Christ. He notes furthermore that the concept of mission is

5. Manfred Linz, *Anwalt der Welt: zur Theologie der Mission* (Stuttgart: Kreuz Verlag, 1964).

often narrowed to include only oral proclamation while the deeper dimensions receive scant attention.

Linz believes that preachers often fail to see the real point of Mark 13:10 and Matthew 24:14. The real question, he believes, is not "When will the end come?", but rather "Why has it not come yet?" Mistaking this, preachers view the missionary task as one of preparing for the end rather than of making the coming kingdom a reality.

The author ends his analysis of the classic missionary texts by discussing their actual meaning within the contexts as the newer exegetes who employ the methods of form criticism understand them.

In his fifth chapter Linz offers his own theology of mission. After extensive research of the biblical text, he sets forth his definition of mission: "Mission is God engaging the church as a partner in his work in the world. Through mission Christ establishes and exercises his Lordly rule. Mission frees men for discipleship in every area of human life and thereby offers active hope for the final goal of God's creation to be reached." Linz thus sees the work of the church within the perspective of the *missio Dei*; the church herself is mission. Her mission to those outside is only one element of her missionary calling, for there is a close relationship between what was once called "internal mission" (to those within) and "external mission" (to those outside). Moreover, Linz's definition spells out more clearly than previous missiologists the deep unity between oral proclamation of the gospel and works of service done in the name of Christ. He treats extensively the way mission, history, and the kingdom of God are closely related. Mission is the service which Christians — yes, lay Christians too — perform on the world's behalf. And, claims Linz, wherever Christians perform this service in and for the world, there the kingdom of God is coming.

Allow me several comments on Linz's ideas. One detects immediately that Linz put heavy emphasis on the note of the church's involvement with God in his mission. In fact, he hit this theme so hard that he excluded every other one. Motives such as the rescue of lost human beings, love for those who are lost, obedience to the missionary command, and preparation for Christ's return are cast aside as irrelevant. Moreover, though I am happy for Linz's deep insights into the call to Christians and to the church to cooperate with God in his work, I wonder whether his phrase "cooperative enterprise" may not have been ill-chosen. As I see it, I Corinthians 3:9 and II Corinthians 5, when read in context, do not speak of cooperation between God and man, but rather of men themselves being co-workers with other men within their joint relationship to the one God, from whom, through whom, and to whom are all things. I am not trying to detract from the rich insights Linz provides, but I do believe he is over-reacting to those earlier missiologists who developed all manner of motives for mission when he subsumes the whole of the missionary enterprise under the single rubric of "cooperation." Is this monistic urge even necessary? Is it not true that the Bible allows room for all the other motives we mentioned?

My second comment concerns Linz's interpretation of the relationship between salvation history (*heilsgeschiedenis*) and world history. In his concern to emphasize the deep unity between the two and thus to prevent a Christian escapist attitude toward the events of world history, Linz is accenting an important biblical point seriously neglected by Christians. But again, has Linz not yielded to the urge to put everything under one heading? Is world history really a close partner of salvation history, as he says, or are the tensions between them much greater than their unity?

Linz obviously was irritated by apocalyptic speculations and to a great degree discarded them in favor of concentrating on human responsibility in the here and now. But have not recent New Testament scholars warned that one fails to understand the work of Jesus except he place it within the coordinates of a new heaven and a new earth? To be sure, the author's ardent opposition to cheap apocalyptic speculation is justified, but he goes overboard. Apocalypticism is present in the Bible as a reaction to late Jewish apocalypticism, and we must reckon with it as we seek to solve the puzzle of history. Are not, for example, the arch-rivalries between the kingdom of God and the kingdom of darkness, between Babel and the New Jerusalem, between God and Satan crucial to our view?

I have one other criticism quite unrelated to the above. Linz is right in claiming a great deal of missionary preaching failed to be concrete in its vision of the world; yet he has fallen prey to the same error in his view of the young churches of Africa and Asia. Reading Linz, one could infer that cooperation in the *missio Dei* is restricted to the West, but this is of course untrue. He completely disregards that cooperation today means precisely cooperation between churches in West *and* East.

The book's title, *Anwalt der Welt* ("Advocates for the World"), reveals the author's purpose. He summarized it with these words:

> The title expresses a hope and expectation. As the war goes on between those who either curse or bless the world with their words, who either withdraw from it or else subject it to their own visions of the future, what the world really needs are human beings who cherish and prize it for what it really is: God's creation. Desacralizing and secularizing the world are not enough; the oft-honored cool and sober Christian assessment of the world is often nothing more than cultural pessimism whose roots are quite different from those of Biblical realism. Some Christians do display their own specific brand of a "desire to perish." There are critics of the world aplenty; what we need are advocates for the world. The farther we go in experiencing the world through history, the more inescapable becomes our responsibility for it. Jesus Christ, who is the realization of God's faithfulness to the earth, makes us able to accomplish our task. Therefore, brothers, be faithful.

Hans Werner Gensichen

Hans Werner Gensichen, professor of missiology and the science of religion at Heidelberg, is today one of Germany's most prominent missiologists. After performing a variety of tasks in postwar Germany, he went to India in 1952, serving as teacher first in Tranquebar and later in Madras. In 1957 he was appointed to his present post at Heidelberg. In addition to his teaching, Gensichen served as assistant director of the Theological Education Fund from 1961–1964, a London-based fund which operates under the auspices of the Commission for World Mission and Evangelism of the World Council. During these years he supplemented his knowledge of Asia with a firsthand acquaintance with Africa, serving as advisor to the theological schools there. Gensichen is a prolific writer and was one of the founders of the International Association for Mission Studies. In 1974 he became its first chairman.

DUTCH MISSIOLOGY

There are so many Dutch missiologists, both present and past, whose outstanding contributions deserve extended treatment here. Think, for example, of only two of the many individuals: J. Blauw with his book *The Missionary Nature of the Church: A Survey of the Biblical Theology of Mission* and A. T. van Leeuwen with his book *Christianity in World History: The Meeting of Faiths East and West.* Although for brevity's sake we must omit many individuals who made unique contributions, we shall single out two figures from the line of Netherlands missiologists for special attention, the two figures who without a doubt had the most profound impact on the development of Dutch missiology. We select Dr. Johan H. Bavinck and Dr. Hendrik Kraemer for special attention because each has had close contact with both the local church and the worldwide church and because those who have worked on the mission fields have testified to the help, stimulus, and understanding which these men have given.

Dr. J. H. Bavinck (1895–1964)

In 1965 a memorial book bearing the title *Christusprediking in de Wereld* ("Proclaiming Christ in the World") was published by the J. H. Kok Company in Kampen, Netherlands.[6] In it Dr. A. Pos records Bavinck's life history, Dr. J. van den Berg analyzes his scholarly work, and A. Wessels provides a complete bibliography of his writings. I do not intend to repeat what they have already done, but I do wish to record a few personal impressions I have of Bavinck's life and work in order to amplify and illustrate what the memorial book says.

A Transparent Christian
Wherever Johan Bavinck lived and worked, he emitted a special influence. What was his secret? Was it not due to the fact that by God's grace he had become a saint through and through? He was not the Light itself, but was rather a witness of the Light, Jesus Christ, and that Light shone through him completely. He had been brought out of the power of darkness into the kingdom of the Son of Man, who is also the Son of God (cf. Col. 1:13, 14). And how keenly did he know of the powers of darkness, even in his very own life!

The genius of his transparent Christian devotion lay in his act of repeatedly and radically surrendering himself to Christ. Through this he became an integrated, harmonious human being. In surrender his whole being was joined to

6. Johan Bavinck, *Christusprediking in de Wereld: studieën op het terrein van de Zendingswetenschap gewijd aan de nagedachtenis van prof. dr. J. H. Bavinck* (Kampen: J. H. Kok, 1965).

Christ: his heart, his lucid understanding, his deep emotional life, and his special aesthetic capacity.

His radical devotion to Jesus was also the source of his deep sensitivity toward the needs of his fellow human beings. He had utmost respect for human beings and loved them all — people of every race and station in life, children, and young people. His extraordinary courtesy and friendliness toward everyone were not for him mere acquired rules of social intercourse; they flowed from the sensitivity to people which he ever and again was learning through union with Jesus.

His radical surrender to Jesus was the deep well from which flowed his ecumenical inclinations. He was ecumenical, not because he felt forced to be showy or stylish, but simply because with childlike simplicity he thankfully and joyously recognized the Spirit of Jesus Christ in whichever human beings and church communions He was revealing Himself.

Some Notes on Bavinck's Life and Work

Born on November 22, 1895, Bavinck was the son of a preacher from Rotterdam, Rev. C. B. Bavinck, brother of Dr. Herman Bavinck. Stimulated by both theology and philosophy during his years at the Free Reformed University of Amsterdam, Bavinck continued his education in philosophy at the University of Erlangen after finishing his candidate degree work in theology at the Free University. The topic of his thesis for the doctor's degree gave early indication of Bavinck's later interest. He wrote on the mysticism of the medieval mystic Heinrich Suso; throughout his life Bavinck was intensely involved with how the powerful gospel waged war against the alluring forces of monistic mysticism. In addition to his theological and philosophical interests, he also developed a fascination for psychology. Involved in the Student Christian Movement in a variety of ways, Bavinck showed an interest in how to bring a Christian witness to the intelligentsia both during and after the First World War.

Minister for the Dutch-speaking Churches in Indonesia (1919–1926)

The Reformed churches of the Netherlands *(Gereformeerd)* had begun to organize the ecclesiastical work among the Dutch people in Indonesia more fully after the First World War. Dr. W. G. Harrenstein industriously pioneered this effort on the east coast of Sumatra (Medan), and he prevailed upon the young Bavinck to become his ministerial assistant in this rapidly expanding work. However, Bavinck's stay was brief in Medan, for this gifted assistant minister very soon received a call to become minister for an affiliate of Medan in Bandung, a city whose educational institutions attracted many young people. Bavinck accepted the call to Bandung and went there after his marriage to Tine Robers, a woman whom he had come to know in Medan. Until her death in 1953 she, by her blithe spirit and practical sense, solidly supported Bavinck in his work. Bavinck became one of the first ministers of the Dutch Reformed *(Gereformeerd)* church in Bandung (July 3, 1921). Many times I have stood on the grounds near that lovely church in Van Deventer Park and read the inscription stating that Johan Bavinck laid the first stone.

Bavinck worked chiefly among the Dutch. But he opened their eyes to the Indonesian and Chinese societies in which they were dwelling and inspired them to serve those societies. But already then Bavinck was gaining the attention of the Indonesian world; every Sunday many young Indonesians and Chinese came to hear him preach. President Sukarno told me of the time when he was being held as a political prisoner in Suka Miskin prison in Bandung during the colonial era. Preachers and officers in the Salvation Army came occasionally to speak or offer him some reading material. Then he confided: "While there I often listened to the melodious voice of the harmonious young Bavinck!" Even among those conditions he could both recognize and acknowledge in Bavinck a genuine human being and an authentic Christian.

In Bandung Bavinck acquired many contacts with the Indonesian and Chinese world, and thus his time of service in the "Dutch congregation" was preparing him for the missionary service which would follow.

Preacher in Heemstede (1926–1929)
Having returned to the Netherlands from Bandung, Bavinck became affiliated with the church at the Dutch town of Heemstede. His remarkable personality and unique style of preaching caught the attention of those outside his own congregation. During his ministry at Heemstede he also concentrated on studying psychology. His book *Inleiding in de Zielkunde,* which first appeared in 1926 and was revised by Dr. A. Kuipers in 1935, was a marked achievement in the field for that time. Hard work and study made it possible for him to move with apparent ease in this area when he later became professor of practical theology at the Free University. Already at that time many fully expected that he would be offered a position in this area at the Free University. For the time being, however, he did not get it; the climate in the Reformed (*Gereformeerd*) church after 1926 was not favorable for granting an ecumenical figure like Bavinck a position. But even here one can see the truth of the adage *Hominum confusione, Dei providentia*, for this time marked the beginning of great growth in Bavinck's life. The congregation in Delft called him to become a missionary pastor in the Indonesian city of Solo.

The Solo Period (1930–1933)
Bavinck's missionary work began in Middle Java in the very heart of Javanese culture. Solo, a city of palace-forts, old nobility, and feudal culture, was also a city with its middle-school youth and a growing national movement. The city also was a center for a teacher-training school which in those years educated young people from all over Indonesia. The school was headed by the famous pedagogue H. Meyerink. Bavinck was put in charge of the youth work, a work to which he gave himself totally. He wrote a small book describing it, *Youth Work in Middle Java* ("Jeugdwerk in Midden Java"). After reading it, one is simply amazed at the variety of work done among those young people. It was a remarkable period, indeed, for it was the springtime of rising national consciousness and of blossoming Indonesian churches. Bavinck's crucial task, as he saw it, was, through vital contact with the Bible, to bring the young people close to the very fount, Jesus Christ himself. He wrote guidebooks to the Bible, which were later included in a little summary volume in Dutch, *Hoe kunnen Wij de Here Jezus vinden.* The

book is still going through repeated printings in Indonesian translation. Some learned people deem themselves too learned to write simply. Bavinck was one of the rare learned few who was humble enough to serve his fellowman by speaking and writing with childlike simplicity for specific groups of people. This volume and others like it from his pen are among the best of his collection.

A unique organizational feature of Bavinck's work among the young people was his "little clubs of five" (*Pantja-saudara*). Intuitively, Bavinck felt that taking over the number "five" (*pantja*) from the ancient mysticism and applying it to group formation could be of real service in proclaiming the gospel. (A key term in Bavinck's missiology is *"possessio,"* by which he means "adopting, taking over, taking possession of.") These little groups, by using one of Bavinck's guidebooks, made a thorough study of the Bible. Sitting in a holy circle, as it were, they learned to discuss, not in some detached fashion, but in deep communal engagement, searching out God's promises and demands. These little groups had an untold influence upon some young people who would later be called to shoulder heavy responsibilities in a young and independent Indonesia.

While in Solo, Bavinck also strengthened his personal contact with the older intellectual elite, in particular with Javanese mystics. Bavinck engaged with them in study and made good use of his formidable knowledge of the Orient. One time Hendrik Kraemer told me, "I never had a student who caught on to Javanese mysticism more quickly or understood it more thoroughly than Bavinck."

A notable mark of his missionary communication with the mystics was Bavinck's little Javanese book, *Soeksma Soepono*. All of his images and concepts come from the half-Muslim, half-Hindu mystical milieu in which he was living. He compares the soul to a palace-fort with its many entrances, ports, and canals; through them come both the divine as well as the demonic influences to rouse the "powers of the soul." The "powers of the soul" he describes with language borrowed from Ghazali. But every one of these images and concepts is made to serve Bavinck's central theme: when Jesus enters the fort, at first there is wrestling, then capitulation, and finally full surrender to him.

One may argue whether Bavinck succeeded in his attempt. Some claim he did not. But looking back on how Bavinck worked himself into the surrounding milieu and how he proclaimed the gospel, we see an example worthy of our emulation. To try to copy him would be both stupid and impossible. But well might we pray for the ability to display some of his charisma in a manner now appropriate to Asia and Africa.

From a number of sources I get the impression that Bavinck's time in Solo was his most fruitful missionary period. One is still struck by the deep influence on Indonesia which Bavinck made during that time. Its effects are still visible today. In the meantime, the General Deputies of the Reformed Mission called Bavinck to teach at the theological school in Jogjakarta. Bavinck gladly accepted, but not before doing some preparatory work. He took a leave of absence, and it goes without saying that for Bavinck a leave meant a study leave.

Study Leave
Bavinck made thorough preparation for his future work in Jogjakarta by studying at Leiden University. During that time he also finished his famous book, *Christus*

en de Mystiek van het Oosten ("Christ and Eastern Mysticism"), which was published in 1934. Although this book went through only one edition and was never revised, I do not hesitate to call it Bavinck's most important publication. In addition to a competent description of Hindu and Muslim mysticism, especially in its Javanese forms, we also find a confrontation between the gospel and mysticism which to my knowledge is unique and highly original. More than 120 of the finest pages ever written on the subject of confrontation are included in this book. Through his intense study Bavinck developed an appreciation for the attracting power of monistic mystical life and thought as few others have. With a smile he once made the comment, "I was born with an Eastern soul." He felt the monistic urge to identify God with the cosmos. He himself wrestled with this urge and through it developed gratitude for a completely different vision of God, man, and the world which the gospel of Jesus offered him. God's Light illumined his view of man and the world, and it dispelled the delusions of mystical speculations. He explained his position so lucidly to the mystic that he became his comrade and carried him along in the direction of that Light through which Bavinck had found freedom. Bavinck developed this theme in hundreds of later readings and lectures and especially in personal conversations with the mystics.

The Jogjakarta Period (1935–1939)

The youth pastor from Solo became teacher at the theological school in Jogjakarta to join his colleagues in training preachers for the Javanese and Chinese congregations. In retrospect, I wish to point out three facets of that period.

First, Bavinck enriched the school's curriculum by strongly emphasizing a *theologia in loco*. Together with Dr. A. Pos he zealously set forth the study of Java's cultural and religious milieu by careful attention to its literature and other cultural expressions. He also became a close associate of Dr. Barend Schuurman, who made a similar attempt in Bale Wijoto in East Java.

Second, in those years Bavinck teamed up with Dr. F. L. Bakker to write *Geschiedenis der Godsopenbaring* ("History of Divine Revelation"). Bavinck did the New Testament section. The book was translated into both Javanese and Indonesian, and while today it is somewhat dated, pastors, teachers, and evangelists still use it with appreciation and profit.

Third, Bavinck's lectures, travels, and publications during those years generated support for his manner of appearance, his great erudition, and his loyalty to the gospel.

He, too, is partially responsible for the heavier flow of ecumenical traffic between Indonesian churches in that era. Bavinck, D. L. van Doorn, and Hendrik Kraemer cleared the way for ecumenics. In Bavinck's judgment, the need for ecumenical openness was self-evident, and he practiced this openness in countless ways during those years.

Professor of Missions (1939–1964)

In 1939 at the Free Reformed University of Amsterdam and at Kampen Theological School there was a growing awareness of the need for a separate chair for missiology and related studies. Presently every Dutch university offers missiology, but the Reformed institutions of higher learning can claim the honor of being first in this area in Protestant Netherlands. Bavinck, decisively chosen as the first Dutch Protestant occupant for this chair, began his teaching at the Free University and Kampen toward the end of 1939 by delivering an imposing inaugural lecture entitled *ChristuspVediking in de Volkerenwereld* ("Proclaiming Christ to the Nations").

Bavinck's great impact as professor is best measured by the stream of dissertations on missions which flowed from the pens of students stimulated by his teaching. Bavinck never served his students by carefully weighing every line they wrote; the secret of his influence lay in things which are harder to pinpoint. He was a "guru" for his students, an Eastern guru.

In 1955 Bavinck gave up his post at the Kampen Theological School and became full professor at the Free University. The university had offered him a position as teacher of missiology and practical theology. He was now in a position to serve students by his wide pastoral and missionary experience, his psychological insight, and his homiletical gifts. Two of his books *Religieus Besef en christelijk Geloof* ("Religious Awareness and Christian Faith") and *Inleiding in de Zendingswetenschap* ("Introduction to the Science of Missions") attracted attention. Bavinck's careful, delicate analysis of the morphology of religions is striking in the first-mentioned book, so striking, in fact, that the world's greatest scholar in morphology of religion today, Mircea Eliade, invited Bavinck to the University of Chicago to lecture to his students. Bavinck's *Introduction* will continue to be important for its theological principles of missions even though the picture it gives of missionary work in many respects derives from an earlier period and therefore must be supplemented by the work of later scholars.

While a professor Bavinck paid several visits to South Africa. His last visit was in January, 1964 to offer a course for teachers in Bantu theological schools. As I see it, Bavinck did two important things in South Africa: he inspired the Calvinist churches to greater missionary effort among the black Africans, and by his word and example he gently pricked many consciences into seeing the injustice of the "small" and "great" apartheid policy between the races. Perhaps both are needed to combat apartheid in South Africa. At any rate, Bavinck's priestly ability to identify with the feelings of whites and blacks alike led many to closer introspection.

Bavinck's years at Kampen and the Free University placed hundreds of theologians in his debt. His lectures, his informal conversations, and his inspiring example enriched them. A Brazilian student who was studying with Bavinck when the professor had already become extremely fatigued and worn out told me one time, "He doesn't have to say much; just to see him once in a while is for me a fount of inspiration!" Bavinck spoke by his life, his words, and his deeds. And when his power to speak was gone, his life still spoke.

His Departure

A serious kidney ailment had been sapping Bavinck's strength for a long time. Bavinck's second wife, F. van der Vegt, whom he married in 1956, stood by him during this severe time about which few knew.

Bavinck worked while it was yet day and even ventured a trip to South Africa in 1964 as we noted above. Finally his bodily strength gave way and hospitalization became necessary. The kidney problem clouded his spirit. When he was coherent, he spoke with a love which drives out all fear of death; he told what Jesus meant to him in life and death. At times, while teetering on the edge of unconsciousness, he recalled incidents from the past. Those at his bedside heard him once address some former students in Javanese; at other times he spoke English to black teachers!

As death approached he was conscious and bade farewell, one by one, to the members of his family. Then he bowed his head and died. He died as he lived: a transparent witness of the Light who is eternal.

Hendrik Kraemer (1888–1965)

Childhood Years

Kraemer's ancestors came from Westphalia to Amsterdam after the war of 1870. Kraemer was born in one of the slum quarters of Amsterdam in 1888. He often retold his mother's story about the bullet that flew through his cradle during the "eel-fracas."

Kraemer's father died when he was six, and his mother, who worked to support the family, died two years later. The orphaned Kraemer was placed in a family that strongly identified with the socialist movement's pioneers, Domela Nieuwenhuis and P. J. Troelstra. Kraemer's exposure to this movement is indirectly responsible for his lifelong burning interest in political and social issues. To his dying day he was a follower of the Christian Socialists. Later he was cared for by a family with church contacts. When he was thirteen, he was placed in a Reformed (Hervormd) church orphanage.

Conversion

In Kraemer's own words, at age fifteen he experienced a conversion that set the course for the rest of his life. He discovered the Bible as the word of the living God. The very Bible which had been read in the cold, hard, routine style of an orphanage supervisor had now become the means through which he met the Lord Jesus Christ. He was the living Lord and the only rightful owner of people's lives, as Kraemer was so fond of saying. Through this Lord he was born again, Kraemer said of himself, borrowing a vintage biblical term. He received a different vision about God, himself, and human beings. Many times he said that no biblical book had as profound an impact upon him during his youth as did the Acts of the Apostles. He was deeply convinced of the need to carry on the acts of Christ in this world, and he wanted to participate. Impressed by encounters with specific missionaries and with specific missionary publications, he was seized with the desire to enter missionary service.

Meanwhile, the first school of missions in the Netherlands had been established in Rotterdam. At first he was turned down, but somewhat later he passed his entrance exams with honors and was admitted. His phenomenal aptitude had finally come to light.

His meeting with the great leader of the International Missionary Council, Dr. J. H. Oldham, stands out during Kraemer's years at the Rotterdam school. Chosen for his mastery of foreign languages to give Oldham a tour of the Nether-

lands, Kraemer got a fresh vision of world mission from Oldham. It is striking how
often such contacts have played important roles in the lives of missionaries.

Young Kraemer was chosen to continue his studies at the university level.
He went to the University of Leiden, which was famous for its oriental department, and spent ten years studying Eastern philology and cultural history (1911–
1921). The Netherlands Bible Society supported him during this time, for it
wanted to send him out later as its language expert. Kraemer studied under the
Islamics scholar, Professor Snouck Hurgronje. The professor had great respect
for his student's abilities, but he always felt that Kraemer divided his attention too
much to become and remain a pure scholar in one area. Snouck Hurgronje was an
agnostic, and I can still recall Kraemer simply yet profoundly telling him the good
news as the professor approached the end of his life. In 1921, Kraemer concluded
his studies with this famous Islamics scholar by writing his dissertation, *Een
Javaanse Primbon uit de 16e Eeuw*. Kraemer did something in his dissertation
which had never been tried before; he tried to bring some order and organization
into the confusing array of Javanese Muslim mysticism. It was a stepping-stone
for later similar studies and is still being consulted today.

Kraemer, the Dutch Student Christian Movement, and the World Federation of Christian Students

During many of his student years Kraemer was chairman of the Dutch Student
Christian Movement. Both during and after the First World War the movement
played a highly important role in Dutch student life and had close affiliation with
the World Federation of Christian Students headed by Dr. John Mott. Kraemer
had close ties with Mott and became greatly indebted to him. With Kraemer at the
head, the members of the movement acted as shock troops for the kingdom of God
in the university world. The moral and spiritual influence of the movement has
been mighty.

As often happens to students of culture and religion, Kraemer passed
through a period of deep spiritual crisis. The skepticism and relativism which had
withered so suddenly in his youth revived to threaten his faith. It was his meeting
with the missionary-linguist, Dr. N. Adriani, he often recalled, which brought him
through the crisis. Kraemer subsequently wrote a book about Adriani, who
worked for the Netherlands Bible Society in the Posso region of the Celebes in
Indonesia. Adriani was the spiritual father of the Toradja church. Kraemer related
his problems with the gnawing skepticism to Adriani; Adriani, in turn, simply
confronted Kraemer with the crucified and risen Lord and urged him to give total
allegiance to this Lord and his unique and absolute message. From then on
Kraemer's loyalty grew considerably.

Kraemer on the Threshold of Active Service

As his study period was coming to a close, Kraemer increasingly thought about his
future work and discussed it with the man who was then chairman of the Netherlands Bible Society, Professor P. D. Chantepie de la Saussaye. In the professor's
judgment, the times and situation of the Dutch-Indonesian churches demanded
more than mere linguistic expertise; the churches needed an advisor to guide them
through the stages leading to complete independence. Today we would call such

work *implantatio ecclesiae.* Chantepie de la Saussaye ended his talk with Kraemer by issuing him a challenge: "Kraemer, you must be the man." And Kraemer did become that man.

During this time Kraemer married Hyke van Gameren. How they met is so striking that it bears telling. As editor of the Liberal Student Union newspaper she had written an article describing her postwar feeling that nothing was stable any more. There was nothing to which a person could cling. In his reply in the newspaper of the Dutch Student Christian Movement, Kraemer criticized her "groundless subjectivism." The publicity generated by these articles led to a personal discussion, and the discussion in turn led to marriage. It was not an easy marriage, but a blessed one nonetheless; each gave the other a great measure of support. When Kraemer pressed his physical and psychical powers to their very limits, she stood by him with her support. Kraemer worked too hard for a while during his student days, and he paid for this for the rest of his life by being plagued with long bouts of total insomnia. His wife understood the torment and often revived him by her patient love. On the other hand, he supported her as she passed through frequent periods of deep psychological crisis when she required all his attention. Standing at Kraemer's grave, Arend van Leeuwen once said that in human marriage there is something that transcends the marriage itself. I agree with him and believe that their marriage had a specific role to play in God's plan for them.

Kraemer as a Friend

Kraemer had the gift of being a deep and faithful friend to both men and women alike. Owning and working in a cheerless old printing shop in Solo, Middle Java, was a young Chinese fellow with only an elementary education. Kraemer was struck by his outstanding abilities and personally took it upon himself to contact the University of Leiden to learn its entrance requirements. For a whole year Kraemer tutored the young man so he could pass the tests and enter the university. He was subsequently admitted and became the first oriental professor who graduated from Leiden. His name was Dr. Tjan Tju Som, a professor in Indonesia until he died in 1970.

I recall, too, his deep friendship with Suzanne de Diétrich, who with him directed the Ecumenical Institute in Bossey. He was deeply grateful for her extraordinary contribution to the institute's development, and they were closely knit in their work. The same story of Kraemer's friendship with various men and women could be repeated hundreds of times.

Kraemer in Indonesia

Kraemer worked in Indonesia from 1922 to 1928 and from 1930 to 1935 and in a few brief intermittent stints later. Kraemer knew Islam well and wrote several books on it: his dissertation; his little book, *Het Raadsel van de Islam* ("The Puzzle of Islam"); and his book written in Indonesian, *Agama (Islam)*. Even in the last months of his life he was busily writing down his final thoughts and insights about Islam in a summary book. Kraemer did this in other areas of his interest too, but he did not live to complete his book on Islam. He had become too weak.

Kraemer's knowledge of Islam and the Islamic fellowship is of course legendary, but what was even more striking was his appeal for Christians not to avoid contacts with Muslims but to seek such contacts and to do missionary work among these people. During his whole active life Kraemer did just that, maintaining many contacts with both simple and highly learned Muslims alike. He began his active service with an intense and packed visit to Cairo, and he never let up. In fact, one year before he died he visited Lebanon to keep up his strong involvement with the Muslim world. He left an example for many of his students to follow. Then too there is Kraemer's work as a linguist. And though it is not possible at this point to go into details about Kraemer's linguistic work for the Netherlands Bible Society in Indonesia, I do want to mention several facets.

First of all, Kraemer realized more clearly than anyone else that the Malesian language would become the lingua franca of an independent Indonesia or a "bahasa Indonesia," as it is presently called. While the Netherlands Bible Society was devoting its major attention to the various regional languages, Kraemer was chiefly interested in producing a fresh translation of the Malesian Bible. Along with the German scholar, Rev. Bode, and Mrs. Bode, Kraemer completed this pioneer effort which later became the foundation for the new Indonesian Bible which is now complete and was made under Indonesian directors.

Second, Kraemer emphasized the need for providing reading material which was relevant to the modern issues facing Indonesia. Although he restricted himself far too much to the subject of planning, this does not detract from the fact that he saw the need and thus made it possible for others to carry out the work and thus fulfill the need.

Another feature of Kraemer's work in Indonesia was his assistance in the churches' drive for independence. Kraemer's studies and advice played an extraordinary role. A summary of his studies which have since become classics can be found in the collection of essays entitled *From Mission-field to Independent Church* (1958).[7] They concern the Moluccan church, Minahassa church, Batak church, and the churches of East and West Java. Kraemer never despised the imperial church or its leaders, but with his patient and hopeful love he encouraged and inspired them to bend and renew the structures of the church. I shall try to state Kraemer's principles regarding the churches' drive for independence as succinctly as possible.

(1) The church must ever anew be redeemed from her Babylonian captivity. It could be a captivity to colonial authorities, as for example in the regions of Ambon and Minahassa. It could also be a captivity to myths and customs or to ideologies and the religious powers.

(2) Let the church be the church of Jesus Christ, living in total dependence on him and his law and gospel rather than on any other power.

(3) Let the church be no potted plant artificially set in a foreign environment; let her rather grow naturally by wrestling with her surroundings. In this connection, Kraemer continually wrestled with the problem of syncretism and urged what he later called a confrontation with the environment surrounding the church.

7. Hendrik Kraemer, *From Mission-field to Independent Church: Report on a Decisive Decade in the Growth of Indigenous Churches in Indonesia* (The Hague: Boekencentrum, 1958).

(4) Let the obedience which flows from faith cover one's whole life, and let the church so train its members that they live Christianly in all areas of their lives.

(5) Local congregations and regional churches must learn to live in ecumenical alliance with the whole people of God on earth. Dr. Visser 't Hooft strikingly summarized it as "an uncompromising, Christo-centric theology combined with a patient and loving concern for the life of the people who hear the Gospel." This dialectical tension is an apt summary of Kraemer's church-building efforts.

A fourth feature of Kraemer's Indonesian efforts was his work in preparing the Indonesian churches for their mission to a new Indonesia. His work with Dr. Barend Schuurman in founding the theological school in East Java was an attempt, not wholly successful, to develop a *theologia in loco*. Kraemer also established a secondary theological school in Djakarta which in 1953 became a full-fledged theological college. It represented the first attempt to bring theological education to the rising level of training intellectuals. This theological college has always worked and continues to work at a *theologia in loco* as well as at an ecumenical awareness.

Kraemer developed cooperative ventures among churches in many other regions. Along with other Indonesian ecclesiastical representatives he even made an initial try at forming a Council of Churches and Missions. It did not succeed then, but after the Second World War the churches did succeed, without the intervening help of the missions.

An exciting phase of Kraemer's Indonesian activity is summarized in the title of one of his books published in 1933: *De Strijd over Bali en de Zending* ("The Struggle over Bali and the Mission"). The conflict with the government, the subsequent settlement with the resident Jansen, the founding of the Bali church by tying in the East Java churches, and the conflict with the culture specialists Goris, Bosch, and Stutterheim could fill a book. But Kraemer's views can be summarized in two brief points: the church's call to mission is universal, and Bali is gradually coming to feel the influence of Western civilization. Hence, to fail to proclaim the gospel to Bali would be a denial of love.

Kraemer's interest was in no way restricted to the church and its efforts to become independent. He was fully involved in the struggle for national self-expression in Asia. He held a distinguished position amid the tensions developing between the Western imperialist faction and those who sought for Asian national self-expression.

Kraemer's Position during the Time between the Two World Wars
After his thorough preparation in philology and cultural history at Leiden University, Kraemer was ready to be sent out by the Netherlands Bible Society to the Orient to serve as its linguist and to become advisor for churches and mission in Indonesia. He worked there primarily from 1922 to 1935. But he also traveled to many other Asiatic countries during those years. These were not merely casual stopovers; he tried to come to grips with the vital issues in each of the places he visited: Egypt, India, Ceylon, China, Japan, Singapore, Hongkong, and Lebanon.

Anyone who follows his career closely during this time immediately becomes impressed with Kraemer's vital and loving concern for what was living and growing in the Asiatic world. His beautiful and incisive surveys in the missionary periodical *De Opwekker*, which he wrote to describe the religious, cultural, and national shifts taking place in India and Indonesia during those years, attest to Kraemer's unbiased openness and interest. For that day his attitude was something completely new. He stood in the very center of the stormy tensions between colonialism and the drive toward national self-expression, and every page that he wrote, every talk that he held, and every public deed that he did give testimony not only to his interest but also to his ardent desire for this drive to end in complete national self-expression. Kraemer was a man who struggled and worked with the peoples of Asia in their attempt to achieve a normal status and determine their own destiny rather than consign it to the colonial authorities. The best description of his position was the criterion he set for it himself: prophetic criticism and priestly service.

Charged with prophetic courage and honesty Kraemer time and again exposed the underlying motives of imperialism, namely, the urge to use other peoples for the sake of the great colonial powers. With prophetic clairvoyance he saw the day coming when the Asiatic peoples would recover their ability to choose for themselves.

Kraemer also assumed the role of the serving priest. He assisted in the push for national self-expression, not only through his help to Indonesian churches becoming independent, but also in offering priestly service for what the colonial government was doing to help the native population. He always said that the West, too, was bothered by a nettling thing in the whole issue of colonialism: it had a Christian conscience which called for service to others and thus was working from within to refute colonialism. Wherever he saw this conscience coming to the surface, he did his best to keep it vibrant and alive.

In those days Kraemer's prophetically critical posture was uncommon. Missionaries did not yet possess it, for in that era they were largely inspired by a pietistic vision of their work. Kraemer not only set the pace by his personal example, but he also did much to nourish the churches and missions. His 1929 lecture entitled *De houding van zending en Christendom in Indië* ("The Relationship of Mission to Christendom in India") is a worthy example of his chastising and nourishing efforts.

Kraemer's testimony gained such wide attention that he finally was in a position where he could forthrightly speak to political and governmental authorities. A striking example is his review of De Kat Angelino's three-part book *Staatkundig Beleid en Bestuurszorg in Nederlands Indië* ("Political Leadership and Administrative Care in Dutch India"). Kraemer devoted two numbers (three and four) in his series of *Koloniale Studiën* ("Colonial Studies") to a thorough review of this book.

De Kat Angelino sang the praises of paternalistic, ethical, and colonial politics. Kraemer hit the bull's-eye with his charge that De Kat Angelino and his allies displayed no real understanding for the power and the right of nationalism. I cite but one passage from his critique:

> De Kat Angelino apparently can't stand it that the Orientals view the
> colonial governors as anything other than noble supporters and unspotted

stimulators of native power. As he sees it, there is only one serious possibility. The administration has the synthesis movement completely in hand. Only it can and may act. Whoever does not work within its harness has forsaken his obligations. He is sterile. But, by Jove, is Gandhi at this moment living in vain?

Gandhi is living proof that in the long run a people can better provide its own redemption than the most well-intentioned colonial government, even though this people does not have an organization as good as the colonial one. Seriously, the well-willed striving of another never measures up to a really aroused creative force. Take careful note: the growing pride and the dominant, constructive work of several nationalistic groups can do much more to bring about a genuine synthesis than all the pseudo-syntheses of the so-called cooperators. I say this in spite of the antithetical aspects which these nationalistic groups display and however much or little they are given to cooperating with the European powers. . . .

Rarely during the colonial period was the actual issue stated so pointedly. Time and again Kraemer pounded on the issue of clarity, and for him clarity meant that the colonial authority, without beating around the bush, steadfastly adhere to the avowed goal of independence. This meant too that the colonial power must give elbow room to those forces and people who eventually would sit in positions of responsibility after independence had come.

Interest in Kraemer's ideas spread beyond Indonesia. It comes as no surprise to note that in 1935 Kraemer was invited to address the first International Student Missionary Conference on the topic *Mission between Imperialism and National Self-Expression.* I, along with many young people from Asia, had the opportunity to attend this conference.

Kraemer's topic was as thorny as it was urgent. But the lines he drew in that lecture left a deep impact on both sides and gave each a much greater sense of direction. Do not think that Kraemer's views made him popular; they did not. Instead his prophetic criticism and his priestly bearing rendered him suspect on both sides. He simply went his own way, however, facing every good and evil rumor free and unafraid like one who knows himself called to be a servant of his Lord.

Kraemer's Position after the Second World War

Both during and after the Second World War it gradually began to appear that the fullness of times which Kraemer had mentioned in 1931 had arrived for the peoples of Asia. Kraemer made a journey to Indonesia with a specific mission in mind. The thunder of the conflicts was shocking everyone in those days, and the unclear policies of the Dutch government had become well-nigh unbearable for all concerned. By fulfilling this mission Kraemer made an important contribution to soothing the tensions and preparing for a transfer of sovereignty.

Perhaps the question arises how Kraemer assessed what the new Asiatic and African nations have done with the freedom they seized. Many of the erstwhile progressives have now become cynics since freedom did not take the course they had desired. Kraemer never degenerated into a cynic as he viewed the history of these young states. He never had any romantic illusions about human nature and how human beings conduct themselves collectively. Nor did he ever idealize nationalism, for he knew that it could be seized and gobbled up by human egoism and the types of self-eroticism displayed by men like Sukarno and Nkrumah. He knew the ever-present danger of self-intoxification, of exploitation, and of self-glorification. On the other hand, he was not a defeatist. He simply persevered in his prophetic and priestly posture as always. Thus, his attitude to the very end of his life was open, critical, gentle, wise, honest, patient, and loving.

If I were asked to name those Dutchmen who best understood the nationalist drive for self-expression and whose service to the cause was the most pure, I would name three: the socialist D.M.G. Koch, the Jesuit father, van Lith, who was missionary to Muntila, and the missiologist Kraemer. Each in his own way and out of different convictions made his worthy contribution while facing both hostile opposition and admiring approval. Many on both sides were deeply suspicious of each of them, and yet each was also trusted, loved, and respected by those on either side who could feel the hunger and thirst for righteousness and a society of free and equal people.

A Few Brief Notes on the Final Phase of Kraemer's Life
(To save space I shall write these notes in telegram style.)

(1) Kraemer's role in international missions, the ecumenical movement, and missiology and the theology of religions. Kraemer, along with Karl Heim and Karl Hartenstein, was present at the Jerusalem conference of 1928. Joined with Heim and Hartenstein to oppose the tendency to relativize missiology. Against the value-theory of missions. John Mott discovers Kraemer. Kraemer mandated to write a study book in preparation for the next IMC conference. Result: in 1937 Kraemer finished his renowned book, *The Christian Message in a Non-Christian World*, published in 1938.

Some of the book's seminal ideas:
   (a) Emphasized the unique character of the Bible's message. Biblical realism. Bible characterized as "the recitative of God's saving acts in Jesus Christ."
   (b) The relationship between God's revelation in creation and through Jesus Christ. The problem of continuity-discontinuity.
   (c) The young churches in their sociological and religious context.

Kraemer gave the biblical theology of religions and a theology for church-building in this book.

Kraemer at the Tambaram conference in 1938. Much opposition.

Contact and friendship begun with Dr. D. T. Niles and Bishop Kulandran. Another trip to India and Ceylon.

Kraemer's later writings. *Religion and the Christian Faith* (1956) — an elaboration of his theology of religion, an important declaration of Kraemer's views on general and special revelation, also contains Kraemer's analysis and critique of Tillich's theology as well as his struggle with syncretism. His great book, *World Cultures and World Religions, the Coming Dialogue,* published 1960. The book is a veritable storage containing the harvest of years of research and study. For basic information about the religions, extremely valuable. But our study of how religions and cultures develop must continue; the situation is ever changing. Book still structured along the lines of East-West relationships; thus is somewhat dated; we must now study the worldwide church in a secular setting and the worldwide character of religions.

(2) Kraemer's homefront activity. His outstanding informational work among those at home-base, such as his little books *Waarom Zending Juist Nu?* ("Why Missions Now?"); *De huidige stand van het christendom in Ned. Indie* ("Christianity's Present Status in Dutch India"); and *Ontmoeting van het christendom an de wereldgodsdiensten* ("Christianity's Confrontation with the World Religions").

His work in reviving mission organizations, his influence on the Dutch Reformed church (*Hervormd*) to de-emphasize the ecclesiastical character of its mission. His work to renew the educational aspect of missions. His proposals to dissolve the Missionary Study Council and to alter the design of the Netherlands Missionary Council.

(3) Professor at Leiden University from December 3, 1937 until the outbreak of the Second World War. Inaugural speech on syncretism. Kraemer a nontheologian in a theological faculty.

Kraemer's posture toward theologians and theology. Worked continually as layman among theologians. Always reminded theologians of the danger of failing to accompany words with deeds in proclaiming the gospel. The danger of merely declaiming the truth rather than revealing it.

Post of professor at Leiden of short duration. Leiden University the first university closed by German authorities because of the University Senate's opposition to the firing of Jewish professor Meyers.

His work of church-building in Netherlands done jointly with Rev. Gravemeyer and Professor Banning.

Following the war, participation in building up Dutch ecclesiastical and political life.

(4) Kraemer, the leader of the Ecumenical Institute in Bossey, Switzerland, 1948–1957. Communication of the Christian faith in the world of journalists, politicians, artists, philosophers, etc.

(5) Eve of his life in Driebergen, Netherlands, filled with writing, teaching and advising. Interrupted by travel to Hongkong, Indonesia, Japan, and America.

The approaching end: gravely bothered when writing was no longer possible; conversation and interest remained clear, fresh, and up-to-date to the very end.

I now add a few comments about Kraemer the human being to show that he was a missionary through and through.

Kraemer the Human Being

Kraemer's body was very weak physically; psychologically, he lived amid tremendous tensions. He struggled his whole life with vexatious periods of insomnia. The famed Christian psychiatrist from Switzerland, Dr. Maeder, taught him how to cope with this problem. During the time when he was being helped by Maeder, Kraemer wrote a book about the doctor himself which includes essays by Maeder. Kraemer is probably one of the first to underscore the importance of psychoanalysis and psychotherapy as useful tools in caring for man's psyche. It is remarkable that a man who physically and psychically was so fragile could nonetheless achieve so much through God's strength.

As regards Kraemer's character, Van Leeuwen describes it as a combination of phlegmatic and choleric. Perhaps one might better say it was patience and deep love that typified Kraemer, although at times he could give vent to that slowly brewing holy indignation within him. His words, which usually flowed calmly and clearly from his lips, could at other times be as sharp as a two-edged sword, especially when he witnessed a lack of truth or of ecumenical inclination coming through.

The secret of Kraemer's remarkable life lay in four features:

Loyalty to his Lord. I can remember the time when Kraemer told of how he was simply overwhelmed at one point in his life by the gracious Lordship of Jesus Christ. He was always quick to add that those moments had taught him always to be completely loyal to his Lord, and the loyalty of which he spoke was evident not only in his daily life, but also in his life of prayer. To hear him pray reminded one of the Waldensian prayer: "Ton serviteur, mon Dieu." Or perhaps he was echoing Isaiah: "Here am I, Lord, send me." He was always urging young people to continually give themselves in obedience to the only lawful ruler of human life, Jesus Christ.

Total service. His whole life with all of its talents he offered in service to his Lord. Without exception every gift he had received he gave back in service to his Lord and his fellowman. Nowadays the key word used to describe the Christian lifestyle is *disponsibilité*, that is, availability for service. Such a term is a fitting description of Kraemer, whose formidable knowledge and vast insights he shared unreservedly with others.

Deep humility and strong sense of call. Every time I read the Pauline letters or the story of Luther and Calvin's lives I am again struck by the deep humility and strong sense of call that each had. Kraemer, too, had both of these in combination; his life and work gave ample evidence.

Work for his Lord on the frontier of church and world. Impelled by his sense of call and clothed with humility, Kraemer became a man sent to the very borders of church and world. His acute awareness of being sent can be observed from two features of his life and work.

First, Kraemer was not a reclusive scholar, nor was he merely a man of practice. He was both scholarly and practical and related his study to his work. At times he would suddenly disappear into his study to try to crack open a tough problem. But he did not stay there; he would re-enter the church and society in which he lived and worked and take steps to implement his new insights.

Second, his sense of being sent showed itself in his patience with and fidelity to the empirical church. Unlike many others, Kraemer never despised the empirical church, but rather completely gave himself to her to the very end of his life. He never wanted to walk separately on the path which leads to the kingdom of God.

Kraemer's Place in the Missio Ecclesiae

Kraemer was a missionary statesman and strategist, a builder of genuine ecumenical spirit, and a prophet and doer of the Word.

He can and must serve as an example for us all in how he joined word to deed, in how his missiological insights took concrete form in his actions, and in his ecumenical vision and conduct. Kraemer termed this unity between theory and practice a "theology of obedience." He used the phrase, not to deny other phrases such as "theology of grace" or "theology of glory," but rather to underscore the fact that he who claims to live by God's grace and for his glory must show it in obedience. Hendrik Kraemer, a servant of God, showed each of us what such obedience really means by his life, his words, and his deeds.

J. C. Hoekendijk

Concluding our servey of Dutch missiologists, we wish to take note of the dissertation of J. C. Hoekendijk. While Hoekendijk, who was born in Garut, Indonesia, was serving as secretary of the Netherlands Missionary Council, he wrote a famous dissertation, *Kerk en Volk in de Duitse Zendingswetenschap*. Hoekendijk's dissertation had a profound impact upon German missiology as it went through the process of reorientation after the Second World War. Hoekendijk's influence was especially strong on men like Freytag and Hartenstein. He received his doctoral degree from the University of Utrecht in 1948. In 1952 Hoekendijk was appointed professor at Utrecht and from 1965 to 1975 he taught missiology and ecumenics at Union Theological Seminary in New York. He passed away suddenly in 1975.

In his dissertation Hoekendijk radically tested against the biblical norms the *Volkstumideologie*, which has been so prominent in German missiology from Gustav Warneck to Christian Keysser. He clearly showed how romanticism and neo-romanticism had infected the German view of missions, how these had grown into a full-fledged *Volksideologie*, and how all of this had been given a biblical window-dressing by a misunderstanding and misapplication of the biblical concept of *Volk*. He measured the tension between the gospel and the *Volksideologie* in the writings of a whole series of missiologists. His study clearly shows that while some missiologists firmly withstood the tendency to relax the tension, others like Gutmann and Keysser allowed the gospel to be completely swept along and swallowed up by the *Volkstumideologie*.

Hoekendijk concluded his dissertation by giving a compact outline of his own missiology. He began by discussing the biblical context of missions, claiming that the work of missions is a direct implication of the doctrine of eschatology. The work of missions is apocalyptic, apostolic, and directly connected with the events of salvation history. He followed this with a study of the biblical meaning of the phrase "people of God" and clearly distinguished this vintage biblical phrase from any notion of *Volksideologie*. "This people of God has no analogy. It is a sociological impossibility. It is the 'third generation' in which peoples whose natural bent and customs are so divergent yet become bound together in a unity of disposition and manner of living."

Hoekendijk completely repudiated the idea of organizing a congregation along the lines of some *Volkstum* notion. He wanted the congregation to take shape in the *oikos*, that is, in the ecological milieu which is fashioned and structured by the people and places which make it up. He principally rejected any idea of a church which is based on *Volk* or, as it is sometimes called in Dutch literature, a *taalkerk* (a church whose language is its chief identity). "Paul thought in terms of provinces," said Hoekendijk. That is to say, Paul always reckoned with the concrete societal structures as he found them.

Finally, Hoekendijk deemed it both impossible and irresponsible to hermetically seal off the various local cultures from the "great society." Rather than seal them off we must prepare the peoples of Asia, Africa, and Latin America for participation in the "great society."

This can only happen if one sees the need for a *comprehensive approach*. Congregations must begin to function as centers of social integration and as much as possible must involve themselves in every aspect of society simultaneously. Hoekendijk pleaded for an approach that was both comprehensive and simultaneous. The various services required to carry out this task were not merely ancillary, in his judgment. Each was a full-fledged and equal component of the total program.

ENGLISH MISSIOLOGY

One of the noteworthy features of Anglo-Saxon missiology is that it is rarely a mere academic enterprise; in the United Kingdom missiology usually flows out of the direct concerns of missionary practice and/or missionary administration. A telling example is Henry Venn.

Henry Venn (1796–1873)

Henry Venn never worked in Asia or Africa; in fact, he never even visited there. In spite of this, he was secretary of the renowned Church Missionary Society for 32 years and through this had a mighty effect on missionary thinking and administration in the nineteenth century.

Venn was born on February 10, 1796 in Clapham. He studied at Cambridge and while there struck up a friendship with William Wilberforce. In 1821 he became an Anglican priest and served under the bishop of Norwick. In the following year he became a member of the board of the Church Missionary Society and was appointed as its secretary in 1841. In this capacity he served as editor of the *Christian Observer*. He resigned his secretarial post in 1872 and died on January 13, 1873.

The only biography of Venn is *Memoir*, written by William Knight and first published in 1880. Dr. John Taylor is at work on a new biography in which he hopes to show Venn's important contributions to missiology. Venn's name is usually mentioned in the same breath with his American colleague and contemporary, Rufus Anderson, who served as secretary of the American Board of Commissioners for Foreign Missions while Venn was secretary of the English society. In many respects their ideas are remarkably similar, though Venn's thoughts bear a definite episcopal stamp and Anderson's reflect his congregational background. Max Warren published a selection of Venn's essays and letters in his book *To Apply the Gospel*.[8]

Venn's chief contribution stems from his vision of how young churches become independent. Both he and Rufus Anderson coined the famous phrase

8. Max Warren, ed., *To Apply the Gospel: A Selection from the Writings of Henry Venn* (Grand Rapids: Eerdmans, 1971).

which has now become much misused and heavily criticized: "the three-self formula." The phrase means that the chief goal of Western missions must be to build churches which are self-supporting, self-governing and self-propagating. In this connection, we refer the reader to the chapter on the goal of mission. One can really see how the colonial policies of the British empire were strongly influenced in those years by what was called "ethical politics."

A knowledge of Venn is also important for a good understanding of the ecclesiastical and political developments in West Africa in the nineteenth century. Prof. J. A. Ajayi of the Nigerian Ibadan University explicitly stated this in his book *Christian Missions in Nigeria 1841–1881*, published in 1965.

Without question Venn ranks high among the great nineteenth-century missionary strategists, but he was also one of the most clairvoyant. His special interests were the purpose of mission, the special calling of the missionary, and the special function of the missionary society. Although the Church Missionary Society has always worked within the framework of the Church of England, the society's leaders have always adamantly maintained that its role is primarily substitutionary; the work of the society represents the call which comes to the whole church to engage in missions. Even today, though the church has largely taken over and replaced the mission work of the societies, the notion of societies acting as substitutes for and representatives of the churches shines forth in the vision of the present-day Church Missionary Society missiologists, Dr. Max Warren and Dr. John Taylor. The idea appears in refined form, of course, but it is there nonetheless.

Roland Allen (1868–1947)

An English missiologist whose writing draws constant attention is Roland Allen. He was an Anglican missionary to China sent out by the Society for the Propagation of the Gospel. He went through the Boxer Rebellion and saw his mission post become completely devastated. This rebellion and the subsequent tension it caused, the deep resistance to foreigners, and the Chinese belief that Christianity was foreign led Allen to question the policy which the society and virtually all other boards had employed up to that point, namely, the setting up of mission stations. He underwent a revolution in his thinking, and in his stimulating book, *Missionary Methods: St. Paul's or Ours?*, published in 1912, he called for a fresh approach. Like Paul, who from the very beginning endowed the earliest Christians with spiritual authority so that the building up of the churches became *their* responsibility and calling, Allen pleaded for a casting off of paternalism and ecclesiastical colonialism. He wanted the churches to be built up by the new Christians themselves who were led by the Holy Spirit. Allen never tired of reiterating that the nineteenth-century methods lacked the elements of spontaneity and simplicity. He called for a return to following once again in the footsteps of Paul. See, for example, his book *The Spontaneous Expansion of the Church and the Causes Which Hinder It* (1927). Allen claimed that mission posts only serve to underscore the foreign character of the gospel. We must do everything in our power to make the churches "indigenous." He found little response to his appeal from the society itself, but the progressive World Dominion Press was willing to publish his books. Today they are known throughout the whole of the missionary world.

After ten years in China and five years of service in England, Allen became a "voluntary clergyman." In that capacity he traveled to India, Rhodesia, East Africa, South Africa, Canada, and other places to test his ideas and to deepen his practical experience. He died in Kenya in 1947.

Allen was a man ahead of his times. His ideas met with great opposition and resistance. His views on the need for native churches to be independent, his call for ecumenical cooperation, and his appeal for responsible lay participation in building up the churches bespeak his deep insight and prophetic courage in going against the paternalism of his day.

For thirty long years Allen pleaded with the authorities to give the native churches a chance to stand on their own feet. He did not mean simply allowing them to be boss in their own house, so to speak; rather, he was calling for a respect for congregations who have received the gift of the Holy Spirit and who are aware of what it means to be led by the Spirit.

In 1960 the World Dominion Press of London published a representative selection of Allen's most famous writings under the descriptive title *The Ministry of the Spirit*. The book was edited by D. M. Paton.

Allen's writing stimulated many others. Later missionary figures like Dr. Hendrik Kraemer (as he began his work in Bali), Dr. Harry Boer in Nigeria, Donald McGavran, and others willingly attest that Allen's ideas influenced their methods. Not, of course, that they dutifully followed everything that he said, for the questions of what Paul's methods were and how we must follow them today are more involved and complex than Allen pictured them. He gave too little thought to the question of whether Paul's methods are applicable in every situation. Moreover, he underscored the independence of the young churches too heavily and the interdependence of all churches within the one body too lightly. The financial problems of the young churches are more weighty than Roland Allen imagined; they are more closely tied to world economic conditions than he realized. But that he was the guiding genius of many none can contest.

Dr. M. A. C. Warren

Max Warren was the son of an Irish missionary to Northern India. After finishing his theological education at Cambridge, Warren was sent to Nigeria by the Church Missionary Society. His stay was cut short by tuberculosis, and through this illness he lost one of his eyes. Although he is recovered, his physical condition since then has been rather unstable. Considering all this, his work output has bordered on the phenomenal.

In 1942 Warren was appointed secretary of the Church Missionary Society and thus had great opportunity for travel, study, and writing. He is one of the most widely traveled and experienced missiologists of the twentieth century. In 1963 he stepped down as secretary to become a canon in Westminster Abbey. Countless people the world over still seek his advice.

Warren's missiological publications are extensive. They clearly reflect his travel experience and the changing situations in the world and the church during the time he wrote.

At this point we shall cite only the most important of Warren's writings. His books *The Gospel of Victory* (1955), which discusses the book of Galatians, and *The Truth of Vision, a Study in the Nature of the Christian Hope* (1948), provide his view of the biblical foundation. Missions are placed in an eschatological perspective, and to accent the eschatological nature of the missionary enterprise he uses the key phrase "Expectant Evangelism." *The Christian Mission* (1955) and *The Christian Imperative* (1955) discuss the fulfillment of the missionary mandate. Three of his books contain a wealth of information on the subject of missions and their relationship to colonialism: *Caesar — the Beloved Enemy, Three Studies in the Relation of Church and State* (1955), and *Social History and Christian Mission* (1967). *Partnership, the Study of an Idea*, a treatment of the watchword of the Whitby conference, and *The Functions of a National Church* (1964) are both important studies of the relationship between Western churches and those in Asia and Africa. An imposing study of the English contribution to missionary work is *The Missionary Movement from Britain in Modern History* (1965). Dr. Warren's influence also spread through his famous *C.M.S. Newsletter*, a monthly, four-page letter compiled by him which is one of the richest sources of missionary information ever written. His successor, Dr. John Taylor, took over the *Newsletter* in 1975 and brings to it the same high and exacting standard for quality.

Max Warren belongs to the evangelical wing of the Anglican church. His genuine ecumenical spirituality and practical wisdom have contributed greatly to establishing and maintaining relations between Western churches and those in Asia, Africa, and Latin America. Postwar missiology is deeply indebted to this man who so closely joined theory and practice that it became second nature to him.

In 1974 Warren finished his autobiography with its arresting title, *Crowded Canvas*. It is a record of a life full of rich experiences and is as instructive as it is inspiring, for it contains a wide cross section of missionary activities.

Warren passed away on August 23, 1977, at the age of 73. His last two publications were a book entitled *I Believe in the Great Commission* (Eerdmans, 1977), which can be viewed as a last testament summing up his thinking and work and indeed his whole life as well as his hopes and desires for the mission of Christ's church; and an important essay, completed less than one month before his death, entitled "The Fusion of the IMC and WCC at New Delhi: Retrospective Thoughts After a Decade and a Half."[8a]

Stephen Charles Neill

One of the most productive of the English missiologists and a man who also doubles as church historian and expert in ecumenical affairs is Stephen Charles Neill. Here are several pertinent biographical details about Neill's life:

1924–1945: missionary to India
1939–1945: Angelican bishop of Tinnevelly and highly involved in the union movements which led to the founding of the Church of South India

8a. Translator's note: Warren's essay will appear in the Fall of 1978 as a chapter in a book honoring Professor Verkuyl upon the occasion of his retirement.

1949–1951: associate general secretary of the World Council of Churches who worked closely with Dr. W. A. Visser 't Hooft; subsequently worked with Miss Ruth Rouse on *A History of the Ecumenical Movement, 1517–1948*, first published in 1954; for the benefit of churches in developing countries he planned the series *World Christian Books*, short but important writings by theologians throughout the world which may be duplicated and translated without copyright and are designed to build up the body of theological literature

1962–1967: professor in Hamburg, a post vacated by the late Walter Freytag; also director of *World Christian Books* since 1962

Stephen Neill has written extensively in the area of history of missions and young churches as well as on the problems of world mission. Here is a brief sample of his publications: *The Unfinished Task* (1957), *Creative Tension* (1959), *Christian Faith and Other Faiths: The Christian Dialogue with Other Religions* (1961), *A History of Christian Missions* (1964), *Colonialism and Christian Missions* (1966), and *The Church and Christian Union* (1968).

Neill also worked as one of the editors of *A Concise Dictionary of the Christian World Mission*, published in 1970. The dictionary surveys all the missionary activity and the related issues of the last five centuries.

Lesslie Newbigin

Bishop Lesslie Newbigin is a Scottish missiologist who has the rare gift of being able to combine theoretical reflection with actual missionary practice. Born of Presbyterian parents, he worked for years among the young churches of India and was fully involved in the negotiations culminating in the founding of the Church of South India. Newbigin became one of the first bishops of the new church. In the interim period following his missionary service and preceding his assuming the office of bishop of the South India church, he spent some productive years as Director of the Division of World Mission and Evangelism of the World Council of Churches. In 1974 Lesslie Newbigin returned to England to take up a teaching post at Selly Oak Colleges.

Newbigin's writings bear the marks of a shepherd as well as of a theologian. *One Body, One Gospel, One World: The Christian Mission Today*, written in 1958 while Newbigin was the first director of the new Division of the World Council, is a thorough investigation of the goals of the Division. *The Relevance of the Trinitarian Doctrine for Today's Mission* (1963) reflects one of the chief ideas coming out of the Willingen conference, namely, the *missio Dei*. Newbigin accords this doctrine its full status; he speaks of the *missio Patris, Filii, et Spiritus Sancti*. A major portion of Newbigin's writing deals with ecclesiology and the building up of churches. See, for example, *The Household of God* (1954) and *The Reunion of the Church* (1948).

Newbigin threw himself into the "Honest-to-God Debate" which was unleashed after Bishop John Robinson wrote his famous book *Honest to God*. Newbigin's response to the so-called God-is-Dead movement is his little-known but nonetheless important book, *Honest Religion for Secular Man*, published in 1966.

A book which so clearly shows the relevant way Newbigin went about doing his theology and his meditation is his collection of addresses which he gave at a medical conference in India. The collection is entitled *Christ, Our Contemporary* (1968).

The Finality of Christ (1969) is Newbigin's exciting contribution offered in preparation for the Uppsala assembly of the World Council. He discusses the finality of Christ in an age which is asking questions about the universality of history.

John Foster

John Foster may not be omitted in this survey of English missiology. He is professor both at Selly Oak Colleges in Birmingham and also at the University of Glasgow. He views missiology as an integral part of the discipline of church history and wants it treated as such; furthermore, like Latourette before him, Foster sees church history as one indivisible whole and urges that it not be restricted to Europe and America. But in my judgment, his greatest contribution is his suggestion that to fully understand the situation in which the young churches live and work, it is helpful to compare them with the early church. Like Kraemer, he continually argues that a study of the early church will make one's teaching of Asian, African, and Latin American church history richer and more productive.

Foster's publications include *Then and Now, The Historic Church and the Younger Churches* (1944), *Chinese Realities: The Chinese Church in Action. The Church of the T'ang Dynasty* (1939), and *After the Apostles: Missionary Preaching of the First Three Centuries* (1951).

Foster taught people to think in terms of a "world church" and "world-churchmanship." See his book *World Church*, published in 1945.

R. K. Orchard

R. K. Orchard is an English missiologist who has made a great contribution in the area of administration as well as in the theoretical view of mission work. His influence has extended over many years and continues into the present. He began as secretary of the London Missionary Society, continued as one of the secretaries of the former International Missionary Council, and later worked for the World Council of Churches when the IMC became a branch of the World Council. He presently serves as General Secretary for the British Council of Foreign Missions of the British Council of Churches.

Orchard's writings are valuable because he is so fully involved in the practical affairs of mission work. His position as secretary puts him in daily touch with the actual work.

Part of Orchard's work at the Mexico City conference of the Division of World Mission and Evangelism held in 1963 was seeing the official reports through to publication. They appeared in 1964 and were entitled *Witness to Six Continents*. Many of the themes which came out of the Mexico City conference Orchard treated more fully in his famous book *Mission in a Time of Testing* (1964). In a day when the missionary enterprise is being radically tested, Orchard returns to the

Scriptures to discover anew the place of missions. He scans the radically changed geographic, cultural, and political context of missions today, pointing out such things as the dissolution of the *Corpus Christianum* and the basic changes in church-state relations which face young churches. He seeks to show how pluralistic societies arise.

One of the questions Orchard raises is the matter of continuing Christian schools and colleges in developing countries. He is skeptical of their continued usefulness and prefers that pupils and students be influenced through the secular governmental schools. As I see it, this is no either-or affair; we need both. Where possible, we ought to support Christian education, but we ought also to assist in the governmental education. But Orchard's arguments are well worth listening to. In chapter seven of his book he discusses the role of the Western missionary in the developing countries. He calls for an "order of missionaries" regulated by a "simple common rule" and serving the world over, mobile and available to go anywhere. He makes an impassioned plea for an ecumenical approach in helping young churches, and he actually organized the plan for bringing real help for actual projects in developing countries. The plan is called Joint Action for Mission and began after the Mexico City conference. Orchard compiled background information on the project and published it in many publications of the Division of the World Mission and Evangelism. In fact, Orchard is so fully involved in the present-day work of missions that we shall come across his name again in other chapters of this book.

John V. Taylor

Nor must we overlook the name of John V. Taylor in our survey, even though he is still in his very prime and many of his contributions have yet to be made. Taylor began his work with a period of missionary work and research in various parts of Africa and later succeeded Dr. Max Warren as secretary of the Church Missionary Society. In this post he serves as editor-in-chief of the renowned *CMS Newsletter*. He has several imposing studies to his credit.

One of the books in the "Christian Presence" series is Taylor's *Primal Vision*, a study of armchair religiosity in African religious systems. Along with the books by Tempels and Mbiti, it is one of the most impressive books on African religiosity. It is indispensable for intelligent participation in the current discussion about the value of this religiosity. He has also put the conclusions of two of his research projects into book form, both of which are model ecclesiastical and sociological investigations of the young churches: *The Growth of the Church in Buganda* (1958) and a book which he coauthored with Dorothea Lehmann, *Christians of the Copperbelt* (1961). One more of his publications deserves mention here, *For All the World: The Christian Mission in the Modern Age* (1966).

Dr. John Taylor is one of the most influential missiologists of our era, a person whose friendships the world over and close contact with the practical aspects of missions are a vital stimulus to advance the work. His relation to the evangelical tradition as well as his involvement in the ecumenical movement make him a bridge builder. A good example of his stature in ecumenics today is that he was chosen to compile the much-discussed report, *Renewal In Mission*.

In 1974 Taylor resigned his position as secretary for the Church Missionary Society.

SCANDINAVIAN MISSIOLOGY

The churches of Sweden, Norway, and Denmark have not only participated significantly in modern missionary work, but they have also produced a number of missiologists who made important contributions. Greatest among the Scandinavian contributions is undoubtedly the scholarship in the area of theology of religions and science of religions. Since they belong in those areas and not in the realm of missiology, I must restrict myself to mentioning in passing the names of men like Nathan Söderblom and Tor Andreae. In the present context I shall treat only those who significantly added to *missiology* in the strict sense of the term.

Bengt Sundkler

For years Bengt Sundkler worked in South Africa. He followed this by serving as Lutheran bishop in Bukoba, Tanzania, East Africa. At present he is professor of young churches and mission at the University of Uppsala. His contributions to missiology are rich and varied.

First, I would mention his work on the biblical foundation for missions. In 1936 he published an essay in the *Revue d'Histoire et de Philosophie religieuse*, "Jésus et les Païens."[9] The article was later reprinted in *Arbeiten und Mitteilungen aus dem neutestamentischen Seminar zu Uppsala* (no. VI, 1937). In it he skillfully traces the centripetal and centrifugal lines through the Old and New Testaments as they touch on the "paiens." He introduced the terms "centripetal" and "centrifugal" to do away with the notion of an apparent antithesis between particularism and universalism in the Old and New Testaments. Since then, other authors like J. Blauw in *The Missionary Nature of the Church* have borrowed Sundkler's terminology. Sundkler's article recently got new attention when Dr. David Bosch from Praetoria discussed it in his essay "Jesus and the Gentiles — a Review After Thirty Years." Bosch's essay was part of a festschrift for Bengt Sundkler published in 1969, *The Church Crossing the Frontiers*.

Second, Sundkler made a pioneer study of the independent church movement in Africa. Scholarly interest is presently growing by leaps and bounds, but Sundkler was busy when no scholar was paying these movements the slightest attention. His book *Bantu Prophets in South Africa* (1948) provided the impetus for others.

Sundkler's third contribution was his study of African ministry, *The Christian Ministry in Africa* (1960).

He also wrote a concise handbook for missiologists bearing the title *The World of Mission* (1965). He treats topics such as the biblical foundation for

9. Bengt Sundkler, "Jésus et les Païens," *Revue d'Histoire et de Philosophie religieuse* 16 (1936): 462–499.

missions, the relation between church and empire through the ages, and young churches in their socio-religious-historical milieu.

Sundkler's energetic involvement in both missionary practice and theory have earned him the attention of all who are engaged in the worldwide missionary enterprise.

Carl F. Hallencreutz

Hallencreutz, once a student of Bengt Sundkler, now serves as lecturer in missiology at Uppsala. His writings are models of clarity and pose stimulating questions. Hallencreutz wrote his doctoral dissertation in 1966 on the missionary approach of Hendrik Kraemer, *Kraemer towards Tambaram*. He wrote an outstanding summary of the post-Kraemer discussion on this topic in *Research Pamphlet No. 18*, published in 1970 under the auspices of the World Council of Churches. The title of the pamphlet is *New Approaches to Men of Other Faiths*.[10]

For the Uppsala assembly of the World Council Hallencreutz provided an exciting and informative survey of Swedish missionary history.

Hallencreutz's budding career has just gotten underway, but he is a man worth watching.

Olav Guttorm Myklebust

O. G. Myklebust is missiologist at the theological seminary in Oslo which trains preachers for the Lutheran state church but also for the "free churches." In addition, he serves as head of the renowned Egede Institute for Missionary Studies and was the first secretary of the International Association for Missiology.

Myklebust wrote a two-volume work entitled *The Study of Missions in Theological Education*. He published the first volume in Oslo in 1955 and the second in 1957. Myklebust is a leading expert in this field. His other publications include *An International Institute of Scientific Missionary Research*, written in 1951, an article in a festschrift for Walter Freytag, "Integration or Independence," and a summary of his missiological studies, *Misjonskunnskap* (Science of Mission), which appeared in Oslo in 1976.

Myklebust's ten-year stint as missionary in South Africa continues to provide him contact with numerous experienced missionaries.

Johannes Aagaard

I choose Johannes Aagaard as representative of the Danish missiologists. Aagaard teaches missiology at the University of Aarhus. The title of Aagaard's dissertation is *Mission, Konfession, Kirche: Die Problematik ihrer Integration im 19. Jahrhundert in Deutschland* (1967). Aagaard is centrally involved in the latest missiological trends. His ecumenical disposition and his willingness to listen to those who are asking deep social questions qualify him as one of today's leading Danish theologians.

10. Carl F. Hallencreutz, *New Approaches to Men of Other Faiths, 1936–1968: A Theological Discussion, Research Pamphlet No. 18* (Geneva: World Council of Churches, 1970).

SWISS MISSIOLOGY

Karl Barth (1884-1968)

Of course, when one mentions the name of Karl Barth in theological circles, everyone thinks immediately of systematic theology. However, Barth's *Church Dogmatics* (III:2 and IV:3 in particular) provides some insights which are of crucial importance to missiology. In these passages Barth discusses the *missio Dei* and refers to the church's call to be God's earthly witness as the *missio Dei continuata*. Barth develops his ideas about the church's call against the backdrop of the church's election, reconciliation, promise of the Spirit, call, mandate, and service. If the church fails her missionary obligations, she is no longer church. Like Christ, the church has been sent into the world not for her own welfare but for the world's.

Hans Schärer

One of the most exciting Swiss missiologists was Hans Schärer. Following his education at Basel, he went to Kalimantan, Borneo to work among the Ngadju-Dajak people in the delta region of the Katingan River. He labored there for seven years, from 1932 to 1939. Using material he had gathered during this time, he came to Leiden University to study cultural anthropology under Dr. Josselin de Jong from 1939 to 1944. He wrote a dissertation which later became famous: *Die Gottesidee der Ngadju-Dajak in Süd-Borneo*, a case study dealing with the classification systems for the archaic religions. It was published in Leiden in 1946.

During his stay in the Netherlands he also wrote two brochures: *Die Begründung der Mission in der Katholischen und Evangelischen Missionswissenschaft* (1944) and *Die missionarische Verkündigung auf dem Missionsfeld* (1946).

He returned to the Dajak church and died in 1947, the victim of blood poisoning.

Johannes Dürr

Johannes Dürr was a missionary to Java for several years and was appointed an adjunct professor at Bern University to teach missiology and related subjects. His dissertation, *Sendende und werdende Kirche in der Missionstheologie Gustav Warnecks*, was published in 1947. Recently he has devoted many articles in the *Evangelische Missions Magazin* to problems relating to missions, diaconal work, and development. An example is his article "Moderne Missionsprobleme" (1958); still another is his contribution to the symposium *Hilfe für technische unentwickelte Länder* (1959).

Werner Bieder

Werner Bieder, a native of Basel, taught at the university there until 1976. During his career he served intermittently as short-term teacher in Ghana and India. He occasionally presents guest lectures at the mission, but he presently serves as director of the Basel Mission itself and is involved in training missionary personnel.

Bieder's specialty is the study of the New Testament. He concentrated his work on developing a biblical foundation for mission, and the following books are the results of his efforts: *Gottes Sendung und der missionarische Auftrag der Kirche nach Matthäus, Lukas, Paulus und Johannes* (1965), *Die Apostelgeschichte in der Historie: Ein Beitrag zur Auslegungsgeschichte des Missionsbuches der Kirche, Das Mysterium Christi und die Mission: Ein Beitrag zur missionarischen Sakramentalgestalt der Kirche* (1964), and *Grund und Kraft der Mission nach dem ersten Petrusbrief* (1950).

Jacques Rossel

Jacques Rossel is the present chairman of the Basel Mission and a member of various commissions of the World Council of Churches. Though he comes from French-speaking Switzerland, he is equally at home with the German language. He served a theological school in India for thirteen years and also worked in various administrative capacities for the Basel Mission. The University of Bern accorded him an honorary doctorate.

One of his best-known publications is *Mission dans une société dynamique*, which was printed in Geneva in 1967 and appeared in a German translation as *Dynamik der Hoffnung* in Basel during the same year. It seeks to apply Jürgen Moltmann's theology of hope to the principial and administrative questions facing the mission enterprise today. The first part of the study is a close-up view of the world today; it pays special attention to the developing countries which the author has visited frequently. The second part treats the present missionary mandate, and the third enlarges upon the missionary service (*der missionarische Dienst*). The book is practically oriented and helps the reader ponder the difficulties and challenges as well as the hope for world mission today.

FRENCH PROTESTANT MISSIOLOGY

French Roman Catholic missiologists comprise a rather sizeable contingent while, numerically at least, French Protestantism is not very strong. Nevertheless, French Protestants have made an important contribution to mission, especially in French-speaking Africa, through the Mission de Paris. In places like Madagascar, Cameroon, Congo, Burundi, and Ruanda, the Mission de Paris does its part to fulfill the worldwide call to mission. Meanwhile, the mission was thoroughly restructured and now goes by the name *Département Evangélique Français d'Action Apostolique* (DEFAP). In a wider context the DEFAP works cooperatively with *Communauté Evangélique d'Action Apostolique* (CEVAA).

We shall look only briefly at several theologians who have written detailed studies relating to missiology and end this section with a slightly fuller treatment of Marc Spindler's summary missiological study.

Raoul Allier (1862–1939)

Raoul Allier's first two books described the development of the Japanese and Chinese churches. They are entitled *Les troubles de Chine et les missions chrétiennes* (1901) and *Le Protestantisme au Japon: 1859–1907*, published in 1908. For many years Allier was dean of the Protestant theological faculty in Paris and influential in the administration of the Mission de Paris. Some of his later works are in the area of psychology of religion: *La psychologie de la conversion chez les peuples non-civilisés* (1925); *Le non-civilisé et nous* (1927), and *Magie et religion* (1935).

Roger Mehl

Mehl is a well-known theologian and philosopher from the *Faculté de Théologie Protestante de Strasbourg* who teaches history of missions and missiology and is an administrative official of the former Mission de Paris and the World Council of Churches. He wrote *Décolonisation et missions Protestantes*, which was published in 1964.

André Roux

Pastor André Roux belonged to the administrative staff of the Mission de Paris and was also involved in training missionary personnel. He published a spate of promotional literature, among which is *La prière pour la mission, à l'origine de la Société des Missions Evangéliques de Paris et aujourd'hui* (1956).

Roland de Pury

The French theologian Roland de Pury, best known for his homiletical and exegetical work, also wrote a book about missions. Its chief focus is the island of Madagascar and is entitled *Les églises d'Afrique entre l'Evangile et la Coutume*.

Marc Spindler

In our survey of missiologists who write in French, I want to make mention of Marc Spindler's summarizing book, *La Mission, combat pour le salut du monde* (1967).[11]

Spindler organizes his missiology christologically. Jesus Christ, he says, is living and active in three relationships:

The first relationship involves Christ and God the Father. Reflecting on this relationship, Spindler can see a doxological dimension to mission work. One purpose for missions is to exalt and honor God. "In his work of missions Jesus Christ exalts God the Father in the (power of) the Holy Spirit." The doxological dimension keeps mission from veering too much in the direction of this world.

11. Marc Spindler, *La Mission, combat pour le salut du monde* (Neuchatel: Delachaux & Niestle, 1967).

The second relationship is antagonistic. Proclaiming the good news necessarily involves a struggle with the demonic idols present in the various religious systems. Spindler goes into great detail as he describes the weapons for warfare against the demonic elements. One of the weapons is prayer. Owing to this battle, the way of mission always involves the cross. Mission suffers apparent defeat at the hands of idolatry.

The third relationship involves Christ and the world. This is the soteriological dimension of mission. Spindler discusses the concept *Salut du monde,* connecting the biblical *soteria* to two other biblical terms. Following Hoekendijk's example, he joins *soteria* to the biblical idea of *shalom* to avoid any danger of pietistically reducing it to individual salvation. He also connects it to the element of joy (John 15:11; I John 1:4). Mission is not some sort of spiritual imperialism, but rather the sharing of the joy of salvation while we eagerly await its all-embracing and full disclosure.

In 1974 Spindler was appointed the successor of E. Jansen Schoonhoven at Leiden University and also director of the missiology branch of the Dutch Inter-University Institute for Missiological and Ecumenical Research.

MISSIOLOGY IN THE UNITED STATES

Rufus Anderson (1796–1880)

For the first two hundred years, American missionary organizations operated without a solid theoretical base, according to Pierce Beaver, editor of *To Advance the Gospel,* a book of selected writings by Rufus Anderson. Both Beaver and Robert Speer describe Anderson as the first American to provide a theoretical view of missions, and they claim that his ideas prevailed in America for the next 100 years. Anderson's influence in America paralleled Henry Venn's in England.

In 1826 Anderson was appointed assistant secretary and in 1832 became senior secretary of the American Board of Commissioners in charge of contact with all board personnel working in foreign territory. Through his work Anderson came to the conclusion that the primary goal of all Western missions should be the "development of self-supporting, self-governing, and self-propagating churches of Christ." Commonly called the "three-self formula," this view was developed by Anderson and his English counterpart, Henry Venn, and was explicated in several of Anderson's publications: *Tracts, Outline of Missionary Policy,* and in a book printed in 1869, *Foreign Missions: Their Relations and Claims.* Moreover, a number of histories of specific American missionary societies are credited to Anderson.

By his "three-self formula" Anderson was reacting to the pietistic view which emphasized individual salvation to the neglect of church-building and to the trend of building native churches as "colonial outposts of Western churches." He strongly opposed ecclesiastical colonialism which is more than satisfied to make carbon copies of Western churches in Asia, Africa, or among the Indians.

As for the missionary mandate, Anderson strongly claimed that it comes to each and every missionary. Churches and boards exist "to carry out the purpose of the missionary." The deepest motivation for mission comes from love, that is, a response of "Love to Christ." He formulated the goal of mission as follows: "Missions are instituted for the spread of a Scriptural, self-propagating Christianity."[12] This goal involves four aspects: the conversion of lost men, organizing them into churches, giving the churches a competent native ministry, and conducting them to the stage of independence and (in most cases) of self-propagation.

In Anderson's mind, schools should be established only to help in the primary work of missions. Their chief function is to train "native teachers and preachers." The real work is to build up the young churches, and he states this time and again in his writings. In many respects we are indebted to Anderson for the concept of an "indigenous church."

Anderson was obviously a man of his time. He could not at that time see clearly the problems which would arise between church and society. What is more, the ideal relationship between Western churches and the young churches, as he saw it, was marked by paternalism. Then too, by today's standards his view that education and what we call "diaconal assistance" are merely supportive of the main work of orally proclaiming the gospel is somewhat narrow.

Rufus Anderson's influence lasted for one hundred years. Hundreds of missionaries came under his sway, and mighty transformations in mission policy occurred under his leadership. Old "mission stations" were replaced by young churches, and native preachers were trained and ordained to staff them. Schools were used less as a means of evangelism and more as a means of training the laity. Young churches were given a greater voice in administrative affairs and decision making.

"There was no rival theory of missions set forth in North America during the nineteenth and first half of the twentieth century," says Pierce Beaver. And Robert Speer, who later became director of the future Student Volunteer Movement, wrote of Anderson: "Rufus Anderson was the most original, the most constructive and the most courageous student of missionary policy whom this country has produced."

One publication which has appeared on Anderson and his work, *To Advance the Gospel: A Collection of the Writings of Rufus Anderson*, is edited by and contains an introduction by R. Pierce Beaver (1967). In a collection of essays commemorating the life of J. H. Bavinck, *Christusprediking in de Wereld*, Beaver included a piece on "Rufus Anderson's missionary principles." In it he wrote:

> A brief summary of Anderson's thought may be a fitting contribution to a volume in memory of Professor J. H. Bavinck. Both these servants of Christ in the mission of His Church had the same comprehensive concern for the totality of mission and they found the source of their insights in the Bible. Unlike Professor Bavinck, Dr. Anderson never systematized his theory.[13]

12. Rufus Anderson, *Outline of Missionary Policy* (Boston: The American Board of Commissioners, 1856), p. 3.
13. R. Pierce Beaver, "Rufus Anderson's Missionary Principles," in *Christusprediking in de Wereld, pp. 43–44.

Kenneth Scott Latourette (1884–1970)

Kenneth Scott Latourette was a leading American authority on the history of missions and young churches. He died in an auto accident in 1970, but prior to his death he was involved in both history and theology, first as teacher in China for several years and then at Yale University from 1921 until his retirement in 1953.

Supported and assisted by a small army of local and corresponding collaborators, Latourette came out with the famed seven-volume series *A History of the Expansion of Christianity*. The volumes appeared between the years 1937 and 1945. He added to it a series of five volumes, *Christianity in a Revolutionary Age — A History of Christianity in the Nineteenth and Twentieth Centuries*, published from 1958 to 1962. Each series has become classic in the study of the history of the expansion of Christianity.

Latourette's books display a rare combination of detailed knowledge, sense of reality, and earnest sobriety. But Latourette did not only have a phenomenal knowledge of church history in general; he knew Asian history very well and wrote much about China and Chinese history. His works on Asia include *A History of Christian Missions in China* (1929), *The Chinese, Their History and Culture* (1934), and *A Short History of the Far East* (1946). Latourette joined with W. Richey Hogg to write an exciting account of the world missionary conference held at Whitby, Canada, in 1947. They entitled it *Tomorrow is Here* (1948).

Latourette set forth a statement of his theological point of departure in a publication he called *The Unquenchable Light*, published in 1941. Though Latourette has not made a profound theological impact, his detailed historical knowledge has made his books indispensable sources of information for those who see church history in ecumenical perspective rather than restrict it to two continents. His autobiography, *Beyond the Ranges,* was published in 1967.

R. Pierce Beaver

A native of Hamilton, Ohio, R. Pierce Beaver ranks as one of the most influential American missiologists. Following missionary service in China and internment during World War II, he was director of the Missionary Research Library in New York from 1948 to 1955 and during that time also served as research secretary for the Division of Foreign Missions of the National Council of Churches. From 1955 until 1971, when he retired, he served as professor of missiology at the University of Chicago Divinity School. He was director of the Overseas Ministries Study Center in Ventnor, New Jersey, from 1973–1976.

Beaver is a specialist in the history of missions. Some of his historical works are *Ecumenical Beginnings in Protestant World Mission, a History of Comity* (1962), *To Advance the Gospel, Selections from the Writings of Rufus Anderson* (1967), *Pioneers in Mission: The Early Missionary Ordination Sermons, Charges and Instructions* (1966), and *All Loves Excelling, American Protestant Women in World Mission* (1968). He also wrote a stirring book about the mission to the American Indians: *Church, State, and the American Indians* (1966).

But Beaver also writes on the vital and concrete questions facing missionaries today. His book *The Missionary between the Times: a Christian En-*

counter with a World in Upheaval discusses some of these: "Why the vocational crisis? Why send missionaries? Who should go? How do others see the missionary?" He also touches upon subjects like "Renewal in Mission," "Communicating the Gospel in Dialogue," "The Missionary and the Indigenous Church," and "The Missionary and His Home Church." His final chapter, "Between the Times," faces us squarely with the issues of today: "The Coming of World History," "East and West," "Agrarian and Industrial Ages," "Western Mission and World Mission," "The Gospel for all Times: the Missionary Message," and "The Nation and the Individual."

Beaver is one of the most scholarly and stimulating missiologists of our era. He enjoys the confidence and trust of "evangelicals" and "ecumenicals" alike. Under the auspices of the Theological Education Fund he toured Asia, Africa, and Latin America to lay the groundwork for libraries in many theological schools. In 1971 he was honored by a festschrift, *The Future of the Christian World Mission*, edited by W. J. Danker and Wi Jo Kang.

Donald Anderson McGavran

Donald Anderson McGavran is a highly influential American missiologist among both evangelicals and non-evangelicals. Born to American missionaries to India, McGavran labored for thirty-one years in the land of his birth as a missionary commissioned by the United Christian Missionary Society of the Christian Churches. The society is the missionary arm of the Disciples of Christ church to which McGavran belongs. McGavran worked in India primarily in the realm of education.

After his return to America in 1954, McGavran resolved to devote the rest of his life to think through what made his many missionary projects either successes or failures and thus to arrive at a good methodology and strategy for mission work. His first book on this subject was *Bridges of God* (1955). To encourage research in this area he founded the School of World Mission and Institute of Church Growth with its headquarters at Fuller Theological Seminary in Pasadena, California, where the faculty includes Arthur F. Glasser, C. Peter Wagner, Charles H. Kraft, and Paul Hiebert.

But McGavran produced many other works besides *Bridges of God*. His latest book is *Understanding Church Growth*, published in 1970. Moreover, he edits a bimonthly *Church Growth Bulletin*. Under his guidance students and assistants are hard at work producing numerous case studies of acceleration and deceleration in church growth throughout the world. We shall look at only a few of the many themes McGavran discusses in his missiology.

People's Movements

McGavran believes that a good missionary strategy takes full account of existing social relationships and works for the conversion and transfer to Christianity of the whole "homogeneous unit." This could be a tribe, an urban middle class, a caste, an extended family, subgroups, etc. It is any group whose members self-consciously belong together.

"Multiplying Churches" and Encouraging "Growth of Churches"
McGavran writes in the *International Review of Missions*: "What the fantastically mounting population of this world needs is fantastically multiplying churches."[14] By using tables and charts McGavran and his assistants seek to pinpoint the causes for receptivity to the gospel and growth in the churches in certain areas and for rejection, resistance, stagnancy and even decline in other areas. They look for spots where growth and receptivity are most likely to occur. McGavran believes that missionary organizations ought to concentrate on these areas and give the highest priority to building up the churches there. Any other work (diaconal assistance and developmental projects, for example) is secondary or even tertiary, for in his eyes "the spiritual is more important than the physical and the soul more important than the body." Diaconal programs and projects must serve only one end — church growth. If they do not, they must be terminated.

"Discipling" and "Perfecting"
A basic theme to which McGavran often refers is that one must begin by winning vast numbers of disciples. Only then must they "learn all that Jesus commanded." Jesus' two commands in Matthew 28 become for McGavran two phases of a single strategy: "Make them my disciples and teach them to obey everything I have commanded you."

The above-mentioned themes are sufficient to give the flavor of McGavran's ideas. His methods and strategy have had great power. The Wheaton Declaration of 1966 by the Interdenominational Foreign Mission Association bears traces of his ideas. His biting article written just prior to the Uppsala assembly of the World Council of Churches, "Will Uppsala Betray the Two Billion?", had both a negative and positive effect on members of the section responsible for writing the report "Renewal in Mission." But it was a telling effect nonetheless. His institute's case-study reports were widely read along with the quite different depth-studies in the "Churches in Mission" series put out by the World Council of Churches. McGavran's passionate appeal to proclaim the gospel to the millions who have not heard has caused an echoing and universal response. His emphasis on church-building is being criticized for its one-sidedness, but there is no denying that it is at least one of the tasks of the world missionary enterprise.

Discussion of McGavran's ideas is in full swing, and a host of questions are being posed. Can McGavran be charged with ecclesiocentrism in failing to understand that the church must be paired with the kingdom? Are "people's movements" and "ethnic churches" tenable in the light of the New Testament givens? Is McGavran not judging the growth of churches too much by quantitative standards and too little by qualitative ones? Are not even the apparently "unsuccessful" attempts and "little churches" significant in God's eyes? May we judge by the standard of success? Does not a persecuted church reduced to almost nothing (for example, the Chinese church) show a closer similarity to the *crucified* Lord than those coming out of mass movements and people's movements? Are social work, rural mission, development projects, medical work, etc.,

14. Donald McGavran, in *International Review of Missions* (1965), p. 459.

mere means to serve the goal of church growth? Does McGavran not slight the material world in favor of the spiritual in his view of the kingdom of God?

As many scholars have noted, McGavran has called attention to many issues that are biblically warranted — a passion for souls, an emphasis on the Word of God, and a concern for the expansion of Christ's church. Moreover, he has contributed many valuable insights into the practical work of missions. His efforts to counterbalance other missionary trends would have been even more beneficial, however, had he not become so unbiblically one-sided.

The Church Growth School is moving at full speed, and as we discuss contemporary questions we shall meet it often, both in criticism and in praise.

Eugene A. Nida

A native of Oklahoma City, Dr. Eugene Nida is director of the translation department of the American Bible Society and the United Bible Societies. Although his training was in linguistics and cultural anthropology, this American Baptist's worldwide contacts with Bible translators through the years have made him one of the finest experts in interpreting and communicating the gospel, especially to primitive societies.

Nida's best-known books are *Customs and Cultures* (1954), *God's Word in Man's Language* (1952), and *Message and Mission: The Communication of the Christian Faith* (1960). In *Message and Mission* Nida sets out to analyze the obvious communication problem. In chapter two he analyzes religion and communication, and in chapters three and four he illuminates the structures and meaning of communication. After studying the relationship between communication and the structures of archaic societies, he takes note of the dynamics of communication as they are particularly manifest in the rise and fall of religious mass movements. His ninth chapter treats the problems one faces in Bible translation and revision. He concludes by delineating what he sees as the theological basis for communication and by drawing out its practical implications.

Nida's books should be required reading for anyone who intends to translate or be a consultant for such work. But anyone who is interested in the principles and procedures of communication (as every theologian should be, for is not the theologian a communicator?) can find a wealth of friendly advice from the writing of this amiable Baptist who has helped hundreds of translators throughout the world. His works are extremely valuable for the practical work of mission and evangelism.

Gerald H. Anderson

Gerald H. Anderson, not to be confused with the German missiologist Wilhelm Andersen, was professor of church history and ecumenics at Union Theological Seminary in Manila, Philippines, working there as a United Methodist missionary from 1960 to 1970. Then in 1974, after three years as the president of Scarritt College for Christian Workers in Nashville, he went to the Overseas Ministries Study Center in Ventnor, New Jersey, where he is now the director. Anderson organized and edited a trio of symposium-studies to which I call the reader's attention.

The Theology of the Christian Mission (1961)

This book brings together varied and controversial views from a mixture of ecclesiastical traditions — Protestant, Anglican, Greek Orthodox, Roman Catholic, and even those from the younger churches. Its introduction was written by Lesslie Newbigin, the former director of the Division of World Mission and Evangelism of the World Council of Churches and presently a lecturer at Selly Oak Colleges in Birmingham, England. In part 1, G. E. Wright, J. Blauw, Oscar Cullmann, Karl Barth, Donald G. Miller, and F. N. Davey present essays on the biblical basis for mission work. Part 2 contains historical studies by scholars such as André Seumois, a Roman Catholic, and William Richey Hogg. Part 3 offers some highly controversial approaches to the question of "Christianity and Other Faiths" by such men as Hendrik Kraemer, Paul Devanandan and Masatoshi Doi. One of the essays, written by Frank Wilson Price, discusses the encounter with communism. The "Theory of the Mission" is the subject of part 4 and contains essays by Max Warren, Pierce Beaver, Paul Tillich, Christian Baëta from Ghana, and Wilhelm Andersen.

Nearly all of the essays are of rather high caliber, but those looking for a single, unified and specific position shall be disappointed; such was not the purpose of the book. But it is a useful source of information for those seeking to keep abreast of the current discussion in missiology.

Christian Mission in Theological Perspective (1967)

The second book is completely different from the first, for all its contributors are Methodists and their writing shows an obvious Methodist stamp. Though all are Methodist, this fact does not stop them from openly and honestly facing the issues which confront both young and old churches alike. The contributors include John Godsey, on "The History of Salvation and World History"; D. T. Niles, on "The Work of the Holy Spirit in the World"; A. Roy Eckhardt, on "Christian-Jewish Encounter"; and Walter G. Meulder, on "Christian Responsibility with Respect to Revolution." The essays by Everett Tilson and S. Paul Schilling seek to restate "the aim of mission."

Sermons to Men of Other Faiths and Traditions (1966)

In preparation for his third book the assiduous Anderson requested a number of experts to write a "sermon addressed to men of other faiths." One sermon, by C. Eric Lincoln, is for the Black Muslims in the United States; another is written specifically for communists by Lochmann; another, to Hindus by Professor Moses from Nagpur, India; another, to Muslims by Kenneth Cragg; and still another, to modern existentialists by Martin E. Marty. In all there are fifteen sermons.

Whatever one may think of such a book, the important question still remains: "What does the Christian have to say to the Muslim, the communist, etc.?" Though the reader may not always find the answers this book gives to be completely satisfying, they are nonetheless interesting, valuable, and instructive for one who wants to do more than just approach the questions from the narrow confines of his study. More recently Anderson has co-edited with Thomas Stransky, C.S.P., the useful series of volumes on *Mission Trends* that is widely used in seminary classes in North America.

Norman A. Horner

I wish to call the reader's attention in this survey to the deep discussions currently going on between the "ecumenicals" and "conservatives" on the "approach to world mission." This discussion, which began in America, has so swelled that its reverberations are being felt elsewhere. Therefore it is important that missiologists everywhere take careful note of the book edited by Dr. Norman A. Horner which appeared in 1968 entitled *Protestant Cross-Currents in Mission: The Ecumenical-Conservative Encounter*. A former Presbyterian missionary in Africa and the Middle East, Horner is now associate director of the Overseas Ministries Study Center in Ventnor, New Jersey.

Dr. Horner, like many others, believes that both sides have much to offer, and therefore each must try to build bridges toward the other. Evangelicals are gradually coming to see the social, economic, and political consequences of missionary work, while the ecumenicals are attempting to arrive at a fresh understanding of the vertical dimension of the gospel as well as the horizontal one. In Horner's words, "It is time to meet each other."

Horner issued an invitation to both evangelicals and ecumenicals to present their views on various subjects, such as the missionary mandate (James Scherer and Harold Lindsell), the goals of mission (Richard Shaull and Jack F. Shepherd), and the strategy for mission (David M. Stowe and Arthur Glasser). It is a highly interesting book and tries to promote an honest understanding and exchange of ideas between these two groups which traditionally have been polarized in the United States but between whom new attitudes of openness and communication are appearing.

Dr. Horner wrote an earlier book, *Cross and Crucifix in Mission*, a comparative study of Protestant and Roman Catholic missionary strategy. And while serving in the Middle East he wrote *Rediscovering Christianity Where It Began* (1974).

A GENERAL LOOK AT ASIAN, AFRICAN, AND LATIN AMERICAN MISSIOLOGY

Theologians from Europe and North America are far too little aware of the theological developments in Asia, Africa, and Latin America. The longer they continue their ignorance, the more provincial they become.

We shall devote a separate chapter to a citation of the specific theological contributions made by people from these three continents. The compass of the present chapter allows for only a few illustrations of the contributions being made in the field of missiology. Before doing so, however, we must mention that after the Second World War study centers arose on the three continents for the express purpose of making local studies of the various religions and societies in Africa,

Asia, and Latin America where the gospel is being proclaimed. Most of these centers issue bulletins which often contain excellent missiological material.

Here is a list of the study centers and the corresponding address of each:

SRI LANKA (Ceylon)

Colombo
The Study Centre
490/5 Havelock Road,
Colombo 6.

Jaffna
Christian Institute for the Study of Religion
  and Society
Christa Seva Ashram,
Chunnakam.

CUBA

La Habana
Apartado 4179,
La Habana 4.

HONG KONG
Christian Study Centre on Chinese Religion
  and Culture
Tao Fong Shan,
Shatin, N.T.

INDIA

Bangalore
Christian Institute for the Study of Religion
  and Society
P.O. Box 604, 17 Miller's Road,
Bangalore 6.

Batala
Christian Institute of Sikh Studies
Baring Union Christian College,
Batala, Punjab.

Hyderabad
Henry Martyn Institute
P.O. Box 153, St. Luke's Compound, Station
  Road,
Hyderabad 1, A.P.

Rajpur
Christian Retreat and Study Centre
Rajpur P.O.,
Dehra Dun, U.P.

JAPAN

Kyoto
NCC's Centre for the Study of Japanese
  Religions
c/o Kyoto Diocese of the Japan Episcopal
  Church,
Karasuma-Shimothachiuri, Kamikyo-ku,
  Kyoto.

MEXICO

Mexico City   Centro de Estudios Ecumenicos
                            Guty Cardenas 131,
                            Mexico 20, D.F.

NEAR EAST

Beirut   Near East Council of Churches Study Pro-
                            gramme
                            P.O. Box 5376,
                            Beirut, Lebanon.

NIGERIA

Ibadan   Christian Council of Nigeria: Institute on
                            Church and Society
                            P.O. Box 4020,
                            Ibadan.

PAKISTAN (WEST)

Rawalpindi   Christian Study Centre
                            Saifullah Lodhi Road, 128,
                            Rawalpindi.

PHILIPPINES

Manila   Christian Institute for Ethnic Studies in Asia
                            P.O. Box 1767,
                            Manila.

RIVER PLATE

Buenos Aires   Centro de Estudios Cristianos del Rio de la
                            Plata
                            Parana 489, piso 7° — Of. 42,
                            Buenos Aires, Argentina.

Montevideo   Centro de Estudios Cristianos del Rio de la
                            Plata.
                            Casilla Correo 445,
                            Montevideo, Uruguay

TUNISIA

Tunis   39 Avenue des Felibres,
                            Tunis.

SINGAPORE   Christian Institute for the Study of Religion
                            and Society
                            6G Mount Sophia,
                            Singapore 9.

SWITZERLAND

Geneva   Foyer John Knox
                            27 chemin des Crêts,
                            1218 Grand Saconnex Geneva.

We shall now mention a few persons from Asia, Africa, and Latin America who have contributed to missiology both *in loco* and ecumenically.

ASIAN MISSIOLOGY

Paul David Devanandan: Servant of Church and World in India

The last decades have seen India wrestling her way from colonial direction to full independence. The Indian churches meanwhile are struggling out from under domination by Western missions and working toward the development of ecumenical relations and new forms of cooperation with Western churches. In the political sector there were certain key figures who rose to prominent positions of leadership in the transfer of power — men like Gandhi, Nehru, and Radhakrishnan. So, too, in the shift from "mission field" to "churches in and for India" there were certain individuals who saw the situation clearly and came forward to offer their leadership during this transitional period, thus rendering incalculable service to both church and world. Such a person was Paul David Devanandan, whom I single out for special attention because his publications are readily available in English to anyone interested in beginning or continuing an acquaintance with his work.

P. D. Devanandan was born July 8, 1901 in Madras, India, to a father who was both pastor and high school teacher and to a mother gifted in many areas. She by her prayers, her music, and her ability in languages left a deep impression on her son. Devanandan was educated in the humanities and only at a later point in his life did he become a lay theologian. He received his bachelor's degree from Nizam's College in Hyderabad and his master's degree from the University of Madras.

After working for several years as a school teacher, an event occurred which became a turning point in his life. Dr. K. T. Paul, one of India's earliest native Christian leaders who joined the push for India's national self-expression, invited Devanandan to become his secretary. Devanandan accepted and became highly impressed with Paul's attempt to give meaning to and set the tone for the national movement. He was fond of telling how Gandhi, during one of the bloody uprisings between Muslims and Hindus, sent an urgent telegram to Dr. Paul: "Please, help the Muslims to act like *Christians* toward the Hindus!" Events like that shaped Devanandan's life and gave him vision for helping the "churches to fulfill their calling to be agents of reconciliation in India."

As Paul's secretary, Devanandan made a work trip to the United States. He stayed on in the States and studied Hinduism at Yale University to prepare himself for his future work in India. He concluded his study by writing a dissertation entitled *The Concept of Maya*, which was published in London in 1950 and in Calcutta in 1954.

After his return to India, Devanandan married Dr. Paul's daughter and began teaching at the United Theological College in Bangalore in 1932. He taught courses in the Pauline epistles but also — something new for theological colleges in that day — in classical and neo-Hinduism. Up till then United Theological College, like most other Asian theological schools, paid little attention to the science of religion. Devanandan was convinced that theology takes on relevance and becomes more effective when it takes account of the surroundings in which the Christian congregations are active — or perhaps inactive.

Devanandan was a gifted and respected teacher who, though suffering increasingly from deafness, nonetheless maintained much contact with his students. Foreign colleges and universities took note of his teaching abilities; Cambridge, Selly Oak, and Union Theological Seminary invited him to be guest lecturer, and Yale University and the Pacific School of Religion conferred honorary doctorates upon him.

Devanandan did not find it easy to work in a school like Bangalore which still had the heavy and dominating hand of paternalistic Western missions keeping it in tow. Thus, when he got the opportunity, he moved on to work for the YMCA, first as its general secretary for India and then later as secretary in charge of producing reading material, a position that fit him perfectly. In those years the YMCA was a place where Asiatic lay-persons could test and sharpen their leadership skills without certification by a missionary agency. During that time, the YMCA Publishing House in Calcutta was publishing a spate of literature designed to lay the groundwork for independence and to prepare the churches for their task in the new situation.

After independence came, Devanandan began to do much more in the area of research. He investigated neo-Hinduism and the relationship of religion and society. In 1953 he affiliated himself with two institutes interested in these areas. In 1956 the two institutes fused to become the now world-renowned Christian Institute for the Study of Religion and Society with its headquarters in Bangalore. Devanandan was its actual founder and became its first director; M. M. Thomas, who became director after Devanandan's death, was appointed the first associate director.

The National Christian Council, supported by theological schools, colleges, and study centers, gave the impetus for the institute. Its stated purpose is to encourage scientific study and research in the area of religion and society, to develop contact between Christians and followers of other religions, to interpret the social implications of proclaiming the gospel in India, and to support the church members as they seek to discharge their tasks in church and society. Devanandan was placed in special charge of publications, consultations, and courses.

As its pioneer director, Devanandan unfurled his many talents to make contributions that became crucially significant for Indian churches. He was well aware of the scholarly tendency to investigate an issue from the comfort of one's study rather than from within the situation itself. To avoid this he consented to be ordained a deacon and presbyter in the newly united Church of South India. It gave him opportunity to preach and administer the sacraments, duties which he did not take lightly. His sermons, a few of which were published, are some of the most polished pieces in the corpus of his writings. He worked very hard to bridge the distance between chancel, lecture hall, and practical everyday life.

Industrialism was growing apace in Bangalore. Devanandan and Rev. Harry Daniel set up an Industrial Mission to contact and speak with managers, technicians, and labor organizations.

Meanwhile, Devanandan had also become advisor for the Study Department of the World Council of Churches and for the East Asia Christian Conference. He was fast becoming one of the leading spokesmen for Asia in the world church. It was a foregone conclusion that he would be chosen to speak on one of the topics at the New Delhi assembly of the World Council of Churches in 1961.

However, Devanandan's health left much to be desired. Several heart failures warned him of how weak he really was. This did not deter him from his work, however; to him the work was more important than his life. Just prior to his death he worked mainly in the tense state of Kerala by offering seminars for teachers and pastors, for Christians and Hindus.

He died on his way to a consultation. He collapsed at a train station in Dehra Dun and died on August 10, 1962. He knew something like this was going to happen sooner or later. In fact, he spoke about it almost elatedly; he had the joy of a pilgrim who is certain where his journey shall end.

According to a former student and successor, Samartha, three services were held in his memory. One was in Paris at the meeting of the Central Committee of the World Council of Churches, another at the institute in Bangalore, and still a third at a Hindu institute in Gandhi-Gram, where he was eulogized for "his deep concern for the truth and for his genuine humanness." The service in Bangalore ended with these words: "For the life and ministry of thy departed servant, Paul Devanandan, for his love and scholarship, his affection for students, his manifold services to the Church at large and for his missionary zeal: All glory be to thee, O Lord."

What follows is a closer look at the "manifold services" of Devanandan mentioned in this prayer of thanksgiving and praise to God.

Devanandan the Scholar and Researcher

Anyone who lists Devanandan's services to the church and the world in India must begin with his research into Asiatic religions, Hinduism in particular. To understand his approach one needs to know Devanandan's theological orientation. During his early public life he was strongly affected by theological liberalism which actually reduced Christianity to a type of religious philosophy, to a set of ideas. But though his mind accepted it, his heart opposed reducing the gospel to an ethical philosophy.

During this time Kraemer's book *The Christian Message in a Non-Christian World* appeared (1938). This book and a personal meeting with Kraemer which developed into a friendship brought a "conversion" in Devanandan's life and thinking, as he so often said. (Kraemer attended the organizational meeting of the institute in Bangalore.) Kraemer's "biblical realism" and his emphasis on the acts of God in the birth, life, death, and resurrection of Jesus provided a base for rethinking his own views on theology and religion.

But having accepted this new base, he still found a certain rebellion brewing within him against Kraemer's view of continuity and discontinuity and against Kraemer's idea that every element in a religion flows from the very core of that religion and must be seen as such. That may well have been true in the past, but is it still so today? What is the effect of the various religions meeting and influencing each other? Are not even the very basic structures of the religions changing? Are there not elements present in the religions today for which there is no other explanation than to say they have been influenced by Christianity and secularization? Like M. M. Thomas, Devanandan wanted to press on to a post-Kraemer period without destroying what Kraemer's vision had achieved and secured.

In the last months before he died, Kraemer was caught up in a discussion with the leading figures at the institute in Bangalore. Their correspondence was published in the November, 1966 issue of the Bulletin of the Christian Institute for the Study of Religion and Society and is well worth reading.

One can only understand Devanandan's research within the framework of his theological orientation and reorientation. He began with a philological and historical study of the sources and basic structure of Hinduism. His dissertation, *The Concept of Maya*, typifies this stage of his scholarly life. In it he analyzes the various meanings of *Maya* from the pre-Vedic period to today. According to experts, the study is without equal in its field. Although Devanandan later added other research tools to his collection, which we shall discuss later, he nonetheless believed to the end of his life that to make one's way through the labyrinth of a religion demands a philological and historical investigation of that religion. He always encouraged others to study Sanskrit, as he himself had done.

He later supplemented his philological and historical method with sociology and anthropology. For one to know classical Hinduism does not imply that he necessarily understands a modern Hindu. Great changes have come to the Hindu community's world view, attitude toward life, and view of reality. One must take careful note of how the religions influence each other and what the secularizing process is doing to neo-Hinduism. Devanandan never lost sight of all the remarkable shifts of accent and new elements in his description of neo-Hinduism. He noted the shift from the impersonal Brahman to the personal Isvara, from the Mayan world of appearances to Radhakrishnan's talk of "the relative value of reality." He noted too a changed view of man, his equality, and his worth. He saw a change in the view of sin and solidarity in guilt. He noted how modern Hindus talk not only of coercion and determinism in *karma*, but also make room for freedom and responsibility in their explanation. He saw, too, a changed understanding of history coming to the fore. *Moksha* no longer means "being absorbed by an impersonal Brahman"; there is talk of "social salvation." Hinduism is beginning to talk about the meaning and purpose of one's life in history.

Devanandan followed these changes and analyzed them with such careful honesty that Radhakrishnan, a Hindu, could write the preface to Devanandan's book, *Christian Concern in Hinduism*, and pay tribute to his "learning" and "insight."

Devanandan never optimistically and utopianly claimed that there were direct lines between Hinduism and the heart of the gospel like Farquhar did when he described Christianity as the crown of Hinduism. But he did believe that God in his own mysterious and untraceable way was involved in those changes. But the demonic power and the might of error are also present; when the Hindu takes over elements of Christianity, these demons try to blind and immunize him to the real heart of the gospel, Jesus Christ, who alone is Lord.

Devanandan sought to learn how to speak relevantly to the Hindu experiencing these changes, so that he could understand what the gospel says about that for which neo-Hinduism is searching: the living God, the secret of man, the meaning and purpose of life. To this end Devanandan studied, and his scholarship was recognized by all.

But Devanandan did his research to try to find the Spirit of Christ and distinguish it from the spirit of error. He struggled to find the word for today. Thus it was not the arrogance of one who already knows, but the humility of one who must yet learn that made him a genuine scholar.

Devanandan: A Pioneer in Communication

In addition to his scholarly research, Devanandan also served the world and the church by developing a new form of missionary witness. The majority of churches in India were isolated and far removed from the real life of the Indian people. In most cases they had more to do with Western denominations than they did with each other. Sociological research done among the churches in New Delhi showed that not only the older churches like the Syrian Church but also the younger ones which grew out of mission work were far removed from the mainstream and had thus become another caste. Devanandan simply could not stomach this proud, awful isolation in the churches. His series of essays, collected and published in 1964 by the Christian Institute for the Study of Religion and Society and entitled *Preparation for Dialogue*, focuses on the single question of how to break through this unproductive isolation and begin genuinely communicating with the people of India rather than shouting at them from long distance.

What sets us off, Devanandan reiterated time and again, is our way of life: our introverted social relationships and our lack of involvement in what is moving our people. Devanandan was not interested in making the gospel natively Indian, for the gospel is not native to any culture, whether Western or Asian. Rather, the people of God who are responding to that gospel must learn to witness in a way which takes due account of where they are. They must continually inquire whether the forms, the creeds, the words and the confessions the missionary forefathers used still have meaning and usefulness in declaring the gospel in the present situation.

Devanandan called for a new type of communication: dialogue and cooperation. By "dialogue" he did not mean the quest for some kind of cheap agreement. He would have nothing to do with a Gnostic fusion of religions which are fundamentally different. What Devanandan wanted was a deep contact with men of other faiths or of no faith at all in which all the participants got down to the very core questions of God, creation, man, sin and grace. He wanted everyone to face squarely the Man of Nazareth where each would have to decide either for him or against him. Anyone who puts Devanandan in the camp of those who blunt the edge of missions does him injustice, for Devanandan would have nothing to do with this.

Devanandan also urged Christian cooperation with other religious and nonreligious agencies to build up the state and society. He called for a "creatively critical" posture. One must never identify completely with any system or ideology if he expects to make a significant contribution. Cooperation must be critical. Christianity must never allow itself to become annexed to the interests of any ideology. But cooperation must also be creative, for the Christian realizes that history is God's "workshop" and He, with us as His co-workers, is making all things new.

Paul Devanandan thus tried to open up new paths of gospel communication and evangelization and break down the old patterns. The Christian Institute at Bangalore has become a fine model of how and where men of various faiths can meet each other. The question is: Shall the next generation be able to sustain the momentum the Institute had when Devanandan was living, preserving the integrity of the gospel and yet being open?

Devanandan's Theological Contribution

We must make a brief comment on Devanandan's theological ideas. His missiological writing reveals five fundamental motifs. First, Devanandan views evangelism in a cosmic dimension. Though the term itself may not be altogether felicitous, Devanandan uses it to show that God has a claim on all peoples and nations. Following in the train of the Old Testament prophets, Isaiah in particular, Devanandan emphasized that everyone has to do with God.

Second, evangelism concentrates on the unique and exclusive events in all of history — the birth, life, death, and resurrection of Jesus Christ, the Lord both of his church and of all of history.

Third, Devanandan claims that evangelism follows from and flows out of God's "undertaking." Through the work of the Holy Spirit, God is the evangelist.

Fourth, the whole of the people of God is involved in the work of missions and must become actively involved in the movement.

Fifth, this activity of God is directed toward the goal of bringing all things together under the one Head, Christ Jesus. "Summing up all things in Christ; consummation in him" were words which spurred Devanandan on in his work.

Devanandan probed deeply to learn what, if anything, would be preserved of the religious searchings and strivings of men after the purifying effect of God's judgment had passed. What would be carried over into the new earth? He answered his own question:

> In the new heaven and earth we shall not be able to distinguish new from old. We cannot determine what shall be kept nor how, for we do not know how God shall bring his purposes for humanity and the world to their conclusion.
> But to the degree that we identify with the will of God as he reveals it in Jesus Christ, we may be sure that we are working in accord with that goal and not against it.[15]

So Devanandan concluded his address in New Delhi. It was a statement which was characteristic of the whole of his theologizing.

Devanandan lived with the deep conviction that as the Asiatic churches came into living contact with their surroundings they would discover new facets of the one truth which is in Christ. Thus the church would .come to realize more of

---

15. Paul D. Devanandan, *Preparation for Dialogue* (Bangalore: Christian Institute for the Study of Religion and Society, 1964), p. 192.

her universality. But this is not to be done through syncretism or indifference. The only way is by obedience to God's unique revelation in Christ the Lord.

Devanandan: A Voice for Asian Churches in the Ecumenical Community
In addition to his other noteworthy contributions, Devanandan also represented Asia in the ecumenical community. This responsibility has often fallen upon the shoulders of Indians, in part because they speak and write fluently the lingua franca of ecumenical discussion, English. Furthermore, their country is one of the busy intersections in the network of world traffic. Thus it goes without saying that the ecumenical community expects them to be leading spokesmen for Asia in ecclesiastical affairs. The danger is that often these representatives travel so widely that they are seldom home. Their globetrotting diminishes their influence among their own people. Another source of irritation is that the Indian situation is equated with the whole of Asia and the other areas of Asia are not given their due.

By avoiding these two dangers Devanandan rendered outstanding service to the Western churches in ecumenical affairs. His most notable contribution in this context is his little book *Christian Issues in Southern Asia*, which proved so popular among Western readers that when it was published in 1964 it went through a second printing the very same year. It was one of the last manuscripts Devanandan completed before his death.

The first chapter of this little book paints the historical backdrop in the countries of Nepal, Ceylon, India and Pakistan. His second chapter treats the arrival of Western churches in India. In his third chapter he describes the transfer from mission to church. His fourth chapter, entitled "Resurgent Religions: Faith and Nationhood," highlights the contemporary context of the churches in Asia. In chapter five Devanandan traces the churches' struggle to achieve a more united front in their work, while chapter six describes the "Christian contributions to Nation-Building." His final chapter speaks of the relationship of our mission to Christ's.

The issues he discusses bear striking similarity to those which the Western churches are addressing: the content of the gospel, the missionary structure of the congregation, the role of laity, and the relation between the work done by churches and society as a whole. Though the topics are similar, the book is fresh and original in its approach, for it tries to bring to the discussion a voice which is acutely Asian. In a certain sense this final book of his was the culmination of all of his life and work, for in it he represents those Asian churches who have joined the pilgrim people of God in their march toward the kingdom. He is making what proved to be his final plea for the Western churches to joyously accept this Eastern addition to the ranks. He calls all Christians to support each other as they make the journey together.

D. T. Niles

D. T. Niles, a Tamil-speaking Ceylonese, was born in 1908 to Christian parents in the North Ceylon town of Tellipolai, a suburb of Jaffna. In the January, 1971 issue of the *International Review of Mission* W. A. Visser 't Hooft, his mentor until Niles's death, described him aptly as a *pastor oecumenicus* who lived and worked in several geographic spheres. He was active locally in Jaffna as a pastor, theological educator, and ecumenist. Nationally, he was involved in the Ceylon Council of Churches. In a continental dimension, he actively promoted the East Asia Christian Conference, serving first as its secretary and later as its chairman. Globally, he was both secretary and later chairman of the World Federation of Christian Students and concluded his career by serving as one of the chairmen of the World Council of Churches. Prior to his post as chairman of the World Council, he had been Secretary of Evangelism in the council's Department of World Mission and Evangelism. Niles was an extremely gifted man who made an impact in so many areas: in his pastoral work, in evangelism, preaching, ecumenical organization, and theology.

Niles's Contribution to Missiology

Niles wrote prolifically. The few pieces of his writing to which we shall refer have to do with missiology in the strict sense of the word. The one we shall mention first, which presents his theology of mission, grew out of a mandate from the International Missionary Council to organize a series of consultations throughout the world on two topics which had always intrigued him, the relationship between older and younger churches and the relationship between church unity and the work of mission. He wrote his conclusions in his book *Upon the Earth*, which bears the subtitle "The Mission of God and the Missionary Enterprise of the Churches" and was first published in 1962.

The book begins by describing "The Faith" (the ministry of Jesus to persons, the work of the Holy Spirit in the world, the kingdom of the Father, and the obedience of the disciple), and in the second section details "The Enterprise." Here Niles treats several of his favorite topics: "the selfhood of a church," "the integrity of mission," and "the westernity of the base." Niles entitled the third part "Encounter" and in it discussed the confrontation of the gospel with other religions and with secularization.

In Niles's judgment, the base of mission has been in the West for too long. It must also come east — ecclesiastically, politically, and geographically. By ecclesiastical "easternity" he means a sending of missionaries from East to West as well as West to East. Politically speaking, Niles called for a close involvement with the problems facing the young nations rather than grinning at a distance over some of the errors they make. Geographically, the Christian mission must continue to strive for a theology which is relevant to the Eastern culture it confronts.

Niles had a deep interest in theology, not for its own sake, but because he saw it as an aid in pastoral work and evangelism. His main interest was in biblical theology, and in one of his final writings prior to his death, *We Know In Part*, published in 1965, he evaluated Bishop John Robinson's *Honest to God*. In his critique, Niles urgently pleads for a reinterpretation of the gospel to make it meaningful for a modern person, but is equally strong in his warning never to lose the heart of the gospel in an attempt to make it more acceptable. He registers his strong disagreement with Robinson's interpretation of Bonhoeffer and the many others who wish to exploit Bonhoeffer to serve their own ends. He then goes on to give his own understanding of Bonhoeffer, one which in the judgment of Bonhoeffer's friends is much closer to the heart of his ideas than many of the other interpretations on the market. Niles never tried to hide the "offense and foolishness" of the gospel. "The truth is that many who are invited will not come and that the Master will *not* send His invitation to them in a more acceptable form."

Another Niles publication of great value to missiology today is *The Preacher's Task and the Stone of Stumbling*. It contains what one might call Niles's theology of the religions, but not in the usual sense. Rather than searching for a meeting between the several systems of religion, as regularly happens in theologies of religions, Niles searches for a meeting between persons. The book is his answer to three letters which he wrote to three of his friends: a Muslim, a Buddhist, and a Hindu. He asked them to spell out, black on white, at what points they disagreed with the gospel of Jesus Christ. The characters were not imaginary but were actual friends of Niles who responded seriously to his request and received an equally serious reply. This little book is noteworthy for the many pointers it gives for meeting people of other faiths.

A CONTRIBUTION FROM SIERRA LEONE

We have already mentioned that theologians working in Africa clearly favor working out a theology of evangelism or mission. An example of such work is *Creative Evangelism: Towards a New Christian Encounter with Africa*, published in 1968 and written by an Anglican, Harry Sawyerr, professor of theology at one of Africa's oldest schools of theology, Fourah Bay College of the University of Sierra Leone. Many of Sawyerr's writings, but especially this book, seek to develop an answer to the jackpot question which he already was asking in 1959: "How can the church in Africa be both African and yet worldwide?" *Creative Evangelism* begins with a review of the beliefs about God, man, evil, the living and the dead held by African primitive religions as they come to expression in their myths and rites. The author then goes on to ask how one who proclaims the gospel ought to reckon with these beliefs as he brings his message. What "evangelistic considerations" should he take into account?

In answering this question Sawyerr makes special reference to the Old Testament, where one can find the prophets wrestling with the vital elements of primitive religions. But he rejects the idea popular with so many that in his early contacts with tribal peoples the evangelist should limit himself to dealing with the Old Testament. "For the African evangelist the New Testament must be his guide," says Sawyerr.

Chapter three of the book contains Sawyerr's plea for a proper use of the Bible. He calls for "sound doctrinal teaching" which resists treating the Bible like a moralistic book of rules. When the Bible is treated like a book of rules, the gospel is quickly transformed into another law, binding people to a new series of commandments which merely reflect a specific cultural pattern. The proper relationship between gospel and law requires a clear explanation.

Sawyerr emphasizes that the uniqueness of Christ's person must be underlined in a milieu which so quickly tends to syncretism. Furthermore, it is vital, he says, to proclaim the ecumenical and catholic nature of the church amid people whose sense of fellowship is limited to family and tribe.

Chapter five is the important part of Sawyerr's book, for it contains his plea for a "transfiguration" of African liturgy. By means of an outline for the future he attempts to illustrate how, much more than before, we must seriously take into account the "religio-psychological needs of African converts to Christianity." He goes into detail when discussing this new liturgy, singling out the following points for special attention: "the transformation of the African concept of God, the transformation of the African's attitude to the spirits, the transformation of the rationale of the African's sense of worship."

The concluding words of his little book well summarize the whole of Sawyerr's ardent desire: "If we are patient enough to distil from the corpus of African traditional beliefs and practices such factors as are *consonant* with Christianity, we shall ultimately redeem them unto the obedience of Christ. May the Church in Africa be the vehicle of abundant life for all Africans."[16]

Sawyerr's book, like much other Anglican writing on primitive religiosity, displays a bit too much optimism, but its resolute opposition to "potplant Christendom," to borrow Niles's phrase, which is completely cut off from its environment and only becomes a means of ecclesiastical colonialism, makes this an exciting book. With the rapid rise of "independent church movements" Sawyerr's questions shall be commanding much greater attention.

SOUTH AFRICAN MISSIOLOGY

Few countries have as many separate groups within their geographic boundaries as does South Africa. Churches have arisen among these various groups in South Africa, and therefore it goes without saying that the practical work of mission has produced theoretical reflection on mission work as well. In an address to the Congress of Missiologists held in Frankfurt in 1974, David J. Bosch, secretary of the South African Missiological Society and editor-in-chief of *Missionalia*, presented an outstanding survey of South African missiology from which I shall cite some facts.

Missiological Study Centers

South Africa has four organizations which study missiology:

(1) *The Umpumulo Missiological Institute.* Address: c/o Lutheran Theological College, Private bag, Mapumolo 4470. This institute was established in 1965 by the Lutheran churches and holds a number of consultations on missiological topics.

(2) *South African Missiological Society.* Address: 31 Fourteenth Street, Menlo Park, Praetoria 0002. Founded in 1968, this organization has a completely ecumenical cast; its 250 English- and Afrikaans-speaking members are spread among many racial groups. It publishes a periodi-

16. Harry Sawyerr, *Creative Evangelism: Towards a New Christian Encounter with Africa* (London: Lutterworth Press, 1968).

cal, *Lux Mundi,* which prints the work of various congresses. In 1973, under the direction of David Bosch, the society began *Missionalia,* which as far as I know is unique among missiological publications; it publishes abstracts of articles taken from hundreds of missiological periodicals, books, brochures, etc., throughout the world.

(3) *Ecumenical Research Unit.* This organization, headed by Canon T. D. Verrijn of the Anglican church, specializes in the area of ecclesiastical sociology.

(4) *The Lumbo Missiological Institute.* Address: P.O. Box 11, Lacy Frere. A Roman Catholic organization founded by Bishop Rosenthal in 1962, this institute is at work developing a liturgy and catechism which fit the African context.

Missiological Publications

South African authors have published much material on a variety of missiological topics. David Bosch and Hugo du Plessis, among others, have done work on the biblical foundation for mission. Scores of historical studies of the various South African denominations and the Independent Church Movement have been published. In the historical section, Bengt Sundkler broke ground with his widely acclaimed study of the Bantu prophets, and G. C. Oosthuizen, M. L. Daneel, and many others followed in his path. Other authors have given their attention to the relationship patterns existing between the various churches, some calling for a breakup in the mother-daughter relationship, and others calling for a critical study of these relationships. J. J. Durands's doctoral dissertation, *Una Sancta Catholica in Sendingsperspectief,* is an example of the latter. In effect every single area of missiology has received the attention of South African authors. For further references one can turn to the above-mentioned address presented by David Bosch at the missiology congress in Frankfurt.

I wish to call attention to still one other topic being treated by South African authors. One might call it *missio politica oecumenica;* it is a study of the ideology and practice of apartheid.

A few missiologists from the Reformed church (*Gereformeerd*) and the Dutch Reformed church (*Nederduits-Gereformeerd*) have tried to defend apartheid and the effect it has on the church's missionary calling. Hugo du Plessis' *Banier van die Volke,* J. C. Coetsee's *Volk en Godsvolk in die Nuwe Testament,* D. C. S. van der Merwe's *Verbond en Sending,* and W. J. van der Merwe's *Gesante om Christus' Wil* all reflect this tendency.

Happily, there are many other South African studies which refuse to clothe this ideology and its practice with the mantle of God's authority and radically reject it on the basis of God's law and gospel. We shall mention a few of these. Cosmas Desmond wrote a book which the public authorities of South Africa banned: *The Discarded People.* H. Wipio's study is entitled *Kontrak soos die Ovambo dit sien.* Dr. Johannes L. de Vries, a citizen of Namibia who presently serves as Lutheran bishop in this region, wrote a book, *Sending en kolonialisme in Suid-Wes-Afrika.* Then too, there are the publications resulting from the project "On Christianity in Apartheid Society" which was sponsored by the Christian

Institute of Johannesburg and directed by Peter Randall. The project was designed to study the anatomy of apartheid and to suggest alternatives. Though all ten of its publications bear significantly on the *missio politica* in South Africa, I wish to make special mention of *A Taste of Power* and *South Africa's Political Alternatives*.

Finally, I shall mention the book *Essays on Black Theology*, which came out in Johannesburg in 1972 and later was removed from the market. All the essays come from the pens of black theologians, a fact which by itself disproves the claim that scarcely do South Africa's black theologians make a contribution. Those who made such claims would quite conveniently overlook the work of the late Professor Matthews, P. M. Mpumlwana, Dr. G. Setiloane, and many others. The following essay titles, each of which is found in *Essays on Black Theology*, provide a sample of the work and interest of black South African authors: Dr. Manas Buthelezi, "An African Theology or a Black Theology?"; Dr. Adam Small, "Blackness Versus Nihilism"; Mr. Steve Biko, "Black Consciousness and the Quest for a True Humanity"; Mr. Nyameko Pityana, "What is Black Consciousness?"; Rev. Bonganjalo Goba, "Corporate Personality in Israel and in Africa"; Mr. Mokgethi Motlhabi, "Black Theology — A Personal Opinion"; Dr. Akin Omoyajowo, "An African Expression of Christianity"; Dr. Manas Buthelezi, "The Theological Meaning of True Humanity"; Dr. Mongameli Mabona, "Black People and White Worship"; Rev. Fr. Lawrence B. Zulu, "Nineteenth Century Missionaries in South Africa"; Mr. Mokgethi Motlhabi, "Black Theology and Authority"; Dr. D. E. H. Nxumalo, "Black Education and the Quest for a True Humanity"; Dr. Manas Buthelezi, "Theological Grounds for an Ethic of Hope."

It is beyond dispute that black theologians have often remained silent under the oppressive system of apartheid. Whenever someone mentions this, I recall the comment Abraham Kuyper made about the silence and lack of theological work among the Huguenots in France after the Bartholomew's Day Massacre: "Don't complain about silence in the forest after you've killed all the nightingales." Who has the right to complain about scant theological writings from the pens of black South Africans when the strong hand of government censure is put over the mouths of those who do make an effort to break the silence?

LATIN AMERICAN MISSIOLOGY

As was mentioned before, a complete description of theological developments is clearly beyond the scope of this book. We shall mention only a few of the leading people in Latin America who are involved in meaningfully proclaiming the gospel to their area of the world.

Rev. Emilio Castro from Uruguay, a former secretary of the ecumenical organization of Latin American churches (*Union Latino Americano Pro Unidad Evangelica*), sought to apply God's commands and promises to the explosive economic, political, and social situation in Latin America. His essay in a symposium on problems of Latin America, *Explosives Lateinamerika*, which he entitled "Neue Wege zur Evangelisation" ("New Approaches in Evangelism"), describes some of his efforts.

Julio de Santa Ana from Montevideo has written extensively on the social and political implications of proclaiming the gospel in Latin America. At present he works in Geneva in the Commission on the Churches' Participation in Development. Hiber Conteris, another citizen of Uruguay, belongs to that rare group of sociologists and theologians who analyze and criticize the ideologies. Mexican Mauricio Lopez specializes in analyzing cultural developments using the norms of the gospel. Rubem Azevedo Alves from Brazil is engaged in efforts to forge the contemporary emphasis on the theology of hope into an effective tool for Latin America; his book published in 1969 bears the title *A Theology of Human Hope*. Nor should we fail to mention José Míguez Bonino, a professor of theology from Buenos Aires, who has written much in the area of social ethics. Finally, we should also include Adolpho Ham, the Cuban director of a study center supported by churches, who has focused his writing on the work of mission in his native country.

SOURCES FOR THE STUDY OF ROMAN CATHOLIC MISSIOLOGY

Again, it is clearly impossible to give a complete history of Roman Catholic missiology here. This history has been so long and impressive that it would require a whole book even to give a survey. What is more, this history has been done already with such superior quality that to do it again and as well is both unnecessary and impossible. For those who wish to read further in this area, we shall mention a few of these sources.

Dr. Alphons Mulders, monsignor in the Roman Catholic church and the first missiologist ever appointed to a Dutch university faculty, wrote *Missiologisch Bestek*, an accurate and exhaustive study of Roman Catholic missiology from the early Middle Ages to the year 1962.

Another survey is the three-volume work of Professor André Seumois, *Théologie missionaire*, which came out in Rome in 1973 and 1974. One of its attractive features is that Seumois includes the texts of the most important decrees of the church which relate to its mission.

We must not fail to include in our source references a recent study of Roman Catholic missiology written by Ludwig Rütte and published in Munich in 1972. Entitled *Zur Theologie der Mission: Kritische Analyse und neue Orientierungen*, Rutte's study gives evidence of contact with many of the developments in Protestant missiology.

In recent years some of the younger members of the corps of Roman Catholic missiologists have been emphasizing *in loco* missiological study. Following the Latin American theologian, Gutiérrez, they are convinced that when rich experience is complemented by theoretical study and reflection in a specific locality, a consensus forms regarding "definite, universally valid and applicable constants which Christian congregations can use in their common missionary enterprise or in service of the world which is striving for unity and peace."

Throughout the world Roman Catholic and Protestant missiologists have achieved a measure of contact and cooperation which no one at the beginning of this century would have thought possible.

The most recent Roman Catholic introduction to missiology was written by Walbert Bühlmann: *Wo der Glaube Lebt: Einblicke in die Lage der Weltkirche.* In this volume which describes the crucial role of the "third world" in the contemporary political arena, the author makes pointed reference to what he terms the "third church." He firmly believes that the shifts taking place in politics toward the third world shall certainly have an impact on the churches. The book systematically describes the present situation and challenges the Roman Church to respond appropriately.

INTERNATIONAL ASSOCIATION FOR MISSION STUDIES

The year 1968 marked the time of the first "European Consultation" among missiologists held at Selly Oak Colleges, Birmingham, England. A second was held in Oslo, Norway in 1970, at which meeting steps were taken to organize officially an International Association for Mission Studies. Dr. O. G. Myklebust was appointed as its future secretary, the Egede Institute from Oslo assisted with the administrative details, and a provisional committee was named composed of the following members: A. Camps, H. W. Gensichen, O. G. Myklebust, S. J. Samartha, and A. F. Walls.

Membership in this future association would be open to both persons and institutions "which would promote the scholarly study of all questions relating to the missionary dimension of the Christian message, promote fellowship, exchange of information and interdisciplinary cooperation, arrange international learned conferences and stimulate publications (including, hopefully, a journal) and bibliographical activity." While some of the participants in the Oslo Conference preferred to delay the founding of such an association until missiologists from around the world had been polled, its planners nonetheless went ahead, hoping that their Asian, African, and Latin American colleagues would later join the fellowship. A. F. Walls stated his case well when he wrote in 1968, "There is too much for any individual. It is the concern of us all, at home and abroad, scholar, teacher, researcher, missionary secretary and council missionary, tutor and college, working missionary and practical men of every sort. Let us fulfill it together."

At the conference in Driebergen, Netherlands, held in 1972, the association was officially established.

BIBLIOGRAPHY

Aagaard, J. *Mission, Konfession, Kirche: Die Problematik ihrer Integration im 19, Jahrhundert in Deutschland.* Lund: Gleerup, 1967.

Andersen, W. *Auf dem Weg zu einer Theologie der Mission.* Gütersloh: Bertelsmann, 1957.

Anderson, G. H. "The Theology of Mission Among Protestants in the Twentieth Century." *The Theology of the Christian Mission.* New York: McGraw-Hill, 1961.

Beaver, R. P. "North American Thought on the Fundamental Principles of Mission During the Twentieth Century." *Church History* 21 (1952): 345–364.

De Jong, J. A. *As the Waters Cover the Sea: Millennial Expectations in the Rise of Anglo-American Missions, 1640–1810.* Kampen: J. H. Kok, 1970.

Galm, P. M. *Das Erwachen des Missionsgedankens im Protestantismus der Niederlande.*

Oberbayern: Missionsverlag St. Ottilien, 1915.
Günther, W. *Von Edinburgh nach Mexico City: Die ekklesiologische Bemühungen der Weltmissionskonferenzen 1910–1963.* Stuttgart: Evangelische Missionsverlag, 1970.
Hoekendijk, J. C. *Kerk en Volk in de Duitse Zendingswetenschap.* Utrecht: n.p., 1948.
Margull, H. J., ed. *Zur Sendung der Kirche: Material der Oekumenischen Bewegung.* Munich: Kaiserverlag, 1963.
Myklebust, O. G. *The Study of Missions in Theological Education: An Historical Inquiry into the Place of World Evangelization in Western Protestant Ministerial Training with Particular Reference to Alexander Duff's Chair of Evangelistic Theology.* Oslo: Egede Instituttet, 1955–1957.
Rooy, S. H. *The Theology of Missions in the Puritan Tradition; a Study of Representative Puritans: Richard Sibbes, Richard Baxter, John Eliot, Cotton Mather, Jonathan Edwards.* Delft: Meinema, 1965.
Van den Berg, J. *Constrained by Jesus' Love: An Inquiry into the Motives of the Missionary Awakening in Great Britain in the Period between 1698 and 1815.* Kampen: J. H. Kok, 1956.
Verkuyl, J. *God's Initiatief en ons Mandaat: De Betekenis van de Wereldzendingsconferentie in Mexico City.* Amsterdam: Ten Have, 1964.
_____. *Jezus Christus de Bevrijder en de voortgaande Bevrijdingen van Mensen en Samenlevingen: De Betekenis van de Wereldzendingsconferentie voor Zending en Evangelisatie in Bangkok.* Baarn: Ten Have, 1973.

CHAPTER IV

The Biblical Foundation for the Worldwide Mission Mandate

THE INCREASED URGENT NEED FOR A BIBLICAL FOUNDATION

At the 1963 Mexico City world mission conference Dr. W. A. Visser 't Hooft presented a penetrating address, the gist of which was that mission was now in a "time of testing," a period when the modern world was putting the mission enterprise to the test in a variety of ways. "The consensus of the *Zeitgeist* is clear. It is an anti-missionary consensus. And nearly all the signs in the realm of politics and of ideas point in the direction of increasing rather than decreasing unwillingness to recognize the *raison d'etre* of missions. A new testing time for missions has arrived."[1] In a time such as this every foundation which human beings have dreamed up is shriveling up and blowing away; only one based on the living God, the risen Lord, and the Bible can endure.

A variety of these imaginary foundations has of course been built through the years. Think, for example, of how missions were based on "the spread of Western civilization," how they were "to accompany colonialism," and how they were to expand the *Corpus Christianum* in a secularized form of theocracy. But all of these are crashing on the rocks in the wake of the antimissionary storm which is presently raging throughout the world; they are sinking away during this period of thorough testing.

During this "time of testing" we are having to learn to turn back to the Bible and pay fresh attention to the God who in the Old Testament is described as the "sending God" and "on the move" and to Jesus, who in the New Testament is spoken of as "the One sent from the Father." This God speaks to us through the Bible.

THE "HOW" OF A BIBLICAL FOUNDATION

H. W. Gensichen, in his book *Glaube für die Welt* (1971), reminds us that whenever one inquires how the Bible develops its foundation for mission, the

---

1. W. A. Visser 't Hooft, "Missions as the Test of Faith," in *Witness in Six Continents: Records of the Meeting of the Commission on World Mission and Evangelism of the World Council of Churches Held in Mexico City December 8th–19th, 1963*, ed. R. K. Orchard (London: Edinburgh House Press, 1964), p. 26.

matter of how he goes about his search is not unimportant. In the past the usual method was to pull a series of proof-texts out of the Old and New Testaments and then to consider the task accomplished. But more recently, biblical scholars have taught us the importance of reading these texts in context and paying due regard to the various nuances. The proof-text method does not fill the bill; one must consider the very structure of the whole biblical message.

Nor can one do a worthwhile job when he works with the so-called kerygmatic method, for it leads to an arbitrary cropping of the biblical data. W. Holsten's book *Das Kerygma und der Mensch* and Falk Wagner's *Über die Legitimität der Mission* are good examples of this tendency. Holsten, for example, tends to restrict the term "kerygma" to the message of justification, and Wagner sets out on an independent course where the term "kerygma" ends up in philosophical territory.

Our best help comes from biblical studies which are carried out with great attention to the basic structure of the biblical message in all of its nuances as it relates to the mission mandate and which help us relate the message to the present situation by providing hermeneutical pointers in addition to the exegetical material. Are such studies available? There are two which in my judgment are of invaluable assistance.

The first is J. Blauw's *The Missionary Nature of the Church* (1961). The book is the product of Blauw's mandate from the Division of World Mission and Evangelism of the World Council of Churches to critically review and summarize the exegetical and hermeneutical studies done between 1930 and 1960 which relate to the biblical foundation for mission. Though it must be supplemented by other material written since 1960, it is nonetheless indispensable for anyone interested in this field.

The second volume which must be mentioned here was written by A. de Groot, a Roman Catholic theologian skilled in the practical work of missions. H. W. Gensichen noted that traditionally Roman Catholic missiology has been content to base missions on the teaching authority of the church and thus to ignore the biblical foundation. But *Ad Gentes,* the Second Vatican Council's decree on mission, frequently refers to the Bible. In accord with the council, de Groot's study, *De Bijbel over het Heil der Volken (The Biblical View of Salvation among the Peoples),* is a worthy testimony to Roman Catholic missiology's efforts to achieve a biblical foundation for mission work.

What follows is my brief contribution to an understanding of the biblical basis for mission. It must not be understood as an effort to replace any other study but rather to supplement the work done by men like J. H. Bavinck, J. Blauw, A. de Groot, H. W. Gensichen, and so many others. It seeks to accent some points which in my opinion have often been neglected.

THE SIGNIFICANCE OF THE OLD TESTAMENT

The twentieth century has produced a steady stream of literature which regards the Old Testament as an indispensable and irreplaceable base for the church's missionary task among the nations and peoples of this world. As one who has made frequent use of this literature, I wish to look at four motifs in the Old Testament which form the indispensable basis for the New Testament call to the church to engage in worldwide mission work: the universal motif, the motif of rescue and saving, the missionary motif, and the antagonistic motif.

The Universal Motif

The God who in the Old Testament identifies himself as the God of Abraham, Isaac, and Jacob and who discloses to Moses his personal name, Yahweh, is the God of the whole world. The experience of a few patriarchs and later the one nation of Israel with this God expands to include the horizon of the entire world. We shall cite only a few of the Old Testament passages to illustrate this universal motif.

The Table of Nations in Genesis 10

Genesis 10, with its passage listing the table of nations, is important for understanding the universal motif of the Old Testament. Gerhard von Rad described it as the conclusion to the history of the Creation. All of the nations issue forth from the creative hand of God and stand under his watchful eye of patience and judgment. The nations are not mere decorations incidental to the real drama between God and man; rather, the nations — that is, mankind as a whole — are part of the drama itself. God's work and activity are directed at the whole of humanity.

This is one of the fundamental truths of Genesis 1–11, the record of history's beginning; it is also found in the moving account of history's end, the book of John's Revelation. The very God who revealed himself to Israel and dwelt among us in Jesus Christ identifies himself as the Alpha and Omega, the beginning and the ending. He does not lay down his work until "every tongue and nation" and "a multitude without number" have been gathered round his throne (Rev. 5:9–10 and 7:9–17). God is cutting a path directly through the weary and plodding activities of men in history in order to achieve his goals among the nations. In Genesis 10 the nations are as yet only a dotted line, so to speak, but as history progresses, the dots become connected until, entirely in accord with the plan of God, the whole line becomes solid. The protohistory of Genesis points forward to the eschaton of Revelation when God's intentions have become worldwide in their scope.

God's Election of Israel with His Eye on the Nations

After the Bible finishes its account of God's judgment of the nations, so graphically described in the Genesis passage about the Tower of Babel, in chapter 12 it shifts to God's call to Abraham to leave Ur of the Chaldees. The "God of the whole earth" seems at first glance to narrow his interests to the private history of one family and tribe only, but in actuality nothing could be farther from the truth. In de Groot's words, "Israel is the opening word in God's proclaiming salvation, not the Amen."[2] For a time Israel, the "people of Abraham," is separated from the other nations (Ex. 19:3ff.; Deut. 7:14ff.), but only so that through Israel God

2. A. de Groot, *De Bijbel over het Heil der Volken* (Roermond: Romens, 1964).

can pave the way toward achieving his world-embracing goals. In choosing Israel as segment of all humanity, God never took his eye off the other nations; Israel was the *pars pro toto,* a minority called to serve the majority.[3]

God's election of Abraham and Israel concerns the whole world. He deals so intensely with Israel precisely because he is maintaining his personal claim on the whole world. To speak to this world in the fullness of time he needed a people. Countless recent studies are emphazing this very point: God chose Israel in preparation for the complete unwrapping and disclosure of his universal intentions. See, for example, the work of scholars like G. von Rad, Walter Eichrodt, Bächli, and G. E. Wright.

Whenever Israel forgot that God chose her with a view to speaking to the other nations and turned away from them in introverted pride, prophets like Amos, Jeremiah, and Isaiah lashed out at the people's ethnocentric pretension and charged them with subverting God's actual intentions (see especially Amos 7:9–10).

The Breakthrough of the Universal Motif in the Exile

Israel's experiences during the seventh and sixth centuries B.C. opened her eyes to God's universal intentions. As Israel passed through her catastrophic experience of being trounced by the Babylonians and carted off into exile, the prophets came to see how closely the career of Israel was tied in with the history of the nations. Out of the judgment which Israel was feeling there blossomed the eager hope of a new covenant, a new exodus, another Son of David. Jeremiah, Ezekiel, and Deutero-Isaiah all saw the horizon expanding and bore witness that all nations now fall within the spotlight of God's promises.

Traces of Universalism in Post-exilic Apocalypticism

After the exile an apocalyptic theology was formed in the crucible of new oppression; the message boldly underscored some of the universal features of the Old Testament message. The apocalyptic vision of Daniel, for example, predicts the coming of the Son of Man whose kingdom shall put an end to the brutish kingdoms of the world and whose domain shall include all peoples (Dan. 7:1–29).

In this apocalyptic theology the universal lines of Old Testament history and prophecy are so clearly extended that no one can fail to see that the world of the nations mentioned already in Genesis 10 is the final goal — not the point of departure — of all God's efforts.

The Motif of Rescue and Liberation

Yahweh, the Redeemer of Israel

The soteriological theme of the Bible, that is, God's work of rescuing and saving both Israel and the other nations, is tied closely to the theme of universalism. Yahweh, the God of all the earth, displayed his love and kept his word to Israel by freeing her from the bonds of slavery with his strong and outstretched arm (see

---

3. See J. Verkuyl, *Break Down the Walls,* trans. and ed. Lewis B. Smedes (Grand Rapids: Eerdmans, 1973), p. 40.

Deut. 9:26; 13:5; 15:15; 24:18). This was a basic part of Israel's credo and crucial to understanding the first commandment. This God — the one who saves and frees — alone is God. "You shall have no other gods before me" (Ex. 20). This credo transformed Israel from being merely one nation among others into the *qāhāl*, the chosen community which owes its very existence to God's act of deliverance and returns its praises to him in psalms and prayers of thanksgiving.

Yahweh, the Redeemer of the Nations

The prophets of Israel grew increasingly aware that not only Israel would share in God's acts of redemption. God would break in to restore his liberating Lordship over the entire world of the nations.

In their studies Sundkler and Blauw point out that the prophets develop this theme centripetally; that is, after their rescue the other nations make their pilgrimage back to Zion, the mountain of the Lord. The prophets picture the people of the other nations as returning to Jerusalem, where the God of Israel shall appear as the God of all the peoples. (See Isa. 2:1-4; Mic. 4:1-4; Jer. 3:17; Isa. 25:6-9; Isa. 60; Zech. 8:20ff.)

Several psalms chant this theme, too. Psalm 87 proclaims Jerusalem as the ecumenical city whose citizens shall some day include inhabitants of the various nations, even from those nations who once most ardently opposed the God of Israel. They shall join in celebrating God's restored fellowship with the peoples.

God's Method of Achieving Liberation

The Bible also describes the means God is using to bring salvation to Israel and the nations. No other Old Testament passage probes more deeply into this matter than the so-called *Ebed-Yahweh* ("Servant") songs of Deutero-Isaiah 40–55. They are, however, mystifying as well, and Hendrikus Berkhof, the dogmatician, cautions against a too facile interpretation of them from a New Testament perspective without first having considered their Old Testament background.

These Servant songs make unmistakable reference to the spread of salvation through the whole world. The Servant shall carry it to the ends of the earth (Isa. 49:6), and he will not stop until righteousness prevails throughout the earth. The coastlands are awaiting his instruction (Isa. 42:4).

The fourth Servant song in chapter 53 uncovers the secret of *how* the Servant of the Lord shall discharge his mission. This deeply moving passage depicts the Servant becoming a victim of the most savage human butchery. Every kind of mistreatment human minds can devise shall be done to him. However, the Servant also at that point shall be acting as a substitute who is incurring the judgment of God which was properly due not only to Israel but to all peoples and nations.

Rabbi Ignaz Maybaum, in referring to the two characteristics of the Servant mentioned in this passage — victim and substitute — points out in *Trialogue between Jew, Christian, and Muslim* that "wrath is demonic, but substitution brings healing."[4] Of course this author parts ways with the Christian as he goes on

4. Ignaz Maybaum, *Trialogue between Jew, Christian and Muslim* (London: Routledge & Kegan Paul, 1973).

to explain this passage in greater detail, but on one point there is no dispute: as a substitute for both Israel and the nations, the Servant has to walk the path of suffering to bring them freedom. Moreover, this passage describes the nations as Yahweh's gifts to the Servant in return for his willing obedience to suffer death. He achieved the right to bring salvation and healing to all people.

In passing, we must note that Paul, the Apostle to the heathen Gentiles, grounds his call from God to engage in worldwide mission in these very Servant songs taken from the Old Testament (see Acts 13:47).

The Missionary Motif

Connected with the other two Old Testament motifs mentioned previously is the missionary motif. The prophets never tire of reminding Israel that her election is not a privilege which she may selfishly keep for herself; election is a call to service. It involves a duty to witness among the nations. Israel must be a sign to the other nations that Yahweh is both Creator and Liberator. One Servant song (Isa. 49:6) refers to Israel's mandate to become a light to the nations.

Virtually every author who attempts to explain this call to Israel comes up with the concept of presence. Chosen by God to become the special recipients of his mercy and justice, Israel now has the corresponding duty to live as the people of God among the other nations in order to show them his grace, mercy, justice, and liberating power. Time and time again the prophets recorded their deep disappointment over Israel's continual sabotage of her divine calling. But however hot their righteous anger burned against Israel's disobedience, the prophets kept on reminding Israel to the very end of her mandate to be present among the people as distinct people and a royal priesthood.

It is worth noting that since the Second World War a number of missiologists have urged Christian presence as one of the leading methods of engaging in today's mission work. For a variety of reasons and in a variety of manners, they claim that the most suitable form of witness lies in simply being a specific kind of people while living among other people. This is not the place to develop this idea further but only to point out that the idea that presence is witness has deep roots in the Old Testament. The prophets continually claimed that by her very act of living out her divine appointment to serve, Israel becomes a sign and bridge for the other nations.

However, I do not believe it is correct to view the missionary motif only in terms of the concept of presence. I simply do not understand why various writers make such a point of avowing that the Old Testament makes absolutely no mention of a missionary mandate. Blauw, Gensichen, Hahn, and many others do this. In his book *Mission in the New Testament* Hahn says, for example, that the Old Testament bears a "completely passive character." In my opinion this is an exaggeration. Bächli's book *Israël und die Völker* is closer to the truth by noting that the Exodus account and the Deuteronomic tradition distinguish between 'am ("people") and qāhāl ("the religious community") and expressly mention that already in the desert many individuals had joined the qāhāl who had not been original members of the 'am. The heathen people too, who had come along with Israel and dwelt as strangers among God's people, participated in Israel's worship. They heard of God's mighty deeds and joined Israel in songs of praise.

Then there is that striking number of individuals who left their heathen origins and by a word-and-deed witness were won over to trust and serve the living God who had shown them mercy. The stories of Melchizedek, Ruth, Job, the people of Nineveh described in the book of Jonah, and many others in the Old Testament are windows, as it were, through which we may look out on the vast expanse of people outside the nation of Israel and hear the faint strains of the missionary call to all people already sounding forth.

The wisdom literature of the Old Testament is similar in both form and content to both Greek and Egyptian cultures. Without doubt, her own literature served Israel as a means of communicating her beliefs to the other nations.

Moreover there is no other way of explaining the powerful missionary impact of Judaism during the Diaspora than to affirm that those dispersed Jews *from their earliest days* had heard and understood their call to witness directly as well as by their presence.

The Motif of Antagonism

The above list of Old Testament missionary motifs is incomplete. Intricately connected with each of those mentioned above is the antagonistic motif, that is, Yahweh's powerful wrestling against those powers and forces which oppose his liberating and gracious authority. Marc Spindler, in his book *La Mission, combat pour le salut du monde,* goes so far as to claim that it is the leading motif.

The whole Old Testament (and the New Testament as well) is filled with descriptions of how Yahweh-Adonai, the covenant God of Israel, is waging war against those forces which try to thwart and subvert his plans for his creation. He battles against those false gods which human beings have fashioned from the created world, idolized, and used for their own purposes. Think, for example, of the Baals and the Ashtaroth, whose worshippers elevated nature, the tribe, the state, and the nation to a divine status. God fights against magic and astrology which, according to Deuteronomy, bend the line between God and his creation. He contends against every form of social injustice and pulls off every cloak under which it seeks to hide (see Amos and Jeremiah, for example).

The whole of the Old Testament burns with a feverish desire to defeat these opposing powers. There are grand visions of that coming kingdom where every relationship is properly restored and when the whole of creation — people, animals, plants, and every other creature — will perfectly accord with God's intentions for it (see Isa. 2, Mic. 4, and Isa. 65). The Old Testament longs for this kingdom's final revealing and categorically states its promise that Yahweh shall indeed finally overcome. This too is a highly significant theme for missionary participation. To participate in mission is quite impossible unless one also wages war against every form of opposition to God's intentions wherever it be found, whether in churches, the world of the nations, or one's own life.

The Old Testament ties the antagonistic motif closely with the doxological theme: the glory of Yahweh-Adonai shall be revealed among all peoples. Then every human being shall come to know him as he really is, the "gracious and merciful God, slow to get angry, full of kindness, and always willing to turn back from meting out disaster" (Jon. 4:1–2).

Each of these four motifs is basic to understanding and carrying out the work of missions. Of course, each could only be lightly touched upon within the compass of this book. However, there is one passage which I must treat more extensively at the conclusion of this study of the Old Testament, for it reflects the basic themes so clearly. This is the book of Jonah.

The Book of Jonah

The book of Jonah is so significant for understanding the biblical basis of mission because it treats God's mandate to his people regarding the Gentile peoples and thus serves as the preparatory step to the missionary mandate of the New Testament. But it is also important for catching a glimpse of the deep resistance this mandate encounters from the very servant Yahweh has chosen to discharge his worldwide work.

Today there is much talk and writing about "educating the congregation" and "educating personnel" for mission. Jonah is a lesson in educating a person to be a missionary; it reveals the need for a radical conversion of one's natural tendencies and a complete restructuring of his life to make it serviceable for mission.

Background of the Book

Literary genre. Jonah is a book unique among the books of the twelve minor prophets. The other books are collections of the various prophets' words; the book of Jonah is a story about the prophet himself. It is a story written with a specific purpose in mind.

Old Testament scholars claim that the book is a *midrash* — a constructive, homiletical application of a story written for a specific reason. It is not an historical journal of events, but rather a story with a message. Even those who prefer to read the book as an actual account of what happened to Jonah may never ignore the primary message and intention of the writing.

The *midrash* contains eight successive scenes, each one pointing to God's all-embracing plans for the Gentiles and Jonah's futile efforts to sabotage these plans.

Title. The title of the book is the personal name of the unwilling prophet, Jonah, and harks back to the days of King Jeroboam II (787–746 B.C.) when a prophet named Jonah ben Amittai was living. It is obvious, however, that this *midrash* is intended for reasons quite other than detailing the events of this prophet's life. The author uses this personal name to portray for his readers a missionary who has no heart for the Gentiles and who, like the later Pharisees, cannot tolerate a God who shows them mercy. In the words of the Dutch author Miskotte, "the writer intends to picture a person who is the exact opposite of an apostle." The author of Jonah warns his readers against this intolerant attitude and sets before each of them the question of whether he or she is willing to be transformed into a servant who works to accomplish the mandates of God.

Provenance. From evidence in the books of Sirach and Tobit it appears that this book was already known in the second century B.C. Old Testament scholars vary in the date they give to the book, some claiming it was written as early as 600 B.C. and others as late as 200 B.C. H. W. Wolff in his *Studien zum Jonabuch* offers a guess that the *midrash* originated among a group of Diaspora Jews who were convinced of their missionary duty in a heathen environment and wanted to warn against a perverted view of Israel's election.

Position within the canon of Scripture. It is a miracle that Jonah, with its strong warning against ethnocentrism, ever made its way into the canon of Scripture. It squarely sets forth man's attempt to sabotage God's worldwide plans so that its readers — Israel, the New Testament church, and us — can hear what the Holy Spirit through the medium of this little book is trying to tell them.

To whom the book is addressed. As the author sees it, Israel has become so preoccupied with herself that she no longer directs her eyes toward the world of the nations. Israel, the recipient of all God's revelation, refuses to set foot in alien territory to tell the other peoples God's message of judgment and liberation. But the message of the book also is addressed to the New Testament congregation which tries various ways of evading her Lord's command to speak his message to the world.

Jonah's crafty evasion efforts represent a lazy and unfaithful church which does not heed its Lord's command. God has to wrestle against Israel's narrow ethnocentrism which tries to restrict his activity to the boundaries of Israel alone and against the church's ecclesiocentric refusal to go out into the world to proclaim God's message and do his work. The writer is bent on convincing his readers that the radius of God's liberating activity is wide enough to cover both Israel and the Gentiles. Israel, as he sees it, is merely a *pars pro toto* since the God whom she worships, Yahweh, is God alone and no mere tribal god or idol of man's making.

A Short Review of the Book's Eight Scenes

The first scene opens with Jonah receiving the command to go to Nineveh. While the Old Testament usually appeals to the other nations to *come to* Zion, the mountain to God, Jonah, like the disciples of the New Testament (cf. Matt. 28:18–20), is told to *go!* The Septuagint translation of Jonah uses the word *poreuomai* in 1:2–3 and again in 3:2–3, the very same verb used by Jesus in his Great Commission recorded in Matthew 28. Where must Jonah go? To Nineveh, of all places, Nineveh, a very center of totalitarianism, brutality, and warlike attitudes. To Nineveh, notorious for the shameful hounding, vicious torture, and imperialist brazenness it reserved for those who chose to oppose its policies. God wants his servant to warn Nineveh of impending judgment and to call her to repentance. He wants to save *Nineveh!*

But Jonah refuses. He prepares himself, to be sure, but only to *flee* from the face of God who is Lord over all.

In the second scene God responds to Jonah's flight by sending a mighty storm (1:4–16). The wind obeys Yahweh's commands, but the disobedient Jonah sleeps in the bottom of the boat, oblivious of the fact that the storm is directed at him. At times the church, too, sleeps right through the storm of God's judgment passing over the world, assuring herself that the wind outside has nothing to do with her. While the crew vainly searches for the storm's cause, Jonah confesses that he worships and fears the God who made both the sea and the dry land, the one God who is above all nations. This God, he claims, is bringing a charge against him, and the only way to quiet the waters is to throw him into the sea. In this scene the crew represents the Gentiles, a people for whom Jonah is totally unconcerned, and yet who themselves are interested in sparing his life. After a second order from Jonah they throw him overboard and the storm ceases. Scarcely able to believe their eyes, the sailors break forth in praise to the God of Jonah. Their obedience surpasses that of the saboteur Jonah; they are more open to God than the very prophet himself.

The third scene (1:17) describes a large fish which, at Yahweh's instructions, opens its mouth to swallow Jonah and spew him onto the shore at the appropriate time. Jonah simply cannot escape God's missionary mandate. The God who whipped up the stormy winds and directed the sailors to accomplish his purposes now guides a fish as part of his plan to save Nineveh. Yahweh continues his work of reforming and preparing his missionary to be a fit instrument in his plans.

In the fourth scene (2:1–10) Jonah implores God to rescue him from the belly of the fish. He who had no mercy on the Gentiles and refused to acknowledge that God's promises extended to them now appeals for Divine mercy, and by quoting lines from various psalms pants after those promises claimed by worshipers in God's temple.

Yahweh reacts. He speaks to the brute beast and Jonah lands on shore, safe and sound. By his very rescue Jonah was unwittingly a witness of God's saving mercy. Though covered with seaweed (to borrow a phrase from one of Kohlbrugge's Jonah sermons), Jonah was nonetheless a testimony that God takes no delight in the death of sinners and saboteurs but rather rejoices in their conversion.

In the fifth scene (3:1–4) God repeats his order to the man whose very life affirms the truth of what he confessed in the belly of fish: "Salvation is from Yahweh." The Septuagint uses the term *kerygma* in 3:1–2ff. That single word summarizes Jonah's mission: he must *proclaim* that Nineveh, however godless she may be, is still the object of God's fervent concern, and unless she repents, she will be destroyed. His message must be one of threat as well as promise, of judgment as well as gospel.

In the sixth scene (3:5–10) Nineveh responds to Jonah's appeal to repent. The proud, despotic king steps down from his royal throne, exchanges his robes for dust and ashes, and enjoins every man and animal to follow his example. What Israel continually refused to do the heathen gentiles did do; the cruel king of Nineveh stands as anti-type to the disobedient kings of Judah.

The people join the king in repenting. They cease all their devilish work, and the terrifying and coercing engines of political injustice come to a halt. In deep penitence they turn away from idols to serve the God who is Lord of every nation and all creation. All this becomes possible because Yahweh is God. The world of the heathen is a potentially productive mission field for no other reason than this: He alone is God.

The curtain closes on this scene with these amazing words: "God saw what they did, and how they abandoned their wicked ways, and he repented and did not bring upon them the disaster he had threatened." Yahweh is faithful to his promises. Still today his will for Moscow and Peking, for London and Amsterdam, is no less "gracious and full of mercy" than it was for Nineveh. To borrow from Luther, who loved to preach from the book of Jonah, the left hand of God's wrath is replaced by his right hand of blessing and freedom.

The seventh scene (4:1–4) recounts the fact that the greatest hurdle to overcome in discharging the missionary mandate was not the sailors, nor the fish, nor Nineveh's king and citizenry, but rather Jonah himself — the recalcitrant and narrow-minded church. Chapter 4 describes Jonah, who has long since departed the city to find shelter east of the borders. The forty-day period of repentance has passed, but since God has changed his mind about destroying it, the city continues to be nourished by Yahweh's grace and mercy. Jonah is furious that God has extended his mercy beyond the borders of Israel to the Gentiles. He wanted a God cut according to his own pattern: a cold, hard, cruel nature-god with an unbending will set against the heathen. He cannot stand to think of the Gentiles as part of salvation history.

This is Jonah's sin, the sin of a missionary whose heart is not in it. He who once pleaded with God for mercy from the desolate isolation of a fish's belly now is angry that this God shows mercy to the nations. He vents his fury in the form of a prayer found in 4:2, the key text of the whole book: "And he prayed to the Lord, 'This, O Lord, is what I feared when I was in my own country, and to forestall it I tried to escape to Tarshish; I knew that thou art a "gracious and compassionate God, long-suffering and ever constant, and always willing to repent of the disaster." ' " Part of the text comes from an ancient Israelite liturgy which every Israelite knew by heart and could rattle off in worship at the temple or synagogue while half asleep (cf. Ex. 34:6; Ps. 86:15; 103:8; 145:8; Neh. 9:17). But Jonah cannot stand to think that this liturgy is true not only for Jerusalem, the location of God's temple, but for other places as well — Nineveh, Sao Paulo, Nairobi, New York, and Paris. Sometimes the church shows the same narrowness in adamantly insisting that there is no salvation outside her walls.

Why is Jonah really so angry? For no other reason than that God is treating those outside his covenant the same as he is those within. But Jonah's anger in effect is putting himself outside the covenant, for he obstinately refuses to acknowledge the covenant's purpose — to bring salvation to the heathen. He had not yet learned that Israel could not presume upon some special favors from God. Both Israel and the Gentiles alike live by the grace which the Creator gives to all of his creatures. So God comes to his prophet, but no longer as a covenant partner; he comes as the Creator and asks his creature: "Do you have a right to be so angry?"

In the eighth and last scene (4:5–11) one can see God still working to teach his thick-skulled missionary his lessons. He did not catch the point of the storm, the sailors, the fish, and Nineveh's conversion because he did not want to. Now Yahweh tries one more approach — the miraculous tree. A climbing gourd springs up quickly, offers Jonah protection against the beating sun, but as quickly withers and dies, the victim of an attacking worm. Jonah is peeved.

At that point God again turns to his missionary-student, using the tree as his object lesson. The very God who directs the whole course of history, who rules the wind and the wave and turned Nineveh's millions to repentance, now asks tenderly: "Are you so angry over the gourd? You are sorry about the gourd, though you had nothing to do with growing it, a plant which came up in a night and withered in a night. And should not I be sorry for the great city of Nineveh, with its hundred and twenty thousand who cannot tell their right hand from their left, and cattle without number?"

God spares and rescues. Jerusalem's God is Nineveh's as well. Unlike Jonah, he has no "Gentile complex." He worries about that self-willed center of power, chauvinism, and heathen practice. He agonizes over those masses of human beings whom theologians for so long have labeled *massa perditionis,* the multitude of the lost. And while he never forces any one of us, he tenderly asks us to put our whole heart and soul into the work of mission. God is still interested in transforming obstinate, irritable, depressive, peevish Jonahs into heralds of the Good News which brings freedom.

The book ends with an unsettling question which is never answered: "God reached his goal with Nineveh, but what about Jonah?" No one knows. The question of Israel and the church and their obedience is still an open one.

The question is one which every generation of Christians must answer for itself. Jacques Ellul closes his book *The Judgment of Jonah* with these words: "The Book of Jonah has no conclusion, and the final question of the book has no answer, except from the one who realizes the fulness of the mercy of God and who factually and not just mythically accomplishes the salvation of the world."[5]

The New Testament church must pay close heed to the message of Jonah's book. Jesus Christ is "One greater than Jonah" (Matt. 12:39–41; Luke 11:29–32). His death on the cross with its awful cry of God-forsakenness and his resurrection with its jubilant shout of victory are signs of Jonah for us, pointing to the profound meaning of his whole life and clearly attesting that God loved the *whole* world so much.

If a person draws his lifeblood from the one greater than Jonah and yet declines to spread the good news among others, he in effect is sabotaging the aims of God himself. Jonah is father to all those Christians who desire the benefits and blessings of election but refuse its responsibility.

Thomas Carlisle's poem "You Jonah" closes with these lines:

And Jonah stalked
to his shaded seat
and waited for God
to come around
to his way of thinking.

And God is still waiting for a host of Jonahs
in their comfortable houses
to come around
to his way of loving.

---

5. Jacques Ellul, *The Judgment of Jonah* (Grand Rapids: Eerdmans, 1971), p. 103.

THE INTERTESTAMENTAL PERIOD

Research into the period of the Jewish Diaspora has uncovered evidence of a Jewish effort to proselytize, which, in turn, definitely stamped later missionary work carried on by the Gentile as well as the Jewish Christians. The Septuagint (the Greek translation of the Old Testament) went through the whole of the civilized world and was explained in the synagogues. Diaspora Judaism's missionary impact was far greater than many realize. What is more, Judaism affected early Christianity, for the Jewish Christians kept close contact with the synagogue communities. The synagogue played a crucial role, for it attracted not only proselytes (Gentiles who adopted the complete range of Jewish beliefs and practices, including circumcision) but also a class it termed "God-fearers" (Gentiles who accepted most of Judaism's ethics and some of its cultus, but refused circumcision).

In spite of the connection, however, the Jewish message was quite different from the New Testament gospel of God's kingdom and the Christian belief that Jesus was the Messiah. Palestinian Judaism required that the heathen be assimilated into the Jewish fellowship and made every effort to achieve this transfer. Jewish communities outside of Palestine, on the other hand, laid their emphasis on monotheism, a belief which the pagan world, weary with worshiping many gods, found highly attractive. They spiritualized the cultus and decried the decadent lifestyle of the Gentile world. Their message was to a great degree auto-soteric — a person could save himself. Both the Sibylline oracles and book of Joseph and Asenath make the claim that a person, by properly maintaining the ethical and ritual requirements, can reconcile himself to God. By affirming that God's people can only patiently wait for him to undertake his work among the heathen, late Judaism proclaimed an eschatology which lacked missionary perspective, and by proclaiming that a person's own attitude and efforts can save him their mission was without an eschatology.

Jesus was quite possibly aiming his sharp words of Matthew 23:15 against these specific elements in the Jewish message when he lamented: "Alas for you, lawyers and Pharisees, hypocrites! You travel over sea and land to win one convert; and when you have won him you make him twice as fit for hell as you are yourselves." Paul joins Jesus in rebuking the Jewish legalism and efforts at self-justification in Romans 2:17–24.

Jesus and Paul were not opposing Jewish missions to the Gentiles per se. In fact Paul views his own work among them as continuing what the Jews in the Diaspora had already started among the Gentiles. But they do object to what the Jews said. Therefore, when Jesus began to proclaim his own message, he did not go back to late Jewish traditions for support, but back to the Old Testament itself.

THE NEW TESTAMENT: BOOK OF WORLD MISSION

From beginning to end, the New Testament is a book of mission. It owes its very existence to the missionary work of the early Christian churches, both Jewish and Hellenistic. The Gospels are, as it were, "live recordings" of missionary preach-

ing, and the Epistles are not so much some form of missionary apologetic as they
are authentic and actual *instruments* of mission work. We cannot discuss every
detail which would underscore the New Testament's importance for the foundation and practice of mission, but we do nevertheless wish to examine a few of
them.

Jesus, the Savior of the World

All the various Old Testament motifs converge in the person and work of Jesus of
Nazareth. The episode on the Mount of Transfiguration underscores how the
universal, messianic, and missionary motifs come together in his life. In the
account of Mark 9:2–13 Moses and Elijah are mentioned along with Jesus. But by
announcing that he who is in the midst of those three disciples, Peter, James and
John, is greater than any Moses or Elijah, the passage is claiming that Jesus does
more than simply pull all of the Old Testament together and fulfill it in his own
person; he is marching forward to announce that God has a concern for the whole
world. The promises which he carries in his own person and work make the Old
Testament indeed old and mark the beginning of the New Testament. As Hendrikus Berkhof so aptly puts it, "we believe that Christ is the next and decisive
step which God took along the lengthened section of a path he had already been
traveling with Israel." The half-Gentile Samaritan citizens of the town of Sychar
are the first to speak of this when they say in John 4:42: "We know that this is
indeed the Savior of the world [*sōtēr tou kosmou*]."

The Arrival of the All-Embracing Kingdom of God

At the outset of his ministry, Jesus came to his hometown of Nazareth. Having
gone to the synagogue to worship on the Sabbath, the leaders accorded him the
honor of reading the Scriptures. As he concluded his reading of the prophet
Isaiah's message in chapter 61 and had set the scroll down, he added a comment
which brings incalculable hope to many but at the same time deeply offends those
who reject him. He said: "Today in your very hearing this Scripture has been
fulfilled" (Luke 4:21).

The coming salvation to which the prophets bore witness came true in
Jesus Christ. Salvation has arrived, and therefore the good news which Jesus
proclaims describes a kingdom which had both *already come* and is *yet coming*.
Applying the words of Isaiah 61 to himself, Jesus says the Spirit of the Lord is on
him. He marks the beginning of God's kingdom and introduces the "acceptable
year of the Lord" in all of its rich variety. The kingdom's first appearing was
provisional and still awaits its final fulfillment, but when Jesus made his daring
claim — "He has sent me to bring good news to the afflicted, to proclaim liberty to
the captives, and recovery of sight to the blind, to set at liberty the oppressed, to
proclaim the acceptable year of the Lord" — the kingdom had really come and the
hour for decision had been reached. In Jesus Christ God was holding before men
his gracious saving work more directly and urgently than ever before. The shape
of things to come, his kingdom, became exceptionally clear in the person, the
words, and the deeds of the Messiah. He powerfully subdued those sinister forces
which were destroying the souls and bodies of men and renewed those who were

the victims and servants of those forces. He called people to repentance.

The whole of the New Testament speaks the language of fulfillment. God's gracious and saving work has *already appeared* for all people (see Titus 2:11; Eph. 1:10; Gal. 4:4–5; Heb. 1:1–4). But it also affirms that the final appearing of this kingdom is *yet coming*. There is an air of expectation in the New Testament as well.

In the Gospels these motifs switch back and forth. The one presupposes the other. According to the Gospels we now live between the *already* of the kingdom which has come and the *not yet* of its final manifestation, between the promise of Luke 4:21 ("Today in your very hearing this Scripture has been fulfilled") and the anticipation of Matthew 24:14 ("And this Gospel of the Kingdom will be preached throughout the whole world, as a testimony to all nations; and then the end will come").

The Manner of the Kingdom's Coming

Jesus' miracles and parables provide special help in understanding how the kingdom is revealed in this world. John's Gospel calls the miracles signs which point to the approaching kingdom and the majestic character of the Messiah. These miracles address every human need: poverty, sickness, hunger, sin, demonic temptation, and the threat of death. By them Jesus is anticipating Easter. Each of them proclaims that wherever and whenever in God's name human needs and problems are being tackled and overcome, there God's kingdom is shining through. Likewise, the parables Jesus told — for example, the parables of the seed, the fishnet, the harvest, the mustard seed, and the leaven — tell how the message about this kingdom shall reach all nations and peoples (see Matt. 13; Luke 8; Mark 4).

"On the basis of Jesus' own preaching one may claim that the apostolic work of the Church throughout the whole world is the very reason for the interim period between Jesus' ascension and his return as the Son of Man."[6]

Jesus and the Gentiles

There has been much talk about whether or not Jesus purposely directed any of his work to the Gentiles prior to his death and resurrection. In his book *Mission und Ausbreitung* (I), Adolph von Harnack tried to show that a mission to the Gentiles lay entirely outside the horizon of Jesus' thinking. To disprove Harnack's contention, Bengt Sundkler published an essay which later became famous, "Jésus et les Païens," and thirty years after the Sundkler essay David Bosch followed it up with one of his own, which, though denying certain of the details in Sundkler's treatment, nonetheless supports the main contention.

In Sundkler's view, every one of Harnack's followers goes wrong by working with a particularism-universalism schema and then proceeding to assign Jesus to the class of particularists. Sundkler totally rejects the schema and replaces it with one of his own — centripetal-centrifugal. At first Israel's relationship to the other nations is centripetal: the *gôyim* come to the mountain of the Lord in Jerusalem, Mount Zion. But after the Old Testament is fulfilled and all the various

---

6. "Report of the Netherlands Missionary Council on the Biblical Foundation for Mission," *De Heerbaan* 4 (August, 1951): 197–221.

strands meet in the Man from Nazareth, and following a short time of concentrating on Israel, the relationship becomes centrifugal. The lines fan out and the path to the heathen is made ready.

Ferdinand Hahn's *Mission in the New Testament* provides a helpful summary of the many studies on this issue in a section entitled: "Jesus' Attitude toward the Gentiles." He looks at the occasions when Jesus met Gentiles: the Syro-Phoenician woman (John 4), a Roman centurion (Matt. 8:5–13), and a delegation of Greeks (John 12:20–36). He also recalls some of the other things Jesus said and did: his visit to the northern reaches of Palestine, including the territory of the Gadarenes (Mark 5; Luke 8:26–56), and his reminder that the Gentiles shall someday become pilgrims making their way to the feast (Isa. 25:6–12; Matt. 8:11).

My own little book *Break Down the Walls*, which deals with the issue of race relations, discusses these encounters of Jesus with Gentiles. In them I see Jesus itching with a holy impatience for that day when all the stops shall be pulled as the message goes out to the Gentiles. For a time he restricts his message to the lost sheep of the house of Israel, knowing that certain conditions must be met before the message goes out to the *gôyim*. Israel must hear first (Matt. 10), and the blood of the Lamb must be poured out to bring forgiveness "to many" (Mark 10:45; 14:24).

Cross and Resurrection — The Foundation for World Mission
On his cross Jesus vicariously endured God's judgment which was properly due to Israel and the Gentiles. His resurrection likewise brought about a liberating rule, and the lines thus become extended to reach the whole worldwide community of nations and peoples. Jesus' cross and resurrection are the bases for a worldwide mission. For this reason interspersed with reports of his cross and resurrection are the mandates to carry the message to all peoples. This mission will be accomplished only when "the fullness of the Gentiles has entered and the kingdom of God has fully come."

I now wish to give closer attention to the several ways in which the Gospels present the missionary mandate.

The Missionary Mandate in the Gospel of Matthew

New Testament scholars claim that Matthew's Gospel is composed of catechetical material gathered and organized mainly to instruct recent converts about Jesus' work, person, and coming kingdom but also to assist them in spreading the message to others.

To a great degree Matthew used Mark's Gospel as the source for his stories about Jesus' deeds, but his own unique contribution was to collect a ninefold series of Jesus' words. Matthew's Gospel thus becomes a textbook for missions.

Scholars disagree on the date the book was written, some claiming it comes from about A.D. 75 and others preferring a slightly later date, perhaps somewhere between the years 80 and 100. If they are right, we must then keep in mind that this Gospel reflects a period in the early church when both Jewish and Gentile Christians were powerfully broadcasting the good news. One can easily understand then that this Gospel issues a strong call to communicate the faith in Jesus the Messiah to both Israel and the non-Jewish nations and peoples.

Communication of the Gospel to the People of Israel

Matthew 10 records Jesus' command to his disciples to proclaim the message to Israel. Note that the striking words of verse 5 — "Go nowhere among the Gentiles and enter no town of the Samaritans, but go rather to the lost sheep of the house of Israel" — are from the very same book which in chapter 28 includes the Great Commission to go to *all* peoples. The final editor made no attempt to "reconcile" these two passages. As he saw it, none was necessary, for the two complement each other and remain equally valid. When the Gospel of Matthew was written, there were Jewish Christians living in Palestine who opposed any mission to the Gentiles because they anticipated certain other events happening first. The author-editor of this Gospel, quite possibly a member of the Jewish Christian community in Syria, wrote his textbook with the strong conviction that the call to proclaim the message to Israel had to be paired with a mission to the non-Israelite peoples. The synchronization, he believed, was an implication from the Lord Jesus' command. As the writer saw it, the preresurrection concentration on Israel was a matter of *strategic* significance.

A segment of Jewish Christendom played off the mission to the Jews against the mission to the Gentiles, believing that the second should not be undertaken until another event of eschatological importance had first transpired, namely, the gathering of "the sheep of the twelve tribes." Only then would the "way to the Gentiles" be open.

But the writer of Matthew 10 disagrees. For him the event which opened a way to the Gentiles was Jesus' resurrection. Prior to that, all the attention is focused on Israel, but the cross and resurrection are both the base for a worldwide mission and the signal to begin. Jesus' words recorded in Matthew 10:23 — "Truly I say to you, you will not have gone through all the towns of Israel, before the Son of man comes" — are a covert reference to his resurrection. The fundamental epiphany of the Son of Man is the Christophany of the risen Lord.

Ferdinand Hahn beautifully exegetes the relationship between Matthew 10 and 28. The two passages are concentric circles and synchronize the Christian mission to Jews and non-Jews. While the earthly Jesus, himself a messenger to Israel, called the church to continued contact with the old people of God, the risen and exalted Lord of the whole world issued the command to go to all peoples. "What Matthew wants to assert in his own way is the priority of the mission to Israel and the permanent obligation towards it — for without Israel as the center there would indeed be no salvation. This mission, however, is only carried out rightly if at the same time the universal commission is observed by working among all nations."[7]

Chapters 10 and 28 in Matthew's Gospel are therefore not contradictory. On the contrary, they make clear the historical situation in the time after the resurrection when the disciples were called to engage in mission. Any study,

7. Ferdinand Hahn, *Mission in the New Testament* (London: SCM Press, 1965), pp. 127–128.

therefore, which like Joachim Gnilka's claims that the *góyim* or *ethnē* take the place of Israel is only repeating an age-old misunderstanding.[8] Taken together, the two passages remind us that the doors are now open to everyone.

The Great Commission of Matthew 28

That only Matthew contains a mandate for engaging in worldwide mission is a popular and stubborn misconception. The following pages will make amply clear that every Gospel, as well as the book of Acts, presents it. But there is no doubt about it: the concluding verses of Matthew's Gospel express it the most forthrightly.

Not only is the conclusion to Matthew's Gospel extremely powerful compared to the others, but the final verses form a climax and present a summary of what was written before. They are the key to understanding the whole book.

In these concluding verses Jesus, the risen Lord, standing atop one of the mountains in Galilee — could it be the same one from which he delivered his Sermon on the Mount (Matt. 5:1)? — proclaims a three-point message to his disciples.

(a) *Jesus' authority.* He mentions his authority in language reminiscent of Daniel 7:13–14 and of his own words before the Sanhedrin recorded in Matthew 26:64. The divine work of judging and liberating is now placed in the hands of the crucified one who has arisen. He who once had no power has now received full authority. All power has been given to him. "There are therefore not such things as natural law, natural power, asserting their own domain over against Jesus, deserving homage, trust, fear and obedience in their own right."[9]

No area, people, or culture now lies outside the domain of his power and authority. The missionary command which follows is directly connected to this report of the risen Lord's coronation. Having arisen, he now has exalted authority over the whole world. Thus, the mission mandate is not the basis for his enthronement. Rather, the reverse is true: the mandate *follows from* the fact of his authority. However the several recorded missionary mandates may vary, they all in unison proclaim this one truth: a saving and liberating authority proceeds from him, the victim who became a victor. He is the crucified Lord who now rules. His power is not that of a despot bent on destruction; instead he uses his power for our healing and liberation and accomplishes these goals by love, reconciliation, and patience.

(b) *Jesus' continuing mandate to mission.* After his enthronement the crucified and risen Lord issues his mandate to mission. The time between his resurrection and second coming is not simply an empty interim but rather a period during which the discharge of this command is included in the process of enthronement. Philippians 2:5–11 contains a strong parallel to this truth stated here.

What does the enthroned Lord command his disciples to do? He says, first of all, "Go therefore." The author chooses the Greek word *poreuthentes*, which

8. Joachim Gnilka, "Der Missionsauftrag des Herrn nach Matthäus 28 und Apostelgeschichte I," *Bibel und Leben* (1968): 1–9.
9. Karl Barth, "An Exegetical Study of Matthew 28:16–20," in *The Theology of the Christian Mission*, ed. G. H. Anderson (New York: McGraw-Hill, 1961), p. 61.

means "to depart, to leave, to cross boundaries"—sociological boundaries, racial boundaries, cultural boundaries, geographic boundaries.

This point is most important to one who carries on the task of communicating the gospel. It affects work done in his own area as well as in faraway places. The missionary must always be willing and ready to cross boundaries, whether they be at home or away. The word *poreuomai* in this text reminded the early Christian church of a peripatetic Jesus and his disciples who were continually crossing boundaries to reach out to the other person.

Jesus also commands his followers to "make disciples of all nations." The author makes the Greek noun *mathētēs* into a verb. The verbal form of this word occurs four times in the New Testament (in Matt. 13:52 and 27:57, in Acts 14:21, and here in Matt. 28:20). To become a disciple of Jesus involves sharing with him his death and resurrection and joining him on his march to the final disclosure of his messianic kingdom. He commands us to *make* disciples, that is, to move them to surrender to his liberating authority and to volunteer for the march already enroute to a new order of things, namely, his kingdom.

We are to make disciples of "all nations" (*panta ta ethnē*). These words have often been confused with what the Germans call *Volkstum* — "ethnic units." It is, however, a technical term referring to the whole humanity from which God is gathering his people. Even as the phrase "ends of the earth" refers to people of every geographic location, so too the words "all nations" refer to all human beings. The Gospel must go out to all human beings wherever they live. They must be gathered as the firstfruits of a new humanity.

This new fellowship composed of both Jews and Gentiles transcends every limit imposed by family, clan, tribe, ethnic group, nation, and culture. This new people is a seed of the new humanity.

As promised, the proclamation shall lead to baptism. "Baptizing them in the name of the Father, and of the Son, and of the Holy Spirit" implies a change of status. A slave submitting to proselyte baptism became a free person. This baptism in the name of the Father, Son, and Holy Spirit affirms one's passage from the realm where one is held captive by sin, death, and demonic powers to the realm of the messianic kingdom.

The trinitarian form of Christian baptism sets it off from Jewish proselyte baptism and the Gnostic purification rites. It also makes explicit what is contained in the power conferred by Jesus: the love of God the Father, the grace of his Son, and the fellowship of the Holy Spirit.

Our Lord does not call his disciples to proclaim the message of an "anonymous Christendom" but rather to make known the name of the Father, Son, and Holy Spirit. We may not preach liberation while failing to mention the Liberator or peace without speaking of the one who himself is peace.

Jesus also says, ". . . teaching them to observe all that I have commanded you." Although Mark also occasionally uses the Greek word *didaskein* ("to teach, to instruct"), no one uses it as frequently as does Matthew in his catechism. When Jesus talks here about teaching, he does not mean instruction prior to a person's baptism, but rather training and guidance to help the newly baptized ones on their way. Baptism denotes the fact and nature of being a disciple while teaching (*didachē*) points out the paths along which this discipleship can come to expression. The function of teaching (the New Testament Torah) is to clear a path through the wilderness.

People must learn everything that Jesus has commanded. This includes his law and his gospel, his commands as well as his promises. Matthew presents a series of nine collections of Jesus' teachings as though they are being recorded live before an audience of catechumens. But his *didachē* is most clearly expressed for us in his Sermon on the Mount (Matt. 5–7). In it one can hear God tolling out the beautitudes of his liberating promises as well as his radical and liberating demands.

Matthew included Jesus' Sermon on the Mount in his Gospel to show us how we in like manner must teach what Jesus has commanded us. We do not fulfill Jesus' mandate simply by repeating what has been said before; we must rather delve into and analyze the contemporary era and only then go on to point in the direction of the Law and the Prophets, the Sermon on the Mount and the teaching of the Apostles. Only then will we be of any real help in telling our fellow human beings which way to take.

Didaskein does not merely involve disseminating information. It likewise involves initiation and a thorough introduction to what participation in the cross and resurrection of Jesus involves. The real aim of *didachē* is to get catechumens walking along Jesus' way and then to nourish them with the necessary victuals from the law and the gospel.

(c) *Jesus' promise.* When Jesus adds the concluding words of promise "Lo, I am with you always, even to the close of the age," he is reminding his disciples that he will be present among them in a new manner.

The promise holds true for all time. Note in passing how often the word "all" occurs in this text: all power, all peoples, all the commandments, and finally, the word "always."

The presence of the hidden and exalted Lord within his church is both her richest gift and her real genius. It is Christ's final and grandest promise, which is good even to the very present time. Through his Spirit Christ abides with his churches in every continent on earth as they encounter apocalyptic distresses and all manner of alluring temptations. He is with declining churches and growing churches both.

The Son of Man marshals his vast power to be with his congregation, always bearing her up and leading her on as she makes her way through the ages. But his promise does not discontinue when history stops. Only in the eschaton itself will it be fully realized. His sovereign presence and activity in the missionary church today are but an inkling and a pledge of what is to come.

Christ promises to be with his church during "all of her days." As she discharges her missionary calling, the church must forever be asking "What kind of day is it today?", for no two days are alike in her history. But however much the days and ages may change as the church carries on her mission in the six continents, one fact never changes: Jesus Christ is urging on his church to complete her missionary calling as he guides her to her final destination. And this missionary movement which emanates from him will not cease until the end of the world. Thus even though the methods of carrying it out must be changed continually, the task itself remains the same.

The new school of exegetes has made an intense study of the concluding verses of Matthew. Rudolf Bultmann and many of his followers view them as having arisen from a specific need for catechetical material in the early church. However, I believe that Hendrikus Berkhof was right in claiming that in the early church tradition was not subject to the interests and needs of the congregations but stood under the authoritative control of Apostles and eyewitnesses who possessed the Spirit of Jesus. And as John 16:12–15 promises, it is this Spirit who takes Christ's words and renders them into the various languages spoken by the congregations.

While the conclusion to Matthew's Gospel most surely dates from a time when missions to the Gentiles were already going full-speed and thus reflects certain aspects of this period, it nevertheless breathes fully the actual Spirit of Jesus.

Karl Barth's study of this passage contains these striking words: "Both as recapitulation and anticipation, by revealing the hidden reality of the eschatological community, the Great Commission certainly is the most authentic of Jesus' sayings."[10]

The Missionary Mandate in the Gospel of Mark

The most influential New Testament scholars believe Mark was written approximately forty years after Jesus' death and resurrection. Most likely written in Gentile surroundings by a Jewish Christian, John Mark, the book thoroughly reveals its author's purpose. He intended it as a useful instrument for winning human beings over to Jesus and his kingdom. His opening words, "The gospel of Jesus Christ," clearly show "that in his own mind he is convinced that he by writing is doing the very same work as the missionaries were doing orally."[11] By setting forth and interpreting the facts about Jesus' life, death, and resurrection, he wished to call people to a faith decision for Jesus the Christ. Thus, even though Mark's Gospel should lack an explicit missionary mandate, its whole tone is missionary.

However, this Gospel does have an explicit command to mission in verses 15 and 16 of that much-disputed concluding section of the book. "And he said to them, 'Go into all the world and preach the gospel to the whole creation. He who believes and is baptized shall be saved; but he who does not believe will be condemned.' " The missionary mandate and its accompanying charge to baptize is unique in Mark's Gospel, for the phrase in Matthew "to all nations" is replaced by the words "into all the world." The connotation of these words is that the disciples are to journey the world over seeking to make converts. Moreover, deciding for or against the Messiah is no take-it-or-leave-it matter; it is a decisive issue which involves either salvation or condemnation.

Scholars view the concluding section as an addition which was made to the original Gospel after the question of the canonical Gospels had been settled. Whoever added it compiled his material from that of other gospel writers who did

10. Ibid., p. 67.
11. C. H. Dodd, *The Founder of Christianity* (New York: Macmillan, 1970), p. 24.

include the missionary mandate. Therefore, though these verses in Mark are a compilation and do not really belong in the Gospel, they are based on and presuppose reliable traditions which are found in other Gospels. The rest of Mark's Gospel is obviously missionary in spirit and nature, as appears from the manner in which it tells people of the kingdom which has come in Jesus' person and work and calls them to a new life.

The Missionary Mandate in the Gospel of Luke and the Acts of the Apostles

Scholars believe that originally the Gospel of Luke and the Acts of the Apostles were written as two parts of what was intended as a single book. The time difference between the two parts was quite possibly A.D. 75 for the first and A.D. 95 for the second. Everyone agrees that their author was Luke, a Greek medical doctor and member of Paul's "staff."

Both parts were written with a missionary purpose in mind. In his Gospel, Luke begins by reminding his readers that he has carefully examined and studied the incidents in Jesus' life and is attempting to record them as accurately as possible in order that the readers may believe. His writing is his own attempt to obey the missionary mandate, and one of his main sources was the Gospel of Mark.

Luke includes the mandate in the accounts of Jesus' resurrection. Both in the Gospel and in Acts he connects the appearance of the risen Lord to the call to mission. The mandate was part of Jesus' address to his disciples prior to his ascension and is recorded in Luke 24:46–47: ". . . he said to them, 'Thus it is written, that the Christ should suffer and on the third day rise from the dead, and that repentance and forgiveness of sins should be preached in his name.' "

Both Luke 24 and Acts 1 single out Jerusalem as the starting point for proclaiming the good news worldwide, a message which is based on the suffering, death and resurrection of Christ.

Luke took pains to tie the call to mission not only to Christ's resurrection but also to the promise of the Holy Spirit. In Acts 1 there is an immediate charge to wait for the coming of the Holy Spirit.

The author of these volumes views the events in Jesus' life recorded in the first book as the base and starting point for the work of the early church described in the second. In Acts, too, the call to mission is placed in one of Jesus' talks with his apostles prior to his ascension. "So when they had come together, they asked him, 'Lord, will you at this time restore the kingdom to Israel?' He said to them, 'It is not for you to know times or seasons which the Father has fixed by his own authority. But you shall receive power when the Holy Spirit has come upon you; and you shall be my witnesses in Jerusalem and in all Judea and Samaria and to the end of the earth' " (Acts 1:6–8).

There are some unique features to this statement of the missionary mandate. First, the author specifically notes that the horizon of this mission is as wide as the world itself. In its final form it shall include not only inhabitants of Israel but people from every part of the globe.

Second, the disciples are mandated to go with a specific message; they are to proclaim the events of Jesus' suffering, death, and resurrection as decisive for every person. A genuine witness is no mere tape recording or museum guide who yawns his way through a tour of ancient monuments and documents; he is rather one whose whole life is caught up in those events which happened on Calvary's hill and in the grave of Joseph of Arimathea.

Third, there is mention of a specific order the apostles are to follow as they go to the whole world. They must begin at Jerusalem, go on to Judea and Samaria, and finally cover the whole world. The author follows this as an outline for his book of Acts; chapters 1–7 describe the spread of the gospel in Jerusalem, chapters 8–9 describe its spread in Judea and Samaria, and the rest of the book treats the whole world with special emphasis on Rome as the center.

A fourth feature of this passage is that it reflects Jesus' unwillingness to discuss the "times and seasons" of his return. He dismisses idle speculation by simply saying, "It is not for you to know. . . ." God, the King of all ages, holds the chronometer in his hands; we do not.

Finally, this version ties the giving of this mandate to another event which is soon to follow — the coming of the Holy Spirit. The account of Jesus' ascension and the promise of the Holy Spirit clarify for us how these two belong together. When Jesus leaves this earth to go to heaven, the Holy Spirit arrives to aid men in discharging the mandate.

The Missionary Mandate in the Gospel of John

Many contemporary New Testament scholars believe John's Gospel became a part of the Easter tradition in a way quite different from the other Gospels. In both form and content it stands separate from the other three. Most experts believe it was the last Gospel to be written although the time span between it and the others is now believed to have been much less than once thought. At any rate, it was written before A.D. 100.

The author may quite possibly have written his book while living in Ephesus, and his selection of material about Jesus reveals his missionary aim. He wanted to reach the people living in the cities of Asia Minor. He had three goals in writing this Gospel and his three Epistles: to bring people to faith in Jesus Christ (John 20:31), to keep them steadfast in their confession that Jesus "has come in the flesh" (I John 4:2–3), and to continue the fellowship which believers have in Christ (I John 1:3). Within that framework all of the Johannine literature reflects a deep interest in the disciples' call to world mission (John 4:35–38; 13:20; 17:18).

John orients the call to mission not only around the person of Jesus Christ and his work, but around God himself. Standing behind Jesus, the Apostle or Sent One, is none other than God himself who does the sending (John 13:20). The Father sends the Son who in turn sends his disciples forth to gather one flock from all peoples and to bring the scattered children of God's family together again (John 10:16; 12:32; 17:1–26).

After Jesus had said these things, we find him giving the actual command to engage in mission in John 20:21–22: " 'As the Father has sent me, so send I you.' And when he had said this, he breathed on them, and said to them, 'Receive the Holy Spirit.' " Here too the mandate is tied closely to the appearance of the risen Lord. Surely John 20:19–23 and Luke 24:36–39 are separately written variants based on a source common to both. But John alone among all the Gospels makes that striking analogy between the Father's sending his Son and the Son sending forth his disciples, an analogy also found in Jesus' high priestly prayer in John 17:18.

When Jesus breathes his Holy Spirit into his disciples, it fulfills a promise he made to them when he told them of his imminent departure (John 14).

New Testament scholars of today are continually advising us not to draw sweeping conclusions about the whole of the Bible from a few specific texts but rather to heed the existence of separate traditions and layers of material within the New Testament. In my judgment, they are correct. When we follow this redaction-history method and distill what is distinct from each of the separate accounts, there is more than enough material to make a summary. This I shall attempt to do, taking courage from the fact that I am following in the footsteps of one who is highly skilled in this area and who has tried it before me, namely, F. Hahn.

The several forms of the missionary mandate as we have them in the Gospels and Acts are but the final deposit of a much richer tradition before them. To understand the mandate in all of its richness, therefore, we must gather all of the variations and view them as one whole. Which of the variants is the most original and how Jesus actually stated the command are questions of secondary importance. All the variants are part of a proper understanding and thus form the basis for our present conclusions.

(1) Every one of the four Gospels and Acts has its own way of stating the missionary mandate.

(2) In every one of them the command is given by the risen Lord. Belief in the Lord's resurrection and obedience to his missionary command belong inseparably together. An emphasis on these two elements links the Gospel writers to Paul, for he, too, throughout his letters claims that God was pleased to reveal his Son to him "in order that I might preach him among the Gentiles" (Gal. 1:16).

(3) Although John 20:21 states it the most directly, all the accounts connect Christ's mandate to his Apostles to the fact that he himself had been sent into the world. When the disciples begin their work and cross boundaries, they are only continuing a work which, though begun by Christ among the Jews, actually knows no limits or borders.

(4) Every account connects the discharge of this order with the coming of the Holy Spirit. Christ issues the command; the Holy Spirit enables the disciples to obey. Matthew alone mentions the continuing presence of the Lord himself; the others mention the presence of the Holy Spirit.

The Holy Spirit, sent by both the Father and the Son, empowers the disciples to proclaim the message by both word and deed (Mark 16:20) and accompanies the church as she discharges her missionary calling. And when the church refuses to heed Christ's command and neglects his orders, it is the work of the Spirit which for a time is thus being frustrated and sabotaged.

One final comment to conclude this section. As appears from Christ's call, mission is not merely one among the many aspects of the church; it belongs to the very core of her being. Therefore Hendrik Kraemer's penetrating comment, "A

Church without a mission is a galvanized corpse," is certainly in full accord with the Gospels and Acts.

The Importance of Paul for a Biblical View of Mission

By way of concluding our treatment of the New Testament material on mission, we shall discuss a missionary without peer in the early Christian church, a person whose very life was an obedient response to his Lord's call to mission — the Apostle Paul. We shall restrict ourselves to a few brief observations.

In his doctoral dissertation on the missionary nature of the early Christian congregations as seen in the writings of Paul and Peter, D. van Swigchem noted that nowhere do either of these Apostles remind the churches of their missionary mandate.[12] It was a matter beyond dispute and a duty for which they needed no prodding. "She was not an army whose leader had to repeatedly issue his command; she did it voluntarily because this call to mission had become part of her very flesh and blood." Strikingly, whenever Paul mentions the mandate, it is to remind *himself* of his obligation. He deems himself entrusted by God with a specific mission (I Cor. 1:17; Gal. 2:7), mentions the "necessity" resting upon him (I Cor. 9:16), and underscores how he is a "debtor" to all people (Rom. 1:14).

Though he is aware of his calling to the Jews, his own people (Rom. 10:1), Paul sees himself called especially to be an apostle to the Gentiles. Passages like Galatians 1:15-16, 2:7-8, and Romans 1:5 show that his chief aim was "to bring about the obedience of faith for the sake of his name among all the nations."

When Paul brings his message, he makes use of the full range of his abilities to reach people of varying tongues and cultures. Recent studies of Paul's life and work clearly show that he could employ Palestinian-Jewish concepts, Hellenistic-Jewish concepts, and Hellenistic-Gentile concepts as the occasion required. His example is incalculably important not only to Bible translators today, but to any person who communicates the gospel.

As for the matter of strategy, Paul always made it a point to visit the vital centers of trade and culture, knowing that each of them radiated an influence on the surrounding area. Not that he ignored the villages, for connecting cities to surrounding villages were permanent lines of communication.

Of course, this strategy is not normative for today. But though we do not need to imitate him at this point, two other elements of his strategy are important for missionaries of any era: he was always open to the beckoning call of the Holy Spirit, and he consciously sought to know the will of God in his work.

As a general rule, Paul preferred to pioneer rather than to build upon the work of others. But when he did come into an area where others had already worked, he did not engage in the practice of stealing sheep as so many others have done throughout Christian history. Rather, he tactfully and cautiously connected his own efforts with those of others in an attitude of give-and-take (see Rom. 1:8-15). If only *all* missionaries would follow his example.

12. D. van Swigchem, *Het missionaire Karakter van de Christelijke Gemeente volgens de Brieven van Paulus en Petrus* (Kampen: J. H. Kok, 1955).

Paul offered his powerful intellectual capacities in the service of his missionary vocation. It is both improper and impossible to read his letters as sheer dogmatic treatises. He was not a systematic theologian; he was a missionary, and his letters breathe a missionary spirit. Each of them is practically oriented and deals with concrete problems and issues in the church to which it is addressed.

Because Paul was the first theological thinker in the early church, his writings had a profound effect. Very early in her history, the church took steps to collect his letters and circulate them among the various congregations. Thus they also enjoyed early entrance into the canon and down through church history have continued to have a decisive and reforming effect upon both individuals and Christian communities.

This Diaspora Jew, a convinced Pharisee and disciple of one of the most famous rabbis of his day (cf. Phil. 3:4–6; Gal. 1:13–14; Acts 22:3), a man who had drunk deeply at the fount of Hellenistic learning, was also a man who directed all the vast resources of his knowledge and theological erudition toward unlocking and explaining the secret of God's revelation in Christ.

Like Paul, those who today seek to reveal the secret of this revelation must not rest content with simply repeating what has been said and done before; by keeping abreast of theological developments, by producing reading material, by the use of modern means of communication — in effect, by every available means — they must uncover the secret for a new age.

The final act in Paul's career was his martyrdom. By giving his heart, mind, gifts, time, and even his own life in the service of the gospel, he became an example of total dedication for those who followed him in history. However, though Luke quite possibly knew of Paul's martyrdom, he gives no report of it in the last verses of Acts 28. Nor does any other New Testament writer mention his death. Paul's only interest was in continuing the work of spreading the good news, and therefore his last reported act was one which has encouraged men and women to press on in every age: ". . . [He] welcomed all who came to him, preaching the kingdom of God and teaching about the Lord Jesus Christ quite openly and unhindered" (Acts 28:30–31).

BIBLIOGRAPHY

1. *General*

Bavinck, J. H. *An Introduction to the Science of Missions.* Translated by David Hugh Freeman. Nutley, N.J.: Presbyterian and Reformed Publishing Co., 1964.
Berkhof, H. and Potter, P. *Keywords of the Gospel.* London: SCM Press, 1964.
Beyerhaus, P. *Allen Völkern zum Zeugnis: Biblisch-Theologische Besinnung zum Wesen der Mission.* Wuppertal: Brockhaus, 1972.
Blauw, J. *Goden en Mensen: Plaats en Betekenis van de Heidenen in de Heilige Schrift,* Groningen: J. Niemeyer, 1950.
_____. *The Missionary Nature of the Church: A Survey of the Biblical Theology of Mission.* New York: McGraw-Hill, 1962.
De Groot, A. *De Bijbel over het Heil der Volken.* Roermond: Romens, 1964.
Eastman, A. T. *Chosen and Sent: Calling the Church to Mission.* Grand Rapids: Eerdmans, 1971.
Lapham, H. A. *The Bible as a Missionary Handbook.* Cambridge: Heffer, 1925.
Love, J. P. *The Missionary Message of the Bible.* New York: Macmillan, 1941.

May, P. "Towards a Biblical Theology of Missions." *Indian Journal of Theology* (1959): 21–28.

Peters, G. W. *A Biblical Theology of Missions.* Chicago: Moody Press, 1972.

Rosin, H. H. *The Lord is God: The Translation of the Divine Names and the Missionary Calling of the Church.* Den Haag: Nederlandsche Boek- en Steendrukkerij, 1955.

Warren, M. A. C. *The Gospel of Victory.* London: SCM Press, 1955.

2. The Old Testament

Bosch, D. "Der alttestamentliche Missionsgedanke." *Evangelische Missions Magazin* 100 (November, 1956): 174–188.

Brunner, E. *Die Unentbehrlichkeit des A.T. für die missionierende Kirche.* Basel: Evangelische Missionsverlag, 1934.

Eichrodt, W. "Gottes Volk und die Völker." *Evangelische Missions Magazin* 86 (September, 1942): 129–145.

Ellul, J. *The Judgment of Jonah.* Grand Rapids: Eerdmans, 1971.

Hempel, J. "Die Wurzeln des Missionswillen im Glauben des A.T." *Zeitschrift für die Alttestamentliche Wissenschaft* 66 (1954): 244–272.

Kaiser, O. "Wirklichkeit, Möglichkeit und Vorurteil: Ein Beitrag zum Verständnis des Buches Jona." *Evangelische Theologie* 33 (1973): 91–103.

Martin-Achard, R. *A Light to the Nations: A Study of the Old Testament Conception of Israel's Mission to the World.* Edinburgh: Oliver and Boyd, 1962.

————. "Israel's Mission to the Nations." *International Review of Missions* 51 (October, 1962): 482–484.

Rosin, H. *The Lord is God: The Translation of the Divine Names and the Missionary Calling of the Church.* Den Haag: Nederlandsche Boek- en Steendrukkerij, 1955.

Rowley, H. H. *The Missionary Message of the Old Testament.* London: Carey Press, 1945.

Sellin, E. "Der Missionsgedanke im Alten Testament." *Neue Allgemeine Missions Zeitschrift* 2 (1925): 33–45, 66–72.

Von Rad, G. *Old Testament Theology.* Translated by D. M. G. Stalker. New York: Harper, 1962.

Vriezen, T. C. "De Zending in het Oude Testament." *De Heerbaan* 7 (1954): 98–110.

Wiersinga, H. A. *Zendingsperspectief in het Oude Testament.* Baarn: Bosch en Keuning, 1954.

Wolff, H. W. *Studien zum Jonabuch.* Neukirchen: Neukirchener Verlag, 1965.

Wright, G. E. "The Old Testament Basis for the Christian Mission." In *The Theology of the Christian Mission.* Edited by G. H. Anderson. New York: McGraw-Hill, 1961.

3. The Intertestamental Period

Bamberger, B. J. *Proselytism in the Talmudic Period.* New York: Ktav Publishing Co., 1968.

Braude, W. G. *Jewish Proselytizing in the First Five Centuries of the Common Era.* Providence: Brown Univ. Press, 1940.

Charles, R. H. *Religious Development Between Old and New Testament.* London: Williams & Norgate, 1914.

Dalbert, P. *Die Theologie der hellenistisch-jüdischen Missionsliteratur unter Ausschluss von Philo und Josephus.* Hamburg: Evangelische Verlag, 1954.

Derwachter, R. M. *Preparing the Way for Paul: The Proselyte Movement in Later Judaism.* New York: Macmillan, 1930.

4. The New Testament

Barth, K. "An Exegetical Study of Matthew 28:16–20." In *The Theology of the Christian Mission.* Edited by G. H. Anderson. New York: McGraw-Hill, 1961.

Bieder, W. *Grund und Kraft der Mission nach dem 1. Petrusbrief.* Zurich: EVZ Verlag, 1950.

————. *Die Berufung im Neuen Testament.* Zurich: Zwingli Verlag, 1961.

————. *Gottes Sendung und missionarische Auftrag der Kirche nach Matthäus, Lukas, Paulus und Johannes.* Zurich: EVZ Verlag, 1965.

Bornhäuser, K. B. *Das Johannesevangelium: Eine Missionsschrift für Israel.* Gütersloh: Bertelsmann, 1928.

Bornkamm, G. "Der Auferstandene und der Irdische. Mt. 28:16–20." In *Zeit und Ge-*

schichte. Dankesgabe an R. Bultmann zum 80. Geburtstag. Edited by E. Dinkler. Tübingen: Mohr, 1964.

Bosch, D. J. *Die Heidenmission in der Zukunftsschau Jesu: Eine Untersuchung zur Eschatologie der synoptischen Evangelien.* Zurich: Zwingli Verlag, 1959.

Bussman, C. *Themen der Paulinischen Missionspredigt auf dem Hintergrund der spätjudisch-hellenistischen Missionsliteratur.* Bern: Lang, 1971.

Cullmann, O. *The Early Church: Historical and Theological Studies.* London: SCM Press, 1956.

_____. *Christ and Time: The Primitive Christian Conception of Time and History.* Philadelphia: Westminster Press, 1950.

DeRidder, R. R. *The Dispersion of the People of God: The Covenant Basis of Matthew 28:18–20 against the Background of Jewish, Pre-Christian Proselytizing and Diaspora, and the Apostleship of Jesus.* Kampen: J. H. Kok, 1971.

Du Preez, J. "Mission Perspective in the Book of Revelation." *Evangelical Quarterly* 42 (1970): 152–167.

Eichholz, G. "Der Ökumenische und missionarische Horizont der Kirche. Eine exegetische Studie zu Röm. 1:8–15." *Evangelische Theologie* 21 (1961): 15–27.

Fuller, R. H. *The Mission and Achievement of Jesus.* London: SCM Press, 1954.

Green, M. *Evangelism in the Early Church.* Grand Rapids: Eerdmans, 1970.

Haas, O. "Das Missionsziel des Apostels Paulus." *Zeitschrift für Missionswissenschaft und Religionswissenschaft* 48 (1964): 1–4.

Hahn, F. *Mission in the New Testament.* London: SCM Press, 1965.

_____. "Mission im Neuen Testament und in der frühen Kirche." *Neue Zeitschrift für Missionswissenschaft* 27 (1971): 161–172.

Harman, A. M. "Missions in the Thought of Jesus." *Evangelical Quarterly* 41 (1969): 131–142.

Hengel, M. *Die Ursprung der Christliche Mission.* Leiden: E. J. Brill, 1971.

Jeremias, J. *Jesus' Promise to the Nations.* Naperville, Ill.: Allenson, 1958.

Kasting, H. *Die Anfänge der Urchristlichen Mission.* Münster: Kaiser Verlag, 1969.

Kilpatrick, G. D. "The Gentile Mission in Mark 13:9–11." *Studies in the Gospels: Essays in Memory of R. H. Lightfoot.* Edited by D. E. Nineham. Oxford: Blackwell, 1955.

Knak, S. "Neutestamentische Missionstexte nach neuer Exegese." *Theologia Viatorum* 5 (1954): 27–50.

Kuhl, J. *Die Sendung Jesu und die Kirche nach dem Johannes-Evangelium.* St. Augustin: Steyler Verlag, 1967.

Liechtenhahn, R. *Die Urchristliche Mission.* Zurich: Zwingli Verlag, 1946.

Lohmeyer, E. "Mir ist gegeben alle Gewalt: Eine Exegese von Mt. 28:16–20." In *In Memoriam Ernst Lohmeyer.* Edited by W. Smauch. Stuttgart: Evangelische Verlagswerk, 1951.

Luck, U. "Herrenwort und Geschichte im Mt. 28:16–20." *Evangelische Theologie* 27 (1967): 494–508.

Manson, T. W. *Jesus and Non-Jews.* London: Athlone Press, 1955.

Meinertz, M. *Jesus und die Heidenmission.* Münster: Aschendorff, 1925.

Miranda, J. P. *Der Vater, der mich gesandt hat: Religionsgeschichtliche Untersuchungen zu den Johanneischen Sendungsformel. Zugleich ein Beitrag zur Johanneischen Christologie und Ekklesiologie.* Bern: Lang, 1972.

Moulton, H. K. *The Mission of the Church: Studies in the Missionary Words of the New Testament.* London: Epworth Press, 1959.

Munck, J. *Paul and the Salvation of Mankind.* Richmond, Va.: John Knox Press, 1960.

_____. *Christ and Israel; an Interpretation of Romans 9–11.* Philadelphia: Fortress Press, 1967.

Oehler, W. *Das Johannesevangelium eine Missionsschrift für die Welt.* Backnang (Württ.): Buchhandlung der Ev. Missionsschule Unterweissach, 1957.

Pieper, K. *Paulus: Seine missionarische Persönlichkeit und Wirksamkeit.* Münster: Aschendorff, 1929.

Rengstorff, K. H. *Die Mission unter den Heiden im Lichte des Neuen Testamentes.* Hermannsburg: Missionshandlung, 1936.

Rétif, A. *Foi au Christ et mission d'après les actes des Apôtres*. Paris: Ed. du Cerf, 1953.

Ridderbos, H. N. "Zending in het Nieuwe Testament." *De Heerbaan* 7 (1954): 133–142.

Schille, G. "Anfänge der christliche Mission." *Kerygma und Dogma* 15 (1969): 320–339.

Schoeps, H. J. *Paul: The Theology of the Apostle in the Light of Jewish Religious History*. London: Lutterworth Press, 1961.

Schürer, E. *Geschichte des jüdischen Volkes im Zeitalter Jesu Christi*. Leipzig: Hinrich's, 1909.

Spitta, F. *Jesus und die Heidenmission*. Giessen: Töpelmann, 1909.

Stoodt, D. "Mission im Selbstverständnis der Urgemeinde." *Evangelische Missions Zeitschrift* 21 (1964): 1–21.

Sundkler, B. "Jésus et les Païens." *Revue d'Histoire et de Philosophie religieuse* 16 (1936): 462–499.

Van Swigchem, D. *Het missionaire Karakter van de Christelijke Gemeente volgens de Brieven van Paulus en Petrus*. Kampen: J. H. Kok, 1955.

Wasmoes, F. "La Vocation de saint Paul selon les notices des épîtres Pauliniennes." *Revue du Clergé Africain* 23 (1968): 373–398 and 24 (1969): 229–248.

Wilckens, U. *Die Missionsreden der Apostelgeschichte*. Neukirchen: Neukirchener Verlag, 1961.

CHAPTER V

The Communication of the Gospel to the Church and the Jewish People

Recently missiologists coined an apt phrase to describe the word and deed Christian witness: "Mission to six continents." In subsequent chapters we shall be turning our attention to the several individual continents, but before doing so we must first study the Christian duty to join with Jews who confess Jesus as Messiah in order to bring the gospel to the people of Israel.

In the last chapter we noted that the book of Matthew enjoins believers to proclaim the message to both Jews and non-Jews alike. Matthew 10 (the command to preach to the Jews) and Matthew 28 (the call to go to the whole world) belong together. And while Paul, who was born a Jew, called himself the "Apostle to the Gentiles," he did not forget or turn his back on his native people even for a moment. "First the Jew, then the Greek," he said in Romans 1:16.

Churches often try to avoid meeting with Jews. This is wholly unbiblical. Rather than trying to evade them, the churches ought to be sensitive to their tasks as the Bible describes them and confront the perplexing Jewish people.

The Jew himself, as he brings to mind his own people's long nomadic wandering over the face of the earth, sighs for divine liberation and rest. Christians and the Christian church may never rest from their ceaseless search to solve this perplexing mystery of the Jewish people. But of all the people who are intrigued by this mysterious people, unbelievers must be the most amazed, for the phenomenon of the Jewish people simply cannot be explained by historical factors alone. In fact, Karl Barth went so far as to say that the continued existence of the Jews through so many stormy eras is the only real proof for the existence of God.

Since the Second World War, however, European Christians have been so gripped by a collective feeling of guilt that they have avoided meeting with Jews whenever possible. Christians began to realize that it was precisely they who for a significant portion of their history had caused the Jews so much agony and left a deep scar on their collective consciousness. European Christians had previously wiped clean their own memories of these deeds. But not any longer. What happened during the Second World War has so seared Christians' consciences and opened their eyes to the past that any meeting between Jew and Christian cannot evade this issue.

But Christian guilt feelings were heightened by the fact that during the war many of them kept silent and refused to intervene when Hitler, the very incarnation of a vile hate for Jews, was burning them in the gas chambers. As for the Dutch attitude during the war, while many did protest, a great many others did not.

Rev. J. M. Snoek, who ministered for years in Israel, collaborated with the Israelis and various church agencies in producing a book which details the attitude of the churches prior to and during the Second World War. He entitled it *The Grey Book: A Collection of Protests Against Anti-Semitism and the Persecution of Jews Issued by Non-Roman Catholic Church Leaders During Hitler's Rule.* Uriel Tal, professor at the Hebrew University in Jerusalem, in the introduction to this volume acknowledges the work of the Dutch Reformed church *(Hervormd),* which was the first in the Netherlands to publicly protest Hitler's measures against the Jewish people. But he wonders whether or not public protests were the most appropriate form of helping in that situation. Could not the churches have been of more help by supporting and being active in the underground movements? Could the churches not have given the Jews more encouragement in their efforts to resist? Were the ecclesiastical protests really revolutionary, or were they only so loud as was necessary to ease the Christians' consciences? The Hebrew professor is asking questions here which apply not only to the situation back then but are strikingly appropriate for some situations today as well.

The shame which many Christians felt after the Second World War produced in them a new perspective on the relationship between the church and the Jewish people. Out of it arose the immediate question "How must the church communicate the gospel to the Jewish people?" In view of all that transpired, would it be better to keep silent about the message and simply be present among the Jewish people, helping them in any way possible? Is there still room for a "mission to the Jews," or should one speak instead of cooperation between church and synagogue? In an ecumenical era, would it not be preferable to speak of dialogue rather than mission? These and similar questions are being posed all over Europe, and Asia, Africa, and Middle East Arab Christians are inescapably facing them as well.

After a quick look at a few statistics on Jewish society provided by the *Jewish Yearbook* of 1973, we wish to delve into some of these questions.

The total number of Jews worldwide in 1973 was 14,236,000. Of these 2,632,000 were living in Israel while over half of the total lived in North and South America. In the Americas there are great pockets of Jewish people; for example, 500,000 live in Argentina, 300,000 in Canada, 150,000 in Brazil, and 20,000 in Uruguay. The greatest concentration, however, is in the United States where in New York City alone 2.4 million Jews reside.

The Soviet Union has 2.5 million Jewish inhabitants, while Western Europe has approximately one million. The other places which have anything more than a token number of Jews are: South Africa, 117,900; Iran, 80,000; Morocco, 35,000; India, 14,500; Ethiopia, 12,000; Tunisia, 8,000; Syria, 3,500; Lebanon, 2,500; Iraq, 2,500; and Egypt, 800. Many countries do not have a single Jewish citizen.

These statistics are important for they give us a clue to where in the world the dialogue with the Jewish people must receive high priority. Theologically speaking, the church's call to be concerned about the Jews should always receive top priority (as the biblical evidence cited below will show); however, since many areas of the world have few or even no Jews in them, the dialogue in these places is quite obviously impossible.

THE NEW TESTAMENT "PEOPLE OF GOD" AND THE
OLD TESTAMENT "PEOPLE OF PROMISE" IN ROMANS 9–11

The writings in Romans 9–11 have played a powerful role in the history of theology. In them Paul, the Tarsus-born Jew, with deep faith in God and probing powers of discernment examines the relationship of the gospel of Jesus Christ to the Jewish people. Because Paul speaks the language of election and predestination in these chapters, both opponents and defenders of these doctrines have been quick to garner more ammunition from these verses which they supposed could reinforce their position. The manner with which they hurl these texts about as if to slug their opponents makes one wonder whether they really understand the passages in the first place.

Paul did not write these chapters to arm either defenders or opponents of predestination. Rather they came from the pen of a Jew who believed that Jesus was the Messiah and was puzzled why his fellow Jews did not also believe. He is struggling for Israel to be converted and is pleading for their hardened hearts to be melted. He is inquiring what his and our posture should be toward these people and what hope to entertain for this ancient, God-chosen people.

We shall now attempt to summarize Paul's answer to these burning questions. For a complete analysis of his whole argument one must turn to other commentaries, for we are concerned here only with the marrow of his message.

At the time of writing these chapters Paul has already completed a great amount of work among Jews and Greeks and other ethnic groups who were living in western Asia and eastern Europe. He now desires to press on to Rome and from there to go on to Spain. In this letter to the fellowships of Christians living in Rome, Paul gives them an account of the message which he is bringing in obedience to his Lord to both Jews and Gentiles.

As Paul sees it, the Jew illustrates a problem which is deeply entrenched in every man. To be human involves partnership with the God who made man his partner. This partnership is a basic feature of man's humanness. But when human beings subvert this sense of partnership and do not live up to its full potential, they are calling their very humanness into question. Whether he is aware of it or not, man is a rebel against God and is the one who broke the partnership.

But the marvel of the gospel is that while man himself is both unable and refuses to restore the partnership with God, God from his side offers righteousness free of charge and so restores the partnership. But Paul observes that many Jews ardently oppose this gift of God's righteousness, preferring rather to believe that they can achieve the necessary obedience to their Covenant Partner on their own (Rom. 3:9–21).

According to the Apostle, the Jews are bringing on themselves impending and permanent judgment for rejecting the proffered gift. Paul himself in Romans 6–8 is addressing his readers from the perspective of this righteousness. He speaks of rebels being declared innocent, of those imprisoned by guilt being set free, of covenant breakers recovering their lost status. These new people set free by God's grace have now become his volunteers who responded to his call to place their whole life in the service of righteousness.

With this as background Paul now goes on to try to unlock the puzzle of the Jewish people, some of whom have staunchly opposed the good news.

When Paul the Jew mentions that new people which lives by the grace of Jesus the Messiah, does this imply that he is separating himself from his own people, or that God — and Paul too — has written them off? In the strongest language possible Paul refutes this. God has absolutely *not* rejected his people (11:1). He has not withdrawn his gracious and inexhaustible promises from them; whenever they wish, his people may lay claim to them.

But why did a part of the Jewish people spurn Jesus Christ and reject the good news which they heard? That is the question with which Paul wrestles, and his struggle leads him on to discover a depth of wisdom and knowledge hitherto unknown. Suppose, he says, that the people of Israel *did* accept the gospel of the Messiah in those earliest years; if they had, then the church and the community of the faithful would have been a completely Jewish matter. But since a part of Israel has temporarily rejected the gospel, the messengers have gone throughout the world.

Perhaps I can illustrate what Paul meant. To hurl a stone a great distance one has to rear back as far as he can in order to achieve the distance. In like manner, God has temporarily withdrawn his hand from Israel in order to propel the gospel farther into the regions of the Gentiles. As one shooting an arrow must stretch back the bowstring, so too God has pulled back his bowstring to give the arrow of his gospel greater distance. But this does not mean God has relinquished his claim on his own people. Rather, the people of God now has a twofold form: the Old Testament people of Israel and the New Testament people gathered from all nations.

While individual branches have been trimmed off from the tree to make room for grafting new branches on, the old tree itself has not died (11:21–24). We, the Gentile Christians, have been grafted into the main stock of Israel. This is a truth which so many Christians consistently forget, and it has led them into believing that Israel is no longer to be seen as an integral part of God's people since the New Testament community developed. What is more, many Gentile Christians misunderstand another point. They believe that if any Jew is saved at all nowadays, he is grafted onto the main trunk of Gentile Christians. Actually, it is the reverse; we, the Gentiles, are the engrafted ones.

Does Paul cherish any hope for his own Jewish people? By all means. Even as the temporary hardening which Israel endured produced an incalculable benefit for mission to the Gentiles, so, too, when Israel once again believes — as it most certainly will — the Jews' acceptance will be a blessing to all peoples (11:24). Paul views the conversion of individual Jews like himself as preview of a complete and final turning for the whole people (11:26). He is full of optimism.

Exegetes have gone around and around in their discussion of what the clause in Romans 11:26 means: ". . . and so all Israel will be saved." All their talk strikes me as rather futile. Rather than talking we ought to be hoping and praying.

Paul ties his grand hope for Israel to the work which those who confess Jesus as Messiah must do. Though they have neglected it to their shame, they by their lifestyle were to show the Jews what it meant to be the objects of God's protecting care and thus make them jealous. The Gentile Christians had to stimulate the Jews into desiring the very same freedom and messianic grace which they were enjoying and thus enlist them for the march to the messianic kingdom.

Many people aver that Christians ought not to use direct speech as a means proclaiming the gospel to the Jews. In my judgment their exegesis of this passage makes little sense at all. In his own ministry the very Paul who wrote these two chapters in which he calls for Christians to arouse the Jews to jealousy had but one overarching goal — to communicate the message about Jesus the Messiah to both Jew and Gentile alike and to build up the messianic community wherever he went.

Paul closes these three chapters with a doxology. He casts a backward glance over the course of history and notes both God's faithfulness to his people and the infidelity of both Jew and Gentile alike. He detects hardening, blindness, and rejection. But he lifts up his voice in a spirit of praise, for cutting through all human failure he sees a highway passing through the important events of Christ's death and resurrection and extending on into the world of the Gentiles. But the road does not dead-end there. It continues on and shall end in unspeakable blessing for both Jew and Gentile. "For from him and through him and to him are all things. To him be the glory for ever. Amen" (Rom. 11:36).

Paul began the three chapters with an anguished cry of distress, but ends with this moving hymn of praise to God. He praises the God of Israel and of the Gentiles and is confident that in spite of all of Israel's unfaithfulness God will remain faithful. This hope inspired Paul, and through this he aroused other believers to join him in the task of bringing the good news to Israel too.

JEWS AND CHRISTIANS IN EUROPE UNTIL THE CLOSE OF THE SECOND WORLD WAR

In view of the above, an appropriate question arises at this juncture. Given that Christians have the job of arousing the Jews to jealousy and of communicating to them the gospel, how well have they done it?

Karl Barth answers as follows:

> The recurrent Jewish question is the question of the Christian and the Church which has not been and cannot be answered by any of its ministries. It stands as an unresolved problem, and therefore as the shadow behind and above all its activity in foreign missions (*Church Dogmatics,* IV/3, p. 878).

In all honesty and candor the Christian church must admit that the history of her contact with Jews is a shameful one. Occasionally there was an authentic relationship, while at other points there was no relationship at all. But the typical attitude toward the Jews was one of suspicion — a far cry from what Paul called for in Romans!

In this section I wish to give a short historical review of how Christians and Jews have related to each other. It is quite impossible to do this exhaustively, and therefore we shall be content to refer to specific books anyone who wishes to pursue this subject in depth might consult.

Speaking generally, one might claim that Jews and Christians have been ambivalent in their attitude toward each other. Judaism could not speak in the Western world without at least mentioning Christianity, and Christians cannot talk about themselves without also drawing in the issue of the Jews.

From the New Testament to the Reformation

Heinrich Rengstorf and Siegfried von Kortzfleisch are presently coauthoring a well-documented survey of Christian-Jewish relationships throughout history. Only two of the projected several volumes have yet been published and are entitled *Kirche und Synagoge*. We shall be referring to this book frequently in the early stages of our survey.

Rengstorf's first chapter examines the period of the New Testament and the Apostolic Fathers. In commenting on the so-called anti-Semitic tendencies of the New Testament which have been claiming so much scholarly attention lately, Rengstorf calls it a strictly internal Jewish tension, not unlike the tension between the Pharisees and Sadducees within Judaism. The Jewish Christians had joined to form a separate entity, and this generated tension between the church and the synagogue, the obvious point of tension being the question whether or not Jesus who was crucified and rose again was indeed the Messiah. But as for the Christian rites and liturgy and lifestyle, they showed a close resemblance to Judaism. One exception was the Christians' celebration of Passover in which they referred directly to Jesus' death and resurrection.

With the advent of the age of the Apostolic Fathers, Jewish-Christian relationships took a turn for the worse. In his Easter homily, Bishop Melito of Sardis (ca. 190) accused the Jews of deicide, a term that Christians were quick to use throughout history but which is as untrue as it is crude. The Roman Catholic Second Vatican Council in the early 1960s finally decided to abolish this word from any of the decrees which they promulgated.

In the second chapter which covers the period from 200 to 1200 (the patristics and early Middle Ages), Bernhard Blumenkranz details the pre-Constantinian Christian polemic against the Jews as it is expressed, for example, in a man like Tertullian. But though he was sharp in his criticism, Tertullian was not hostile toward the Jews.

In the pre-Constantinian era Judaism was a *religio licita* (religion permitted by the public authorities) and thus had a certain appeal for Christians who were being persecuted for practicing a forbidden religion. Though the early church fathers warned against the Jewish religion, they moderated their tone, not wanting to add the wrath of the Jewish community to that which they were already incurring from the government. Christians opposed heretics inside their community much more strongly than they did Jews outside.

As Christianity became a *religio licita* through Constantine's Edict of Milan in 313 and gradually came to acquire those features which would one day make her a monopoly, the attitude of the church fathers toward the Jews also changed along with it. For example, Ambrose (339–397) urged the Emperor Theodosius not to replace a Jewish synagogue which had burned. And Augustine (354–430) began to lay the groundwork for a theology which viewed the Jews as no longer part of the people of God — a doctrine which has carried through to the present with tragic results.

Blumenkranz labels Western Christianity's attitude a "theoretical hostility" which at that point did not spill over into practice but which would do so in the Middle Ages. On the Eastern front, however, both before the reign of Justinian and after, anti-Jewish sentiment had reached a fanatical pitch. Though his name means "golden-mouthed," Chrysostom (354–407) did not live up to it when he spoke of the Jews. He hated them with a passion.

Meanwhile the era of the so-called *Corpus Christianum* dawned with the reign of Justinian (527–565). At this time Christianity became mixed with Roman ideology, and the bitter mixture was forced — sometimes gently, sometimes harshly — onto the citizens and subjects. Justinian's *Corpus Juris Civilis* is full of anti-Jewish statutes and thus offered a legal sanction for discriminating against the Jews, the effects of which lasted long into the eighteenth century. This is not to imply that the discrimination was continuously sustained, for there were periods of rather peaceful coexistence between Jews and Christians during the early Middle Ages. But all this came to a screeching halt during the period of the Crusades.

Contrary to popular opinion, the Crusaders' hatred for Jews appeared already during the first Crusade, not only during the third. The first Crusade, initiated by Pope Urban II in 1095, began as a Jew-hunt during which "Christians" tracked down and slaughtered Jews. When the Crusaders conquered Jerusalem in 1099, they gathered all the Jews into the synagogue and set it afire.

Any Jew living in the ghettos of eastern Europe was fair game for the Crusaders enroute to the Holy Land. To be sure, there were individual voices of protest (the weak voice of Bernard of Clairvaux and the much stronger voice of his theological opponent, Peter Abelard, who wrote *Dialogue between a Jewish and Christian Friend of Wisdom*), but they merely bounced off the thick wall of Roman ideology called *Corpus Christianum*.

Willehad Paul Eckert's chapter on the later Middle Ages describes a dark phase in Jewish-Christian relations. Several popes like Gregory VII protested the false charges which were trumped up as an excuse for hounding Jews, such as, for example, the charge that the Jews engaged in ritual murder. Others protected them against forced belief and the Inquisition. Pope Leo X (1513–1521) even encouraged the study of Hebrew, and during his time some Christians were converted to Judaism. But these were all exceptions. When Pope Innocent III at the behest of the Fourth Lateran Council (1215) ordered the Inquisition, he cast a heavy pall over Jewish-Christian relations. People were forced to accept the Roman ideology of the *Corpus Christianum* rather than being allowed to hear and freely accept the pure claims of the gospel.

Jews felt the effects of the Inquisition most bitterly in Spain. After the Jews had enjoyed a measure of freedom to express their beliefs and culture under the Omayad rulers, the fanatical Berbers took over and tracked down and murdered Jews, sometimes in wholesale fashion (1066). When the Christians recaptured Spain, they initiated the notorious Spanish Inquisition which made life for Jews so difficult.

Jewish converts to Christianity were divided into two groups: *conversos,* who changed only after being coerced, and *marranos,* who changed for practical expediency. But not even this relaxed the relentless persecution on them. The threat of death hung heavily over the heads of those who chose to remain faithful to their religion and culture. And once the marriage of Ferdinand to Isabella had welded Spain into a unified and smooth-functioning whole, a decree went out in 1492 calling for the complete extermination of the Jews from Spain, an effort to be started in Granada and later applied throughout Spain. This edict was finally lifted officially in 1968, even though it had become a dead letter long before that. In fact, by the time of the Second World War Spain had become a haven for many Jewish refugees.

After the edict took effect, many Jews fled, some going north to places like Amsterdam and others returning to the land of Israel. Even though Spanish persecution was both the most intense and most extensive of all the European countries, there was not a single country a medieval Jew could visit without suffering to some degree at least the effects of uncertainty and social ostracism.

In reaction to the Christian persecution, the Jews during the Middle Ages tried to articulate an answer, an answer which in many respects was shaped by the coercive atmosphere in which they were living. They attacked the Christian understanding of the Old Testament, condemned the person of Jesus, and even offered their own polemical commentaries on the New Testament. For further references to this issue consult Erwin Rosenthal's chapter on the Jewish medieval response to persecution included in the book mentioned above.

Until now, we have been following rather carefully the historical survey in Rengstorf and von Kortzfleisch's *Kirche und Synagoge.* In the following section on the Reformation we shall take our leave of this excellent guide in order to shorten our survey somewhat and to refer to treatises and statements which are not already covered in the extant volumes of Rengstorf.

Luther and Calvin on the Jews

A knowledge of the Reformers' position is important for our study since Luther — regrettably — had such a formative influence on Germany's later attitude.

One can detect two phases in Luther's attitude. Prompted by a missionary spirit, Luther initially expressed an interest in the Jews, but later, having been disappointed in their response, his love turned to fierce rejection.

In the early years of the Reformation Martin Luther hoped that the Jews who had endured the deep trauma of mistreatment by the medieval Roman Catholic church would welcome his efforts for church reform and join him. Not only did Luther collaborate with certain Jewish scholars and make ample use of their knowledge of Hebrew; he even wrote a treatise to win the Jews for the Reformation cause: *Dasz Christus ein geborener Jude sei.*

But the Jewish synagogue communities spurned Luther's attempts to court them and by their refusal put him in a different frame of mind. His polemical writings against the Jews can be found in one volume of the Luther collection,

Schriften wider den Juden. In many respects this book contains thoughts unworthy of a Christian leader and though I do not intend to reproduce them here, I do wish to note at least four basic themes in the book which with some variation occur in later history and produce tragic consequences.

1. God's wrath is resting on the Jewish people. Only he can lift it.
2. Jews are strongly resistant to conversion.
3. Judaism is essentially anti-Christian.
4. Christians who oppose the doctrine of *sola gratia* become as Jews and join them in guilt. "But the Jews are even more crafty than our Roman and Scholastic opponents."

In 1970 Walter Holsten, a Lutheran missiologist, wrote that Luther by his unbridled and relentless repetition of the first three themes and his vicious attacks on the Jews produced the right conditions for a later anti-Semitism to spring to life.

In 1963 the Dutch pastor Rev. A. J. Visser wrote a short piece entitled *Calvijn en de Joden.* In it he noted that while Calvin was not gripped by the anti-Jewish passion which overwhelmed the more choleric spirit of Luther, theologically he differed little from his Reformation counterpart. In all candor, one must admit that though Calvin was French, in his esprit he could at times revert to a medieval penchant for abusive name-calling. His description of Jews was shameful.

During the sixteenth-century Reformation a consensus grew among its leaders regarding the Jews. Though they may have had different individual accents in their theological positions, they agreed on two points:

1. The Jews are no longer God's people; the church has replaced them as God's elect.
2. The church of the New Testament has now become the main branch into which a few Jews become engrafted, not vice versa as Romans 11:17 so clearly states.

Such ideas persisted up to the time of the Second World War and are even held by a number of Protestant Christians today, though the time both during and directly after the war marked a great change in belief and attitude.

Increased Tolerance and Recognition of Jewish Rights during the Eighteenth and Nineteenth Centuries

When the coercive nature of the *Corpus Christianum* became increasingly clear during the eighteenth and nineteenth centuries, Europe's collective conscience was pricked. European society was becoming more pluralistic and room had to be made for religious and ethnic minorities. A number of factors contributed to increased tolerance. For example, Puritans, Pilgrims, Independents, and Anabaptists in England, North America, and elsewhere aided in bringing medieval culture with its tactics of political coercion to an end and assisted in the development of an ecclesiastical, social, and political environment amiable to the rights of minorities.

But secular currents such as the Enlightenment, rationalism, humanism, liberalism, and the French Revolution were also influential in creating a greater tolerance for and recognition of the rights of Jewish communities. John Locke, the father of liberalism, in the first of his famous *Letters on Toleration* argued for the rights of Jews, and the rationalist John Toland in 1714 wrote his *Grounds for Granting Jews the Rights of Citizenship in Great Britain and Ireland*. Gotthold Ephraim Lessing, a relativist who had been acquainted with and influenced by Moses Mendelssohn, argued for continued dialogue and mutual respect between Jews and Christians in two of his writings, *Die Juden* (1749) and *Nathan der Weise* (1799).

These religious and secular streams of thought gradually found their way into law. The Virginia Bill of Rights of 1776, which later had a deep influence on the United States Constitution, and the Declaration of the Rights of Man, which came out of the French Revolution in 1789, both granted Jews the rights of citizenship. After this, most countries in western Europe and in Latin America joined in granting the full rights of citizenship to Jews whose presence in a country had theretofore only been grudgingly or ungrudgingly tolerated.

Revived Anti-Semitism at the Close of the Nineteenth and the Beginning of the Twentieth Centuries

Not even France was free from an intolerant anti-Semitism, as appeared from the famous essay by the French nobleman Gobineau, written in 1855 and entitled *Essay sur l'inégalité des races humaines*. In it he proclaimed the superiority of the Aryan over the Semitic race. Sometime later the sinister contours of a latent anti-Semitism came to light in the Dreyfus affair which, though it ultimately proved the Jewish officer innocent of any wrongdoing, nonetheless so deeply shocked the Jewish community that the pace of the incipient Zionist movement accelerated. Theodor Herzl, founder of Zionism, was a journalist covering the story of the Dreyfus affair, and when he saw what had happened, he became convinced in his own mind that such latent anti-Jewish tendencies as had surfaced at the trial would only keep bursting forth throughout Europe. In his judgment, the founding of a separate Jewish state was the only answer.

During the struggle between clerical and anticlerical factions which was so common to France, the clerical faction frequently flirted with anti-Semitic sentiments during the late-nineteenth and early-twentieth centuries.

In Germany, too, anti-Semitism revived after 1870. Jews were made the scapegoats for the economic chaos which followed the war between Germany and France. The theories of Max Müller, an English historian of religion whose roots were in Germany, were twisted by others into an argument for Aryan superiority. H. H. Chamberlain, who became a naturalized German citizen, "applied" Müller's theories in his writings.

In 1872 the pseudo-ethnologist Friedrich von Hellwald came out with his dreadful book, *Zur Charakteristik des Jüdischen Volkes,* and a few years later (1879) Wilhelm Marr continued to develop von Hellwald's "theory" and used and tried to defend the term "anti-Semitism" in its racist sense.

During Bismarck's *Kulturkampf* against the Jews and others, Adolf Stöcker, the court preacher (1835–1917), tried to lend anti-Semitism an air of religious respectability by his "Christian Social Party." The first Christian social conference of 1890, which he organized, and his writings and speeches were all efforts to tie the gospel to a nationalist ideology. "Christentum, Kaisertum, Preussentum" were all mixed together to produce a frothy nationalist brew. Jews, he believed, were not fellow citizens but strangers. He pressed for a clear demarcation between "we Germans" and "those Jews" which later became such popular phrases in the vocabulary of German Lutheranism.

Adolf Stöcker clearly had an influence on Abraham Kuyper of the Netherlands. To be sure, there are heart-warming passages in Kuyper's writings which refer to Jews as God's ancient covenant people, and he maintained many fine personal contacts with Jews. Regrettably, however, like Stöcker, Kuyper viewed the Jews as guests and strangers in the Netherlands. His approach to the "Jewish question" described in a series of articles in *De Standaard* (1878) was strikingly similar to Stöcker's in Germany. To be sure, there were corrective influences at work in Kuyper's thinking, but the suspicious elements were there as well and may not be camouflaged or denied. Fortunately, Kuyper's Calvinist descendants in the Netherlands showed little trace of this smirch of anti-Semitism, as became clear during the Second World War.

Anti-Semitism in the Third Reich of National Socialism (1933–1945)

Until the time of the Third Reich of Hitler, Goebbels, Rosenberg, Streicher, and those of similar ilk, Europe had always shown an ambivalent attitude toward the Jews. Thank God for a bothersome Christian conscience which continuously hounded her! But when Nazism came, it broke with Christianity, at first secretly but later quite openly, and gushed forth a venomous stream of hate toward Judaism. The religious, economic, and political factors which had traditionally contributed to anti-Semitism were given a racist cast in Nazi Germany. One must never forget that Nazism was a thoroughly racist ideology which demagogically employed the mass media to whip up the people into an anti-Jewish frenzy after the *Kristallnacht* and the Nuremberg laws of 1935. It was against this form of racism that the planning conference for the World Council of Churches held at Oxford in 1937 did battle. Later the Uppsala conference of WCC would come up with a program to combat all types of racism, but we should always remember that it was the anti-Semitism of the 1930's which was the first of the battles to be fought in this many-fronted war.

Nazism's goal of exterminating the Jews chills one's bones. With methodical precision the Nazis managed to eliminate six million Jews in the infamous holocaust before they were finally stopped. Though experts today may say that an atomic war would slaughter so many millions of people as to make Auschwitz seem like child's play, that such a pogrom could occur in a nation calling itself civilized is so scandalously shameful that we may never — even for a moment — forget it. It must stand as a continuous warning for us of the dastardly effects of every form of anti-Semitism.

The Jews in Russia

It is common knowledge that the Jews in Eastern Europe, particularly in Poland and Russia, have endured extreme hardship for centuries.

In a piece written for the weekly Jewish newspaper *Nieuw Israelitisch Weekblad,* Dutch professor Dr. Louis de Jong noted that it was not mere chance which led the Russian Jews to organize a Zionist movement in 1886, no less than thirteen years *before* the first Zionist congress in Basel. Or again, the fact that Israel's first three presidents, Weizmann, Ben Zwi, and Sjazar and its premier, Golda Meir, were all Russian Jews is more than happenstance.

The word *pogrom* is Russian, and during the Czars' regime the Jews were continually the target of discrimination and persecution. But at least the Czars, unlike the present communist authorities, allowed the Jews to leave, and between the years 1880 and 1914 no less than two million did depart.

After the Russian Revolution of 1917 it appeared that Jews were in for a better day. Every anti-Jewish law was annulled, and Jewish culture and religion thrived. In fact, seven Jews held seats in the central governing body. However, by 1920 the oppression revived; thousands of Jews were shipped off to exile in Siberia and hundreds of thousands lost their lives in a civil war. Yiddish schools were banned and every Jew had to carry an identification card on his person. Though Jews fought alongside other Russian soldiers in attempting to stop the Nazis, who at the war's end had killed two million Russian Jews, after the war had stopped, cultural discrimination against Jews continued.

Toward the end of his life Stalin spread the lie that Jewish doctors had laid a plot to poison him to death, a lie which resulted in a series of threats against the Jewish community.

After the Stalin era, the deepest distress of Russian Jews was and still remains the pressure of forced assimilation into the mainstream of Russian life and culture. Though Jews in Russia today, within well-defined limits, have freedom to make a career, they are not free to express their Jewishness. Hence, many desire to emigrate to Israel or elsewhere. Russian Jews, like many other groups, are the targets of a genocide of the spirit, and anyone who has endured a similar distress can understand their clamorous call: "Let our people go!"

The foregoing material comes as a reminder to the Christian churches of Europe that they have seldom, if ever, attempted to fulfill their task of arousing the Jews to jealousy. We should never lose sight of this shameful fact as we later attempt to state some things about the method of communicating the gospel of Jesus the Messiah and his kingdom to the Jewish people.

But the above material is also a reminder that anti-Semitism (perhaps anti-Judaism would be a preferable term) can again spring to life at any moment. Whenever serious difficulties arose in Western societies, there was an urge to make the Jews the scapegoat. For disorders, inflation, unemployment and any other ill, both extreme rightists and leftists sought out the Jews for blame. Hidden behind the more visible motives for such drives is the religious motive; such people are bent on opposing the religion of Israel and the God of Israel.

THE WORLD COUNCIL OF CHURCHES, THE ROMAN CATHOLIC CHURCH, AND JUDAISM AFTER THE SECOND WORLD WAR

After the Second World War Christians searched for reorientation and new patterns of relationship with the Jews. In this connection it is well to pause briefly and note the efforts of the World Council of Churches and the Roman Catholic church vis-à-vis the Jews.

The World Council of Churches and Israel

Rev. Johan Snoek, former secretary of the World Council's Commission, The Church and the Jewish People, is an expert in the field of Jewish-Christian relations from whose writing I shall borrow and make supplementary comments of my own.

Before the World Council was ever organized, a "Committee on the Approach to the Jews" was organized in 1929 under the auspices of the International Missionary Council. In 1961 that committee was disbanded and its work assumed by a new committee of the World Council, the Committee on the Church and the Jewish People (abbreviated CCJP). Since 1974 this committee has been part of the World Council's division called Dialogue with Representatives of Contemporary Religions and Ideologies. The first secretary of CCJP was a Mr. Tjerding, who was followed in 1975 by Rev. Snoek.

The work of the CCJP is in the continual process of reformulation. Its most recent mandate, written in 1973, is as follows:

1. To help churches to understand Jews and Judaism better and to encourage discussion of topics which are fundamental to the relation and witness between Christians and Jews.
2. To assist churches, missionary organizations, and councils in consulting with each other and thus to clarify their understanding of the essence and content of their witness about Jesus Christ to the Jewish people.
3. To advance dialogue and reconciliation between Christians and Jews, to cooperate in preventing every form of religious discrimination, and to work with people of other faiths for social justice and peace.
4. To encourage the production and circulation of appropriate literature on Jewish-Christian relationships.
5. To urge the churches on to biblical and theological study of the goal of history and the experience of the Jewish people in modern times.
6. To cooperate with other divisions of the World Council of Churches to achieve these goals.

Anyone who keeps abreast of the work of this committee through its regular newsletters knows that it is seriously involved in trying to accomplish these diverse tasks. I shall give but a few illustrations of its work.

In 1973 the committee invited a team of Jewish scholars to join with Christians in exploring "the relevance and authority of the Old Testament." One of its study projects was devoted to an exposition of the Bible's message for Christians seeking to determine their position on events transpiring in the Middle East.

The CCJP also pays careful attention to any expression of revived anti-Semitism. The World Council, through a liaison committee, maintains permanent contact with six Jewish organizations, among them the World Jewish Congress. Thus, through consultations, Jews, Christians (including Arab Christians), and sometimes even Muslims are meeting each other and discussing not only the theological questions common to them but also the tensions which arise in the Middle East from time to time. The World Council has contact with both sides in the conflict and seeks, where possible, to reconcile the differences. The task of the CCJP in keeping the lines of communication open is a most imposing one and often invites misunderstanding from both sides, but this is all the more reason for the member churches of the World Council to surround its committee and its efforts with concern and prayer.

Snoek closes his brochure explaining the work of the CCJP with a text from Proverbs which continually inspires both him and his co-workers to carry on: "In all your ways acknowledge him, and he will make straight your paths" (Prov. 3:6).

The Roman Catholic Church and the Jews

In his book *Machet zu Jüngern* the Roman Catholic missiologist Ohm called for a total Roman Catholic reorientation toward the Jews. It was especially the honest and irenic person of Pope John XXIII which led to a turning point and renewal in Roman Catholic-Jewish relationships. Even more than the documents of Vatican II themselves, certain specific events in John's career illustrate the renewal. I shall cite a few.

While receiving a delegation of American Jews in an audience, he made a play on words, making reference to his own name (Joseph). He said, "When I see you all standing before me, I recall the incident of Joseph in Egypt who hid his true identity from his brothers for a long time. But finally he could not any longer and confessed: 'I am Joseph your brother.' "

After the Second Vatican Council had removed the offensive medieval prayer "Oremus pro *perfidis* Judais" from the liturgy, a thoughtless canon leading a Good Friday service inadvertently slipped it in. John stopped the service and pointed out that this section had been removed.

Finally, just a few days prior to his death Pope John XXIII penned a prayer pleading with God for forgiveness of sins committed against the Jews.

> We now realize that for many, many centuries our eyes have been so blind that we could not see the glory of your chosen People nor discern the special status of our brothers.
>
> We have come to realize that the mark of Cain is inscribed on our foreheads. For century after century our brother Abel lay in blood and tears due to the misdeeds of us who had forgotten your love.
>
> Forgive us for the curse which we have unjustly laid on their Jewish name. Through them and in their flesh we have crucified you again; forgive us, for we did not know what we were doing.

The Second Vatican Council's declaration on the Jews in the decree *Nostra Aetate* and Cardinal Bea's accompanying commentary on the decree are also important for keeping abreast of the changed spirit in Roman Catholic-Jewish relations.

Originally, a number of theologians wanted the question of the church's relationship to the Jews included in the decree on ecumenism. They viewed the issue as an ecumenical matter. However, this proposal was properly rejected in favor of including it in the decree on non-Christian religions *(De ecclesiae habitudine ad religionas non-christianas)*.

To avoid political misinterpretations and to concentrate on the inter-religious nature of the relations, the decree does not speak about the Jewish people but about Jewish religion. It condemns every form of anti-Semitism and goes on to claim that "neither every living Jew back then nor any Jew from our time may be reckoned" among those responsible for what happened during the time of Jesus' suffering and death. "The Jewish people may not be deemed as rejected by God." Rather, the decree calls for a manner of preaching and catechesis which conforms more to the gospel at this point. The heart of the gospel is the message of the cross, a message which, according to the decree, includes the following themes:

1. The beginning of faith and the election of the church at the time of the patriarchs, Moses, and the prophets;
2. The position of the Jewish people regarding the trial and death of Jesus;
3. The position of the Jewish people in the people of God under the New Covenant;
4. The mystery of the cross;
5. The church's practical relations with the Jewish people.

The council spelled out concretely what it intended by the last point. It called for continued vital contact with the Old Testament, a realization that we Christians share a common heritage with the Jews, biblical and theological studies, and cooperative ventures into many areas. Though the document itself never expressly used the term "cooperation," its intent was clearly apparent.

We shall now cite a few salient passages from the decree itself. The first quotation, given in the exact words of the decree itself, reflects the council's efforts to scrap the word "deicide" when referring to the Jews' involvement in Jesus' death. According to Cardinal Bea, the term was avoided for reasons of "pastoral caution and Christian love." "True, the Jewish authorities and those who followed their lead pressed for the death of Christ; still, what happened in his passion cannot be charged against all the Jews, without distinction, then alive, nor against the Jews of today."

It is worth noting that the phrase "God's people" is used only in reference to the Jewish people before Christ, not after. Moreover, as we mentioned earlier, the decree prefers to speak of the Jewish religion and not the Jewish people. And the condemnation of anti-Semitism in the final form of the decree is weaker than it was in the original draft. But even so, the decree is an important phase in the process of reorienting the Roman Catholic church to the Jewish people.

Relations between the Vatican and the modern state of Israel have been difficult since the Vatican has not yet recognized Israel. In fact, when Golda Meir visited the Vatican in 1973, the Vatican newspaper, *Osservatore Romano,* took immediate steps to remind its readers that this unique occasion did not imply formal recognition of the Jewish state.

Perhaps the most important follow-up material to the Vatican decree yet to appear came from the French bishops who set about to enact some very urgent reforms in their religion. On April 16, 1973 a committee of bishops, headed by Archbishop Msgr. Elchingen, issued a document on Jewish-Christian relations that gained wide attention and was even translated into German. In 1974 it was introduced for consideration to the West German Roman Catholic episcopate by Cardinal Hoffner. The chief West German rabbi gave the piece a very positive review.

Of all the countries in Europe, France is second in the number of Jewish inhabitants (600,000). Therefore, the outstanding way in which the French bishops sought to extend the guidelines of *Nostra Aetate* for the French situation was extremely important.

The French bishops did not view *Nostra Aetate* as the final word on Christian-Jewish relationships, but rather as a turning point. They strongly emphasized that the very existence of the Jewish people poses a question to the Christian community. The document mentions the "ongoing calling of the Jewish people" and makes a plea for a greater Christian understanding of Jewish existence and tradition and for mutual understanding and respect.

The document very carefully poses the question of the need for Jews to return to the promised land.

> The world conscience cannot deprive the Jewish people which has passed through so many catastrophes in the course of history of the right and the means for its own political existence. However, it has equally little right to refuse the very same possibility to those who because of local conflicts and the return of the Jews (to the promised land) are daily being added to the number of victims of a grievously unjust situation.
> A vital question for both Jews and Christians is whether the gathering of a people who were dispersed throughout the world and were threatened with destruction by ceaseless persecution and the struggle of political powers may yet prove to be one of the means God uses to display his righteousness to both Jews and other peoples in spite of the many tragic incidents that have been connected with this return.
> How could Christians ever remain indifferent to what is happening in that land today?

On the question of the church's relationship to the Jewish people, the document explicitly states that the church and Israel are not complementary institutions. The very fact that they still stand opposite each other is evidence that God's plan is not yet fully accomplished, for both are looking toward the messianic era.

The document concludes by expressing the desire that both sides "put away their old adversary relationship and turn to the Father in one and the same movement of hope which shall contain a promise for the whole earth."

This document is the most penetrating piece yet to appear since the Vatican Council on this subject and has been partially responsible for improved relations between Jews and Christians in France.

NEW IDEAS ON THE RELATIONSHIP OF JEWS TO CHURCHES

It is noteworthy that both during and after the Second World War the phrase "Mission to the Jews" and the practices implied in it were dropped by almost everyone involved. Prior to that, it had been a stock-in-trade phrase among churches in both Europe and the United States. It was reported at the famous world missions conference held in Edinburgh in 1910 that no less than ninety-five societies were at that time sending out 804 people engaged in mission to the Jews. A number of these societies later joined to form the International Missionary Council's Committee on the Christian Approach to the Jews, among them the International Hebrew Christian Alliance.

There is ample reason to hold these stalwart Christian missionaries — both Jew and Gentile, both men and women — in the highest respect for their work. Many of them attained a level of knowledge about the Jews coupled with a sincere desire for their conversion that is worth emulating and has rarely been matched. I am thinking of people like Dr. Franz Delitzsch, Gustaf Dalman, and J. Jeremias, who had to close his institute in 1933 because of pressure from Hitler.

When the work was resumed among the Jews both during and after the war, the phrase "Mission to the Jews" was scrapped for at least two reasons. Not only did the Jews' long acquaintance with coercion and psychic pressure make them sensitive to it, but the Christians themselves came to realize that the phrase is theologically incorrect. According to the Old Testament, the Jewish people were chosen by God to be the bearer of his revelation. Christians and Jews therefore are involved in the same covenant with God, and any relation between them must take the form of a dialogue, as Paul so clearly indicates in his chapters in Romans.

Almost all agreed that the phrase should be dropped, but they did *not* agree on what was the appropriate relationship and method of communication with which to replace it. Opinions varied widely. It may be of some use to set forth some of these ideas in order to come to some conclusions of our own on this matter.

Proposals to Make the Relation of Church to Synagogue Both Ecumenical and Cooperative

(1) Shortly after the Second World War, James Parkes, a fast friend of Israel and ardent opponent of anti-Semitism, was one of the first to propose recasting the old relationship more ecumenically. His book *The Foundation of Judaism and Christianity,* published in 1960, argues for such a revised pattern; to be sure, he maintains, "Sinai and Golgotha" are in tension, but their actual relationship to each other is ecumenical in nature. As he sees it, the only essential difference between Judaism and Christianity is that whereas the former is geared to man as a social being, the latter singles out man the individual. Parkes borrowed this (in my judgment) untenable proposition from Martin Buber's book *Zwei Glaubensweisen.* According to Parkes, every human being has a variety of religious needs and the several channels of divine revelation correspond to these needs. Parkes glaringly omitted any talk about the resurrection and thus avoided one of the most fundamental differences between the two religions.

(2) Both by his personal contact with Jews and by his academic study of Judaism Reinhold Niebuhr has done much in the area of Jewish-Christian relations. His book *Pious and Secular America* argued against doing mission work among the Jews. Not only is it futile; it is also wrong. Judaism and Christianity have enough in common for Jews to find God within their own tradition rather than demanding that they switch over to Christianity, an act which, whatever the advantages, has always been viewed as a coercive measure imposed by a cultural majority. Throughout history Christians have so sullied the image of the real Christ that Jews no longer can see him as he really is. Says Niebuhr, "Practically nothing can purify the symbol of Christ as the image of God in the imagination of the Jew from the taint with which ages of Christian oppression in the name of Christ tainted it." Though he admits in other writings the deep difference between the Jewish and Christian understandings of the Messiah and his role in the kingdom of God, he nonetheless cautions against proclaiming the gospel to Israel.

Niebuhr was fond of reminding Christians how much they could learn from the Jews in their struggle for justice. Commenting on his early years as pastor, he says, "In Detroit it was the rabbi who acted so Christianly in the struggle for justice in the Ford factories." Some of his later writings carried through this same point, such as his article in the *Central Conference of American Rabbis Journal,* "The Relation of Christians and Jews in Western Civilization" (April, 1958), and his book *Godly and Ungodly* (London, 1958).

(3) Paul Tillich's position was akin to Niebuhr's. His writings in the book edited by Gerald Anderson, *The Theology of the Christian Mission,* and in the periodical *Christianity and Crisis* argue for the need for "cross-fertilization" between Judaism and Christianity. Christians must discover within Judaism the contours of a "latent church."

Tillich pleads for openness among Christians in their personal contacts with Jews. He comments, "I myself, in the light of my many contacts and friendships with Jews, am inclined to take the position that one should be open to the Jews who come to us wanting to become Christians. Yet one should not try to convert them; rather, we should subject ourselves as Christians to the criticism of their prophetic tradition."

Though Tillich claims a willingness to keep an open mind on these question, he also freely admits his skepticism regarding any attempt to purposely go out and proclaim the gospel to Jews.

A Protest from Jewish Christians

A number of Jewish Christians rose up to dispute the positions of men like Parkes, Niebuhr, and Tillich. One of the most prominent spokesmen for this company was Jacob Jocz who wrote *Christians and Jews: Encounter and Mission* (London, 1966). In times past, claims Jocz, the church attempted to force her belief onto unwilling Jews. When those Jews resisted, the "Christian" community responded with even more force. The result is that now the church is so overwhelmed by shame for her past doings that she has for the most part reduced her meeting with Jews to mere conventionality. Church and synagogue, however, are not really addressing each other if they do not talk about what really counts, namely, the issues of faith. In Jocz's opinion, a church without a message for the Jews lacks one for the Gentiles as well.

Jocz does not believe that Christians have exhausted their mandate when they have spoken to the Jews verbally only. "There is but one way to proclaim the Gospel and that is by *living* it."

Jocz takes special exception to Niebuhr's suggestion that Christians refrain from mentioning Jesus Christ to Jews. In his book *The Jewish People and Jesus Christ,* he issues an impassioned plea for regarding witness to Jesus Christ, the Son of Mary and Messiah of Israel, as an inescapable obligation.

In spite of protests from people like Jacob Jocz, the position represented by people like Niebuhr and Tillich has gained some popularity. In the November 28, 1973 issue of *Christian Century* Robert Osborn repeated the familiar arguments for not communicating the gospel to the Jews and closed with this pious outburst: "If God wishes a Jew to become a Christian, it is for God to see to it. Of the Christian he asks only that he be Christian — to the Jew above all." That being a Christian might have something to do with the call to witness apparently did not cross this writer's mind.

Dialogue with Israel

In the years since the Second World War the churches in the Netherlands have been searching for a new phrase to describe more accurately their relationship to the Jews. In 1942 the Hervormde Kerk established a Council on Church and Israel and stated in its church order that the church discharges her apostolic mandate toward Israel "by means of conversation." The Gereformeerde Kerken also dropped the phrase "Mission to the Jews" and replaced it with "Gospel Proclamation among (the people of) Israel," wishing thereby to underscore their contention that conversation is the primary means by which Christians and Jews should introduce the issue of the gospel.

I must bring this section to a close, but not before stating that I, too, believe the relationship of the church to Israel is dialogical. The churches must listen intently and learn much, but they must also never fail to bring up the matter of Jesus the Christ and his kingdom which both has come and is yet coming. The next sections will attempt an answer to some of the questions which naturally follow from this position: Who must do the communicating to the Jews? How must they do it? What must they say?

WHO MUST COMMUNICATE THE GOSPEL TO THE JEWISH PEOPLE?

The Jewish People Who Confess the Messiah

Gospel communication began with Jews in and around Palestine who confessed Jesus as Messiah. The earliest Christian congregations were Jewish as were the Apostles of Jesus, and it was primarily the work of both Palestinian and Hellenistic Jews which made possible the spread of the gospel throughout Palestine and beyond it to the whole Roman Empire.

Simon Peter, who at first believed that the gospel was intended for Jews only, was corrected by the Holy Spirit and hence crossed the border separating Jews from Gentiles when he baptized Cornelius. But this in no way obviates the fact that Peter and his fellow Apostles, Paul excepted, saw their primary mission as being to their own people.

Hellenistic Jews spread the gospel to their Jewish neighbors dispersed throughout the Roman Empire. In some areas these newly converted Jews set up independent Jewish Christian congregations, though in other areas (Antioch, for example) the congregations were a mixture of Jews and Gentiles. The Acts 15 account of the Jerusalem Council reflects an early Christian attempt to maintain the unique identities of both the Jewish and Gentile elements of the Christian fellowship and yet to maintain the fellowship between them.

It is rather strange that scarcely any effort was made in the subsequent long tradition of Christian history to establish uniquely Jewish Christian congregations. Von Zinzendorf (1700–1760), a great pioneer in world mission, called for a "Jewish ecclesiola" which would reflect the Jewish dimension of the church. Then too, there was the Herrnhut missionary, Samuel Lieberkühn, who made such an earnest effort in this area that the Amsterdam Jews called him Rabbi Samuel. And today there is a congregation in Baltimore, Maryland which is trying to preserve the existence of Jewish rites and yet interpret them from a New Testament perspective. But these were individual exceptions to the general rule, and one can only wonder what the impact would have been if Christians had put forth greater effort to establish strictly Jewish congregations. Fortunately, even at this late hour, some are beginning to show some interest in this question. In 1966 the World Council's Commission meeting at Glion concluded: "In specific situations it is proper to form special groups composed primarily of Jewish Christians."

We must not fail to mention the stellar contribution some Jewish Christians have made as members of Gentile congregations, for they often played key roles in communicating the gospel to their fellow Jews. I think of such honorable figures as Prof. P. Kohnstamm, Rev. J. Blum, Dr. Reëmi, Dr. Jacob Jocz, Simone Weil, and Levitin Krasnow who each in his or her own unique way made such an outstanding contribution. Nor must I fail to mention Mrs. Flesseman–van Leer, a Jewish Christian theologian whose work in the World Council of Churches increasingly is serving as a bridge between the Israelis and the Arabs.

Allow me to make an observation. Jewish Christians often have the feeling of being a segment with which no one else wants to associate. Other Jews look upon them as suspect, and they feel that other Christians by not using their presence in the churches actually deem them of little worth. All of us do well to listen to the voice of one who was present at a meeting between Jewish Christians and non-Jewish Christians in the Dutch city of Doorn in 1973:

> God will join us together, and toward this goal we must work. I plead with you gentile Christians, move over a bit so that your Christ-confessing Jewish brother can find room. And to my Christ-confessing Jewish brothers and sisters I come with this plea: By God's grace accept the position honorably which He has given you in your own congregation and it shall prove to be a blessing to both you and the congregation.

The Gentile Christians

Of course none of the above section is written to imply that Gentile Christians
have no part in the work of approaching the Jews. By their common human
contacts with Jews at work, in scientific study, in social and cultural life, in
politics, in journalism, and in interreligious dialogue, Gentile Christians can do
much. Above and beyond this, however, the church needs people whose special
training in Judaism equips them for their work of being a bridge to the Jewish
people.

CHANGES IN JUDAISM WHICH AFFECT THE COMMUNICATION OF THE GOSPEL

Christians often fail to remember that the faith confessed by Jews today is not
identical with that described in the Old Testament. Hendrikus Berkhof points this
out in his book *Het Christelijk Geloof.* According to Berkhof, the Talmud is the
deposit of Jewish faith. "The Talmud is a parallel to the. New Testament. Both
integrate the material of the Old Testament into their own worlds of belief and read
the Old Testament within a completely different hermeneutical framework."[1]

In the Talmud, the covenant and its messianic kingdom depend upon
God's covenant partner for their realization. By obeying the Torah, God's covenant partner acts in concert with God himself to bring the covenant and the
kingdom to realization.

Christianity, on the other hand, admits the failure of the partner to live up
to God's covenant demands but trusts in Jesus who, acting as a substitute for us,
reconciles us to God and fulfills God's law. In him the kingdom of God both has
come and is yet coming, for the Christian awaits its final manifestation through the
Holy Spirit. Anyone who wishes to communicate the gospel to the Jews must take
serious account of the fundamental differences between his own belief and theirs.

Furthermore, no one can dispute that within the basic framework of
Judaism there are various nuances and differentiations which one must observe as
he works with Jews. Jewish communities are far from homogeneous. What follows is no exhaustive discussion of the several Jewish streams of thought. It is
written only to alert the reader to the fact that the different nuances do exist.

Liberal Reform Judaism

Reform Jews call for a reinterpretation of the Jewish faith in the modern era.
Though they oppose a wholesale departure from the traditional tenets of Judaism
such as occurred after the ghetto-like atmosphere enveloping Judaism had been
destroyed in the French Revolution, they do nevertheless call for revision. Reform Jews are selective in their ritual observance and are more flexible in their
views on the Sabbath. They call for a freer application of Judaism's Halachot and
carry on a modern form of pastoral and educational ministry which seeks to
reckon with the issues of the day. The members of the synagogue are allowed to

1. H. Berkhof, *Het Christelijk Geloof* (Nijkerk: Callenbach, 1973).

advise in determining the Halachot. Gentiles may take the vow of bar mitzvah.

In the modern state of Israel liberal Jews receive official opposition to their work. Liberal Jewish rabbis, for example, may not perform marriage or funeral services. And yet, for all the opposition they receive, liberal Jewish fellowships have been rather positive in their assessment of the Israeli state, especially in recent years.

Orthodox Judaism

Orthodox Judaism is interested in maintaining the orthodox faith in the state of Israel and bringing the faith of Jews dispersed throughout the world more into line with the teachings of the Talmud. As the Orthodox see it, assimilation poses the single greatest threat to their faith, and therefore they resist the marriage between Jews and Gentiles. They seek to recall those who have wandered from the faith and revive those who fell away during the war's holocaust.

Except for solidarity in crisis situations like the state of Israel or the persecution of Russian Jews, liberal and Orthodox Jews have little contact with each other.

Secularized Jews

Secularization has penetrated Judaism deeply. Thousands of Jews have been assimilated into the mainstream of the society in which they live and have thereby both inwardly and outwardly come to adopt the lifestyle and thought patterns of liberal Western society. Many have turned to communism or socialism for inspiration, finding a welcome from Karl Marx, who argued for solving the "Jewish question" by encouraging their participation in the incipient Socialist movement and thus assimilating them into the whole of society. One has only to recall names like Edward Bernstein, who laid the foundation for democratic socialism, Lassalle, Rosa Luxemburg, and many others to note how many Jews have responded to Marx's words of welcome.

But even apart from any external enticement a number of Jewish Socialists from the very start have wanted to wed socialism to a reinterpreted Judaism. Moses Hess, whom Marx and Engels ironically named "the Marxist rabbi," was an early leader in this movement within Judaism. He wrote his "Rome and Jerusalem" in 1862, attempting to reinterpret the Torah socialistically and to tie in Marxist ideas about land division with his own views about the holy land.

Many of the founders of the largest political party in the state of Israel, the Socialist party, in which David Ben Gurion played such a prominent role, have followed in the spirit of Moses Hess.

Many secularized Jews are humanists. The Zionist movement too can find some secularized Jews among its ranks, though of course not every Zionist is a secularized Jew.

Jewish Mysticism

Judaism also has within it many mystical streams. The most famous Jewish expression of mysticism is Chassidism, which arose in eastern Europe in the eighteenth century and took its place alongside the Pharisees and Saducees as an independent wing within Orthodox Judaism. The word *chasid* means "pious" and Chassidism has within it many charismatic rabbis as well as "saints" and charlatans. It is a curious mixture of deep piety, fundamentalism, superstition, magic, and a particularly strong belief in miracles.

Though Martin Buber was not himself a Chassidic member, his summary and reinterpretation of its complicated teachings and beliefs have given this movement a measure of prominence.

Freudian Streams within Judaism

Judaism also has its Freudian streams. The liberal Jewish rabbi Richard Rubinstein is a prominent representative. In his book *After Auschwitz,* he beckons his fellow Jews to forsake the unique faith of their fathers who ardently believed that God acts in history and to return to a worship of the Baals and the Ashtaroth. The God of history did not intervene in Auschwitz, says Rubinstein, and therefore in view of this God's silence the Jews must return to a modernized form of Baal worship. Baal is a nature god, a god most suitable to Rubinstein's dictum: "Gather rosebuds while ye may."

Jürgen Moltmann answered Rubinstein's shocking challenge in his book *The Crucified God.*

> After Auschwitz theology would have been altogether impossible if the "Shema Israel" and the Lord's Prayer had not been offered and God himself had not been suffering along with those who were being martyred and killed. Any answer other than this would be blasphemy. An absolute God would make us indifferent and a "God of actions and success alone" would cause us to forget the dead who may not be forgotten.
>
> But God lives now and lived then with those who entered the gaschambers in a *"unio sympathetica."* In his memoir about Auschwitz, *Night,* Eli Wiesel recalls the thoughts which he who was then but a boy had as he experienced the holocaust of suffering. The rest of the prisoners were forced to look on as two Jewish men and one boy were hanged. The two men died quickly, but the boy clung to his life. Then someone said: "Where is God?", but I did not reply. After a half-hour, he again asked: "God, where is God?" A voice speaking within me said: "He is hanging there on the gallows."[2]

As we Christians speak with Jews, it is vitally important that we do not shun any of the various expressions of Judaism today, but rather that with deep emotion and interest we listen to what they are saying.

What Makes a Jew a Jew

As one surveys the broad spectrum and endless variety within Judaism today, he inevitably asks himself, "What really makes a Jew a Jew?" Many have tried their hand at answering this difficult question, and on the basis of what I have heard and read from them, I shall give my own answer.

2. Jürgen Moltmann, *The Crucified God* (New York: Harper, 1974).

A Jew is a Jew by virtue of God's special relationship with the people of Israel in history and the polar relationship every Jew since then has borne or now bears to that history. Whether a Jew stands positively or negatively over against this history, whether he delights in it or disdains it, he is nevertheless related to it. Or, as Markus Barth said, "A Jew is a member of a people chosen by God for special service whom He will not allow to fall from His hand."[3]

HOW TO COMMUNICATE THE GOSPEL TO JEWS

There is no better means of communication to be found anywhere than the means of personal friendship; that is, one becomes so interested and involved in the life of the other person (in this case, the Jew) that he actually suffers along with him in times of crisis and tension and comes to the alert when a dread anti-Semitism once again bares its ugly head. In this connection, Christian cooperation in ventures which strive to change the fate of Jews in places like Russia and Syria means very much.

To provide an opportunity for contact with Jews deeper than mere personal friendship, study centers have been set up in many areas where Jews and Christians can meet each other in genuine dialogue. Then too there are the formal and informal discussion groups formed for the purpose of increasing Jewish-Christian contact.

Still another method of communication being tried is Christian presence. Nes Ammim is an imposing Christian project whose aims, according to its Declaration of Principles (issued June 24, 1970), are:

1. To meet the Jewish people in their own land;
2. to assist both Jews and Christians in understanding each other's positions and learning from each other;
3. to promote a type of dialogue in which each side respects the other's identity;
4. therefore, Nes Ammim's goal is to renounce both practically and in principle any pretension to engage in missionary proselytism (that is, efforts to make Jews members of the Church).

When I was reading the Declaration of Principles, the fourth of Nes Ammim's goals caught me by surprise. I must register my disagreement, for it strikes me that it calls Christians to do something which is principially impossible and never allowable. No Christian community may ever vow to give up its missionary activity. Nor do I think that such a promise was necessary in view of the fact that the state of Israel guarantees freedom of religion in its constitution. Let me say therefore that I hope that this promise which Nes Ammim made for the time being can ultimately be withdrawn as it discusses its function with the Israeli government. As for the rest of the work which Nes Ammim does by contributing to the Israeli economy and building bridges of understanding between Jews and Christians, I have nothing but the deepest admiration and respect.

3. Markus Barth, "De Jood, Jezus, en het Geloof der Joden," *Verkenning en Bezinning* (December, 1972).

To be sure, this project is not perfect, but until the day dawns when Jewish Christians will be able to return to their homeland and live in the peace they so earnestly desire, it does deserve our sympathy, our prayers, and our money for what it seeks to do.

There are other means which I could discuss here, but I desist. Genuine love always finds a way, and if we really love the people of Israel as we ought, we shall never be without means of reaching them.

What Can Christians Learn through Contact with Jews?

Christians who have engaged in dialogue with Jews continually attest that both sides stand to gain much through the encounter. Allow me to make a few observations of my own on this point.

Christians commonly make the mistake of equating Judaism today with the brand of Pharisaism which is criticized in the New Testament. Jesus had harsh words for holiness which was but a sham and for those whose beliefs did not spill over into their practice. He scorned those who piously sought for positions of honor and whose emphasis on law made them stiff and unbending. In fact, some of his own disciples today could well be on the receiving end of his attacks as the Pharisees were then.

Christians often caricature Jews and Jewish religion. If they depict Christianity as a religion of love, then its anti-type becomes Judaism, a religion of fear. If Christianity is a religion of mercy, then Judaism is a religion of wrath and vengeance. Such generalizations and caricatures do untold harm and impede any efforts at genuine listening and can only be dispelled by intense study.

Learning from Jewish Interpretations of the Tanach

A heartening note in Jewish-Christian relations is the increased collaboration between Jewish and Christian scholars in the study of both the Old and New Testaments. It goes without saying that there are profound differences between them on the interpretation of Jesus of Nazareth, but there is also much to gain by such cooperation. I shall give but one illustration where such cooperation can help.

Jews see the Torah as God's invitation to join him in walking a path and living a life of responsibility and caring for each other. Torah is full of *halaḥôt*— pointers for life's way.

We Christians often forget that the New Testament has similar material, for example, Jesus' Sermon on the Mount. We have often thought the only purpose for such passages was to force us to our knees with a confession of our sin and with a prayer for forgiveness: "Lord, be merciful to me, a sinner!" But the Sermon on the Mount actually was written to help us to get in step behind Jesus as we, his disciples, follow his leading. The Sermon on the Mount calls for performance. The fresh element in it is the resonant chime of grace and freedom which peals forth in the Beatitudes (Matt. 5:1–12), but this in no way detracts from the fact that we, with this chime of grace ringing in our ears, are expected to go on and live by the new *halaḥôt* which Jesus gave in the rest of the sermon.

Learning from Jewish Life in the Diaspora

If, as some scholars are predicting, Christians and Christian communities are moving into an era where they shall be living in diaspora on all six continents, then we have an unbelievable amount to learn about the challenges and the temptations of such a lifestyle from the Jews.

Jesus' prayer in John 17 bespeaks his awareness of the challenges and dangers which his disciples shall encounter when they are spread over the whole earth. On the one side is the danger of the ghetto; on the other, the danger of total assimilation. Who of us does not have anything to learn from the Jews and their experiences in this area?

Learning from the Jews' Emphasis on the Messianic Kingdom

Throughout its history Christianity has so spiritualized and individualized its understanding of the messianic kingdom that it is in need of a good lesson from Judaism, which tries to give some shape and form to the kingdom in *this* world by emphasizing justice and righteousness in the here and now. Fortunately, the message is now getting through to at least some Christians.

Learning from Judaism's Emphasis on Desacralized Nature and Culture

One of the most profound lessons which Judaism has to teach us is that nothing in the created world is divine and worthy of worship. Heathen religions take either a part or the whole of the created world (whether in its natural form or as a product of man's culture) and turn it into a cultic object. Israel broke away from this tendency; the created world, she continually asserted, was *under* God and every product of culture was man-made. Much has been made of this point in the last years in the so-called theologies of secularization.

However, many of these theologians of the secular fail to catch another point that the Jews always made; when they emphasized a desacralized nature and culture, the Jews dedicated both nature and culture anew to the Creator of heaven and earth. We must learn both of these lessons equally well!

I must limit my discussion of what Christianity can learn from Judaism to what is mentioned above. But I cannot end this section without at least mentioning that when we Christians enter the schoolhouse of Judaism, we would do well to be modest and attentive. Let every Christian remind himself that the synagogue is the mother of the church and that we Gentiles continually need the Jews lest we fall back into the "ways of the heathen."

Jewish-Christian Discussion about Joshua of Nazareth

When Jews and Christians talk together, they neither can nor may avoid the subject of Joshua (Jesus) of Nazareth. In fact, many Jews are quite willing to talk about him.

In his article on Jesus in the *Encyclopedia Judaica* David Flüsser from Jerusalem mentions that the figure of Jesus forms a bridge linking Christianity with Judaism, but that the question of who he really is arouses tension between them. Another Jewish writer hit the nail on the head when he said that the biggest religious event in the history of the West was, is, and ever shall be the Jews at work interpreting the person and work of Jesus Christ. After two thousand years of adventurous detours, the world has finally gotten back onto the track and is ready to start again its original and most important discussion.

Most Jews see Jesus as a carefree person who acted as though the unredeemed world were already redeemed. But many are calling for a striking reevaluation of the old attitudes. The New Testament scholar from the Hebrew University in Jerusalem whom I quoted above also went on to say this about Jesus: "I wish to remind my readers of one thing: the fact that Jesus both lived and died as a good Jew ought to fill every last one of us with pride."

The religion of Judaism is willing to acknowledge that the rabbi from Nazareth was a prophet and a teacher — perhaps even the best teacher ever. It recognizes him as a true Jew and son of Israel. Martin Buber, Franz Rosenzweig, Leo Baeck, Hans Joachim Schoeps, Scholem Asch, and others describe Jesus as a brother and a mediator who brought the Gentiles closer to the God of Israel. The enlightened rabbis were even making this claim back in the Middle Ages. But each of these Jewish authors refuses to accept the Pauline and Johannine confession that Jesus, the messianic Son of David and Son of God, is also God's Word to Israel. In their opinion, such a confession does damage to the Jewish belief that God is one.

The unavoidable question is this: Who is the Savior *(sōtēr)*, Israel or Jesus? Who is the Way, the True Vine, the Door, the Light of the world? Is it Israel or Jesus? Are both we and Israel together a fellowship of sinners who live only by the grace of our one Redeemer, Jesus Christ, or are we not?

All these expressions, images and symbols appear in the Old Testament and the rabbinic literature and refer to the people of Israel. But in the New Testament both in the parables he told and in the "I am" passages in the fourth Gospel, Jesus is clearly referring to his own person and work.

In his magisterial book, *Images of the Church in the New Testament*,[4] Paul Minear writes:

> All these associations are profoundly Christological in orientation, for they make clear how the story of Christ has converted their earlier meanings. All of them express the conviction that the whole history of Israel has been summed up in the person and work of Israel's Messiah and that he is therefore the living link between Israel and the church.

The question "Who is Jesus?" is the line which divides synagogue from church. It is our crucial task as Christians to explain as carefully and as clearly as we can why we do not consider him merely as one messiah among many others, but as the only one, the very Son of God who was sent from the Father. But when doing so we must not fail to mention one oft-neglected aspect. For us too, as Markus Barth reminded his synagogue audience in New York, the final coming of this Messiah is in the future. We too await the final manifestation of a Messiah who has already come to us and is now enroute to us again.

4. Paul S. Minear, *Images of the Church in the New Testament* (Philadelphia: Westminster Press, 1960), p. 48.

In a broken world full of guilt and tragedy, frustration and death, Jesus' life seems more like a single exception than that of a universal Lord. But, as Barth said, Jesus, the "one who is coming," is the "Man of the Future." He is our hope and God's guarantee to us of our own future.

Thus Christians and Jews both agree that we are underway. But Christians know that there is but one goal and one way. Though we Christians cannot offer any final solutions to the endless number of problems which presently perplex our unredeemed world, we have nonetheless discovered in Christ's resurrection the direction in which God is leading us. And that is what keeps us from laying down our arms in our fight for renewal. "This is more modest than we have often been, but it is nonetheless real and it is enough."

Jewish-Christian Discussion about the Death and Resurrection of Jesus

In Jewish-Christian dialogue the significance of Jesus' death is an unavoidable question. David Flüsser in his *Encyclopedia Judaica* article points out that Judaism is willing to concede that the deaths of martyrs do have atoning significance. Thus, if one believes that Jesus is the Messiah, it is easy to understand why he would accord Jesus' death a cosmic significance.

One often hears that the idea of a substitutionary or vicarious atonement is un-Jewish. Nothing could be farther from the truth. As one surveys the history of the Jewish interpretation of Isaiah, he notes that all along the scholars view the Servant's suffering as vicarious in nature. The real question between Jews and Christians is whether Jesus is the real Messiah and whether his suffering and death thus has cosmic significance or not. Is it true, as Christians claim, that what happened to Jesus, the Son of David, happened once for all; did he, the one, die for the many, as his resurrection certified?

More and more Jews are focusing their discussions with Christians on the decisive character of Jesus' death and the question of his resurrection. Though they may give an answer that differs from the one given by the church down through the ages, it is nevertheless significant and moving to note that they are involved with the same questions as captured the attention of the early disciples and the people of Israel who had heard about the events on Golgotha and in the garden of Joseph of Arimathea.

Jewish-Christian Discussion on the Kingdom of the Messiah

Discussion about the Messiah inevitably leads to further discussion about this Messiah's kingdom. I recall so vividly an evening I spent at the house of a Hebrew University professor in Jerusalem. The several lines of our discussion finally converged on the figure of Jesus. The professor spoke with deep respect about Jesus and said that the feeling was growing within him that Jesus could not be fully explained from within the Jewish tradition. He borrowed a sentence from Goethe: "There is something incomparable about Him." I immediately recalled the verse from Isaiah and, applying it to Jesus, I asked the professor, "With whom then shall you compare Him?" He shot back immediately with a challenge of his own: "But supposing that Jesus is the Messiah, show me his kingdom." That is an honest question which the Jews are asking, and it is one which we Christians have too often ignored. In our proclamation the person of Christ strongly overshadows his kingdom; we idolize Jesus while we ignore his kingdom.

But Jews often go to the other extreme where the kingdom takes precedence over the Messiah himself.

The Bible, however, never is one-sided on this issue. The New Testament Gospels proclaim both the Messiah and his kingdom which has come and is yet coming. Paul too speaks of the growth of Christ's body among the peoples and the coming fullness of the Gentiles. He charts the course of the kingdom with its start in the cross and resurrection of Jesus, the coming of the Holy Spirit along the way, and the final destination in the consummation itself.

With these New Testament data our dialogue with the Jews must deal. We shall have to tell them that our hope for the final display of that kingdom rests only and alone on Jesus' promises to us. And we shall have to show them by some anticipatory acts of our own that we really expect a new earth in which righteousness shall dwell.

I so fervently hope that through a common friendship, through mutual recognition and understanding, and through conversing many Jews will turn to the Messiah of Israel "in one and the same movement of hope, which shall be a promise for the whole earth."

ZIONISM

Before making some notations on the modern state of Israel in the following pages, I must pay due heed to Zionism which gave rise to the Israeli state. By the term "Zionism" we mean the efforts of a great many Jews to achieve a political, cultural, and religious identity of their own. The term was coined by the famous painter, poet, and orator Nathan Birnbaum, who was also the long-time editor of the paper *Zion* and who wrote a brochure in 1983 entitled *Die nationale Wiedergeburt des Jüdischen Volkes in seinem Lande*. But the fervent desire for a political and cultural identity and a return to what they believed to be their own land burned in the hearts of many Jews long before the term "Zionism" was invented. In fact, ever since the destruction of Jerusalem in A.D. 70 and during the long period of exile and diaspora, this one prayer taken from the Jewish Pesach has been on their lips: "Here now, (but) next year in Jerusalem."

For twelve centuries the rabbis dealt with the issues involved in a return to the land of the patriarchs. But in the nineteenth century the pressure to deal with them much more concretely increased vastly.

Jochanan Block's book *Judentum in der Krise* accords the title "spiritual father of Zionism" to two specific individuals. As an Orthodox rabbi, each pressed hard for returning Palestine to Jewish control. The first individual, Alkalai (1798–1878), already in the year 1834 called for establishing Jewish colonies in Palestine "as a condition we must meet before God provides his deliverance." And the second, Zwi Kalischer (1795–1874), both by his book *Zions Herstellung* and through direct intercession with the powerful Rothschilds requested permission from the several involved governments for gathering the scattered children of

Israel together in Palestine. Although modern political Zionism breathed and thrived on some of the nationalistic spirit which was in the air during the nineteenth century, this does not totally explain its phenomenal rise. In addition there was always present the religious notion of "a chosen people for a chosen land."

Most scholars view Moses Hess (1813–1872), the "communist rabbi" whom we mentioned above, as the direct precursor of modern political Zionism. Though Hess himself differed substantially from Marx on the solutions to the perplexing issue of the Jews — Marx pleading for the whole Jewish community to totally identify with the rest of humanity's quest for Socialist emancipation rather than doing it by itself — both were nonetheless agreed that Marxist socialism was the answer. Hess interpreted the Torah in a Marxist spirit, speaking, for example, of "Mosaic, that is Socialist, principles." Understandably, the ideas of Moses Hess have had a deep impact on the Socialist-minded wing within the Zionist movement today.

Leo Pinkster, a medical doctor from Odessa, is often credited with being one of the first to give the incipient Zionist urge in Jews some actual shape. In response to the pogroms in Russia, he wrote anonymously his book *Auto-emancipation*, which bore the subtitle "A Warning Call from a Russian Jew to His Brothers." The book was his call to Jews to take their old fatherland back and once again make it their own. To implement his ideas, he formed "Friends of Zion" societies which would in turn encourage the establishing of Jewish colonies in Palestine.

I have already noted the contributions of Nathan Birnbaum (1864–1937), who coined the term "Zionism" and thus rallied the Jews around the cause. Since I have previously mentioned his writings and activist work, I shall not treat him more extensively here.

Zionism got a hefty push forward from Theodor Herzl (1860–1904), who as a reporter at the Dreyfus affair in France got an inkling of the deep anti-Jewish feelings which were then living in the souls of Frenchmen. He wrote a book, *Der Judenstaat* (1896), but also took steps to contact various Western governments and the Ottoman regime to determine the possibility of actually establishing a separate Jewish state in Palestine. With Max Nordau assisting him, Herzl convened the first Zionist Congress in 1897 in Basel which transformed Zionism from a latent feeling burning in the hearts of so many Jews into an actual organization with specific and concrete goals. The Basel congress set its sight on one goal only: a judicially guaranteed area in Palestine in which Jews could dwell.

When negotiations with the Turkish government broke down and offered very little hope of success, Uganda and Argentina were suggested as alternative spots for a Jewish state. In view of the situation, Herzl made no objection to considering them as temporary measures to relieve the problem of dispersed Jews, but for a permanent Jewish residence he had only one place in mind — Palestine.

The Zionism of those years also had a cultural dimension in addition to the political dimension which we have been discussing. One of its most gifted representatives was Martin Buber (1878–1965) who in the years 1909–1911 offered in Prague a series of three lectures which later became famous: "Judaism and the Jews," "Judaism and Humanity," and "The Renewal of Judaism."

A whole series of Jewish writers was active in the cultural renaissance of the Jewish people. One only has to mention names like Jacob Wassermann, Max Brod, Hugo Bergmann (rector of the Hebrew University and author of *Die Heiligung des Namens*), and Franz Kafka (whose *Letters to Felice* bespeak his longing for Israel to gauge the impact of this cultural renaissance. Another imposing figure in this movement was Asher Ginsberg, who described Jerusalem as the center which radiated a spiritual and cultural influence; he personally believed that this center of radiating influence could be revived without engaging in political negotiations.

The successor to Theodor Herzl as chairman of the Jewish congress, Chaim Weizmann (1874–1952), tried to synthesize the political and cultural elements within Zionism. During his early efforts, however, he received far less than full support from his fellow Zionists.

The rise of Zionism took a great many Jews by surprise, for they sought for a solution to the "Jewish question" either through humanism or through a "new religious thinking." Only after the opponents of European Jews became more strident did political Zionism gain momentum. The Orthodox Jew, Dr. Isaac Urma from Germany (1872–1948), tried to give political Zionism a religious foundation: "The land of Israel is the orthodox Jew's real hope for the future." Said he, "We have a mandate to settle in Israel." And from the liberal wing within Judaism Leo Baeck (1873–1936) in his book *Das Wesen des Judentums* saw the return to Palestine in terms of the old Jewish hope for a messianic kingdom: "The ancient idea of God's exaltation and of his Kingdom are again living and real."

But the greatest interest in returning to the land of Palestine came from eastern European Jews who wanted to flee the pressure coming from their own governments and set up the first of the many later socialist *kibbutzim*. Heading one of these kibbutzim was the future president of Israel, Ben Svi, and still another kibbutz led to the founding of the city of Tel Aviv, whose name harks back to Theodor Herzl's novel with the same title.

During the First World War the Turks persecuted the Jews who had established colonies in Palestine, for since the Turks were fighting against the allied forces, they naturally were suspicious of Jews. In that connection a Jewish detachment formed in the United States and London for the express purpose of fighting the Turks. Chaim Weizmann, the Russian Jewish chemist, had meanwhile won the respect of the English cabinet and was asked to assist in developing war material in England. He earned the respect and sympathy of Lord Balfour and Sir Mark Sykes, the secretary of the English cabinet during the war, and thus through this acquaintance and Weizmann's mediation the famous "Balfour Declaration" was issued which guaranteed Jews a national home in Palestine on the condition that the civil and religious rights of the Palestinians would not be violated.

General Allenby began capturing Palestine and Syria the very same day the declaration was issued. At war's end, the Treaty of Versailles mandated England to carry out the provisions of the Balfour Declaration, which meanwhile had been included in the peace treaty with Turkey. The very words of the mandate to the English laid the groundwork for a future Jewish state: "Recognizing how closely the history of the Jewish people is intertwined with Palestine, the mandatory is responsible for creating the proper political, administrative, and economic conditions that shall guarantee the existence of a national home for the Jewish people."

After some time England withdrew from Palestine because of the turmoil caused by the Balfour Declaration. Not only had England given promises to the Jews, but both England and France had made big promises to the Arabs. And after the war the spirit of Arab nationalism was rising rapidly.

It is not my purpose to rehearse the whole of the very ambivalent history of Palestine under British rule, but several factors need to be mentioned. First of all, Jews started legally and illegally immigrating to Palestine because of what was happening to them time and again in western and eastern Europe. They were continually being threatened with extermination. For example, after 150,000 Jews were murdered in the Ukraine, thousands of others streamed toward Palestine at the close of the First World War. Or again, when German Jews saw the specter of national socialism rising after 1930, thousands of them fled to Palestine, so that by spring of 1936 no fewer than 400,000 Jews were already in Palestine. The "death ships" transported people who had been living under a cloud of futility and threat and were now seeking a spot in the sun where both they and their children could have a future. Both during and after the Second World War thousands of escapees from the hellish concentration camps left Europe for Palestine to join those who had immigrated earlier. Anyone who forms a judgment about Zionism and the Israeli state without remembering the "holocaust" which gave rise to them simply is not being fair. The Jews were fighting for their very survival.

A second factor worth noting is that the Zionist leaders themselves are deeply divided on a proper approach to the Palestinian Arabs. A small group of highly qualified Zionists sternly warned the Jewish people who themselves had suffered so much injustice not to act in kind toward the Palestinian Arabs. Judah Magnes (second rector of the Hebrew University), Martin Buber, Ahad Ha Am, Moshe Smilansky, Ernst Simon and many others called for Jews and Arabs to live together in peace in a binational state. The kibbutzim supported their efforts. Shortly before his death Martin Buber took the occasion of his eightieth birthday to tell how disappointed he was that this ideal had not yet been realized. The failure was in part due, he said, to the unwillingness of most Jews to make the plan work, but even more than that, the recent holocaust had rendered a peaceful building up of relations between Jews and Arabs impossible for a time. He still expressed his hope for a binational state which would federate with the other states in the Middle East.

Other moderate figures such as Chaim Weizmann and Ben Gurion supported a plan proposed by the United Nations to divide the land between Jews and Arabs. Even after the State of Israel had been constituted, Ben Gurion continued to declare his support for the idea which had been rejected by the Arab nations.

Still other people believed that the whole of Palestine on both sides of the Jordan River had to be annexed and thus serve as a place of refuge for millions of Jews. Heading this group was Vladimir Jabotinsky, who organized a Jewish militia in Jerusalem (Haganah) and whose ideas finally won out. Other military organizations came into existence as well (for example, Ezel and Lechi), and all of them joined hands in opposing the presence of the British as well as the storm troops of the Great-Mufti of Jerusalem. The military groups became so strong that even the former supporters of a binational state finally joined them.

These military groups were so tightly coordinated that they made British rule completely impossible. In 1946 the King David Hotel, center of British operations in Palestine, was blown up. In 1947 the United Nations proposed still one more plan to divide the land. But meanwhile "Exodus 1947" had begun; the British were going through with evacuating their troops.

On May 14, 1948 Ben Gurion proclaimed the state of Israel officially organized. Very soon thereafter both the United States and Russia recognized the new state, as did the United Nations to the degree that it had promised a specific area to Israel under the plan it had proposed to divide the land.

Several days after the English high commissioner had boarded ship in Haifa, Egyptian, Syrian, Lebanese, and Iraqi troops accompanied by the Arab Legion crossed the border into Palestine. The Israelis had their backs to the sea, and the bloody fighting was about to begin.

Judah Magnes predicted long before the fighting erupted that such armed conflict with the original inhabitants of Palestine, with the thousands of refugees who had left the land amid all the confusion and tension, and with the neighboring Arab states would only spiral once it began. Alas, his words have proven all too true.

The first war the Jews waged against the Arab league ended with both sides agreeing to cease hostilities, an arrangement worked out by Ralph Bunche of the United Nations. The state of Israel could now begin its work of building. The Zionist movement had achieved one of its primary goals — a national rebirth of the Jewish people in the land of Israel.

THE STATE OF ISRAEL

In 1950 when the state of Israel began to breathe a bit more easily, it passed a law which granted every Jew the right to immigrate to this newly established state. "Every Jew who came to the land of Israel before this law went into effect, and every Jew born in the land whether before or after the law went into effect, enjoy the same status as any other person who moved (there) on the basis of this law."

Meanwhile state and society set about to build up the cultural, social, economic, and political life of the citizenry, achieving results that are nothing short of amazing. The state of Israel has become a creative center of Jewish culture and a model of social and economic progress.

But the plight of the refugees in the surrounding lands remained an unresolved problem, and the armed conflicts between the Israelis and the Arab nations spiraled alarmingly. The Sinai expedition of October 29, 1956 spelled great victory for Israel but only increased the ill-will among the Arabs. On May 18, 1967, at Egyptian President Nasser's request, Secretary-General U Thant of the United Nations withdrew the UN contingent from the Gaza area. The Six-Day War soon began and once again ended with Israel capturing vast areas of former Arab territory. By now the Arab urge for revenge had reached a boiling point.

Though the United Nations passed Resolution 242 calling for Israel to return the captured areas, she refused. In 1973 the Arab nations, led by President

Sadat of Egypt, fought back quickly, and even though the Israeli state again "won" in this so-called Yom-Kippur War, the awful fighting so stymied her self-confidence and at the same time increased Arab self-consciousness that Israel in a very real sense stood before another beginning. Once again she was asking the question she had posed earlier: What should be Israel's relationship ethically, culturally, politically, and pragmatically to her neighboring states, and how can the rights of the Palestinian Arabs be guaranteed to them? The higher the spiral of armed conflict, the clearer it becomes that force is no solution; the right acquired by way of military strength only paves the way to chaos and the devastation of both sides. Reconciliation must come, and to make this possible, the voice of the Palestinian Arabs must also be heard.

THE PALESTINIAN QUESTION

If one's interest in this complex dispute extends only to the State of Israel and excludes concern for the rights of the Palestinian Arabs living in Israel and in the refugee camps, he cannot hope to offer a genuine Christian service of reconciliation.

In the words of a Palestinian Arab, Dr. Suudi, "Today's Palestinian Arab is a descendant of the Philistines, Canaanites, and other earlier peoples such as Greeks, Romans, Arabs, Mongols, and Turks. He is thus a product of mixture."

At the close of the First World War Palestine was an Arab land. Its population of 700,000 consisted of 574,000 Muslims, 70,000 Christians, and 56,000 Jews. During the fight against the Turkish Ottoman Kingdom which failed at the end of the First World War, Arab thirst for self-expression grew apace. To insure Arab support, England promised Hussein, the great sharif from Mecca who after the war became King of Hedjaz, that she would quest for, recognize, and support the independence of the Arabs "in all those areas within the boundaries requested by the Sharif of Mecca." (Cf. the McMahon letter of 1915.) Arab hopes for national self-expression soared with the promise.

But the Balfour Declaration and the Sykes-Picot Agreement annulled this English promise and retarded the progress toward the goal of self-expression. The Arabs felt they had been deceived, for rather than having become a Palestinian Arab state, the area had been turned into a mandate region in 1920. At that time ninety-two percent of Palestine's citizens were Arabs, and this ninety-two percent owned ninety-five percent of the land.

Meanwhile, though Palestine did not receive her freedom, her neighboring Arab states (Trans-Jordan, Iraq, Syria, and Lebanon) did become free. Moreover, from 1920 to 1948, the time the mandate was in effect, Palestine had to cope with still an additional problem — the steady stream of Jews who had come to Palestine to escape persecution in Western and Eastern Europe.

I shall not rehearse all the charges the Israelis and the Palestinian Arabs hurled back and forth during those years, nor shall I detail how the Palestinians lost their land and their houses and either ended up in refugee camps or felt reduced to second-class citizens within the state of Israel. But anyone who has objectively studied the facts and the charges must admit that the Palestinian Arabs felt deeply frustrated in their quest for national self-expression. They had suffered a heavy blow to their human self-esteem, and in reaction they organized resistance movements. Al Fatah (the national Palestinian freedom movement) proposes to take the destiny of the Palestinian Arabs into its own hands. But in addition to Al Fatah, there are several other resistance movements: the Democratic Front for the Liberation of Palestine; the People's Front for the Liberation of Palestine, led by Dr. George Habash; and *Sā'iqua,* supported by the Syrian Baath-party.

In October, 1974, the Arab top conference held in Rabat granted Yasser Arafat and his Palestine Liberation Organization (PLO) the right to represent the Palestinian Arab people, and in this capacity Arafat was given the opportunity to address the United Nations in the same year.

The question of the Palestine Arabs is no longer seen as merely one of what to do with the refugees; there are political issues involved, and this dimension is being recognized more and more. Palestinian participation is absolutely indispensable in the search for a solution. For, as the World Council of Churches declared in Canterbury in 1969, "By lending their support to the founding of the state of Israel, the great powers have also done a great injustice to the Palestianian Arabs, and this must be rectified."

Paying such heed to the Palestinian side of the problem is often misinterpreted as anti-Judaism. One may not view the state of Israel as being above and beyond any and all law; such an attitude would be a poor service done to the Israeli cause. While the Palestinian Arabs must quit dreaming about devastating the state of Israel, the Israelis must learn to pay due regard to the rights of the Palestine Arabs and, by creating for the Arabs a place to live, rectify the injustice done to them. The Jews have been oppressed too long in this world to now begin wearing the mantle of the oppressor.

Judaism's best representatives have always understood this truth. In those momentous days after the Yom Kippur War, Abel Herzberg said that the only genuine solution to those seemingly insoluble problems would come when the sons of Abraham, Israel and Ishmael, recognized each other's rights and made the appropriate concessions. Shortly before he died Chaim Weizmann said, "Israel shall be judged by what it does *for* the Arabs."

History teaches that what one people does *for* another is not determinative. In the future both Israel and the Palestinian Arabs shall be judged for what they *together* do to secure each other's rights. Will the Palestinians from their side show understanding for the earnest Jewish desire to find a safe domicile after centuries of exile and diaspora? And will the Israelis in turn be prepared to make concessions to the Palestinian Arabs in order to satisfy their desire for recognition and a feeling of worth? These are the real questions which must be answered if genuine reconciliation is ever to take place.

THEOLOGICAL INTERPRETATIONS OF THE MODERN STATE OF ISRAEL AND OF THE MIDDLE EAST

As churches throughout the world seek to communicate with the Jewish people, specific theological interpretations many of them have about current developments in the Middle East often serve either to retard or to advance such communication efforts. I wish to consider these interpretations, many of which contradict each other, hoping thereby to discover a path which shall lead to a service of reconciliation.

Such attempts at theological interpretation as have arisen are not only inescapable; they are both permissible and proper. Anyone who confesses that God acts in history must look for signs of his leading. But to be complete, such attempts must seriously reckon not only with what happened to Jews both during and after Auschwitz and as they established the state of Israel, but they must also pay due regard to the Arab refugees who had to flee when the Israeli state was born.

Trying to Tell the Time on God's Clock of History

Throughout history but especially since the Jewish return to Palestine many people have been speculating about God's eschatological time schema. Believing that the Jewish return directly fulfills specific prophecies made by Ezekiel and Ezra, they try to determine the "time and the seasons" through which God will be passing as he makes his way to the end of history and begins the complete revelation of his kingdom.

In my judgment such attempts are completely at odds with the teachings of Jesus. In the first chapter of Acts he disallows his disciples' questions about the time of the kingdom. The timepiece is in God's hands alone, said Jesus, and since this coming kingdom will embrace the whole earth, he gives his disciples the command to communicate the gospel worldwide (Acts 1:1–8). Such work is quite different from continually speculating about what time it is on God's clock.

A Hebrew University professor reminded those who engage in such speculation of the real purpose of prophecy. It is not fortune-telling but rather a radical testing of events in history to see whether they conform to the high standards of the Law and the Prophets.

As I see it, this kind of speculative juggling of the prophets' words in no way contributes to the service of reconciliation; it uses the Jews and Israel only as the pointer hands on God's clock of history and does not really engage them as partners in the search for reconciliation.

Theological Zionism

In an interpretation even more serious than the above, certain Christians are trying to provide the Zionist ideology with a foundation and a touchstone in Christian theology. In one man's words, this is "theological Zionism," and in my judgment there is no clearer representative of it than F. W. Marquardt, who wrote an essay in *Evangelische Theologie* (28:638, 1969) entitled "Christentum und Zionismus." For theological or, to be more specific, for christological reasons he believes a Christian must support the state of Israel. Says he: "My Christology makes a renunciation of my solidarity with the Zionist Nationalism completely out of the question." Not because he is driven by some spontaneous emotional attachment to the Jewish state, but rather because he has "heard the proclamation of Christ," he feels he must accept the claims of the Zionist movement.

Claude Duvernoy, a French Protestant theologian, goes even further than Marquardt in his claims. His essay in *Foi et vie* (July/August, 1964) entitled "Essai du théologie Zioniste" without any critical reserve whatsoever identifies with the intentions and claims of Zionism.

Though the Dutch Reformed (*Hervormd*) church's report "Israel, Volk, Land, Staat," written largely by two individuals, Dr. Hendrikus Berkhof and Dr. E. Flesseman-van Leer, is a much more modest offer than those described above to shake hands with the Jews, there are nonetheless traces of theological Zionism in it which I must question and which I think can only hinder open participation in the service of reconciliation.

I shall restrict my discussion of the report to three basic statements with which I have difficulty. First, the report claims that if the election of Israel and the related promises are still valid, then it naturally follows that the close connection between people *(volk)* and land is divinely sanctioned. Of course, I wholeheartedly agree that the people of Israel together with the New Testament people of God are elect, but does this mean that the promise of land in Palestine as contained in the Old Testament is also still in effect? I agree with the New Testament scholar van Iersel, who says that while there is a direct tie between people and land in the Old Testament, this is no longer true in the New Testament because the messianic promise now extends outward from the "land of Israel" to cover the "ends of the earth." Asks van Iersel: "Have the authors of the report wrestled long enough with the New Testament?"

Of course, one must try to understand what it means for the Zionists to be able to return to Palestine after two thousand years of dispersion, and one must join them in rejoicing. But in my judgment it is improper to assign a special theological significance to the land of Palestine and view the Jewish return as a fulfillment of God's promise to Abraham. Such ideas can only produce unacceptable consequences. For example, many Israelis view the western shores of the Jordan River as "God's gift to Abraham" and therefore reject any Palestinian claim to this land. Does not the danger lurk here of clothing the claims of any ideology with the mantle of authority of the God of Abraham? Land promises in the Old Testament had a *pars pro toto* quality to them. In the New Testament there is talk of the rights of all people throughout the whole earth.

My second problem with the report is that it claims that anyone who believes in God's promises must thereby also accept a separate Israeli political state. I too believe that until both Jews and Arabs together decide the future shape of their society in Palestine the present state of Israel must be accepted. But is it proper to base the existence of such a political order on biblical and theological grounds?

My third difficulty with the report has to do with the question of the role of Jerusalem in the eschaton. While the report is much more cautious on this score, it does incline to view Jerusalem as specially significant in the eschatological fulfillment. Is that defensible in view of the fact that the New Testament speaks of the "new Jerusalem," God's ecumenical city whose inhabitants come from every nation and spot on earth (Rev. 21)?

When Jesus tells the Samaritan woman that the time will come when the question of whether to worship God on Mount Gerizim or in Jerusalem will be irrelevant, is he not hinting at something the rest of the New Testament carries through, namely, the removal of the geographic boundaries of Jerusalem from their once special position of importance? Does not such sacralizing of Jerusalem as the report contains actually impede the search for realistic solutions by both Jews and Arabs living in the city?

Anyone who is oblivious to the deep Jewish attachment to the city of Jerusalem cannot understand the Jewish people; but when one provides these deep feelings with a theological foundation he runs the risk of encouraging idolatry.

The Palestinian Arabs and the Theology of the Poor and Oppressed

While some opt for the state of Israel because of their theological Zionism, others choose for the Palestinian Arabs and against Israel because of a theology of the poor. Many Arab Christians and even a few Jewish Christians who know firsthand about the problems the Arab refugees encounter and about their attempts to rectify the injustice through resistance movements claim God is on the Arabs' side, for Yahweh is the God who sides with the poor and oppressed. The New Testament too is solidly linked with the plight of those who are the victims of power politics and have no hope.

Hans-Ruedi Weber from Geneva, Switzerland, inquires how we ought to view both of these positions stated above. Is the one true prophecy and the other false? Or do they complement each other? Or perhaps does the tension between them correct the excesses of each and enrich them both? Before we can answer these questions, we must approach the issue from a different direction.

RECONCILING ISRAELIS AND PALESTINIAN ARABS

The polarizing interpretations discussed above do very little to reconcile the opposing sides in the Middle East. Would it not be far better to work together toward reconciliation by paying close heed to the social-psychological, moral, and juridical factors operative on both sides?

Whoever wants to help must understand something of the expectations as well as the bitterness carried by both sides. The Jews are eager for safety and certainty after two thousand years of uncertainty, while the Arabs in Palestine want a recognition of their human value and worth and a control over their own destiny. They are increasingly anxious about the steady stream of Jews immigrating to Palestine, for they see every step the Jews take forward toward expansion as a step backward in the Arab quest for self-determination.

The Jewish Desire for Safety

As the Jewish writer David Polish once wrote, no one can fathom the deep attachment both religious and secular Jews have for the land of Israel without understanding what two thousand years of exile and semi-exile have meant for them. It meant living outside the land they believed was promised to them and outside the protection afforded by their own community. The urge for national self-expression did not begin as recently as the nineteenth century; it began the very moment the Romans drove the Jews out of Palestine. The very dynamic of Jewish existence throughout the centuries involved a restoration of the community to its place of origin. The paradigm of all Jewish history is the exodus from Egypt — an ardent desire to escape the bonds of exile and to return to Jerusalem and the land of Israel.

In this sense Auschwitz and Jerusalem belong together. Except for Auschwitz, the great powers who recognized the state of Israel would never have looked the other way while so many Jews returned to Jerusalem and the state of Israel. The experience of Auschwitz would have been absolutely unbearable if the Jews who endured the suffering had not also been fired with the dream of returning to Jerusalem and the land of Israel. And if that dream had not later become a reality, there would have been a moral collapse of incalculable proportions among the battered Jewish people. This dream and hope kept the Jews standing on their feet as they passed through the hell of Nazi tyranny.

No one would want to be so bold as to claim that the state of Israel today is the fulfillment of the long-held Jewish hope for a messiah, but there is no denying that after the agony of Nazi terror it was deeply significant for Jewish identity and for the conviction which lives deep in the heart of every Jew that he and the whole community are involved in the unique genius of ongoing Jewish history. Rabbinic Judaism held the Jewish people together during the Diaspora; in like manner the state of Israel ought to function today as the unifying force which drives on Jewish history.

Many Jewish thinkers such as Einstein, Buber, and Judah Magnes hoped for a situation to develop in the Middle East where the Jews could live peacefully and in freedom and develop their Jewish ways *without* necessarily calling into existence a separate state of Israel. They hoped for a binational state in which both Jews and Palestinian Arabs could peacefully coexist, but regrettably these Jews were in the minority. Most believed a separate state was practically necessary to defend and guarantee Jewish safety. This is not for us as outsiders to decide; however, to understand the Israelis one must have a feeling for their deep desire for security, which finally led them to establish a separate Jewish state and to maintain that state amid the enormous tensions today.

The Palestinian Arabs' Desire for Recognition of Their Human Dignity

For five hundred long years the Palestinian Arabs were dominated by the Ottoman Turks. When they became free of the Turkish yoke at the end of the First World War, they were ruled by British mandate for another twenty-five years. At the end of this period they fully expected that their long-awaited freedom could finally begin as it had been promised to them in 1947 by the major powers.

However, the founding of the state of Israel obstructed the construction of an independent Palestinian state. Thousands of Arabs fled from Palestine and landed as refugees in neighboring Arab states, and still other thousands, both Muslims and Christians alike, who chose to remain felt reduced to the status of second-class citizens in the land of their birth. The Arabs were most deeply pained by the recognition of the west bank of the Jordan River after the Six-Day War in 1967 and by the Israeli annexation of the Arab part of Jerusalem.

One must understand Jewish attachment to the land of promise, but no less must he empathize with the Arabs who also feel strongly attached to the land where both they and their forefathers lived. He must identify with the feeling the Jews throughout the world have for the city of Jerusalem, but he must be equally concerned about the Arabs' desire to control Jerusalem, the site of the Arabs' imposing mosque, The Dome of the Rock. One must understand that after the ordeal of Auschwitz the Jewish desire for security was both untameable and irresistible, but he must equally understand the thoughts and feelings of the Palestinian Arabs when the existence of a completely new state was proclaimed right in their very own territory without in the least reckoning with their rights or consulting with them whatsoever. As soon as one realizes that both the Israelis and the Palestinian Muslims have legitimate claims he will come to see the need for a service of reconciliation between them and will encourage the start of dialogue.

Many are asking: Is it proper to urge this on the Israelis? Is this not to invite holocaust against them? Does not flexibility in the Israeli position spell their doom?

To be sure, reconciliation at Israeli expense is quite out of the question, but it is also quite unreal if peace is made at the expense of the Palestinian Arabs. Someone has written: "The life of a nation, in this case Israel, is a non-negotiable item." Of course it is, but the particular shape such a nation takes *is* negotiable, and one must be flexible as he searches for a solution which will be just to the cause of the Palestinian Arabs.

Concrete Possibilities for Reconciliation

When one considers the present thorny and bitter situation, is not a call for reconciliation simply a waste of breath? After all, reconciliation seems completely out of the question. But in this futile situation it just could be that what seems impossible is actually the only possible way out of the hopelessness, as Abel Herzberg once commented.

One does well to recall that the Palestine liberation movement has never made a Jewish departure from Palestine one of its official demands. The slogan "Israel must be thrown into the sea" now has much less currency in the Arab world than heretofore, and the famous resolution of the United Nations issued in 1967 (Resolution no. 242) which calls for both a return of the Israeli-occupied west bank and other areas to the Arabs as well as the tacit recognition of the state of Israel by Egypt, Jordan, and Lebanon is now being mentioned more frequently.

Some of the most progressive young Arabs are increasingly becoming aware of the need for a form of coexistence. Through personal contacts many of them are arguing for a federative union between a Palestinian Arab state and the state of Israel.

In the long run Israelis and Palestinians are first going to have to learn to live together with open borders between them, sharing a certain customs-union,

and then ultimately to live in a political federation itself. But each side must begin
by breaking through the deep suspicion and fear it harbors toward the other side
and approach the other side in a spirit of goodwill.

There must be a solution somewhere for the problem of the west bank of
the Jordan and for the problem of how to establish the Palestinian Arab component of a political state. It must be possible somehow to solve the refugee problem
as United Nations Resolution no. 242 calls for by liberally compensating those
refugees who do not return and by returning and resettling others. There must be
some way possible to reform the governing of Jerusalem so that the concerns of
both the Israelis and the Palestinian Arabs are taken into account.

Sydney Bailey, the well-known Quaker historian of the United Nations,
made six specific suggestions regarding Jerusalem:

1. Jerusalem must remain an undivided city.
2. Jerusalem must consist of separate Jewish and Arab neighborhoods.
3. Whether done bilaterally or under United Nations auspices, both sides
   must determine policies which will make cooperation between the
   Jewish and Arab neighborhoods possible in administrative affairs.
4. The Arab section must serve as the capital city of the Palestinian Arab
   state, while the Israeli section must serve as the capital for the Israeli
   state — as is presently the case.
5. The city must be recognized internationally as an open, unprotected
   city having no armed military force present in it.
6. Each of the three main religious communities (Jewish, Muslim, and
   Christian) must have free access to the holy places. There must be
   freedom of conscience and religion. Every person must have the right
   to express his religious convictions in public worship, practice and
   education and submit to such limits as may be necessary to protect the
   fundamental rights of others. By such means the cultural and religious
   variety within Israel must be guaranteed.

After twenty-five years of pent-up emotions, even to suggest such recon-
ciling measures as these seems to indicate that one is out of touch with reality. But
really, is this not the only way to arrive at a solution in a situation so explosive and
dangerous not only for the opponents themselves in the Middle East but indeed for
the whole world? We must hold before both sides the standards of truth, justice,
and mercy. One does not set about doing this by yielding to all the demands of the
Zionist ideology nor by uncritically adoring all claims of the Palestinian resistance
organizations. Rather, churches and governments can serve both sides by lovingly
and patiently maintaining relations with them and not giving up until both sides
gather round a conference table to try to hammer out a just solution.

In the October 13, 1973 issue of *The Times,* James Parkes, a proven friend
of Israel, wrote the following:

> To achieve peace the Israelis and the Palestinians must be reconciled with
> each other. For both of you security and power are not dependent on
> geographic boundaries, but rather on the attitude of those who dwell on
> the other side. We are convinced that neither of you can achieve perma-
> nent gain or security by war, and we shall do everything in our power to
> help you to arrive at peace and a guaranteed protection for each side.

It strikes me that the World Council of Churches through its Commission on International Relations and its Commission on the Relation Between the Church and the Jewish People is continually performing just such a service of reconciliation. In my judgment, such work better serves the cause of promoting the gospel of reconciliation than all the various Christian positions which tend to polarize both sides by either providing theological Zionism a Christian base or by propping up Palestinian Arab ideology with Christian arguments.

The World Council maintains close contact with both sides and by straightforward social-psychological and legal means attempts to induce them to adopt measures that seriously reckon with the rights of each.

Let us hope and pray that the Israelis will renounce the hard-line attitude they displayed between the Six-Day War and the Yom Kippur War. And let us hope and pray that the Arab peoples will cease their radical rhetoric which only impedes the search for concrete solutions. And finally, let us Christians be ready in any way we can to promote reconciliation between both sides.

BIBLIOGRAPHY

1. Judaism in General

Baeck, L. *Das Wesen des Judentums*. Frankfurt: Kaufmann, 1926.
Bloch, J. *Das Judentum und der Krise*. Göttingen: Vandenhoeck & Ruprecht, 1966.
Boertien, M. *Het Joodse Leerhuis van 200 voor tot 200 na Christus*. Kampen: J. H. Kok, 1974.
Buber, M. "Het Geloof van Israel." In *De Godsdiensten der Wereld II*. Edited by G. van der Leeuw and C. J. Bleeker. Amsterdam: Meulenhof, 1956, pp. 161–300.
————. *Gottesfinsternis: Betrachtungen zur Beziehung zwischen Religion und Philosophie*. Zurich: Manesse, 1953.
————. *Der Jude und sein Judentum: Gesammelte Aufsätze und Reden*. Cologne: Melzer, 1963.
Miskotte, K. H. *Het Wezen der Joodse Religie*. Haarlem: Holland, 1967.
Palache, J. L. *Inleiding in de Talmoed*. Haarlem: Bohn, 1954.
Soetendorp, J. *Symboliek der Joodse Religie*. Hilversum: De Haan, 1966.
Vriezen, T. C. *De Godsdienst van Israël*. Zeist: De Haan, 1963.

2. History of Judaism and the Churches' Response to Anti-Semitism
History of Judaism
Epstein, I. *Judaism, a Historical Presentation*. London: Penguin Books, 1959.
Kupisch, K. *Das Volk ohne Geschichte: Randbemerkungen zur Geschichte der Judenfrage*. Berlin: Lettner Verlag, 1953.
Kuyper, A. "Het Joodse Probleem." In *Om de oude Wereldzee I*. Amsterdam: van Holkema en Warendorff, 1907, pp. 239–324.
Kwiet, K. *Van Jodenhoed to gele Ster*. Bussum: Unieboek, 1973.
Marcus, J. R. *The Jew and the Medieval World*. New York: World Publishing Co., 1961.
Parkes, J. *The Conflict of the Church and the Synagogue: A Study in the Origins of Anti-Semitism*. London: Soncino Press, 1954.
————. *A History of the Jewish People*. Harmondsworth: Penguin Books, 1962.
Runes, D. D. *The War Against the Jew*. New York: Philosophical Library, 1968.
Sartre, J. P. *Réflexions sur la question Juive*. Paris: Gallimard, 1962.
Snoek, J. M. *The Grey Book*. Assen: Van Gorcum, 1969.
Tillich, P. *Die Judenfrage: ein christliches und ein deutsches Problem*. Berlin: Weiss, 1953.
The Churches' Response to Antisemistism
Albinski, M. *Antisemitisme in ons?* The Hague: Pax, 1964.

Berdjajew, N., et al. Die Gefährdung des Christentums durch Rassenwahn und Judenver-
    folgung. Lucerne: Vita Nova Verlag, 1935.
Bernstein, F. Der Antisemitismus als Gruppenerscheinung. Berlin: Judischer Verlag, 1926.
————. Over Joodse Problematiek. Arnhem: van Loghum Slaterus, 1935.
Bloch, J. S. Israël und die Völker. Berlin: Härz, 1922.
Brunner, C. Der Judenhass und die Juden. Berlin: Oesterheld und Co., 1918.
Coudenhove, H. Antisemitism Through the Ages. Westport, Conn.: Greenwood Press, 1935.
Duehring, E. Die Judenfrage. Karlsruhe: Reuter, 1880.
Glock, C. Y. and Stark, R. Christian Belief and Anti-Semitism. New York: Harper, 1966.
Guardini, R. Verantwortung: Gedanken zur Jüdische Fragen. Munich: Koselverlag, 1952.
Hoch, W. Kompass durch die Judenfrage. Zurich: Zwingli Verlag, 1944.
Kohnstamm, P. Psychologie van het Antisemitisme. Amsterdam: ten Have, 1933.
Leschnitzer, A. Saul und David. Heidelberg: Schneider, 1954.
Maurer, W. Kirche und Synagoge. Stuttgart: Kohlhammer, 1953.
Poliakov, L. Harvest of Hate. London: Bestseller Library, 1960.
————. Histoire de l'antisémitisme. 3 vols. Paris: Calmann-Levy, 1956–68.
Reichman, E. Hostages of Civilization. Westport, Conn.: Greenwood Press, 1950.
Sulzbach, W. Die Zwei Wurzeln und Formen des Judenhasses. Stuttgart: Kohlhammer,
    1960.
Thieme, K. Judenfeindschaft. Frankfurt: Fischer Bücherei, 1963.
Valentin, H. Antisemitism Historically and Critically Examined. Freeport, N.Y.: Books for
    Library Press, 1936.

3. Zionism and the State of Israel

Buber, M. Israel und Palestina: Zur Geschichte einer Idee. Zurich: Artemis Verlag, 1950.

4. Jewish Literature on Christianity

Andermann, F. Das Grosse Gesicht. Munich: Ehrenwirth, 1971.
Ben Chorin, S. Die Anwort des Jona: Zum Gestaltwandel Israels, ein geschichts-
    theologischer Versuch. Hamburg: Reich, 1956.
————. Je Broeder Israël. Amsterdam: ten Have, 1968.
————. Broeder Jezus. Amsterdam: ten Have, 1971.
————. Paulus, der Völkerapostel in Jüdisch Sicht. Munich: List, 1970.
————. Mutter Mirjam: Maria in Jüdisch Sicht. Munich: List, 1971.
Brod, M. Der Meister. Gütersloh: Bertelsmann, 1951.
Carmichael, J. Leben und Tod des Jesus von Nazareth. Munich: Szczesny Verlag, 1966.
Finkel, A. The Pharisees and the Teacher of Nazareth. Leiden: E. J. Brill, 1964.
Flüsser, D. De Joodse Oorsprong van het Christendom. Amsterdam: Moussault, 1964.
Isaac, J. Jesus and Israel. New York: Holt, Rinehart and Winston, 1971.
Kabak, A. The Narrow Path. Tel Aviv: Institute for the Translation of Hebrew Literature,
    1968.
Klausner, J. Jesus von Nazareth. Berlin: Jüdischer Verlag, 1934.
Lapide, P. E. Jesus in Israel. Gladbeck: Schriften Missionsverlag, 1970.
Van Praag, H. De Boodschap van Israël. Amsterdam: Wereldvenster, 1952.

5. Christian Literature on Israel

Barth, K. Church Dogmatics. Edinburgh: T. & T. Clark, 1957.
Barth, M. Israel und die Kirche im Brief des Paulus an die Epheser. Munich: Kaiser Verlag,
    1959.
————. Jesus, Paulus und die Juden. Zurich: EVZ Verlag, 1967.
Bergema, H. Rondom Israël. Kampen: J. H. Kok, 1957.
Daniélou, J. Théologie du Judéo-Christianisme. Tournai: Desclée, 1958.
De Ridder, R. R. The Dispersion of the People of God. The Covenant Basis of Matthew
    28:18–20 against the Background of Jewish, Pre-Christian Proselytizing and Diaspora,
    and the Apostleship of Jesus Christ. Kampen: J. H. Kok, 1971.
Hartenstein, K. Israel im Heilsplan Gottes: Eine Biblische Besinnung. Stuttgart:
    Evangelische Missionsverlag, 1952.

Koole, J. L. *De Joden in de Verstrooing*. Franeker: Wever, n.d.

Mulder, H. *Geschiedenis van de Palestijnse Kerk*. Kampen: J. H. Kok, 1968.

Ridderbos, H. N. *Israël in het Nieuwe Testament: In het bijzonder volgens Romeinen 9–11*. The Hague: 1955.

Tillich, P. "Missions and World History." In *The Theology of the Christian Mission*. Edited by G. H. Anderson. New York: McGraw-Hill, 1961, pp. 281–290.

Visser, A. J. *Calvijn en de Joden*. The Hague: Boekencentrum, 1963.

Vriezen, T. C. *Die Erwählung Israels nach dem alten Testament*. Zurich: Zwingli Verlag, 1953.

6. The Relationship between the Church and Israel throughout History

Rengstorff, K. and von Kortzfleisch, S. *Kirche und Synagoge: Handbuch zur Geschichte von Christen und Juden*. Stuttgart: Klett, 1968, Vols. 1 and 2.

Schoeps, H. J. *The Jewish-Christian Argument: A History of Theologies in Conflict*. New York: Holt, Rinehart and Winston, 1963.

7. Dialogue Between Christians and Jews

Baeck, L. *Judaism and Christianity: Essays*. New York: Atheneum, 1970.

Boon, R. *Ontmoeting met Israël: Het Volk van de Thora*. Kampen: J. H. Kok, 1974.

Buber, M. *Zwei Glaubensweisen*. Zurich: Manesse Verlag, 1950.

De Beus, C., et al. *Op het Spoor van Israël; Studie ten Dienste van het Gesprek met Israël*. The Hague: Boekencentrum, 1961.

Eckhardt, A. R. "Toward a Theology for the Christian-Jewish Encounter." In *Christian Mission in Theological Perspective*. Edited by G. H. Anderson. Nashville: Abingdon Press, 1967, pp. 125–146.

Gollwitzer, H. *Israel und wir*. Berlin: Lettner Verlag, 1958.

Gollwitzer, H. and Sterling, E. *Das gespaltene Gottesvolk*. Stuttgart and Berlin: Kreuze Verlag, 1966.

Grolle, J. H. *Dit Komt U tegen in Israël: Ontmoetingen met Joden en Christenen*. The Hague: Boekencentrum, 1963.

————. *Open Vensters naar Jeruzalem*. The Hague: Boekencentrum, 1969.

Israël en de Kerk. The Hague: Boekencentrum, 1960.

Jocz, J. *The Jewish People and Jesus Christ: A Study in the Relationship between the Jewish People and Jesus Christ*. London: SPCK, 1949.

————. *A Theology of Election: Israel and the Church*. London: SPCK, 1958.

————. *The Spiritual History of Israel*. London: Eyre and Spottiswoode, 1962.

————. *Christians and Jews: Encounter and Mission*. London: SPCK, 1966.

Marquardt, F. W. *Die Entdeckung des Judentums für die christliche Theologie: Israel im Denken Karl Barths*. Munich: Kaiser Verlag, 1967.

Miskotte, K. H. *Das Judentum als Frage an die Kirche*. Wuppertal: Brockhaus, 1970.

Rosenberg, S. E. *Antwoord van een Rabbijn*. Nijkerk: Callenbach, 1966.

Von Balthasar, H. U. *Einsame Zwiesprache: Martin Buber und das Christentum*. Cologne and Olten: Hegner, 1958.

8. Bibliographies

Bergema, H. "Kerk en Synagoge." *Vox Theologica* 35 (1965). (This article includes an extensive bibliography.)

Holsten, W. "Judentum, Heidentum, Christentum." *Theologische Rundschau NF* 35 (1970): 65–86, 94–163, 181–195.

Jackson, H. C. *A Select Bibliography on Judaism, Jewish-Christian Relations, and the Christian Mission to the Jew*. New York: Missionary Research Library, 1965.

9. Periodicals

Christian News from Israel. Edited by C. Wardi. Publication of the Government of Israel, Ministry of Religious Affairs, Jerusalem.

Christlich-jüdischer Forum. Mitteilungsblatt der chr. jüdischen Arbeitsgemeinschaft in der Schweiz. Basel.

Christus en Israël. Publication of the Roman Catholic Council for Israel, St. Willibrord Society, Driebergen, Netherlands.

Emuna Horizonte. Deutsch-Israelische Gesellschaft. Frankfurt am Main.

Evangelie en Israël. Publication of the Deputies of the Gereformeerde Kerken in the Netherlands to aid in proclaiming the gospel to Israel. Wilhelminalaan 3, Baarn, Netherlands.

Freiburger Rundbriefe; Beiträge zur Förderung der Freundschaft zwischen dem alten und dem neuen Gottesvolk im Geiste beider Testamente. Edited by K. Thieme. (The second volume [1959–60] contains an extensive bibliography.)

Immanuel: A Semi-Annual Bulletin of Religious Thought and Research in Israel. Published by the Ecumenical Theological Research Fraternity in Israel. P.O. Box 249, Jerusalem.

Judaïca, Beiträge zum Verständnis des Jüdischen Schicksals in Vergangenheit und Gegenwart. Zurich.

Kerk en Israël. A monthly publication of the Reformed (Hervormde) Council for the Relationship between the Church and Israel. Wilhelminapark 60, Utrecht.

The Bridge. Edited by J. M. Oesterreicher. Yearbooks of the Institute of Judaeo-Christian Studies in Newark, N. J.

The Church and the Jewish People. Quarterly newsletter from the WCC Committee on the Church and the Jewish People. (This newsletter is a continuation of *Quarterly News Sheet of the Christian Approach to the Jew,* produced from 1931 to 1960 by the International Missionary Council.)

The Hebrew Christian. Publication of the International Hebrew-Christian Alliance, 19 Drycott Place, London S.W. 3.

Verkenning en Bezinning. A series of essays on the relationship of the Church to the Jewish people. Published by J. H. Kok, Kampen, Netherlands.

Koole, J. L. *Tenach of Oud Testament.* No. 1, March, 1967.

Smeenk, B. D. *De Verkiezing van Israël.* No. 2, June, 1967.

Wytzes, J. *Antisemitisme in de antieke Wereld.* No. 3, September, 1967.

Van der Woude, C. *Gesprek met Israël in de tweede Eeuw.* No. 4, December, 1967.

Bavinck, C. B. *De Verhouding van de Kerk en het Joodse Volk.* Vol. 2, No. 1, June, 1968.

Mulder, M. J. *Iets over de Farizeeën.* Vol. 2, No. 2, September, 1968.

Bergema, H. *Verbroken Eenheid.* Vol. 2, No. 3, December, 1968.

Koole, J. L. *Jesaja 53.* Vol. 2, No. 4, March, 1969.

Mulder, H. *De Synagoge in de N.T.-ische Tijd.* Vol. 3, No. 1, June, 1969.

Van den Berg, J. *Joden en Christenen in Nederland Gedurende de 17de Eeuw.* Vol. 3, No. 2, September, 1969.

Dijk, J. *Uitverkoren en vervolgd (Gedachten over het Lijden van Israël).* Vol. 3, No. 3, December, 1969.

Popma, S. J. *De Lastendrager.* Vol. 3, No. 4, March, 1970.

Snijders, L. A. *Het Verhaal van Abrahams Beproeving.* Vol. 4, No. 1, June, 1970.

Bakker, R. *Van Israël en de Heilshistorie.* Vol. 4, No. 2, September, 1970.

Steendam, H. *Het nieuwe Verbond.* Vol. 4, No. 3, December, 1970.

Dijk, J. *Niet zonder Israel.* Vol. 4, No. 4, March, 1971.

—————. *Uit Joden en Heidenen.* Vol. 5, No. 1, June, 1971.

Slomp, J. *Joden, Christenen en Muslims: Een Driehoeksverhouding?.* Vol. 5, No. 3, December, 1971.

Smeenk, B. D. *Het Joodse Volk en zijn Land.* Vol. 6, No. 1, 1972.

Klijn, A. F. *Het Proces tegen Jezus.* Vol. 6, No. 2, 1972.

Barth, M. *De Jood Jezus en het Geloof der Joden.* Vol. 6, No. 3, 1972.

Dijkstra, M. *25 Jaar Erets Israel.* Vol. 6, No. 4, 1973.

Mulder, H. *Fiscus Judaicus.* Vol. 7, No. 1, 1973.

—————. *De Joodse Christenen onder Trajanus en Hadrianus.* Vol. 7, No. 2, 1973.

Oosterhoff, B. J. *De Beloften aan de Aartsvaders.* Vol. 7, No. 3, 1973.

Snoek, J. M. *De Wereldraad van Kerken en Israël.* Vol. 7, No. 4, 1974.

CHAPTER VI

Motives for Fulfilling the Missionary Task

If it be true that missions generally are in a "time of testing," then it is certainly true that motives for which people engage in mission are being radically inspected and "sifted like wheat" (cf. Luke 22:31). Not only are the actual motives of missionaries today and the possible ones of those tomorrow being investigated, but even those of the past are being recalled for testing. In the biographies of great missionaries one can often detect a certain romanticized glorification of their missionary motives. The biographies remind one of the medieval "holy lives"; biography seems at times to turn into hagiography and the missionary's motives appear to have sprung completely from the Holy Spirit himself, completely unspotted with other less noble ones.

But for every biographer who idolized his subject there are others who misunderstood the missionaries' motives and actually slandered their persons. Bernard Shaw described English missionaries as covert imperialists interested more in the British empire than in the kingdom of God. Johannes Schütte, a competent missionary to China, wrote a dissertation on the picture of mission described in the Red Chinese press, *Die Katholische Mission im Spiegel der Rotchinesische Presse* (1956). It is a shameful book, one filled with slander, stereotypes and cliches about the Christian mission. But by looking into the mirror of the Red Chinese press as Schutte does, one can find much that calls for reexamination and change. African missions too have come under a barrage of criticism, some of it well-intentioned, some of it fashionable, and some of it downright slanderous. Missionary agencies are accused of everything, including cultural aggression, ecclesiastical colonialism, spiritual imperialism, and escapism from the situation back home.

Sometimes demonic forces so obviously control the sifter that both the proper and improper motives dance about as chaff and wheat together, and the bad is not finally sifted off from the good. But at other times it is God himself at work trying to teach us to distinguish chaff-filled motives from worthy ones and thus to lead us to self-examination, humility and reorientation.

Two questions will command our attention in this chapter. First, what should be the deepest motives for communicating the Christian faith throughout the six continents of this world? Second, what impure motives have hindered the missionary task in the past and still threaten it today? For, quite frankly, throughout the history of the Christian mission pure and impure motives have been as mixed through each other as the clean and unclean animals of Noah's ark.

PURE MOTIVES

First I wish to consider those motives which should fill the heart of every member of every Christian church throughout the world. I shall stick as closely as possible to the New Testament Epistles' description and praise of the several motives for mission, motives which have received increased accent in the history of the newer mission and which are now at work among churches in every continent since the day of one-way traffic in missions has come to an end.

The Motive of Obedience

In the chapter on biblical foundations we discussed the various forms of the missionary mandate and also noted how Paul in his letters indicates a certain duty which he feels toward the will of God (I Cor. 1:17; Gal. 2:7). He speaks of an inner necessity (I Cor. 9:16) and of being "under obligation" to all people (Rom. 1:14). The motive of obedience plays a very definite role throughout the apostolic literature. Fulfilling the missionary task is nothing more than obedience to the command of the Lord.

This motive has inspired countless thousands to dedicate their whole lives to the missionary task. When William Carey came to see that limiting the missionary mandate to the age of the Apostles was completely wrong and actually violated its very meaning and sense, he wrote a piece entitled *An Inquiry into the Obligation of Christians to Use Means for the Conversion of the Heathen.* I am happy to say that thousands of people, when critically asked, "But *why* do you do mission work?", responded with a curt "Just because!" and then went on to support their answer with the deep yet uncomplicated affirmation: "It is the will of the Lord!"

Hendrik Kraemer believed that missiology should more and more become a *theologia oboedientiae,* a theology of obedience. While on a furlough during a crisis in Dutch missions, he wrote his famous series of pamphlets, *Why Mission Just Now?* and *Church and Mission.* In them he stridently countered the antimission tendencies of his day by claiming that if one gives up mission both at home and abroad, he is being disobedient to his Lord.

Though other writers such as O. Noordmans and G. C. Berkouwer have quite properly uttered warnings about perceiving this motive of obedience in too legalistic a manner, I think there is every reason today for underscoring its importance. Some Christians today have the idea that mission is a voluntary affair, a hobby some people have, an activity to be done by people who are interested in that sort of thing. Such people must hear once again the strong call to obedience.

As I noted above, D. van Swigchem's dissertation shows that the early Christian congregations scarcely had to be reminded of their missionary calling. Their whole existence was caught up in mission. Such is not true of most churches today. Today churches on every continent need to be reminded of their need to obey the command of the Lord, but especially our European churches, infected as they are with laziness and the quest for a comfortable life, and with skepticism and relativism.

The Motives of Love, Mercy and Pity

The Bible strongly accents the motives of love, mercy and pity in mission work. Jonah, who was rescued because God loved and had mercy on him, was accused of lacking these qualities. Paul describes those who do not live in the light of God's promises as estranged from the living God and having no hope in the world (Eph. 2:1–10). Time and again he mentions that he, too, in spite of his religiosity and legalism, was once such a rebel against God, a criminal whose perverted piety cut right at the very heart of God who revealed himself in Christ. Throughout his letters Paul simply could not stop talking about what God's love meant for him!

Paul goes on to tell the congregation to whom he is writing that they too were once strangers to God, people who loved the darkness and who were in danger of being destroyed. But they who have been rescued and now live by the love of God must now reflect that very same love to others through the work of mission. The objects of God's mercy and pity must now become the instruments and communicators of that mercy and pity to others. Christ wants to reach out to others via his congregation. But the church can only act as God's bridge to the world if she is filled with the very same love, mercy and pity as she herself has received from God.

One can see from a text like I Thessalonians 2:8 the depth of Paul's mercy: "So, being affectionately desirous of you, we were ready to share with you not only the gospel of God but also our very own selves. . . ." But individuals and churches who do not feel the call to communicate the gospel in their own environs and in distant lands are lacking in love and mercy and impede the flow of God's love to these people. But once the sediment of guilt is dredged from men's hearts so that the stream of the Holy Spirit can again flow freely, he shall again open up the springs of love, mercy and pity from which a genuine concern for mission has always arisen.

The Motive of Doxology

Praise to God's name is another of the motives for mission found throughout the New Testament. Paul says his concern is that ". . . the word of the Lord may speed on and triumph" through the whole world and that ". . . every tongue [might] confess that Jesus Christ is Lord, to the glory of God the Father" (II Thess. 3:1; Phil. 2:11). Or again, after he has reflected deeply on the task of proclaiming the gospel to both Jews and Gentiles and has opened up some mighty perspectives, Paul ends his three-chapter discussion (Rom. 9–11) with a doxology: "O the depth of the riches and wisdom and knowledge of God. . . . For from him and through him and to him are all things. To him be the glory forever" (Rom. 11:33, 36).

This motive of *gloria Deo* is not only present in virtually every theoretical treatment of the motives for mission, but it also inspired the life and work of many missionaries themselves who during the centuries have participated in the missionary enterprise.

What is the heart of doxology? Some people mistakenly suppose that God is one who eagerly goes out in search of praise and glory. In direct opposition to the biblical message, they portray him as a little Greek god, a Narcissus who is always preoccupied with self, or as a little Roman god who ever loves himself. Nothing could be further from what the Bible says about God.

What is God's glory? We can best begin by describing what it does to human beings. God's glory drove the shepherds to their knees beside the crib in Bethlehem when they saw that God had looked with favor on mankind. God's glory moved Simeon to cry out in praise as he stood on the temple's marble floor shortly before he died. God's glory filled Mary with awe as she carried Jesus in her womb and pondered shortly after his birth all the things which had been spoken about her newborn son. God's glory is what the disciples beheld at the wedding in Cana when Jesus saved the celebration by performing his first miracle (John 2:11).

Jesus spoke of God's glory when he offered to die for human beings: "Now is my Father glorified and the Son is also glorified" (cf. John 17 and John 12:20–36).

God's glory is the fullness of his divinity. It is the unveiling of the manner of his existence. To see God's glory is to bask in the wonder that God is pro-mankind and that he takes great delight in freeing human beings so that they can make their lives a celebration with him and with each other, Or, as Karl Barth said: "God's glory is the appearance, the expression, and the manifestation of everything that God really *is.*"

The phrase "God's glory" summarizes all of his features — his holy love, his grace, his mercy and justice. This then is the very heart of the doxological missionary motive — a burning desire that all men may come to know God as he really is.

Paul claims in Romans 1 that human beings perversely exchange their knowledge of God as he really is for idols of their own making. God is pronounced dead by many ideologies; he is so ignored, minimized, misinterpreted, slandered, ridiculed, and caricatured that many people simply do not know him as he really is. The doxological motive implies that people who know the true and living God discover that he is such a delight that they want others to get acquainted with and live in fellowship with him as well. For genuine human life is learning to live with him and thus also with each other in fellowship. In the high priestly prayer which is replete with the exaltation of the Father, the Son says to the Father: "This is eternal life, that they may know thee the only true God. . . ." Thus, as we come to live and work with others and as with every breath that we take we fellowship with him, from whom and through whom and to whom are all things, our authentically human life begins to bloom.

The Eschatological Motive

The motive of the kingdom plays an important role in the Gospels. The second petition of the Lord's Prayer, "Thy kingdom come," expresses this central motive succinctly.

Though Paul switches terms, the same motive comes through in various ways. Paul and his co-workers were driven by the desire for the "fulness" (*plērōma*) of the Body of Christ. Especially in Ephesians and Colossians, he emphasizes how he wants all peoples to share in the "Body of Christ" (*sōma tou Christou*).

Missiologists like J. C. Hoekendijk and E. Jansen Schoonhoven throughout their writings note how important this motive was to the pioneer missionaries. Von Zinzendorf cannot be understood without it. The Student Volunteer Movement was full of it.

We could go on reciting still others, but this is unnecessary. Only one truth still needs stating: any church which does not eagerly long for the kingdom and for the "fulness of the heathen" to come into it is no longer a church; it has become an exclusive club. Churches on every continent must begin to feel the throbbing desire to gather all people under one Head, Jesus Christ, the only rightful owner of human lives.

The Motive of Haste

The motive of haste is closely tied to the motive of expecting the kingdom. Mark's Gospel uses the phrase "and immediately thereafter" no less than thirty times in describing the events of Jesus' life. Jesus was serene yet at the same time intensely hurried as he discharged his divine mandate in the cities and villages he visited. Paul too showed an inner security about his faith and yet was driven by a deep compulsion to get the message out quickly. The Apostle continually warned his readers to make the most of their time since the days are evil. "Don't be indifferent," he cautioned, ". . . but do good to everyone while there is still time" (cf. Eph. 5:16–17; Col. 4:5; Gal. 6:10). Time is a gift from God, and our lifespan is limited. Therefore we may never despise it or fritter it away but must use it in the service of the Lord (cf. the parable of the talents recorded in Matt. 25).

Anyone acquainted with the biographies of the pioneers in world mission knows of their strong drive to get the message out quickly. But no generation of Christians may ever be without it, and therefore Karl Barth could cite sluggishness as one of the major sins of the church today. This sluggishness can take so many forms: theoretical analyzing which fails to put ideas into practice, inertia, indecision, lack of vision and inventiveness, passing up opportunities, and planning without implementing the plans. One can observe this sluggish attitude in churches on every continent.

We must as Christians be alert to what the New Testament calls the "times and seasons" *(chronoi kai kairoi)* and take appreciative advantage of them while it is still daylight, for the night is coming when no man can work.

One could easily write a book on the history of world mission with the title "A Record of Lost Opportunities." But there is still time; the King of all ages still holds the timepiece of history in his hands. The motive of haste must ever drive us on.

The Personal Motive

Finally, I must make mention of what Paul says in I Corinthians 9:23: "I do it all for the sake of the gospel, that I may share in its blessings." When Paul refers to this as a motive for mission, he is pointing to an established fact of human experience, namely, that he who rouses others to belief strengthens his own faith as well.

D. T. Niles never tired of mentioning this motive. Stagnant waters turn
into a morass, but if one keeps on communicating, his own stream will also remain
fresh and flowing. The one who shares the gospel with others discovers for himself
that it is a "spring of water welling up to eternal life" (John 4:14). He is overwhelmed with joy. But Christians and churches who are no longer impelled by this
motive for mission become introverted and disputatious.

IMPURE MOTIVES

Not a single missionary in whatever area he works is prompted only by those pure
motives described above. Impure motives have also been clearly discernible
throughout the history of the Christian mission, but in this recent "time of testing"
they have received increased attention often from those who operate from an
ideological bias and are quick to point an accusing finger at Christianity. Many
times such critics either generalize or else fantastically exaggerate the problem.

However, no one can deny that shady motives have been operative, and in
this section I shall single out those which in our day are being subjected to the
sifting process of criticism.

The Imperialist Motive

One of the most frequent criticisms made of missionary work, particularly of
missions originating in the West, is that it was done for imperialist reasons. By
imperialism I mean the attempt by one state to use another people or state as a
means to achieve its own goals. Imperialism for centuries came in the form of
colonialism, but it does not absolutely depend upon political domination of
another people in order to function. Colonialism can also be economic in nature,
as for example was and still is the case in Latin America after the political
revolutions of the nineteenth century.

The question is: Were imperialist motives present in the work of missions
throughout history? The answer is clear: Yes, beyond the shadow of a doubt.
During the fifteenth and sixteenth centuries Popes Nicholas V and Alexander VI
instructed first Spain and later Portugal to extend their political influence to Asia,
Africa, and the recently discovered America but also to be zealous for extending
the domain of the Roman Catholic church. By so doing, these Popes tied missions
tightly to political authority and to the work of the conquistadors who worked not
only in the Antilles and in Latin America but also elsewhere to establish "Royal
Patronage" in the fifteenth and sixteenth centuries. The results of this are well
known.

In the last few years we have seen the last vestiges of this close connection
between mission and patronage gradually disappear as the African areas of
Mozambique, Angola, and Guinea-Bissau gained their independence. Though
concordats between the colonial governments and missionary organizations had
disappeared in other areas long ago, Portugal and the missions in these three areas
still had them up until recently.

However, we do the thousands of missionaries who worked during the era of Spanish and Portuguese colonialism a great injustice if we see them only as the willing tools of imperialism. Anyone who knows the life of Francis Xavier (1506–1582) can only be deeply impressed with his willingness to serve. Imperialism always has been and still is a power which seeks to *be* served. But Xavier's life reflects much more the features of him who came not to be served, but to serve.

Bartholome de las Casas (1474–1566) ran directly counter to the spirit of Spanish imperialism when he rose to defend the rights of the Indians. Nor did he stand alone; to make a long leap to the twentieth century, those Roman Catholic missionaries who left Mozambique during the last few years because they found it impossible to work in the framework of medieval concordats were in the company of people like las Casas who either secretly or openly resisted colonial interference.

During the sixteenth and seventeenth centuries the imperialist motives played a definite role in those churches which came into existence as a result of the English and Dutch East-India Companies. Hendrik Kraemer was still busy clearing away the ballast of colonialism in the early twentieth century when he argued for the independence of the Moluccan and Minahassan churches; he was ardently opposed by a number of ecclesiastical authorities. But once again, one may not generalize, for there were many missionaries both long before and during Kraemer's time who refused to become the willing accomplices of a mercantile imperialism and who, though it cost them dearly, identified with the cause of the people among whom they were working.

During the nineteenth and twentieth centuries when modern colonialism led to the establishment of all sorts of small and large domains throughout the world, once again the imperialist motive was clearly present among the mission enterprises which accompanied the colonial spread. For example, the "mother churches" often restricted their mission interest to the colonial area held by the motherland; Dutch churches worked in Dutch territories, English in English, Belgian in Belgian, German in German, and so on. The argument was often heard: "Mission attaches the governed to the governors."

But once again, beware of easy generalizations about modern nineteenth- and twentieth-century missions. Many of the missionaries came to witness and serve in their respective fields long before the colonial powers came along to seize power for their own ends. One only has to mention famous names like Morrison, Taylor, and Carey, and many others who went to work in areas not yet in the clutch of colonial authority.

During the era of the so-called ethical politics, these missionaries cooperated more closely with the colonial authorities, but chiefly to raise the level of education and health among the people as high as possible. Many of the missionaries never realized that this very education would one day be the very lever of national self-expression among those people, but the clairvoyant few encouraged this process of national expression and gave their heart and soul in hoping and wishing and working with the people to give it birth.

Today, criticism abounds of the motives of those earlier missionaries, much of it very generalized and much of it coming from the lips of those whose own willingness and vision for missionary service cannot stand in the shadow of those whom they criticize. But for those who want to get an accurate picture of this very ambivalent era in the history of mission, several good books are available, including the following: H. Kraemer, *Godsdiensten en Culturen,* The Hague, 1968 (see especially his section on "Ambiguity during the nineteenth century 'colonial' era"); Stephen Neill, *Colonialism and Christian Mission,* London, 1966; Max Warren, *The Missionary Movement from Britain in Modern History,* London, 1965; Max Warren, *Caesar, the Beloved Enemy;* and Alphons Mulders, *Missiegeschiedenis,* Bussum, 1957.

After reading books such as these one can only admit that it is a caricature of missions and missionaries in the nineteenth century to depict them only as slaves to colonialism. In fact, men like Shaftesbury, Wilberforce, Livingstone, Monroe, Alexander Duff, John Mott, Adriani, Kraemer, John Smith, J. H. Oldham and thousands with them aided the drive for national expression. They were living within the structures of colonialism and knew that counter-pressure had to be applied.

It would be silly to suggest that missionaries alone were responsible for the nationalist spirit. In large part, the strength for this fight for social, cultural, spiritual, economic, and political freedom flowed from another source, namely, a deep inner resistance to domination from the outside. But that thousands of missionaries assisted in giving this spirit definite shape and form no one can deny.

On the other hand, the imperialist motive was so obviously present in nineteenth-century missions that there is no sense trying to camouflage or sweet-talk it out of existence. By now, however, colonialism has been sent to its grave in most areas of the world. From 1945–1960 forty nations with a combined population of eight hundred million people acquired their independence. To cite but one example, China forcefully cast off the shackles of its centuries-long semi-colonial status. The Bandung Conference held in 1955 was the clear signal that Western domination was everywhere being rejected.

But does this mean that that page from the lesson book of mission history is now superfluous and merely academic? By no means. Though it may seem that the arrival of political independence has signaled an end to Western imperialism, this is not the case. Economic imperialism, now free from the burden of colonial administrations, has become even more agile. Consider Latin America today as a case in point. When one considers the tight economic grip many of the larger nations of the West have on these Latin American peoples, no wonder figures like Emilio Castro and Julio de Santa Ana are probing how much churches and church structures assist neocolonial forces and actually become agents of "dependence" rather than independence. These churchmen are also searching for new ways for the churches to become first independent and then later to arrive at a responsible interdependence among themselves.

It is to the honor of the Presbyterian churches in North America that they are now working with the Latin Americans to search out every trace of neocolonialism with a disarming amount of honesty and candor.

A warning against imperialism may never be considered old-fashioned or out-of-date, for the danger is always present. Our generation too must be reminded that *every* people and *every* state are by their very nature imperialist. Not only West Europe and North America, but in equal measure Russia and Japan — to name but a few countries — face the continual urge toward imperialism, and the respective churches in those countries often willingly or unconsciously jump on the bandwagon.

The Cultural Motive

During the nineteenth century, cultural motives often supplanted genuine biblical motives for mission. That is, mission work went hand in hand with a transfer of the missionary's culture.

The cultural motive came dressed in various guises. The coryphees of cultural Protestantism in the nineteenth and early twentieth centuries viewed missionary work as primarily a means of transmitting the values of Western culture. Schleiermacher believed that missionaries should go only to those areas where Western culture is penetrating and seek to transmit and transfer to those people the "deeper values" of this culture. The goal of the missionary is not to present the gospel of salvation to them, but to try to "carry his fatherland with its laws and customs along with him and to look upon the higher and better things of life wherever he goes."[1]

Though Schleiermacher had been trained in a school run by the Herrnhutters, had learned much about non-Western cultures, and thus was willing to admit that there were "gigantic differences" among them, he nonetheless believed that mission work was primarily a cultural enterprise and accompanied a general transfer of culture. Mission involves cultural extension.

Another prominent representative of this position was Ernst Troeltsch, a philosopher of religion whose views are gaining increased attention. He bases the phenomenon of religion in his theory of the religious a priori. All of the various religions which have appeared throughout history are but specimens of the one phenomenon called religion. The Christian religion is but one stage along a way which shall lead to a "higher form of religiosity." Within this relativist and historicist framework he saw mission as contributing to a coming world civilization. In an article which he wrote in 1906, *Die Mission in der heutigen Welt,* he claimed that missionaries have the right to work among people in primitive societies whose religions will not be able to stand as the incoming tide of world civilization rushes over them.

As for the relationships and attitudes that the higher religions and religious fellowships should sustain toward each other, Troeltsch called for replacing the Christian mandate to mission with mutual understanding and cultural and religious exchange.

William Hocking expressed the same spirit. The report *Rethinking Mission,* issued in 1932 and written by a committee of which he was chairman, and Hocking's own books, *Living Religions and a World Faith* and *The Coming World Civilization,* both argue for replacing the missionary mandate with mutual understanding in order the better to prepare for the coming world society.

No one denies that world mission has a role to play in getting various cultures to meet one another. Nor may one deny that mission ought to take careful note of the global spread of a civilization which bears a heavy imprint of technol-

1. Friedrich Schleiermacher, *Reden über die Religion,* p. 190.

ogy and the exact sciences. In fact, A. J. Toynbee warns of the disastrous results
which will certainly ensue if mankind allows this civilization to spread globally
without paying due heed to the religious and ethical problems which it poses.
A. T. van Leeuwen has continually issued similar warnings. But this does not
mean that the cultural motive can become the central motive for mission. Cultural
Protestantism fails to realize that the mandate to engage in mission does not issue
from a given culture, but from Christ himself. When Paul claims in II Corinthians
5:20 that "we are ambassadors of Christ," he is no mere cultural attaché.

Moreover, the spokesmen for cultural Protestantism like Troeltsch and
Hocking were filled with optimism as they tried to join Christianity to a specific
culture. However, the experience of two world wars has made us better able to
see that sharp and glistening scythe which shall cut through the harvest field of
every culture. Perhaps we from our vantage point can see better than the
coryphees of cultural Protestantism that the field of Western culture, though filled
with rich grain, is horribly weedy as well. And we today know better than did
those apostles of cultural Protestantism that there is a kernel of truth to the charge
heard from Asia, Africa, and Latin America that missionaries are often cultural
aggressors.

As world mission seeks to discharge her Christ-given mandate she shall
have to adopt a critical posture toward each and every culture and thus act priestly
and prophetically as an ambassador of Christ in the world. This cannot be done if
the missionary sees himself as a purveyor of French, English, American, or any
other Western culture; it is only possible if the missionary listens keenly to all that
the Lord himself is saying to his disciples who live within those cultures. The
recent pronouncements of the Bangkok conference of the Division of World
Mission and Evangelism of the World Council of Churches on the subject of
"conversion and cultural identity" are most relevant to this subject (1972/73).

Africa's shocking cry to preserve her cultural identity ought to put us on
guard against trading in too quickly and easily the deeper and genuine mission
motives for the cultural one. Throughout the history of mission, the new identity
one receives in Jesus Christ "has often been confused with other secondary
identities whose origin lay much more in the mission than in the Gospel itself."
Now, during this time of general house-cleaning, it is a good thing that the cultural
motive is being swept out the door.

The Commercial Motive

Though the turbid commercial motive never dominated, it often became an accessory motive and a point in the "propaganda" for mission. As J. van den Berg
showed in his essay on David Livingstone, this man wove genuine missionary
motives with commercial interests. To be sure, he pleaded for a legitimate commerce devoid of any ignominious slave traffic, but Livingstone's approach and
vision were nevertheless quite naive.

> Thus, toward the end of his life, we hear Livingstone talking less
> than before about the connection between commerce, Christianizing, and
> the war against slavery. He had suffered deep disappointment. His effort
> to open up the heart of Africa had provided the slave-traders easier access.

He stood lonely and powerless against the forces of slave trade which were continually crossing his paths. His great ideal of opening up a path for both Christianity and commerce into Africa passed before his eyes almost like a mystical beam but it only disappeared again into the mists.[2]

At various times the promotional literature written by missionaries made an appeal to the commercial interests of its readers. When John Williams, a man whom no one could accuse of having commercial interests only, sailed to the Pacific in 1877, he included this sentence in a letter he wrote to interest others in his work: "Anyone interested in furthering the commerce of his land is hereby called to engage in the work of mission." In commenting on this poor argument, Max Warren in his book *The Missionary Movement from Britain in Modern History* reminds his readers to remember the spirit of the times. Business companies were opposing missions because they thought missions did harm to their commercial interests. (Such opposition surfaced time and again throughout history and still does whenever the companies get into a bind.) For this reason Williams resorted to his bad argumentation. Adds Warren wittily: "Bad arguments often arouse bad counter-arguments."[3]

Though there are many other illustrations I could give of how missionaries joined mission and commerce, I shall desist. William Danker, an American missiologist from the Lutheran Church Missouri Synod, has written an historical survey of all the attempts to bind the two. It strikes me that his *Two Worlds or None* is too optimistic in its judgment of the attempts. To be sure, Danker is right when he notes the social and economic consequences of mission. But for this very reason one ought to inspect very carefully the tie between mission and commerce. History has taught us this lesson time and again.

The Motive of Ecclesiastical Colonialism

The final impure motive I shall cite is what the Christians in Africa and Asia strikingly call ecclesiastical colonialism. Ecclesiastical colonialism is the urge of missionaries to impose the model of the mother church on the native churches among whom they are working rather than give the people the freedom to shape their own churches in response to the gospel.

Especially during the nineteenth century the Anglican church imposed its ecclesiastical structures on the churches of Africa and Asia. The result was that these churches looked more like the national Church of England than like the congregations of the New Testament. Though with the advent of the twentieth century there is much more room for self-expression within the Anglican fellowship of churches, not every trace of this colonialism is yet obliterated.

But this is not the only example. Confessionally and structurally, the so-called mother and daughter churches in South Africa are so similar. Europe and America have exported their various denominations to other continents. And

2. Johannes van den Berg, "Een Open Pad voor Handel en Christendom — David Livingstone's Inzichten betreffende de Introductie van 'Commerce and Christianity in Africa'," *Christusprediking in de Wereld* (Kampen: J. H. Kok, 1965).

3. Max Warren, *The Missionary Movement from Britain in Modern History* (Naperville, Ill.: Allenson, 1964), p. 46.

though the confessional families such as Methodists, Lutherans, and Calvinists have helped to dispel the isolation some churches feel by keeping them in contact with others of like confession, the disadvantage is that many of these churches often maintain closer contact and have more to do with other churches within the confessional family than they do with other churches in their own backyard.

The churches in Asia and Africa are now getting behind the effort of the regional councils of churches and assisting them in trying to wipe out the vestiges of ecclesiastical colonialism.

I believe that the various confessional fellowships such as the Lutheran World Federation, the Presbyterian Alliance, and the Reformed Ecumenical Synod should pay close heed to the cry of the various churches around the world for a greater opportunity to be themselves. In the future these bodies should consider it as part of their task to assist these churches in their efforts and thus to strive for more mature ecumenical relationships.

Though I admit my list has been selective rather than exhaustive, I have nonetheless tried to discuss some of the pure and impure motives for mission. If they show anything, they definitely show that the churches on every continent must continually test their motives, asking questions like "What are we doing? Why are we doing it? What actually motivates us and what ideally should motivate us? Where is reform necessary?" But while we are posing these questions to ourselves, one more is indispensable: "Are we perhaps not being moved to mission at all?" Recall that at the Mexico City conference Visser 't Hooft described mission as the touchstone and the test of faith.

If there is no spiritual wind to drive us forward, we stand off to the side in embarrassment, indifference, or actual opposition to world mission and world diaconate. It is high time to inquire what sort of spirit really inspires us. Perhaps the antimission spirit has reached us, too, making us slothful and sickly. It is our task to continually test and retest our motives, distinguishing the pure from the impure motives for mission and making sure that we are indeed being led by the Spirit of God. As Visser 't Hooft said, "Tested missions defend nothing else than the right to bring the gospel to all men."

When Peter began to preach, the high council summoned him and ordered him to cease talking about Jesus. Peter's answer shows that he and the other disciples saw their work of mission and preaching as absolutely crucial and indispensable, for, said Peter, "there is no other name under heaven given among men by which we must be saved" (Acts 4:12).

We in our generation are again in need of this deep motivation for our task. In his beautiful book *The Missionary Between the Times*, Pierce Beaver says that as the wellsprings of participation in world mission begin to flow again, we will be moved also to communicate the gospel in our own environs.

Throughout history the argument was often used that we ought to engage in world mission only when our task at home had been completed. Though there is nothing new about it, it is being offered again today as though it were brand new. It is, in fact, as old as mission history itself. But Kraemer had the best answer to this argument: churches are never done with their work, wherever they may be involved. Whoever thinks that they are is only revealing his poor eyesight.

Participation in world mission and in mission at home always go hand in hand. The urgent need for this hour in the history of missions is a new motivation to engage in both.

CHAPTER VII

The Goal and Purpose of Mission

The goal of mission is an inescapable issue and one of great practical importance, for it determines missionary strategy and the choice of means and methods. Various answers have been offered throughout the course of mission history, and each of them has had important consequences for missionary practice.

In this short survey I shall limit my discussion to the various positions proposed during the modern history of mission only. After this I shall return to the Bible and attempt to formulate the biblical view on the goal of the *missio Dei* and *missiones ecclesiarum*.

THE GOAL OF SAVING INDIVIDUAL SOULS

Ever since the seventeenth century many missionary agencies have viewed their task as essentially one of saving individual souls. There have been many variations on this one theme.

Early Pietism

The fathers of early Pietism, Philip Jacob Spener (1635–1705) and August Herman Francke (1663–1727), geared their work largely to reach the individual. In his *Pia Desideria* Spener spelled out the classic goal of Pietist reform, while Francke was in the forefront of those who tried to carry it out. Both these men laid the accent on true piety, on confessional activity, on the importance of small gatherings of "devout Christians," on worship services held in people's houses, on religious discussion and Bible-reading at mealtimes, on singing and prayer, and on the priesthood of the individual believer. In their theological education they laid great emphasis on the crucial role of devout faith in the lives of their students and took steps to insure their conversion. He who had experienced no *Busskampf* showed that he was not converted and was no genuine Christian. The early Pietists stressed good works as a preparation for grace.

Such ideas were typical of the early Pietists. From their center in Halle these leaders, in cooperation with the Danish court, sent out scores of missionaries whose approach had been learned at the feet of their masters. But once they had become involved in the work itself, many of these missionaries broadened their vision considerably — a fact often overlooked by critics of early Pietism.

Take for example Bartholomeus Ziegenbalg (1682–1719) and H. Plutschau, the first Protestant missionaries sent out cooperatively by Francke and the Danish court to the region of Tranquebar in India. A study of their careers shows very clear traces of the early Pietism which they had acquired at Halle, for they were genuinely interested in the saving of individual souls. But both of them came to realize that an emphasis only on this goal is unbiblical. Hence, they took up projects in education, social work, and medical care, and when the General Secretary of the Danish Mission sent them a letter admonishing them "only to preach" and "not to become engaged in merely earthly affairs," they were quick to reply that a concern for souls also requires a concern for bodies. A Christianity that has become so spiritualistic that it is unwilling to be of service in "earthly affairs" is lopsided and bad.

While the chief emphasis of these two missionaries continued to be the saving of individual souls, we do them injustice in thinking that they limited the scope of their work to this alone. In fact, the early Pietists in Europe itself also broadened their horizons. Along with their emphasis on personal salvation, contrition, and the quest for penitence, the fathers of early Pietism provided the stimulus for establishing hundreds of sanitoriums, charitable institutions, schools, etc. — a precedent to which Ziegenbalg and his co-workers could have appealed for support.

Later Pietism

The early Pietism of Spener and Francke was replaced by the later Pietism of Count Nicolaus von Zinzendorf (1700–1760) and the hundreds of missionaries sent out both by him and the *Unitas Fratrum* to such faraway places as Greenland, Labrador, Alaska, the Himalayas, Egypt, Abyssinia, West India, and South Africa.

As he bade farewell to the first Herrnhut missionaries sent out, Zinzendorf spoke these words to them: "Go forth then in Jesus' name, and see if there be souls among the Moors who can be led to the Savior." Such words were typical of Zinzendorf, who from his youth had been deeply conscious of what he called "the great love and condescension of this God and Savior Jesus Christ, even to the death of the cross." His time spent at Halle and the cumulative experiences which followed only served to deepen this awareness. In response to the love of Christ for him, he felt a burning desire to win human beings for the Lamb or, to borrow his phrase, "to bring souls to the Lord."

When Zinzendorf spoke these words, he was thinking primarily of individuals, the firstlings of those gathered from all the peoples and nations on the earth. He spoke of "Cornelius-souls" and the ingathering of the "firstlings"; or again, he used terms like *ekloge* ("the calling out of individuals") and *aparche* "getting a start"). While referring to I Samuel 25:29, he says that the work of mission comes down to "binding one more soul into the parcel of those who live in fellowship with the Lord God."

Zinzendorf had a term to describe his work: *Einzelbekehrungen* ("conversion of individuals"). Says he: "The very meaning of the term Apostolate implies this: 'More souls must be saved. Come, heathen! Come, Christian! Come, people! As for us, we can do nothing more than preach the Good News.' "[1]

Of course, Zinzendorf never intended that these recent converts simply fend for themselves. Both he and his followers laid definite plans for bringing them within a spiritual fellowship once they had been converted. He organized small "cores" of believers to receive these new converts.

On his deathbed Zinzendorf told of how the "mission to the heathen" had grown to a size far exceeding his original expectations: "My invitation went forth only to the first of the heathen, but already now the number of those who surround the Lamb as a caravan of travellers has reached into the thousands."

Thus, it would be true to say that though these missionaries emphasized the saving of individual souls, wherever they worked national churches appeared. Think, for example, of the congregations of the Brethren in Surinam and the southern Caribbean. While these fellowships reflected to a great degree the genius and features of the people who comprised them, the missionaries were adamant and insistent on "issues of the heart," as they called them. *Ecclesiolae in ecclesia* were arising.

The example of Zeisberger, Hutterite missionary to the Indians, is rather typical. Fearing that their decision was superficial, Zeisberger at first denied entrance into the fellowship to those Indians who in a tribal council had chosen for Christ. Later in his ministry, however, he came to accept such mass conversions and even went so far as to write a regulation governing the entrance of such groups into the fellowship. He thereby contributed to the development of *ecclesiolae in ecclesia*.

Henry Martyn (1781–1812)

Henry Martyn was a missionary for the Christian Missionary Society of the Anglican church and a pioneer evangelist among the Muslims. He felt led to win individuals among this group for Christ. When he arrived in India, he entered the following statement in his journal: "Until now I have not been very useful. Let me now burn out for God." While closing out his life working on a Bible translation in Persia, he won one single Muslim for Christ, and one of his last missionary acts was baptizing this lone individual. Such incidents typify his view of the goal of mission in the household of Islam, but anyone who on that account would charge this man with having tunnel vision ought first to recall that Martyn did stellar work in the study of important languages of the Muslim peoples: Arabic, Persian, and Urdu. Furthermore, he translated the Bible with the aid of native assistants, and, by his famous debates with Muslim scholars, he set the stage for later Muslim-Christian dialogue. His biographer, C. E. Padwick, described these discussions as "the first meeting after centuries (Martyn's immediate predecessor as a Christian apologist to Muslim India was a Portuguese Jesuit named Hieronymo Xavier, confessor of Christ at the court of the great Akbar) of two gigantic spiritual forces all unguarded and unaware, coming together

1. Karl Müller, *200 Jahre Bruder Mission I*, p. 275.

with a first rude clash, unsoftened by intercourse and interaction of thought."[2]

Of course, no one today would try to converse with his opponent in the same way as Martyn did, but the courage he displayed in trying to bridge the gap created by centuries of animosity and misunderstanding reveals his deep religious conviction and his passionate love. Amid all the flurry of language study, translation work, and debates, he never lost sight of his ultimate goal — the concern for the individual. He commented after some years of ministry among them, "I have lost all hope of winning Muslims by argument. I know of nothing else to do but to pray for them." Or again, "A deep concern for their souls is something quite new to them; it arouses within them a corresponding earnestness of spirit." He repeatedly refers to intimate contact with individuals as the single most suitable tool for tilling the missionary fields.

William Carey (1761–1834)

William Carey, like Henry Martyn, also strongly emphasized the theme of individual salvation, but we do him an injustice if we think this was his sole interest. Dr. M. M. Thomas, a recent chairman of the World Council of Churches, attempted to dispel this caricature of Carey in an article printed in the January, 1971 issue of the *International Review of Missions*. As a young man in Leicester, Carey waged war against slavery and organized a boycott against sugar imports from West Indian slave plantations. While in India, he established an "agrihorticultural society" to improve the food situation, encouraged the humanizing of relations between people there, and fought against the caste system. In Serampore he initiated the study of the Sanskrit language which made possible the later scholarly investigation of the classic Hindu texts. For these reasons William Carey is now properly seen as a transitional figure whose life and work made a newer and broader vision of mission work possible. He is the cornerstone of the newer missiology.

In 1806 he and his fellow workers in Serampore published a *Form of Agreement*, which would guide the brothers in their approach to the non-Christian fellowships. The primary goal of mission, as the *Form* states, is the "winning of individuals," but along with that the document also calls for the "founding of churches and organizing of schools."

The Student Volunteer Movement

As a final example of those missionaries and missionary organizations which emphasized the salvation of individuals, I must mention the American Student Volunteer Movement, an organization which during the latter part of the nineteenth century and the early part of the twentieth roused many American and European students to offer their lives in the service of mission in Africa and Asia. Leaders of this movement were people like John Mott, Robert Speer, and Herman Rutgers. Its influence was so profound that it really deserves its description as

2. C. E. Padwick, *Henry Martyn, Confessor of the Faith* (London: SCM Press, 1923), p. 204.

"the greatest missionary movement since Pentecost." Its missionaries spread out over all six continents, and still today traces of its influence are clearly visible in the churches of Asia, Africa, and Latin America.

In 1886 this movement formulated its aims: "As an evangelical and ecumenical gathering of disciples and workers, we invite all who believe in Christ to unite in the communal task of bringing God's Word of salvation to a humanity living amid spiritual and moral chaos. Our purpose is none other than the evangelization of the whole of mankind in this generation."

Evaluation

Allow me to make several comments on the goal of mission which the above individuals and organizations represent.

(1) A genuine interest in the salvation of individual souls may never be absent in mission work. Even though the latest missionary conference held in Bangkok in 1972 viewed the scope of God's liberation in Christ as much broader than the individual soul's salvation, it took pains to explicitly state that when mission fails to address individual need — the deep loneliness of the human heart, the threat of sin, demons, death, and the devilish condition of doubt and hopelessness — then that mission has failed its calling.

Jesus Christ, who was so deeply touched by the multitudes, who wept for Jerusalem and who bore the heavy burden of the whole world upon his own shoulders, was nonetheless the very same Jesus who took time for individuals — for a Nicodemus, for a Samaritan woman, for a blind man along the way, for a robber hanging next to him on a cross. If, therefore, churches ever neglect the needs of the individual as they seek to discharge their missionary calling, they in effect sabotage the commands of Christ.

(2) Though certain missionaries and the organizations they represented sometimes had a lopsided theoretical concentration on certain needs within the individual, especially the spiritual and moral ones, they did not ignore the other needs in actual practice. Early Pietism gave rise to many institutions of mercy. The Hutterites stimulated social and educational activity wherever they went. And the Student Volunteer Movement did untold work in developing schools, universities and theological seminaries.

(3) Nonetheless, we must honestly admit that the goal of mission as these men and movements stated it is too narrow. They viewed the liberation effected by Christ in a perspective which was too individual. As one of their spokesmen said: "Our theology does not wrestle with cultural problems and our ethic does not concern itself with the totality of human activities."

(4) Not only the early Pietists but the later ones as well erred in making their own form of piety the norm for everyone else. In the tradition of Francke early Pietists raised the struggle of the soul to find penitence to an almost normative level and frequently directed more of their attention to the battle within the soul than to Christ and to his kingdom. Later Pietism, however, broke away from the tendency to impose this on everyone; Zinzendorf accented the note of joy within the gospel and jubilantly declared that Christ had done the wrestling for us.

But even later Pietism and Methodism tended to generalize and require of all people what is in fact only a particular form of piety and one type of conversion. For a good description of nineteenth-century criticism of this aspect of Pietism see Fritz Blanke's essay "Evangelische Missionskritik im 19. Jahrhundert." Ernst Friedrich Langhaus's book, too, *Pietismus und Christentum im Spiegel der aüsseren Mission,* though at other points it may not ring true to the Bible, is right on target when it treats this issue.[3] Langhaus faults the Pietists for their occasional sin of complacency and pride, for their involvement with self rather than with the urgent needs of the world, for their making conversion only a matter of the emotions rather than seeing it as touching all of life, for their replacing a renewal of all of life by a flow of tears, etc. All of these phenomena which Langhaus describes have indeed occurred in both early and later Pietism.

(5) In our own day many missionary organizations both in theory and in actual practice restrict the goal of mission to the saving of individual souls. Counteracting them, still other missionary organizations view their missionary goals as being broader, deeper, and more encompassing.

Regrettably, through the years these points of difference between them have tended to polarize the two groups so that in the United States, for example, one side can be labeled by the confusing term "evangelical" and the other side by the no less confusing term "ecumenical." To bridge the unfortunate gap Norman Horner has written a most helpful book, *Protestant Crosscurrents in Mission.*

One leading evangelical wrote, "It is time to meet." One can sense this readiness everywhere. And as leaders from both sides begin to talk with each other, none may ever forget that the present worldwide missionary movement originated with those who saw its very purpose for being as the salvation of individuals. Though we today certainly need to broaden the purpose of mission beyond that of the early pioneers, it would be sheer mockery to honor their memory with flowery words of praise if we were to give up that for which they lived and died.

ECCLESIOCENTRIC GOALS

I began this chapter by examining those movements and groups which saw the salvation of the individual as the only goal of mission, for this was the dominant trend at the beginning of the nineteenth century, the "great century of missions." But now I must turn our attention to those people and movements which emphasized the implanting of churches as the main purpose of mission. Such aims appear in Roman Catholic missiology and also in early Reformation statements, though the latter were substantially revised from the Roman Catholic position.

Roman Catholic Views on *Plantatio ecclesiae*

Thomas Aquinas, whose ideas on the purpose of mission influenced not only Roman Catholic missionary work but also the missionary theory of Gisbertus Voetius, speaks in his *Summa Theologica* of the apostolic office of church plant-

---

3. Ernst F. Langhaus, *Pietismus und Christentum im Spiegel der aüsseren Mission* (Leipzig: Wigand, 1864).

ing. As Aquinas sees it, the purpose of mission work is to so thoroughly root the church with all of her monarchical and hierarchical structure in the various cultures and societies that it serves as an instrument to salvation and good. Furthermore, through preparation for the various papal encyclicals which have been circulated as well as through the later reflection which these documents stimulated, the Roman Catholic church has continued to develop the concept of implanting.

Missiologists such as Father Henry P. Löffeld, Père Pierre Charles, S.J., of the Louvain school, T. Ohm and Joseph Glazik and others from Münster point out that the church can never be said to have been definitively implanted; her status always has a degree of uncertainty to it. The task of implanting must therefore forever go on. Divine grace is never something definitive for either individuals or for societies, but rather it constantly goes forward, needing ever to be planted and rooted in other soil.

H. P. Löffeld puts heavy emphasis on the local church as the partial realization of the monarchical-hierarchical church. Says he: "In the phenomenon of the local church the Church catholic manifests itself. It is Christ's chosen way to gather humanity to himself and share with it his redemption. Through the local church the Church both expands (extensive catholicity) as well as deepens by forming its own clerical order and laity (intensive catholicity)."

The schools of Münster and the Louvain[4] had a direct influence on Pope Pius XII's mission encyclical, *Evangelii Praecones,* issued on June 2, 1951, as appears from the following citation: "The final goal toward which we must strive and which must ever remain before our eyes is the firm establishment of the Church among the peoples, each [local church] having its own hierarchy chosen from the ranks of the native clergy." Scholars such as Couturier, Seumois, and Daniélou have worked out this approach in greater detail.

In 1962, A. De Groot, writing in the *Yearbook of Catholic Theologians,* took note of recent exegetical work and emphasized the eschatological dimension of mission. He accented more the mystical nature of Christ's body, a point which theologians generally have been underscoring since the Second Vatican Council. Here in part is what de Groot says:

> The mission of the Church, enjoined by God as her response to his own sending of the Logos and the Holy Spirit, is an eschatological event which involves proclaiming the Gospel to all non-Christians. Missionaries proclaim the lordship of Christ in the hopes of making disciples and establishing among the hearers the whole Christian economy of salvation in a manner that is native to them and yet stable and will serve as a constant offer of redemption. The ultimate goal is to complete the contours of the mystical body of Christ, to the glory of the Father through the Son and in the Holy Spirit.[5]

The Second Vatican Council's decree on mission, *Ad Gentes,* describes the goal of mission as follows: "The specific aim of this missionary activity is to preach the Gospel and plant the Church among peoples or groups in which it has

---

4. Initially the Louvain school accented the institutional aspect of the mission while the Münster school underscored the individual aspect.
5. A. de Groot, in *Jaarboek van de Katholieke Theologen,* p. 108.

not yet been established."[6] In its formulation this statement differs little from the thoughts of Thomas Aquinas, *Evangelii Praecones*, and another encyclical promulgated on January 15, 1957, *Fidei Donum*. However, if one reads *Ad Gentes* in its totality and views it along with *De Oecumenismo* ("The Decree on Ecumenism"), *Nostra Aetate* ("On the Relationship of the Church to the Non-Christian Religions"), and *Gaudium et Spes* ("On the Church in the World Today") as part of the total effort of the council, he can detect some striking shifts of accent. A deeper ecclesiology is at work in these decrees than has been traditional in Roman Catholicism. It is less monarchical and hierarchical. Rather than being completely Vatican-oriented as was traditionally the case, these decrees view the church as the people of God who are as pilgrims enroute to the kingdom of God. Features of this pilgrim people mentioned in the decree itself are peace, fellowship, brotherly love, and justice.

Roman Catholic missiology since Vatican II has gone in two directions. Some missiologists have tended to revive and underscore anew the pre-conciliar Vatican-centered view of mission. A typical example of such efforts is André Seumois's two-volume work, *Théologie missionaire*, published in Rome in 1972. He devotes the whole of volume one to a delimitation of the missionary function of the church and in it rehearses the classical and scholastic goal of Roman Catholic mission — the implanting of the church. On the other hand, some Catholic scholars are going the route of emphasizing the coming of God's kingdom in history and describing in fuller detail its features to which *Ad Gentes* referred. These theologians are developing an ecclesiology which is connected closely with the kingdom and which calls for humans to participate in the events of history, all the while remembering that the eschatological kingdom of God is coming near and that they belong to a pilgrim people of God who are enroute to this kingdom. Ludwig Rütti, one of the many who are urging the Roman Catholics in this new direction, issued his *Zur Theologie der Mission* in 1972, the same year as Seumois's *Théologie missionaire*.[7] But his conclusions are substantively different; as he sees it, the traditional implanting theory is far too restrictive and narrow. As he put it, "The mission of the Church is genuinely apostolic only when her structure and tradition handed down from the Apostles is geared to communicating the message that in the Kingdom of God lies the world's universal future. As she proclaims this message the Church in every historical situation transcends every boundary and even her own mode of existence."

The Roman Catholic missiologists who are working in this direction feel a close ecumenical bond with Protestant missiologists with similar ideas.

Plantatio ecclesiae in Early Protestant Missiology

Following the Reformation of the sixteenth century, Gisbertus Voetius, who lived in the Low Countries and therefore knew about the growing mission work in the

---

6. Roman Catholic Church, "Decree on the Missionary Activity of the Church," *The Teachings of the Second Vatican Council* (Westminster, Maryland: The Newman Press, 1966), p. 392.

7. Ludwig Rütti, *Zur Theologie der Mission: Kritische Analysen und neue Orientierungen* (Munich: Kaiser Verlag, 1972).

East Indies, developed his own missiology in his *De Missionibus ecclesiasticis*. H. A. van Andel, who would later become a pioneer missionary in Central Java, analyzed Voetius' theory of mission in his dissertation *De Zendingsleer van Gisbertus Voetius* (1912). In this study, van Andel examines Voetius' goal of mission *(ad quid mittendi)*. Actually there are three goals:

1. The conversion of the heathen is the immediate goal.
2. The planting of a church or churches comes next.
3. The glory and manifestation of divine grace is the final and highest goal.

Voetius notes that conversion is valuable in and by itself, but implantation of churches without the prior conversion of individuals in worthless. Conversion itself leads to the second goal of implanting, for it involves a growing into fellowship with Christ *(conversio salutaris et per fidem communio Christi)*.

Plantatio ecclesiae involves the gathering together of those who have come to believe. *Infideles* ("unbelievers") become *auditores* ("hearers") who in turn become *catechumeni* ("students whose instruction shall lead to their baptism"). But Voetius extends the line even farther: *catechumeni* become *competentes* ("those who request baptism"), and *competentes* finally become actual *membra ecclesiae* ("members of the church").

How striking that in his theory of mission Voetius did not get all wrapped up in the theological dispute about hardening and reprobation in which some of the figures of the later Reformation became so exaggerated in their claims. Voetius rather put all his emphasis on the glory of God who was disclosing his liberating grace and on the praise which was due him for extending that grace.

J. H. Bavinck in his *Introduction to the Science of Missions* ties his own ideas closely to those of Voetius before him. But he, more than Voetius, emphasized the close connection between the three goals and added this noteworthy sentence: "It must be emphasized, however, that these three purposes are not distinct and separate but they are in fact three aspects of a single purpose of God: the coming and extension of the kingdom of God."[8]

Toward the close of this chapter I will pick up this line of thought and develop it further. But first I shall discuss several other theories of mission which actually are variations of the ecclesiocentric theory.

THE "THREE-SELF" FORMULA

During the nineteenth century a reaction to the one-sided individualist approach developed. It took due regard of the need to build up the corporate life of churches. Two prominent leaders, each of them associated with very well known missionary agencies during that time, began about the same time to articulate a goal for mission that called for the building up of "self-governing, self-supporting and self-extending units of the church universal." These men were the Anglican Henry Venn and the American Congregationalist Rufus Anderson, who, though

---

8. Johan H. Bavinck, *Introduction to the Science of Missions* (Nutley, N.J.: Presbyterian and Reformed Publishing Co., 1964), p. 155.

each had come up with his idea independent of the other, nevertheless collaborated much after hearing of each other's work.

Henry Venn (1724–1797)

Canon Max Warren, one of Venn's successors, edited some of Venn's addresses, articles, letters, and instructions and had them published in 1971 under the title *To Apply the Gospel: Selections from the Writings of Henry Venn*. The book is an indispensable source for the study of the missionary principles and practical guidelines developed by the man who for thirty-one years — from 1841 to 1872 — served as secretary of the largest missionary organization of the Anglican church — the Church Missionary Society.

As one reads these documents, he cannot fail to be impressed with Venn's sure grasp of the issue facing the Western missionary agencies in their relationship with the developing native churches. He is aware of the ever-present danger of keeping these churches too dependent and not allowing them to become and be themselves. Terms which today have become stock-in-trade for missiologists already then were the very warp and woof of his thinking. He senses how paternalistic Western missionaries are in their attitudes, how they pose as "supervisors," "directors" and "paymasters" toward the people in Asia, Africa, and the Caribbean. He knows that an excessive reliance on "mother churches" or on missionary societies can immobilize the young churches.

As he reflected on all of this, Venn came to formulate a new goal for mission. But before we discuss his actual views, we must add a prior note of caution. Let no one assume that Venn, by offering these administrative proposals, thought he had the last word on missionary goals. Venn himself was an "evangelical" within the Anglican church who had been strongly influenced by the "Awakening." Do not think, therefore, that his ecclesiology necessarily directly corresponds to what he propounded in his three-self theory. Venn—and for that matter, Anderson too — was far from being a proponent of a purely institutional ecclesiology. In their judgment, the institutional aspect of the church had always to be paired with its essential nature as the people of God.

Having made this comment, we can now allow Venn to speak for himself.

> Regarding the ultimate object of a Mission, viewed under its ecclesiastical result, to be the settlement of a Native Church under Native Pastors upon a self-supporting system, it should be borne in mind that the progress of a Mission depends upon the training up and the location of Native Pastors; and that, as it has been happily expressed, the *"euthanasia* of a Mission" takes place when a missionary, surrounded by well-trained Native congregations under Native Pastors, is able to resign all pastoral work into their hands, and gradually relax his superintendence over the pastors themselves, till it insensibly ceases; and so the Mission passes into a settled Christian community. Then the Missionary and all Missionary agencies should be transferred to the "regions beyond."[9]

9. Max Warren, *To Apply the Gospel: Selections from the Writings of Henry Venn* (Grand Rapids: Eerdmans, 1971), p. 28.

Not content with developing mere theory, Venn worked for two generations with great zeal to implement his ideas. By appointing native bishops (Samuel
Crowther of Nigeria, the first native African bishop, was one of those whom he
appointed), by training native clergy, by appointing natives to positions on various
councils, by transferring administrative authority over the schools to the natives,
etc., Venn tried to insure that the people in a given territory would themselves
take over the reins of leadership.

But Venn was also flexible enough to realize that his ideas could not be
carried out in doctrinaire fashion. When one of the Church Missionary Society
missionaries noted that a certain native diocese was not conforming to the principles espoused by Venn and therefore proposed to cut off all financial aid to it,
Venn called such a measure a gross injustice and compared it to throwing someone
into the water who had not yet learned to swim. Venn indignantly reminded
everyone involved that such a rigorous and abrupt application of his principles
could do untold harm rather than good. Nevertheless, he adamantly insisted that
from the very time they began a new mission, the missionaries had to keep in mind
the long-term goals as they developed the organizational machinery. As he put it,
"It is expedient that the arrangement which may be made in the missions should
from the first have reference to the ultimate settlement of the Native Church, upon
the ecclesiastical basis of an *indigenous* Episcopate independent of foreign aid or
superintendence."[10]

Rufus Anderson (1796-1880)

Pierce Beaver edited a companion volume to Max Warren's on Venn and entitled
his *To Advance the Gospel*. Beaver's book is a select compilation of the essays
and instructions of the most influential American theorist and strategist of mission
during the nineteenth century — Rufus Anderson.

Like Venn, Anderson was secretary of a missionary organization, the
American Board of Commissioners for Foreign Missions, a post he filled for no
less than forty years (1826–1966). His *Outline of Missionary Policy*, which he
issued in 1856, is of special interest to us.

Such differences as did exist between Venn and Anderson are partially to
be explained by the fact that Venn was Anglican and Anderson was Congregationalist. Hence, their views on church polity differed substantially. But this
does not detract from the striking similarity between their views, especially on the
need for building up independent and indigenous churches through the efforts of
Western missions. The following quotation is taken from Anderson's *Outline of
Missionary Policy:* "Missions are instituted for the spread of a scriptural, self-
propagating Christianity. This is their only aim. But it includes four elements: 1.
converting of lost human beings 2. organizing them into churches 3. providing the
churches with competent native ministers 4. conducting the churches to the stage
of independence and (in most cases) of self-propagation."[11] As means to achieve
these goals Anderson specified "oral proclamation, education, and literature."

10. Ibid., p. 69.
11. Rufus Anderson, *Outline of Missionary Policy* (1856).

In commenting on Anderson's theories, Beaver noted that for two hundred years prior to Anderson, American missions had been operating without any principial guidelines; Anderson was the first American to develop a theory and carry it out in practice.

He earnestly strove to have the missionaries view their work as basically "the gathering and developing of local congregations each having its own presbyters to engage in pastoral care."[12] As he made his visits to the missionary fields, he did not come to check on how many huge "mission stations" had been erected; rather, he encouraged the spread of independent village churches and neighborhood congregations. Breaking with tradition, he put heavy emphasis on "lay training" as the most suitable means of equipping congregations to discharge *their* task.

The "three-self formula," as Anderson and Venn's ideas later came to be called, would go on to receive wide acclaim. In fact, as N. G. Clark, Anderson's successor, noted in a memorial address for Anderson, his theory and formula "later became the common possession of virtually very mission agency throughout the entire world."[13] Beaver himself points out that the theory spread from England and the United States to achieve a leading position from the mid-nineteenth century to the mid-twentieth century. Until the time of the Second World War, which inaugurated a new era in world mission, practically all English-speaking missionaries and their respective agencies have at the very least paid lip-service to Anderson and Venn's ideas.

But the influence of their ideas did not stop there. German missions acknowledged them. In the Netherlands one can see clear traces of their influence on the acts of the missionary conference held in 1890, especially in the position taken at that conference by Abraham Kuyper. Kuyper himself was deeply influenced by Anderson and Venn in spite of the fact that he rejected the concept of *societal missions* (which Venn so passionately defended) and favored rather *ecclesiastical missions*.

Evaluation

As I attempt my hand at evaluating this theory, I must begin by admiring the important truth which it expresses. Just as God in the Old Testament called the people of Israel to be the instrument for presenting the message of his liberating work to other peoples and nations, so too God in the New Testament era of salvation history is working to gather and equip his church, the new people of God, to become a "chosen race, a royal priesthood, a holy nation" (I Pet. 2:9). In the Acts of the Apostles we catch a glimpse of the church in the process of formation, and the apostolic letters give a glimpse of the Apostles and their helpers hard at work calling out churches from the ranks of the peoples to whom they are preaching. The anti-institutional strain in much of recent missiology tends

12. Rufus Anderson, *Foreign Missions: Their Relations and Claims* (New York, 1969), p. 45.
13. Cf. the essay by Pierce Beaver on Anderson in *Christusprediking in de Wereld* (Kampen: J. H. Kok, 1965), p. 44.

to downplay the importance of this work, but figures such as Venn, Anderson, and all those who follow in their train stand as a continual reminder to us all that the task of inviting individuals to fellowship with the people of God and then forming them and equipping them as congregations is an indispensable aspect of our missionary calling.

But this theory is also valuable from a sociological standpoint. The famous Nigerian church historian, Ajayi, makes this point in his book *Christian Missions in Nigeria 1841–1891: The Making of a New Elite* (London, 1965). Ajayi describes Venn as a great missionary statesman whose vision not only stimulated the growth and development of independent churches in West Africa but whose emphasis on self-reliance and independence aided — quite unbeknown to him — in giving birth to the young national states now found in that area.

In spite of its numerous strengths, however, the theory is somewhat lopsided and weak at several points. First of all, it is too ecclesiocentric. The Bible always relates the building up of the church to something much deeper and broader, namely, the kingdom of God. In the Bible the kingdom stands central, not the church. Second, the note of self-support is accented so strongly in this theory that one would think it is one of the distinguishing features of a true church. But the New Testament nowhere accords it that position of honor. On the contrary, it resolutely calls the prosperous churches to aid without grudging or reproach the poorer churches who cannot yet support themselves. As one reads Venn and Anderson, he almost gets the impression that the heavy budgetary burden their societies bore nudged them in the direction of elevating "self-support" to the status of a principle. Obviously, one may not turn poverty into virtue, but neither may he allow his budget to mold and dictate his principles.

In the third place, the danger is more than illusory that the three-self formula could be exploited to justify a dismantling and severing of existing relations between churches. Think, for example, of how the churches in China, operating with the "three-self" idea, were forced to break off their contact with other churches throughout the world. They later justified this measure which was forced upon them by an appeal to the three-self formula. Obviously, it was a misuse of the theory, but unfortunately it does lend itself to misuse.

One final criticism: while Venn and Anderson pressed for the building up of independent churches throughout the world, in the West they held that mission was properly the work of *missionary societies,* not churches. Their theory would seem to argue for churches to engage in mission. And though there may have been a multitude of historical reasons to explain why societies rather than churches engaged in mission, nevertheless the fact that Venn and Anderson argued so forcefully for societies over churches poses an internal contradiction within the whole of the theory.

THE GOAL OF CHURCH GROWTH

The "Church Growth School"

In 1960 Donald McGavran established the School of World Mission and Institute of Church Growth with its headquarters at Fuller Theological Seminary in

Pasadena, California. As the title suggests, the leaders of the school view church growth as the chief goal of mission.

McGavran has developed his ideas in a whole series of publications which include the following: *The Bridges of God: A Study in the Strategy of Missions* (London, 1955); *How Churches Grow* (London, 1959); *Understanding Church Growth* (Grand Rapids, 1970); and an interesting symposium study, *Church Growth and Christian Mission* (New York, 1965), which includes a contribution by McGavran and a reply by Eugene Nida.

Not only has McGavran himself published extensively, but his co-workers at the school have done case studies of how effectively these missionary principles and strategies have worked throughout the world. These reports have been published as parts of a series entitled *Church Growth Studies*. In addition, the school regularly publishes its "Bulletin of Church Growth."

I shall attempt to present the main features of this influential school by concentrating on the ideas of McGavran himself. I single out McGavran because, as I see it, the views of some of his colleagues such as Arthur Glasser and A.R. Tippett do not fully correspond with his own.

The Life and Thought of Donald McGavran

Born in India as the son of a missionary, McGavran himself after finishing his education commenced his career as a missionary sent out by the Disciples of Christ. For thirty-one years, from 1923 to 1954, he labored in India and became an expert in the field of education and the organizing of medical work, which, incidentally, makes even more striking the fact that he pays these missionary tasks scant attention in his present theories.

McGavran returned to the United States in 1954, disappointed at the scant church growth his thirty-one years in India had produced, but determined to find out why. In what follows, I shall summarize the most important elements of his theory.

(1) As churches discharge their missionary calling, they must gear all their efforts to produce numerical church growth. Quantitative expansion is a top-priority item of "church business." However successful educational activities and social programs may be, if they do not contribute to church growth, they are without significance. McGavran believes that churches' involvement or, as he calls it, "preoccupation" with matters such as peace, justice, development, and the struggle against disease, poverty and ignorance is actually misplaced. When they struggle against racism, become enmeshed in political diaconia, etc., the churches are fleeing their genuine responsibilities. Churches have only one main job — to multiply themselves. Everything else must be subordinated to it.

(2) Churches should employ mass movements to multiply themselves. According to McGavran, the churches should take careful note of the existing patterns of social relationship as they begin to work in a certain region in order to root any future church the more firmly in its native soil. Any church which is genuine is a movement of the people, the term "people" being taken in the sense of a "homogeneous unit." The unit can take various forms; it could be a tribe (as in Africa), or a middle-class group (as often occurs in Japan), or a caste (as in

India). But whatever it is, McGavran believes that it must serve as the church's vehicle for spreading the gospel.

As a missionary begins his work among a people, he selects the key families who hold the leadership. Since all of the families within the homogeneous unit are interlocked, if one can get the leading ones to respond, it will produce a snowball effect until eventually all of the families respond. While remaining intact, whole groups, societies, and castes must be won for Christ, for these existing social patterns can serve as "God's bridges" which he traverses in order to gather the peoples to himself. In the final analysis, McGavran is pleading for nothing more than the establishing of ethnically defined churches. If one faithfully performs this first step, inter-church relations will follow by themselves.

(3) As mission strategists survey the landscape, they ought to be on the alert for tribes, groups, or castes which are "now winnable," to borrow McGavran's phrase. Thus, the churches ought to focus their attention and regulate their budgets on the basis of which fields seem especially ripe for harvest. Fish where the fish are; don't bother plowing on the rocks; work where the harvest promises to be the best. Quit fooling around with such modern forms of mission as dialogue with and presence among people who are inimical to the gospel. Go rather to people who display an eagerness and readiness to hear and obey the gospel.

(4) In connection with his strategy of first achieving rapid quantitative growth and only thereafter turning to qualitative issues, McGavran makes a noteworthy distinction in the words of Jesus' Great Commission recorded in Matthew 28. He claims that Christ distinguished two separate tasks; the first is to make disciples, and the second is to perfect them in keeping his commandments.

(5) All missionary research must be designed to answer two questions: what factors and methods yield successful church growth, and which ones retard such growth? In answering such questions the mission strategist can profitably engage the assistance of sociologists and cultural anthropologists.

McGavran has compared the growth of churches to that of apples and pears in an orchard. Just as the farmer tries to figure out why his fruit in one field grows into luscious produce while that in the other field is miserably disappointing, so too the mission strategist must attempt to discern why missionary efforts in one area are blessed with a bountiful harvest while in another area the response is meager.

This is precisely what the *Church Growth* series attempts to do. Having done their research and programmed all their various data into a computer, these scholars then disseminate their results and findings so that missionaries the world over may learn how to organize their own work more effectively.

(6) Missionary organizations must set and constantly review their priorities in the light of the principles of church growth. They must give even greater support to programs which enhance church growth but scrap whatever fails to do so.

Evaluation

We ought not to overlook the powerful influence which the Church Growth theory has had on the contemporary mission scene, especially among that group in the

United States known as the conservative evangelicals. Moreover, the Iberville conference convened under the auspices of the World Council of Churches in Quebec province in 1963 shows evidence of being influenced by McGavran's ideas, as does the Wheaton Declaration of 1966 promulgated by the Interdenominational Foreign Missions Association.

To be sure, the emphasis upon the growth of churches is an aspect of mission which may not be neglected. The New Testament book of Acts frequently mentions it, in fact so frequently that Abraham Kuyper, as we noted in our first chapter, proposed "auxanics" (the study of church growth) as a suitable term to describe the function of missiology.

However, there are several serious objections which one must make toward the manner in which McGavran poses the issue of church growth. His own colleague, A. R. Tippett, has admitted that quantitative growth has received too much emphasis in McGavran's thinking, while what Tippett calls "organic growth" unfortunately has been relegated to the periphery of his concern. In the same vein Eugene Nida, in the symposium mentioned above, responded to McGavran in his cautious and sympathetic way by warning him against a too heavy emphasis on the numerical. Nida, the capable secretary of the United Bible Society, points out that often a rapid growth curve for a church will in due time fall just as rapidly; it is important therefore for the church's leaders, even while the curve is rising, to take steps to cushion its eventual fall not only by *discipling* but also by *perfecting*. The tasks are inseparable, and if one remembers this as he goes about his mission work among a given people, he will be of greater service and actually erect a firmer platform for future church growth than one who is interested in initial numerical growth alone.

But others have been more biting in their criticism. Writing in the July, 1968 issue of the *International Review of Missions*, Rev. Matthew P. John from India claims that McGavran has become too wrapped up in the mentality of American business where sums, profit, numerical growth and success play such large roles.

Permit me to add a couple of comments. If Bonhoeffer had inquired whether his political pronouncements would help or hinder the numerical growth of the church, he obviously would have kept his mouth shut. But it was precisely his prophetic words before he sacrificed his life that incalculably deepened the *quality* of the church's witness during that critical time. Or, to give another example, if Dr. Beyers Naudé and his colleagues at the Christian Institute in South Africa simply reckoned the effect of their witness in terms of quantitative church growth, they would keep silent. But because they dare to speak, they vitally increase the qualitative dimension of the church's existence.

Then too, those who assist those smaller churches which must bravely face plowing on rocky soil often render more valuable service than those who work and live amid the huge masses which are turning to Christianity. I do not say this to denigrate the importance of the latter's work, but merely to set the work of a Dr. Paul Harrison on the border of Saudi Arabia, for example, into proper perspective. For twenty-five years this man worked among the Arabs, and, as far as numbers go, he was quite unsuccessful, for only twenty-five Arabs were converted to Christ. But Harrison's very presence and work was a mighty sign of

God's patience with human beings. If we ever desert those lonesome, despised and tiny churches which, humanly speaking, do not have a very good chance of growing numerically, in favor of better prospects elsewhere, we shall most certainly hear the voice from Gethsemane speaking directly to us: "Could you not watch with me one hour?"

Moreover, McGavran's contention that the tribe, class, and caste are the most suitable vehicles for spreading the gospel is open to serious question. No one denies that ethnically defined churches often expand rapidly and that groups whose social structure corresponds rather closely to the church which is seeking to address them are usually relatively "easy" fields in which to work. Examples of this truism abound. Nevertheless, any keen observer will have to admit that in such situations there is a high risk that the old exclusivism of the tribe or caste will return to haunt the newly established church; when that happens, the attempt to integrate the church fully into the ecumenical people of God runs into almost insurmountable obstacles. Experiences with tribal churches in Asia and Africa show how the church can often serve as a convenient vehicle of a reinvigorated tribalism or a new caste system. McGavran passes too lightly over these difficulties, and hence can denigrate the efforts of those who seek to establish ecumenical contacts and build up church unity. May we ever strive so earnestly for church expansion along ethnic lines that we rend the unity of Christ's body in the process?

McGavran's method of setting priorities is one-sided and unbiblical. For him the top priority is always growth. But in the New Testament the priorities vary according to the situation. In some instances, the issue of hunger receives top priority; in others, sickness; in others, the struggle for justice; and in still others, the proclamation of the gospel. Mission strategy must always remain flexible and alert to the hints God provides along the way (cf. Luke 10).

McGavran tends to divide human existence into two parts, the "spiritual" on the one side and the "social, political, economic, etc." on the other. He claims that concern with what he calls "temporal projects" only serves to deflect one's attention from the more important issues of eternal redemption and the soul's salvation. But where in either the Old Testament or the New does one find warrant for such a fissure between soul and body, between eternal and temporal?

McGavran views the church solely from the perspective of her relationship to her Lord. But the church also has a posture toward the world which it must maintain, and this McGavran forgets. The church is *in* the world and must there fulfill her calling through him who is both her Head and the world's Lord.

Though we have accused this school and especially its leader of being one-sided in their approach, we must maintain contact with them to keep both of us from becoming lopsided in our emphasis. It is encouraging, therefore, to note that individuals like Tippett and Glasser have fully committed themselves to the dialogue from which all of us can greatly profit.

THE GOAL OF FORMING A CHRISTIAN SOCIETY

Throughout history the Christianizing of society has frequently been stated as the goal of Western mission. Gustav Warneck, for example, in his three-volume

Missionslehre repeatedly mentions this as the aim. "When Jesus speaks of the need to Christianize all peoples *(panta ta ethnē)*, he means that they must be made Christian on the basis of their natural distinctiveness as a people" ("auf Grund ihrer völklichen Natureigenart").[14] J. C. Hoekendijk has thoroughly analyzed these ideas of Warneck in his famous dissertation, *Kerk en Volk in de Duitse Zendingswetenschap.* He claims that Warneck is operating on two levels: "On the upper level are the living memories of the Kingdom which place mission before its eschatological mandate — the saving of souls. On the lower level history exercises its 'holy prerogative' and demands that mission not only engage in the building up of churches but also the Christianizing of peoples."[15]

Elsewhere in his book Hoekendijk analyzes the kindred "folk-organic" *(volksorganische)* missionary methods which B. Guttmann applied in East Africa and the "folk-pedagogical" *(volkspädagogische)* method of Christian Keysser in German New Guinea. Hoekendijk ends his study by holding before the advocates of these "volkstümliche" views the biblical purpose of mission—the kingdom of God. He adds these words: "Amid the array of confusing relationships which are almost impossible to analyze and facing a future which is most uncertain, we shall have to make our way step by step toward a new social order. But he who tries to construct it on the notion of *Volkstum* runs the risk of pouring new wine into old wineskins."[16]

It is worth noting that without exception every German missiologist writing since the Second World War has given up this naive notion of Christianizing the *Volk;* in fact, they resolutely avoid even using the term.

A. A. van Ruler, Hoekendijk's teacher and subsequently his colleague, also mentions Christianization as a goal of mission. But unlike many others, he never did so naively. He never tired of repeating that even in Christianized cultures God "rules in the midst of his enemies" and "amid the dark history of the human race."

However, in spite of all the chaff which exists even in the Christianized world, Van Ruler nevertheless insisted that the purpose of mission went beyond the mere building up of churches; it included the Christianizing of culture too. Writing in his book *Vaart en Visie,* he said:

> The Church is the divining-rod of world history which passes over the earth and points out where new cultures of humanity are beginning to arise; such cultures have Jesus Christ as their mid-point and are therefore Christianized. They are suited to set the tone for the world community and to be the bed on which the stream of world history will flow forward.[17]

All van Ruler's writings indicate that he deemed European and American cultures to be expressions of the kingdom of God and that therefore to extend this culture throughout the world in effect amounts to propagating the kingdom itself. In my judgment, van Ruler proves himself an untrustworthy guide at this point. His whole plan seems to be built on the dream of a return to some form of Christian theocracy on the one hand and on the culture-Protestantism of Ernst

14. J. C. Hoekendijk, *Kerk en Volk in de Duitse Zendingswetenschap* (Amsterdam, 1948), p. 93.
15. Ibid., p. 95.
16. Ibid.
17. A. A. van Ruler, *Vaart en Visie* (Amsterdam, 1947), p. 162.

Troeltsch's *Social Teachings of the Christian Churches* on the other. Troeltsch's book, incidentally, commanded van Ruler's deep interest. All these things misled van Ruler into initially opposing the decolonizing process and into believing that "Christian colonialism" is Christ's Lordship being reflected in the broken mirror of constitutional law.

But Christianization of peoples can never become the ultimate goal of mission, for when such attempts are viewed from the perspective of the coming kingdom of God, they are seen for what they really are — a complete and total compromise. Moreover, as the world becomes ever more pluralistic, we ought not to strive for domination but rather follow him who washed his disciples' feet and took the way of the cross. Our goal is not some secularized theocracy but rather Christocracy. Emilio Castro, director of the World Council's Division of World Missions and Evangelism, made this clear in an address he gave in 1974 on the role of the church in a pluralistic and revolutionary age; the church, he said, must never seek to dominate other cultures in triumphalist fashion but rather to fulfill her prophetic and priestly role amid all the oppression and injustice.

In fact, the church reflects her Lord more accurately when she is oppressed than when she dominates, for though Christ most certainly rules, never forget that he rules as a Lamb. The reins of his Lordly rule do not meet at some *Arc de Triomphe* but at a cross. Therefore, only as she takes the form of a servant does the church command the right to speak.

THE GOAL OF THE "SOCIAL GOSPEL"

At the close of the nineteenth century and the beginning of the twentieth a movement started in the United States as a reaction to the exclusive emphasis of some on individual conversion and of others on the ecclesiocentrism found in much of traditional home and foreign missions. The reaction was both theological and practical in nature and went under the label "Social Gospel."

The people in the forefront of this movement were men like Walter Rauschenbusch (1861–1918), author of *Applied Christianity* and *Christianity and Socialism;* and Harry Emerson Fosdick (1878–1970), who exerted a deep influence not only by his books but also by his sermons preached at New York City's Riverside Church.

W. A. Visser 't Hooft's dissertation, *The Background of the Social Gospel,* though a bit one-sided at certain points, does a very good job of identifying the seeds of this movement. The book notes the influence of the Enlightenment, the social sciences (especially the work of William James and John Dewey), revivalism, Puritanism, and the American pioneer spirit with its firsthand acquaintance with tackling social problems and establishing small communities.

Rauschenbusch loudly called for an energetic effort at "Christianizing the social order," while Fosdick viewed world history as a "progressive manifestation of the loving purposes of God." The Social Gospel, said Fosdick, is "dynamic, active, transforming, [and] evolutionary." It seeks to bring the kingdom of God into reality in social affairs.

But Fosdick was not blind to the obstacles which blocked the pathway to this kingdom. Social progress does not just happen naturally and automatically. Human beings need conversion, but a type of conversion which produces deeds of concrete social reform.

We are especially interested here in the impact of the Social Gospel on American missions. Its influence has been great and continues to the present day, even though American missions have now shifted from the theological base provided by the Social Gospel.

J. S. Dennis, who wrote his three volumes entitled *Christian Mission and Social Progress* between 1879 and 1906, charts in detail the considerable impact of the Social Gospel on missionary practice. He lists a host of social evils found in Africa and Asia in such diverse areas as the family, the community, the nation, commerce, and religion and then gives numerous illustrations of where missionary agencies were in the forefront of the attack against them. His final volume is a tabulation of the results.

As one reads over the long list, he might well inquire whether those missionaries who were so quick to spot the evils present in the non-Christian world were sufficiently aware of the evils to be found in the Christian world and whether they had any feeling for the positive elements in the older societies in which they were working. In any event, Dennis's book is a stark and impressive account of the festering wounds in those societies at the turn of the century and of the first Western attempts to combat them with a combination of prophetic moralism and modern belief in progress which so typified the missionaries inspired by the Social Gospel.

Evaluation

Noting first of all this movement's positive aspect, I must point out that the rise of world diaconate simply could not have happened without the stimulus provided by the Social Gospel, for it strongly emphasized deeds, the fruits of conversion, and the social implications of Christian faith. Until then orthodoxy, by exclusively emphasizing doctrine, had neglected orthopraxy, and Pietists could only talk about their "experience" and not about social obedience and justice.

But the Social Gospel detected the presence of collective sins firmly rooted in microstructures of society. From then on, according to Walter Rauschenbusch, people could respond in one of two ways; they could try to do some changing or simply and fatalistically accept the status quo.

I must, however, also make some negative judgments about some elements within the Social Gospel. Sometimes the Social Gospellers have been unfairly criticized, especially by evangelicals who could have learned so much from those whom they condemned and who just now are gradually coming to realize how grievously they themselves have neglected the social dimensions of their faith. But the criticism was not unfounded, for both in theology and in practice the Social Gospel was far too optimistic. It paired the kingdom of God with a belief in progress derived more from the Enlightenment than from the gospel itself. Reinhold Niebuhr, who came from the school of Rauschenbusch, unmasked and tried to correct this easy optimism while at the same time he never lost sight of the movement's positive contributions.

Moreover, the Social Gospel disregarded the eschatological dimensions of the kingdom. During the movement's apogee, its ambassadors often unwittingly substituted the American way of life for the kingdom itself. The founders of a magazine like *The Christian Century* quite romantically, naively, and uncritically embraced this brand of Americanism; this is no longer true, however, for the magazine's present editors are now some of the most profound critics of this way of life.

Finally, the Social Gospellers realized far too little that the microstructural evils which they attacked are often buttressed by evils in the macrostructure. It took the Niebuhr brothers, Reinhold and Richard, to point this out later.

I do not want to end this section on a negative note, for though it may have based its appeal to the churches on grounds that were theologically weak, the Social Gospel did call them to a most important duty — to war against the evils in society both at home and abroad. Both by theoretical ethical reflection and by actual practice this movement's advocates made important strides in overcoming the individualism then found in evangelism and missions and aroused the churches to identify solidly with the victims of injustice. It would be too much to claim that the movement's goals correspond to the deepest goal of mission, but the effort to overcome social ills does certainly belong to the inclusive goals.

THE GOAL OF IMPROVING THE MACROSTRUCTURES

In recent times many have called for mission to join in the worldwide cooperative struggle for better social structures and greater human rights. They accuse nineteenth-century missionaries of doing nothing about the macrostructures.

As I see it, these critics are unfair, for at that time the Christian communities were very tiny minorities in Africa and Asia who did not yet have available to them the skills of those trained in sociology and politics and who could thereby influence those macrostructures. Missionaries worked on a small scale among rather small social groupings.

One can, however, claim that those early missionaries were laying the groundwork for what would later be incorporated into the macrostructures of those lands. Prominent men like Nehru, Sukarno, Nyerere, Kaunda and a host of others have repeatedly said that missionary efforts in such diverse areas as education, health care, care for the blind, the orphaned, and the hungry did much to insure that such concerns would later become part of the macrostructural programs. Even in China, which, for reasons quite understandable, has reacted the most strongly against influence from the West, there are those whose eyes have not been blinded by ideological shrouds and who can therefore see the positive influence which missions have had in their country.

But in spite of all these positive influences of the past, it goes without saying that we today must devote much more of our attention to macrostructures themselves. Billy Graham remarked to me on one occasion that the Apostle Paul did not visit the Roman Caesar to talk about macrostructures in the Roman empire, but I replied that we live in an age which is much different from his. Countries who pride themselves on having democratic ideals have today a crucial opportunity to influence the macrostructures in other countries, and if we as Christians within those democracies pass these opportunities by, we are failing our prophetic and priestly task. The Christian church can join the discussion provided she indeed has sufficient desire and courage. All sorts of agencies stand ready to offer their help. The Conference on Church and Society organized by the World Council in 1966 is but one example.

The church has a *missio politica oecumenica*. She must respond to her call to become involved worldwide in the quest for development and the struggle to throw off the shackles of economic exploitation and political and racial oppression. Not only theologians, but sociologists, political scientists, anthropologists, journalists, and servants of a world diaconate have their roles to play within the one *missio Dei*. Thus, I conclude that work on the macrostructures of society belongs right alongside work on the microstructures and the building up of churches as one of the inclusive goals of mission.

But let me make a twofold warning. First, we may never emphasize macrostructures at the expense of the other inclusive goals, for to do that would violate the spirit of Jesus the Messiah. We then lose sight of the individual person and suffer from a form of roofpeak psychosis which has lost touch with real life and real persons. Second, the improvement of macrostructures must never become the deepest and ultimate goal of mission. It is, however, a constituent element within the ultimate goal.

THE GOAL OF GOD'S MISSION AND OURS AS SEEN IN THE BIBLE

The Kingdom of God as the Goal of the Missio Dei

As a fitting conclusion to this chapter, I wish to return to the Bible and pose this question: What really does God intend for the world to which he has revealed himself in Jesus Christ? What is the ultimate goal of the *missio Dei*? The answer is easy to find; in both the Old Testament and the New, God by both his words and deeds claims that he is intent on bringing the kingdom of God to expression and restoring his liberating domain of authority. From the countless biblical images and symbols which describe God's intentions I select this one as the clearest expression of God and his purposes.

Biblically speaking, what is the kingdom of God? Some exegetes frequently narrow its borders to include only the inner life of the individual. Their interpretation is not wrong; it is, however, inadequate, for the preaching of Jesus so obviously treats issues which extend beyond the individual soul.

Other people restrict the kingdom exclusively to the church. Kingdom and church are for them interchangeable terms. But many scholars are quick to point out that the terms *basileia* and *ekklēsia,* though related, are anything but synonymous. Still others claim that the kingdom has come when man's spiritual needs are satisfied; kingdom involves the forgiveness of sins. But the New Testament nowhere spiritualizes the kingdom of God or limits it to the spiritual side of man. The kingdom to which the Bible testifies involves a proclamation and a realization of a total salvation, one which covers the whole range of human needs and destroys every pocket of evil and grief affecting mankind. Kingdom in the

New Testament has a breadth and scope which is unsurpassed; it embraces heaven as well as earth, world history as well as the whole cosmos.

The kingdom of God is that new order of affairs begun in Christ which, when finally completed by him, will involve a proper restoration not only of man's relationship to God but also of those between sexes, generations, races, and even between man and nature. This is the message of the prophets, and this is what John saw in his visions recorded in the book of Revelation. This too is the testimony of the Apostles who join Peter in affirming, "We await a new heaven and a new earth in which righteousness dwells" (II Pet. 3:13).

What then is the kingdom? It is the creation which has achieved its goal. Chaos will be overcome, every antimessianic tendency will have been erased, and God's liberating acts will have reached their final goal. The whole of the church's deep and wide mission agenda must receive its focus and orientation in this kingdom perspective.

The first three petitions of the Lord's Prayer summarize so well the deepest and ultimate goal of mission: "Hallowed be Thy name; Thy kingdom come; Thy will be done on earth as in heaven" (Matt. 6:9–10).

The Importance of This Goal for the Missionary Mandate Today

Leading People to a Belief in Jesus as Messiah and to a Confession of Him as Lord

When we inquire into the practical consequences of viewing mission from the perspective of the kingdom and its structures, one of the first things to mention is our God-given call to invite human beings to come to know Jesus as the Messiah of that kingdom. Throughout the Gospels, the Epistles, and indeed all of history, the whole missionary enterprise has always begun with this. The New Testament itself arose as a result of the deep urge of his disciples to tell the story of Jesus.

Today there is widespread neglect of this basic task. Missionaries look beyond it to other dimensions and end up with a kingdom without Jesus; they speak of peace without mentioning him who himself is peace. They quest for righteousness but in a way that completely skirts him. Such a tendency is perhaps at least understandable in view of the fact that in times past people often held up for honor some syrupy-sweet notion of Jesus without ever mentioning the messianic kingdom which he began and the promises and demands which follow from it. But though this may suffice as an historical explanation, this overreaction is certainly not justifiable. For this reason I rejoice in the fact that leading figures in world mission today are increasingly emphasizing the importance of telling the story of Jesus, the crucified and risen Lord.

Two things are necessary in order to lead people to the Messiah and to invite them to confess him in word and deed. In the first place, they must come to know what the New Testament says about him. All the New Testament witnesses agree that Jesus is Messiah, but they also agree that this Messiah was quite different from what they had anticipated. Men must come to know this Jesus, whose very life and work are an open window letting us see the very heart of God who has come to us. God has employed many means in the course of time to reveal something of himself, but in Jesus he has truly communicated himself. Said

Jesus: "Anyone who has seen me has seen the Father" (John 14:9).

But in this Jesus, through whom God disclosed himself, we also meet the Son of Man — that is, the authentic and new man as God intends him to be. In John's Gospel we read that various individuals tried to make Jesus conform to their own purposes. But the Apostle goes on to say that "Jesus for his part would not entrust himself to them, . . . for he could tell what was in a man" (John 2: 24–25). And because Jesus could not facilely be shaped to fit into their idle dreams and plans, he was rejected and nailed to a cross. Yet God acknowledged Jesus and by his resurrection confirmed him as the Lord of the new kingdom. We may withhold from no one an opportunity to meet personally this Jesus who comes to us in the clothing of Scripture.

The second thing necessary as we lead people to the Messiah is for each of us to recall that the living Lord is actually present. As Dr. Gerhard Hoffmann said: "We who tell the story of Jesus are not simply acting as historians who dig out the rich spiritual treasures from a bygone era; rather we are ambassadors of a ruling Prince."[18] We represent a living Messiah who is enroute to the final revealing of his kingdom. Therefore every generation discovers fresh aspects about him and confesses him in a new manner. I must only remind my readers of the multitude of new christological themes which have recently been developed — themes like *Christus Liberator* which is so popular now in the world of Asia, Africa, and Latin America, or the Christology being articulated by advocates of "black theology," many of whose experiences as humiliated and oppressed people led them to grasp new insights into the person of Jesus. The danger of trying to annex Christ to one's own ends remains ever present, and therefore we must continue to strip off those myths and dreams in which he has been wrapped. People everywhere must hear the clear invitation to know him as the Savior and Liberator of the world — Muslims, Buddhists, Hindus, Marxists, Leninists, Maoists, scientific humanists — indeed everyone.

Precisely because we have accepted the kingdom as the frame of reference and point of orientation for our missionary task, we must go on to claim that a call to conversion must necessarily follow our proclamation. This is fundamentally important, for confessing Jesus without following him as his disciples makes no sense at all. This *imitatio Christi* is what the New Testament calls *metanoia*. To it I now turn my attention.

The Kingdom and Conversion

Within the framework of the kingdom, conversion has been viewed properly as one of the inclusive goals of mission. To see how this goal applies, we must return to the New Testament itself, for so many people have such diverse conceptions that it becomes necessary once again to inquire what Jesus really meant when he declared: "The Kingdom of God is upon you; repent, and believe the Gospel" (Mark 1:15).

Conversion is the answer Christ requests and expects from those who take his message of the kingdom seriously. C. H. Dodd, the British New Testament scholar, claims that in times past *metanoia,* or "conversion," had a negative ring

18. Gerhard Hoffmann, *Monthly Letter of Evangelism,* February-March, 1974.

emphasizing a sorrow for sin. But in the New Testament it is used positively. *Metanoia* literally means "to think again" or "to have second thoughts." It therefore involves a total reorientation of one's thinking, will, and emotions and results in a new style of living and new conduct. These are the fruits of conversion to the message of the kingdom, a message in which Jesus confronts us in all of his splendor. Of course, the negative element of sorrow and repentance, of *fletus,* as Augustine termed it, is not absent, but the stronger accent falls upon the turning to God and orienting oneself anew to the standards of his kingdom.

Two aspects require special attention. First, *metanoia* embraces all of one's life, his life in society included. Therefore, anyone who divides personal conversion from participation in the life of society makes an unbiblical separation. Second, conversion is not a once-for-all event; it is a continual process of renewing one's life, or reorienting himself to the kingdom as he, Christ's disciple, confronts new and changing situations. Emilio Castro continually emphasizes that conversion as the New Testament describes it is no "agency of escapism." Conversion requires that Christ's disciples stand with both feet in the cold, hard, tough world and continually reorient themselves to persons and structures within that real world. When seen in this light, conversion is indeed one of the inclusive goals of mission.

The Messianic Kingdom and the Messianic People
According to the New Testament, proclaiming the messianic message must always be accompanied by gathering, preserving and adding to the people of God. When Jesus invites us to become his disciples, he calls us to join a community and become members of the people of God, not to stand isolated and alone. He calls Zacchaeus a "son of Abraham" (Luke 19:9) and the woman whom he healed in the synagogue, "Abraham's daughter" (Luke 13:16). His interest was not merely in converting individuals but in forming a new people. Having seen that the synagogue "establishment" rejected him, he immediately began to form a new community and called the Apostles out from the ranks of his disciples to become the founders of this new fellowship (Luke 6:13).

The Apostles carried on the work begun by Jesus. They established a new community of faith among the various peoples whom they met. It was a community which bore the stamp of God's own possession. The factors which united this people were not the economic or political or cultural ties which usually bind human communities together; this people emerged from the ranks of Israel and the Gentiles by the words, deeds, and Spirit of the Messiah and existed only in complete dependence on him, its shepherd and king. He calls it, cares for it, and frees it through the forgiveness of sins and the renewal which proceeds from him. Furthermore, he desires to employ this people as the means of realizing his world-embracing plans.

Listen to the words of I Peter 2:9–10: "But you are a chosen race, a royal priesthood, a holy nation, God's own people, that you may declare the wonderful deeds of him who called you out of darkness into his marvelous light. Once you were no people but now you are God's people; once you had not received mercy but now you have received mercy."

Since God's call and mercy are so basic to the life of this people, it becomes rather obvious that human beings are not the ones to trace out who does and who does not belong to it. The Messiah himself determines the boundaries, and in doing so, he is guided by grace. The Bible constantly claims that the people of God which we now see taking shape before our very eyes is but the small beginning of a completely new humanity (see II Thess. 2:3; James 1:18). God's purposes extend much farther than we can see at any moment in time. The firstfruits will in due time yield a bountiful crop, and workers are needed to reap the harvest (Matt. 9:37–38). Here is where the people of God fits in, for it, like the Messiah whose mark it bears, is called not to be served but to serve (Mark 10:42–44). As he lay three days in the grave and then arose, so this people must fall into the ground and die like a grain of wheat in order that it might later produce a rich harvest (John 12:24–25). Just as he carried his cross, so his disciples must deny themselves, take up their crosses and follow him (Luke 14:26–27). When this people identifies itself with its Messiah in this manner, it will discover that God the Father is pleased to grant it his kingdom (Luke 6:20).

My concern here is not to present an elaborate ecclesiology. For this one can refer to such books as Paul Minear's *Images of the Church in the New Testament,* which carefully details the various images depicting the new people of God. My only concern here is to show that if we take the message of the kingdom as the frame of reference and point of orientation from which to view our missionary task, we shall come to see the work of forming a church as an essential aspect of our larger calling.

Much ink and many words have been wasted on the question of whether we ought to think in terms of the triad God-church-world or the triad God-world-church. All this is needless bickering, for those whose life and thinking are oriented around the Messiah and his kingdom will learn to see the church within the wider perspective of the kingdom, even though they may differ among themselves on the arrangement of the details. Missiology must always save a spot for ecclesiology and for the study of churches in their own environments, but the essential question each of these studies must forever ask remains the same: To what degree do these churches contribute to the messianic kingdom? Numerical and qualitative growth and the equipping of churches must never become ends in themselves, but must always serve the Messiah who is making his way "to the ends of the earth."

The Kingdom and Our Participation in the Struggle against Every Form of Human Ill

Viewing our missionary task within the wider perspective of the kingdom will lead us to still another insight: participation in the fight against every vestige of evil plaguing mankind is an intrinsic part of our calling. According to the Bible the kingdom does not belong to the future. It is a present reality which, though not yet fully revealed, does nevertheless show definite signs of being underway. When John the Baptist's disciples came to Jesus and asked whether he were the Messiah or whether they should look for another, Jesus answered with these remarkable words: "Go and tell John what you hear and see: the blind receive their sight and the lame walk, lepers are cleansed and the deaf hear, and the dead are raised up, and the poor have good news preached to them. And blessed is he who takes no offense at me" (Matt. 11:4–6). Jesus was thereby indicating that the kingdom both has already come and is yet coming. It is both present and future. Between these two points, said Jesus, one can detect signs of the ongoing fight being waged against those forces and powers spreading human suffering.

The message of the kingdom as Jesus described it makes sense only if we take careful note of these powers and forces and strive to discern the shapes which they take today. Liberation makes sense only if we first understand what keeps men in bondage. And once we realize how deep this evil really is and how profound are the saving acts of God in Jesus the Messiah, we shall inevitably and inescapably hear God calling us to participate in uprooting every vestige of evil and suffering from human society. In this chapter I shall only make brief mention of the range of human ills and needs.

Physical and psychical distress. In the quotation from Matthew 11 Jesus acted not only as a preacher but also as a healer. Rembrandt's famous "Hundred Guilder Print" catches this aspect of Jesus so well. As the shadows of evening approach, Jesus stands amid children and adults caught in the grip of physical and psychical distress; Jesus' messianic presence and their needs and yearnings seem to interpenetrate; God himself condescends to concern himself with the ills of people, to heal their sicknesses, and to still their confusion.

God calls his messianic people to wage war against sickness and every form of psychic disorder with every weapon in its arsenal. Hence, the call to mission includes an appeal to engage in social and medical work.

The burden of ignorance. Ignorance is an evil which paralyzes not only the individual but society as well. People often toss about the easy slogan "What you don't know won't hurt you," but that is a lie. Ignorance can hurt. Indonesians have a choice word to describe the plight of those who can neither read nor write; they are "letter-blind." Indeed, illiteracy is a handicap, and a lack of proper facilities for training and educating people only perpetuates the problem. Therefore, part of our missionary calling is to correct this deficiency and thus to restore sight to the blind and healing to the lame. The very glow of messianic light surrounds this noble enterprise.

The burden of poverty and hunger. Jesus knew that many of the poor people were inexorably bound to that iron wheel of necessity called poverty. He identified with their needs and earnestly desired that the banners of his kingdom be jubilantly unfurled for all the poor and hungry to see. Once again, when we join the war against poverty and hunger we are working in the halo of his messianic light.

The burden of racial discrimination. As this century has progressed, we have gradually opened our eyes to the fact that millions of human beings pass their days caught in social structures which discriminate against them because of their race and thus compromise their human dignity. Jesus himself constantly moved in the midst of those whom others rejected and despised. He solidly identified with them in his own life and earnestly desires his disciples to follow in his path.

The struggle for cultural identity. The Bangkok conference of the World Council of Churches in 1973 paid close heed to the desire of millions of people for cultural identity. Hundreds of societies have inbuilt structures which hinder the people from achieving their own cultural expression and thus rob them of their identity. They feel themselves deprived and others avoid them as though they were leprous. When the liberating power of the gospel is unleashed in such situations, it frees men to be themselves within the kingdom. A black South African commented some time ago: "When I become one with Christ, the new Man, he grants me the freedom to express my new-found humanity in my own way."

The threat of approaching death. How wonderful that God responded to the deepest and final need of man and through his Son freed us from the threat of even death itself. Hence, we can say in the words of I John 3:2: "What we shall be has not yet been disclosed, but we know that . . . we shall be like him." Human beings the world over are crying for a solution to the approaching specter of death, and we as Christians engaged in world mission and evangelism must give them the answer which can allay their fears.

In a Bible study prepared for the Bangkok conference Paul Minear wrote: "The deepest cry which the Holy Spirit arouses in man is the yearning cry for heaven, for direct contact with God's throne, for a victory of God over his demonic enemies, for an invitation to the marriage feast of the Lamb." How remiss we would be if we failed to attend to this heartrending cry and ignored our task of extending invitations to this marriage.

It is gratifying to be able to note at the end of this study of the goal of the *missio Dei* and our concomitant mission that missiology is more and more coming to see the kingdom of God as the hub around which all of mission work revolves. One can almost speak of a consensus developing on this point. I take the liberty of ending this chapter by citing several authors who view mission in this perspective.

Max Warren was one of the first to formulate the purpose of mission in this way in his book *The Truth of Vision,* published in 1948 and subtitled "A study in the nature of Christian hope."

After the Evanston assembly of the World Council of Churches convened in 1954 under the theme "Christ our Hope," Hans Jochen Margull wrote his book *Hope in Action.* D. T. Niles devoted a chapter to this same theme in his missiological treatise, *Upon the Earth.* Then, of course, there is Jürgen Moltmann, who has written copiously on the theme of hope in essays and books such as "The Aim of Mission," *Theology of Hope,* and *The Crucified God.* For the Roman Catholic theologian Rütti, hope is the basic theme of his whole theology. I might also mention in this connection Ludwig Wiedemann's full-length study published in 1963, *Mission and Eschatology.*

The theme which I have been treating is of great practical significance. If it be true that we who practice mission must take the kingdom of God as our constant point of orientation, it is imperative that we pay close heed to the whole range of burdens and evils plaguing mankind. Our priorities may change as the situation demands. At certain times the accent will fall on poverty and hunger; at others, on ignorance; and at still others, on sickness, racial injustice, economic exploitation, or a variety of others.

The churches on all six continents need to be alert to changing needs and set their priorities accordingly. But even so they must present the entire message of the kingdom and not reduce it to just one point. We would be most inhuman if we should treat only the most acute and pressing needs of a people and deprive them of the full range of God's promises by failing to mention the Messiah himself.

It would be sheer pride and impudence to imagine that *we* will establish the kingdom and bring it to completion. This is the work of God alone — the Father, Son, and Holy Spirit. At the same time, it would be a sign of sinful sloth and indolence if we were not to attempt in faith, together with the children of the kingdom throughout the world, to erect in the midst of the wide range of human burdens and evils signs and signals of that which is coming. He who prays "Thy kingdom come, Thy will be done" is thereby called to aid in spreading the kingdom of God over the length and breadth of the earth.

CHAPTER VIII
Ways and Means

Now that we have inquired what the goal of God's mission in this world is and discovered that all of his activity is geared to the coming of his kingdom, we shall investigate the ways and means God chooses to achieve his goal. God does not select these means because he has to, but simply because they are the route he chooses to take to realize his world-embracing plans. While speaking about the hiddenness of the kingdom, Jesus touched on the issue of ways and means. He told a parable about how a sower went out to sow his seed and how the seed of the gospel was planted on earth (Mark 4:1–20). Paul too, in unraveling the mystery of the approaching kingdom, inquired how people of all nations would come to believe in this kingdom and answered his own question by saying that belief comes through hearing, and hearing through the "word of Christ" (Rom. 10:17).

God uses means and engages men in communicating his good news. These means may never become the goal itself but must be used in service of the genuine goal — the kingdom of God. The Bangkok conference of 1973 made this point very clearly. In discussing the choice of media, programs, and projects to proclaim the "Good News of liberation" it stated that all of these must be "salvation-oriented," that is, geared to bringing rescue and healing in situations and circumstances which so desperately need them. Altering the language of Bangkok a bit, one might say that all of our ways and means must serve the kingdom of God in which peace, righteousness, and an all-embracing wholeness and healing come to expression.

Missiology has paid remarkably little attention to the question of ways and means up to now. In fact, Alphons Mulders in his *Missiologisch Bestek* makes the point that the first book dealing with the issue of missionary methods has yet to be written. Protestant missiology too is sadly lacking in this area.

My book *Daar en Nu,* another on which I collaborated, *Onze blijvende Opdracht,* and the little book published by the Dutch Missionary Council, *Hier en Daar: Zending en Werelddiakonaat in de Jaren Zeventig,* are my attempts to give some attention to this sadly neglected topic. The present chapter in this book complements what I have written there.

A fourfold division is often made when discussing the matter of ways and means: means of communicating the gospel, means of fulfilling diaconal responsibility, means of establishing fellowship, and means of serving the cause of righteousness and justice. Though each is related to the others, the distinction is useful, and I shall comment on each of the categories.

MEANS OF PROCLAIMING THE GOSPEL OF GOD'S KINGDOM

The New Testament arose as a result of the communication of the gospel by the earliest Christian congregations. New Testament scholars never tire of saying that each of those congregations saw this communication as its inescapable responsibility and fulfilled it in a variety of ways.

Kerygma ("proclamation") was the form the congregations used to tell those who had never heard the good news of God's messianic kingdom, while *didachē* ("teaching") was their way of leading those who had already heard along the path leading to that kingdom. Dialogues were started on the subject of the good news. Letters and treatises were circulated to communicate the gospel in written form.

The church today faces this very same elementary task of communicating the message over the whole globe with whatever means are useful and serviceable. Eugene Nida, translation secretary for the United Bible Societies, in his excellent book *Message and Mission,* described what it means to communicate the message of Jesus Christ amid the tremendous cultural variation found in the world today; he underscored the vital importance of listening to those people of other cultures so that when one opens his mouth to communicate the gospel, he transmits the real gospel. Missionaries often ascribe rejection of the gospel to apparent hardness of hearts or the presence of Satanic influences, etc., when the real culprit is faulty communication. One thing is becoming increasingly clear: however helpful foreigners may be in communicating to a given culture, the best communicators come from within that culture itself.

A second obvious factor is the shift in accent when the gospel is transmitted to a different culture. If one looks carefully, he can find great differences of accent already in the New Testament, and as we communicate the gospel, we shall have to make allowances for such shifts of accent.

Third, genuine gospel communication requires that we make use of a whole variety of means. Walter Hollenweger, a famous missiologist from Birmingham, England, maintains that these means are not restricted to the traditional preaching, catechesis, tract distribution, etc. And Nida makes the same point. In fact, in some tribal societies chanted stories, dramas, and liturgical dances seem to be more effective than the traditional forms. Or again, "sowing weeks," held, not in an official church building, but at those spots where the people normally and routinely convene, often are more successful in moving inhabitants of Asian and African societies closer to the eternal kingdom than are gatherings in church buildings.

The symposium study edited by Roland Scott from India, *Ways of Evangelism,* contains twenty-three chapters filled with a tremendous number of possibilities for communicating the good news in cities and villages. Though I of course cannot describe here all the means presently being used, I do want to make a comment about the ecumenical efforts being made to spread the gospel through theological education, Bible translation and distribution, and through the use of electronic media. And in connection with these I will comment briefly about the urgent need for planning for mission.

Theological Education

In *Daar en Nu* and *Onze blijvende Opdracht*, I indicated the vital importance of theological education as one way of equipping individuals for their pastoral and missionary work. I told of the important role the Theological Education Fund (established in 1957 at the Ghana assembly of the International Missionary Council) was playing in supporting theological education. In those books I explained, too, that the goals its organizers set for the fund are incorporated in its first and second mandates: improvement of buildings, help for libraries, improvement of curricula, exchange of teaching personnel, student recruitment, etc. As a supplement to the material I gave in those other books, I now want to discuss the third mandate given to the fund in 1973/74.

The third mandate discusses more than the first two what we now call "contextuality." The fund's 1973 publication, *Learning in Context,* provides the direction for understanding this new accent. Contextuality takes due account of the fact that in theological education we are waging war on two fronts. On the one hand we are answering the call of God which comes to us in the demands and promises of the Bible. But on the other hand we are called to respond to the challenges confronting the churches in every country throughout the world today. That is to say, while we theologize, we must keep our eye trained on the special context and situation in which we find ourselves. Our chief concern is to achieve relevance in teaching the revelation of Jesus Christ.

In a later chapter I hope to provide a guide to the literature being published on the current varied theological developments. But one thing is certain: theological educators absolutely must take account of the great contextual changes now happening about them. A *theologia perennis* which needs only to be repeated and perpetuated by the succeeding generation simply does not exist. Students throughout the world must learn to construct theologies in a way which is obedient to the gospel as well as responsive to the situation of the church within their own land. There is no hard and fast rule on how to carry on theological education.

Theological education is an ongoing process. If it is carried on properly, it is not done in immovable cathedrals, but in portable tents which can be transported by the pilgrim people of God. Theological educators must not become too firmly attached to one place or way of doing things, but must be ever ready to change and adapt as the situation may require.

The little book put out by the Theological Education Fund includes contributions from Latin America (which is at the vanguard of the search for new forms), the Philippines, the former Australian New Guinea, and Africa.

People the world over are coming to see that a fruitful tie exists between a *theologia in loco* and an ecumenical theology.

We are also coming to realize increasingly the growing need to allow lay-persons to share the benefits of theological education. Around 1960 in Guatemala theological educators experimented with offering extension courses for laity whose gifts, qualities, and experience indicated that they would benefit from such training. Such extension training is still being offered in scattered regions, usually in one of two ways: either by offering weekend courses at the seminary or theological school itself or else by sending out the teachers to the local spots where the need exists.

We also need to increase communication and exchange between the various theological schools. In Asia, Africa, and Latin America more than twenty associations of theological schools have been established to achieve this goal.

Fortunately, Western theologians are beginning to see that Europe and America are not the norm or standard against which theologians in other parts of the world must judge their own "theologies in context." European and American theology is merely one expression of a theology in context; Western theological institutions must be flexible as any other, and Western theologians must be willing and able to learn from theologians in other parts of the world.

Whether a fourth mandate for the fund shall follow the one now in effect is at this time not yet settled.

By discussing the Theological Education Fund here I do not want to create the mistaken impression, of course, that what happens to it is what is really important in the realm of theological education. The schools themselves in places like Jakarta, Ambon, Bangalore, Umpumulo, Campinas or Lagaweng are the real centers of activity and much more important. It is simply impossible within the limits of this book to parade each of them before us for inspection.

Bible Translation and Distribution

I have asked A. de Kuiper, who presently serves as the contact man between the Dutch Bible Society and the United Bible Societies and is himself fully involved in the work of Bible translation, to provide information on the most recent developments in the work of Bible societies throughout the world. He graciously consented, and to him I am indebted for the following data and information.

Dynamic equivalent translations in colloquial languages. For many years Eugene Nida, the amiable supervisor for Bible translation work of the United Bible Societies, has been calling for missionary translations of the Bible in the daily language of the people in addition to translations whose chief aim is to give the accurate and precise meaning. A good example of such a colloquial translation is *Good News for Modern Man.* In de Kuiper's words, "In such translations our first concern is not strict formal agreement with the original but rather a very lucid reproduction of the *message,* a task which often requires extensive restructuring of the language forms."

Such translations are regularly appearing in Asia, Africa, and Latin America today. They have become a well-nigh indispensable help and blessing for missionaries.

Helps in Bible reading. In the past, Bible societies avoided publishing "helps" at all costs lest they unleash a storm of arguments and disagreements because of the inevitable interpretation which they contain. The Dutch Bible Society, however, took the first step, and now every society within the United Bible Societies is doing it too. By "helps" I mean such things as: explanatory comments preceding the biblical passage, maps, short introductions to the biblical books, footnotes to the text (nondogmatic and purely informational), clarifying word lists, etc.

The Bible societies also now publish anthologies, selections, and books about the Bible. The purpose of all this material is only to make the Bible itself an open and understandable book. The producers have a role similar to Philip who helped the Ethiopian understand the Bible (Acts 8:26–40).

Help for illiterates and beginning readers. Approximately 783 million people cannot yet read or write. Thus, however excellent a translation may be, for them the Bible is still a closed book. For this reason the Bible societies have become involved in the fight against illiteracy not only among young people but old people too. But even though an older person may have taken some initial strides in learning to read, this does not mean he can already handle a thick book with small type like the Bible. For these people the societies are coming out with selections from the Bible accompanied by small vocabulary lists printed in large type.

Man-to-man Bible distribution. In recent years the Bible societies have worked hard at supplementing Bible distribution through commercial bookstores and depots by emphasizing man-to-man distribution. When personal contact develops into something more than casual meeting and leads to an involved conversation on spiritual matters, it makes sense to offer a Bible as a gift to that other person. Of course, such gestures are nothing new, but it is good that the Bible societies are now taking official cognizance of such actions. In our personal contacts we are so seldom alert to such opportunities for Bible distribution.

Use of audiovisual aids. Millions of men and women cannot yet read or write, but there are millions more who have forgotten how to read or write. Moreover, in the West many people, though literate, now choose to hear and see rather than to read. Simply stated, many today have become post-literate beings. This phenomenon has caused the Bible societies to reflect on the connection between words, sounds, and pictures. They are experimenting on a large scale with slide presentations, movie films, and cassette Bible recordings. In the near future they will also be using the video recorder in their effort to transmit the biblical message.

Continuation of classic Bible translation work. One must not mistakenly infer from reading about all of the new developments and experimental work being done by the Bible societies that they are simply dropping everything they have done through the years. On the contrary, the Bible societies themselves are working with no less than 647 translation committees. This number does not include the hundreds of translation teams sent out under the auspices of the Wycliffe Translators. Reliable sources fix the number of Bible translations in 1975 at 1530.

Radio, Television, and Literature

I have already underscored the importance of the churches' efforts to communicate the message of Christ through regional distribution of Christian literature and through the use of electronic media such as radio and television. I have noted too the several ecumenical organizations which were organized to aid in these developments. For example, the world missions conference meeting at Mexico City in 1963 established the Christian Literature Fund to train and encourage writers and publishers, to improve means of publication, and to organize a network of distribution centers for the sale of books, periodicals, etc. After the mandate of the CLF had expired, a new organization took its place, the Agency for Christian Literature Development. There is also a parallel ecumenical agency for radio and television, the World Association for Christian Communication.

Though the agencies are separate, practical experience dictated that the Agency for Christian Literature Development and the World Association for Christian Communication keep a close working relationship. After all, each treats the same core issues: what, how, and to whom shall we communicate? Thus, in 1974 the leaders of both of these ecumenical agencies decided to merge their separate organizations into one World Association for Christian Communication and appointed Albert Devasirvatham Manuel, an Indian with great experience in both areas, as its first general secretary. He began his work in 1975 with the inception of the new organization.

The new association still maintains the two separate departments (one for printed media and the other for electronic media), but it differs from earlier organizations in that it keeps in contact with related organizations not only in Asia, Africa, and Latin America but also in Europe and the United States.

Once again, what happens on the local and regional levels in terms of actual communication through radio and television and distribution of literature is much more important than all the supportive work on the ecumenical level. But if this brief treatment of the ecumenical agencies serves as a display window through which to see hundreds and thousands of men and women hard at work communicating the gospel, it will have achieved its purpose.

Planning for Mission

The late Bishop Azariah, first native bishop of South India, was in the habit of asking every adult person he baptized this question: "Are you willing to state publicly, 'Woe is me, if I preach not the Gospel'?" Indeed, this is a task which comes to the whole church and to every member in her. Pity her if she neglects her duty!

When the International Missionary Council was organized shortly after the first missionary conference in 1910 at Edinburgh, it adopted as one of its statutes the goal of stimulating gospel proclamation "so that all people might be saved." During its many years of existence the IMC contributed an indescribable amount toward achieving this goal. It appointed experts not only to gather data on the progress or decline of gospel proclamation in specific areas but also to locate unevangelized areas and to discover ways in which churches could cooperate in evangelizing those areas.

The International Missionary Council has now disbanded but its work has been taken over by a separate division of the World Council of Churches, the Commission on World Mission and Evangelism, and this commission has acknowledged in its statutes the same goal as its predecessor.

The plenary meetings of the commission in Mexico City in 1963 and in

Bangkok in 1972 and 1973 show that concern for gospel proclamation is not lacking in the commission, but in the future it will have to devote much more attention to what its study-secretary, Thomas Wieser, termed "Planning for Mission."

Technologically and scientifically speaking, the world is daily growing closer together. Industrial civilization is now global. Sociology and political science reckon in terms of one common humanity. And, as Lesslie Newbigin said, missiology has to do with "One Lord, One Body, One World." Therefore it is incumbent on sociologists of the church, missiologists, and administrators of the respective ecumenical organizations to put their heads together and come up with a global strategy for communicating the gospel today.

Vast regions of the world have not yet heard the sounds of the gospel. Though the Lausanne conference held in 1974 may have been a bit shallow in the statistics and data it gave, there is no denying that in some parts of the world the task has not yet even begun. In other regions doors have been shut. Think of once-Christian northern Africa overrun now by Islam, western Asia dominated by other religions, and Eastern Europe where since the Second World War the church has been reduced to the status of *ecclesia pressa* ("persecuted church") under the force of a specific ideology. Think too of China and of central and eastern Africa where gospel communication is severely restricted. A person has to be blind and deaf to his Christian calling to say that the task is now finished or that it can be suspended or discontinued. Millions have not yet heard God's gracious invitation to join his kingdom. But to get the job done properly takes planning, ecumenical planning, in which all churches have their input. What we need now is a new *élan,* a missionary revival.

MEANS OF FULFILLING DIACONAL RESPONSIBILITY

Though I have written before on the subject of diaconia, I want to bring the previous material up to date here.

God's goal in his mission is his messianic kingdom. The kingdom does not only address the spiritual and moral needs of a person, but his material, physical, social, cultural and political needs as well. For this reason Jesus came not only as one who preached but also as one who served *(diakonos).* He made the signs of that kingdom appear: the blind saw, the crippled walked, lepers were healed, the hungry had food to eat, and the lonely discovered they were no longer alone.

When the New Testament congregations came into existence, they very quickly instituted the office of deacon. In II Corinthians 9 we read about the first instance of what today we call inter-church aid. Here Paul supports his plea for help for the impoverished church at Jerusalem with an imposing theological rationale for giving and assisting other congregations. His argument lays the groundwork for a worldwide diaconia. God, says Paul, is our example; he did not give only something, or even much, but he gave everything. "Thanks be to God for his unspeakable gift" (II Cor. 9:15).

How did God give? He solidly identified with human needs. He became one with people so that now each of us may take strength from the divine "sympatheia," to borrow a term from Jürgen Moltmann's *The Crucified God.*

Seen in this light, one can understand how Paul considers diaconal responsibility an implication of one's Christian confession. Note what he says in II Corinthians 9:13: "Under the test of this service, you will glorify God by your obedience in acknowledging the gospel of Christ. . . ." For us confessing Christ has to do with something verbal; we think immediately of documents and tracts. But for the early church the matter of confession had to do in the first place with serving. In a church with a genuine confession diaconia blossoms forth, for a deed is the measure of one's love.

To rehearse the complete history of worldwide diaconia since the Second World War would be totally superfluous, but I do want to give a snapshot view of the work today and thus provide a glimpse of the several forms of diaconia.

Education

Education ranks as the oldest form of diaconia in the modern history of missions. It goes without saying, of course, that no longer are Western missionary agencies primarily responsible for this work; agencies and organizations within the developing nations themselves have taken it over.

In many of these nations the enterprise of Christian education is now completely impossible to carry out. Think, for example, of communist countries where the government monopolizes the educational process and assumes the right to feed minds from their earliest years on up through their university training on a steady diet of its own ideology. Then too, there are countries like Saudi Arabia and Afghanistan where a non-Christian religion prevails in the realm of education. In other lands, however, the declaration of human rights is honored and a freedom exists to establish schools which heed God's commands and trust his promises. Such ventures deserve the support of Christians everywhere, and it is gratifying to note the number of organizations which support such undertakings.

Worldwide diaconia has a great role to play here. Take a look at the list of projects receiving diaconal support and note especially the number of agrarian and technical schools receiving assistance. Such schools are vitally important in the present phase of development, even though it is often extremely difficult to secure the proper teaching personnel and equipment to outfit them.

Social-Medical Diaconia

Both in the Old and New Testaments the close connection between word and deed comes to no clearer expression than in the relationship between proclamation and healing. Wherever Jesus went, he earnestly tied his preaching to his healing sick people. Furthermore, the Hebrew word for rescue or liberation is *yasha,* and in the Old Testament it often meant a physical liberation from sickness or fear of death as well as spiritual liberation. But it could also mean social and economic liberation for the imprisoned, the oppressed, the errant, or the accident-prone.

The word *therapeuein* (from which we get our modern word "therapy") occurs 45 times in the New Testament and can mean both healing and rescue from sin and death. The same is true, only even more strongly, of the Greek verb *sōzein*, from which we get words such as *sōtēria*, *sōtēr*, salvation, Savior, Liberator, and Rescuer. Twenty-one times in the New Testament *sōzein* occurs in the context of healing; 24 times it refers to deliverance from the threat of physical danger; and 104 times it refers to deliverance from the grip of sin, demons, and death.

But in addition to all this lexicographical proof, Jesus' very life and work offer a prime example of the close tie between proclamation and healing. He was driven by the urge to give his life as a "ranson for many" *and* to proclaim the good news to the poor while healing their every disease and infirmity (Matt. 9:35–38). He sent his disciples out to both preach and heal (Matt. 10).

Jesus was not interested in healing alone. Whenever he healed, he was concerned to point out to the patient or the friends of the patient (Mark 2:1–12) the need of a faith relation between that person and himself. Thus, for Jesus, healing is only one part of the total picture. He had come not only to heal men's bodies or spirits, but to bring them total liberation from all their needs.

In that remarkable account of the lame man beside the pool of Bethesda (John 5:1–18) we observe that Jesus ignored that man just long enough so that he came to realize that he needed Jesus. In many other instances, too, Jesus so regulates the situation that the suffering person at the proper moment must choose whether to invest all his heart and trust in the Man standing before him.

But I must not go on. I must only once again restate what every reader of the New Testament can verify for himself: our witness and our help for those caught in the trauma of physical distress and psychical anguish are inseparably connected. Furthermore, the whole of church history indicates that the church understood this connection; think, for example, of the role European monasteries played in caring for the ill.

When one considers all this, it is not strange that "medical missions" accompanied modern missionary initiatives from the very outset. Some elements both then and now have viewed medical missions as aberrant from the real work to which the Lord calls us, namely, the verbal proclamation of the gospel. But the great majority within the modern missionary enterprise view social and medical assistance as an integral part of the work and bearing the closest possible relation to the motives and goals of God's saving activity.

One might well ask the question, however, whether or not this particular form of diaconia has not received a rather one-sided emphasis throughout history. A medical missionary, the late Dr. C. van Walraven, wrote me a letter one time in which he stated his belief that the reason Jesus spent so much time healing the sick was simply because sickness was the most pressing need in those days and therefore he naturally gave it so much attention. One must therefore never use Jesus' example as an excuse for not attending to so many other needs of mankind today. So many other needs too cry out for our attention: socioeconomic, cultural, political, and socio-psychological needs — all caused by unjust structures of power in this world.

I could not agree more with Dr. van Walraven. In the prewar period medical missions often claimed an undue amount of attention, and we may not repeat the same mistake today in this new situation. With all due regard to this word of caution I still must maintain that though there are so many areas of a person's life which cry out for justice and righteousness, medical assistance ought to remain high on our list of priorities for the simple reason that the people of the developing nations often give it high ranking in their hunger and thirst for righteousness.

Once one begins to see social and medical efforts within the coordinates of God's coming kingdom, it is not difficult at all to determine its precise position within that kingdom. Social-medical work is an elemental form of diaconia alongside all the other forms. It is not subservient to the important work of proclaiming the gospel but has its own important position alongside the work of proclamation.

Social-Medical Diaconia throughout Missionary History

Judging social-medical missionary activity in the light of the position developed above, one must admit that it has often been misplaced thoughout history. Though I do not have an opportunity here to develop fully the exciting story of this work, I do want to make several comments on how people throughout history viewed its role.

In the nineteenth century medical doctors accompanied missionary personnel, who were constantly threatened with fatal infections and sicknesses. Let it be said to their honor: those missionaries were concerned not only for their own physical well-being, but requested those doctors to attend to the needs of those living in the vicinity of the mission compounds. Gradually, from about 1870 on, a type of regional health care developed, and medical work came to be seen as a means of achieving goodwill and of making the native people receptive to the gospel. Medical mission was thus an ancillary service, a means of more effectively achieving the real goal of gospel proclamation. Against this conception many medical doctors quite properly protested by claiming that concern for another's physical health is a mandate coming out of the New Testament as clearly and strongly as the call to proclaim. The status of social-medical work is not derived from the work of proclamation; it is independent and has its own authority.

Then came the era of the so-called ethical colonial politics when thousands of small and large mission hospitals replaced their public counterparts and took the form of regional hospitals. During this time there was a real danger of giving more jurisdiction to Caesar than God's Word properly consigned to him. In China there was a sharp popular reaction shortly after the Opium Wars and during the rise of the communist regime. For even though the work of medical missions was extensive, it was not so vast that it could totally replace their public counterparts.

Since the time of the Second World War virtually every state which had but recently achieved independence developed its own national health-planning agency. This too has brought medical missions as well as so many other agencies of proclamation and diaconia into a time of testing. Should social-medical work be discontinued in the developing countries as well as in Europe and America? Or should medical missionaries try at all costs to hang on to that work formerly done by the mission hospitals? Or should they search anew the age-old motives and goals of the gospel for new ways of giving medical service and help? Out of the swirl of such questions the World Council of Churches created an agency to tackle such issues, The Christian Medical Commission. The commission began its work in September of 1968, and it is still going strong.

I shall end this section by quoting from the preamble of this commission's statement which it formulated both to guide itself and to explain its purpose to others:

> The ministry of healing is motivated for all Christian churches in terms of Jesus Christ.
>
> Christ's command to love our neighbour commits us to the compassion He has shown for all who suffer, demands that we see in our neighbour the dignity of one who is created in the image of God, and leads us to serve our fellow man in the imitation of Christ.
>
> In this healing ministry the whole people of God is committed to reflect Christ the Saviour in the fullness of His divinity (cf. Col. 1:19–20) and in the servanthood of His being man (cf. Phil. 2:5–11). Through this healing ministry the congregation witnesses to the salvation which Christ offers to man whether in health or in death and testifies to the unshaken hope in the resurrection of Christ.
>
> No man alone can heal the total brokenness of the human condition. Rather through a variety of talents, gifts and disciplines the whole man is healed with God's grace. For both, individual man and the community, Christ has brought salvation. In this healing ministry both the individual and the congregation live by God's mighty power working in Jesus Christ.

Social-Medical Diaconia in a New Situation

The pioneering days of medical missions are now past. Gone is the time when missions had a virtual monopoly on hospitals on the mission field. Such shifts call us to once again assess the situation to determine the best way of discharging our God-given mandate. A steady stream of literature, to which I shall refer at the end of the chapter, has flowed from the pens of many writers on this subject. I shall restrict myself to a very few comments on what I judge to be the most important elements in the present situation.

First of all, missions must coordinate social-medical diaconia with the national health-planning agencies of the respective governments. Now that government has taken over the major burden of providing proper medical care for its citizens in almost every young nation and has incorporated its efforts into the total overall plans for social and economic development, mission agencies must quit pretending that they are still in the pioneer stage when medical help was their virtually exclusive domain. Today advanced medical education, which was initiated by mission agencies, is usually an integral part of the public university's curriculum. Education of medical assistants, advances in natal care for mother and child, centers for rural and urban health care, dissemination of health information to the public, industrial health, wars on national epidemics — all of these have now been permanently taken over by the regional and national governments.

In many countries this in no way means that there is no room left for medical work with a Christian orientation. It does mean, however, that private initiatives must be coordinated with public efforts — at least if one proceeds on the assumption that medical help must be available to anyone in the whole society who needs it. In this way medical care becomes a joint effort. In the past, too many medical mission agencies have ignored this most elementary rule.

Second, I believe that Christian medical agencies must remain flexible as they lend their aid to the total effort to combat disease and illness. For example, medical missions ought not to become too doctrinaire in what types of work they will and will not perform in their role of assisting the government. Some have said that Christian medical missions may participate in curative medical help but not in preventive medicine; I question such arbitrary divisions. If the government is carrying out a program of medical prevention, very well. Let the mission not duplicate the government's efforts. But in many areas the government is devoting all of its resources and personnel to curative medicine and neglecting the preventive aspect. Why should a Christian agency not be allowed to take up the slack?

Then, too, I believe that Christian medical agencies must remain flexible enough to search out and discover the areas which are being neglected by the government. It could be the fight against leprosy; it could be natal care for mother and baby; it could be rehabilitation work; it could be gerontology. But whatever it is, there must be flexibility so that love can find those neglected areas and begin to tackle the problems.

I believe too that Christian medical diaconia should give priority to programs and projects which allow us to address persons in the totality of their existence. If healing is but a part of Christ's total program of salvation and rescue, then obviously programs and projects in which we can communicate with persons, families and whole societies on a wider range of issues than just their physical condition ought to take precedence.

Christian medical diaconia can also perform a very valuable task in not only applying medical help to people in need but also in interpreting such help for them. Everyone knows of the deeply ingrained views and attitudes toward sickness, healing and death prevalent among devotees of traditional primitive religions. Deep suspicions and resistance still prevail toward modern medicine. Christian diaconia is in a unique position to patiently explain to these people the significance of modern medicine by setting it within a different framework of God, man, the cosmos, sin, sickness, life, and death. To perform this service close teamwork between medical doctors, cultural anthropologists, and theologians is of utmost importance.

Allow me one final comment on this matter of flexibility: I want to remind those involved in social-medical diaconia that care for the poor must remain at the center of their efforts and not be shoved off to the side. No one can charge Christian medical centers with favoring rich people, for many of them are in financial trouble. But if Christian hospitals in developing countries should ever turn into places where medical personnel treat only the elite with good credit and refuse the poor, then it would be better to scrap the name "Christian." For then they are paying homage to that awful idol mammon and have fallen into the hands of medically trained people whose chief concern is business.

Not only must medical diaconia coordinate its efforts with the public health-care plans and not only must it remain flexible, but I must also remind those involved in this facet of the Christian mission that their best efforts are never enough. We must involve ourselves in the struggle for healing and recovery with the best means presently at our disposal. Sometime ago Dr. Lambourne, an English psychiatrist, made the point in an address to the Hongkong Council of Churches that God never speaks to his church without reckoning with the time. He always calls his people at a specific point in time and arouses them to do the good with the measure of insight and the means which they have at their disposal at that time and in that situation. "True knowledge," said Lambourne, "is dependent on being obedient to what they know *today*. If they are not obedient to what they can already know, they become blinded to the truth for tomorrow."

How right he is! New vistas of medical science are opening daily. Leprosy sanitoria have replaced the leprosy asylums of yesterday only to be in turn replaced by leprosy wings in modern hospitals where powerful medicines are producing remarkable results. Antibiotics and insecticides have sharply reduced the incidence of many tropical diseases. But in this war against sickness, we do not simply need medical help. We need the *best* medical help available at the time.

I must also make a fourth comment on social-medical diaconia in the modern situation. It is so obvious that it scarcely needs repeating: our advances in medical science must be paired with advances in responsible medical ethics. I would not even make the point except for the fact that we are not doing very much hard thinking in what is today called medical "macro-ethics." We today are in a better position to study how medical help is distributed over this globe, and the statistics show it: the division is lopsided and unjust. The same is true in areas of technology and cultural bounties, but when this injustice involves the matter of medical care and attention, it hurts most — in the most literal sense of the word.

Take for example the situation in London as compared with central Africa. London has one doctor for every four hundred people while central Africa has only one for fifty thousand. And in the developing countries themselves, the situation is far worse in the rural areas than in the cities. Consider India and Indonesia, for examples.

May we let the situation go on like this? In the words of Dr. Lambourne, "What kind of morality is it where we are consuming the health care of others?"

Another issue of medical macro-ethics is whether it is fair to pour vast sums of money into highly specialized clinics (for example, those which perform heart transplants) and thus deprive other clinics which provide basic medical care of badly needed funds.

One thing is certain: God's liberating activity reaches out to cover all mankind, and for that reason medical care must also become available to all men everywhere. This means that both the individual doctor and the ecumenical medical agencies must respond ethically to the medical statistics.

A fifth comment on medical diaconia in a new and changed situation has to do with the Christian congregation. The Tübingen Consultation of 1964 published its report in 1965 in Geneva: *The Healing Church.* The very title is a plea for a "comprehensive understanding of the church's concern with all forms of healing" and a warning against a fragmented approach to medical care which results from over-specialization. Recovery of health and victory over death are not totally separate entities. One could conceivably fail to recover his physical health and yet discover an inner integrity, a unity of life, and authentic human existence which the Bible calls "life." The reverse is also possible: one could be delivered from his physical pain and yet continue to be plagued by a much deeper ailment. Thus total care for a patient involves so much more than attending to his physical needs. A patient facing death may need reassurance that the gates of the eternal kingdom are open wide to receive him. Recovery includes a mental as well as a physical dimension.

This is part of what we mean by a "healing church." "Healing church" does not refer to the necessary contact between a Christian hospital and the Christian congregation in its vicinity. It does not merely mean that Christian congregations maintain regular contact with patients, both Christian and non-Christian, in governmental facilities. It rather means that the whole congregation must strive to become a genuinely human fellowship of people whose members are concerned about the health and welfare of each other.

Someone warned about speaking too romantically about the church as a healing community; sober inspection will force anyone to concede that some congregations seem more like prisons than healing communities. Many congregations are themselves in need of healing. All this is true, and yet in spite of the often deplorable present situations, it is good to be reminded of what the congregation ought to be. For this most important work the church must marshal every gift, both discovered and as yet undiscovered, which its members possess.

In this regard, the churches of Asia and Africa have much to teach the rest of us. I have often been struck by how deeply involved not only families but also whole churches become in the suffering and lot of those who are sick. They attend them with a genuine spirit of helpfulness, intercessory prayer, love, friendship, and kind concern.

Patients need a "healing community" in addition to all the technical medical assistance. When Christian doctors and nurses who themselves are part of the community of Christ Jesus seize the opportunity of witnessing to their patients about the hope which is in them, then medical diaconia can achieve a richness and depth which many former patients in Christian hospitals on mission fields can still so vividly recall. It is still being done today both here and abroad and is a blessing to many.

Other Types of Diaconia

I can only briefly summarize a few other types of diaconia. First of all, there is disaster help, which at present comprises a very sizeable share of inter-church aid. This has always been the case, but it is even more true today in view of the fact that we now try to respond not only to victims' immediate needs but also their long-range ones: acquiring a new dwelling, providing for education, getting a job, etc.

Another area of diaconia is refugee help. Here too, there is increasing emphasis on longer-range questions of resettlement and possible return to the refugees' land.

A third type is help for political prisoners and their families. Work centers on three areas: the social-pastoral area, the social-economic area (for the prisoner's family) and the political-legal area (defense of the prisoner's rights before the political authorities).

Another important area of service is aid to victims of unjust power structures in society. When injustice is vested in the basic fibers of a society, minority groups turn out to be the losers. Worldwide diaconal agencies have become much more sensitive to this now than before. In fact, when Leslie Cooke attended the Swanwick Consultation of 1966 shortly before he died and added this category to the list of traditional diaconal concerns, it was something brand new.

I would mention too the financial aid which supports small-scale projects in local areas to raise the social and economic level of the populace. The list of causes is too numerous and varied to mention; help for farmers, fishermen, animal breeders, small businessmen, industrial artists, and manual laborers are but a few examples.

With life expectancy rising, another area that is demanding increased attention in developing countries is help for the elderly. Many diaconal agencies are already doing exemplary work in building homes for the elderly and training personnel to staff them.

I must not fail to mention help for the orphans, the handicapped, the invalids, and others similarly deprived. So little is yet being done by the governmental agencies in the developing countries. But so it was too in nations like Germany and the Netherlands in the nineteenth century. Only after certain societies and organizations had taken the plight of these disadvantaged people upon themselves did the government finally recognize the need and include the care for these folk in its programs. So too in the new nations world diaconal agencies in cooperation with concerned individuals may provide the impetus for a more official recognition of these persons' needs.

This kaleidoscopic list is of course far from complete. In fact if each of us could scan the complete range of needs and challenges which require our attention, all of our diaconal help would seem like a drop in a bucket. Not that I am ungrateful for what is being done. On the contrary, I am deeply grateful that a veritable army of men and women and diaconal agencies working in ecumenical cooperation are tackling problems on a scale which far surpasses both in quality and in quantity anything mission agencies in the prewar days did do or even tried to do.

I must add one comment before I conclude this section: at present there are development projects which involve a whole geographic region and the entire population within that region. I shall be treating these later on in the book but must at least mention them here because they are receiving the support of worldwide diaconal agencies.

Church Participation in Movements for National Development

During the recent decades the feeling has been growing among the ecumenical fellowship of churches that they ought to be doing more than merely participating in world mission and world diaconia. They have felt the urge to participate in the whole process of development in the broader sense of that word — not as something totally divorced from their traditional activities but in close connection with them. Since I have written about such involvement elsewhere, I shall merely report here how matters stand at present at the ecumenical level. Once again, the most important work in this area is being done at the local level, but reports on such activity can best be handled through monographs and not in full-length books.

At an ecumenical consultation in Montreux in 1970 dealing with matters of development, the delegates provided the impetus which led to the founding of the Commission on the Churches' Participation in Development (CCPD). The title of its report is *Fetters of Injustice* — a report well worth reading. The chief goal of the CCPD is to render aid to churches who are in the process of development and liberation. This does not mean that churches now want to take on projects which only governments and the international organizations of the United Nations can properly handle, but it does mean that these churches, while recognizing their limited capacities and paying due regard to their special calling, do nevertheless want to participate in the process of development, emancipation, and liberation.

CCPD activities focus on three interrelated goals: justice, independence, and economic growth, with the first goal being primary. It seeks to call the attention of the officials within newly formed governments to the plight of the poor and neglected within their borders and to encourage and help them in the struggle for human dignity, independence, and social and economic welfare. It strives to achieve its goals by issuing detailed studies on trade relations, ecclesiastical investments, applied elementary technology, the organized efforts of emancipation movements, etc., which enable the authorities to analyze the situation and begin tackling the problems.

The CCPD also makes available its technical experts to aid in regional planning. Its most important contributions occur, not in the headquarters at Geneva, but throughout the world where it has established counterpart groups with the assistance of the local churches. Such groups operate, for example, in Cameroon, the Caribbean, Ethiopia and Indonesia. Regional consultations determine the priorities and then take on projects in the areas of agriculture, district development, employment, etc.

Where projects and movements are already underway which coincide with CCPD goals, this organization lends its technical assistance. Take, for example, the CCPD help to Rosca in Colombia, to the agricultural development organizations in Turkey, to the work with cooperatives in Uruguay, and to the centers for regional development in Venezuela.

The CCPD held its second conference at Montreux in December, 1974 to review its efforts and develop guidelines for future projects. It called for closer cooperation between the CCPD and the various agencies involved in worldwide diaconia and made a special plea for concerted effort to help the uprooted, the despised, refugees, workers from foreign countries, political prisoners, prisoners being rehabilitated, etc. The CCPD's involvement in alleviating the destruction caused by both natural disasters and warfare received special scrutiny; the organization resolved to meet not only the immediate and acute needs of the victims but also to create for them a future filled with hope.

The CCPD has proposed that the churches in rich countries set aside two percent of their total yearly income to fund projects of the CCPD. Although the proposal has met with stiff opposition from the side of the churches, it can teach them that to become involved in the work of development and liberation — as well they should — will cost *them* something.

I recently had occasion to again become familiar with the life and work of Camillo Torres from Colombia, who was shot and killed in 1966 while working among a guerilla group. What so estranged this Roman Catholic priest from his church? He was offended that the church could become so wrapped up in work of charity but did not — at least then — lift a finger to help the victims of structural poverty. (That had to wait until after his death when the bishops met in conference at Medellin in 1968.) Torres accused his church of failing to show love which issued in concrete deeds and of an unwillingness to seriously assess the situation and then cooperate with others to achieve development and liberation.

The life and death of people like Torres has kindled the hope that churches will never again face their servants with a dilemma such as he faced, but rather back up what they confess in both worship and proclamation by genuine words and deeds. There are evidences that both Roman Catholic and Protestant churches are coming to see the light. The very existence of the CCPD is one symptom. Once churches themselves have begun to show love and justice they will acquire the right to examine and judge the motives and goals of the governments' developmental schemes and to stimulate them "to loose the bonds of wickedness, to untie the knots of the yoke, [and] to let the oppressed go free" (Isa. 58:6).

MEANS OF COMMUNICATING THE GOSPEL THROUGH FELLOWSHIP (KOINONIA)

Witness and diaconia are not the only ways of telling the good news about God's coming kingdom. Another very important way is through fellowship ("koinonia"). Not only did Jesus proclaim the gospel to people and serve them by performing signs and wonders; he also built up an incalculably deep fellowship with them. He searched out and found the individual and built up contact with the multitudes. He participated with people in their worries, their disappointments, their joys, and their suffering.

In Jesus the Word became flesh (John 1:14), and that does not mean that he barely touched our human condition like a bird who skims the water and touches it with its wingtips. No, Jesus pitched his tent among us. In revealing God to us, Jesus walked the hot, stuffy roads of ancient Palestine and so lived with his disciples that he could claim at the end of his life: "He who has seen me has seen the Father" (John 14:9). And now this same Jesus comes to his disciples today and calls them to totally give themselves to their fellow human beings who are living in jungles, villages, and cities.

Life begets life. Fellowship is the means par excellence of introducing people to Jesus the Messiah and to the messianic community which the Bible calls ecclesia ("church"). Therefore, we must stimulate new ways of creating fellowship, and this search for fellowship must take institutional shape as we engage in the work of communicating the gospel. The history of the gospel's spread and the consequent rise of the young churches shows how important all of this is. Permit me to give several illustrations.

Ashrams in India. The Christian ashrams in India, which now number 150, have played a very important role in increasing contact and fellowship between Christians and adherents of other religions during the last fifty years. With their emphasis on prayer and meditation, an ascetic lifestyle, the peaceful atmosphere, and the openness and courtesy, these centers of fellowship are an important bridge between Christians and Hindus.

Programs of Christian presence. After the Second World War with its horrible campaign in Algeria had given official Christendom a very bad image in North Africa, Jacques Ellul, a French Christian from Bordeaux, stated the case for programs of Christian presence which would communicate the gospel more by serving presence than by verbal proclamation. The World Federation of Christian Students picked up Ellul's phrase and used it frequently in many conferences. D. T. Niles and Philip Potter, who became the chief spokesmen for this idea, were right in their claim that only after a person has listened to people may he claim the privilege of speaking to them about the gospel. Of course Niles and Potter did not mean that one must simply keep his mouth shut. Niles was a fiery communicator to his dying day, and no one can rightly charge Potter with not proclaiming the gospel. Later exponents of this idea often created the mistaken impression that they were pleading for Christian presence to avoid the risk of being called religious fanatics. Moreover, one must frankly admit that some of this idea's defenders were exporting an ideology more than an idea of genuine *Christian* presence.

At any rate, one thing is certain: with God's blessing, Christian presence for the sake of Christ can serve as a profound representation of the gospel of God's kingdom; genuine love is so adept at discovering means of reaching out. Throughout the world there are Christians who have received the gift of being able to build bridges of fellowship between themselves and those they meet. One can discover people with such gifts in every continent, especially in Asia, Africa, and Latin America. I am personally acquainted with highly capable missionaries who seldom preached a sermon or gave a speech but who were veritable artists at establishing friendships and through this made a profound impact.

Finally, I would mention that for those who have been won over by and for the gospel to experience genuine koinonia, the fellowship of the Christian congregation is absolutely indispensable. Those who are being swept along by the current reckless anti-institutional tendency neglect this altogether. Of course it is good to heed the oft-repeated warning not to overemphasize the institutional; but one can also go to the other extreme. If a person really believes that certain ecclesiastical structures must change before he can in good conscience invite others to participate, he should not press for de-institutionalization but rather for renewal of the present structures.

The worldwide study project on structures for a missionary congregation produced two things: it proved that existing church structures can be barriers which hinder a person's achieving fellowship, and it unleashed a mighty appeal to renew those structures, as happened, for example, at the Bangkok conference.

No one can thrive on messianic faith all by himself. People need each other as together they travel the road to the kingdom. For this reason koinonia is indispensable and ought to be encouraged at all costs.

MEANS OF CONTRIBUTING TO JUSTICE

The well-known Old Testament scholar, C. J. Labuschagne, wrote that in response to her meeting Yahweh, Israel made a confession that was revolutionary: Yahweh alone is God (Deut. 6:4). Why? Because, in the words of Psalm 82, "He defends the widow and fatherless, and gives justice to the poor and despised by delivering them from the hand of the wicked." Says Labuschagne, "He alone is God who stands for right and justice for the weak and poor. Whoever cannot is not God. With that fundamental perspective Israel looked out on the world of the other religions."[1]

The same characteristic is uniquely applicable to Jesus Christ and the messianic kingdom. The kingdom is a new earth in which righteousness dwells. For this reason anyone who lives on and is nourished by the conferred righteousness of Christ ought automatically to aid the cause of righteousness and justice where injustice prevails.

Even though candor compels us to admit that the Christian church has often almost totally neglected this responsibility and opted for mercy at the expense of justice, we may note with gratitude to God that churches and individuals are increasingly recognizing their obligation to serve the cause of justice. Recall, for example, the support worldwide diaconal agencies are giving to programs which strive for justice. Think too of the CCPD's involvement in political diaconia and the World Council's "Program to Combat Racism."

In the final chapter of this book I shall focus in on the *missio politica oecumenica* and there try to show that our service in the cause of justice must be as wide as the range of injustice which now prevails. Christian churches the world over must be alert and ready to serve this noble cause. But here I want to state that it is not only the big, spectacular programs which aid in fulfilling this calling of ours; multitudes of Christians working without fanfare on the local level can do much to root out injustice. Practically speaking, however, it seems that Christian churches need a lot more training than they have been receiving to prepare them for participation in the struggle. A well-known lawyer, given a long sentence in an Asian prison for his protest against injustice, once wrote me that so few of his fellow prisoners were aware of the wide range of means available to them to insure themselves and others of their rights.

This is true not only in Asia, but everywhere. It is here that Latin Americans like Paulo Freire, Dom Helder Camara, Ivan Illich, and many others are doing so much to equip and train their fellow citizens for the fight for justice. In the future, however, we shall have to expand this education, especially in areas where injustice is the most extreme and where acquiescence has too long been proclaimed.

One of the merits of the World Council's fund for combating racism is that many of the appropriations go directly to institutions run by the oppressed them-

1. C. J. Labuschagne, "De Godsdienst van Israel en de Andere Godsdiensten," *Wereld en Zending* 3 (1975): 8-9.

selves; in this way the Indians, Eskimos, aboriginals, and many others get a
chance to put their own hands to the plow in the quest for justice.

This chapter is so fragmentary and incomplete that I scarcely need to
mention it. However, I never intended to be exhaustive. I had two goals: first, to
show that anyone who becomes aware of the goals of the *missio Dei* and the
missiones ecclesiarum must be ready to use the ways and means designed to
achieve those goals; and second, to show that one must be flexible and willing to
vary his methods in accord with changing times and different cultural situations.

But I want to state one more thing. In spite of all the means and instruments, programs and projects, the attitude of the men and women who discharge
them is still so crucially important. To vary the words of I Corinthians 13: "Even
though I had tremendous expertise, could work with all sorts of media and had
mastered the most advanced communication techniques, but had not love, I would
be nothing." That too is what Paul meant when he talked about different strategies
for different situations. "To the weak I became weak, that I might win the weak. I
have become all things to all men, that I might by all means save some. I do it all
for the sake of the Gospel" (I Cor. 9:22–23).

BIBLIOGRAPHY

1. Theological Education

World Council of Churches, Commission on World Mission and Evangelism, Theological
    Education Fund. *Learning in Context: The Search for Innovative Patterns in Theologi-
    cal Education.* London, 1973.
————. *Ecumenical Responses to Theological Education in Africa, Asia, Near East,
    South Pacific, Latin America and Caribbean: A Report from the Theological Education
    Fund.* London, 1974.

2. On Proclaiming the Gospel

Gensichen, H. W. *Glaube für die Welt.* Gütersloh: Mohn, 1971, pp. 186–216, 214–244.
Hollenweger, W. J. *Evangelisation, Gestern und Heute.* Stuttgart: Steinkopf, 1973.
Nida, E. *Message and Mission: The Communication of the Christian Faith.* New York:
    Harper & Row, 1960.
Scott, R., et al. *Ways of Evangelism.* Mysore, India: Christian Literature Society, 1952.
Wieser, T. *Planning for Mission.* London: Epworth Press, 1966.

3. On Worldwide Diaconate

Berg, H. C. C. *Ökumenische Diakonia.* Berlin: Lettner Verlag, 1959.
Cooke, L. *Bread and Laughter.* Geneva: World Council of Churches, 1968.
Hendriks, J. *Overal waar Mensen wonen, een diakonale Gemeente.* Kampen: J. H. Kok,
    1973.
McCord, J. I. and Parker, T. H. L., eds. *Service in Christ: Essays Presented to Karl Barth
    on His 80th Birthday.* London: Epworth Press, 1966.
World Council of Churches, Commission on Interchurch Aid, Refugee, and World Service.
    (From its headquarters in Geneva this commission publishes an annual project list on
    inter-church aid. In addition, the reports of the diverse consultations held by this
    commission offer a glimpse of the developments in this area.)

4. On Church Participation in Development

World Council of Churches, Commission on the Churches' Participation in Development.

Fetters of Injustice: Report of the Montreux Conference. Geneva: World Council of Churches, 1970.

————. *Activity Report, No. 1.* Geneva: World Council of Churches, 1971.

————. *Activity Report, No. 2.* Geneva: World Council of Churches, 1974.

————. *Papers of the Second Montreux Conference.* Geneva: World Council of Churches, 1974.

5. On the Quest for Justice

Adler, E. *A Small Beginning: An Assessment of the First Five Years of the Programme to Combat Racism.* Geneva: World Council of Churches, 1974.

Verkuyl, J. *Break Down the Walls.* Translated by L. B. Smedes. Grand Rapids: Eerdmans, 1973.

Winter, J. A. *The Poor: A Culture of Poverty or a Poverty of Culture?* Grand Rapids: Eerdmans, 1971.

CHAPTER IX

The Study of Asian, African, and Latin American Churches

THE TREND TOWARD DECOLONIZING HISTORIOGRAPHY

In this chapter I want to focus our attention on the shift in approach to studying the young (and old!) churches in Asia, Africa and Latin America. Our point of departure is no longer Western missions and their agencies, but rather the existence of full-fledged churches themselves in the above-mentioned continents. This calls for a change in our approach.

Of course this shift in approach to church history is closely connected to specific trends in historiography generally. With help from UNESCO, historians from Asia and Africa are hard at work with historians from the West in what they call a first order of business — decolonizing historiography. There is a dawning awareness that we no longer live in the era of Disraeli and Bismarck, and he who persists in his Europocentric attitude as he writes history will produce a piece that is inevitably provincialistic. A new phase has come upon us, an era of *universal history* when Asia, Africa and Latin America are no longer colonized and submissive continents but full partners in the interplay between societies on the six continents. This is a revolution of Copernican magnitude, and both Western and Asian, African and Latin American historians were beginning to sense its future impact on historiography long before UNESCO became officially involved. Arnold Toynbee's *The World and the West* is a striking example of the change. Nehru's *Discovery of India* made a clean break with Europocentric historiography, and Panikkar's *Asia and the Western Dominance*, though rather one-sided, made the new trend quite explicit. One Latin American example is the historian Arcieniegas, who since 1944 has been describing the history of his continent with the aid of this new perspective. See his books *The Green Continent: A Comprehensive View of Latin America by Its Leading Writers* (1944) and *Latin America: A Cultural History* (1966).

It was UNESCO, however, which gave the real push toward accepting the new approach to historiography. Geoffrey Barraclough with his two books, *History in a Changing World* (1955) and *An Introduction to Modern History* (1969), set the tone for change. Toward the close of his second book he wrote:

> The European age — the age which extended from 1492–1947 — is over, and with it the predominance of the old European scale of values. Litera-

ture, like politics, has broken through its European bonds, and the civilization of the future, whose genius I have tried in the preceding pages to
trace, is taking shape as a world civilization in which all continents will
play their part.[1]

Through these books he received the commission to go to Africa and aid African
historians in writing a general history of the continent. An appointed committee
divided this monumental work between historians of various African universities,
and the goal is to produce a complete history of Africa in eight volumes.

Rather than extending this section, let me simply make three statements.
First, the revolution occurring in writing the history of young churches stands in
close connection to the revolution in writing general history. Second, in the
writing of church history the point of departure is now in the lands themselves and
no longer in the motherlands of Western missions. Third, there is a mutual
interaction in the matter of methodology.

REPLACING THE HISTORIES OF WESTERN MISSIONS WITH
STUDIES OF YOUNG CHURCHES

The work of describing Western missions extends over many years and fills the
reader with respect. One who wants to become familiar with the spread of
Christian faith in Asia, Africa, Latin America, and the Caribbean and Pacific
islands must wade through countless monographs and summarizing books. It is
both desirable and likely that still more of these studies will appear. I shall
mention only three summaries of the work of Western missions. The first is
Kenneth Scott Latourette's monumental seven-volume standard, *A History of the
Expansion of Christianity*. It has an exciting approach: it covers the entire travel
of church history in every continent from the perspective of the spread of Christianity. However, when it describes the spread of Christianity in Asia, Africa and
Latin America, it focuses on the work of Western mission agencies and personnel.

A book that displays an amazing mastery of material is Stephen Neill's *A
History of the Christian Mission*. Some time ago the author wrote that if he had to
do it again, the book would be quite different because of all the shifts which have
taken place, but there is no denying that even in its present state, this is a very
important and useful book.

Finally, I would mention Alphons Mulder's *Missiegeschiedenis*, which
describes Roman Catholic mission activity through the years and details with
amazing accuracy the involved work of the *Congregatio de Propaganda Fide*.

Though all these and similar studies are useful and good, we desperately
need studies which choose their point of departure within the land under investigation itself. Histories of Western missions cannot take the place of histories of
young churches. The African historians J. F. Ade Ajayi and E. A. Ayandele
made this point convincingly in their chapter in the book honoring Bengt
Sundkler, *The Church Crossing Frontiers*. About the same time Ajayi and Ayan-

---

1. Geoffrey Barraclough, *An Introduction to Modern History* (Middlesex: Penguin
Books, 1969), p. 268.

dele's essay appeared (1969), Stephen Neill made the same point from the Western side in his essay "The History of Mission: an Academic Discipline," which appeared in *The Mission of the Church and the Propagation of Faith.* The same point has been made countless times since.

Why is Western mission history no substitute for histories of "young" churches? There are several reasons. First of all, because Western mission histories always start off with the land from which the missionary personnel came and not the land in which Christian faith spread.

Second, most of these studies restrict themselves to describing only certain mission societies or Western church missions which worked in what used to be termed "mission terrain." Think, for example, of the studies on Anglican mission, on the Basel mission, on the Moravian missions, etc. As imposing as all of these studies may be, they simply do not and indeed cannot allow the unique form of the native church to come to expression.

Third, Western mission history is frequently quite "hagiographic," to borrow Stephen Neill's sharply critical term. These books often breathe a spirit of hero worship. Genuine heroism is nothing other than being faithful to the work at hand in spite of all obstacles and difficulties, and there have been many true heroes throughout the course of mission history. But these heroes would be the first to admit that it was really the Lord who was faithful in spite of all their own personal weaknesses and errors.

Fourth, the involvement of native Africans, Asians, and Latin Americans in planting, spreading and developing churches is often underemphasized in Western histories of mission. In my judgment, this is one of the most glaring weaknesses, for there was scarcely a Bible translated, medical care extended, education offered, diaconal work done, or the gospel transmitted without these native people playing a decisive and indispensable role.

Fifth, Western mission histories often pay little attention to the whole context in which church growth takes place. They often depict the churches as merely residing *in* Africa or Asia but not being through and through African or Asian in character. Topics like the church's relationship to society, its role in the tension between colonialism and national self-expression, and later on the connection between "church-building" and "nation-building" often receive scant attention.

Sixth, churches and movements which totally withdrew themselves from the influence of Western mission or never felt it in the first place were either omitted from attention, condemned outright, or measured by the standards of Western ecclesiastical practice. There was crying need for a new approach to the phenomenon of the so-called independent church movements.

Seventh, though the motives which inspired Western missionaries to share the gospel received careful attention, those which moved people in the other three continents to accept it did not.

Eighth, in their research the authors of Western mission histories often worked to investigate, arrange and systematize the archives of the Western agencies but failed to employ methods suited to the milieu in which the young churches arose.

Forerunners of the New Trend

When Kraemer complied with the request of the Netherlands Bible Society to provide it with reports on various churches in Indonesia, he responded with what today we would call sociological studies of churches. His reports were collected and issued in shortened form in a book, *From Missionfield to Independent Church* (1958), and contain information on the Moluccan church, the Minahassa church, the church of East-Java, the church of West-Java and the Batak church. The reports themselves are a combination of socio-historical and "ecological" analysis and sound administrative advice. He always kept one question central in his examination: Has the church of Jesus Christ become manifest here and now? What factors and structures either aid or subvert its coming to expression, and what specific advice is required to bring about in a church both independence from and interdependence with other churches as it grows in its reliance upon the Lord? Kraemer's studies became models for later studies.

After completing an extensive tour of Asia the capable and sensitive German missiologist Walter Freytag wrote a book that caused no small stir, *Die junge Christenheit im Umbruch des Ostens,* subtitled "Vom Gehorsam des Glaubens unter den Völkern." Freytag was one of the first missiologists to look at the activity of the young churches from the perspective of the "obedience of faith among the heathen" rather than from the viewpoint of Western missionaries. His questions are stimulating to students of the young churches.

The Churches in Mission Series

The Willingen conference of the International Missionary Council held in 1952 set in motion a planned series of studies on various *Churches in Mission.* The idea for such a series was inspired in part by the forerunners mentioned above, for Freytag was a member of the board of the International Missionary Council. The purpose of this series was to examine the life and growth of young churches, and its results are in many respects exemplary and indeed pacesetting. The proposal of the IMC reads as follows: "to commission studies in the realm of the life and growth of the young churches."[2]

The Danish missiologist Erik Nielsen, at that time one of the IMC secretaries, worked out the details of this proposal, and this led to the first case study on the growth of the church in Buganda by J. V. Taylor. This study was later published as a book, *The Growth of the Church in Buganda: An Attempt at Understanding.*

What is so different about this study compared with all the previous case studies? It consistently keeps the church which is under examination as its point of departure and insures that its methods of investigation conform to this. The primary focus of the study is how the people of a certain region respond to God's

2. Notes of the International Missionary Council enlarged meeting held in Willingen, Germany, 1952.

revelation which they heard and what particular shape and form this response takes as the church meets and interacts with its surrounding environment.

Nielsen and Taylor compiled a long list of questions which were designed to measure in six different areas how the church interacted with its environment. The first area was how the Christian fellowships reacted to the old religion and the congeries of myths, rites and customs. Second, how were the fellowships responding to the secularization process which slowly but surely was penetrating their community? Third, what attitude did the fellowships take toward the process of regional self-expression and subsequently toward national self-expression? Fourth, how is the church herself functioning in both her "misery and grandeur?" Fifth, how extensive is the influence of foreign mission workers? Sixth, to what degree is the tradition of Western churches flowing through foreign missionaries into the church?

Of course J. V. Taylor, Dorothea Lehmann, Busia, Debrunner, Van Akkeren and so many others who carried out such studies continued to make use of missionaries' letters, diaries, travel journals and the various other material in Western archives, but these were secondary to African and Asian source material, including the oral tradition which, though it must be used cautiously, is nevertheless an absolutely indispensable source of information in the study of young churches.

These new studies also gather information through interviews and questionnaires and thus reach much more closely to the life of the people and provide a more vivid description of the ecclesiastical leaders than did the previous mission histories.

I shall include the title of each of the books in this series in the bibliography at the end of the chapter. As one can see, even Western churches are being studied in this new way.

After this series of studies was temporarily halted, Steven Mackie, a secretary for the Division of World Mission of the World Council of Churches, gave a summary evaluation of the series' impact up to that point in *Research Pamphlet* no. 17: "Can Churches Be Compared?" What did we learn in the process that was useful for writing the history of young churches and advising them on their future course? In December, 1968, the complete staff of the Division of World Mission and Evangelism discussed Mackie's evaluation and came up with seven "clues," as they called them. These seven clues, though latent, were present and operative from the very beginning, but now that they are patent, they form a fine summary of the harvest of all these studies:

1. At whatever level we seek to compare different churches (whether at the congregational, the denominational or at an intermediate level) we find a basic diversity which outweighs superficial resemblances. Each church is the Church of the Lord Jesus Christ in its own individual way.
2. This individuality is particularly evident in a church's interaction with its surrounding culture. A church's awareness of itself is inevitably in terms of that culture and may change considerably with changes in the environment.
3. External criteria such as the traditional signs of Word, Sacraments and Discipline only define a church imperfectly. It is the evidence of God at

work within a particular community (the work of grace in the hearts of sinful men, of love in their actions towards their neighbours, and of fellowship binding them together) that authenticate a church as the Church of the Lord Jesus Christ.

4. This authentication may be present even where there are errors of doctrine and irregularities of order, judged by Western theological concepts, and a failure in standards, judged by Western moral codes. The response and faithfulness of a particular church can only be assessed in terms of a theology and a Christian ethic sensitive to the norms and aspirations of the surrounding culture.

5. Foreign missionaries have played different roles in church history. They have not been the only bringers of the Gospel. In general, the first interpreters of the Gospel message in terms of a particular culture have belonged to that culture itself. The majority of Christians have heard of Jesus Christ from their own countrymen. But the foreign missionary will remain alien even when the Gospel has been assimilated.

6. For most Christians the Church is an immediate rather than a universal reality; international and ecumenical links are regarded as secondary. The significance of the link between a church and a foreign mission agency will be understood differently in the two countries concerned. The limiting aspect of such historic links may well bulk larger than their potentiality as signs of the catholicity of the Church.

7. To talk of mission in terms of strategy, even a strategy with a diversified six-continent approach, is to forget that the primary strategy of mission is with God himself and that, through the Holy Spirit, he retains the initiative even when we forget to leave room for it. The details of his strategy, when he chooses to reveal them to us, may surprise and humble us.[3]

Norms and Criteria

Western church history has gradually become completely descriptive in character. Church historians today synchronically and diachronically inspect every aspect of ecclesiastical life in its historical context, but rarely do they test the churches against the biblical norms for their existence. Strangely enough, when it comes to a study of the sects, church historians do not hesitate to evaluate; but they do not evaluate churches. I suspect there are two reasons for this hesitation. First, throughout European history everyone understood that the church is a fellowship of people with a unique character; no further proof or examination of this was necessary. Second, in societies where a pluriformity of churches exists the testing and evaluation of these churches against the standards of the New Testament became so difficult and confusing that many church historians simply surrendered the task to systematic theologians. But I believe that in writing the history of the young churches the element of normativity is vitally necessary.

In continents where the church is still young, ecclesiastical fellowship is

3. Division of World Mission and Evangelism, World Council of Churches, "Seven Clues for Rethinking Mission," *International Review of Missions* 60 (July, 1971): 325–327.

something brand new. The so-called older churches in Asia and North Africa lack
this element of the strange and unfamiliar and fit right into the traditional social
patterns. The Mar Thoma church in India has become a caste. The same is true for
the Greek Orthodox and the Maronite churches in the Middle East. But the young
churches are in a situation similar to the church in New Testament times. These
fellowships could not be explained in terms of the old social ties; their tie with the
Lord was their only *raison d'etre,* and he used them to discharge his missionary
purposes. The early fellowships simply stood out in traditional society, open and
flexible, and expressed a great willingness to serve. They were the new Israel
spoken of by the Old Testament prophets, that third people made up of Jews and
Gentiles who had risen from the dead. We can find this people's own interpretation of its existence and calling in the many letters and parables in the New
Testament. Paul Minear analyzed these various self-portraits in his book *Images
of the Church in the New Testament.*

I firmly believe that these passages are not merely "images" of the church
back then but must become the criteria against which people in every age test the
mettle of their own churches. Freytag's questions were good, but these New
Testament "images" are even better tests. Are churches today really the "salt of
the earth" and "the light of the world?" Are they "ambassadors of reconciliation" (II Cor. 3:2–3), and the Body of Christ (I Cor. 12)? Have they really taken
on the form of a servant (John 13)? In my judgment responsible historiography will
deal with questions like these.

When historians begin treating questions like these in their histories of the
young churches, they become involved not merely in objective description but
also in offering advice for the future. Let me give but one example. J. F. A. Ajayi
gave his book *Christian Missions in Nigeria* (1841–1891) this subtitle: ' The
Making of a New Elite." His book is a thorough investigation of the strong and
weak points of the Christian mission to the Ibo people. There was a drive toward
forming an elitism among the Ibos, and this inevitably led to Ibo domination over
other people in Nigerian society, leaving violence such as occurred in Biafra in its
wake.

If we are serious in our resolve to make scientific investigation relevant to
human society, we must not fail to offer at least some parenetic conclusions,
however few they may be. Historiography of the young churches is the most
empty of empty occupations if it does not serve the work of examination and
renewal. Anyone who checks the prescribed goals set forth by those who headed
up this new series of history books will notice immediately how sensitive the
directors were to all of this. Erik Nielsen wrote in 1953 that the intent of this new
historiography was to face the sociological phenomenon of church armed with a
series of theological questions. Victor Hayward wrote in much the same manner
when he was coordinator of this project in 1967. James Scherer may have a point
when he cautions against dogmatizing too much on what are the criteria of a
healthy church, but does this mean that we in a spirit of "humble agnosticism"
can simply do without the New Testament standards which mark the people of
God? In my judgment the real worth of so many of these studies in the series lies
precisely in the fact that they did not skirt such questions and criteria.

The Study and Mastery of Oral Tradition

Only recently have scholars been making regular use of the fund of oral tradition in their work. That this should have come about only so recently in historiography is hard to understand, for the early church was filled with it and even the Gospels themselves arose through it. Moreover, one must remember that people who are nonliterate often have a keenly developed memory, much more developed than those who can read.

The few church historians who have dared to go beyond the archives of Western missionary societies and get into the whole fascinating world of oral sources were rewarded with a view of history which was deeper and headier than those of other historians. I am thinking of studies done by such scholars as Ajayi and Ayandele and Sundkler.

To be sure, one must be careful in his use of these sources. In his standard work, *Oral Tradition: A Study in Historical Methodology,* J. Vansina warns against the many possible pitfalls which an uncritical use can cause. In discerning fact from fancy one must keep the categories of "eyewitness," "rumor," and "oral tradition" clearly before his mind and weigh what he is hearing in terms of them.

I believe the possible pitfalls in using oral sources for writing histories of young churches are far fewer than for writing histories of the tribal religions (which were the main focus of Vansina's study) for the simple reason that the young churches are of much more recent origin. Their roots do not disappear into prehistory. Yet even here one must carefully separate the mythical from the historical, as, for example, Eugene Rubingh has done in his book *Sons of Tiv* with the witnesses from Akiga in the Tiv region of Nigeria. An example of one who failed to do this is Boubou Hawa from Niger; his *Recherche sur l'histoire des Touang Saharians et Soudanois* calmly intersperses solid fact with myth and saga and makes no effort to distinguish between them.

In spite of the dangers, no one can deny that the fund of oral tradition is a *sine qua non* of complete historical investigation. Therefore it is gratifying to see the history departments in Africa hiring research assistants in oral tradition. The famous Ibadan School of History is a leader in this field.

The Study of Why a Region Becomes Christian

At the beginning of this chapter I mentioned that the motives for engaging in mission have been thoroughly studied. But this must be supplemented by an investigation of the motives which have contributed and are still contributing to the acceptance of Christianity by a people. The School of World Mission at Fuller Theological Seminary in California, sometimes called the Church Growth School, makes this issue the object of special study.

The Study of Phases in the History of Young Churches

J. F. A. Ajayi and E. A. Ayandele are two historians who posed the question of phases in the history of young churches. In their essay "Writing African Church

History," included as a chapter in the book honoring Bengt Sundkler, *The Church Crossing Frontiers,* they propose the following phases for study: the precolonial period, the colonial period, and the postindependence period.

Keeping these three phases in mind would at least deliver one from the fashionable (but false) claim that the timespans of mission history and colonialism exactly coincide throughout the whole world. There was a precolonial phase, and Ajayi and Ayandele earnestly plead with their readers to discard this traditional misconception.

The authors remind their readers that each of these phases must be studied in its own context and urge them not to overlook important studies done by African scholars. *Mutatis mutandis,* I would offer the same advice for those who wish to study Asian churches.

The Study of "Independent Church Movements"

Church movements in several parts of Africa, particularly South Africa, which withdrew from the protecting authority of Western missionary agencies in the nineteenth century have again been springing up in the twentieth century and have attracted a good measure of recent attention. This was not always so, for even some of the most formidable African church historians like Christian Baeta kept themselves at arm's length from these movements. But now scholars like Sundkler, Turner, Barrett, and Oosthuizen are pressing for deeper and closer contact. David Barrett's standard book, *Schism and Renewal in Africa* (1968), is the product of his investigation of no less than 6000 of these movements.

M. L. Daneel is one of the first historians to not only write about these movements but actually to involve himself in the life of these people and cooperate with their leaders. Nor must I fail to mention in this connection the work of William H. Crane who just prior to his death established contact with the Kimbango Christians in Zaire and paved the way for them to become members of the World Council of Churches. He gave an account of his efforts in his article "De Kerk der Kimbanguisten en het Zoeken naar authentieke Katholiciteit" ("The Kimbango Church and the Quest for Genuine Catholicity). In it he held before both the older churches in the West and these young churches the mirror of the New Testament church and urged each to join the other in a common quest for a genuine expression of the one holy catholic church.

Thus, we attain responsibility in our study of the young churches only when we with these other churches and movements allow ourselves to be included in the circle of those to whom the Word of God speaks and when we "with all saints everywhere" respond to God with that Word through prayers and songs of praise, in expressions of thanksgiving, in fellowship, and in deeds of justice.

Institutes for the Study of Young Churches

In Africa C. P. Groves, the author of the four-volumed *The Planting of the Church in Africa,* is chairman of the Society for African Church History. Some of the other members of this society are C. G. Baëta, M. Timkulu, K. Onwuka Dike,

E. A. Ayandele, J. S. Mbiti, and J. F. A. Ajayi — all of them Africans who have earned their stripes and charted new paths.

As for Asia, I want to mention the largest study project heretofore undertaken in this field being directed by F. Ukur and an American sociologist-theologian, F. Cooley. Through extensive interviews conducted by theologians in various regions approximately forty different studies of various Indonesian churches are being carried out. Through this project books will be coming out in the Indonesian language both to inform and to advise the local churches, and along with them will come short English surveys whose main goal is to inform. Sponsor for the project is the Institute for Research and Study of the Indonesian Council of Churches.

BIBLIOGRAPHY

1. Methodology

Ajayi, J. F. A. and Ayandele, E. A. "Writing African Church History." In *The Church Crossing Frontiers: Essays on the Nature of Mission in Honour of Bengt Sundkler.* Uppsala: Studia Missionalis Uppsaliensia, 1969.
Gensichen, H. W. *Missionsgeschichte der neueren Zeit.* Göttingen: Vandenhoeck & Ruprecht, 1961.
Gottschalk, L., Kluckhorn, C., and Angell, R. *The Use of Personal Documents in History, Anthropology and Sociology.* New York: Social Science Research Council, 1945.
King, N. Q. "African Church History in the Making." *Journal of Ecclesiastical History.* October, 1967, pp. 237–241.
Turner, H. W. "Problems in the Study of African Independent Churches." *Numen* 13 (1966): 27–42.
Vansina, J. *Oral Tradition: A Study in Historical Methodology.* London: Routledge & Kegan Paul, 1965.
Verkuyl, J. "Enkele Aantekeningen over nieuwe Trends in de Historiografie der 'Jonge Kerken'." *Wereld en Zending* 1 (1972): 44–58.
Webster, J. D. "Source Material for the Study of the African Church." *Bulletin of the Society for African Church History* 1 (1963): 41–49.

2. Model of the New Approach: The World Studies of Churches in Mission
General
Mackie, S. G., ed. *Can Churches Be Compared? Reflections on Fifteen Study Projects.* WCC Research Pamphlet No. 17. Geneva: World Council of Churches, 1970.
Africa
Andersson, E. *Churches at the Grass Roots: A Study in Congo-Brazzaville.* London: Lutterworth Press, 1968.
Debrunner, H. *A Church Between Colonial Powers: A Study of the Church in Togo.* London: Lutterworth Press, 1965.
Taylor, J. V. *The Growth of the Church in Buganda: An Attempt at Understanding.* London: SCM Press, 1958.
Taylor, J. V. and Lehmann, D. A. *Christians of the Copperbelt: The Growth of the Church in Northern Rhodesia.* London: SCM Press, 1961.
Asia
Hayward, V. E. W., ed. *The Church as Christian Community: Three Studies of North Indian Churches.* London: Lutterworth Press, 1966.
Lee, R. *Stranger in the Land: A Study of the Church in Japan.* London: Lutterworth Press, 1967.

Luke, P. Y. and Carman, J. B. *Village Christians and Hindu Culture: Study of a Rural Church in Andra Pradesh, South India.* London: Lutterworth Press, 1968.

Van Akkeren, P. *Sri and Christ, A Study of the Indigenous Church in East Java.* London: Lutterworth Press, 1970.

Latin America

Lalive d'Epinay, C. *Haven of the Masses: A Study of the Pentecostal Movement in Chile.* London: Lutterworth Press, 1969.

Oceania

Tippett, A. R. *Solomon Islands Christianity: A Study in Growth and Obstruction.* London: Lutterworth Press, 1967.

Europe

Busia, K. A. *Urban Churches in Britain: A Question of Relevance.* London: Lutterworth Press, 1966.

Freytag, J. and Osaki, K. *Nominal Christianity: A Study of a Hamburg Parish.* London: Lutterworth Press, 1970.

North America

Wilkinson, T. S. *Churches at the Testing Point: A Study in Rural Michigan.* London: Lutterworth Press, 1970.

3. The "Church Growth School" and the "Church Growth Books"

General

McGavran, D. *Understanding Church Growth.* Grand Rapids: Eerdmans, 1970.

Tippett, A. R. *Church Growth and the Word of God.* Grand Rapids: Eerdmans, 1970.

Africa

Grimley, J. B. and Robinson, G. E. *Church Growth in Central and Southern Nigeria.* Grand Rapids: Eerdmans, 1966.

Kwast, L. E. *The Discipling of West Cameroon: A Study of Baptist Growth.* Grand Rapids: Eerdmans, 1971.

Olson, G. W. *Church Growth in Sierra Leone.* Grand Rapids: Eerdmans, 1969.

Wold, J. C. *God's Impatience in Liberia.* Grand Rapids: Eerdmans, 1968.

Asia

Braun, N. *Laity Mobilized: Reflections on Church Growth in Japan and Other Lands.* Grand Rapids: Eerdmans, 1971.

Shearer, R. E. *Wildfire: Church Growth in Korea.* Grand Rapids: Eerdmans, 1966.

Tuggy, A. L. *The Philippine Church: Growth in a Changing Society.* Grand Rapids: Eerdmans, 1971.

Latin America

Enns, A. W. *Man, Milieu and Mission in Argentina.* Grand Rapids: Eerdmans, 1971.

Read, W. R. *New Patterns of Church Growth in Brazil.* Grand Rapids: Eerdmans, 1965.

Read, W. R., et al. *Latin American Church Growth.* Grand Rapids: Eerdmans, 1969.

Middle America

Bennett, C. *Tinder in Tabsco: Church Growth in Tropical Southeast Mexico.* Grand Rapids: Eerdmans, 1968.

McGavran, D. *Church Growth in Mexico.* Grand Rapids: Eerdmans, 1963.

4. General Information on Churches in Various Areas of the World

Bavinck, J. H. and van den Berg, J. *De jonge Kerken op het Zendingsveld.* Vol. 9 of *Geschiedenis van de Kerk.* Edited by G. P. van Itterzon and D. Nauta. Kampen: J. H. Kok, 1967.

Beaver, R. P. *Ecumenical Beginnings in Protestant World Mission: A History of Comity.* New York: Nelson, 1962.

Enklaar, I. H., et al. *Onze blijvende Opdracht.* Kampen: J. H. Kok, 1968.

Gensichen, H. W. *Missionsgeschichte der neueren Zeit* Göttingen: Vandenhoeck & Ruprecht, 1961.

Latourette, K. S. *A History of the Expansion of Christianity.* 7 vols. New York: Harper, 1937–1945.
Neill, S. C. *History of Christian Missions.* Baltimore: Penguin Books, 1964.
Warren, M. A. C. *The Missionary Movement from Britain in Modern History.* London: SCM Press, 1965.

5. Other Studies

Asia
Anderson, G. H., ed. *Studies in Philippine Church History.* Ithaca: Cornell Univ. Press, 1969.
Clark, W. H. *The Church in China: Its Vitality, Its Future?* New York: Council Press, 1970.
Drummond, R. H. *A History of Christianity in Japan.* Grand Rapids: Eerdmans, 1971.
Gössmann, E. *Religiöse Herkunft — profane Zukunft? Das Christentum in Japan.* Munich: Max Hueber Verlag, 1965.
Kraemer, H. *From Missionfield to Independent Church.* The Hague: Boekencentrum, 1958.
Müller-Krüger, T. *Der Protestantismus in Indonesien: Geschichte und Gestalt.* Stuttgart: Evangelisches Verlagswerk, 1968.
Rullman, J. A. C., Sr. *De Gereformeerde Zending in Midden-Java.* Baarn: Zendingscentrum van de Gereformeerde Kerken, 1969.

Africa
Abruquah, H. W. *Der Alte aus Ghana: ein Katechist erzählt sein Leben.* Stuttgart: Evangelisches Missionsverlag, 1967.
Ajayi, J. F. A. *Christian Missions in Nigeria, 1841–1891: The Making of a New Elite.* London: Longmans, 1965.
Ayandele, E. A. *The Missionary Impact on Modern Nigeria, 1842–1914: A Political and Social Analysis.* London: Longmans, 1966.
Baeta, C. G. *Christianity in Tropical Africa.* London: Oxford Univ. Press, 1968.
Beetham, I. A. *Christianity and the New Africa.* London: The Pall Mall Library of African Affairs, 1967.
Groves, C. P. *The Planting of Christianity in Africa.* 4 vols. London: Lutterworth Press, 1948–1964.
Kessler, J. B. A. *A Study of the Older Protestant Missions and Churches in Peru and Chile.* Goes: Oosterbaan & Le Cointre, 1967.
Pauw, B. A. *Religion in a Tswana Chiefdom.* London: Oxford Univ. Press, 1960.
Rubingh, E. *Sons of Tiv.* Grand Rapids: Baker Book House, 1969.
Sales, J. M. *The Planting of the Church in South Africa.* Grand Rapids: Eerdmans, 1971.
Taylor, J. V. "Processes of Growth in an African Church." IMC Research Pamphlet No. 6. London: SCM Press, 1958.
Von Sicard, S. *The Lutheran Church on the Coast of Tanzania 1887–1914.* Lund: Gleerup, Studia Missionalia Uppsaliensia, 1970.

The Caribbean
Gonzales, J. L. *The Development of Christianity in the Latin Caribbean.* Grand Rapids: Eerdmans, 1969.
Schalkwijk, J. M. W. "Oecumenische Samenwerking in het Caribisch Gebied." *De Heerbaan* 19 (1966).
Van der Linde, J. M. *Het Visioen van Herrnhut en het Apostolaat der Moravische Broeders in Suriname 1735–1863.* Paramaribo: Kersten, 1956.
Zeefuik, K. A. *Herrnhutter Zending en Haagse Maatschappij 1820–1867.* Utrecht: Elinkwijk, 1973.

6. Studies on "Independent Churches"

Barrett, D. B. *Schism and Renewal in Africa: An Analysis of Six Thousand Contemporary Religious Movements.* London: Oxford Univ. Press, 1968.

Daneel, M. L. *The Background and Rise of the Southern Shona Independent Churches.* Den Haag: Mouton, 1971.

Foster, R. S. *The Sierra Leone Church, A Contemporary Study: An Independent African Church.* London: SPCK, 1961.

Haliburton, G. M. *The Prophet Harris and His Work in Ivory Coast and Western Ghana.* London, 1966.

Hayward, Victor E. W. "African Independent Church Movements." *Research Pamphlet No. 11, Commission on World Mission and Evangelism.* Geneva: World Council of Churches, 1963.

Hollenweger, W. *Pentecost Between Black and White.* Belfast: Christian Journals Ltd., 1974.

Knoob, W. *Afrikanisch-Christliche Bewegungen unter den Bantu.* Diss. Univ. of Cologne, 1961.

Martin, M. L. "Prophetism in the Congo: Origin and Development of an Independent African Church." *Ministry Theological Review for Africa* 8 (October, 1968).

Oosthuizen, G. C. *Post-Christianity in Africa: A Theological and Anthropological Study.* Grand Rapids: Eerdmans, 1968.

————. "The Misunderstanding of the Holy Spirit in the Independent Movements in Africa." In *Christusprediking in de Wereld.* Kampen: J. H. Kok, 1965.

Sundkler, B. G. M. *Bantu Prophets in South Africa.* London: Oxford Univ. Press, 1961.

————. *The Christian Ministry in Africa.* London: SCM Press, 1962.

Turner, H. W. *An African Independent Church: The Church of the Lord.* 2 vols. Oxford: Clarendon Press, 1967.

————. "Problems in the Study of African Churches." *Numen* 13 (1966).

————. "Profile through Preaching." *Research Pamphlet No. 13, Commission on World Mission and Evangelism.* Geneva: World Council of Churches, 1965.

Webster, J. B. *The African Churches Among the Yoruba: 1888–1922.* London: Oxford Univ. Press, 1964.

Welborn, F. B. and Ogot, S. A. *A Place to Feel at Home: A Study of Two Independent Churches in Western Kenya.* London: Oxford Univ. Press, 1966.

CHAPTER X

A Brief Survey of Ecumenical Organizations in Asia, Africa, Latin America, the Caribbean, and the Pacific Islands

Having discussed in the last chapter the matter of how to write the history of "young" churches in the various continents, a natural sequel would be to give a survey of the history of these churches in the present chapter. This being obviously impossible in an introduction such as this, I can only refer the reader to the survey books and specialized studies I have already mentioned. I do want to give, in however brief compass, an overview of the various regional conferences and councils of churches which have been formed in these continents. I do not do this because I believe the heart of church life beats there. Local churches are the real centers, and ecumenical organizations, though they can modestly aid in stimulating local churches, may never become their substitutes. For that matter, large numbers of churches, especially in Africa and Latin America, are not even affiliated with these organizations. I do this only because as far as I know such a survey has never been done.

THE CHRISTIAN CONFERENCE OF ASIA

Hans-Ruedi Weber's outstanding book *Asia and the Ecumenical Movement 1895–1961* provides a look at the events both before and shortly after the founding of the Christian Conference of Asia. As in many other parts of the world, the ecumenical youth organizations such as the World Student Christian Federation, the YMCA and the YWCA gave rise to still other ecumenical organizations. John Mott, whose name is associated with so many ecumenical and missionary organizations, paid a visit to China in 1895 and for the rest of his life was fully involved with the developments in Asia. Twelve years later, in 1907, the World Student Christian Federation held its first Asiatic conference in Tokyo, Japan, and still another in Peking in 1922.

Asians who were part of the staff of the WSCF and who later encouraged greater Asian participation in the ecumenical movement include:

> *Sara Chakko* (1905–1954): leader in the emancipation of women in India and later one of the presidents of the World Council of Churches.

M. M. Thomas: staff member of the WSCF from 1947 to 1950; later chairman of the executive committee of the World Council of Churches.

T. H. Ting: staff member from 1948 to 1951; presently Anglican bishop of Nanking and unofficial contact person with the ecumenical movement.

U Kyaw Than: from 1950 to 1956, administrative member of the World Federation; subsequent to that, secretary of the East Asia Christian Conference.

H. Daniel: from 1951 to 1953, staff member of the World Federation; later, secretary for Urban and Industrial Mission for the East Asia Christian Conference; since 1973 adjunct general secretary of the Christian Conference of Asia.

D. T. Niles: once chairman of the World Federation; in the years preceding his death in 1970 a chairman of the World Council of Churches; leading figure in the birth of the East Asia Christian Conference.

Though there are a host of other names which could be mentioned, I singled these people out to show that the World Student Christian Federation was an excellent breeding ground and training school for later participation in the ecumenical movement. This fact is nowhere more obvious than in the remarkable first regional conference of the World Federation held in Tjiteureup, Indonesia in 1933. In many ways this meeting was a precursor of the East Asia Christian Conference. Moreover, as Weber's book so clearly shows, the YMCA and YWCA were also important crossroads in the regional ecumenical traffic, especially in India, China, and Japan. The YMCAs were halfway houses between church and world, training grounds for future native leaders, launching pads for new initiatives, and places for manifesting Christian unity. Among the leaders in the YMCA organization in Asia were T. Z. Koo from China, who served as secretary first for the YMCA and later for the World Federation; K. T. Paul from India; and Leung from Hongkong who laid important groundwork for the future East Asia Christian Conference.

Years of Preparation

Already prior to the Second World War the International Missionary Council tried to set up a Far Eastern office under the leadership of Dr. Warnshuis, one of its American secretaries. The attempt failed, however, because Asiatic Christians resented it as another Western initiative.

The events of the Second World War, the Japanese occupation in eastern Asia, and the acceleration of home rule in other parts of Asia — notably India — all brought about a fundamental turning point in ecclesiastical developments in Asia.

The moratorium on relations with the West which the pressure of events forced upon many churches in Asia served to increase the desire to forge much closer regional ties once the war was over. In 1948 Dr. Rajah B. Manikam, a highly capable Indian leader who later became a Lutheran bishop in India, was appointed to prepare for the formation of a joint committee composed of people from the East Asia Commission of Churches and the World Council of Churches. At the first preparatory conference held in Bangkok December 3–11, 1949, Manikam received official confirmation of his appointment and thereafter with great dedication set about his work of "gathering the scattered people of God together."

The conference in Bangkok was a poignant moment for the Asiatic churches; it was the first time they could convene and share with each other the recent hellish experiences of the Japanese war. The delegates were pained to learn that Bishop Ting and other Chinese delegates could not attend; their government had denied them passports. The pain of an absent Chinese delegation continues to this very day among the ranks of Christian Conference of Asia members.

One more preparatory conference was held in Prapat, Sumatra, in 1957 before the East Asia Conference of Churches officially came into existence at a meeting in Kuala Lumpur, Malaysia, in May, 1959. The official purpose for the existence of the EACC reads as follows:

> Believing that the purposes of God for the Churches in East Asia is life together in a common obedience to Him for the doing of His will in the world, the EACC is hereby constituted as an organ of continuing cooperation among the Churches and National Christian Councils in East Asia within the framework of the wider ecumenical movement.[1]

It shares with the World Council of Churches the same confessional basis.

This regional organization of churches bears no official relationship to the World Council of Churches. Some churches who neither are nor cannot yet become members of the World Council have been accepted into the ranks of the EACC members. But lack of official connection does not imply lack of close unofficial cooperation between the two organizations.

The former EACC (which now goes under the official name "The Christian Conference of Asia") has formed a whole range of commissions to take charge of a host of activities designed to bring about regional ecumenical cooperation. The chief areas of activity are: inter-church aid, regional international affairs, affairs relating to church and society, cooperation in proclaiming the gospel, stimulation of lay work, cooperation between men and women, and Christian literature and mass communication.

The CCA's domain of influence reaches as far west as Pakistan, north to Korea and Japan, and south to Australia and New Zealand. From the very beginning the churches of Australia and New Zealand were invited to join this ecumenical effort; having accepted, they have contributed a wealth of leadership talent throughout the years. The Rev. Alan Brash, who later became general secretary for inter-church aid in Geneva, for many years fulfilled a similar role for the EACC. Commenting on the presence of Australia and New Zealand, M. M. Thomas publicly declared at the Bangkok conference in 1964: "And let us hope that these churches will remain members of the fellowship of churches in Southeast Asia even when the tensions between rich and poor nations increase and the vast unpopulated areas of Australia are compared to the population explosion in Asia."

1. East Asia Christian Conference, *Constitution of the East Asia Christian Conference*, in *Witnesses Together: Inaugural Assembly of the East Asia Christian Conference*, ed. U Kyaw Than (Rangoon: East Asia Christian Conference, 1959), p. 17.

Activities

In the course of its short history the number of member churches in this conference increased from forty-eight to ninety-two so that it now represents Christians
numbering more than 38 million.

Here are some of the key figures in the preparatory years and the
first years of EACC existence. Dr. Rajah Manikam from India laid the real
groundwork for the organization from 1951 to 1956. Thereafter he served as
Lutheran bishop in Tranquebar until his death in 1970. The EACC's first chairman
was Dr. Enrique C. Sobrepena; his successor was Dr. D. J. Moses from India,
who still holds the title of honorary chairman. Dr. D. T. Niles from Ceylon also
exerted strong influence in his position as secretary during the decade from 1957 to
1967 and as chairman from 1967 until his death in 1970. U Kyaw Than from
Burma, previous to his work with the EACC, was professor of history in Rangoon
and a staff official for the WSCF. In 1967 he took over Niles' post as secretary and
served until 1973. During Than's time of service the secretariat's home office was
located in Bangkok.

Though I have no space to provide a complete report of the work being
done through all the various secretariats, I must single out two of the CCA's
activities for special attention, in part because they deserve much more attention
than they have up to this point received.

1. One of the most impressive CCA functions is its middleman work in
providing for the exchange of missionary and diaconal personnel among the
churches in Asia. In recent years many churches have been sending some of their
personnel beyond their own national borders to do missionary and diaconal work
elsewhere. Churches from India, Burma, Japan, the Philippines, and South Korea
are helping other churches in specific ecclesiastical tasks. The assumptions on
which this work is based are that sometimes Asians in one country understand
those in another country better, and furthermore that the tasks involved are often
so similar in both countries that the people from one can learn from the experience
of people in the other. See Kosuke Koyama's book *Waterbuffalo Theology* for
some striking illustrations of this truth. Financial support for such exchanges of
personnel comes from sources within the sending country, whenever possible, but
non-Asiatic missionary agencies also contribute to a fund designed to cover
situations where no money is available.

2. During the awful years of war in Southeast Asia, the EACC set up a
diaconal agency, the East Asia Christian Service, which brought help to people in
both North and South Vietnam, Laos and Cambodia. Through this unsung agency
Asian Christians bravely ignored the hazardous circumstances to bring medical
help, organize cooperatives for the fishermen of the Mekong delta region, help
villagers with agriculture, assist women with earning an income, etc. And when
the horrors of war had somewhat subsided there, this noble band in the East Asia
Christian Service offered its help to the victims of the confusion and danger in
Bangladesh.

One of the most poignant expressions of help in Vietnam was made by a
Japanese student who went to Saigon and organized aimless boys into a team of

shoe polishers. Their only means of identification was a sign on each of their boxes: East Asia Christian Service.

The world press never made much of the service's efforts; therefore I want to record them here lest they be forgotten.

EACC Becomes CCA (1973/74)

At a meeting in June, 1973, a resolution passed both to change the name of the East Asia Christian Conference to the Christian Conference of Asia and to make some other administrative changes. For reasons of age Professor Moses resigned his post as general chairman and Dr. T. B. Simatupang from Indonesia succeeded him. In June 1970 he was succeeded by the Rev. John Nakajima from Japan, who together with three other presidents holds the presidium.

Dr. Yap Kim Hao from Singapore has taken over U Kyaw Than's post as secretary, and he is now assisted by Rev. Harry Daniel from India and Rev. R. O'Grady from New Zealand.

Even the headquarters of the organization is no longer the same. The new offices of the CCA at 480 Lorang 2, Toa Payoh, Singapore 12, were officially opened on May 4, 1974. At the dedication Chairman Simatupang reminded his audience that the situation of the numerous churches throughout eastern Asia which function as minorities among the majority religions and ideologies is in many respects similar to the situation the New Testament churches faced. But there is one marked difference: churches today live in times of dynamic change which is shaking cultures and religions to the very foundations. It is possible, he added, that in years to come churches will have a threefold calling:

1. To persevere in spite of the various threats and temptations common to dispersed fellowships amid other religious communities and pressure from certain ideologies.
2. To exhibit a freedom and a unity based on love.
3. To join other people in the common struggle for freedom and unity by bringing to it a dimension which never even occurred to the others but comes only from the very heart of the gospel.

To borrow Simatupang's words, the CCA is no ecclesiastical Ministry of Foreign Affairs but rather a clearinghouse, a place to exchange information and render mutual service for the ambassadors of Christ in the countries of Asia and throughout the world.

THE PACIFIC CONFERENCE OF CHURCHES

The Oceanic islands in the Pacific consist of three separate groups: Polynesian islands in the east, Melanesian islands in the west, the Micronesian islands north of the equator. John Williams was the pioneer missionary to this region, beginning his work in 1817 and ending it in 1839, the victim of murder in the New Hebrides.

Following Williams's initial work Roman Catholic and Protestant churches sprang up throughout these hundreds of islands.

This extremely isolated region of the world only really became involved in ecumenical trafficking among the churches after American soldiers stationed there during the Second World War had become acquainted with these Christians and churches.

In 1961 both churches and missionary agencies working in Oceania convened at Malua in Samoa. It was a meeting which paved the way for a more permanent organization. The conference appointed a continuing committee with Rev. Vavae Toma as its temporary secretary. During his one-year appointment Toma toured the whole Oceanic region visiting churches and eliciting their interest and support for an official regional ecumenical organization. Finally, from May 25 to June 7, 1966, the Pacific Conference of Churches was officially inaugurated at a meeting in Lifou, a city in the Loyalty islands. The conference appointed Rev. Setareki Fiulovone, the president of the Methodist church on the Fiji archipelago, as its secretary and Dr. Sione A. Havea as its chairman. Since 1975 Rev. Posenai Musu has taken over as secretary.

The conference administration is made up of people from five different denominations from five different geographic sectors and has stimulated cooperation in such activities as education, the production of literature in both English and French, urban work, marital and family problems, and the Christian attitude toward custom and tradition.

Two events stand out during the days of inaugural celebration. First, the delegates paid a visit to Mau, the place where Rao, the Karotongan evangelist, began his work of bringing the gospel in the Lefau archipelago. It is noteworthy that churches in these islands were planted by evangelists from the Pacific itself. Second, an inter-insular and inter-church theological school was officially opened in Suwa, thanks largely to financial help from the Theological Education Fund. A school such as this can do much to answer a problem which the churches in these far-flung islands have faced from their very beginning — a lack of communication.

The Papua churches from the former Australian New Guinea (now Niugini) did not participate in the inauguration of the PCC since they chose to be represented in the recently organized Melanesian Council. Since then, however, they have taken up contact with the PCC.

PCC is still a fledgling organization which in days to come will have to translate its words into deeds.

THE MIDDLE EAST COUNCIL OF CHURCHES

In 1906 a group of Christian missionaries convened in Cairo to discuss their work among the Muslims. A second (in Lucknow, 1911) and third conference (on the Mount of Olives, 1924) followed, and these two conferences in turn gave birth in the year 1927 to the Council for West-Asia and North America. In 1929 the council was rechristened the Near East Christian Council for Missionary Cooperation.

Since the member churches of the Near East Council were independent, there was considerable pressure to change it into the Near East Council of

Churches. Since 1964 this council of churches has been headquartered in Beirut, Lebanon. Its secretary is a Coptic Evangelical Christian pastor, Rev. Albert Isteero.

The NECC has made substantial contributions in such areas as theological education, Christian literature, medical work, and — its important specialty — communication with the Muslim community through a study program. For three years the famed Kenneth Cragg served as full-time director of this program and thereafter on a half-time basis. His books *The Call of the Minaret, The Rock and the Dome, Sandals at the Mosque,* and *The Privilege of Man* were born out of his living contacts with the Muslim world in the Middle East. Under his inspiration other scholars are now continuing Cragg's work.

The NECC until recently has been plagued with one glaring weakness: the ancient churches of the Middle East such as the Greek Orthodox, Coptic Orthodox (not to be confused with the Coptic Evangelical church), etc., refused to have anything to do with the undertaking, and therefore its only members were those churches which Western missionary agencies founded in the nineteenth century.

This situation caused no small irritation among Middle Eastern churches and often frustrated NECC efforts. Finally, after years of patient and careful preparation done by Mr. Laham from the Greek Orthodox side and by so many others, in ceremonies held from May 28 to 30, 1974, the Greek Orthodox church and the Oriental Orthodox church (which included the old Egyptian Coptic church) joined with the other smaller churches who had comprised the NECC. Bishop Samuel of the Coptic church spoke at the inauguration of the new organization now called the Middle East Council of Churches. Recalling that the NECC roots lay in that preparatory conference on the Mount of Olives in 1924 headed by foreign missionaries, he said: "That day is now past. The time has come to form a fellowship of churches in which the national churches participate." No less than ninety delegates and advisors from twenty different churches attended this organizing meeting in Nicosia on the island of Cyprus.

The work of the MECC officially began on September 1, 1974. Rev. Isteero, who had already given ten years of service as secretary for the NECC and worked so diligently for its expansion, continued in the same post for the new organization. Plans are to hold a general convention every three years, though an executive committee of fifteen members from five denominations will make the decisions which call for more immediate attention.

During its short life the MECC has already become involved in work among Palestinian refugees, in dialogue and witness, in radio (carried on jointly with the Radio Voice of the Gospel in Addis Ababa), in Christian education, in worldwide diaconia, and in work among young people and students.

The MECC was born during explosive times in the Middle East. Bishop Samuel, commenting on this situation, said:

> Together we must pray and work hard to determine the spiritual and material needs of our fellowships and devise plans for churches in our region of the world to meet these needs. We must offer to our fellow men the Gospel of our Lord and thus give concrete expression to his liberating service, his saving call, and his healing power over soul and body. In this

way we shall be training the beams of his enlightening Word on the needs of repressed people.

THE ALL-AFRICA CONFERENCE OF CHURCHES

In Africa as in Asia it took many long years of preparation to finally bring about a continental organization of churches. In his book *Ecumenical Beginnings in Protestant World Mission: A History of Comity*, R. Pierce Beaver describes the many comity agreements which the various missionary organizations concluded between themselves in Africa toward the end of the nineteenth century and at the beginning of the twentieth. "Comity" comes from the Latin word *comitas*, which means courtesy, politeness, friendliness. When applied to missions, comity refers to those agreements between the missionary organizations to not transgress the geographic boundaries of each mission's work and, where possible, to arrive at a division of labor on the one hand and cooperation on the other in certain activities. These agreements were the first steps, however hesitant and unsure, to bring an end to all the division and confusion and achieve a more unified church.

Without a doubt these comity agreements provided the initial stimulus toward organizing ecclesiastical fellowships in western, southern, and particularly eastern Africa. Nevertheless, their nature was more of accord between the western mission boards than of genuine ecumenical relations between African churches who view their calling to the whole of their own continent.

The missionary councils which arose in response to the Edinburgh Conference in 1910 and the International Missionary Council several years later provided additional stimulus toward cooperation. From C. P. Grove's report in Volume 4 of his *The Planting of Christianity in Africa*, one can see the influence of these councils in such places as Sierra Leone, Gold Coast (now Ghana), Nigeria, Congo, Tanzania, Kenya, South Africa, Southern Rhodesia, Northern Rhodesia, Nyassaland, etc. All of these councils were in one form or another affiliated with the International Missionary Council.

It is so easy many years later to fault these missionary councils for their paternalistic structure — one can be so wise after the event! — but anyone who cares to make these accusations must also realize that these bodies in their various regions contributed greatly to the feeling among Christians that they were one fellowship in their continent and also had ties with the worldwide fellowship. It is true, however, that the deep experience of the Second World War and the process of political decolonization made church leaders realize that an ecclesiastical decolonization was also the order of the day. These councils had become obsolete, were disappearing, and had to make way for a new structure allowing for genuine regional ecumenism.

Zachariah K. Matthews

One of the first to sense that such developments were necessary was Professor Z. K. Matthews, a pioneer crusader for a new All-Africa Conference of Churches. In fact, he was the presiding chairman at the inaugural meeting of this new regional ecumenical body in Kampala, Uganda, on April 20, 1963, and also gave an address as a visiting delegate from the World Council of Churches. Matthews along with Pastor Pierre Benignus (the leader of French-speaking African churches in this movement) were the actual guiding geniuses of this new movement.

In an earlier stage of African ecclesiastical history few people ever viewed Africa as a single and complete entity and dreamed and worked to bring about a corresponding unity among African churches. One of the lonely exceptions was J. H. Oldham (1874–1969), the Scottish mission strategist, whose labors in the International Missionary Council and later in the Phelps-Stokes Commission of Education contributed so much toward bringing African churches together in the final days of colonialism and preparing them for the new days ahead.

I must also mention in this connection James E. K. Aggrey (1875–1927) from Ghana who toured Africa frequently, seeking to raise the level of education, to improve race relations, and to stimulate cooperation among African churches for the benefit of the whole continent.

Both of these men belonged to the end of the so-called ethical-political era; Western missions still controlled African churches.

But a new era arrived when numerous new independent African states arose and independent churches confronted the task of reorienting themselves to be ready for the new days ahead. Z. K. Matthews was a real leader during this transition. Since so little of Matthews's life and work is generally known, I shall try to sketch both areas briefly.

Matthews came from the Xhosa tribe and was the son of a diamond mine worker in Kimberley, South Africa. After his elementary schooling in Kimberley and secondary education in Lovedale, he enrolled as one of the first black students in the South African Native College in Fort Hare in the little town of Alice. During my visit in 1970 to the federal theological seminary in Alice (home also of Fort Hare University), I saw in the Anglican chapel a stained-glass window depicting a black student intently listening to his white bishop explaining the Bible. The student was Z. K. Matthews and the bishop was Edmund Smithe who had such a profound impact on Matthews's life.

In 1925 Matthews was appointed director of Adams College in Natal. Meanwhile he continued his studies in law at the University of South Africa, and in 1934 with the help of Dr. Loram received a scholarship to Yale University where he earned a master's degree in cultural anthropology. The Yale experience was Matthews's first stepping stone toward acquiring one of his hallmarks — a worldwide orientation. Some time later Matthews took a study leave to do work with Malinowsky, an anthropologist at the University of London.

Matthews's great intellectual distinction brought him an invitation from Union Theological Seminary in New York to spend a year there as visiting lecturer. After his return to South Africa he first became lector in native law and cultural anthropology and then later professor and head of the department of African Studies in Fort Hare.

Matthews's political activity during those years brought him into conflict with the recently introduced apartheid policy and the Bantu Education Act. Matthews's political involvement reached back to the days when Jan Smuts was president of the Union of South Africa and Matthews was member of the Native Representative Council whose job was to advise the government in matters relating to black Africans. But once Matthews became convinced that the government was not taking the advice of this moderate body seriously, he resigned and joined the African National Congress, the Luthuli party. Matthews headed the party's Capetown division and openly opposed apartheid. Matthews was not one of those black political leaders who wanted to exchange one form of apartheid for another, replacing all-white power by all-black power; to his dying day he called for cooperation in working to achieve a mutual respect for the rights of all. He was the farthest thing from a demagogue; he was a servant of reconciliation between races. But this posture made him suspect on both sides, the apartheid people seeing him as a communist and the more radical blacks judging him as too moderate.

Once the apartheid law had passed, especially its provisions for education, Matthews and the government entered a period of sharp conflict. He (along with many others) was arrested and tried for high treason (1956); during this long, drawn-out affair he maintained a deep spirit of inner contentment and confidence and finally was pronounced totally innocent of the charges. Through this, however, he and eight of his colleagues lost their positions at the university and the pension rights connected with them.

Matthews then set up his offices as a "people's lawyer" and also accepted the position of vice president at the Institute for Race Relations in Johannesburg. In 1961 he delivered his famous address, "African Awakening and the Universities," in which he argued that prior to the Bantu Education Act the South African universities had cooperated in producing leaders for the whole of Africa but apartheid had now rendered this task completely impossible. Thereafter he left his native South Africa, feeling deeply disappointed at being forced to exile but hoping that he could still in some way help his continent and its people. His wish came true far beyond the reaches of his wildest imagination and prayers, for he became African secretary for the Division of Inter-Church Aid, Refugee, and World Service of the World Council of Churches. He now had a better-than-ever opportunity to gain firsthand knowledge of the various churches and societies throughout Africa and to assist them in preparing for the coming AACC. Traveling with Sir Hugh Foot (later Lord Caradon), the United Kingdom's ambassador to the United Nations, Matthews visited almost every country in all of Africa and drafted for them the Ecumenical Program for Emergency Aid. In that capacity he represented the World Council at the founding of the AACC in Kampala on April 20, 1963.

Matthews's years working for the World Council were busy and eventful. He became a respected member of the Commission for International Affairs and a valuable resource person on African matters. He coordinated the symposium study, *Responsible Government in a Revolutionary Age,* and delivered it to the Conference on Church and Society in 1966. By this time he had become an internationally respected lawyer, anthropologist, teacher, statesman, and ecumenical visionary and strategist.

But all of his efforts would not have been possible without the support of his sympathetic and intelligent wife, Frida. She was, like Matthews, also a black African, but from a different tribe. According to all the authorities, Sotho-speaking tribesmen simply have nothing to do with their Nguni-speaking counterparts, but Matthews and his wife joyously bridged the gap together. Matthews was a firm believer in detribalization, not retribalization.

Then in 1966 Matthews's former student in Fort Hare, Sir Seretse Khama, who had become president of Botswana, invited his one-time teacher to become his country's ambassador to both the United Nations and the United States; he accepted these appointments convinced that they would place him in a position where he could do much for Africa and become a spokesman for change in South Africa. Regrettably, his health deteriorated while in America, and in 1968 he died during an operation. The President of the United States made his own airplane, Air Force One, available to transport Matthews's body back to Botswana, where a completely unexpected host of friends awaited its arrival and accompanied it to the burial on May 17, 1968.

Matthews was a pioneer in so many respects — in ecumenical relations, in the African quest for self-expression, and in the relations between church and society.

The Preparatory Period

Shortly after the International Missionary Council held its world missions conference in Ghana (Achimota) in 1958, a group of African church leaders from twenty-five nations met in Ibadan, Nigeria, along with representatives of the World Council who were invited guests. These leaders came from as far west as Sierra Leone, as far east as Ethiopia, as far north as the Sudan, and as far south as South Africa. Z. K. Matthews and Pierre Benignus were the guiding geniuses, and under their leadership the conference appointed a committee with Sir Ibiam from Nigeria as chairman and Dr. Donald J. S. M'Timkulu from South Africa as secretary, to implement the conference's decision to press ahead with plans for an All-Africa Conference of Churches.

For Africa, 1963 (the year of the AACC founding) was a long way from 1958. In 1958 only Ethiopia, Liberia and South Africa were independent. By 1961 twenty-two states representing a combined population of 130 million people had achieved independence, and this fact which loomed large in the background of the committee deliberations continually confronted it with the question "What role should the churches play in this formative stage?" During these years the committee organized a series of special conferences on literature and education.

The All-Africa Conference of Churches was officially inaugurated on April 20, 1963, in Kampala, Uganda, exactly 150 years after the birth of David Livingstone. At the inaugural Z. K. Matthews spoke these eloquent words: "This is the closing of the circle; now we are coming together again. In Livingstone's time the different denominations, the different churches and missions were established on the African continent. Now the circle is closed. We have come together again."[2] Throughout the assembly hall African drums beat jubilantly to announce the founding of the conference.

---

2. From Z. K. Matthews's speech to the inaugural assembly of the AACC, included in *Drumbeats from Kampala* (London: Lutterworth Press, 1963), p. 10.

In the first general meeting of the conference which followed, M'Timkulu was elected chairman of the General Committee of seven members elected from various regions and churches throughout Africa. Dr. Samuel Amissah from Ghana became the general secretary in 1965, and in that same year the headquarters was transferred from the extreme south (Mindolo, Zambia) to a much more central location (Nairobi, Kenya).

Here are a few facts about this ecumenical organization from the year 1974:

Membership: More than 100 member churches and councils from thirty-one countries.

Basis: "The All Africa Conference of Churches is a fellowship of churches which confess the Lord Jesus Christ as God and *only* Saviour according to the Scriptures and therefore seek to fulfill together their common calling to the glory of the one God, Father, Son, and Holy Spirit."[3]

Like the Christian Conference of Asia, the AACC has taken its basis from the World Council of Churches.

Functions:

1. To keep before the churches and National Christian Councils the demands of the Gospel pertaining to their life and mission, for evangelism, for witness in society, for service and for unity, and to this end to promote consultation and action among the churches and Councils.
2. To provide for a common programme of study and research.
3. To encourage close relationships and mutual sharing of experience among the churches in Africa through visits, consultation and conference, and the circulation of information.
4. To assist the churches in finding, sharing, and placing personnel and utilizing other resources for the most effective prosecution of their common task.
5. To assist the churches in their common work of leadership training, lay and clerical, for the task of the churches today.
6. Without prejudice to its own autonomy, to collaborate with the World Council of Churches and other appropriate agencies in such ways as may be mutually agreed.[4]

General and regional secretaries. Working out of the AACC headquarters in Nairobi, the general secretary of the organization, who at present is Canon Burgess Carr from Liberia, coordinates all activities of the AACC. Under him there are divisions for administration and personnel matters. The AACC also maintains a regional secretary for French-speaking Africa whose headquarters is in Togo. James Lawson, the associate general secretary, holds this position and travels the whole of French-speaking Africa in his work.

Though the language and cultural barriers between French- and English-speaking Africans at first made cooperation slow and cumbersome, the sense of cohesiveness between the two has become much stronger in recent years.

3. *Drumbeats from Kampala,* p. 63.
4. Ibid., pp. 63–64.

Activities

The AACC spreads its work among diverse "clusters," as it calls them, each with its own secretary. The first cluster involves questions and issues relating to the expression of the Christian faith in Africa and patterns of relationship between the churches there and in other parts of the world. This subject is increasingly coming into the limelight of discussion. This cluster also treats the question of the AACC's approach to the so-called independent churches — a matter which Canon Carr is emphasizing much more than did his predecessor, Dr. Amissah.

The second cluster includes the secretariats for family life, refugees, development and education, and work in urban and industrial society. Until September, 1968, baroness C. M. van Heemstra held the post of Secretary for Marriage and Family Life. Her book, *Thuis in Afrika (At Home in Africa),* is her exciting report of the various aspects of African family living and its attendant problems — bride price, choice of partner, polygamy, etc. The work done by this secretariat led to a very important consultation held from February 12 to April 10, 1963, in the ecumenical center in Kitwe, Zambia, on "The Christian Home and Family Life." Its report was published in Geneva in 1963 and is filled with advice to the churches on virtually every facet of this thorny issue. The present secretary of this division is Mercy Aguta.

The third cluster is related to the training center for work in radio, television and journalism. Its secretary is Canon Y. Olumide.

The AACC has increased its role in the political situations in Africa. For example, in 1969 the president of the Sudan, Numayeri, appealed to the AACC to join with the Commission on International Affairs of the World Council in serving as mediators between the official government in Khartoum and an organization of blacks in the south, the Anya' nya. It worked: an accord was reached on February 27, 1972 and signed on March 12, 1972. To be sure, the situation remains explosive and is much more complicated than many realize; nevertheless, peace was reached, and rehabilitation began on a massive scale in the southern region through the team efforts of the AACC and the appropriate agencies of the World Council.

In another political dispute the AACC took a much clearer stand against Portuguese colonialism and in favor of national expression for Guinea Bissau, Mozambique, and Angola. It also sided with the black people of Zimbabwe (Rhodesia) and Namibia.

At its general assembly meeting in Lusaka the AACC gave clear support to a solution to the disputes between Portugal and her colonies which would insure their ultimate independence from the former colonial power. As for Namibia and Zimbabwe, the AACC has come out in favor of structural changes which would put an end to the suppression of the black majority by the white minority. On the South African situation the AACC is joining its voice with many others both inside and outside the country in calling for full participation of all groups in the real centers of power and responsibility.

The General Assemblies

Though the most important work of the AACC is being carried on through its various secretariats and its network of relations throughout the whole African continent, the general assemblies are in a sense the high points of all the continuing work and set the course for the following years.

The first general assembly, as was mentioned above, was held in Kampala in 1963 subsequent to the inauguration. The second meeting convened in French-speaking Africa in the Ivory Coast city of Abidjan in 1969 under the theme "Working with Christ in Africa Today." Its official report was issued from Abidjan in 1969: *Engagement: la deuxième assemblée de la Céta.* In one of the most important speeches delivered at the assembly Dr. Eteki Mboumoua spoke on "Working with Christ in the Cultural Revolution." He incisively exposed how the top layer of African society has become an elite which shares in a culture that at its core is either Anglo-Saxon or French in nature while the great masses of people are scarcely allowed any cultural expression at all. The real questions are: How can we work to insure cultural expression for all people and serve to advance a culture that takes account of both the ancient native culture, seeking to preserve what is valuable in it, and the developments in a world civilization which is more and more being stamped by technology and science? In all of this how can Christians best carry out their work as critics of culture?

I shall close this survey of the AACC with a few brief notes on the third general assembly meeting in Lusaka in 1974. A general report of the proceedings can be found elsewhere; I want only to point out some of the most important aspects of what is called the "engagement of Lusaka."

Lusaka and the Struggle for Racial and Political Justice

The Lusaka assembly emphasized much more than the previous two the need for actual participation in the struggle for racial and political justice. The delegates met in Zambia, itself one of the first bridgeheads of a free and independent Africa. Kenneth Kaunda, freedom fighter, Christian humanist, and president of the nation of Zambia, not only addressed the convention meeting in his country but continued to exert great influence on its proceedings. Representatives of the freedom movements were present.

The delegates met on the eve of the revolution in Portugal and the talks which would lead to independence for all its former colonies: Guinea Bissau, Mozambique, and Angola. The AACC supported the work of the freedom movements and made an earnest appeal to Portugal to take steps to hand over the reins of power, and called its member churches to support pastoral and missionary efforts in the freedom movements' ranks "in order that the message of Christ's total liberation may also be heard." It coupled this with an appeal to Christians both within and outside Africa to discontinue all political, economic, military, and any other form of help to structures which house oppression, for "these structures form an obstacle to the fulfilling of God's plan for full freedom and justice for all humanity."[5] With the crisis between Portugal and her former colonies now past, it

5. Lusaka Conference of the AACC.

is evident that the cutting edge of these declarations must now be applied to the situations in Namibia (Southwest Africa), South Africa and Zimbabwe (Rhodesia).

Lusaka and the Struggle against Tribalism

The Lusaka general assembly probed more deeply than ever into the nettlesome problem of tribalism, a phenomenon which throughout Africa continually threatens to explode and destroy the wider bands which hold men together. The general assembly did not categorically condemn tribal allegiance, for it recognized that a feeling of kinship with one's people gives a person a certain anchor, a feeling of identity and belonging. But this feeling of belonging often turns into "tribalness" (a closed tribe feeling) and tribalness in turn degenerates into "tribalism" (an exaltation of one's tribe and its expressions to the denigration of others).

Lusaka did not support an effort to stylishly explain tribalism in terms of class opposition. It rather saw the roots of tribalism in an "underdeveloped vision of man" which sees him only as a member of the tribe but not of the whole human family. Furthermore, this assembly noted the typical features of tribalism: a stiff opposition to renewal and change and an excessive attachment to traditional customs which results from lack of openness 'o developments outside the tribe.

It also suggested possible ways of counteracting the unhealthful effect of this strong allegiance by toning down the language; for example, by replacing the word "tribe" with the phrase "smaller fellowship." Other suggested antidotes were the teaching of languages other than one's own tribal language, devising exchange programs for the young people of the tribes, the planning of joint activities between tribes sponsored by the churches, and the development of an adequate view of man based on the only worthy norm of genuine humanity, the gospel of Jesus Christ.

Lusaka acted properly in not evading this touchy issue. But we from our side in Europe and America must not make the common error of thinking that tribalism is unique to Africa. In many respects National Socialism in Germany was an old German tribalism revived and cloaked in modern garb. The same is true for state Shintoism in Japan. Every people and community must learn to put away that awful tendency toward self-exaltation which comes to expression in countless old and new forms of tribalism.

Lusaka and the "Independent Churches"

The Lusaka assembly was much more open to the independent church movements than Abidjan had been. Many of these churches have become members of the AACC, and from the AACC side there is an increasing willingness to join with these churches in reviewing the positive worth and value of the ancient African tribal religions which, when reborn and properly integrated into the framework of Christian faith, can do much to enhance the Christian liturgy through dance, music, and other artistic expressions.

Lusaka and the Appeal for a Moratorium in Receiving Foreign Financial and Manpower Assistance

An appeal for a moratorium such as Lusaka issued is nothing new. The world missions conference held in Bangkok the year before issued the same appeal, even though the echo was not so loud. In fact, many Asian churches have in the past suspended relations with foreign Western churches — in effect, proclaiming a moratorium. During the Second World War this happened, and when the war was over, these relations were restored — but with one important difference: the paternalistic structures were gone. In China a moratorium came in cold, brutal fashion, from the top down. No church in Asia wants that ever to happen again. Moreover, Asian churches are tiny minorities among the millions of people surrounding them; they need help, and any financial assistance they receive from the outside is interpreted not as an urge to dominate but as a gesture of hearty friendship.

But Africa has not experienced many of these changes; for her the structures have remained much more paternalistic. Therefore, Lusaka gave a drumbeat call for moratorium.

When we think of a moratorium, we must not interpret it as a permanent abolition but as a temporary suspension needed to achieve new patterns of relationships.

Candidly speaking, the language of their appeal often makes it appear that these Africans are calling for the relationships to be put to death rather than for them to be suspended temporarily. Dr. John Gatu, the chairman of the AACC, repeatedly and emphatically denied this. The goal of this new course is more mature relationships, not a total abolition of them.

In the Lusaka statements on this issue I detect two factors. One of them deals with the matter of self-reliance. The moratorium debate was designed to bring about a sense of self-reliance in the African churches so that through it they could gain a new understanding of the catholicity of the church. In the words of the secretary-general, "Too long the catholicity of the church has been identified with the technological and mercantile culture of the West." Genuine catholicity will emerge only when the African churches become aware of their own unique and worthwhile place within the worldwide church. Genuine exchange and communication depends on African churches recovering their stolen identity.

The second factor I detect involves the matter of redistributing financial sources. Burgess Carr, the secretary-general, cited the example of West Africa where no less than sixty-one percent of the churches' budget goes toward paying foreign missionary personnel. In this context, the moratorium means an appeal to invest these monies into programs of a more local nature run by Africans rather than to earmark it for foreign personnel.

It would be folly for us in the West to think that this moratorium means that Western money and personnel are no longer desired or necessary. The real purpose is to set out on a course which will bring about a reorientation in inter-church aid. Carr concluded by saying that the whole idea is useless without Africa from her side taking steps to train leaders and to generate a sense of self-sufficiency. It is a simple fact that Western churches are still being asked and will continue to be asked for their financial and manpower assistance. The very fact that the AACC requested help with its own budget is a good example. Furthermore, it is well to remind ourselves that organizations such as the AACC do not in the final analysis make the decisions for their member churches in areas such as this.

THE UNION LATINO AMERICANA PROVISORIA PRO UNIDAD EVANGELICA

Up to this time numerous obstacles have blocked efforts to build up a strong network of ecumenical relations in Latin America. There are many reasons for this; I will cite but a few.

At the world missionary conference in Edinburgh in 1910 the Anglican church, considering Latin America a bulwark of Iberian Roman Catholicism, advised the conference — rather unwisely, in retrospect — not to incorporate the Latin American churches in the network of relationships being constructed among the Protestant churches. These advisors completely disregarded the fact that Brazil already in the sixteenth century and the whole of Latin America by the nineteenth century had received Dutch, English, and North American Protestant missionary agencies. They realized too little that for serious dialogue with the Roman Catholic church to prove to be a blessing depends upon a previously erected ecumenical infra-structure. The upshot of this unwise decision was that less ecumenically inclined, even anti-ecumenical, Protestant organizations moved industriously into Latin America and filled the lacuna. Thus later ecumenical efforts had one strike against them before they were ever undertaken.

Fortunately the Commission for World Mission and Evangelism of the World Council of Churches broke with this unhealthful tradition. Not only did it gather in Mexico City for its general assembly meeting in 1963 as a gesture of new openness to Latin America, but it also gave leading Latin American Protestants like Gonzales-Castillo Cardenas from Colombia, G. Baez-Camargo from Mexico, and Emilio Castro from Uruguay full opportunity to present the needs and challenges of Latin America. This they did in outstanding fashion.

Yet candor compels one to admit that Protestant (and even Roman Catholic) Christianity is polarized worse in "turbulent Latin America," to borrow José Míguez Bonino's phrase, than anywhere else in the world. Tensions between conservatives and progressives, revolutionaries and denominationalists, revivalists and charismatics are increasing, not decreasing. All this hinders ecumenical efforts.

Couple these reasons with the facts of great geographic distances and differences in culture and language in Latin America, and they all spell trouble and difficulty for ecumenical work.

Nevertheless, a modest ecumenical organization has been born. Its title for the time being is *Union Latino Americana Provisoria Pro Unidad Evangelica* (abbreviated UNELAM). The basis for this organization was laid in the "Declaration of Cordoba" in 1963 by six chairmen representing the national councils of churches in Argentina, Brazil, Chile, Peru, Mexico, and Uruguay. The affiliate organizations in Puerto Rico and Cuba lent their moral support. Already in 1949 a number of delegates to the first Latin American Evangelical Conference had expressed the desire for a continental council of churches. But no decision was taken either then or at the second conference held in Lima in 1961. UNELAM was finally born in 1965 but still retained the term "Provisional" in its name. During the stormy period from 1965 to 1972, Rev. Emilio Castro, a former Methodist preacher from Montevideo, served as its secretary, traveling the entire continent to build up contacts and all the while facing denominations which were pitched for battle against each other and against their common opponent, Roman Catholicism.

Castro's dedication led to a third Latin American Evangelical Conference, held in Buenos Aires July 13–19, 1969. Representatives came from forty-three denominations in twenty-three lands, including for the first time a contingent from the Pentecostal movement. The person of Rev. Manuel de Mello from the gigantic Pentecostal church in Sao Paulo is being seen and heard more and more in ecumenical gatherings.

From the very outset the union maintained relations with three other regional ecumenical organizations in Latin America: ISAL (Church and Society in Latin America) which Dr. Julio de Santa Ana both initiated and served as its secretary, the MEC (The Christian Student Movement), and the CELADEC (Latin American Evangelical Committee on Christian Education).

In June, 1970, UNELAM became an official regional organization and dropped the term "provisional" from its official name. It thus became the Latin American counterpart to the Christian Conference of Asia and the All-Africa Conference of Churches. How noteworthy that the decision to organize officially and permanently was taken at the request of the third Latin American Evangelical Conference and that this conference mandated the newly founded UNELAM to prepare for a fourth evangelical conference in Mexico City in 1976.

In his moving letter of resignation, Emilio Castro wrote that UNELAM distinguished itself as an organism that, however tiny, was devoted to "a passionate love for a church which is fully cognizant of its responsibility *in* Latin America and devoted to Christ in the Latin American situation." The Buenos Aires conference expressed this so well in its theme taken from Romans 1:14: "Indebted to All." This sense of becoming debtors to Latin American society led UNELAM to underscore the need for freeing churches from the colonial shackles of North American domination and making them other than extensions of North American activity. It also led UNELAM to devote serious attention to the social and economic problems plaguing Latin American society and to the search for a new relationship with the Roman Catholic church which is now in such ferment. This theme led UNELAM to greater contact with the new movement among Roman Catholic priests striving for a worthier expression of social justice. And finally, it led to a proclamation of the gospel through new means and with increased allegiance.

Rev. Castro and his assistants had to row against a strong anti-ecumenical current in their work. As Castro himself described the situation, "There was the fear of an imagined ecclesiastical imperialism imposed from the outside, a suspicion that church unity would be forcibly imposed. Others feared that modernism would control the course of theological thinking. Some organizations raised their voices in alarm against a movement that was out to create a Latin American conscience." To their credit, the members of this staff confronted these obstacles and slowly but surely worked to overcome them. Finally many Latin American churches came to see that striving for one's own identity within the worldwide fellowship absolutely does not proceed from a nationalistic desire to reject others but rather "from a genuine desire to cooperate *more deeply* than ever before."

UNELAM is active in many areas. Alberto Franco Diaz industriously leads a team of people devoted to publishing and distributing Christian literature and to coordinating efforts in the fields of books, periodicals, radio, television, and audiovisual aids. Furthermore, the members of ISAL are fully engaged in the fight on various fronts against economic exploitation and oppression.

Because UNELAM itself embraces a vast geographic territory, several sub-organizations have arisen in places like the Andes mountain range (headed by Dr. A. Fernandez Arlt), in Colombia and in Venezuela (headed by Juan Marcus Revera). Ever since 1974 Rev. Luis P. Bucafurco has been chairman of the main organization. Ever since Emilio Castro vacated his post as secretary-general to become director of the Commission for World Mission and Evangelism of the World Council in Geneva, Rev. Angel Luis Jaime has been secretary. Rev. Wilfrid Artin is treasurer.

UNELAM is still a very young organization, but it has grown enough to allow churches of the Reformation their positions within the worldwide body. And all this is happening in a day when both the Roman Catholic church and the churches of the Reformation are finally learning that their goal is not to fight each other but rather to join in answering God's call to serve his people on the Latin American continent and to work for his messianic kingdom.

THE CARIBBEAN CONFERENCE OF CHURCHES

For sixteen long years J. M. W. Schalkwijk, a former worker in Surinam who now teaches at the theological school in Jamaica, functioned as a temporary secretary who paved the way for a future Caribbean Conference of Churches. All his personal efforts in addition to those of many area churches were crowned with success when during November 13–16, 1973, the Caribbean Conference was inaugurated.

The Caribbean area is geographically vast and spread out. It embraces no less than fourteen separate lands and peoples whose roots lie in such diverse places as India, Africa, Indonesia, Spain, Portugal, the Netherlands, France, and England. Major religions abound — Hinduism, Buddhism, Islam, and Christianity — but the countless forms of magic and mysticism (including the Voodoo cult of Haiti) are also present. The Caribbean is indeed a microcosm of peoples.

The CCC itself is composed of sixteen different denominations spread over thirty islands and represents eight million Christians. The Roman Catholic church itself was involved in the planning for a future CCC, and when this new ecumenical organization was inaugurated, it joined the ranks and stood on par with all the other regional ecumenical bodies already discussed.

The theme of the inaugural conference was "God's Right Hand," and during those days Dr. Philip Potter, the present secretary-general of the World Council of Churches who himself was born in the Caribbean and worked there for years, spoke about God's judgment on the fact that his churches have abdicated their common prophetic role and consigned it to secular writers. Among the topics discussed at the conference were redistribution of power, development, and reconciliation. Thus, one can observe a definite accent on the struggle for social justice and human dignity.

The leaders of this regional ecumenical body desire to maintain close ties with Asia (via the Hindustans) and especially with the AACC in Africa. The present administration is comprised of three chairmen: Archbishop Samuel Carter from Jamaica; Dorinda Sampath, a Presbyterian from Trinidad; and Rev. Claude Cadagan, a Methodist from Antigua. Rev. Roy G. Neehall, a Presbyterian from Trinidad, is the secretary-general.

All of the regional organizations which I have attempted to describe in this chapter are still very young and therefore really only beginning to formulate their ecumenical initiatives.

The World Council of Churches has established a special secretariat to establish and maintain contact with the various national councils of churches and the regional bodies which were described in this chapter. During June and July of 1971, Rev. Victor Hayward, the World Council's secretary for these matters, called the delegates from these various regional and national organizations to a consultation to find better ways for these bodies to share experiences with each other and help each other to fulfill their common responsibility.

In bringing this chapter to a close I wish to categorically affirm that communication between Western churches and those in the regions discussed is the very elementary *ABC* of authentic ecumenical fellowship. Up to the Second World War too much traffic went in one direction. Delegates to the Oxford conference on church and society in 1937 had become so preoccupied with Western problems that finally Devanesen aptly commented that it appeared as though the delegates' interest stopped at the Bosporos and Dardanelles! But we now live in one world, a world which all of us together are coming to realize is basically an indivisible whole. To quote André Dumas, "Never before has mankind been so conscious of belonging to a family of brothers, brothers who ofttimes fight, but unavoidable brothers nonetheless and not strangers." One can mark the truth of his words in areas such as economics, the military, and ideology.

The world has grown to become interdependent and now confronts the choice between global self-destruction and survival. Through no decision or choice of their own the Christian churches dwell in this world which is fast becoming one, and if they do not work together in a worldwide fellowship, they neglect their calling. God, the Lord of both his church and his world, calls the church to represent mankind. To again borrow from Dumas, "Only when the church represents mankind can she *present* God to mankind."

This means that churches must set about searching for ways to communicate with each other throughout the world to fulfill their calling. Alas, the desire to do so is far less evident than one might reasonably expect. All our Western talk about the "third world" notwithstanding, we in the West simply have not taken seriously our responsibility to communicate. A deep bond must begin to grow, a sense that we simply cannot do without each other (Heb. 11:40). These regional organizations need contact with the worldwide *oikoumenē* represented by the World Council, but the World Council also needs them, lest its perspectives become too

Western, American, or European. And should those churches in the areas of the world discussed in this chapter, so recently delivered from the shackles of colonial domination, threaten to become snatched away into a new form of ideological exile, we in the West must warn them.

At certain times in history the pressure of events forced the church to abandon communication. Think, for example, of the ancient Syrian churches, the Millets, the closed fellowships in the Middle East, the Maronites, Nestorians, Copts, Greek Orthodox, Armenian Apostolic church, and so many more. For centuries they kept their distance from everyone else, but to both their joy and ours they are now beginning to flow with the ecumenical traffic. Now the pressure of isolation has come in new form upon the church in China and, in still different form, in Burma. But such isolation is abnormal. Churches living in vital union with their Lord, Jesus Christ, must talk with each other in all their rich diversity. When we do this, we in the West shall discover that we have so much to receive.

Churches in the West are crumbling. It may well be that churches in other areas of the world can help us in the West to quicken our steps as we search for church renewal. What is more, we in the West have so much to learn from the hearty faith and devoted lifestyle of so many Christians in other parts of the world. Listen to John Taylor, one of the most knowledgeable persons on African and Asian Christianity:

> Many people feel that the spiritual sickness in the West with its symptomatic division between the sacred and the secular, between the reasonable and the intuitive, and with its lonely individualism may perhaps be able to be cured by a rediscovery of the wisdom which the Christians in Asia and Africa have not yet discarded. By obediently answering God's call, the young churches can become a means by which the Holy Spirit desires to instruct his people everywhere how to be both in Christ and yet fully-involved participants in humanity, how to be completely wrapped up in the bundle of human living and yet one with the Lord our God.

Indeed we need each other to understand even a tiny bit of the length, height, breadth and depth of God's love which surpasses all our knowledge; to the same degree we need each other as we link arm in arm to serve as agents of reconciliation, instruments of forgiveness, and fighters for justice among mankind and as we become channels through which Jesus Christ brings people together into one body with him as its head (Col. 1:15, 18).

BIBLIOGRAPHY

1. The EACC/CCA

Ideas and Services. A Report of the EACC, 1957–1967. Bangkok, 1967.

Takenaka, M., Carlton, A., and Than, U. K. *Christ's Ministry and Ours.* The John Mott Memorial Lectures delivered before the EACC at Bangalore. November, 1961. Singapore: East Asia Council of Churches, 1962.

Than, U. K., ed. *Witnessing Together: Being the Official Report of the Inaugural Assembly of the EACC Held at Kuala Lumpur, Malaya, May 14–24, 1959.* Rangoon, 1959.

Visser 't Hooft, W. A. "The Significance of the Asian Churches in the Ecumenical Movement." *The Ecumenical Review* 11 (July, 1959): 365–376.

Weber, H.-R. *Asia and the Ecumenical Movement, 1895–1961*. London: SCM Press, 1966.

2. The Pacific Churches

Beyond the Reef: Records of the Conference of Churches and Missions in the Pacific, 1961. London: n.p., 1961.

Burton, J. W. *Missionary Survey of the Pacific Islands*. London: World Dominion Press, 1930. (This book provides background information on the churches in the Pacific.)

3. The Middle East Churches

Horner, N. *Rediscovering Christianity Where It Began: A Survey of the Contemporary Churches in the Middle East and Ethiopia*. Beirut: MECC, 1974.

Malik, C. H. "Die geistige Situation der nahöstlichen Christenheit." In *Theologische Stimmen aus Asien, Afrika und Lateinamerika I*. Munich: Kaiser Verlag, 1965.

Webster, D. *Survey of the Training of the Ministry in the Middle East*. Geneva: World Council of Churches, 1962.

Wysham, W. N. "Partners in Christian Quest." *Presbyterian Life*, February 1, 1959.

4. Africa

Beetham, T. A. *Christianity and the New Africa*. London: Pall Mall Press, 1967.

Drumbeats from Kampala: Report of the First Assembly of the All Africa Conference of Churches. London: Lutterworth Press, 1963.

Hastings, A. *Church and Mission in Modern Africa*. London: Burns and Oates, 1967.

Van Heemstra, C. M. *Thuis in Afrika*. Utrecht, 1970.

5. Latin America

Christians and Rapid Social Change in Latin America: Findings of the First Latin American Consultation on Church and Society. Geneva: World Council of Churches, 1961.

E Christianismo Evangelico en la America Latina: Informe y resoluciones de la primera conferencia evangelica Latino Americana. Buenos Aires: 1949.

Jacobs, M. *Die Kirche in ihrer Geschichte: Die Kirchengeschichte Südamerikas spanischer Zunge*. In Schmidt, K. D., ed. *Die Kirche in ihre Geschichte*. Göttingen: Vandenhoeck & Ruprecht, 1969.

Mackay, J. *The Latin American Churches and the Ecumenical Movement*. New York: Committee on Cooperation in Latin America, 1963.

Rycroft, W. S. and Clemmer, M. M. *A Factual Study of Latin America*. New York: Committee on Cooperation in Latin America, 1963.

6. The Caribbean

Atkins, H. L. Jr. "The Church in the Spanish and French Caribbean." *International Review of Missions* 60 (1971): 192–195.

Chaplin, David. "Caribbean Ecumenism." *International Review of Missions* 60 (1971): 186–191.

Schalkwijk, J. M. W. "Mission in the Micro-World of the Southern Caribbean." *International Review of Missions* 60 (1971): 196–205.

CHAPTER XI

A Brief Guide to the Literature on Black Theology and on the Theological Developments in Asia, Africa, and Latin America

I do not intend this chapter as an explanation of the theological developments in the continents mentioned in the title, for that would require many volumes. My goal is very modest: to give those interested in those theological trends a few directions to the literature which can help them. I am convinced that my efforts are not superfluous, for most of the discussion carried on in Western periodicals is limited to European and North American issues. Granted, the horizon has expanded to a certain degree; German periodicals no longer restrict themselves to intranational discussions between German theologians as in the prewar years. The same goes for France, the Netherlands, and the United States. There is openness to developments in other countries. In spite of this, however, Western theology which has finally made a slight breakthrough in its narrow provincialism has not yet opened itself very wide to developments beyond other countries of the West. Even the most ecumenically trained scholars usually leave their non-Western colleagues outside the discussion. One reason for this is lack of acquaintance with the appropriate non-Western theological literature, and therefore, at the request of many, I am writing this chapter to fill the need.

But I have a second reason for writing this chapter. Many misconceptions and delusions tenaciously cling to the theological work being done in the continents of Asia, Africa and Latin America — many of them born out of ignorance. One often hears that such theology is merely a Western import, a reproduction, and a potted-plant variety. Such generalizations are as ungrounded as they are unfair and often are only intended as cloaks under which to conceal one's lack of interest. To be sure, there are reproductions and imports among the theologies being produced in these continents, but there are also genuine attempts to do theology in an Asian, African, or Latin American context, as the case may be. And these deserve much more attention.

As long as the history of churches in those continents was deemed a mere appendix to the history of Western missions, there was no genuine interest in such theological enterprises. But fortunately the study of the young churches and their history is vastly changing. We are coming to realize that these churches have a tradition worthy of separate mention and study, and with this change we may hope that the day is not far off when we in the West also become interested in the unique contribution to theological discussion which these churches and their theologians can bring.

THE MEANING OF INDIGENOUS THEOLOGICAL SUBJECTS

An old Buddhist legend from Ceylon (Sri Lanka) is so apropos and instructive here. The great Indian prince, Asoka, had a son whose name was Thera Mahinda. In the third century before Christ, Thera Mahinda brought the Buddhist teaching (Dhamma) to Ceylon and persuaded not only the king, Devamampya Tissa, but also thousands of other people to accept its teachings. One day the king asked Thera Mahinda whether he thought Buddhism was now fully established on the island. Mahinda replied, "O great king, Buddhism is established, but its roots are not yet deep enough into the soil."

"And when will that come?" inquired the king.

Mahinda said, "When a man, born in Ceylon of Ceylonese parents, becomes a monk in Ceylon, studies the Vinaya in Ceylon and recites it in his own language, then the roots of Buddhism have penetrated deep into the soil of Ceylon."

In a certain sense the same in true for Christianity. Only when the native sons and daughters of a certain land fully assimilate the gospel and begin to communicate it in the language(s) of that land has Christianity taken deep root in that land.

Examples abound throughout history of where this failed to occur. The gospel was kept estranged, could develop no roots and therefore quickly disappeared. Only when the gospel is proclaimed by word and deed in a way uniquely appropriate to the land in which it has entered and the sons and daughters of that land continue to pass it on do the contours of an "answering church" begin to emerge.

Constructive theological work is a very important element in any church's attempt to respond to the gospel in ways appropriate to the context of its life.

Having made these prefatory comments, I shall now seek to provide a guide to the theological literature itself. I could not have completed this work without the help of so many others who provided some orientation. Moreover, what I offer here is only a selection, since the literature is so extensive. I have made no mention in my guide of Westerners' efforts to produce a theology native to non-Western lands. Such efforts abound; they extend from the Jesuit de Nobili in India to Barend Schuurman in Indonesia, from Patrice Tempels in Africa to Western colleagues who oppose his efforts. I believe that these Western theologians neither can develop a native non-Western theology nor may forcibly hasten the day of its birth. By no means do I say this to deny the important contributions which Western theologians have made in Asia, Africa, and Latin America but only to underline the fact that their valuable work did not constitute native theology. Furthermore, when they did try their hand at this, their efforts were neither successful nor appreciated by the natives.

THEOLOGICAL TRENDS IN ASIA

At a consultation on theology in 1967 the East Asia Christian Conference issued the following statement:

A living theology must deal with the burning questions which Asians in the midst of their dilemmas, their hope and frustration, their aspirations and achievements, their suspicions and suffering, are posing.

A living theology must also relate its pronouncements to the answers offered by Asiatic religions and philosophies, both in the classical form and the new forms generated by the impact of western ideas, secularism and science. Christian theology in Asia shall have fulfilled this mandate only when Asiatic churches begin to function as servants of God's Word and Revelation in Jesus Christ and to speak *in* the Asiatic situation and *out of* involvement with it.[1]

It is of course completely impossible within the compass of this book to cite all of the literature dealing with the theological developments throughout the whole of Asia. I shall restrict myself to three areas: India, Indonesia, and Japan. Let no one get the impression from this that nothing worthwhile is going on anywhere else. That is far from true; limitations of space, however, have forced me to make a selection.

India

The best introduction to what is going on in Indian theology is the book that Robin Boyd from Northern Ireland wrote on the basis of his many years in India: *Introduction to Indian Theology* (Madras, 1969). In the preface M. M. Thomas lauds this book for two reasons: first, because it describes the development of Indian theology as a continuously flowing stream from the time the gospel reached India — at times it was more visible than others, but it was always there; and second, because this book avoids the pitfall of measuring Indian theology by Western standards and laying it on the Procrustean bed of Western thinking. Instead, it assesses Indian theology in the light of the future task of the churches of Asia. In that connection, Thomas cautions his readers not to expect another *Summa* or *Kirchliche Dogmatik* from the pens of Asian authors but to look for more modest theological forays, fragments, and treatises on single topics (such as Western authors too are producing at the moment).

Boyd begins his book by describing the work of several authors (such as Ram Mohan Roy, Keshab Chandra Sen, Upadhyaya) from the Indian Renaissance period who never became fully converted to Christianity but were nevertheless deeply influenced by it and incorporated various Christian elements into their own thinking.

Our chief concern here, however, is not with them but with Christians who tried to articulate the gospel against the backdrop of their own environment. Boyd discusses the well-known trio of Appasamy, Chakkaray, and Chenchiah extensively. All of them interpreted the gospel in the light of surrounding Indian culture, but each made his own individual selection of the trends and accents inherent in that culture and tradition as he interpreted the gospel.

---

1. This quotation is a translation from the Dutch. The original quotation in English was unavailable to the translator.

A. J. Appasamy (b. 1891)

While Chakkaray employed the terminology of *Avatara* to articulate his theology, Appasamy identified more with the *bhakti* tradition. While Chenchiah tended in the direction of the monistic framework of Sri Aurobindo, Appasamy inclined toward the more personalist and dualist thought frames of Ramanuja.

A. J. Appasamy, writer, teacher, pastor and bishop, wrote an exciting account of his religious and theological pilgrimage in his book *My Theological Quest* (1964). His most famous books are *Christianity as Bhakti-Marga* (1928) and *What is Moksha?* (1931).

There is not a hint in Appasamy's writing of a tendency to concede the central biblical concepts of redemption and salvation by replacing them with the Hindu concept *moksha* or opting for the mystical self-surrender of the *Bhakti-Marga* in favor of biblical faith. But without becoming Ramanuja's disciple he did employ the terminology of his personalist mysticism to communicate the Christian gospel of salvation. Chakkaray did the same with *Avatara* terminology.

Herwig Wagner's book *Erstgestalten einer einheimischen Theologie in Südindien* (1963) lays Appasamy's work on the Procrustean bed of Augustana theology, and G. C. Oosthuizen measures its value by the standards of the Calvinist confessions in *Theological Battlegrounds in Asia and Africa* (London, 1972). In my judgment these are not fruitful approaches, for theology such as Appasamy wrote is evangelism-in-action. Valid criticism of it therefore requires that the critic be thoroughly familiar with the communication of the gospel among the Hindus. If he is going to be constructive, the critic must be prepared to suggest better alternative terms and methods. Who from the West is in a position to do that?

Vengal Chakkaray (1880–1958)

Chakkaray's parents were high-caste Indians. His father lived by the *vedantic* tradition and his mother by the *bhakti*.

When he was a twenty-year-old student at Madras College, Chakkaray became a Christian, and after his schooling, he became a lawyer and lent his full support to the drive for political independence. In 1941 he became mayor of Madras and in 1951 the chairman of the All-India Trade Union Congress.

Chakkaray wrote *Jesus the Avatar* (1927) and *The Cross and Indian Thought* (1932) and submitted articles regularly to the *Guardian*.

Some key concepts in Chakkaray's theology are the *avatars*, the Holy Spirit, and *bhakti*. Hindus believe in *avatars* — thousands of flighty appearances of divinity which disappear as fast as they come. For Chakkaray, Jesus is the one and only *Avatar*. Time and again he emphasizes this point: we see God in the face of Jesus. God himself is the unrevealed one, but he becomes visible in Jesus, the revealed God. God is *Sat*; Jesus is *Cit*. Only when the Hidden One reveals himself — *avyakta* becoming *vyakta* and *Brahman, Ishvara* — do we come to know him as he really is. One can come to know God not through *Jnana* ("Gnostic illumination") but only through *bhakti* ("loving surrender").

Through *bhakti* one comes to experience the immanence of God in Christ, the lotus of the heart, the singing bird in its nest, the beam of light in one's eye. In Christ transcendence and immanence meet.

According to Chakkaray this *avatar* in Christ Jesus comes through the dynamic work of the Holy Spirit, who is the risen Christ. Christology and pneumatology are coterminous. In this same train of thought, Jesus Christ revealed through the Spirit is the *antaratman*, the permanent mediator between *atman* ("man") and *Paramatman* ("God").

Though this summary of Chakkaray's theological contribution has been brief, I hope it sufficiently indicates how he tried to use the vocabulary of *Bhakti-Marga* to confess the cardinal Christian truths that Jesus Christ is both the *Avatar* ("incarnation of God and man") and *Antaratman* (mediator).

Pandipeddi Chenchiah (1886–1959)

The third man in this trio of Indian theologians was a layman, P. Chenchiah. He was both a distinguished lawyer and a judge and, like the other two individuals, left Hinduism to become a Christian. One of his most important writings was his book *Rethinking Christianity in India*.

Like the other two men, Chenchiah too found an instrument within the Hindu religion which he used to express Christian faith — *yoga*. In one of his memorable comments, he said: "In Jesus God created a new man. Hinduism searches for God in order to have him superabundantly fulfill the old man. Hinduism offers a so-called complete man, but Christianity a radically new one. Hinduism strengthens the Mahasakti of nature and man. Christianity develops the new sakti of the Holy Spirit. Jesus is the firstborn of a new creation. Hinduism is the last harvest of the old."[2]

Chenchiah describes Christian faith as yoga from the Holy Spirit designed to bring to light a new humanity which bursts forth from the Spirit-directed encounter with Christ.

In line with the purpose of this chapter I shall refrain from analyzing these theological topics developed by this trio of writers but rather refer only to literature by and about them.

In India a series of little books is being published entitled *Confessing the Faith in India*. The first book to appear was an exhaustive analysis of Chenchiah's work by D. A. Thangatamy, *The Theology of Chenchiah*. The second was written by P. T. Thomas, *The Theology of Chakkaray*. This series was not intended in any way to canonize the theological work of these three Indian authors but simply to show how they were intently striving to confess Christ in thought patterns meaningful to people living in India during their time. One catches a glimpse of writers in serious dialogue with the religious and secular culture around them and giving responsible account of the truth and importance of Christian faith. To be sure, they were not infallible, and therefore criticism is proper. But any communicator of the same faith today will discover in these predecessors not only a source of inspiration but also examples of errors to avoid in his own attempts.

This series, done by Indian authors only, is a useful addition to analyses made by Western writers. Since no separate volume has yet appeared on Appasamy, one can best turn for an introduction to his thought to his own book, *My*

---

2. Pandipeddi Chenchiah, *Rethinking Christianity in India* (Bangalore: Christian Institute for the Study of Religion and Society, 1939), pp. 181, 187.

Theological Quest. This book is itself the first publication in another interesting series entitled *Indian Christian Thought*, which, like the series mentioned above, is being published by the Christian Institute for the Study of Religion and Society in Bangalore.

Recent Theological Topics

Chapter eleven of Boyd's *Introduction to Indian Theology* offers a clear overview of the topics of recent interest to Indian theologians. It discusses Surjit Singh's *Preface to Personality,* a highly captivating book which withstands the suction of Indian monism by clearly articulating the Christian claim that God is God and he wants man to be man.

Boyd's book also reviews *The Meaning of Grace* by the Ceylonese bishop of the Church of South India, S. Kulandran. The book amply bespeaks its author's rich personal experience with and deep knowledge of the Hindu environment.

M. M. Thomas

I want to conclude this section on India by mentioning two figures who in my judgment have contributed most profoundly to the development of Indian theology — Paul Devanandan and M. M. Thomas. For material on Devanandan I refer the reader to my notations in Chapter Three.

M. M. Thomas has led a varied and interesting career, working originally as a chemist, sociologist, philosopher and only later as a lay theologian. The University of Serampore recognized Thomas's theological contributions by awarding him an honorary doctorate in theology, and the University of Leiden followed suit in 1975. In my judgment such honors were most appropriate, for M. M. Thomas is one of the most productive Christian thinkers in all of India as both his writings and his work as director of the Institute for the Study of Religion and Society in Bangalore so eloquently attest. His method of teaming up with other scholars to tackle a wide range of issues and his efforts to involve young people in the research mark him as unique. Even though I shall mention only two books among his many writings, I believe that any student of Indian theological trends must take note of the work of this man who has so strongly influenced the course of Indian theology.

I shall begin with Thomas's *The Christian Response to the Asian Revolution* (1966). Not confining his study to India but including the whole Asian scene, Thomas sets forth the several factors producing revolutions and transforming traditional societies into modern states throughout the continent. Then, with radar-like sensitivity he fixes upon the suggested new spiritual foundations, analyzing them and recommending to the churches their proper response.

At no point does Thomas ever identify the work of God with the events taking place in secular history, for secular history is too ambiguous. But in spite of the ambiguity, Christians would be traitors if they failed to testify of the liberating person of Jesus Christ to their Asian brothers. To do this one must participate, for "only participants can be prophets." Thus this book combines sober analysis of the situation with a passionate appeal to Christians in union with Christ to forsake their ghettos and begin to take part in the struggle for personal dignity, social justice and national self-expression.

Thomas also makes an appeal to Western missionary and diaconal agencies not to limit their help to the personal and ecclesiastical spheres but to stand behind the drive for social, political and economic emancipation.

The second book by Thomas which I wish to mention is *The Acknowledged Christ of the Indian Renaissance*, which discusses various Indian Renaissance leaders' views on Christianity and the person of Jesus Christ. He includes such figures as Rammohan Roy on "The Christ of the Precepts," Keshub Chunder Sen on "The Doctrine of Divine Humanity," P. C. Mozoomdar on "The Oriental Christ and the Unfolding Spirit," Vivekananda on "Christ as Jivan Mukta," Mahatma Gandhi on "Jesus, the Supreme Satyagrahi," and many others.

Each of these analyses is particularly valuable, for through them Thomas is trying to show the Hindus' fascination with Christ and their attempt to find him a home within their pantheon. All their efforts notwithstanding, this still leaves Christ a "displaced person."

All the attention which these Hindus give to Christ inevitably raises the question which C. F. Andrews, the great missionary and friend of Gandhi, asked: "Where are all the Christians who should be at work taking the Christian faith out of the wraps of western theology and by their life and work making it real to their Hindu neighbors?"

Indonesia

Students of Asian theological trends often skip over Indonesia because of a language barrier. Indonesian theologians usually write in their own Indonesian language and thus escape attention because, regrettably, only treatises written in English, French, Spanish, or Portuguese attract a significant degree of interest.

It would be committing an unpardonable sin, however, if I, a Dutch author, were to omit Indonesia and its theological developments. Once again, I shall mention only the works of Indonesians themselves, and since so many Indonesian "lay" theologians have made valuable contributions, I shall begin with some of them.

T. S. G. Mulia (1896–1966)

Among those lay theologians who have made outstanding contributions, T. S. G. Mulia ranks as a leader. Combining work in the fields of cultural anthropology, law, economics, and teaching with his efforts on behalf of the Indonesian Council of Churches (organizer and first chairman), the theological seminary in Jakarta (chairman of the board), and Indonesian Bible Society (chairman), Mulia was amply worthy of his honorary doctor of theology degree from the Free University of Amsterdam in 1966.

Mulia was the first Indonesian who from the time of the Jerusalem conference of 1928 was continually involved in the flow of ecumenical traffic. In an essay, Simatupang wrote of Mulia and his theological influence: "It is more lived out and acted upon than written about."

Mulia was so important to Indonesian theology because his life and work underscored the bearing of God's commands and promises upon the total range of human existence — including its cultural and political dimensions. He learned much from his good friend, Hendrik Kraemer, in this regard. Simply stated, Mulia was a remarkable pioneer who encouraged many young people to shoulder their responsibilities and to undertake new initiatives during an age which faced a future full of exciting developments for their own country and the world at large.

O. Notohamidjojo

Notohamidjojo is a lawyer, philosopher, and former rector of the Christian University in Salatiga who has always had a strong interest in theology and contributed importantly to forming the structures of theological thought. He too received an honorary doctor (of law) degree from the Free University of Amsterdam in 1972.

Notohamidjojo's writings bear a strong interdisciplinary stamp which reflects his own interests in the several fields of law, philosophy and theology. I shall cite only a few of his works: *Iman Kristen dan Politik* ("Christian Faith and Politics"), 1951; *Tanggung Djawab Gredja dan Orang Kristen Di Bidang Politik* ("The Responsiblity of Christians and the Church in Politics"), 1969; *Demokrasi Pantjasila*, 1970; *Makna Negara Hukum* ("The Significance of the Constitutional State"), 1970.

T. B. Simatupang

T. B. Simatupang is the most influential lay theologian in all of Indonesia today. Shortly after Indonesia became independent, he was chief of staff of the Indonesian army charged with organizing it into a viable modern fighting unit, and through this experience he saw how little Indonesian theology touched the social and political issues of his land. After he and President Sukarno had a falling out and he thereby lost his job, Simatupang became one of the chairmen of the Indonesian Council of Churches. At present he is also serving as chairman of the Christian Council of Asia and as a member of the Executive Committee of the World Council of Churches.

Throughout his life Simatupang has acquired a thorough knowledge of ecumenical theology, especially as it applies to issues of church and society. In spite of a continually packed agenda, he manages to find time to write articles and books in his renowned crystal-clear style for both professional and accomplished lay theologians. I shall mention only some of his publications: *Membangun Manusia* ("The Development of Man"), *Pelopor Dalam Perang, Pelopor Dalam Damai* ("Pioneer in War and Peace"), *Laporan Dari Banaran* ("A Biographical Sketch on Guerilla Warfare"), *Tugas Kristan Dalam Revolusi* ("The Christian Responsibility in Revolution"), *Dari Edinburgh Ke Jakarta* ("From Edinburgh to Jakarta").

I could cite the names of many more lay theologians in Indonesia, but limitations of space require that I now move on to discuss the work of Indonesia's professional theologians.

The Theological Schools of Jakarta and Jogjakarta

Through the initiative of Hendrik Kraemer a theological college was first founded in Bogor and then transferred to Jakarta, where it now stands. It has always been ecumenical in scope, attracting students from the whole archipelago. Since the

Second World War it has received university status, including the right to confer doctoral degrees.

After the Japanese had invaded and occupied Indonesia, many of the students of Jakarta Theological College took on leadership roles in the churches which the invaders had taken away from Western missionaries, and through this valuable experience they learned much that would help them during the struggle for independence soon to begin. They had learned to take upon themselves the responsibility for building up the churches in the young state which achieved its independence in 1945.

From this and a more recent group of students graduating from the theological colleges in both Jakarta and Jogjakarta has come a new generation of theologians who not only deeply involve themselves in practical church life but also make their own contributions to theological developments. We may hope that in the years to come many will follow in the train of Dr. F. Ukur, the first theological student to earn his doctorate in Indonesia at the theological college in Jakarta. Until now, as the following pages will show, most of Indonesia's theologians did graduate from either Jakarta or Jogjakarta but for their doctorates went on to either Europe or America.

Old Testament Scholars

It is gratifying to observe a number of Indonesian theologians doing specialized work in the field of the Old Testament after completing their studies at either Jakarta or Jogjakarta. I am thinking of scholars such as Dr. Oei (name later changed to S. H. Widyapranowo) who did his doctoral work at Edinburgh. Then too there is Dr. Ihromi who specialized in Semitic languages under Dr. Christoph Barth and began his teaching career at Jakarta with a significant address entitled "Solidarity with the People as Seen in the Prophet Jeremiah." Dr. A. A. Sitompul earned his degree at the University of Mainz and began teaching at Nommensen University in 1973. Dr. Nico Radjawane also studied under Dr. Christoph Barth in Mainz and thereafter began to teach at the theological school in the Moluccan islands.

All of these individuals thus comprise a team of young Old Testament scholars which can be expected not only to produce commentaries but also actually to do Old Testament theology, which is so relevant and important to the context of Indonesia.

New Testament Scholars

Dr. Liem Khiem Yang was the first Pentecostal Christian to study at the theological college in Jakarta. He followed this with post-graduate work in Bonn, West Germany, and a dissertation completed in 1963 on the letter of Philemon. He began his work as professor of New Testament at Jakarta by delivering his inaugural address, "Allowing God's Saving Deeds to Happen in Us," which he published in 1973. His incisive exegesis and hermeneutical experimentation are already bringing a fresh dimension to the development of New Testament theology.

Dr. Rudi Budiman is a professor of New Testament at Jogjakarta who in 1971 culminated his work at the Free Reformed University of Amsterdam with a fine dissertation, *De Realisering der Verzoening in het menselijke Bestaan* ("Achieving Reconciliation in Human Existence").

Systematic Theologians

Though many non-Indonesian authors have published numerous systematic theological books and articles while working in Indonesia, I shall cite only the works of Indonesian dogmaticians themselves.

Dr. R. Soedarmo studied at the Free Reformed University of Amsterdam, earning his degree under G. C. Berkouwer with a dissertation on Gogarten, *In de Wereld en Niet van de Wereld* ("In, but Not Of the World"). Soedarmo ultimately rejected Gogarten's theology because of its accommodation to the existing culture and national context. After his doctoral study Soedarmo returned to Indonesia to teach in the Theological College of Jakarta. In 1965 he produced his own systematic theology, *Ichtisar Dogmatica*.

Dr. S. A. E. Nababan graduated from the Theological College of Jakarta and pursued post-graduate work at Heidelberg which he finished in 1962 with a dissertation entitled *Kyriosbekenntnis und Mission bei Paulus*. The thesis sets out to prove that both the unity and the worldwide mission of the church are grounded in the liberating Lordship of Christ over the whole world. Even though his dissertation is exegetical in nature, the author's main interest is in systematics, and therefore I include him here.

Nababan is now serving as secretary-general of the Indonesian Council of Churches and as chairman of both the Commission for World Mission and Evangelism of the World Council of Churches and the World Lutheran Federation. Both he and T. B. Simatupang have been leading spokesmen for Indonesian churches in ecumenical circles and have also tried to introduce an ecumenical dimension to Indonesia in their work among the churches there.

The last dogmatician I mention here is Dr. Harun Hadiwyono, professor at the theological college in Jogjakarta. His dissertation reflects both his past and present focus of study — Javanese mysticism *(Man in the Present Javanese Mysticism)*. In 1973 Hadiwyono published his own dogmatic theology, *Iman Kristen*, which paid far greater heed to the Indonesian context than many previous studies.

Church Historians

Dr. Fridolin Ukur's roots lie in the Evangelical church in Kalimantan, known better in the West as the Dajak Church of Borneo. Ukur's work has many facets and ranks him as one of the leading church historians in Indonesia. First of all, he recorded the history of the Evangelical church in the region of the Dajak tribes and published it in 1960 under the title *Tuaiannja sungguh banjak* ("The Harvest is Indeed Great"). Then too, he worked for his doctor's degree in Jakarta, concluding his work in 1971 with a study of why Dajaks became Christians: *Tantang-Djawab Suku Dajak* ("The Answer of the Dajak Tribes"). Finally, I would mention his cooperative venture with Dr. Frank Cooley to head an extensive survey team studying Indonesian churches. By 1974 this team had already produced no less than twenty-two stenciled surveys of Indonesian churches which are now being prepared for publication in the Indonesian language with summaries in English.

The first book of this great series to appear was S. H. Widyapranowo's *Benih jang tumbuh* ("The Seed That Grew"), a history of the Gredja Kristen Indonesian Church on Middle Java. Even though Widyapranowo's field is Old Testament, he, like most theological professors in Asia, is intensely involved with his home church, and therefore he undertook to write this book.

Social Ethicists

Dr. P. D. Latuihamallo began teaching social ethics at the theological college in Jakarta after finishing his doctoral work under Dr. John Bennett. In his dissertation, *The Relations of Church and World in the Writings of Hendrik Kraemer,* Latuihamallo describes what he sees as two poles in Kraemer's work, the church and the world, to both of which the dictum applies: *semper reformanda*. Thus there must be continual "encounter" between the two.

Latuihamallo himself is concretely applying Kraemer's theme through his present work as professor, his former work as parliamentarian, and his close involvement with countless practical programs and issues. From the earliest days of Indonesian independence this Moluccan Christian has taken very seriously his responsibilities as a *minister verbi Dei* to build up the church and the nation.

Then too there is Dr. W. B. Sidjabat who earned his doctor's degree in 1960 from Princeton Theological Seminary with a thesis on *Religious Tolerance and the Christian Faith,* later published in Jakarta. It is an exciting Christian perspective on the problems of religious tolerance within the context of the Indonesian philosophy of state.

Still another person who cannot be omitted from this list is Dr. Sutarno, whose doctoral dissertation, written at the Free Reformed University of Amsterdam, is an effort to explain the model Christian political organization developed by the former Dutch theologian, professor, and statesman, Abraham Kuyper, and to critically examine whether it can aid one in coming to a Christian understanding of the relationship of faith to politics in the situations of Indonesia and the Netherlands today. One may hope that Sutarno, who now serves as rector of the Christian University of Salatiga, will now pursue these questions which he posed in his doctoral study and apply them to the situation as it now exists in Indonesia.

Practical Theology

One of Indonesia's most prolific theological writers is the present chairman of the Indonesian Council of Churches and professor of practical theology at the theological college in Jakarta, Dr. J. L. Abineno from Timor. Abineno did his doctoral work at the University of Utrecht under J. C. Hoekendijk and completed a dissertation on the liturgical forms and patterns found on his native island. He has been a highly productive scholar, not only as author of a number of handbooks on practical theology but also as director of a new Indonesian translation of the Bible.

Abineno's first book on practical theology *(Sekitar Theologia praktica I)* discusses homiletics, while his second *(Sekitar Theologia praktica II)* treats the theology of the apostolate. He also wrote a book on pastoral care, *Pelajanan Pastoral*.

Even though Abineno with his typical precision is carrying on dialogue with Western theologians, his work is anything but a duplication of Western handbooks. Rather, it bears the stamp of his own Indonesian soul and reflects the issues which the practical theologian confronts in Indonesia.

Another well-known Indonesian practical theologian is Dr. Andar Lumbantobing from Nommensen University in the Batak lands. He did his doctoral work in Bonn, West Germany, and wrote his disseration on the offices within the Batak church. Lumbantobing has primarily been dealing with the problems, work, and challenges confronting the biggest church in all of Asia, the Batak church (HKBP), which in many respects bears nationalist traces. Lumbantobing and many others have been critical of this, and their protests have led to schism. Presently he serves as moderator of the new church, the Protestant Christian Church of Indonesia, which separated in 1964. In spite of this painful turn of events, both sides are still cooperating at Nommensen University, and this holds forth the hope of a complete healing of the disturbed relations.

Finally, I must mention the little book by Dr. Eka Darmaputera, *Toleransi, kerukunan, pembangunan, Paskah* ("Tolerance, Peace, Edification and the Message of Easter"). Most of the theologians have written their books in conscious relation to the trends of Western theology. Darmaputera's book is different, for he belongs to that new breed of theologians who have felt less of the impact of Western theology and are developing a *theologia in loco*. One could call his little book the first evidence of contextual theology in Indonesia.

All of us have reason to rejoice when we note the great amount of theological work being done in Indonesia. In fact, Ivy Chou of the Theological Education Fund said some time ago that more autochthonous theological books are being written in Indonesia than anywhere else in Asia.

The theologian's task of creatively and critically examining the relationship between gospel, church and society as he stands under both the divine commands and the promises is as risky as it is important. May God bless and strengthen those who undertake the work.

It is regrettable that no book is available which summarizes the many theological developments in Indonesia. There is, however, a fine essay by T. B. Simatupang written for a 1969 Asian consultation of the Theological Education Fund, "Toward Creative Maturity."

Japan

Japanese Contributions to Christian Theology

Though Carl Michalson, an American Methodist theologian, does not know the Japanese language, he has served several times as guest lecturer at Japanese theological schools and with the help of several bilingual friends produced a book, *Japanese Contributions to Christian Theology*, which the Japanese scholar Dr. Kitagawa described as "incisive" and "on target."

Michalson begins by explaining the so-called non-church movement

(*Mukyokai*) founded by Kanzo Uchimara in reaction to the paternalistic air of Western missions in Japan. It is one attempt to arrive at a genuinely Japanese expression of the Christian faith. Those affiliated with this movement come together in houses, factories, schools, etc., to study the Bible and to determine concretely the meaning of obedience in the society in which they are living. They appoint no officers, celebrate no sacraments, and have no organization.

Through his visits to Japan, Emil Brunner learned to know these groups and became one of their enthusiastic supporters. Michalson too gives them sympathetic treatment in his book even though he does not totally share Brunner's assessment. He recognizes that this is the first movement in Japan to catch the eye of Japanese intellectuals and admits that in a certain respect it serves as a corrective to the church; but he believes that lack of theological reflection cuts off the possibility of a complete impact. Moreover, in Michalson's judgment, the existence of a church is not merely a fancy but useless accessory, but is a clear implication of obedience to the Lord.

Michalson follows his discussion of the non-church movement with a treatment of another Japanese theologian, Zenda Watanabe, who has developed his own doctrine of the Bible (*Seisho-ron*). When it canonized the Bible, the church was acknowledging the fact that the Bible claims to be a guideline for faith and life. Watanabe proceeds to develop a biblical hermeneutic on which to build his view of the church, which he sees as a "third people" called out by its Lord, God himself, to reveal itself as a genuine *ekklēsia* in the world. The boundaries of this "third people" are coterminous with no other nation or people on earth.

Michalson also discusses the theology of Yoshitaka Kumano, who wrote *Eschatology and Philosophy of History, Outline of Christianity,* and *Dogmatics.* The focus of his thought is on the relation between tradition and church. Kumano rejects the traditional Roman Catholic two-source theology on the one hand and the non-church movement on the other. Kitagawa charges the Calvinistically oriented Kumano with ecclesiocentrism and with offering little impetus for erecting a theology of culture — the very thing which one might expect Calvinism to provide. Moreover, claims Kitagawa, though Kumano has succeeded in combining the several theological insights of historic churches into a serviceable instrument for Japanese churches, his theology does not take due account of the Japanese religious and cultural context.

Both Michalson and Kitagawa express the highest respect for the work of the recently deceased Seiichi Hatano, a professor at the University of Kyoto. Michalson calls him the most erudite Christian Japan has ever known. Hatano's specialty was the relationship between Christian faith and philosophy, specifically the problem of time. Hatano claimed that every person is joined to the very structure of time by a series of loves: *epithymia* ("desire") for the time of his natural life, *eros* for the time of his cultural life, and *agapē* for the time of his religious life. With this as his fundamental claim, Hatano went on to develop a philosophical ethic of *agapē,* which both guides and judges *epithymia* and *eros*.

Hatano thus tried to enrich philosophy of religion with Christian perspectives and cautioned his fellow Japanese intellectuals against the then current tendency to facilely discard Christianity as a Western religion. One who searches for the deepest truth simply may not fail to take account of the gospel.

Kazoh Kitamori

Kitamori is a popular theologian in Japan whose fame has spread far beyond the borders of his own country. His most important book, *Theology of the Pain of God,* appeared in English translation in 1966 with an introduction by John Taylor, and, much to Kitamori's surprise, it has been in the center of ecumenical discussion. The book was originally published in 1946.

Kitamori himself was born in 1916 to non-Christian parents in southern Japan. During his secondary school years he requested Christian baptism and joined the Lutheran church. He began to study theology, was profoundly influenced by Luther, and thereafter took up the study of philosophy. His philosophical terminology shows clear marks of Zen Buddhism, neo-Hegelianism, and Bergsonianism. To understand Kitamori one must also consider the events of Nagasaki, Hiroshima, and the complete collapse of Japan. As he reads the book one must also reckon with a certain Buddhist accent on a life of suffering. All these experiences and features combined to produce Kitamori's attempt at a *theologia in loco.*

Kitamori's core concept is pain and suffering — specifically, the pain and suffering of God. He borrows this language from Jeremiah 31:20 where the Bible speaks of God as "moved in his deepest parts and will most certainly have mercy on him." Another similar text is Isaiah 63:9: "In all their affliction he was afflicted." These and similar texts in the Bible Kitamori summarized by the phrase "the pain of God." He concludes his fourth edition with these words: "Theologia *doloris* serves for *ecclesia doloris* through existentia doloris." Isaiah came to realize God's holiness; Hosea, God's faithfulness; Amos, God's justice; and Jeremiah, God's pain. Actually, the suffering of God is a combination of "love and pain together," which, via an "analogia doloris," reflects itself in the pain which comes to Christ's disciples. Our pain and suffering with Jesus as we follow him do not have any soteriological importance, but pain is nevertheless inherent in the nature of discipleship and is a sign of union with him. We meet God in the midst of the suffering and needy humanity (Matt. 25), and by addressing these needs we act as servants of God.

These are the two key points of Kitamori's theology. He borrows his hermeneutical material from the time of deep need both during and after the Second World War, and his terminology comes largely from his encounter with traditional Japanese and Buddhist concepts, especially the Japanese tragedies. For example, he confronts the Japanese concept of *tsurasa* ("sacrifice of oneself") with his own interpretation of the pain of God. He tries to show that the Japanese spirit by its very nature is wholly incapable of understanding how one could offer himself as a sacrifice for his enemies who are entirely unworthy of his love. Kitamori claims that *tsurasa* is devoid of ethical connotation in the Japanese tragedies, and he urges Japanese theologians to underscore a point which is so meaningful in a Japanese setting — the "pain of God." Geographically, Japan is the spot where this truth will come to be understood, and the *kairos* ("appropriate time") for it to emerge was during the dark and trying days at the close of World War II. At one point Kitamori boldly claims, "The pain of God is an eternal truth, but one which would not have been discovered without Japan as a medium."

The travel of the gospel among the peoples of this world followed a line from the Greeks to the Germans to the Japanese, says Kitamori.

I do not have the space to explain how Kitamori develops each of his daring ideas. I have devoted rather extensive coverage to his book primarily because of the great discussion it aroused not only in Japan, but also in such places as Switzerland and Germany where such formidable figures as Karl Barth and Heinrich Ott participated. One can find the results of this discussion in Keyi Ogawa's book printed in 1965 under the title *Die Aufgabe der neueren Evangelischen Theologie in Japan.*

Ogawa lauds Kitamori's effort for two reasons. First, it is an attempt to break through the denominational division in Japan and to do theology for all Japanese churches. Second, it is a concerted attempt to pay due heed to the Japanese context within which Kitamori did his theology. Ogawa, however, believes that in his attempt to be relevant to Japan Kitamori did not escape the danger of "japanizing" his theology, that is, of making the gospel primarily an interpretation of Japanese experience. In Ogawa's opinion a radical openness to the Word of God is the best guarantee of openness to one's own situation, not vice versa.

In both Kitamori's predilection for the dialectical philosophy of the Kyoto school and his enthusiastic acceptance of the Greek-German-Japanese triad, Ogawa, like Barth, senses an inclination to capture the gospel in nationalistic categories. However that may be, I believe that few theologians have worked as intensively as Kitamori to produce a *theologia in loco*. His book shows how difficult such a work really is. I am encouraged by the rare amount of ecumenical discussion this book has precipitated.

Masao Takenaka

One contemporary Japanese theologian supersedes even Kitamori in his efforts to produce a theology appropriate to the Japanese situation — Masao Takenaka. While Kitamori's experience and disposition inclined him to deal primarily with the Japanese situation both during and directly after World War II, Takenaka is in the very midstream of contemporary developments such as urbanization and industrialization and the struggle to discover the role of the church in such a fast-changing society.

Takenaka is both theologian and economist. He now holds the post of professor of Christian social ethics at Doshiha University in Kyoto and was a former vice-president of the World Federation of Christian Students and a member of several commissions of the World Council of Churches. His books and articles have brought him universal fame.

His book *Reconciliations and Renewal in Japan* is in my judgment the most important description of the postwar situation in Japan. It depicts the incredible growth of industrial production with its dehumanizing results, the Japanese attempt to discover a *modus vivendi* between communist China and the Western nations, Japan's tendency to orient its life more toward the West than toward the other countries of Asia, the revival of Japanese militarism, etc. He then follows this with a description of the role of the Protestant churches in a land where both Protestants and Catholics together comprise less than one percent of the total population and where new religions are continually sprouting up like weeds. Takenaka shows how the impact of Christians on Japanese society is far greater than their small numbers might indicate. This book is a must for anyone desiring to become familiar with contemporary Japan.

Takenaka has also written an exciting book on social ethics which not only shows its author's erudition and thorough acquaintance with the Niebuhrs, John Bennett, and Karl Barth but is also a probing independent analysis of his own society.

Not content with remaining on the level of theory, Masao Takenaka has been closely allied with the large training center in Kansai, one of Japan's great industrial areas, where a team of preachers and lay persons has been active for more than thirteen years in both factories and the labor movement.

Masao Takenaka is one of those precious Japanese theologians who brings a vast knowledge to his task of rowing against the current of popular Japanese policy and thinking. He is calling Japan to a moral orientation by asking "Why do you cast your lot primarily with the rich countries of the West rather than try to serve the poor peoples of Asia, Africa and Latin America?"

AFRICA

I turn now to the continent of Africa and attempt to describe the recent efforts of African theologians to develop an African Christian theology.

Africans themselves caution against hasty generalizations, for Africa is a continent of no less than 300 million inhabitants and 1000 ethnic groups. Countries like Ethiopia, Zambia, Mali, Liberia, Cameroon, Namibia, etc., are so different from one another in almost every respect. Then too there are the language sectors — French, English, and Arabic. But in spite of all the diversity, there is even greater talk in Africa than in Asia about a continental approach to theology and about a *theologia Africana,* which, though it may be variously expressed by different authors, nevertheless shows the same features at its core.

Theologia Christiana Africana

The phrase "African Christian Theology" has been around for the past twenty years or so and has been studied by at least three consultations of the All-Africa Conference of Churches (Ibadan, 1966; Abidjan, 1969; Kampala, 1972) and one study project conducted by the World Student Christian Federation. Descriptions of such a theology abound. John S. Mbiti wrote in his preparatory study for an AACC consultation: "Doing theology is a universal and crucial responsibility which Christian faith confers. When African theologians contribute their share to the universal work of the church by developing their own theology in response to the situation in Africa, then we have what may be termed 'African Christian Theology.' " A study report of the World Student Christian Federation expressed the same idea in different words: "African Christian theology can be genuinely Christian only when it is systematized and articulated by Africans who take due account of the religious experience of their own people." At another point the report underscores what many Asians too are saying: only natives and not foreigners can undertake the work. "Africans are the only ones who can determine their priorities and experiences relative to the Gospel of Jesus and other aspects of life."

The Function of African Theology

It goes without saying that African theology does all the things which theology in general does, but in African theology (as in Asian) all these other functions are embraced in the missionary or communicative function. It is not primarily an intra-ecclesiastical exercise, but a discipline whose practitioners keep one question central: How can we best do our theology so that the gospel will touch Africans most deeply?

Of course decolonization and nation-building provided African theologians the impulse to undertake their disciplines in this way. Theology too needs to be stripped of its colonial allegiances. Thus, throughout Africa one can sense a repudiation of theology "made in Canterbury or Rome or New York," and a glad welcome to theologies of specifically African design.

The interconfessional character of these new theologies strikes one immediately. Whereas in times past the theologies current in Africa were usually mere duplications of the "mother churches" in the West, now African theologians maintain wide bands of fellowship with their colleagues throughout the continent and contribute essays to symposium studies, most of which are interconfessional.

Study Centers

That various study centers and periodicals are important to the production of genuinely African theology is so obvious as to require no explanation. I shall include some of them here for information.

A number of universities throughout Africa — for example, Makerere, Fourah Bay, Ibadan, Legon, Nsukka, Salisbury, Nairobi, Kinshasa, and Kisangani — maintain theological faculties and departments of religious studies.

Among the more important theological journals are: *Flambeau, African Ecclesiastical Review, Africa Theological Journal, Bulletin of the A.A.C.C., The Ghana Bulletin of Theology, Ministry, Orientations Pastorales, Au coeur de l'Afrique, Revue du Clergé Africain, Sierra Leone Bulletin of Theology, Présence,* and *Searchlight.* The last two are periodicals put out for the African region of the World Student Christian Federation.

Themes in African Christian Theology

Perhaps the best way to gain insight into the work of African theologians is to inquire about some of the leading themes they are treating. I shall attempt to describe a few of the most important and most discussed among them.

Theological reflection on the "traditional religions." One of the most striking features of African theology is its intense study of what are variously called tribal religions, traditional religions, archaic religions, etc. Statistically speaking, these religions are declining, but they are still a "ferment," as John Mbiti so frequently reiterated, and their influence is indeed increasing. For this reason virtually every African theologian is insisting that a study of these religions is absolutely necessary.

For years the study of these religions was the exclusive province of Western researchers, and, with the exception of such scholars as Father Schmidt, Nathan Söderblom, and Andrew Lang, most of them were horribly one-sided in their evaluations. Okat p'Bitek's book, *African Religions in Western Scholarship*, is a good example of the recent angry African response which this one-sidedness evoked. Now Africans are being encouraged to undertake the study themselves, for only a researcher familiar with the language of the group he is studying can hope to arrive at a proper evaluation. The sociologist and politician from Ghana, K. A. Busia, ever since 1955 has been urging church leaders and theologians to pay far greater heed to these tribal religions and the myths, rites and customs which back them up, for, said he, it would be fantasy to think that these religions and the old world view have no further impact on a person once he becomes a Christian. In Busia's opinion, the church would more profitably serve the African people by such studies than by merely underscoring the authority of the new religion, Christianity. The Christian gospel will never penetrate the total life of the African people unless those who proclaim it reckon seriously with the African world view.

Of course it is improper to make sweeping generalizations about these religions for they differ from tribe to tribe, as the various local studies clearly prove. But amid the diversity there are some features and expressions which all share. Without in any way pretending to present a complete list, I shall cite a few of these features which African theologians are now studying.

The first feature worth mentioning is the tribal conception of God and the gods. All of these religions reveal a picture of a supreme deity whose power is both beneficent but also terrifying and dangerous. This supreme deity is in turn connected with various levels of lesser deities which influence specific events in the lives of human beings such as birth, marriage, sickness, and death and which can bring good or evil. Then too there are those intermediary beings: good and evil spirits, witches, and magical powers.

Western scholars have studied these phenomena for years, but recently Africans themselves have started to analyze the conceptions of God which their fellow inhabitants share. The symposium study headed by the Ghanan, Dr. Kwesi Dickson, and Dr. Paul Ellingworth, *Biblical Revelations and African Beliefs*, begins — significantly — with an essay entitled "God" by E. Bolaji Idowu. This same Professor Idowu also wrote two other books, *God in Nigerian Belief* and *God in Yoruba Belief*. J. B. Danquals wrote on *The Akan Doctrine of God* and Gabriel M. Setiloane on *The Image of God Among the Sotho-Tswana*, to name only a few of the many studies.

Africans vary widely in their evaluation of these traditional beliefs about God. All of them reject the notion that God is Deus Otiosus, but whereas Idowu discovers traces and features in the African supreme deity similar to Yahweh of the Old Testament, John Mbiti speaks more cautiously of the African conceptions as a *praeparatio evangelica* for a true understanding of the Supreme Being.

Many fear that after such a long period of too close attachment to Western confessions of faith Africa will now go too far in the other direction by developing a new form of syncretism. As I see it, there is no cause for alarm; Africans have scarcely begun to assess their traditional religious heritage, and it could well be that these studies will serve to immunize them rather than to lead them on to neo-syncretism. When Israel confronted the other religions of the Middle East, she not only thereby adopted certain elements from those cultures but also deepened her strong conviction that Yahweh alone is God. In like manner it could just be that by soberly and openly assessing these religions rather than by dodging them or rejecting them outright, Africans will achieve a confession of God that is both different and richer than they had before.

Another typical feature of African traditional religions is the worship of ancestors. Even after individuals and tribes become Christian, this belief still continues. There is an unbreakable bond of fellowship between the dead, the living, and the yet unborn. By prayers, sacrifices and ritual meals the living can keep in contact with their deceased ancestors. All this is connected to a system of norms and customs which is cloaked in the mantle of ancestral authority and compels obedience by threats and judgments.

Throughout its history Western missions either disregarded or summarily condemned these expressions of ancestor worship. The result of this policy is that many African Christians, both urban as well as rural, both educated as well as uneducated, now feel themselves living in two separate worlds. Fortunately, African theologians are taking a close second look at this belief and treating it in an open manner. They are viewing it not as the exclusive province of sociologists and anthropologists but are themselves working through the material provided by these other disciplines and then posing their own questions. K. A. Busia, Harry Sawyerr, Vincent Mulago, Kagame, Baëta, Lufuluabo, Mbiti, Adegbola, and Zoa are just a few of the many theologians who are actively researching this area. Their individual approaches are far from uniform.

Here is a sample of the questions such scholars are posing. If ancestor worship is the vessel from which Africans have been drinking for so long, should Christians smash it to pieces and offer another in its place or merely fill the existing vessel with new water? In the light of Hebrews 12:1–2 which speaks of a great cloud of witnesses gathered around Jesus, the pioneer and perfecter of faith, is not a strong emphasis on the *communio sanctorum* warranted by this passage and required in Africa today? Would not such an emotional Christocentric accent serve to counterbalance the polycentric religiosity of the ancestor cults and at the same time represent a unique and valuable African contribution to the worldwide Christian church? As one can see, the Africans view the early church's emphasis on the *communio sanctorum* much more in terms of a fellowship between the living and the dead, the *ecclesia militans* and *ecclesia triumphans*, than does Western Christianity.

Whatever African Christians may finally decide about this extremely delicate issue, it is well that their theologians are talking openly and freely about it. In many instances the independent churches of Africa are setting the pace; in fact it is precisely some of them who by discussing it openly have developed the most ardent opposition to it!

Another feature of African religions which has attracted the attention of many Western researchers is the veneration of spirits and related practices such as witchcraft, fetishism, divination, sorcery, witch hunts, etc. One need only to mention the names of Wilhelm Schmidt, D. Westermann, Ernst Damman, Phoebe

Offerberg, Walter Sangree, Martin Southwold, M. G. Smith, P. H. Gulliver, James L. Gibbs, Lorna Marshall, Colin Tambull, L. M. Lewis, D. Stenning, and so many others to gauge Western scholars' fascination with the subject.

But what about African scholars and theologians? Have they shown a similar scholarly interest and a concern to battle the evil effects of such a veneration of spirits and all the practices associated with it? No, they have not. They evaded the topic for a long time because many of them were still so closely involved with the phenomenon that it was difficult to break free and write about it objectively. Then too, the Christian congregations which they served were often unwilling to become involved in such a delicate matter.

But current African publications prove that this time of hesitation is past. In fact, many African theologians do not hesitate to mention these phenomena by name. In fact they believe that such an exposure is a modern form of exorcism. What I find so exciting is that Africans — much more than Asians, by the way — are tackling this issue together and seeking for a common response to it. For example, in 1955 Christians got together (in Accra, Ghana) to discuss the phenomena of witchcraft and sorcery and later published their findings in a book, *Christianity and African Culture.*

We in the West have often been reminded by authors such as Harvey Cox, A. W. Kist, and William Stringfellow that evil "powers" are at work in our social, political, and institutional structures; except we unmask them and cast them out, they tend to dehumanize our lives. But we Westerners often forget that these "powers" are also at work in African and Asian society in the form of witchcraft, sorcery, fetishes, divination, etc., and they too need to be expelled.

Stephen N. Ezeanya, E. Awuku Asamoa, Bernard Mangematin and M. Unegbu are only several of the many African theologians who are writing about this issue. I detect two different approaches. I hear some of them saying that we must not deny the reality of the world of the spirits but rather victoriously shout forth "Jesus is Victor!" An author like E. Awuku Asamoa says, for example, that Jesus rules with liberating authority over everything and everyone which has power (Col. 2:9–10).

Others take a different approach. They claim it is not so much a question of whether the world of the spirits is real or not, but rather a person's *feeling* himself connected to it — his fears, the related psychic complexes, the group hysteria, the mass suggestion, the vicious circle which causes people to wander about in darkness. It is the Christian's responsibility to challenge these fears in a person and shake them loose by confronting him with the liberating message of Christ. This was the emphasis of the Accra conference.

Whatever may be an individual author's approach, the important point is that this issue is no longer being sidestepped.

John Mbiti has been a real leader in this field. One of his essays broaches a subject that deserves much fuller treatment — the African world of spirits as interpreted in the light of the New Testament and the early church. Some newer Western dogmatics books totally fail to even mention the issue of demons and angels because, say the authors, there is a lack of factual material; but we do well to remind ourselves that Jesus and his Apostles, Paul included, took the existence of these beings seriously within their world view. This does not mean that we should simply absolutize that world view, but rather that we with new tongues should seek to proclaim, both to secularized human beings and to those who are much closer to the world view of Jesus and his contemporaries, the truth that Jesus is Victor.

Theological reflection on time and the eschaton. Another topic African Christian theologians are treating is the meaning of time and the eschaton. Many in Africa believe that Christianity becomes important to a person only after he dies. Many view it therefore as a mere Sunday-religion having little to do with daily life. For meaning in this latter area the Christians revert to their traditional religious systems.

But Seth Nomenyo wrote in an article for *Flambeau* in 1970 that a religion with a message only for the time after a person dies will never be able to dislodge and replace traditional African religions. "If the God of Revelation alone is true, he must then have to do with every man and the whole of man."[3] And to that sentence one might well add "with all his days and the whole of his time."

I am happy to see an increasing number of African theologians reflecting on the gift of time which God gives to man and the eschatological dimension to our life in it. The African student magazine *Présence* countered the excessive traditional Christian emphasis on the hereafter with an equally excessive opposite emphasis on the "now" element in Christianity; it reduced the gospel's whole emphasis on future liberation to temporal terms. John Mbiti takes a much more biblical approach to the question of time and its significance in his books *African Religions and Philosophy* and *Eschatology in an African Background.*

According to Mbiti, time is a key concept in all African religions. Time for an African is two-dimensional; past and present play a role, but the future does not. The distant past, denoted by a variety of terms in the African languages, is the stuff of which the present is made and determines its course in the future, for all the present is becoming past. Mbiti's discussion is so exciting because he analyzes the biblical concept of time against the backdrop of African concepts and proceeds to show how the eschaton and God's coming kingdom are real entitities which do not merely become important to a person after he dies but touch him right now and become the standard for his words and deeds.

Some people accuse Mbiti of being one-sided, but at least he attempted to do something never tried before in Africa: to understand the relation of time to eternity.

African Contributions to Christian Ethics

African theologians today face the great task of building up a system of Christian ethics. Of course no Christian ethical system anywhere can ultimately answer the question "What must we do?", for only God himself by means of his Word can answer that. But Christian ethics can provide arrows pointing to where one can find such an answer.

Africans object to the way ethics has traditionally been taught in seminaries, for instructors took little account of the manner in which African

3. Seth Nomenyo, in *Flambeau* 27 (1970): 127.

ethical consciousness came to expression in traditional culture. Ethics courses in seminaries simply transmitted the deposit of Western material to Africans without trying seriously to engage in dialogue. Since every traditional African religion is a composite not only of myths and rites but also of customs which prescribe certain patterns of behavior, and since those customs are circumscribed by a whole range of taboos, anyone who wishes to teach ethics in an African setting must come to know this background before he proceeds to the fountain from which the gospel's new ethos flows. It is heartening to see a number of African theologians, often writing in the African languages, treating the tension between traditional African adherence to custom and renewal of life in Christ.

One of the most profound African analyses was written by the Nigerian ethicist, E. A. Adeolu Adegbola, *The Theological Basis of Ethics*. He begins his book by providing a case study of the Yoruba understanding of sin, norms, and sanctions and then confronts it with the message of forgiveness and renewal disclosed in the New Testament. The main question around which everything revolves in the Yoruba system, as indeed among so many other African religions, is how to restore order in the universe once the harmony has been disturbed. How can the head, stomach, heart, body — indeed, the whole person — of the sinner be restored? For this one thing the devotees of the archaic religions are eagerly longing. Adegbola concludes his study with these words: "For this these people are waiting. And Christ through his cross has done it, uniquely, absolutely, and finally."[4]

Not only are African theologians and ethicists beginning to develop a theological basis for their ethics, but they are also dealing with concrete ethical issues and problems in African society. One of them is the role of family and marriage in African society. I have already mentioned the book by C. M. van Heemstra, *Thuis in Afrika* ("At Home in Africa"), in which she discusses issues such as polygamy vs. monogamy, the expanded family vs. the single family (in the urban areas), bride price, rearing of children, children of unwed parents, emancipation of women, the status of the unmarried, etc. The question I want to deal with briefly here is: What contributions are African theologians making toward solving some of these problems?

We are all aware that Western missionary agencies seldom consulted the findings of cultural anthropologists when they imposed a system of marriage and family morals on the people to whom they were ministering. Rather, the system bore a greater similarity to a specific cultural phase in the West — for example, the Victorian era — than to an *in loco* reflection on the biblical criteria for marriage and family. African church history is full of tragic conflicts caused by these issues. In fact, the rise of the so-called independent church movements can be explained in terms of them.

But now African theologians themselves are beginning to tackle these problems. To confirm this one need only note the large number of monographs written by both theologians and Christian sociologists. The Roman Catholic theologians Inpongo, Zoa and Lufuluabo focused in on polygamy and bride price.

---

4. E. A. Adeolu Adegbola, *The Theological Basis of Ethics*, p. 136.

Zoa himself sharply attacked the bride price custom. Inpongo wrote *Pour une anthropologie Chrétienne du marriage au Congo* (1968).

I shall name only a few Protestant writers who are addressing these issues. K. A. Busia, the well-known Christian sociologist and politician, contributed an essay, "Married Life and the Family," to *Church in the Town* (1951). C. H. Dodlo wrote *Christianity and Family Life in Ghana*. Gabriel Setiloane and Harry Sawyerr have each written a book in the context of his own community in Africa to clear up the many Western misconceptions about traditional African marriage and to explain the more recent views of marriage.

Nor must I fail to mention the various consultations which local councils of African churches have planned and held in cooperation with individual African sociologists and theologians. The proceedings of these various consultations are now contained in reports which, of course, are too numerous to receive further attention here.

There is, however, one seminar which I do want to expand upon here. It is the first continent-wide consultation ever held in Africa on the topics of Christian marriage and family life. It was an impressive gathering of Christians in Kitwe, Zambia, in 1963 and in my judgment represents one of the most important attempts to provide wise and prudent direction in these delicate matters.

To partners in a polygamous marriage who wish to become church members the seminar said:

1. The polygamist has a social responsibility for his wives. To demand that he put them away, whether with or without their consent, is to place them in a difficult social position, and to expose them to moral danger, including that of prostitution.
2. To permit baptism to the polygamist but to refuse him Holy Communion is contrary to Holy Scripture. Polygamists might be entered on the list of "adherents," and be permitted to partake of the Holy Communion, but not allowed to hold posts of responsibility in the Church.[5]

Of course no one claims that every church in Africa is now falling into line with these statements and determining its policies by them, but it is an important effort to reach a consensus, a consensus which seems to be more in the spirit of Paul than do all those rigorous demands of the "purifiers" of the Victorian era.

The consultation's advice about the bride price custom is also balanced:

We recommend
(i) that the system be not condemned in itself of its acknowledged abuse; that the abuses be countered by sound teaching on the meaning of persons and of marriage and, where necessary, by restrictive (but not prohibitive) legislation by the State;
(ii) that the traditional exchanges be "Christianized" into a token of the covenant between the partners and their families, as part of the integration of custom with Christian marriage rites.[6]

5. All-Africa Church Conference, "Report of the All-Africa Seminar on the Christian Home and Family Life, Held at Mindolo Ecumenical Centre, Kitwe, N. Rhodesia, 17 February to 10 April, 1963" (Geneva: n. p., 1963), p. 20.
6. Ibid., p. 56.

In its resolutions the Christian Home and Family Life Seminar also made powerful pleas for parents to show responsibility in matters of family planning and its relationship to population growth and development.

The seminar addressed the whole range of problems in African marriage and family life, and those with further interest in this topic can best turn to the report itself, *All Africa Seminar on the Christian Home and Family Life* (Geneva, 1963).

African Christians are also beginning to tackle the areas of social-economic and political ethics. In 1963 Z. K. Matthews presented a surprising address to the conference on Inter-Church Aid. African churches, he said, are now taking the responsibility for solving the countless problems they face which were formerly "solved" for them by foreign rulers. The most striking example he used was the churches' accepting responsibility for building up new and politically independent states. "Gaining freedom and independence has not spelled the end of difficulty for the African people. On the contrary, Africans realize that not only must they now do the tasks which others used to do for them but they must also tackle the problems which colonial authorities simply left untouched." This all-around gifted man was one of the first Africans to become deeply involved in the whole range of problems which we summarize in two short words: *ethica politica*. No wonder that the Church and Society Conference of 1966 dedicated its symposium study, *Responsible Government in a Revolutionary Age,* to him.

But other groups and individuals aided the cause of "black Africa." Christians not only participated in the struggle for liberation in Angola, Mozambique and Guinea Bissau but through their participation became more deeply aware of the economic, social and political dimensions of ethics. As is always the case with subjects such as these, students did much of the writing. In this case it was the African wing of the World Student Christian Federation and its magazine, *Présence*. One of the authors writing in this magazine stated: "Economic liberation is equally important as spiritual devotion. And political liberation is equally important as eternal salvation in an 'African theology.' To disregard the material, as most missionaries have tended to do, is to actually denude the spiritual."

These sentences are typical of trends in the area of social, economic and political ethics. Experts claim that Africa does have the necessary help available, and yet in spite of that its people remain poor. More and more young theologians are asking why this should be and are trying to gain an understanding of the neocolonial structures which contribute to this deplorable situation.

Africa is beginning to develop a "theology of liberation" which will be able to counteract the internal and external powers tending to hinder human beings from leading complete and productive lives. Social and political liberation is an important aspect of this total theology.

Adeolu Adegbola from Nigeria has dealt intensively with these issues, not only in his own Yoruba language but also in English. He contributed to the series produced by the Church and Society Conference of 1966, *From Tribalism to Nationhood.* and also to a study on the Christian interpretation of the African revolution which was published in the *Consultation Digest* of the department of Inter-Church Aid of the All-Africa Conference of Churches.

African Contributions to Liturgics

To be complete in my report about liturgy in Africa, I would have to include the great amount of work both Roman Catholic and Protestant Africans are doing in this area. Since space does not permit this, I shall include only a few brief notations and hope that they are sufficient to indicate the high priority I attach to this work.

Anyone who has attended a worship service in a so-called historic church in Africa is immediately struck by the European or American shape of the liturgy. In fact, one of my friends who attended an Episcopalian service in Accra commented that the African service was even more Episcopalian than those in the United States. The same holds true for Presbyterians and the other various denominations.

How different are the worship services of the so-called independent churches where music, dance, recitation and rhythm are such integral parts of worship and seem to flow naturally from the African soul! A recognition of this striking difference has been partially responsible for the recent efforts to give a new shape to the African liturgy.

J. N. van Pinxteren did a survey in which he indicated the wide range of liturgical activities which are receiving a new mold: funeral services, birth and christening rites, prayers, music, dance, exorcism, healing, thank offerings, etc. He cited the following leaders in this effort: Mbunga, Moeng, Inpongo, Kalanda, and Sawyerr.

At a conference on public worship held in Kampala Rev. John Gatu, the present chairman of the All-Africa Conference of Churches, argued for the use of ancient African ritual in the church's worship. He attributed the collapse of communal feelings in many African societies to the lack of respect for traditional values and rituals. But his proposals for change, such as the substitution of flesh and water for bread and wine in the celebration of the Lord's Supper, encountered stiff opposition.

One often hears the charge that by making the agrarian African past, which is so tightly connected with traditional African rituals, into a frame of reference, the needs of city dwellers are being ignored. This may be partially true, but at any rate, the development of new liturgies and the critical reflections upon Western liturgies are so urgent because they are so intertwined with the larger question of a new identity.

LATIN AMERICA

With the assistance and information which Latin American theologians have given me I hope to help my readers find their way through the recent theological developments which both have taken place and are continuing to occur in Latin America. For those searching for a deeper understanding of the trends than these pages provide, I hope to point out the appropriate sources.

In 1967 John Sinclair compiled his *Protestantism in Latin America: A*

Bibliographical Guide, which in spite of its extensive coverage ignores the literature of the evangelicals.

C. Peter Wagner compiled a rather extensive catalog of authors' names and book titles related to Latin American theology. He distributed this catalog in stencil form from the University of Southern California Graduate School of Religion in May, 1974. Then too, Orlando Costas wrote a general orientation to the Latin American scene, *The Church and Its Mission.* Though Costas himself is an evangelical, the tone of his writing marks him as one of the bridge builders between the evangelical and ecumenical camps in Latin America. His comments and footnotes beginning on page 121 of his book I found especially helpful for gaining an orientation.

Latin American Theology before the Rise of the New Theology

Rogier van Rossum, one of the most knowledgeable Dutch students of Roman Catholic Latin America, called the theology of Latin America before the rise of the new theology "subsistence theology," meaning thereby that it suffered from malnutrition. José Comblin, the famous Belgian priest who became a Latin American and now is heavily involved in the theology of liberation, points out in a review of van Rossum's work that the storehouses of Latin American theology were filled with translations of works by European Roman Catholic authors. Juan Luis Segundo, who became so involved in creating a genuinely Latin American theology after the Medellin conference, wrote during the 1960's that a unique Latin American theology is the pressing need of the hour if Latin American theologians are ever to become even branch managers in an industry largely controlled from European headquarters. Even as recently as the 1960's theological education was patterned largely after the model of the French seminaries, and the textbooks were based mostly on material from foreign authors, usually either Belgian or French.

But the bishops' conference held at Medellin in 1968 was a turning point. Latin America had now fully and consciously entered a revolutionary era; the conference shocked the bishops into an awareness of this fact, and thereafter the tiny seed of liberation theology sprouted and grew very rapidly.

Protestant theology has taken a quite different course from Roman Catholic theology. In spite of a few limited forays into Latin American territory during the sixteenth century, Protestantism only really came to this area in the nineteenth century through immigration. It was always a minority, at times tolerated (as in Argentina, Uruguay and Brazil) and at times persecuted. When the situation finally began to loosen up a bit around the turn of the century, genuine Latin American Protestant congregations such as the Methodists, Baptists, Presbyterians, Pentecostals, etc., began to form. These in turn began to consolidate with each other under the impact of the great Latin American Protestant congresses of Panama (1916), Montevideo (1925), and Havana (1928). Through I in no way intend to rehearse the complete history of Latin American Protestantism, I do want to mention that once again, as in the case of Roman Catholicism, there was a dearth of native theological literature.

Most Protestant congregations were satisfied with requiring a mere Bible school training for their pastors, which, however valuable it may otherwise be, certainly does not produce creative theologians. In fact, many large groups of Protestants actively opposed intellectual training. What little theological energy was generated was often spent in polemics, usually against the dominant Iberian Roman Catholic church. The Protestant literature of those years veritably overflowed with attacks against the doctrines of transubstantiation, immaculate conception, infallibility of the pope, etc. Such literature is now totally outdated and merely gathering dust in Protestant bookstores.

Even though the Presbyterian and Lutheran churches did not share the anti-intellectual sentiments of some other Protestant groups and therefore attached greater value to theological literature, most of their books were translations of North American and European authors.

But a new day has dawned also in Latin American Protestantism. The increased social awareness of the Latin American people, the changed climate in the Roman Catholic church since the Second Vatican Council, and the impact of the bishops' conference of Medellin have all had an effect on Protestantism.

The Start of New Theological Trends

Three key questions combined as catalysts to produce new theological trends in Latin America. The first is related to the rapidly increasing Latin American awareness of the deep social, economic, cultural and political needs of the continent. In the early nineteenth century, especially from 1810 to 1820, Latin America struggled free from the shackles of Portuguese and Spanish colonialism, but its social structure did not change. In fact, a form of internal semicolonialism then prevailed which was easily translated into an external semi- or neocolonialism when North America began to penetrate the territory of its neighbor to the south. During this phase the old elite element in Latin America faced the addition of another member to its ranks: a new elite composed of farmers and workers rose to prominence, and it was unwilling to tolerate any longer this neocolonial structure. In addition to this new elite vanguard the popular masses also increasingly regarded the existing situation as unacceptable. Sociologists in those years did much to increase the level of popular awareness.

Dr. Orlando Fals Borda, the well-known Colombian Christian sociologist, wrote in his *Campesinos de los Andes* that Latin American villagers used to simply acquiesce with a dull "What's the use?", but now they are asking "What must we *do*?" The dramatic events in Mexico (1910), Bolivia (1952), Cuba (1960), Chile (1970), and Argentina (1973) all point to the Latin American sense of awareness and are symptoms of the present enormous tensions.

Already in 1962 the historian Arnold Toynbee said in a speech in Latin America: "Things are happening in Latin America today which in my judgment will prove to be as historically significant as the Renaissance of the fifteenth century." And John Mackay, a North American Presbyterian who knew Latin America so well, commented that the present situation reminded him of the period just prior to the Reformation, for now, as then, an all-embracing social, political and religious awareness is taking hold of people.

The question avant-garde Roman Catholic and Protestant theologians were increasingly asking was this: How must we with our theology respond to the challenges of the times?

A second question which Roman Catholic theologians especially have been asking for some time already and are asking still is this: How can we translate traditional Iberian Catholicism into an "incarnational Christianity?" That is, how can we assist in doing away with all the superficial clericalism which prevents the laity from coming into its own, the stiff rituals and stuffy dogmas, and turn this dominant tradition into something which meets people where they are in life and transforms them?

Roman Catholics made their first objective critique of their own tradition in a book entitled *Latin American Catholicism: A Self-Evaluation,* and since that time scores of priests and laity have banded together to press for change. I shall mention just a few of them in the succeeding pages.

Protestants too are asking some of the same questions, though from a different perspective. Traditionally, Protestant theology was interested more in heaven than in life here on earth, more in individual salvation than in justice and shalom for life in human society. Recognizing this, Protestants began asking whether they were not simply bypassing the concrete reality of life in Latin America with all its attendant misery.

The third question had to do with ecumenical relations. Iberian Catholicism and Protestantism had always been suspicious of each other and fueled their suspicions with heavy polemics. But during this time when so many monumental and critical changes were transpiring in Latin American society around them, the avant-garde in both the Roman Catholic and Protestant camps felt that not only were such entrenched positions against each other irresponsible; they vitually needed each other to face the challenges of the hour. Especially since the Second Vatican Council, a new climate of understanding and common feeling has come across the avant-garde on both sides. These Roman Catholic and Protestant theologians began to develop a deep and abiding friendship, and their experience is gradually beginning to penetrate the lives of people in their churches. The United Bible Societies have made their own unique contributions to this greater understanding and respect.

To deal concretely with the issues posed by the above three questions Latin Americans developed a large number of social-political action groups. One feature of liberation theology in Latin America is that it arose and continues to exist through its vital contact with these groups. It is a theological reflection on the actual work which these groups are doing to bring about tiny and great changes in society.

Some of the more important of these action groups are: *Oficinia Nacional de Informacion Sacerdotel* (ONIS) in Peru, *Tercermundistas* ("Priests of the Third World") in Argentina, *Cristianos par el Socialismo* ("Christians for Socialism") in Chile primarily, *Iglesia y Sociedad en America Latina* (ISAL — "Church and Society in Latin America"), *Golconda* in Colombia, *Exodo* in Costa Rica, *Rosca* in Colombia, and *Sacerdotes para el Pueblo* in Mexico. All these were the laboratories which discovered and produced the theology of liberation.

Theology of Liberation

The originators of the theology of liberation chose the phrase "theology of liberation" to clearly set it off from another type, the theology of development. Development theology came to Latin America in the wake of the Second Vatican Council and the World Council of Churches' 1966 Conference on Church and Society. However, the avant-garde was not satisfied with development theology, for in the context of Latin America it played too much into the hands of those groups affiliated with the North American "Alliance for Progress." These latter groups strongly inclined toward the efficient techniques of North American capitalists and managers and were willing to make concessions to them as a means of feathering their own nests while the lot of the impoverished masses did not improve. Proponents of liberation theology are not armchair scholars but rather are fully active participants in the work of helping the poor. Liberation theologians realize full well that structural poverty must be tackled in order to bring genuine relief. Liberation theology is "grassroots" theology.

Liberation theology is also interconfessional. Both priestly movements and Protestant action groups like ISAL work with it.

Nor is this theology a static entity. It is continually moving and developing. It is more interested in experiments than in conclusions and makes progress by first bouncing its head against the concrete problems and then through dialogue searching for solutions. While traditional theologies by their apolitical and individualistic posture became actual accomplices of the manipulation and subjugation of the multitudes, this theology is interested in a new exodus which will lead to justice for all.

Leading Liberation Theologians

The leading Roman Catholic exponent of liberation theology is Gustavo Gutiérrez from Peru who wrote *A Theology of Liberation,* which I shall treat more fully in the following section. Hugo Assmann is a Brazilian Jesuit priest who was expelled from his native country because of his social and political activities, later worked in Uruguay and Chile, and served for a time both as a study secretary for ISAL and as an assistant of Professor Metz. Assmann is a prolific writer who is widely quoted and has attracted the attention of European theologians because of outspoken criticism of some of their work. Assmann's most recent book is *Teología desde la Praxis de la Liberación* (1973). Juan Luis Segundo from Uruguay, a fellow Jesuit of Assmann, finished his doctoral work in Paris in 1963 and now leads a center for research in Montevideo. His books include· *A Theology for Artisans of a New Humanity* (five volumes, published in 1973/74) and *Iglesia Latinoamericana Protesta o Profecia,* a symposium study published in 1973. Enrique Dussel is a Roman Catholic philosopher and historian from Argentina whose book, *Historia de la Iglesia en América Latina* (1972), has been described by experts as the most probing analysis of the history of Roman Catholicism in Latin America.

Another Roman Catholic liberation theologian is José Comblin, a Belgian priest who went to Brazil to work, was expelled, and now is active in various Latin American countries. He wrote a fine survey of the situation in the churches of Latin America in *Wereld en Zending* and has most recently written his book *Liberation in Latin American Christian Thinking*.

Segundo Galilea is a native of Chile who once worked at CIDOC (an inter-cultural documentation center) and now is professor at the Pastoral Institute of the bishops' conference of Latin America with its headquarters in Ecuador. Since the important bishops' conference of Medellin, Galilea has developed into a creative writer in the areas of missiology and pastoral theology. In 1971 he published *The Pastoral Situation in Latin America*.

I must also not fail to mention Hector Borrat, chief editor of *Vispera* and a member of ISAL; Alvarez Calderón; J. A. Hernandez; and J. Lozano as additional representatives of Roman Catholic involvement in liberation theology.

Protestants too have contributed greatly to liberation theology. Lack of space prohibits me from mentioning more than a few names. The first Protestant whom I would mention is Julio de Santa Ana, a former secretary of ISAL who now is a part of the Geneva-based Commission of the Churches' Participation in Development. Among his many books are *Id por el Mundo, Estructuras para la Mision* (1966), and *Protestantismo, Cultura y Sociedad: Problemas y Perspectivitas de la fe Evangelica en América Latina* (1970). The latter book is a most important contribution toward developing a social ethic of liberation in Latin America.

Another Protestant whose work I shall treat more extensively in the following pages is Rubem Alves.

Gonzalo Castillo Cardenas is a Presbyterian preacher from Colombia who served for years as secretary of the Presbyterian Alliance in Latin America and now has concentrated his efforts in two other organizations: *Rosca,* which does work among the Indians, and the Camillo Torres Foundation. In his many Spanish and English publications on the frequent Presbyterian consultations and meetings of SODEPAX (to which he belongs), Cardenas has become increasingly radical in his understanding of the churches' social role in Latin America. "Simposio Sombre Teologia de la Liberacion," his article about the symposium on liberation theology held in Bogota in 1970, is of particular importance here.

No list of prominent Protestant Latin American liberation theologians would be complete without the name of Emilio Castro from Uruguay. However, since I have given him and his work rather extensive coverage in another book (see *Jezus Christus de Bevrijder,* p. 107), I shall do nothing more than mention his name here.

José Míguez Bonino is a highly competent professor at the ecumenical seminary in Buenos Aires whose specialty is social ethics. His writings represent important attempts to continue the dialogue between the ecumenicals and the evangelicals (see, for example, his *Que es la Evangelizacion,* published in 1965), between Protestants and Roman Catholics (*Polemica, Dialogo y Mision, Catolicismo Romana y Protestantismo*), and between the more traditional Christians and the young radicals (*Out of the Hurt and Hope*).

Both Emilio Castro and Míguez Bonino especially have played important mediatorial roles among the various factions within Latin American Protestantism.

Examples of Liberation Theology

(1) Gustavo Gutiérrez, *A Theology of Liberation.* Gustavo Gutiérrez is a prominent Roman Catholic theologian who has dared to fill the blank page of a Roman Catholic Latin American Theology with a highly original book which everyone regards as the *opus magnum* of liberation theology. Gutiérrez wrote his book after the Medellin conference where the bishops simply were forced to take account of the social revolution, though the Pope himself tried to close his eyes to it. Gutiérrez was writing his book during the days when the Christian Democratic party of Eduardo Frey in Chile tried to apply the Roman Catholic social teaching of the famous encyclicals, *Rerum Novarum* and *Quadrigesimo Anno,* but found that they were not effective solutions to the concrete social and political problems.

Gustavo Gutiérrez was born in Peru in 1928 and at present is a professor in Lima, chaplain to students, and advisor to the episcopate. He took part in the first Latin American meeting of "Christians for Socialism" held in Santiago, Chile, during the final phase of the Allende regime. He begins his book with these words: "This book is an attempt at reflection, based on the Gospel and the experiences of men and women committed to the process of liberation, in the oppressed and exploited land of Latin America."[7] Gutiérrez is quite obviously referring to the action groups mentioned above. Though his theology clearly shows the influence of European political theologians like Metz and Moltmann, Gutiérrez shares with his Latin American brothers the opinion that the Europeans remain far too abstract and provide little leadership in practical affairs. One act of solidarity with the poor is worth more than any amount of theology, but a theology which helps people to understand their situation and makes them able to respond appropriately is nevertheless worth doing, claims Gutiérrez. His chief concern is not to develop a new theology but rather a new way of doing theology.

After a short analysis of the situation in Latin America, Gutiérrez rejects the theology of development (*desarrollo*) on the grounds that it is too functional and does not strive for structural change. He then proceeds to describe the liberation which must come and inquires into the place of the church in this whole process. Laity receive the highest position, followed by priests, those in religious orders, bishops, etc.

Gutiérrez devotes his final chapter to eschatology and tries to discern how Christians and the ecclesiastical communities together with other people must learn to live out their days knowing the eschaton is coming. Two of his final words summarize the proper attitude: solidarity and protest.

Throughout his book Gutiérrez frequently compares the work of the theology of liberation with the manner in which Marxism leads its proletariat. Though both are alike in their desire for change, the differences are deep and wide. The motivation is different: agapic love versus hate between the classes. The anthropology is different: contrary to Marxism, liberation theology never claims that one is totally free when the oppressive structures have been lifted. And there are differences in each one's understanding of the meaning of history and the eschaton.

7. Gustavo Gutiérrez, *A Theology of Liberation* (New York: Orbis Books, Maryknoll, 1973), p. ix.

(2) Rubem Alves, *A Theology of Human Hope*. The Brazilian Rubem
Azevedo Alves was born in 1933 and studied at the famous and highly respected
seminary in Campinas. He also studied at Union Theological Seminary in New
York and after a few years' practical experience returned to the United States
to do doctoral study at Princeton Theological Seminary. In 1968 he finished his
dissertation which was later published as *A Theology of Human Hope*. He is involved in higher education in the social studies at Sao Paulo and in the "Church
and Society" studies. Alves is also a member of the Faith and Order Commission
of the World Council of Churches.

Rubem Alves's ideas and vision have been strongly influenced by those of
his friend and co-worker in the Christian student movement, Richard Shaull, who
now is a professor at Princeton; and also by those of Charles West, professor of
ethics at Princeton. Another of Alves's friends, Harvey Cox, wrote the foreword
to his book.

The book itself bespeaks its author's great ecumenical erudition. Alves
simply takes it for granted that a scholar such as he will be in contact with the
whole of contemporary theology and philosophy. With the greatest of ease he can
adapt certain features from the sociology of Karl Mannheim and the philosophies
of John Dewey and Thomas Kuhn. He continually engages Western theologians
such as Shaull, Jürgen Moltmann (and through Moltmann, Ernst Bloch), Paul
Lehmann, Karl Barth, and many others in conversation. But he also carries on
discussion with other theologians from his own continent such as Esdras Borgeo
Costra, Paulo Freire, and others.

This broad acquaintance with so many scholars and traditions does not
lead Alves into the pitfall of eclecticism as one might suspect but rather produces a
theology that is both clear in its objective and able and willing to employ every
tool of theology and philosophy to illustrate the unique theme suggested by the
book's title.

The book's setting is, of course, Latin America, and Alves sees the great
masses of people there as but one contingent of a "worldwide proletariat" which
is becoming aware of its plight. Here and there one can see vanguards (of
students, to cite but one group) arising which are increasingly able to analyze the
situation and creatively participate in the liberation process. But people need
power to achieve liberation, and power is a political matter. To one who has this
new awareness politics is nothing less than a new gospel, a new proclamation of
the good news with the message that as man rises up from his passivity and
reflexive attitude a new future can come into existence.

Alves perceives two distinct camps struggling for liberation in Latin
America: a "humanistic messianism" influenced manifestly by Marxism and a
"messianic humanism" which aligns itself with the means and goals of Jesus the
Messiah in the noble quest for humanization.

Alves poses this question: "What sources does the community of faith
possess to make a positive contribution to the historic liberation of man?", and
with this question in mind he treats the work of Bultmann, Karl Barth and Jürgen
Moltmann. In my opinion he is correct in accusing Bultmann of a rather liberal
pietism which can offer absolutely no assistance to a project which is social and
political in nature. He claims that in the early phase of his theology Barth left too

little room for political obedience, while in the second phase Barth restricted the theologian's contribution to humanization almost exclusively to the work of proclamation.

As for Moltmann, no one can deny that in many respects he and Alves are kindred spirits. I believe that Alves himself would concede that he could never have written his book without Moltmann's inspiration. Obviously the similarity in their theologies goes far beyond the title. However, though I do not agree with him at this point, Alves believes that Moltmann's theology of the future remains too transcendental and too seldom comes down to touch the real experience of suffering in history. Criticizing Moltmann, Alves says: "Hope does not make one pregnant, but rather being pregnant does fill one with hope. God is in the present, and He is opening the way to an authentic future. But one can only take hold of this by striving to bring such a future about." Alves goes so far as to charge Moltmann with being content with the bourgeois status quo — to my mind, a totally unfounded accusation when one considers Moltmann's personal efforts for change within his own country.

After his critique of the several theologies, Alves proceeds to develop "the unique language of Messianic humanism." Humanistic messianism such as Marxism, for example, is too optimistic about man and society and therefore flies to pieces, ending up in romantic illusion or in a cynicism which gives up all hope and glorifies force.

But within the framework of messianic humanism, humanization is the very gift of God guaranteed by his mighty acts among the people of Israel and through Jesus Christ. (Note the clear accents of Moltmann!) The God and Father of Jesus Christ keeps man's future secure, and therefore hope and confidence in him spares us from fanaticism and disillusionment. Man can remain man, still hope when every reason for hope seems lost, and confidently await the new future of the divine messianic reign which God will introduce into history for man. This God guarantees not only liberation but also the freedom to live.

Since the promises of God are sure, we may celebrate and enjoy life even while we participate in the struggle for liberation. In chapter five Alves encourages his readers to celebrate the feast of life while enroute to the promised land of complete liberation where both man and society will be everything they were meant to be. No wonder Harvey Cox, author of *The Feast of Fools*, consented to write the foreword to Alves's book; Cox's own call to joy is so clearly evident in Alves's writing. But to see these sentiments coming through from a person in the context of the Latin American situation makes this a sparkling and refreshing chapter indeed.

(3) Hugo Assmann, *Opresion, Liberacion*. Hugo Assmann, another of the proponents of liberation theology, in all of his writings rails against a theology of repetition which preserves the status quo. He combines his appeal for change with a denunciation of European theology for ignoring the social sciences and being too ivory-towered. Even though Metz and Moltmann's influence upon Assmann is unmistakable, he terms their theologies nothing more than prologues, and in their present condition, impractical in the struggle against dependence and for liberation. Concrete experience and reflection are, as he says so often in his book *Opresion, Liberacion*, the *sine qua non* for any theologian.

Dialogue on Liberation Theology among Latin American Theologians

To follow the discussions in which Latin American theologians themselves are engaging makes exciting reading. Scholars such as Bonino and Costas have provided summaries which I shall follow as I add a few critical notations.

The critics have high regard for liberation theologians' efforts to break through the confines of traditional theology, and they admire deeply their intense involvement in the Latin American situation and the wealth of documentation. They respect too the ecumenical spirit in which liberation theologians do their work.

But along with the praise, these critics also alert their readers to some attendant dangers. Bonino, who himself is a liberation theologian, in a profound essay warned against making history a norm of revelation. He believes that at times liberation theologians have fallen prey to the danger of too facilely identifying the direct revelation of God in history with specific revolutionary events. He points to the work of Richard Shaull as an example. Christians, he believes, must keep their critical distance from the philosophy of Teilhard de Chardin and the ideology of Karl Marx, for only in this way can the church retain its prophetic function which must remain part and parcel of the events of salvation history which converge in the death and resurrection of Christ. The church is prophetic only as long as she continues to use salvation history as the criterion and the prophetic witness of the Apostles as the norm for all her own utterances. Nor must the church today forget that she speaks fallibly.

Peter Wagner, who spent years of work in Latin America before becoming professor in the School of World Mission at Fuller Theological Seminary in Pasadena, California, sharply attacked liberation theology in his book, *Latin American Theology: Radical or Evangelical?* Wagner began by surveying the work of several liberation theologians and concluded by discussing the work of four theologians associated with Billy Graham teams in Latin America: Fernando Vangioni, Washington Padilla, José Maria Rico and José Fajardo. Even though Wagner admits that the work of these four theologians is superficial and too brief in some respects, he offers it as a healthful antidote to liberation theology.

Wagner's horribly one-sided book met with opposition throughout the whole of Latin America, even among the evangelicals. One senses in it little effort to provide objective analysis but rather an attempt to inject the old squabble between fundamentalists and modernists in North America into the Latin American situation. James and Margaret Golff from Guernavaca and Dwain Epps, formerly from Buenos Aires and now a member of the Geneva-based Commission for International Affairs, opposed this book for failing to take into account the implications of the gospel for society and for simply perpetuating an attitude of passive acquiescence and a message of individual redemption rather than offering the church in society concrete help in its struggle for social righteousness.

Since the time he wrote it, even Wagner himself has come to realize that his book made absolutely no contribution to the ongoing dialogue.

One Latin American evangelical author who does make a contribution is Orlando Costas. In the final chapter of *The Church and Its Mission* he describes liberation theology as a challenge to pietistic theology to arrive at a real love, at a faith that acts in a society, and at a creative hope. He warns liberation theologians of the danger of situational hermeneutics and a new Pelagianism which threatens to erase the line of demarcation between humanistic messianism and messianic humanism.

The Latin American dialogue on liberation theology deserves our attention. One acquires the right to participate in it only after he has come to feel something of the deep need in Latin America and is willing to think and work with those who are pressing for change.

Other Latin American Theologies

I hope I have not created the impression in the preceding pages that all recent Latin American theology is liberation theology, for this is definitely not true. Some of the theologies being produced there are only remotely related to it and others have nothing at all to do with it. These other efforts too deserve our attention.

Roman Catholic Theology

The documents issued by CELAM, the bishops' conference of Latin America which met at Medellin, are most useful for the serious student of Latin American Roman Catholic theology. The documents themselves have been published in two volumes: *The Church in the Present-Day Transformation of Latin America in the Light of the Council.* The first volume is a position paper, and the second is a list of conclusions. Published in Bogota in 1970 by the general secretary of the bishops, these two books represent an exciting attempt to apply the decrees of Vatican II to the situation in Latin America.

Two writers who have made very constructive contributions to Latin American Roman Catholic theology through the CELAM organizational structure are Jesus Andreo Vela and Dom Helder Camara. Camara is the archbishop of Olinda and Recife in Brazil and a leading exponent of nonviolent demonstrations for social change. Some of his writings are *The Church in Modern Latin America,* an address to the tenth CELAM convention; *The Challenges Confronting Young People,* a letter to the young people of his diocese; "Is Violence the Only Option in Latin America? Violent or Non-violent Revolution," a classic declaration included in the book *Between Honesty and Hope;* "Development Projects and Concern for Structural Changes," included in *Fetters of Injustice;* and *Christians and Marxists Look for Common Ground,* an address delivered in Münster, Germany, on the occasion of his receiving an honorary doctorate.

Another rich source of Latin American Roman Catholic theology is the Latin American Pastoral Institute (IPLA) based in Quito, Ecuador. It is an affiliate of the Latin American bishops' conference and specializes in "socio-pastoral theology." Segundo Galilea, already mentioned in the list of liberation theologians, heads this institute and enjoys wide respect. His many publications include *Espiritualidad y Renovación Pastoral* (1969); *Reflexiones Sobre Evangelización* (1970); *La Vertiente Política de las Pastoral* (1971); *Evangelización en América Latina; Contemplación y Apostolado;* and *A Los Pobres de Les Anuncia el Evangelio* (1972).

The IPLA published a symposium study which ties in to the developments within liberation theology: *Pastoral Popular y Liberación en América Latina*. Contributors are Segundo Galilea, José Comblin, Monica Gonzales, José Marius, and Maria Arroyo.

Protestant Theology

Both the Methodist and the Presbyterian denominations have given birth to a number of productive Latin American theologians. I shall name only a few. Justo L. Gonzales, a Cuban now teaching in Atlanta, Georgia, wrote *History of Christianity in the Latin Caribbean, Historia de Las Misiones,* and *History of Christian Thought* (three volumes). He also compiled in 1965 a symposium study on the need for renewal in theological education: *Por la Renovacion del Entemdimiento la Educacion Teologica en la América Latina*. I must mention one more of his books: *Revolución y Encarnación*.

Lara Brand, another mainline-denomination Mexican Protestant, wrote *We Claim Our Future*.

Martino Arias, Methodist bishop in Bolivia, served as a delegate to the world mission conference in Bangkok and recorded his impressions in a book, *Salvacion es Liberación*. He also serves as a member of the Commission for World Mission and Evangelism of the World Council of Churches. His other writings include *Evangelizacion y Revolucion en América Latina* and *Die hellen Schatten: Evangelische Christen in Südamerika*.

But Protestant theological activity is not restricted to mainline denominations alone. There are a host of evangelical Christians who cut across countless denominational lines, and the "Latin American theological fraternity" within it has given a great stimulus to theological thinking. This fraternity has held no less than four theological consultations since 1971, the most important of which produced a symposium study on social ethics, *Fe Cristiana y America Latina Hoy,* edited by Rene Padilla. It is a notable first step into an area previously shunned by evangelicals.

The International Fellowship of Evangelical Students in Argentina and Peru provides an additional theological stimulus. While the *Movimiento Estudiantèl Cristano* (MEC) is the Latin American affiliate of the World Student Christian Federation which has close ties with liberation theology through persons such as Emilio Castro, the late Valdo Galland, and many others, the Fellowship of Evangelical Students is much more closely attached to the evangelical wing of Latin American Christianity. The writings of theologians such as Pedro Arana, Rene Padilla, and Samuel Escobar who all come out of this camp indicate that they are becoming increasingly involved with the very same problems which are engaging the liberation theologians. I have in mind such books as Arana's *Providencia y Revolucion* and Escobar's *Dialogo entre Cristo y Marx*.

The Latin American Community of Evangelical Ministries is also publishing many studies in the areas of Old and New Testament theology. Wilton Nelson, Irene Faulkes and Ricardo Faulkes are its leading authors.

My last example of evangelical involvement in Latin American theology is the "Evangelism in Depth" movement, begun by R. Kenneth Strachan of the Latin American Mission and now being continued by many Latin Americans themselves. The movement's representatives call its theology "wholistic." This movement seeks to involve every Christian congregation in a local area in a cooperative effort to bring the Christian faith to bear on every aspect of society. Juan Stam wrote in *Evangelismo a Fondo Conno Revolucion Teologica:* "In a sense this is revolutionary theology, for it puts the message and the doctrine in their original context of 'evangelism.' It underscores the effect of the Gospel upon every aspect of human life and develops a theology from that perspective."

Kenneth Strachan and Victor Hayward participated in an exciting exchange of ideas in the April, 1964 issue of the *International Review of Missions*. Later such men of stature as Emilio Castro, José Míguez Bonino and Markus Barth, who was then teaching in the United States, also took part in this discussion which has become almost a classic. The point at issue was the individual versus the structural approach and whether they could possibly be combined; the intensity of the discussion shows signs of increasing rather than decreasing. The study secretary of "In-Depth Evangelism" is Orlando Costas who wrote *The Church and Its Mission*, which appeared in English translation in 1974. His book is an attempt to speak with defenders of the Church Growth School of McGavran *cum suis* on the one side and with spokesmen for liberation theology on the other. Costas is no mere foreigner but an actual son of Latin America engaging in dialogue on the subject of "In-Depth Evangelism's" theology within the actual context of Latin America. How interesting that he should have generated so much more mutual understanding on both sides than the participants in the dialogue ten years before! Costas' input at the Lausanne conference also marked him as a person interested in building bridges of better understanding between the ecumenical and evangelical camps.

Two thoughts press in upon me as I bring this survey of Latin America to a close. First, I could not have done it without the assistance of several Latin American friends, especially Orlando Costas. Second, the survey is highly selective and anything but exhaustive. In spite of its deficiencies, however, I hope that it may serve as a brief guide for that growing band of people who are becoming interested in Latin American developments.

INTRODUCTION TO THE LITERATURE OF BLACK THEOLOGY

I also wish to add a few pages of introduction to the literature of "black theology" in this chapter devoted to theological developments in Asia, Africa and Latin America. Black theology arose among the predominantly black churches in the United States, but its influence has crossed the Atlantic Ocean to reach the whole continent of Africa in general and the country of South Africa in particular. Since its impact is intercontinental, I treat it in a separate section.

As we surveyed the theologies being developed on the continents of Asia, Africa, and Latin America, we could often sense an element of confrontation and combat with "white" Western theology. Nowhere is this accent more evident than in black theology which quite consciously strives to condemn the arrogance of much of Western theology and to articulate its ideas from the position of a suppressed people which is enroute toward liberation. In this survey I begin with the United States and proceed to South Africa.

Black Theology in the United States

Rights of black people in the United States still are not universally respected. Many of them live in ghettos and are unable to find a job. In many respects they feel like outcasts whose genuine human worth and dignity are radically being called into question at every moment of their existence.

With this in mind, black Christians increasingly began to ask: What does the gospel mean for us in our situation? Yahweh, the God of the Exodus, led a slave people out of the land of Egypt, and Jesus Christ lived amid the poor. He belonged to a despised and oppressed people. He himself was humbled, cut off from his own folk, and finally consigned to a cross. But he also arose victorious from the grave as a Liberator. "What does all of this mean for us?" they began to ask themselves.

Negro spirituals and the blues had deeply and inimitably articulated through song the black understanding of Yahweh, Moses, and Jesus Christ. Songs like "Go down, Moses," "Deep River," "O Freedom, Freedom over Me," "Mary Had a Baby," "Were You There?", "Nobody Knows the Trouble I've Seen" and so many more have already been the "sound of soul" for decades. In essence, black theology is an attempt to give theological expression to the "sound of soul" which black people through their spirituals have been singing for years already. Furthermore, Martin Luther King and his co-workers had already been busy translating the eager longing of the spirituals into programs of action. Their writings were clarion calls to become involved. But there was a lacuna in deep theological reflection. Thus black theology arose to fill the gap.

The actual pioneer of black theology is James Cone, who now is a professor at Union Theological Seminary in New York. According to him and his disciples, theology is one's reflection upon his encounter with God who disclosed himself in Jesus Christ in a specific situation and land, at a specific time and to specific individuals and groups. Given this, black theology is the attempt by black theologians in North America who with their fellow blacks have suffered under structural racism and have been struggling for liberation, recognition, and a recovery of their human worth to work through their common experience theologically and to provide inspiration and insight along the way. Thus, black theology does not pretend to be *the* ultimate and universal answer to the gospel; it is one answer arising from a specific situation. It is and wishes to be "contextual."

James Cone's *Black Theology and Black Power* was the first book of this kind published. Throughout this book and the many other writings which he produced since then, some of which I will mention in the end of this section, he continually charges white theologians with taking special pains to extend themselves to agnostics, atheists, the secularized and those who in Western society have drifted from the church, while at the same time they scarcely have a word for the poor, despised and oppressed people living in ghettos.

•   But not only does black theology try to reflect the situation in which black people find themselves; it also attempts to read the Bible with a view to addressing that situation. In so doing it has picked up many nuances of the biblical message which white theologians until now have completely overlooked. It has come to perceive that sin has structural dimensions; liberation is not from spiritual powers alone; conversion has societal implications; reconciliation involves healing between various races; and living with one's eye on the eschaton also requires his participation in the struggle for justice here and now. All these themes black theology picked up and underscored in a manner hitherto unknown.

A third feature of black theology which admittedly is expressed more covertly and cautiously by some black authors than by others is the invitation to white theologians to do more than listen to the black interpretation. There is a call to participate in the struggle. In times past white people used to allow their black slaves serving dinner to sing a spiritual for the white guests. Black theologians today are totally uninterested in that kind of white participation. If there is going to be participation, it must be real. The words of James Baldwin to his white audience keep ringing through the pages of black theology: "As long as blacks are not really free, you are not free!"

Black theology wants deliberately to become a nettlesome "offense" for indifferent whites. It proposes to shock us and call us to conversion. White people once in a while charge Cone and his followers with depicting black people as totally sinless and white people as responsible for every evil and trouble. That of course is a completely unfounded charge. What they *do* say is that sins which are rooted in the unjust structures and proceed from a white misuse of power certainly cannot be charged against those who have no power but only against those who do have it. Black theology is one earnest appeal to us all to open our eyes to such sins.

Though James Cone was the pioneer voice of black theology and still today ranks as *primus inter pares*, other black theologians have joined him. Their approaches vary, especially on the question of appropriate methods in the struggle. Many of these authors are connected with the black studies programs at various seminaries throughout the United States. G. S. Wilmore wrote *Black Religion and Black Radicalism* (1972) and in his book protests the use of the term "black" as a symbol for all the victims of oppression. He recalls those other victims such as Indians who also suffer and urges his readers to rally in Christ's name for them too. Among the Nazis Christ took the form of one who wore the star of David; among the outcasts of India he became a pariah; and in the United States, says Wilmore, he assumes the form of an Indian and a black person.

Major Jones and Deotis Roberts are two other black theologians who argue strongly for the use of nonviolent means in the struggle and therefore counter the tendency toward black-power ideology expressed in the more strident writings of Cone. Vincent Harding somewhat romantically glorifies the African roots of black people and calls for a closer sense of identity with them. Virgil Cruz respects the intentions of his fellow black theologians and attaches great importance to their quest for an authentic theology but as a New Testament scholar questions their interpretation of Jesus. How, for example, did Jesus respond to the militant Zealots? Recalling the studies of Cullmann and Brandon, he reminds his readers that the last word on this subject has not yet been spoken.

Warner R. Traynham's *Christian Faith in Black and White* published in 1973 is one of the most important sourcebooks on black theology. Not only does he treat the current leading themes of black theology such as Liberator and Creator, the black situation, sin and power, power and violence, love and justice, redemption, penitence and reconciliation, etc., but he also includes the most important documents which the black theology movement has produced. These documents include: *Black Power*, the July 31, 1966, declaration by the National Committee of Negro Churchmen; *Racism and the Elections*, a large advertisement which black leaders placed in newspapers in 1966; *The Church and the Urban Crisis* (1967); *The Project of the Theological Commission*, by Gayraud S. Wilmore (1968); *Black Theology*, a declaration by the National Committee of Black Church Leaders (1969); and *The Black Declaration of Independence*, another newspaper advertisement in 1970.

In 1973 black theologians, Latin American liberation theologians, and white theologians came together for an ecumenical consultation in Geneva. One can read the reports of this discussion in a 1973 issue of the periodical *Risk*. Its cover bears the honest and striking title "*In*communication." One gets the impression from reading the reports of the confusing discussions that not much good came from the meeting. However, when James Cone and Herbert Edwards got together for a discussion directed by Jürgen Moltmann, they conducted the talks on a much higher plane. The January-February, 1974 edition of *Evangelische Theologie* contains a report of their probing exchange.

Black Theology in South Africa

Black theologians in the United States evoked an echo response to their writings from black African theologians who are questing for what they term a "theology of decolonization." One must distinguish this from a *theologia Africana* which in an earlier part of this chapter I described as an attempt to incorporate African culture into one's theological efforts. "Decolonizing theology," on the other hand, accents the same themes as black theology in the United States. They, too, see God as "black," that is, as one who identifies with the oppressed, who in Jesus Christ takes their plight upon himself, and who strives for total liberation by calling a halt to the vain delusion of racist ideology.

It goes without saying that such theology has had a deep resonance in South Africa where the apartheid caste system seeks to keep the whites on top and all other people in subjection. The secretaries of the University Christian Movement, which has since then been disbanded, initiated a study project on black theology several years ago. These leaders, Colin Collins, a former priest, and Basil Moore, a Methodist minister, entitled the project "Towards a Black Theology," and the project in turn led to an ecumenical plan to inquire what black theology could mean for black Africans. Black servility to white power and the white interpretation of the gospel which often comes down to "Trust, and take hope for the hereafter" came under sharp scrutiny. White liberals themselves are not in a position to alter the structures. Black theology in Africa is simply the blacks' effort to reinterpret the gospel for their situation by underscoring God's love as the restoring of human dignity, by emphasizing black self-esteem whereas once they were considered mere things, and by standing up for justice in the face of a thousand and one injustices. In time the lordly agents of the white power monopoly will be as afraid of *this* interpretation as the Roman rulers were of the message itself.

The piece by Collins and Moore ends by appealing to the church to identify with the disinherited and to work with the blacks so that in the end each will be able to proudly proclaim: "I am a man" and "Black is beautiful."

The above-mentioned document, important as it was and is, is the product of two white authors. This fact makes the several essays written by *black* Christians and published by the Christian Institute in Johannesburg in 1972 doubly important. Editor Mokgethi Motlhabi reminded his readers that even though black theology was around for a long time already in the independent churches, Collins and Moore provided the real impetus for actual reflection on black theology as a unique discipline.

Dr. Manas Buthelezi, a Lutheran theologian who came under a partial ban and who at least temporarily has recovered his freedom to speak and write, wrote an essay rejecting an ethnological approach to black African congregations, which was developed, for example, by Temple and used by Sundkler. He rather called for an anthropological approach which means theological reflection carried on in the context of the life of black African people. The poet Adam Small rejected apartheid, not because he longs for integration with Western ways and under Western conditions, but simply because, in his words, "we want to survive as *people*. In this situation one either chooses blackness or nihilism."

Steve Biko (who at the time the series of essays appeared served as chairman of South African Students Organization) unmasked the apartheid policy for what it really is — institutional racism. He therefore has provisionally chosen the way of noncooperation; "Black man," he warned, "you are on your own."

Certain essays show definite deviations from the theology of James Cone. For one thing, there is a stronger accent on love for one's neighbor, even though he be an enemy. Buthelezi, for example, makes an impassioned plea for black people to do things for the benefit of white people both to warn them and to call them to repentance so that a genuine community may emerge in place of segregation.

In conclusion I would like to make a few observations. First, we in the West, facing a different set of issues and circumstances from those of fellow Christians in Asia, Africa and Latin America, continually run the risk of too hastily condemning their theological efforts. Through contact with them and their theology we ought to become more aware of the contextual matrix out of which our own theology flows and thus be reminded of its relative character. A *theologia perennis* good for all times and all peoples simply does not exist. No single theology ever reflects by itself the fullness of God's revelation in Christ.

Second, we in the West really need the addition, correction, and renewal which contact with other theological traditions can provide. Fortunately, certain authors are beginning to realize this. I shall mention only two books which reflect this viewpoint. First of all, Robin H. S. Boyd's fine *India and the Latin Captivity of the Church*. Boyd himself hails from Northern Ireland but spent no less than ten years in India. While Boyd was on furlough in Ulster and Belfast, he was shocked by the tragic conflict in his homeland and as a consequence wrote his book. His final chapter summarizes the lessons for the West which he learned from India. He touches upon such things as the coming of a secular state, the freedom for open communication with others, the liberty for churches to join together, freedom for genuine and practical ecumenicity, freedom to throw off the shackles of Graeco-Roman terminology and to express the message in wholly new terms, images, and symbols.

The other book, no less valuable in this respect than Boyd's, is Kosuke Koyama's *Waterbuffalo Theology*. Koyama worked for a long time in Thailand, the land of the buffalo, and is now in Singapore affiliated with one of the most interracial theological institutes in the world. On the basis of rich experience he makes an impassioned plea for producing many theologies, each one relevant to its own context. Furthermore, there must be a mutual influence between these and Western theologies. The *Memoirs* of W. A. Visser 't Hooft rate so high with Koyama for precisely this reason; Visser 't Hooft's whole life displayed an almost unbelievable capacity to live in other situations and contexts and thus to understand the people, but he was also able to hold every situation, current of thought, and new theology at arm's length and to "test the spirits [to see] whether they be of God" (I John 4:1).

Koyama does not call Christians to return to a Crusade mentality but rather to put on the crucified mind of Christ in order to be able to distinguish the "wisdom of men" from the "foolishness of God."

My third observation is simple: acquaintance with other theologies can provide greater insight into the central themes of Christian faith. Koyama points out, for example, that one's view of the Bible, reconciliation, Christology, the eschaton, etc., can be greatly deepened and enriched by such exchange and new orientation.

Fourth, contact with other theologians can at times give rise to a new spirituality. A majority of the theologies in non-Western continents sprang to life after the Christians came into contact with poor and outcast human beings whose situation people in the West scarcely understand, in spite of all their supposedly learned talk. Latin American liberation theology, black theology and the Japanese theology of God's suffering are the clearest examples of theologies which take account of the needs and plight of real people. The very material which Western theologies at times are inclined to discard as anti-theology could perhaps become a condition for their own renewal, as Claude Geffre once said.

BIBLIOGRAPHY

1. General Literature

Allmen, D. "Das Problem einer 'einheimischen' Theologie im Lichte des neuen Testamentes." *Evangelische Missions Zeitschrift* 27 (1970): 51–71, 160–176.

Camps, A. "A Survey of Non-Western Theology with Special Reference to India." *Bulletin Secretariat pro non Christians* 5 (1970): 67–84.

Chandran, J. R. "Das Problem der 'Heimischmachung' christlicher Theologie in Asien." *Theologische Stimmen aus Asien, Afrika und Lateinamerika I*. Munich: Kaiser Verlag, 1965.

Gensichen, H. W. "Einzigartigkeit und Eigenart." *Ökumenische Rundschau* 18 (1969): 469–481.

Metzner, H. W. *Roland Allen: Sein Leben und Werk.* Gütersloh: Mohn, 1970. (See especially chapter four: "Allen's Missions Theologie und das Problem einer einheimischen Theolgie.")

Oosthuizen, G. C. *Theological Battlegrounds in Asia and Africa.* London: Hurst, 1972.

2. India

Appasamy, A. J. *An Indian Interpretation of Christianity.* Madras: Christian Literature Society, 1924.

——————. *Christianity as Bhakti-Marga: A Study in the Mysticism of the Johannine Writings.* Madras: Christian Literature Society, 1928.

——————. "An Approach to Hindus." *International Review of Missions* 17 (1928): 472 ff.

——————. "Sadhu Sundar Singh." *National Christian Council Review* 49 (1929): 120 ff.

——————. "The Ministry of the Church." *National Christian Council Review* 49 (1929): 468 ff.

——————. *Temple Bells: Readings from Hindu Religious Literature.* Calcutta: YMCA, 1930.

——————. *Church Union: An Indian View.* Madras: Christian Literature Society, 1930.

——————. "What is Moksha? A Study in the Johannine Doctrine of Life." *Indian Studies No. 3.* Madras: Christian Literature Society, 1931.

——————. "What is Christianity?" *Guardian,* April 7, 1932–March 16, 1933.

——————. "The Spread of Secularism in India." *International Review of Missions* 22 (1933): 69 ff.

——————. "The Study of Church History in India." *National Christian Council Review* 53 (1933): 123 ff.

——————. *Christ of the Indian Church: A Primer of Christian Faith and Practice.* Madras: Christian Literature Society, 1935.

——————. "The Christian Approach to Higher Hinduism." *National Christian Council Review* 57 (1937): 239 ff.

——————. *Christ Answers Youth's Problems.* Calcutta: YMCA, 1939.

——————. *The Gospel and India's Heritage.* London and Madras: Society for Promoting Christian Knowledge, 1942.

——————. "Christian Theology in India." *International Review of Missions* 38 (1949): 149 ff.

——————. "Christological Reconstruction and Ramanuja's Philosophy." *International Review of Missions* 41 (1952): 170 ff.

——————. "The Christian Pramanas or the Norms of Theological Thought." *Indian Journal of Theology* 2 (1953): 1 ff.

——————. *My Theological Quest.* Bangalore: Christian Institute for the Study of Religion and Society, 1964.

——————. "Erwägungen zu einer Indischer Theologie." In *Theologische Stimmen aus Asien, Afrika und Lateinamerika II.* Edited by G. F. Vicedom. Munich: Kaiser Verlag, 1967.

——————. "The Incarnate Christ and the Vision of God." *Religion and Society* 11, No. 3 (1969).

Bagoo, K. J. *Pioneers of Indigenous Christianity.* Bangalore: Christian Institute for the Study of Religion and Society; Madras: Christian Literature Society, 1960.

Boyd, R. H. S. *An Introduction to Indian Christian Theology.* Madras: Christian Literature Society, 1969.

Bürkle, H., ed. *Indische Beiträge zur Theologie der Gegenwart.* Stuttgart: Evangelisches Verlagwerk, 1966.

Chakkaray, Vengal. "The Historic Church as a Heritage." *National Christian Council Review* 47 (1927): 217 ff.

——————. "Jesus the Avatar." *Indian Studies No. 2.* Madras: Christian Literature Society, 1927.

——————. "Have We a Message?" *National Christian Council Review* 51 (1931): 581 ff.

——————. "What is to Indianize Christianity?" *Guardian,* October 1, 1931–January 14, 1932.

————. "Christian Higher Education in India." *Guardian*, January 28, 1932.

————. "The Cross and Indian Thought." *Indian Studies No. 6.* Madras: Christian Literature Society, 1932.

————. "Should the Indian Christian Community Continue?" *Guardian*, April 7–14, 1932.

————. "Inter-Religionism and Toleration." *Guardian*, May 12, 1932.

————. "Christian Worship and Idolatry." *Guardian*, June 9, 1932.

————. "Review of S. Radhakrishnan, Idealistic View of Life." *Guardian*, October 20, 1932.

————. "Rethinking Missions." *Guardian*, March 30–April 28, 1933.

————. "The Body of Christ in the West — As an Indian Sees It." *Guardian*, October 5–26, 1933.

————. "Karl Barth on Religions." *Guardian*, April 5–19, 1934.

————. "Triennial Meeting of Council (National Missionary Society)." *Guardian*, January 10, 1935.

————. "Church Union." *Guardian*, May 16–23, 1935.

————. "The Oxford Movement." *Guardian*, February 18, 1937.

————. "The Oxford Group House Party at Bangalore: Impressions and Confessions." *Guardian*, October 21, 1937.

————. "The Kingdom of God vs. The Church at Tambaram Conference." *Guardian*, April 6, 1939.

————. "The Challenge of Neo-Hinduism to the Finality of the Christian Gospel." *Guardian*, September 5–26, 1940.

————. "The Church." *Guardian*, February 18–May 6, 1943.

————. "The Resurrection of our Lord." *Guardian*, April 22, 1943.

————. "The Old Testament and Myself." *Guardian*, August 5, 1943.

————. "My Credo." *Guardian*, December 2, 1943.

————. "Indian Christianity and Its Critics." *Guardian*, March 9–April 20, 1944.

————. "Bangalore Conference Continuation 1944." *Guardian*, June 15, 1944.

————. "Some Aspects of Present Day Christianity." *Guardian*, October 31–December 12, 1946.

————. "Rethinking Christianity Continued." Review of *Our Theological Task*, by M. Ward. *Guardian*, April 17–July 17, 1947.

————. "Dr. Kraemer in Madras." *Guardian*, April 5, 1951.

Chenchiah, P. "Christianity and Hinduism." *National Christian Council Review* 48 (1928): 119 ff.

————. "The Holy Spirit: The Meaning and the Significance of Christianity." *Guardian*, June 30–August 11, 1932.

————. "Essentials of Christianity." Substance of Bible Studies, Bangalore Continuation Conference, 1933. *Guardian*, August 10–November 9, 1933.

————. "Christianity Has Changed." Summary of Bible Study, Bangalore Continuation Conference, 1934. *Guardian*, June 28, 1934.

————. "Bangalore Continuation Conference: Spiritual Heritage of India." *Guardian*, June 11, 1936.

————. "*The Christian Message in a Non-Christian World:* An Indian View of Dr. Kraemer's Presentation." *Guardian*, October 6, 1938.

————. "Kingdom of God in India." *Guardian*, May 4, 1939.

————. "The Time Concept in Religion." *Guardian*, June 29–July 6, 1939.

————. "Christian Youth, Non-Christian Faiths and Indian Culture." *Guardian*, July 27 and October 31, 1939.

————. "The Challenge of Modern Hinduism to the Finality of the Christian Gospel." *Guardian*, September 5, 1940.

————. "Programma: The Indian Christian Book Club." *Guardian*, January 9, 1941.

————. "The Future of Christianity in India." *Guardian*, July 10, 1941.

————. "Problems of the Indian Christianity Community." *Guardian*, January 29, 1942.

————. "Paper Poona Theological Conference." *National Christian Council Review* 63 (1943): 63 ff.

————. "Who is Jesus? A Study of Jesus in Terms of the Creative Process." *Guardian,* July 29–August 19, 1943.

————. "Sri Aurobindo–His Message." *Guardian,* September 9–16, 1943.

————. "Master C. V. V. of Kumbakonam and Briktha Rahitha Tharaka Raja Yoga: A Study of a Recent Religious Development in India." *Guardian,* October 14–28, 1943.

————. "Christians and Yoga: A Study of the Technique of Realisation in Relation to the Aims and Objects of Christianity." *Guardian,* March 23–April 20, 1944.

————. "The Dilemma and Dialectic of Religions." *Guardian,* June 8–July 6, 1944.

————. "Indian Christian Theological Task." Review and restatement of *Our Theological Task,* by M. Ward. *Guardian,* January 2–March 5, 1947.

————. *"The Bhagavadgita."* English translation and notes by S. Radhakrishnan. *Guardian,* September 2, 1948.

————. "Sri Kumaraswamiji, The Virashaiva Philosophy and Mysticism." *Guardian,* October 20, 1949.

————. "Christian Message in Hindu Environment." *Guardian,* February 9–16, 1950.

————. "Dr. Brunner and the Indian Christian Reaction." *Guardian,* August 17 and 24, 1950.

————. "Dr. Brunner and the Modern Hindu Mind." *Guardian,* October 19, 1950.

————. "Rayappan D. Immanuel, the Influence of Hinduism on Indian Christians." *Guardian,* October 19, 1950.

————. "My Search for the Kingdom." *Guardian,* February 8, 1951.

————. "Dr. Kraemer, Inter-religious Co-operation and Syncretism." *Guardian,* March 29, 1951.

————. " Prof. Kraemer and Syncretism." *Guardian,* April 19–26, 1951.

————. "Religions and the World." *Guardian,* July 16, 1953.

————. "The Vedanta Philosophy and the Message of Christ." *Indian Journal of Theology,* October, 1955, pp. 18 ff.

————. "Religious Toleration: An Essay at Understanding." In *Religious Freedom.* Edited by J. R. Chandran and M. M. Thomas. Bangalore: Christian Institute for the Study of Religion and Society, 1956.

————. "The Religious Situation in India." *Guardian,* August 9, 1956.

————. "Evangelism in Free India." *Guardian,* August 16–23, 1956.

————. "A Christian Approach to Sarvodaya: Comments and Criticism." *Religion and Society,* June, 1958, pp. 84 ff.

————. "Indian Christians and Co-operation with Non-Christians." *Indian Journal of Theology* 7 (1958): 1 ff.

————. "Indian Christians and Co-operation with Non-Christians." *Guardian,* April 24–May 1, 1958.

————. "Bulletin CISRS IV/1." *Guardian,* July 10, 1958.

————. "K. Narayanasami Iyer, Navina Geetam — New World Songs." *Guardian,* July 17, 1958.

————. "Harris, *Commentary on I Corinthians* in Christian Student's Library Series." *Guardian,* December 4, 1958.

————. "The Cross and Resurrection." *Guardian,* February 26, 1959.

————. "The Destiny of Man and Interpretation of History." *Principal Miller Endowment Lectures, Supplement to Madras University Journal,* 29, No. 1, n.d.

Chenchiah, P. and Chakkaray, V. *Rethinking Christianity in India.* Madras: D. M. Devasahayam and A. N. Sudarisanam, 1938.

Devanandan, P. D. "Trends of Thought in Contemporary Hinduism." *International Review of Missions* 28 (1939): 465 ff.

————. "The Gospel and the Modern Hindu." *Guardian,* September 26–October 3, 1940.

————. "The Theological Task in India." *National Christian Council Review* 63 (1943): 56 ff.

————. "Whither Theology in India?" *International Review of Missions* 33 (1944): 121 ff.

_____. "The Christian Message in Relation to the Cultural Heritage of India." *The Ecumenical Review* 2 (1949): 241 ff.

_____. *The Concept of Maya: An Essay in Historical Survey of the Hindu Theory of the World, with Special Reference to the Vedanta*. London: Lutterworth Press, 1950.

_____. "Trends of Thought in Contemporary Hinduism." *International Review of Missions* 39 (1950): 465 ff.

_____. "The Recent New Testament Scholarship and the Indian Church." *National Christian Council Review* 71 (1951): 484 ff.

_____. "The Challenge of Hinduism." *National Christian Council Review* 72 (1951): 176 ff.

_____. "The Christian Attitude and Approach to Non-Christian Religions." *International Review of Missions* 41 (1952): 177 ff.

_____. "Evangelism and the Christian Institutions in India." *Indian Journal of Theology* 1 (1952): 11 ff.

_____. "The Relevance of the Christian Hope to Our Time." *The Ecumenical Review* 5 (1952): 253 ff.

_____. "The Religious and Spiritual Climate of India Today." *The Ecumenical Review* 9 (1956): 307 ff.

_____. "A Centre for Study of Hindusim: A New Venture on Christian Evangelism in India." *International Review of Missions* 46 (1957): 260 ff.

_____. "Christian and Non-Christian Faith." *Indian Journal of Theology* 6 (1957): 74 ff.

_____. "Christian Participation in Hindu National Festivals." *National Christian Council Review* 77 (1957): 310 ff.

_____. "The Gospel and the Religions." *National Christian Council Review* 77 (1957): 353 ff.

_____. "The Renascence of Hinduism in India." *The Ecumenical Review* 11 (1958): 52 ff.

_____. "Renascent Hinduism." *Indian Journal of Theology* 7 (1958): 40 ff.

_____. "New Frontiers of Faith: A Study of the Meeting Ground of Renascent Religions." *National Christian Council Review* 78 (1958): 302 ff., 356 ff.

_____. "The Christian Concern in Resurgent Religions." *National Christian Council Review* 79 (1959): 219 ff.

_____. "Hindu Mission to the West." *International Review of Missions* 48 (1959): 219 ff.

_____. "Caste, the Christian and the Nation in India Today." In *Basileia*. "Walter Freytag zum 60. Geburtstag." Edited by J. Hermelink and H. J. Margull. Stuttgart: Evangelische Missionsverlag, 1959.

_____. "Resurgent Hinduism, Review of Modern Movements." *CISRS-Pamphlet*. Bangalore: Christian Institute for the Study of Religion and Society, 1959.

_____. "Living Hinduism, A Descriptive Survey." *CISRS-Pamphlet*. Bangalore: Christian Institute for the Study of Religion and Society, 1959.

_____. "The Gospel and the Hindu Intellectual, A Christian Approach." *CISRS-Pamphlet*. Bangalore: Christian Institute for the Study of Religion and Society, 1959.

_____. "Our Task Today, Revision of Evangelistic Concern." *CISRS-Pamphlet*. Bangalore: Christian Institute for the Study of Religion and Society, 1959.

_____. "The Dravida Kazhagam, A Revolt against Brahmanism." *CISRS-Pamphlet*. Bangalore: Christian Institute for the Study of Religion and Society, 1959.

_____. "The Christian Institute for the Study of Religion and Society." *International Review of Missions* 49 (1960): 319 ff.

_____. *Christian Concern in Hinduism*. Bangalore: Christian Institute for the Study of Religion and Society, 1961.

Devanandan, P. D. and Samartha, S. J., ed. *I Will Lift up Mine Eyes unto the Hills: Sermons and Bible Studies*. Bangalore: Christian Institute for the Study of Religion and Society, 1963.

_____. *Preparation for Dialogue*. Bangalore: Christian Institute for the Study of Religion and Society, 1964.

Kulandran, S. "The Significance of Theological Thinking for Evangelism among Hindus." *International Review of Missions* 33 (1944): 390 ff.

──────. *The Great Errand: A Study of Christian Evangelism.* Madras: Christian Literature Society, 1949.

──────. "Theology for a Missionary Church." *Indian Journal of Theology* 1 (1952): 37ff.

──────. "Kraemer, Then and Now." *International Review of Missions* 46 (1957): 171 ff.

──────. "Christian Faith and Hindu Bhakti." *Indian Journal of Theology* 6 (1957): 118 ff.

──────. "Christian Attitude to Non-Christian Faiths and Faith." *Religion and Society* 5 (1958): 7 ff.

3. Japan

Kitagawa, O. "Überlegungen zur Theologie in Japan." In *Theologische Stimmen aus Asien, Afrika und Lateinamerika I.* Edited by G. F. Vicedom. Munich: Kaiser Verlag, 1965.

Kitamori, K. *Theology of the Pain of God.* London: SCM Press, 1966.

──────. "Das Problem des Leiden in der Christologie." In *Theologische Stimmen aus Asien, Afrika und Lateinamerika III.* Edited by G. F. Vicedom. Munich: Kaiser Verlag, 1968.

Lee, R. *Stranger in the Land: A Study of the Church in Japan.* London: Lutterworth Press, 1967.

Michalson, C. *Japanese Contributions to Christian Theology.* Philadelphia: Westminster Press, 1960.

Ogawa, K. *Die Aufgabe der neueren Evangelischen Theologie in Japan.* Basel: Reinhardt, 1965.

Takenaka, M. *Reconciliation and Renewal in Japan.* New York: Friendship Press, 1967.

Yoshinobu. "Reflections on Liberation." *Bulletin of the Missionary Research Library,* 24, No. 4.

4. Africa

Adegbola, A. "Eine christliche Interpretation der Afrikanische Religion." In *Theologische Stimmen aus Asien, Afrika und Lateinamerika III.* Edited by G. F. Vicedom. Munich: Kaiser Verlag, 1968.

Agbeti, J. K. "African Theology, What It Is," *Présence,* 5, No. 3 (1972).

Bosch, D. J. *Missiological Developments in South Africa.* Frankfurt: Janus, 1974.

──────. "Onderweg naar een Theologia Africana." In *Het Evangelie in een Afrikaans Gewaad.* Kampen: J. H. Kok, 1974.

Bürkle, H., ed. *Theologie und Kirche in Afrika.* Stuttgart: Evangelisches Verlagwerk, 1968.

Buthelezi, Manas. *Daring to Live for Christ by Being Human and by Suffering for Others.* South African Council of Churches, 1974.

Christian Council of the Gold Coast. *Christianity and African Cultures.* Accra, 1955.

Dickson, K. and Ellingworth, P. *Biblical Revelation and African Beliefs.* London: Lutterworth Press, 1969.

Mbiti, J. S. "Afrikanische Beiträge zur Christologie." In *Theologische Stimmen aus Asien, Afrika und Lateinamerika I.* Edited by G. F. Vicedom. Munich: Kaiser Verlag, 1968.

──────. *African Religions and Philosophy.* London: Heinemann, 1969.

Mpumlwana, P. M. "Einheimische Kirche und Theologie in Süd Afrika." In *Theologische Stimmen aus Asien, Afrika und Lateinamerika I.* Edited by G. F. Vicedom. Munich: Kaiser Verlag, 1965.

Oosthuizen, G. C. *Theological Battlegrounds in Asia and Africa.* London: Hurst, 1972.

Said, D. W. "An African Theology of Decolonization." *The Harvard Theological Review* 61 (1971): 501 ff.

Sawyerr, H. "Grundlagen einer Theologie für Afrika." In *Theologische Stimmen aus Asien, Afrika und Lateinamerika I.* Edited by G. F. Vicedom. Munich: Kaiser Verlag, 1965.

Thompson, P. E. S. "Die Dämonen in der biblischen Theologie." In *Theologische Stimmen aus Asien, Afrika und Lateinamerika II.* Edited by G. F. Vicedom. Munich: Kaiser Verlag, 1967.

Towards an African Theological Expression — A Follow-up of the Consultation of African Theologians. Working Document for the Second Assembly of the All-Africa Conference of Churches. Ibadan, 1966.

Van der Horst, G. C. J. "Afrikaanse Theologie en Maatschappijkritiek." *Wending* 29, No. 2, 1972.
Van Pinxteren, J. N. *Het Indigenisatie-Probleem in de Afrikaanse Theologie.* Leiden: Interuniversitair Instituut voor Missiologie en Oecumenica, 1971.
Williamson, S. G. *Akan Religion and the Christian Faith.* Ibadan: Oxford Univ. Press, 1965.

5. Latin America

Míguez, J. B. *Doing Theology in a Revolutionary Situation.* London: SCM Press, 1975.
_____. "Politieke Bevrijding en Christelijke Bevrijding." *Concilium,* July, 1974.
Schuurman, L. "Enkele Kerngedachten van de Latijns Amerikaanse Theologie van de Bevrijding." *Gereformeerd Theologisch Tijdschrift* 74 (November, 1974): 213–232.
_____. "Afhankelijkheid en Overheersing." *Allerwegen* 5 (1975).

6. Black Theology

United States
Cleage, A. *The Black Messiah.* New York: Sheed & Ward.
Cone, J. *Black Theology and Black Power.* New York: Seabury Press, 1969.
_____. *A Black Theology of Liberation.* Philadelphia: J. B. Lippincott, 1970.
_____. *The Spirituals and the Blues.* New York: Seabury Press, 1972.
_____. *Black Power, Black Theology and the Study of Theology and Ethics.* Stenciled study document for the Commission on the Churches' Participation in Development.
Cruz, V. "The Black Revolution and the Church." *Presbyterian Outlook,* January 20, 1969, pp. 5 ff.
Jones, M. L. *Black Awareness: A Theology of Hope.* Nashville: Abingdon Press, 1971.
Moltmann, J. "Warum 'schwarze Theologie'?" *Evangelische Theologie,* January-February, 1974, p. 1.
Sleeper, C. *Black Power and Christian Responsibility.* Nashville: Abingdon Press, 1965.
Traynham, W. R. *Christian Faith in Black and White: A Primer in Theology from the Black Perspective.* Wakefield, Mass.: Parameter Press, 1973.
Wilmore, G. S. *Black Religion and Black Radicalism.* New York: Doubleday, 1972.

South Africa
Boesak, A. "Geseculariseerde menselijkheid: Zwarte theologie en de strijd om mensenrechten." *Wereld en Zending* 3 (1974).
Bosch, D. J. "Stromingen in de Zuidafrikaanse zwarte theologie." In *Het Evangelie in Afrikaans Gewaad.* Kampen: J. H. Kok, 1974.
Kouwenhoven, H. J. "Afrikanen op zoek naar een 'theologie van de dekolonisatie'." *Gereformeerd Weekblad* (June 9, June 16 and July 28, 1972).
Motlhabi, M., ed. *Essays on Black Theology.* Johannesburg: University Christian Movement, 1972.

CHAPTER XII

The Vision of Missions in All Six Continents and the Summons to Mutual Assistance among the Churches

THE NEED FOR A NEW RELATIONSHIP BETWEEN CHURCHES

Everyone familiar with the course of missionary progress throughout the world is aware of the striking impact which certain key words and slogans have made at crucial times. "The Evangelization of the World in This Generation," uttered by John Mott at the Edinburgh conference in 1910, and "Partnership in Obedience," the theme of the Whitby conference in 1947, are but two examples.

In the present stage of world missions two such key expressions have surfaced, each of which we shall inspect in this chapter: "Missions in All Six Continents" and "Mutual Assistance Among the Churches."

The Decreasing Impact of the Church in the Western World

European churches are gradually being shaken out of the ideological intoxication of the *Corpus Christianum* and into the stark and humble awareness that they have become groups within a society which no longer determines its course in the light of God's demands and promises. In France it was the book by Father Henry Godin and Y. Daniel, *La France, Pays de Mission,* which finally shook the churches there into realizing that they were facing a situation which was through and through missionary. The report *Towards the Conversion of England* was the first to do the same in that country. J. H. Oldham and Stephen Neill said the situation was even worse than the report mildly indicated. Neill commented: "It is always better to face reality than to live in a world of illusion. But the awaking to reality has been a dreary and discouraging business; and the facts that have to be faced are, from the Christian point of view, exceedingly grim."[1]

In West Germany two books were published: *Warum ich aus der Kirche ausgetritten bin* and *Warum bleibe ich in der Kirche.* The first is polemical against the church, while the second is appreciative though critical. Both these books give a hint of how estranged the church and society have become. The Netherlands too is being subjected to this gradual process of alienation, as numerous studies indicate.

---

1. Stephen Neill, *Anglicanism* (Baltimore: Penguin Books, 1961), p. 389.

Despite the ecclesiastical window dressing, the situation in Scandinavia is even more distressing than in the countries mentioned above. And churches in Eastern Europe are in complete diaspora.

Missionaries to other countries who return on furlough to what used to be called the "homefront" often can assess the radical change more accurately than anyone else. Upon his return from Korea to England, Rev. Samuel H. Moffett wrote: "In the old days, furlough was a temporary withdrawal from the frontier for rest and recuperation in the warm embrace of the heart of Christendom. Christendom does not have a heart anymore, geographically speaking, and coming home is more of an icy shock than a warm embrace."[2]

The Impact of Young Churches

The slogan "Missions in Six Continents" was invented not only to acknowledge the fact that the established churches in the West are losing their dominant position in society but also because the young churches in Asia and Africa objected to the demeaning phrase "daughter churches," which gives the impression that they are mere satellites of established churches in the West. These Asian and African churches have their own identity, are proud of it, and want to divest themselves of the vassal status which Western invasion imposed upon them.

These and similar experiences convinced church leaders that new patterns of relationship were the order of the day. Division of the world into Christian and non-Christian sectors which prevailed ever since the time of Constantine (from the fourth to the eighteenth centuries) has now become quite untenable and must be dropped.

The first world missionary conference in Edinburgh (1910) maintained this obsolete distinction. The Mexico City conference of 1963 finally broke through it and replaced it with the six-continents concept, cautiously and provisionally indicating in the process a few consequences of this call to mutual assistance.

Origin of the Phrases "Mission in Six Continents" and "Mutual Assistance"

Even before the Mexico City conference actually covened, numerous authors were calling for an alteration of the relationships between the churches. They were thus already pointing in the direction of Mexico City. I begin by citing from an article by Paul Devanandan of India which he wrote after the Tambaram world missionary conference in 1938. As early as 1939 Devanandan, who later rose to such fame, could write in the *Guardian:*

> The Tambaram Conference brought to the fore a new sense of solidarity and fellowship, an awareness of the ecumenical dimension to the worldwide fellowship of the universal church within which young churches and old churches work together in a unity flowing out of a common urge to proclaim the Gospel. The chief responsibility of the Church is to function, and to function means to spread the Gospel. In comparison with that common urge, the tendency to preserve our various denominations fades into the background. This accent upon the Church as

2. Samuel H. Moffett, "Cracked Image," *Princeton Seminary Review* 64 (July, 1971): 80.

principially ecumenical, so visible in Tambaram, will gain in importance in the future for it is grounded in a new sense of mutuality of obligations. Within such a perspective, receiving help, whether in the form of money or of personnel, is not something to be ashamed of. Nor is there room for resentment when the churches who receive it claim the right to decide how to use such assistance to best advantage. The important thing is the proper functioning, not the fortifying of the rights of the donor or the recipient. Such a spirit can only lead to an alliance and a partnership with more mutual understanding and a marshalling of Christian forces on the battle-front where the need for militant evangelizing is the most acute.

Lesslie Newbigin wrote in the same vein in his small brochure "One Body, One Gospel, One World." Newbigin, then director of the Division of World Mission and Evangelism of the World Council, consistently and thoroughly developed throughout the brochure the theme which he stated on page 27: "The homebase is everywhere." Newbigin goes on to ask: "What is the precise *differentium* which entitled an activity to be called 'missionary' in the context of the world-wide Church?" He answers: "Nor does the *differentium* lie in the crossing of a geographical frontier. That conception is a survival from the era when there was a geographically identifiable Christendom. *The differentium lies in the crossing of the frontier between faith in Christ as Lord and unbelief.*"[3]

A third publication which strongly leaned toward what later came to be called "Mission in Six Continents" was David M. Paton and Charles C. West's *The Missionary Church in East and West* (1959). These authors discard the distinction between mission (in distant lands) and evangelism (in one's own land) and opt for seeing the church everywhere challenged by one world which is in need of the gospel. The task of churches is now practically the same throughout the world.

Mexico City kept this theme at which previous authors were hinting central in all its deliberations. For the first time in the history of world missionary conferences the obsolete distinction between "Western mission" and "native churches" was abandoned in favor of seeing the homefront as everywhere. The conference ended with delegates issuing a message:

> We affirm that all Christians are called to go forward in this task together. We believe that the time has now come when we must move onwards to common planning and joint action. The fact that Christ is not divided must be made unmistakably plain in the very structure of missionary work. Our present forms of missionary organization do not openly manifest that fact; they often conceal it. The far-reaching consequences for all churches must be faced. . . . We do not yet see all the changes this demands; but we go forward in faith. God's purpose still stands: to sum up all things in Christ. In this hope we dedicate ourselves anew to his mission in the spirit of unity and in humble dependence upon our living Lord.[4]

This vision is so important because it underscores the need to engage in mission-ary work everywhere, because it represents the gradual breakdown of those

3. Lesslie Newbigin, "One Body, One Gospel, One World" (New York: International Missionary Council, 1958), p. 28.

4. R. K. Orchard, ed., *Witness in Six Continents: Records of the Meeting of the Commission on World Mission and Evangelism of the World Council of Churches Held in Mexico City, December 8th to 19th, 1963* (New York: Friendship Press, 1964), p. 175.

paternalistic structures and attitudes which held missions in their grip for so long, and because it — finally — strives to put an end to the one-way traffic from West to East between the churches.

Mexico City was right in admitting that we have just begun to work through the implications of the six-continents concept and mutual assistance. Like little chickens, we have just popped out of our hard shell and are still dragging huge chunks of it along with us. Note for example how we still use obsolete terminology and preserve the relics of antiquated patterns of relationship.

In the rest of this chapter I intend to think through some of the implications of this new understanding for the practical work of missions.

THE BIBLE ON THE RELATIONS BETWEEN CHURCHES

The New Testament contains an image of the church which is so important to our subject: body of Christ. It is interesting to note that Paul never precedes the phrase by a definite article when he uses it to refer to the congregation. For example, Paul never views the church at Corinth to be *the* body of Christ, as though a specific congregation or series of congregations in a certain region comprised the complete body of Christ. A congregation is the stuff or the material of which the universal body is made.

In I Corinthians 12 Paul makes two points which are decisively important to our subject. First, he reminds all congregations of their dependence on the head of the body, Christ himself. Without him no congregation or congregations could exist. The more a congregation grows in its sense of dependence on him, the more it will be able to realize and achieve its purpose. Second, Paul underscores the fact that all members of the body are interdependent. In deep dependence on Christ our head we all are duty-bound to show responsibility toward and to assist each other. This does not mean that each church simply helps the others to maintain their own existence but primarily that all of them together assist the complete body which is the church of Christ to become totally functional in human society. The New Testament talks about members within a specific congregation who bear each others' burdens: "If one member suffers, all suffer together; if one member is honored, all rejoice together. Now you are the body of Christ and individually members of it" (I Cor. 12:26–27).

Therefore, if Western churches, for example, should simply do nothing about the poverty and need in churches in the other two-thirds of the world, and, vice versa, if the churches in the young countries should express no concern over the crumbling churches in the West, both sides would be neglecting their calling.

But I Corinthians 12 also gives powerful directives on what patterns of relationship should prevail between churches. J. D. Gort once commented in an essay that all the normal distinctions like mother-daughter and giving-receiving are always made by a specific church which raises its own position to the level of a norm. A church is then judging another's situation by its own. But the only frame of reference used in the Bible to determine proper patterns of relationship is the body of Christ in which all the members are equal, indispensable, and useful. This being the case, new mobility, new ways of hearing, speaking and expressing love, new types of obedience and work must come. Congregations must show an increasing readiness to exchange gifts and goods in the service of God's kingdom.

Acts 2:44 says of the Jerusalem congregation: "They had everything in common." This too must become true of the church in a far deeper sense than presently exists. In the earliest days of Christianity it was simply assumed that churches would help each other, but later certain churches became estranged from one another and each went its own way — an indication that the Spirit's work was being extinguished.

The present phase of history allows for experiments in expressing ecclesiastical interdependence, and it is our duty to seize these opportunities to become genuine partners in a common work. If we fail to do so, we are actually leaving our partners in the lurch. One of the most frequent Greek New Testament terms for partner is *etairos*. How striking that when Jesus meets Judas Iscariot in the Garden of Gethsemane, he should call him *etairos*, partner, friend. Thus it is possible for one to be called a partner and yet in actuality to turn out to be a traitor and deserter. The same holds true for churches.

REFORMING THE PATTERNS OF RELATIONSHIP BETWEEN THE CHURCHES

Western churches have often been rather paternalistic in their attitudes toward the churches in Asia and Africa (or maternalistic, as in the case of mother-daughter churches in South Africa). Such relations bear the stamp of ecclesiastical colonialism. Even in the new phase they have often tended to be one-sided and only bilateral, with all the advantages and disadvantages that such relationships bring with them. However, in recent years many multilateral relationships have also developed and taken their place beside the continuing bilateral ones. The several world funds such as the Theological Education Fund, the Agency for Christian Literature Development, the World Association for Christian Communication, etc., are all multilateral in the sense that all member churches of the World Council of Churches there interact and cooperate with one another. The same holds true for an organization like the *Europäische Arbeitsgemeinschaft für ökumenische Beziehungen mit Indonesien,* whose European member churches once had historic ties with specific churches in Indonesia but now fully cooperate with other churches active there.

Then too there are the relationships between churches within several separate confessional families, such as the Lutheran World Federation, the Anglican Lambeth Conference, the Presbyterian Alliance, the World Organization of Methodists, etc.

The Roman Catholic church too has experienced definite changes in its patterns of relationship. Especially since Vatican II national episcopates have more freedom within the monarchical hierarchical structure to express themselves; the tensions which this new freedom has brought to the surface are so close that one can virtually reach out and touch them.

But with all these changes in patterns of relationship, we must always be inquiring how the New Testament sense of churches' interdependence can best be expressed. In my judgment, as the situation now stands, this means that we must work for more multilateral relationships without losing the positive benefits which bilateral relationships have offered and can continue to offer, for these latter relationships are important and very worthwhile, as the churches in the developing countries continually reiterate.

It is not hard to understand why churches regard these bilateral contacts so highly. The specific churches which enjoy them have often traveled a common history and therefore throughout the years have come to know each other in countless ways. They have continually conferred with each other and have often reached accords which determined the precise form and manner of mutual assistance.

But if these churches should simply rest content with enjoying these bilateral relationships, they would be at odds with the New Testament call for interdependence. It is so important that all the churches in a given region put their heads together to determine what they can do together in a whole country or region. To cite only two examples, churches in Indonesia must heed the Indonesian Council of Churches' plea for viewing the whole Indonesian area as one mission field, and in Cameroon churches simply cannot allow the span of influence to be set by the action radius of bilateral relationships.

In addition to all the above, the various worldwide agencies must seriously think about the total task of missions in a global perspective. Of course no given church can be concretely involved in every area of the whole world. It is true that "charity begins at home," and we must be ever on our guard against acting like angels in public but devils at home. But none of this discounts the fact that we must sharpen our vision by learning what the New Testament means by "body of Christ" and by coming to think in terms of "one body, one gospel, one world."

As I see it, the Commission for World Mission and Evangelism of the World Council of Churches must be used more and more as a rendezvous where churches together can determine who needs help and how they will divide the work.

But the Conference of Churches in Southeast Asia and the regional Conference of Churches in Africa have repeatedly declared that the "confessional families" in many ways serve to block efforts to express interdependence. I believe they are right. How an organization such as the Reformed Ecumenical Synod could ever possibly contribute toward interdependence simply baffles me. Its uselessness in this regard has been obvious for a long time even though not everyone is willing to admit it. The larger organizations of confessional families like the Presbyterian Alliance, the Lutheran World Federation, etc., have sometimes shown symptoms of "family sickness," even though in the recent years they have been increasingly willing to think and act along with others in stimulating the sense of global interdependence. We ought to do everything in our power to encourage this tendency.

CRITERIA FOR MATCHING NEEDS TO MISSIONARY AND DIACONAL RESOURCES

The question of how to determine which needs in a specific region will receive missionary, diaconal and other forms of assistance must be faced. The mere shouting of a few wild slogans will not suffice. Neither "Missionary, go home!" nor "Now, more than ever, Africa and Asia need thousands of foreign missionaries and diaconal workers" really contribute toward a solution. My primary intent here is not to inquire whether foreign personnel and material help is still necessary but rather to get at the deeper issue of how to discern which needs exist in a certain region or land, always keeping in mind the total responsibility of the church. Is it enough for a young church simply to be able to keep its head above water, or must we think about its total task in a region or country? Who is going to determine the scope of such a church's ministry and its corresponding needs? Moreover, what *are* the real needs? Allow me just a few general observations:

(1) It is urgently important, wherever possible, to appoint teams of experts in the various regions and countries who will research their respective areas to determine their needs. By making this a team effort, we can arrive at an all-embracing and responsible overview and insight.

It is nothing short of amazing that Protestant churches have done so little of this joint research in the past. A quick review of Protestant missionary history will immediately reveal two facts: God has so wonderfully guided his people to tackle fresh areas of missionary work in given regions; yet the manner in which certain areas were chosen while others were neglected and the strategy for working in them often reveal a certain arbitrariness.

The Roman Catholic church with its monarchical and hierarchical structure has devoted much more attention to systematic research and analysis in the recent past. Throughout Asia, Africa and Latin America the Roman Catholic church has established pastoral research institutes, and Karl Rahner has even called for a "world-pastorate" research institute. One can still have deep respect for the vision which gave these research institutes their birth without becoming an admirer of the monarchical ecclesiastical structure of Rome.

Protestants are beginning to undertake joint and systematic research. The studies by the Presbyterian sociologists, W. Stanley Rycroft and Myrtle M. Clemmer, the thirteen *World Studies of Churches in Mission* sponsored by the Division of World Mission and Evangelism, and the gigantic survey of the total church situation in Indonesia by Frank Cooley and F. Ukur are several examples.

It is high time that missionary and diaconal agencies of the young churches and the cooperating Western churches begin to determine their strategy, not by happenstance, rumors or slogans, but rather by thorough research.

(2) We must develop a list of priorities for an all-embracing program of proclamation, diaconia and developmental projects.

(3) We must describe the type, quality, and educational experience necessary for the foreign and native personnel required to carry out the various programs and projects.

(4) We must pay far greater attention to the so-called unreached areas, that is, geographic areas which have never heard the gospel or segments of a society which have heretofore been ignored even though a church has been established there.

Many at the General Assembly of the World Council of Churches in Uppsala thought Donald McGavran was exaggerating his appeal to do mission work when he said that hundreds of millions of people had not yet heard the gospel, but it was precisely John Taylor, author of the Uppsala report, *Renewal in Mission,* who supported McGavran's claim. In fact, he echoed McGavran in his own report.

In spite of these two individuals and others who have joined their voices, the subject is still not getting the attention it deserves. It must become a high-priority item on the agenda of consultations between councils of churches and Western partners.

(5) By prayer, study and consultation we must develop greater insight into how to carry out our work in areas which because of the oppressive hand of total-itarian ideology and because of other various political circumstances are now isolated. I mean China, Vietnam, and North Korea. It is highly unlikely that in the immediate future Western missionary agencies will be able to contact the churches there to learn from them and to inquire what we might do to help them. But Asian churches might receive such an opportunity, and then Western churches, in turn, could help Asian churches to carry it out. The World Council was wise therefore in requesting the Lutheran World Federation to undertake a study project on this subject.

I made the above observations only to indicate that without concrete analysis, research, and consultation, all talk and writing about whether personnel and financial assistance to other churches is still necessary or not come down to mere stylish slogans, a stab in the dark, and, at best, a groping in the mist. Nor must such research be restricted to talking to a few church leaders; the teams must go into local areas and find out what the real needs are. I must add too that I believe the Division of World Mission and Evangelism must do much more to encourage such research and to organize consultations to determine needs and coordinate efforts to meet them.

The old International Missionary Council did much in its day to encourage work in hitherto unreached areas by establishing comity agreements between churches doing mission work. But this was still a rather paternalistic era, and our day is much more ecumenical. The Commission on World Mission and Evangelism has now replaced the former International Missionary Council. In this era of ecumenicity it is incumbent on the commission to become much more involved in the issues described in this chapter. I am happy to note that the Christian Conference of Asia has appointed a special secretariat to study these matters; Western agencies now must respond by creating their own similar posi-tion, for a responsible determination of needs absolutely depends upon thorough research.

PERSONNEL ASSISTANCE

I now turn our attention to what is presently called "manpower planning." To what degree does mutual assistance involve Europe and America's sending per-sonnel to the young churches to help them in their missionary calling? (In a separate section I shall turn the question around and inquire whether churches in the North also need manpower from the South.)

Of course in determining the manpower needs of young churches, the only proper starting point is to respect the independence, autonomy, and separate identity of the young churches but also to sense keenly the interdependence of churches throughout the world who are set before a common work.

Encouraging Native Leadership

I cannot emphasize too strongly that the first and best place to look for personnel is among the local people themselves. Western missionary history and the history of the young churches prove time and again that, humanly speaking, whether a church will expand or decline is so vitally linked to the training and equipping of native leadership. Paul never ceases to amaze me: with his matchless trust in the Holy Spirit he immediately — one could almost say "recklessly" — turned over the reins of leadership for those newly formed churches to the people themselves.

To cite but one modern parallel, when World War II broke out and caused the demise of Western mission leaders, the first graduates of the theological college in Jakarta all at once were thrust into positions of leadership. In retrospect, we can only stand in awe at the amazing guidance of God.

Western missionary agencies ought to make many scholarships available for educating future native clergy and for training the laity. Moreover, the educational institutions in the West ought to open wide their doors to such students and encourage them to undertake post-graduate education so that their churches back home, eventually equipped with doctors of theology, can then take another significant stride toward achieving selfhood.

Making Foreign Personnel Available

All talk about native leadership does not discount the fact that the young churches in certain countries still need foreign personnel to help them. In countries like China, North Korea, Arabia, Afghanistan, Burma, etc., the respective governments have put up "No Entry" signs to prohibit foreign missionary personnel from coming in. Other countries like India, for example, only admit foreign personnel if they are replacements for others who are permanently leaving. Some countries are extremely arbitrary in whom they permit in and whom they deny. Though it is not my intention to treat this issue extensively at this point, I must point out that the United Nations' Declaration on Human Rights which the representatives of so many young nations solemnly endorsed makes provision for these governments to open their doors to permit an exchange of personnel. During the nineteenth century such agreements were hammered out between the colonial authorities and their subjects. To be sure, such coercive measures left wounds which are still festering in countries like China and Egypt, for example, but the changed world situation has caused the World Council of Churches to ponder anew the question of human rights. The voice of those who are appealing to governments to relax their admissions policy must never become muted.

I simply wish to underscore one point. When analyses and consultations conclusively prove that Western nations have available personnel whose qualifications and expertise particularly suit them for service in other countries, then these Western mission agencies ought to recruit these people, train them for foreign service and send them out. Of course, the key word here is caution. Suppose, for example, the highly unlikely possibility that Western missionary agencies would respond to foreign requests for help by sending out an unlimited supply of people; this would of course upset the structure of cooperation and cause Western domination. One can see that the matter of giving and receiving personnel can cause all sorts of problems; to avoid them many meetings and consultations must precede. The exchange of personnel must be completely voluntary on both sides, and each ought to retain the right to call a halt to it in certain situations. The native churches must clearly have the authority to decide how many and what kind of experts they want and where they want to use them. I believe there is every reason to listen attentively to the advice of young sociologists at this point, for without such advice the personnel issue may in the long run prove to be vexatious. In such circumstances, when crises arise, these foreign personnel will be viewed as a heavy yoke to be thrown off.

The above comments are in no way intended to deny the continuing need for foreign personnel in many lands and churches. However, at present there is a big discussion about the manner of assistance these foreign people should offer. Should they be restricted to helping with specific projects and programs, or should they become involved in the long-range life and work of the churches?

In recent years throughout the whole world of missions more and more foreign assistants are being sent forth on short-term service to lend a helping hand on a specific project or program. Such a so-called project system is a more or less technological approach to a carefully defined problem which seeks to achieve definite and limited goals. Obviously the need here is for short-term workers who do not look beyond the day when their specific task is completed; once the job is done, they can then return home. Such projects are usually experimental and therefore definitely terminal. One only has to look about to see the great worth and benefit which some of these projects have yielded.

Yet, good as they are, these short-term projects are not the whole of the matter. The young churches also need people whose friendship and partnership are of much longer duration and who are willing to stand with them amid the temptations, threats, challenges, and storms which swirl about their heads.

Some American agencies have put heavy emphasis in recent years on project systems, while their English and European counterparts — in continual consultation with their young church partners — accent more heavily the long-term stay of foreign personnel. Once in a while this causes tension, but such tensions are useful, for both approaches can complement each other. Perceptive John Taylor once wrote that the American often takes a clinical view of things and tends to look upon the long-term missionary as a bit too sentimental and emotionally involved with those whom he is helping, but that in fact the one person really needs the other. Though many writers play the one side off against the other, neither side needs to be ashamed of the contribution it is making. We must stop such unprofitable and unnecessary bickering.

Short-term Workers

Missionaries who may have already given years of service in a certain area often look disparagingly at the contributions of a short-term volunteer. Many, many studies conclusively show that such attitudes are entirely unwarranted. I can only summarize the findings of such studies here.

(1) Short-term foreign volunteers can render valuable assistance in training programs and technical projects, as administrative and secretarial help, and in breaking in native personnel on jobs that require special skills.

(2) Short-term workers are often more mobile than long-term workers, often adapt easily to their new surroundings, are usually readily accepted because of their obvious competence and lack of ambition for a position of leadership.

(3) Short-term workers often show deep sensitivity for the environment within which they work. They are not usually blind to what needs to be done — a nettlesome problem which all too often plagues the long-term worker who is quite unaware of it.

(4) Short-term workers are often more up-to-date on modern developments throughout the world and therefore better able than long-term volunteers to help in the transfer of knowledge and the transition of cultures.

(5) The postwar generation is often more idealistic than the previous generation which went through the depression and the war; the younger generation believes that rapid changes are indeed possible.

(6) The short-term worker is not equipped for work which requires a thorough knowledge of the native language and people. But if such are unnecessary and the work assignment is clearly spelled out to him, the short-term worker can perform valuable service.

From experience I cannot deny that the short-term worker is particularly susceptible to error. His lack of orientation often leads him to hasty judgments, and often he is not given to heeding the advice of those with more experience.

Long-term Workers

While the short-term worker usually performs service of a complementary or supplementary character, the long-term worker with the appropriate disposition can work himself or herself into the native society much more fully. Long-term workers have greater experience, much deeper knowledge, and often greater patience. One who does not stay for a long period of time is often given to making comparisons, but the long-term worker who totally immerses himself in his work has an opportunity to get to know friends and to develop a deep kinship of faith with them.

But in addition to the above advantages, there are also disadvantages to long-term service. Paternalism or maternalism is not an imaginary danger. Furthermore, in some cases the native leaders feel intimidated by foreigners with long experience. A bishop from Zaire told me one time that natives' feeling toward long-term foreign workers is analogous to a now fully licensed driver's feelings as he takes his former driving instructor for a ride. To be a good long-term worker requires a humble and serving disposition which no one has of his own accord but must rather acquire from Christ who himself came to serve.

In spite of the dangers, long-term workers who have a good command of the language and an adequate knowledge of the people among whom they are working can serve with real profit as pastors, teachers at theological schools, and in training and equipping native people.

Relations between Long- and Short-term Workers

The proper relationship between these two types of workers is difficult to determine and often is the source of no little irritation. But both sides must learn to understand each other. The inexperienced worker on a short-term appointment ought to be willing to learn from his more experienced counterpart. Each must be open to the other's insights and together with their native colleagues they must strive for a *modus vivendi* and *modus operandi*.

Fortunately, workers who go forth to another country on a short-term appointment often became so challenged by their work and the society in which they live that they stay and thus become long-term workers. In fact, they often even become citizens. But what happens even more frequently is that these "short-termers" return to their own country filled with a new understanding and appreciation for the challenges and opportunities in the third world. They are then in a unique position to bring about this same new understanding in their own home congregations, and many have done so.

Pool-Missionaries

Many Western churches, for example, the Anglican Church Missionary Society and the United Presbyterian Church in the United States, keep in reserve a number of what they call "pool-missionaries" with expertise in specific areas whom they can send out on temporary assignment to areas which can profit from their abilities. Of course the missionary or diaconal agencies provide for the full support of these experts. It strikes me as inequitable that these agencies should guarantee these people and their families support only for the period of time during which they are actually on loan. The support must also cover the interim period between times of actual service.

Those churches and agencies who have not yet set up such a pool of standby missionaries but are interested in doing so would do well to consult the fine report of the Anglican Consultative Council whose first meeting was held in Limuru, Kenya, from February 23 to March 5, 1971. It is a model from which all of us can learn.

FINANCIAL ASSISTANCE

We now come to an extremely touchy subject. Dr. Philip Potter in his opening address to the committee meeting of the Division of World Mission and Evangelism of the World Council of Churches expressed in his unique way just how delicate this whole matter is. "There is something demonic about a powerful, rich sending agency negotiating with poor people and poor agencies. How can there be real "partnership" between poor and rich? Partnership was a nice word which we fell into the habit of using, but now we have become afraid of using it because we know what it all came down to in practice."

In these bitter words one can clearly hear the echoing reminder of those unjust salary scale differences between the foreign missionary personnel and the native church workers, and also the power to control the purse strings which the missionaries one-sidedly reserved for themselves. After the debacle of the China mission when the communists took over, Charles West, using the most revealing pseudonym Barnabas, wrote a brochure entitled *Christian Witness in Communist China*. In it he pointed out that the great divergence in living standards between foreign missionaries and the native Chinese aroused deep resentment and stirred up trouble between them. In some instances foreign missionaries were earning six and even ten times as much as their native colleagues.

I regret to say that we have not yet learned the lesson of China; the problem is still with us.

Setting the Salaries of Full-time Native Church Workers

Many people wipe their hands clean of this problem by categorically and without consultation arguing that the amount of financial remuneration a paid ministry staff receives is a completely internal matter to be kept completely separate from any cooperation and help which foreign missionary organizations may provide. In my judgment this is a cheap and irresponsible solution, for I know firsthand of instances in Asia where such an attitude reduced some full-time church workers to pauper status; they were finally forced to give up their work in the church and to take a position in a school, the army, the navy, or in a business simply to provide for their families.

As I see it, one ought to tackle the whole question of financial assistance by first soberly considering what criteria and guidelines are necessary for determining salary scales for full-time church workers. Much has been spoken and written about this question before, but it has recently come to the fore again; therefore it is necessary to spell out as simply as possible the five criteria.

(1) Providing money for full-time church workers is itself a calling and must never be viewed as only or even primarily a means of caring for daily needs.

(2) *Sacrificial* giving is an indispensable dimension of this calling.

(3) Determination of salaries of full-time church leaders must be made on the basis of genuine needs and not on the basis of some unfounded notion of superiority or inferiority.

(4) Even the minimum salary must be sufficient to allow a full-time church worker to live according to I Corinthians 9:14: "In the same way, the Lord commanded that those who proclaim the gospel should get their living by the gospel."

(5) In determining remuneration for full-time church workers other essential needs must be taken into account. By these I mean such things as:

(a) retirement provisions, so that retired workers do not become a burden to other family members or are not put at the mercy of random expressions of good will from other people

(b) satisfactory educational facilities for the children of full-time church workers

(c) opportunity to purchase books and periodicals and to take courses for deeper study and for keeping up in one's field.

It seems to me that we must begin by setting these down as basic and minimal requirements. Only after we have these clearly before us should we begin to inquire about the possible financial sources we can tap to reach them.

We must begin our search for a solution to the problem of financial sources by underscoring the obvious: a lasting solution can come only after the world economy has achieved a more equitable distribution between the rich and poor countries and when every element within a given country has achieved a certain level of prosperity. I know that this fact has been repeated *ad nauseam,* but I thought it needed mentioning here, because many discussions on fund-raising tacitly assume that we can reach a satisfactory solution simply by offering courses in stewardship and by organizing projects to assist the local communities in which churches operate. However important these projects in themselves are, they can never take the place of genuine prosperity and welfare in which everyone in the whole society shares. Many people still take the approach of Merle Davis, who did so much to bring the economic status of local communities in Africa and Asia up to par in the years between the two world wars. Yet, in spite of all the good that Davis and his cohorts did and still do, some have properly charged them with a certain naiveté in supposing that their approach offered a satisfactory solution to the development issue.

I mention this to remind us here in the West that we must keep the question of financial assistance to young churches on our agenda as long as world prosperity has not reached an acceptable level.

Of course it goes without saying that we ought also to do everything in our power to stimulate the local economies within which churches operate so that increased local prosperity can ease the problem of providing funds for church workers. Small-scale development projects, self-help programs, encouragement of local enterprise, designing economic possibilities, stimulating social and economic awareness, etc. — all these are part of the very *ABCs* of a solution which will make native churches more capable of stewardship and ultimately self-supporting.

But what about the time until native church stewardship is finally able to meet the minimum demands outlined above? It seems to me that these native churches have a complete right to appeal for help to churches in the rich countries to pay their full-time workers at least the predetermined minimum. This is an undeniable implication of the biblical idea of interdependence of churches.

Methods of Financial Assistance

In recent years ecumenical agencies both in Geneva and elsewhere have been asking whether it is better to extend financial assistance through other channels than through the traditional support of programs and projects. In February, 1971, ninety-three churches, all members of the East Asia Christian Conference, came from sixteen countries to a conference in Kuala Lumpur to discuss whether or not it would be preferable to send financial help flowing through ecumenical channels. The conference wished "to initiate discussion with all interested churches and cooperating mission boards to provide national ecumenical structures for the transfer of complete responsibilities for the utilization of mission funds to request-ing churches in Asia.''

Such a request proceeds from pure motives, for, as Philip Potter so incontrovertibly pointed out, financial assistance *to* often goes hand in hand with power *over*. The danger is more than illusory that mission agencies could either wholly or — more frequently — in part become the managers of the full-time workers in the native churches and be tempted to manipulate these churches.

In Asia and Africa one often hears the statement ''Money follows a man''; that is to say, mission boards open their pocketbooks only after they have sent forth their own missionary personnel.

In spite of its laudable intention of avoiding a misuse of power, this proposal has met with negative response from the churches. This is understand-able for very practical reasons.

In the *EACC News* of April 1, 1972, Mr. Park from Korea, the secretary for the committee on ecumenical exchange of personnel, made a report in Bangkok of his local contacts. The staff of the EACC heard that both the matter of exchanging personnel and the matter of directing mission funds through ecumeni-cal agencies aroused great fears among the churches. They preferred to keep the channels much closer to home lest they become unmanageable and uncontrolla-ble. When the EACC followed up this report by even deeper contact with local churches it discovered that opposition to this plan was even more strident than at first supposed. The local churches were afraid lest the money become stuck in the treadmill of ecumenical bureaucracy. Everyone agrees: for the present it is better that help to needy churches come from those who through personal experience have become well-acquainted with the situation in those churches.

But I still wonder whether or not it is possible in the long run to channel financial assistance for full-time church workers' salaries through the division of world diaconate. For principial and practical reasons this is the best solution. I realize that such a plan is very difficult to organize. For one thing, it is an open question whether the various divisions of world diaconate can really stand another financial burden, and second, even assuming that they could, are they ready to do so? Before we set about disbanding the traditional ways of extending aid, we had better be clear on an answer to these two questions. Else we can better keep the old way.

One often hears the claim that giving money to young churches only serves to stifle their own initiatives. I have never been swayed by that argument. I shall never forget the comments a well-known Indonesian theologian made after receiv-ing his doctor's degree from a Western university. In saying good-bye to the rich congregation which had courteously received him during his stay, he remarked:

> For a few years now I have become involved in the life and work of congregational members in this rich satellite city. Many of them think that they are doing so much for the church when they regularly write out a check to support its activities. But I am deeply convinced that desperately poor church members in Java, even though they cannot give much to support the local church budget, show much more dedication and love than the members of a rich congregation in a European satellite city such as this.

And this *doctor ecclesiae* was absolutely right.

Other people (especially representatives of "faith missions," but also of some ecclesiastical missions) contend that Western churches ought to stick by the words of Simon Peter: "I have no gold or silver, but I give you what I have; in the name of Jesus . . ." (Acts 3:6). But for rich churches to repeat this text is a downright lie. Peter was poor, desperately poor, and he spoke the truth. The same was true of Western churches at certain times in the past (such as both during and shortly after the Second World War), and it could happen again. They might at that time even require help from the outside. There have also been instances where foreign missionaries in specific countries of Asia were poor, half naked, weak, and were helped as soon as possible by Asian Christians who in the name of Christ shared what they possessed. But to have the devilish audacity to repeat this text today is the height of hypocrisy. Western churches do have silver and gold, and they are now being called to share their largess with churches abroad which are in need, being all the while aware of the dangerous misuse of power which can attend such financial assistance. But could not the national councils of churches get together and search for a solution to this problem?

At the close of this section I wish to point out one aspect of this oft-neglected issue, even though it cannot be concretely worked out here. This is the relationship between rich churches and poor churches *within* a given developing country. Some churches there are relatively prosperous while others are shockingly poor. Examples abound. Obviously any approach to the problem of rich and poor churches which strives to be ecumenical may not overlook this aspect.

Setting the Salaries of Foreign Missionary Personnel

As I mentioned above, the great disjunction between the salaries paid to foreign mission workers and those paid to their native colleagues has been a sore spot which must now be approached candidly. Emerito P. Nacpil who teaches at the United Theological School in Manila did just that in a sensational article published in the *International Review of Missions*. The foreign mission worker, states Nacpil most emphatically, must view himself as functioning within the independence and "selfhood" of the church which he is serving.

> The work that it entails is to be determined as a necessary and urgent expression of the mission of the inviting church and it must be supported primarily by the faithfulness and stewardship resources of that church. If additional funds are deemed necessary to undergird the work, it will be the responsibility of the inviting church to secure the funds from anywhere and anyone. The missionary will be completely and solely responsible to the church that invites him and in whose life and mission he shares in the same depth and intimacy and freedom as is possible to those who are national participants.[5]

I do not think that Nacpil intended by his article to argue for further burdening the native church budgets by requiring that the native churches actually

5. Emerito Nacpil, "Mission but Not Missionaries," *International Review of Missions* 60 (1971): 361.

come up with the funds to pay foreign workers. Rather he was claiming that the funds earmarked for their salaries and the related costs should be deposited in the accounts of the native churches so that they themselves would be responsible for disbursing these monies. At any rate, there must be much more mutual openness in the matter of fixing salaries.

I do not believe the proposal to pay equal salaries to natives and foreigners is tenable. I recall a conversation with D. T. Niles, the late Ceylonese evangelist and ecumenist. His action-packed career had forced him to live not only in his native Ceylon but also in Geneva. He commented: "While in Geneva I received a higher salary than the local people, and this was equitable and just; simply because we were foreigners, living costs for our family were higher than the local workers." Thus foreign workers in Ceylon, Indonesia, or any place else require higher salaries for the simple reason that it is more expensive for them to live in the country than those who were born and reared there. At a meeting of the British Council of Churches which I had the privilege of attending as a representative of the Netherlands Missionary Council, D. T. Niles presented his proposals: "Let there be a responsible but not too extreme differential between salaries of native and foreign workers which will be spent in the land where they work, and let the western mission workers take appropriate steps to cover such overhead expenses as furlough costs, provisions for children, pension, etc." In my opinion, these proposals attest to their author's maturity and independent good judgment which were born of rich and ripe experience.

Financial Help for Churches with No Western Partner

Many churches throughout Asia and Africa carry on no bilateral or multilateral relationships with Western partners. It is highly expedient for Western missionary organizations in cooperation with the appropriate national councils of churches, if possible, to begin making money available to these churches. In the United States the Presbyterian churches have earmarked part of their missionary budget for these churches, and the Reformed (*Gereformeerd*) churches of the Netherlands have done the same for such churches in Indonesia.

Financial Help for the "Fund to Support Mission Work"

The Christian Conference of Asia has established a fund to encourage the exchange of missionary and diaconal personnel between churches in eastern Asia and other places. Many churches in Asia could well use the services of persons from other parts of Asia who are wrestling with the same problems, whose lifestyle is similar, and whose expertise particularly equips them for making a substantial contribution. Already no less than one hundred persons have been exchanged under this program.

In 1972 Rev. Alexander John from Bangalore, a person of vast ecumenical experience, was appointed to the staff of the East Asia Christian Conference and put in charge of organizing this fund and directing its operations. In the beginning it was called "Asian Interchurch Aid for Mission."

In my opinion, this fund is so deserving of our support as to require almost no argument. Through our support we can aid in establishing within a limited context those ecumenical channels of financial assistance and at the same time help Southeast Asian churches to take their first steps toward erecting a joint missionary strategy. In the long run these first steps could lead to a responsible rebuilding of existing missionary structures.

Plugging in the Laity

Until now I have spoken exclusively about full-time workers. To avoid misunderstanding I now wish to make a few comments on the need to involve the church laity of developing countries in the tasks of preaching, catechesis, and contact work. Of course there is no room to detail all that the laity have meant and still mean to the work of building up the young churches throughout the world. Within the context of this chapter I wish to underline only three things. First, we must all start with the assumption that involving many either unpaid or partially paid laity in the task of communicating the gospel is for both principial as well as practical and financial reasons an absolute *sine qua non* of our total missionary outreach. Second, efforts to encourage lay participation must become much more systematic and organized; they must become part of the overall program of church upbuilding. There is wide variation in the degree to which churches strive to incorporate the laity. Third, full-time preachers must devote much more time to serving as trainers for the laity to help them fulfill their God-given duties within the church. Preachers must be leaders, and we ought to be looking over the corps of theological students for individuals who possess the charisma for leadership. Often students were accepted not because they had leadership potential but simply because they had been turned down for other studies and were available.

Laity from intellectual milieus in the cities must be offered organized training. In Latin America several theological faculties have begun presenting weekend supplementary theological education courses to these people to prepare them for undertaking weekend work within their churches which normally had to be done by full-time ministers.

In similar vein the Division of World Mission and Evangelism of the World Council of Churches heralded the slogan about a "tent-making ministry," and David M. Paton compiled a symposium study on "New Forms of Ministry." I shall do nothing more than mention them here and add the comment that I think it is high time that we reckon seriously with those ideas in our total strategy for offering personnel and financial assistance.

ASSISTANCE IN ALTERING THE WORK PATTERNS

Every church tends to simply perpetuate certain traditional ways of doing things without asking whether or not a change of direction is necessary. Church workers sometimes act like dike workers who keep on enforcing the dike at spots where the waters no longer threaten and ignore the spots where the waves are pounding. Obtuseness does not only show up in the ranks of industrial management; it happens to church leaders too.

One area where churches in the West and in developing countries need each other's help is in detecting the need for new ways of doing things and for another focus. When Jesus saw his disciples on the Sea of Tiberias sweating and plodding and yet achieving nothing, he called forth: "Cast the net on the right side of the boat, and you will find some" (John 21:6). Because they could not see where the fish were, they were fishing on the wrong side. I think all churches could learn something from Jesus' instructions in this passage, but we need each other in order to learn how they apply to our situation.

The participants in the sectional at the Uppsala assembly on "Renewal in Mission" were writing a new book of instructions, as it were. They pointed out new foci: urban mission, industrial mission, work among students, work among those in positions of power, contact with revolutionary movements, the use of mass media, etc. We desperately need each other's help in reflecting upon such new avenues of work. If we do begin to take seriously each other's advice, then perhaps we can begin adding to the list developed at Uppsala. Perhaps, for example, we can remind Japan of her neglect of people living in villages and we in the West can be alerted to our need to work among the people of the counter-cultures.

One thing is sure: the Lord of all mission endeavor who looks down upon us from the brim of eternity wants us to become cured of our obtuseness and to be willing to take new instructions.

ADMINISTRATIVE ASSISTANCE

When Philip Potter complained that nothing much had changed since 1947 when the Whitby conference heralded the nice slogan "Partnership in Obedience," one of his complaints was that policy-making in large part still lies in the hands of the donors. Nor is Potter's voice the only one to deplore the situation; the complaint is universal.

In my judgment it goes without saying that churches in a given area must set their own policy if a spirit of genuine interdependence is ever to grow. But there must be room for consultation with others in setting such policy if their advice is requested. Exchange of charismata includes a willingness to trade insights. The days of autocratic policy-setting are past; group dynamics and "brainstorming" now play a much more important role. Churches too must be ready to use these more modern methods.

When the Whitby conference proclaimed "Partnership in Obedience," it laid special emphasis on partnership in administration. If one looks back sympathetically but also soberly upon the period when Whitby was held, he will find absolutely no reason to criticize this statement. The postwar situation made partnership in administration necessary in some countries.

But today in most developing countries there is a strong current of advice against sharing in administrative functions. In fact, in most of these countries the law forbids such partnership in institutes, societies, and other organizations related to churches or Christian communities.

But Western agencies should not disavow partnership for this reason alone. Anyone who wishes to exercise administrative authority will not only quickly run smack into the charge of being a neocolonialist but will also inevitably tend to brake the free development of native leadership, whether he intends to or not.

Nevertheless the question of administrative assistance has not totally disappeared from the agenda, even though in my opinion Westerners must forget about striving for administrative authority and thus also administrative positions. It might yet be necessary to lend a helping hand in improving the administrative infrastructures; for example, by sending out a bookkeeper or secretary who can in turn train others, by helping to organize accounts control, by providing a number of needed office machines, etc. All these can do so much to increase the efficiency of an administration and boost the morale of the people who work in it.

So, to answer the question with which this section began, I would respond "No" when it means participation in the power structures but "Yes" if the administrative infrastructures can thereby be strengthened.

MUTUAL ASSISTANCE

Up to this point I have discussed the problems involved in providing assistance to the churches in Asia, Africa, and Latin America only. But now I want to reverse the roles and inquire into the concrete content implicit in the mutuality idea. Many times such concepts are so beautifully engraved on the walls in calligraphic script, but in actual practice nothing much changes. The real test comes when one attempts to translate the slogans into something meaningful to the everyday life and existence of the churches. I hope that the following pages show that mutuality is already much more than just a slogan, but also that much more remains to be done.

Joint Tasks between Young and Old Churches

There are so many examples one could give of how young and old churches are joining hands in undertaking common work. I shall mention only a few to indicate that the terrain of common undertakings is much broader than most people imagine.

First, there is the care for foreign students who come to the West to study. Many Western churches have long ago organized student pastorates which specially focus on foreign students, but much greater cooperation under the auspices of ecumenical agencies must come in this area. One question that must be answered is whether or not pastors or lay persons from the foreign students' homeland should be brought over to become part of a team ministry with their Western colleagues.

Another area of cooperation is the pastoral care of foreign workers. Already now social and diaconal agencies in the West are becoming increasingly involved, but unless I am mistaken, these agencies have really not tapped as resource persons those other foreigners who are acquainted with the language, customs, and problems of the foreign workers.

Another important expression of care and service is the mission to seamen. Anyone who has the slightest acquaintance through study or experience with that amazing international fraternity of sailors knows that a joint approach to them is required. Even though international contacts have already been developed by the existing organizations as a result of this work, the churches of Asia and Africa must be encouraged to take a much more active role. The organizational vehicle for getting them more involved already exists; in August, 1972, the International Christian Maritime Association was established to encourage a multiracial and multidenominational approach. Now it is time to use it.

Not only have thousands of people from Africa, Asia, and Latin America come to the West to work; thousands of skilled scientists, technologists, businessmen, airline personnel, diplomats, etc., from the West are working abroad. These too must become the objects of our communal pastoral concern. It is gratifying to see the increasing amount of cooperation between Northern and Southern churches in this work. Both the Christian Conference of Asia and the All-Africa Conference of Churches have stated in recent years their sense of joint responsibility with Western churches for these Western foreigners.

Then too there is the care for political refugees. That churches throughout the world must band together to make these hapless people objects of care and concern is so obvious as to require no further discussion. Fortunately, the appropriate diaconal agencies are already translating this insight into action.

In recent years young people have become international travelers in record numbers. The very city in which I am writing these lines, Amsterdam, has become a popular center for these youthful tourists, and this of course presents a challenge which is far beyond the capability of local churches to answer. To do the job effectively requires the insight and manpower from these tourists' homelands, especially from people who are acquainted with the countercultures. Some cooperation is already evident; it must become much more extensive and systematic.

Third World Manpower in Central Ecumenical Organs

Not enough people are aware of how Western churches are increasingly profiting from the presence of Asians, Africans, Latin Americans, and people from the Caribbean on the boards and committees of the World Council of Churches. Ever since the council itself was organized, churches from the third world were involved, but now a very obvious shift in the structures of power has occurred within the ecumenical movement. Figures from the various non-Western continents are playing decisive roles in administration and on committees. One need only mention such important names as M. M. Thomas from India (former chairman of the executive committee of the council), Philip Potter from the Caribbean (secretary-general of the council), S. J. Samartha (member of the committee on dialogue with the world religions), C. I. Itty (member of the committee on development), and so many more to note the strong impact of non-Western leadership.

Both in the meeting of the Central Committee in Utrecht in 1972, and in the outline of the Bangkok Conference of the Division of World Mission and Evangelism in 1972/73, the shift toward the third world is easy to see. No more can anyone charge this ecumenical body with being a courier of Western ecclesiocentrism. More and more it is becoming a genuine expression of the multiracial world church. And this form of mutual assistance has been coming to the fore through the years without a lot of noise and fanfare.

I must quickly go on to add, however, that the work done by the various commissions and departments of the World Council in Geneva and published in various memoranda, reports, study encounters, and as articles in the *International Review of Missions* and *The Ecumenical Review* is too seldom implemented by the churches on local and national scales. In a September, 1972, article in *Anticipation,* Richard Shaull lamented the fact that a majority of young American intellectuals do not have even the vaguest idea of the vast amount of thinking which is being done in Geneva, and if they are aware of it, most ignore it. Shaull is right. In the future the council must take steps to encourage contributions from the local level and then distribute them to the worldwide church of Christ for reaction. More interaction between grassroots and top echelon, between local churches and central agencies, must come, lest all those finely tuned reports of the ecumenical committees simply hang in midair and remain untested on the anvil of hard practicality. Only then shall we come to see that all six continents are facing a common set of problems and issues which in turn call for a cooperative effort to solve them.

Third-world help to the West through representation in top-level ecumenical organizations, though helpful, is nevertheless insufficient. We must strive to develop the instruments for making expressions of help possible at lower levels. I shall suggest some of these possible means in the following few pages.

Manpower Assistance in Adult Education Programs of Western Churches

Most church adult education centers in Africa, Asia, and Latin America include on their staffs one or more Western co-workers who by their very presence are key ecumenical links and valuable sources of information about what is going on in similar ventures elsewhere. The same is true for adult education in Western churches; since interest in the so-called other two-thirds of the world is already keen and growing even keener, we in the West ought to provide opportunity for representatives from these parts of the world to add their input to our programs. Often we allow individuals with little actual experience in the third world to interpret for us what is going on there; but even though they speak from a wealth of experience, it is still important to have one who is born and bred in the third world to offer his own insights and thus to amplify or correct the views of others.

To hear Westerners talk about the third world with which they have so little actual acquaintance reminds me of a medieval monk who finally visited a region which he had previously come to know only through study. He exclaimed: "It isn't *aliter* (different); it isn't *taliter* (like I imagined); it is *totaliter aliter* (totally different)!"

At present, third world input into Western programs is usually restricted to an occasional visit by a non-Western person. For a long time many have been arguing for people from the third world to be included on the staffs of such adult education centers. It is high time that the administrative agencies take appropriate steps to implement this proposal.

Assistance in Western Mass Media Ministry

When ecclesiastical representatives from the third world appear on Western radio or television, they command an amazingly large segment of the listening and viewing audience. Take, for example, the appearance of D. T. Niles in the United States, Philip Potter on the BBC, and Dr. Budiman and Dr. Boesak in the Netherlands. In my judgment we should take a cue from these experiences and invite gifted individuals from the third world over for further guest appearances on radio and television.

Guest Lectureships

Western universities, colleges, and mission seminaries benefit greatly from an exchange of guest lecturers. Even now professors from the third world who are traveling through a given Western country may be invited to give a lecture or to be available for conversation with faculty and students. But I believe that invitations for longer stays are also worthwhile; these would provide full opportunity for an exchange of insights and experiences.

Union Theological Seminary in New York has been presenting such guest lecturers for many years, and other institutions could well learn from their model. Of course, when I suggest the idea of exchanging guest lecturers, I do not mean only theologians but rather the full range of professors in various disciplines.

Assistance in Administrative Functions

As a rule, one can find sitting on the West European mission and diaconal boards very few representatives from the area to which these boards are sending their people. This does occur in the United States. To invite a person from the area where Western churches are sending their representatives to come and serve as an administrative "link" between the two areas could achieve obvious and important advantages. On the one hand he could articulate the feelings, ideas and insights of his own people to the Western agencies, and on the other hand he would be in a better position to understand what is going on in the West and represent it to his own people.

Exchange of Delegations

The organizing and sending out of delegations to pay visits to other churches still occurs rather haphazardly. There must be more careful planning so that experts in various areas such as theological education, training, literature production and distribution, and diaconia are also invited to go along and thus to keep such visits from turning into mere financial strategy sessions. Furthermore, the churches must also be encouraged to so meticulously plan the composition of such delegations that the subsequent deliberations cover as wide an area as possible.

Exchange of Ideas on Theological and Other Questions

West European theology is too one-sidedly Western and in many respects quite
provincial in some of its emphases. To borrow a comment from Devanandan, upon
reading such theology one could get the impression that Western theologians
believed the world of theological thinking ended at the Bosporos and Dardanelles.
Since the world in which we live is rapidly becoming one, theologians absolutely
must acquire a universal orientation in their thinking. In his most recent book, *The
Power to Be Human,* Charles West emphasizes that with our world now more
united and interdependent than ever before and with *oikoumenē* now, as he puts it,
"an awesome reality," we must all undergo *metanoia* and begin to listen to each
other.

     We need each other's help in sharpening our theological thinking and
articulating the "message of liberation in our age." I shall mention only a few of
the many spots at which we stand in need of each other's help.

     Dr. Samartha from Geneva some time ago in a speech made the claim that
Western theologians would never have begun prating about secularization as the
dying away of religions if they had taken the time to listen to theologians from Asia
and Africa. I believe he is right. Men like Karl Barth, Emil Brunner and J. H.
Bavinck realized full well that human beings are ineradicably religious and therefore the secularization process only parades new forms of idolatry across the
stage. Alas, many of their fellow theologians forgot that for a time. They would
never have made this mistake if they had listened seriously to the theological
voices from the world of Asia, Africa and Latin America. Therefore I make bold
to say that a joint study of the results and implications of the secularization
process is not a stylish accessory but something we simply cannot do without. The
flood of mystical and Gnostic thinking which in the West is following in the wake
of this secularization would have been less alarming if we with our non-Western
Christian brothers had analyzed those processes.

     The same holds true for the processes of change now sweeping over the
religions and the religious communities. One can study religions by reading the
classic sources and documents, but he really does not sense the changes which are
taking place until he comes into living contact with both the uneducated and the
experts who are observing these changes daily and experiencing them personally.

     I must make the same point even more strongly about our study of the
impact of ideologies and utopian ideals on contemporary society. In 1972 the
World Council of Churches which had for some time already engaged in dialogue
with Western Marxism mandated the Lutheran World Federation to undertake a
study project on communism in China. The World Council is stimulating interaction by such studies.

"Joint Action for Mission"

Both during and after its Mexico City conference the Division for World Mission
and Evangelism began to spread the slogan "Joint Action for Mission." The
Mission de Paris in cooperation with the churches of West Africa on the one hand
and the French Protestant churches on the other has undertaken the work of

organizing ecumenical missionary teams. Such teams have logged experience in France, Dahomey, and Switzerland.

In an extremely candid report on the response to cooperative ventures in France the two following points were made:

    a. The receiving party in France had a quite different level of expectation from churches like Cameroon which sponsored the team members.
    b. Non-Western team members were thoroughly shocked by the almost complete de-Christianizing process which had swept over Europe.

The upshot of the whole venture was that most thought it was a valuable effort worth continuing but also one which generated some questions and starkly delineated the unresolved problems. From the discussion it did not appear that the basic questions regarding the new approach could be resolved. Nor was there a clear answer as to whether or not the social situations in Dahomey and France were too different from each other for two similarly constituted teams to function equally well in both areas.

I shall never forget the report a representative of the *Mission de Paris* gave in London about the work of both teams. He did not pretend to know the answers to all the perplexing questions which such cooperative ventures raised, but what so struck me from his report was the urgent need to proceed from the notion of "mission in six continents" and to develop a two-way traffic in communicating the Christian faith. I came away from that report realizing that careful selection of the personnel, ample preparation, and an encouragement of team spirit were absolutely necessary to a successful completion of the mission.

Learning from Each Other's Lifestyles

The phenomenal spread of Christianity in the first centuries can only be adequately explained by one factor: the attractive lifestyle of the Christian members within the congregations. The absence of this very same lifestyle today in the West accounts for much of the serious stagnation and lack of appeal which Christianity suffers among the young people.

Those who have analyzed the countercultures tell us that these people strongly reject a lifestyle which today gives little more than the faintest hint of what Matthew and Luke called the *anawim* of Yahweh. The Uppsala General Assembly of the World Council of Churches was concerned about this loss of genuine lifestyle and devoted at least one sectional to a study of the quest for a new one.

It strikes me that as we set about searching for a new lifestyle, the Christians from the third world have so much to teach us. What characterizes their lifestyle? Permit me to mention only a few features.

First of all, they possess a keen sense of God's transcendence which runs so counter to the God-is-dead philosophy prevalent in the West and to the "eclipse of God" which so many people feel within themselves.

They also have a sense of God's immanence.

They totally reject any hint of separating the sacred from the secular.

They possess a lively sense of the miraculous.

They have the gift of listening.

They know the importance of meditation and fasting.

They are less strongly attached to money and material goods.

They have a much more profound sense of the joy which faith produces.

They experience more intimately the tie between the militant and triumphant church.

They sense much more intensely than Western man the deep unity of all human existence. Whether a man is at prayer, at work, or at play there is a deep continuity.

Of course I am not so naive as to allege that each and every Asian or African Christian expresses each of these elements to the full degree. I was merely giving a tally of the prominent features which do indeed show up in the lives of many Christians from those continents. And with John Taylor I make bold to say that the Holy Spirit can use such Christians to again teach us in the West what it means "to be in Christ and not to cease being bound up with men, to be completely wrapped up in the bundle of life and yet to be one with the Lord God."

IN SEARCH OF MATURE RELATIONSHIPS BETWEEN CHURCHES TO COMPLETE THE TASK

The most recent world missionary conference, held in Bangkok in late 1972 and early 1973, discussed thoroughly the subject with which this chapter deals. Bangkok especially underscored the need for mature relationships between the churches on the continents of Asia, Africa and Latin America and those in the North. Voices from Africa sounded forth a clear note of opposition to continued paternalism in the relations, and from the Latin American quarter one could sense an increasing indignation toward those structures which perpetuate regional and local churches' dependence on outside sources for personnel and finances.

The pressure was not for smashing the relationships but rather for revising them. In the discussions and deliberations the term "moratorium" was bandied about, especially by the Africans. The term itself is, as W. A. Visser 't Hooft remarked, most unfortunate, for it connotes the idea of complete cessation of relationships. But those who used it meant something quite different by it. They meant that churches in Africa should temporarily suspend relations with those in Europe and America in order to set their own house in order and then begin anew to build different patterns of relationship. Nor was this term "moratorium" ever used at Bangkok in isolation. It was merely one part of the total reflection on the uncompleted task of world mission. All attention was focused on one question: "How can we by our inter-ecclesiastical relations become a better instrument for completing the work which still needs doing?"

The Proposal for Moratorium

Alas, the moratorium idea became derailed at the Lusaka conference of the All-Africa Conference of Churches held May 8–21, 1974. It was discussed as an isolated topic and was proposed without any prior consultation with the member churches. Here is the actual text of the general proposal:

The African Church, as a vital part of the African Society, is called to the struggle of liberating the African people. The African Church, as part of the World Community, must also share in the redeeming work of Christ in our world. But our contribution must be African. The contribution of the African Church, however, cannot be adequately made in our world if the Church is not liberated and has not become truly national. To achieve this liberation the Church will have to bring a halt to the financial and man-power resources — the receiving of money and personnel — from its foreign relationships, be they in the Northern continents or foreign minor-ity structures within Africa. Only then can the Church firmly assert itself in its mission to Africa and as a part of the ecumenical world.

Thus, as a matter of policy, and as the most viable means of giving the African Church the power to perform its mission in the African con-text, as well as to lead our governments and peoples in finding solutions to the economic and social dependency, our option has to be A MORATORIUM on the receiving of money and personnel.

What does this mean to the structure and programmes of our churches today? What does it mean to our relationship with foreign mis-sion boards and to the structure of those bodies and to sending churches? How can it be evolved in the situation of our individual churches? How does it affect the structure of the AACC itself?

There is no doubt that the call for a Moratorium will be misinter-preted and opposed in many circles both within and without. But we recommend this option to the churches of Africa as the only potent means of coming to grips with being ourselves and remaining a respected part of the one Catholic Church.

The complete halt to receiving of money and personnel will surely affect the structures and programmes of many of our churches today. Many church leaders will cease becoming professional fund raisers in foreign lands and come to face their true role in evangelizing and strengthening the Church at home. Surely election of this option may cause many existing structures of our churches to crumble. If they do, thanks to God, they should not have been established in the first place, and again it would be profound theology, for to be truly redeemed, one must die and be reborn. What would emerge would indeed be African and be viably African. A Moratorium on funds and personnel from abroad will by necessity enforce the unifying drive of churches in Africa.

Should the Moratorium cause missionary sending agencies to crumble, the African Church would have performed a service in redeeming God's peoples in the Northern hemisphere from a distorted view of the mission of the Church in the world. It is evident, however, that the enterprises of sending agencies will seek to manifest themselves in other ways. It is therefore vitally important that a strategy of implementation be carefully worked out. We call on the AACC to associate with member churches in evolving a strategy suitable for each situation.

Such strategies should, in order to succeed, involve the develop-ment of awareness at the grass roots of the African Church. Only then will the Church consciously develop authentic structures, orders and pro-grammes based on the African values and priorities.

This proposal for a moratorium was not thoroughly thought through before it was adopted by the conference; in fact its very initiators toned down and reinterpreted its ideas not long afterwards. Rev. John Gatu, chairman of the AACC and an originator of the proposal, took pains later in 1974 at the Lausanne Conference on Evangelism to give a more precise and somewhat different explanation of his original proposal. At one point he declared: "The African churches are too dependent on the West. But one is misunderstanding the proposal if he thinks that it seeks to stop the flow of personnel and money to Africa as soon as possible." He pleaded for Western churches to cooperate with African churches in developing "strategies which must lead the churches in Africa toward becoming more consciously African and their African representatives toward accepting a greater share of the responsibility for them."

Canon Burgess Carr, general secretary of the AACC, underscored the need for programs which enhance the sense of independence and self-confidence amid all the planning for joint strategies lest all talk about moratorium be idle chatter.

Many member churches of the AACC responded quite unfavorably to the Lusaka proposal for a moratorium. The Lutheran churches of Tanzania and Ethiopia, and various churches from Cameroon, Ruanda, Ghana, and many other places declared that the proposal was ill-prepared. In fact the AACC itself went back on its own proposal, for in January, 1975, Alan Brash, an assistant general secretary of the World Council of Churches, after consulting with financial advisors, in the name of the AACC issued an appeal to Western churches to help alleviate the great financial distress which was plaguing the AACC. Two remarks stand out in Brash's letter of appeal. The first is that the moratorium proposal was not intended for churches in the North but rather designed only to get African churches thinking seriously about the questions of leadership and the receiving of money from foreign countries. Here is what Brash wrote: "A pamphlet from the A.A.C.C. indicates clearly what is meant by the moratorium proposal. It is a summons to churches in Africa, not to churches in rich countries. It is clear that the A.A.C.C. like other organizations at this time is the victim of unjust distribution of funds and cannot continue to exist without outside help for a long time."

I shall now attempt to summarize my own impressions from these and the many other similar reactions to the moratorium idea.

First of all, one must view the proposal as a reaction against the paternalistic structures which still prevail in African churches' relations with foreign missionary agencies or with the "white mother churches" of South Africa and Rhodesia, etc. It furthermore counters the tendency consciously or unconsciously exhibited by many white missionaries to devalue African cultures and religions. Civilization for many of them comes to be identified with their own culture, and this tends to reduce African people to objects rather than to respect them as subjects.

The moratorium is also a protest against the many "faith missions" operative in Africa which pay little heed to insights and strategy of the existing African churches as they set about building on the foundations laid by others. At the Lausanne conference African delegates complained loudly and bitterly about this.

They came to the right place to make their protest, and my impression is that this time it finally hit home.

But the moratorium was not only intended as a negative protest. It was also a positive indication of the deep African desire for self-expression and self-reliance. Africa is fervently asking this question: How can we as churches grow in dependence on the Lord, living for, from, and through him (the actual theme of the Lusaka conference) and at the same time become less dependent on the churches in the North and the white churches in Africa? This fervent desire and prayer ought to arouse a deep echo of response in us all.

Any assistance which runs counter to that desire is improperly designed and merely perpetuates paternalism.

The quest for self-expression is in itself nothing new; mission boards have confessed this as their goal for decades — sometimes with the lip only, but ofttimes with deeds as well. But here is a declaration from the side of African church leaders themselves. It was a rather shocking statement, to be sure, but it was the first from the African side.

But there were also some bad things about the way this proposal was formulated which no one can overlook or deny. I shall summarize some of the black delegates' reactions as they were expressed in articles and speeches.

(1) Caught up in the emotion of the moment at the close of the conference, many delegates tended to ignore the real situation in which African churches find themselves. If this moratorium were concretely applied, it would spell an end in many areas to the work so recently begun. Rather than signifying a rebirth and renewal of the work, it would totally destroy it.

(2) The AACC neither had nor has the right to make decisions affecting churches in a local or regional sphere. No serious consultations or deliberations with these churches preceded this proposal; rather it was more of a manipulation at the top echelons which was then simply thrown into the lap of the local and regional churches.

(3) The proposal created the tragic impression that all relations with the outside now suddenly had to be broken off.

(4) Both for principial as well as practical reasons, the positive phrase of Bangkok, "mature relationships," would have been a much better choice than the rather negative term, "moratorium," for in the final analysis that is what all of us are striving for.

(5) It would be wrong for churches in the northern hemisphere to emphasize the word "moratorium" in describing the contemporary missionary task. Anyone with two eyes in his head can see that not only do Africa and other places need more mature relationships with other churches; they also need help in the very quest they are making for self-expression and identity. Think, for example, of the challenges which the black churches in South Africa and Rhodesia will face in the coming years as they seek to train and educate responsible church leaders. They will be seeking support from churches in the northern hemisphere, and they deserve it. Think too of our need to support the Roman Catholic and Protestant churches in Mozambique, Angola and Guinea Bissau and to help equip them for their work within the young nations. Think too of the vast areas which African

churches have not even begun to touch with the gospel. Recall too that the independent churches in Africa with their millions of members have but recently made an appeal to Western missionary agencies for specific types of assistance. In the face of all these facts, continuing to cry "Moratorium!" solves absolutely nothing. In fact, it obscures rather than clarifies. Africa must absolutely work toward the goal of mature relationships.

Asian Discussion of the Moratorium Theme

The Christian Conference of Asia issued an impressive statement on the manner of fulfilling the missionary task today in its document *Let My People Go*. It certainly does not underscore the theme of moratorium but rather calls the minority churches to give themselves with increased devotion to the inescapable task of presenting the gospel in an area which contains more than half the world's population. This is not to say that the term "moratorium" is left undiscussed, but in response to the plea for such a cessation, the document encourages churches to hold regional consultations to review past interecclesiastical relationships and then to proceed to set priorities, to develop new strategies, and to undertake new experiments for the future. For, says the document, it is wrong simply to continue traditional ways of doing things without paying close heed to the changes in society.

Here are a few priorities as the document lists them:

(1) Increasing local congregations' awareness of the social changes and encouraging them to greater contact with other religious communities.

(2) Increasing programs to achieve social injustice.

(3) Enhancing care for migrants from the villages whose coming to the city poses great personal problems.

(4) Increasing understanding of the culture and society of neighboring countries on the Asian continent.

The report does not urge the Asian churches to discontinue request for manpower from the West but rather it encourages these foreign helpers to work along with the Asian church representatives to establish priorities for the work. It also makes a special plea for an expanded exchange of personnel between the various countries of Asia. Regarding finances, the report appeals to richer Asiatic churches to share with the poorer ones and the urban churches to share with the village ones. As for money from outside Asia, the report advises that such assistance come in the form of block grants, with the receiving churches reserving the right to determine the salary differential between native and foreign personnel.

Obviously the Christian Conference of Asia does not share Lusaka's judgment on the value of moratorium but rather has used the moratorium debate as a springboard for critically reviewing the relationship patterns between the churches and, if necessary, for revising them. "The Christian Conference of Asia calls its member churches to participate in a process of new deliberations and revision. By such a process carried on within their own regional context the various member churches will be able to find their own answer."

The document goes on to call the Asiatic churches to live and think along with the Western churches about the missionary task in their own areas and, when asked, to join with them in carrying out the work.

The Harvest of the Moratorium Discussions

As I write these lines, the discussions are proceeding at full speed. They will certainly be at least provisionally rounded off when the World Council of Churches meets in general assembly in Nairobi, Kenya, in November, 1975. Within the total context of the material presented in this chapter I should like to state what I believe are the central points which have emerged from the ripening harvest of discussions.

(1) The truths derived from I Corinthians 12 and stated at the beginning of this chapter are absolutely inviolable. Declaring in faith that congregations are members of the body of Christ, one must strive to achieve the interdependence of churches who are all related to Christ who is the Head.

(2) Independence of churches from each other is the reverse side of each's growing dependence on Christ the Head. Precisely when the churches achieve maturity in that state of dependence, a sense of interdependence, mutual cooperation, and assistance will follow, as it were, automatically.

(3) New reflection on the nature and the shape which this cooperation must take is continually necessary, but to call a halt to it by proclaiming a general moratorium is, in the opinion of W. A. Visser 't Hooft, "an abstract and generalized approach to a problem that really ought to be handled concretely and on a case-by-case basis."

(4) If the public authorities hinder, forbid, or block such cooperation, they not only violate the Declaration of the Rights of Man adopted by the United Nations but also are at odds with the Spirit and instructions of Jesus Christ to whom all authorities must give account.

Some people tend to create the impression that the expulsion of foreign ecclesiastical personnel and the stopping of transfer of money from countries like China is really a part of the events of salvation history. They pretend that the "No Entry" signs posted on the borders of many countries must really be welcomed as an omen of good. The truth is, however, that the shooing away of those who serve the gospel is anything but that, and responsible agencies must do all they can through ecumenical contacts and cooperation to plead before the public authorities and the United Nations for a change.

(5) The focus of attention should not be on moratorium but on the task which still remains to be done. According to statistics the 1973 world population was around 3.86 billion people. Assuming for the moment that the birth rate stays the same, this means that the present population will double by the year 2007. Hundreds of millions of people stand either wholly or in part outside the range of gospel communication. This is no time to while away precious moments and waste reams of paper in endless debates about moratoriums. We must rather open our eyes to the task at hand and join hands to complete it together. Let the Western world meanwhile remember that her area of the world too is now in a missionary situation, and then together let us as churches strive for more mature relationships

with each other and help each other fulfill our common calling. We have the promise of the risen Lord that he shall blaze the trail for us and be with us as we walk together.

SYNCHRONIZING MISSION WITH EVANGELISM IN ALL SIX CONTINENTS

We have traditionally designated gospel proclamation in Western lands as *evangelism* and in the developing countries as *mission*. Even the recent studies of Margull and Gensichen still claim it is proper to label work done in Europe by terms such as evangelism, *Volksmission,* or something similar, but work done in Africa, Asia, etc., as *mission.*

As I see it, such a distinction is no longer tenable in view of the fact that churches in the West now also confront a missionary situation in their own backyards. And as for Asia, Africa, Latin America, and the Caribbean, they too, just like Europe and North America, now face the challenge of proclaiming the gospel to great masses of people who have once heard it but now have become estranged. The approach to such people must be different from the one used for people who have never heard. Thus, though the categories of "No Longer" and "Not Yet" which scholars such as J. H. Bavinck, G. Brillenburg Wurth, and Karl Barth used to describe various peoples' relationship to the gospel still make sense, the distinction is not a geographic one; both groups are to be found throughout the world.

Churches everywhere must synchronize their efforts to reach those who have never heard and those who have become estranged, for the circles of activity are really concentric. This means that those who work within them must meet together to exchange experiences and ideas and to coordinate their individual efforts. The arm of the World Council called the Division of World Mission *and* Evangelism is quite properly named, for the work of proclamation does have two foci even though the distinction is no longer geographic but synchronic.

In reaction to the traditional distinction, geographically understood, many want to discard the term "evangelism" and speak only of mission or apostolate. I believe that we must come to see that the tasks of each do not exactly coincide; therefore, though the distinction is useful, both tasks need doing in all lands.

CHAPTER XIII

Trends in the Theology of Religions: Types of Contemporary Dialogue

THE NEED FOR A FRESH APPROACH

Ever since Christian churches began to function as witnessing communities among other religious communities — that is to say, from the very day of their birth — they have faced the question of how to relate to these other communities of faith. The churches have engaged in specific types of dialogue and proclamation from their earliest days.

But now the day has come for some fresh thinking about the disciples of other religions and for new experiments in coming into contact with them. Why?

In the first place, modern transportation, news media, and a burgeoning world economy have all contributed to a feeling of togetherness and mutual dependence among all people throughout the world, including people within separate religious communities. During the days of the Enlightenment, even though the great geographic discoveries opened up a whole new world of information about other religions, Western knowledge about these religions remained rather marginal and scanty. Revolution and increased communication have put those days permanently behind us.

Second, religious pluralism within the Western world has also become a simple fact of life. Even as the tedious conflicts and continual interaction between the various Christian confessional communities during the sixteenth and seventeenth centuries finally introduced an atmosphere of coexistence, so too in the twentieth century followers of the various religions are gradually coming to accept the fact of each other's existence. Many books and articles are providing the latest data. Kurt Hutten and Siegfried von Kortzfleisch edited a symposium study entitled *Asien missioniert in Abendland* (Stuttgart, 1972). Michael Mildenberger described the Hindu and Buddhist movements in the West in his *Heil aus Asien?* (Stuttgart, 1974). And Mildenberger teamed up with Muhammed S. Abdullah to produce *Moslems Unter Uns: Situation, Herausforderung, Gespräch* (Stuttgart, 1974).

Just as happened in the first centuries after Christ, many syncretistic streams of religious thought and devotion are accompanying this rise of religious pluralism, eclectically picking out specific features from various religions and fitting them into their own system.

When one keeps in mind that these non-Christian religions are now spreading over the whole globe, it is not hard to see why a new study of them is vital not only in Asia and Africa where they dominate but also in the West.

Third, young people especially have a great fascination for religion today. Those fortune-tellers who were predicting that we were entering a "religionless age" were dead wrong. In fact, Harvery Cox, who as recently as twenty years ago was willing to argue that we were heading toward a postreligious age, now writes in his most recent book, *The Seduction of the Spirit,* about the use and misuse of religion. Harry M. Kuitert's book *The Necessity of Faith* describes the present status of Christianity among the various current religious tendencies. Karl Heinz Ratschow also ardently opposes the notion of a religionless age in his *Von der Religion in der Gegenwart* (Kassel, 1972).

But most young people today are not simply interested in religion generally. They are turning away from their own traditions and toward the Eastern religions with their meditative emphasis. Caught in an authority crisis, these young people are tired of the Western rationalist emphasis and the struggle to achieve.

Fourth, in response to the heavy Western emphasis on technology and the exact sciences, many are searching for what are the genuinely divine and human factors in human existence. They are becoming interested in the quality of life and thus touch upon some of the deepest issues of human existence. In this the drama of God's relationship to man is again coming to the surface.

Fifth, we need a fresh theology of religions since all of these religions, whether their adherents are aware of it or not, are undergoing radical changes precisely because they function in a world that is rapidly becoming one, at a time in history that is so dynamic, and in a situation which both locally and internationally demands of societies vast renewal and change. Every religious community is forced to face the issue of secularization. Add to all of this the incontrovertible fact that every one of these communities is feeling the impact of other religions and ideologies at work in its sphere of influence, and one can see the obvious need for a new theology of religions and new types of dialogue.

Of course, before such dialogue begins, the partners must first take into account the findings of disciplines like the science of religion and philosophy of religion. But a distinctive *theology* of religions is also a vital element in our preparation.

CHANGES IN THE ROMAN CATHOLIC THEOLOGY OF RELIGIONS

I now wish to describe the latest developments in the field of theology of religions, beginning with the Roman Catholics and going on to the Protestants. Since of course an exhaustive treatment is impossible here, I shall be quite selective.

Roman Catholic theology of religions has undergone vast changes throughout its history; perhaps a brief look at each of these phases is useful at this point. Father Aloysius Pieris, a Jesuit father from Sri Lanka, detects four distinct theories, each of which predominated during a specific phase: the conquest theory, the adaptation theory, the fulfillment theory and the sacramental theory. I shall seek to illustrate each of these, emphasizing especially the last two because they were and are being carried through in practice

The Conquest Theory

During the Middle Ages Roman Catholic theologians developed a view of the church which equated it more and more with the very consummated kingdom itself. Pope Nicolas V reflected this triumphalist understanding of the *Corpus Christianum* when he enjoined the Christian kings of Portugal to subject "Saracens, heathen and other enemies of Christ" to the authority of the church and by preaching and baptism "to bring these unbelieving people into the Kingdom of God." Father Aloysius reminds each of us who may wish to criticize — quite rightly — this too facile identification of the church with the kingdom of God and this confusion of the things of Caesar with those of God, of the good people which this age also produced. To be sure, this was the time of horrible perversions by colonial rulers and conquistadors, but it was also the age of Ignatius Loyola, Francis Xavier, and the thousands of others who, walking in their footsteps, were driven by a self-denying and self-surrendering love for Christ and his kingdom, as Xavier so aptly put it in one of his meditations for students at the Sorbonne.

During this phase Africa and Asia were discovered by the West (1500–1600), and Roman Catholic missions expanded into these areas quickly afterwards (1600–1787). Roman Catholic theology of the religions functioned only within the ideological framework of the *Corpus Christianum* and all evangelistic motives and goals were overshadowed and jerked out of shape by it. The vintage phrase *extra ecclesiam nulla salus* ("outside the church there is no salvation") applied strictly to the Roman church only and the kingdom of God was made coterminous with the *Corpus Christianum*.

The Adaptation Theory

The adaptation theory had its heyday during the nineteenth and early twentieth centuries and was developed in reaction to the conquest theory. It did not simply fall from the clouds. On the contrary, Roman Catholic missions became quite involved during the preceding centuries with the question of inter-cultural relations. Recall the conflicts of Rome with Robert de Nobili in India (1577–1656) and Matteo de Ricci in China (1552–1610). But it was only in the nineteenth and early twentieth centuries that the adaptation theory finally penetrated into Roman Catholic thinking and had such a profound practical influence.

The best descriptions of this theory are J. Thauren's *Die Akkommodation im katholischen Heidenapostolat* and Otto Karrer's *Das Religiöse in der Menschheit und das Christentum*. Both these books accept the traditional Thomist doctrine of nature and supranature; *gratia non tollit sed perficit naturam:* special revelation only has to fulfill a person's natural knowledge of God and morality. Through the sacraments it puts one in touch with the supranatural sphere and clarifies what one already knows in the sphere of nature. Thus special revelation connects itself to one's natural knowledge of God and completes it.

Given this framework, Father Thauren is quite willing to admit that Western Catholicism has borrowed many of its ideas, morals, customs, views of justice, and patterns of worship from German paganism. He fully concedes that Western Catholicism in many respects is a striking accommodation or adaptation to both Greek and German pagan thought. This being so clearly the case already, it is a simple and natural step to extend this line of accommodation to Asiatic and African cultures too and to now absorb from them those unique features which Roman Catholicism has not already taken in from elsewhere. A willingness to acknowledge the natural in man and the valuable in heathen religions is, in Thauren's judgment, a direct implication from the catholic character of the church. Therefore, if one a priori condemns as devilish and perverted the religious views, traditions, morals and customs of the people to whom he is bringing the gospel, he is actually violating the very nature of the church. One must seek to understand these people in the light of their history and strive to preserve every valuable kernel of truth which he can find among the myriad of myths and sagas and trash in heathen religions. This laborious effort is worth doing if for no other reason than to strive to trace religious truths back to their common primeval source of revelation and then to proceed to build up a Christianity founded upon a base of pre- and extra-Christian revelation. Since *anima naturaliter Christiana* ("the human soul is naturally Christian"), it is our moral obligation to acknowledge truth wherever we find it in the heathen world.

In his third chapter Thauren treats the limits and scope of accommodation. Provided the *depositum fidei* and good morals remain intact, one may make as many concessions to the heathen life as he pleases, for the question of truth is not primary, but rather the salvation of souls.

> The norm for all the Church's decisions is the salvation of souls. Everything must become subservient to this goal, for it alone gives the Church her right to exist. Every missionary means is justified only to the degree that it serves the primary goal of the apostolate. Consequently when a mission cannot achieve its goal and a tenacious conservatism threatens to consign whole peoples to an existence devoid of Christian influence for ages or to leave them open to modern heresy or unbelief, the mission should not hesitate to make liberal concessions even though they touch upon time-honored morals or customs. Missions are in a life-and-death struggle with heathenism already, and this by itself brings the pagan people enough difficulties without complicating the situation by overemphasizing specific Catholic customs. All the externalities of ecclesiastical life are not worth the price of one soul. Even from its beginning days in the first century but especially during the Middle Ages and in the history of the Eastern rites Christian missions display a willingness to make concessions when the souls of human beings are threatened with serious damage.[1]

Karrer's book developed the same line of argument but went on to add that as long as the heathen live by the *lumen naturale,* they are part of the invisible church and in the forecourt of the visible Roman Catholic church. All heathen who have made use of the gifts God has entrusted to them are children of his kingdom and citizens of the invisible city of God. Though they have not received the

1. J. Thauren, *Die Akkommodation im katholischen Heidenapostolat* (Munster: Aschendorff, 1937).

sacraments, they do have the *votum sacramenti* ("desire for the sacrament") and thereby become recipients of grace. The task of missions is nothing more than enabling these members of the invisible church to transfer to the visible. The church is the mother of all genuine children of God, even though her presence be hidden among the heathen temples and amid the sayings of learned pagans. She becomes manifest in the rich treasure of symbols, images, sacrifice, prayers and idols. The light of Christ beams forth everywhere. The common foundation on which this invisible and visible mother church is built is the discovery of the religious soul which all people have in common.

Certain things immediately stand out in this adaptation theory. First of all, it is too optimistic in its view of man. It does not reckon seriously enough with man's radical rebellion against God nor with the radical nature of the gospel of Jesus Christ. Proponents of this theory do not cry out to the heathen: "Repent, for the kingdom of heaven is at hand!", but rather, "Come under the wings of mother church and she will prepare you for heaven." This is a form of Christian sublimation, an elevation of natural man into the realm of supranature. It seeks to bring about a new man by the discipline of a new law.

Then too, though both of these authors do take seriously into account the cultural treasures of other peoples, Thauren has not in the least attempted to penetrate to those deeper religious questions which produced the various cultures. To his credit Karrer has begun to do this. But both of them talk about *Latin* Roman Catholic Christendom making concessions to the *cultural* expressions of other people; they do not address the real question of what role, if any, these other *religions* play in salvation history. This has to wait until the third and fourth phases of Roman Catholic theology of religions.

The Fulfillment and Sacramental Theories

Since the theories developed during the third and fourth phases are not clearly distinguishable, I shall treat them together. To explain them I shall give a few illustrations of the shifts in Roman Catholic thinking since Vatican II which have profoundly influenced missionary practice.

A good place to begin is at the Second Vatican Council with its decree on the non-Christian religions, *Nostra Aetate,* and two others connected with it: *Lumen Gentium* ("decree on the church") and *Ad Gentes* ("decree on the missionary activity of the church"). *Lumen Gentium* did away with the traditional Roman teaching that the Roman Catholic church and the kingdom of God are identical; rather than developing an abstract metaphysical notion of what the church is, it emphasized that the empirical church is part of the complete people of God who are on the march. Furthermore, it did away with the conquistadors' interpretation of the adage *extra ecclesiam nulla salus,* deeming it to be exegetically and factually untenable.

By introducing these changes the Second Vatican Council "broke through the limited perspective of the theology of adaptation," as A. Camps put it.

Nostra Aetate begins: "In our time, when day by day mankind is being drawn closer together, and the ties between different peoples are becoming stronger, the Church examines more closely her relationship to non-Christian religions."[2] Note that the chief interest of the Roman Catholic church is no longer cultures but religions and religious communities in their totality. This short decree's strong point is its careful and candid approach to the extremely tough questions which this whole issue raises; in fact, the document poses more questions than it actually answers and thereby shows that the Roman church is willing to allow some latitude for developing new theologies of religions and wishes to stimulate local churches to honest dialogue with members of other religions.

> In her task of promoting unity and love among men, indeed among nations, she [the church] considers above all in this declaration what men have in common and what draws them to fellowship. . . . The Catholic Church rejects nothing that is true and holy in these religions. She regards with sincere reverence those ways of conduct and of life, those precepts and teachings which, though differing in many aspects from the ones she holds and sets forth, nonetheless often reflect a ray of that Truth which enlightens all men. . . .
>
> The Church, therefore, exhorts her sons, that through dialogue and collaboration with the followers of other religions, carried out with prudence and love and in witness to Christian faith and life, they recognize, preserve and promote the good things, spiritual and moral, as well as the socio-cultural values found among these men.[3]

In 1964 Pope Paul VI established a Secretariat for the Non-Christian Religions to extend the implications of this decree into actual practice.

I now wish to take a brief glimpse at how a few Roman Catholic theologians, taking advantage of the room for latitude which *Lumen Gentium* offered, have begun developing new designs for a theology of religions.

In Part 5 of his *Schriften zur Theologie* Karl Rahner introduced a series of propositions which he has since developed on numerous occasions. They still are having a profound influence on the world of Roman Catholic thinking. After defending the unique legitimacy and absoluteness of the gospel and the universal significance of the church in his first proposition, Rahner goes on to claim in proposition 2:

> Until that moment when the Gospel actually enters the historical situation of the individual, [his] non-Christian religion contains not only traces of human sin but also of the supernatural which proceed from the grace which has been given because of Christ. Therefore, one can deem such a religion to be legitimate — albeit in varying degrees — without in any way denying the errors and corruption it contains.

Rahner's third proposition is based on the previous one: "If proposition two be correct, then Christianity meets a member of an extra-Christian religion not as a non-Christian but rather as a person who in certain respects can and must be considered an anonymous Christian."

Again, proposition 4 follows directly from the preceding:

2. Roman Catholic church, "Declaration on the Relation of the Church to Non-Christian Religions," proclaimed by Pope Paul VI, October 28, 1965. *The Teachings of the Second Vatican Council: Complete Texts of the Constitutions, Decrees and Declarations* (Westminster, Maryland: Newman Press, 1966), p. 267.

3. Ibid., pp. 268–269.

If it be true that religious pluralism is here to stay and that the Christian may view the non-Christian world as anonymously Christian, then the Church ought not to regard herself so much as an exclusive community of salvation [*exclusieve heilsgemeenschap*] as rather the historically tangible vanguard, the historically and socially constituted explicit expression of what the Christian hopes and knows is also present outside the visible Church in hidden and implicit form.[4]

Of course no one claims that Rahner has spoken the final word on this subject in the Roman Catholic church, but his ideas have attracted wide attention and are stimulating other scholars to make their own responses.

One respondent was Anita Roper with her book *The Anonymous Christian* (1966).

H. R. Schlette made a highly original response in his *Towards a Theology of Religions*. I shall present a few of his conclusions:

(1) The non-Christian religions appeared as "normal" paths to salvation [*heilswegen*] within general salvation history. (Schlette distinguishes between special and general salvation history and between normal and extraordinary paths to salvation.)

(2) The religions possess an inner legitimacy conferred and willed by the living God.

(3) The paths to salvation which members of non-Christian religions follow do indeed lead to the living God, but they pass through darkness on the way.

(4) Only via the extraordinary path of special salvation history (that is, the church) can one understand history's secret that the salvation which those who dwell in general salvation history take "normal" paths to reach is really the salvation provided by Jesus Christ and as such is mediated by the church.

(5) When one passes from a non-Christian religion to Christian faith, he is neither simply extending the former nor totally destroying it; he is fulfilling it dialectically.

(6) None of this violates the absolute claim of the gospel in the least degree. The only way to answer the question of truth and the proper relation to the transcendental secret is in each situation itself.[5]

Raymond Panikkar, another contemporary Roman Catholic theologian, makes much more radical claims than either Rahner or Schlette. Born to an Indian father and a Spanish mother, Panikkar is professor at an Indian university and through his books and multilateral dialogues has come to be regarded as one of the most prominent exponents of the newer Roman Catholic theology of religions, even though not even his colleagues always agree with his ideas.

In Panikkar's many publications one can find the following basic claims:

(1) Each authentic religion is a way to salvation (*heil*).

(2) Though unknown and hidden, Christ is nevertheless genuinely and actively involved in each authentic religion. He is the fullness of each religion.

(3) Thomas Aquinas' thesis, *Sacramenta sunt necessaria ad humanum salutem* ("the sacraments are required for a person to gain salvation"), is true, but

4. Karl Rahner, *Schriften zur Theologie, I-X* (Zurich: Benzinger, 1957).

5. H. R. Schlette, *Towards a Theology of Religions* (New York: Herder and Herder, 1966), pp. 109–118.

in the case of non-Christian religions these are the rites, which function as means of grace.

(4) Christianity is the conversion of each religion. The church, a tree in whose branches the birds of the heavens build their nests, has room not only for theological pluralism, but also for religious pluralism.

Panikkar claims that even as one can speak of an elevation from the level of nature to the level of grace, so too he may hope for an elevation of the religions to the sphere of Christianity. Mission is nothing more than allowing the living water in the other religions to rise to the surface so that these religions can flow into the mainstream of Christianity. That which other religions have merely incognito, Christianity and the Roman church have explicitly.

Hubertus Halbfas was more radical than Rahner and even Panikkar, and, in my judgment, totally subverted the deepest intentions of these two theologians. Halbfas claims that Christian faith indeed does have a right to speak authoritatively and to exert an influence — but only in the West. According to Halbfas, in Hindu culture one ought to have no ulterior motive other than simply to help a Hindu become a better Hindu.

Halbfas's radical ideas have unleashed a storm of protest within the Roman Catholic church. His critics charge that he, rather than bringing about *aggiornamento,* is actually introducing a boycott of the missionary nature of the church.

Still another variation in the theology of dialogue which has come about as a result of Vatican II is contained in Josef Heislbetz's *Theologische Gründe der nicht-christlichen Religionen.* He too takes his starting point in God's will that all be saved and from it goes on to claim that all religions have their place in salvation history. Those people, he says, "who live in insurmountable error regarding the true religion of Christ can nevertheless by virtue of Divine light and grace attain eternal salvation through faithfully following the demands of the *lex natura* which God has inscribed in their hearts." "The non-Christian is duty-bound (!) to accept his own religion." "God does not only allow a plurality of religions; he wills them." "One must see the rites and doctrines of the non-Christian religions as a result of the impulses of grace." A form of salvation history is being enacted through the history of religions. The mission of the church "is to redeem and liberate what is already Christian by giving it complete historical shape in Jesus Christ." "Until Christianity comes and replaces them," says Heislbetz, aligning himself directly with Rahner, "the non-Christian religions serve as the God-ordained means of bringing salvation" to their members.

According to Heislbetz, Christian mission ought not any longer to proclaim that it comes with a solution to mankind's lost and alienated condition; it ought rather to strive to insure that an already-present anonymous Christianity "becomes the official religion of a respective people."[6]

Obviously Heislbetz does not proclaim a gospel which demands decision. Instead, the questions which Vatican II posed for discussion become enveloped in a cloud of speculations lacking solid foundation.

6. Joseph Heislbetz, *Theologische Gründe der nicht-christlichen Religionen* (Freiburg i.B: Herder, 1967).

The Dutch Jesuit, Father P. Schoonenberg, is much more careful in his approach. In his book *Het Geloof van ons Doopsel* (1958), his essay "Heilsge-schiedenis" in *God's Wordende Wereld*, and his essay "Christologie en Theologie der Godsdiensten" in *Wereld en Zending*, he, too, speaks of a general salvation history of grace, sin, and redemption. Man with his fellow men responds to the divine offer of salvation through religions. Within general salvation history, however, there are, according to Schoonenberg, various phases. The church is at the apex; it is God's salvation completed. The missionary task of the church therefore is to invite other religions to join in this complete salvation manifest in Jesus Christ.

Schoonenberg attempted a practical application of this dialogical fulfillment theology in "Versuch einer christlich-theologischen Sicht des Hinduismus," his personal contribution to a symposium study of the concept of revelation in India. He clearly intended his essay as an effort to bring about a dialogue between followers of the religions and revelations in India and the native Christian churches in India who were themselves once members of those religions but now find in Jesus the fulfillment of their deepest aims and intentions.

I must not fail to cite in this short survey those Roman Catholic theologians who are thoroughly involved in the practical experience of meeting followers of other religions and who thus understand better than the purely speculative theologians the deep break which people must make when they transfer from another religion to faith in Jesus.

Henri Maurier wrote *Essai d'une Théologie du Paganisme*, in which he underscored the fact that it is not religions which become converted, but people. He pointed out that for these people *metanoia* takes place, that is, a break and a crisis. Though he rejected the idea that other religions are *praeambula fidei*, he was willing to concede that they may be stepping-stones in the stage of pre-evangelism. The book attests to its author's long experience in Africa.

Another book which counterbalances a too-optimistic understanding of the relationship between gospel and the religions is André Rétif's *Mission — Heute Noch*. He claims that the views of people like Rahner and especially Panikkar tend to paralyze missionary *élan*.

Writing in much the same vein as Retif and filled with a certain degree of indignation brought about by a knowledge of missionary practice, J. J. M. van Straelen, a longtime missionary to Japan, published *Botsing, Vervreemding en Ontmoeting*.

Hans Waldenfels's essay, "Anmerkungen zum Gespräch der Christenheit mit der nichtchristlichen Welt," in *Kirche in der ausserchristlichen Welt*, though a bit more sedate than van Straelen's book, is no less adamant in its position. Waldenfels argues for engaged dialogue, but a dialogue which always "clearly confesses" the heart of the matter.

To reduce the various Roman Catholic theologies of religions produced after Vatican II to some kind of order is not easy. A. Camps, who has intensively examined both the content and the method displayed in these theologies, divides them into three schools. The key word describing the one school is *fulfillment;* God's revelation in Christ fulfills the non-Christian religions. Father Schoonenberg represents this school. Another school emphasizes *deputyship*. The church functions as the *pars pro toto* and as a *signum levatum in nationes*. Schlette and Ratzinger are leading exponents of this position. The third school emphasizes *anonymous Christianity* and is headed by Rahner, Roper and Panikkar.

However widely each of these positions may differ from the other two, they all in one form or another subscribe to the traditional Roman Catholic distinction between nature and supranature. All of them aim for an elevation or sublimation of the human religious accomplishments into the sphere of supranature. The church is the invitation to people to transfer from being *de jure* anonymous Christians to becoming *de facto* Christians, from being Christians *in spe* to becoming Christians *in re*.

Moreover, all these schools powerfully underscore what Pope Paul VI recommended in his encyclical, *Ecclesiam Suam:* the church must enter into dialogue with the world in which she lives. The church is herself word, message and dialogue.

One final comment. Each of these schools has breathed deeply the air of *aggiornamento*, the attempt to modernize the Roman Catholic church, and in its approach to the religions and religious communities each is following the guidelines set down in *Nostra Aetate*.

TRENDS IN PROTESTANT THEOLOGY OF RELIGIONS

In discussing Protestant theology of religions I must again be highly selective in view of the great mass of material. In conjunction with my discussion here one does well to consult the chapter on theological developments in Asia, Africa and Latin America for various data because those theologians are naturally much more immediately involved with members of other religions than Western theologians.

The World Missionary Conferences and Theology of Religions

Man studies have, of course, been made of the theology of religions influential at Edinburgh (1910), Jerusalem (1928) and Tambaram (1938). For the trends developed since World War II, one does well to consult the especially lucid survey by Carl Hallencreutz, "New Approaches to Men of Other Faiths," published as Research Pamphlet no. 18 by the World Council of Churches. Hallencreutz wrote his doctoral dissertation on Hendrik Kraemer's theology of religions (*Kraemer Towards Tambaram*), and he has been following the subsequent developments throughout the world, especially the work being done in the many centers for the study of religion and society throughout Asia, Africa and Latin America.

Then, too, S. J. Samartha's reports of the various consultations sponsored by the World Council's Division for Dialogue with People of Another Faith are extremely valuable.

As supplement to this literature one should also read about the trends in the recent Bangkok conference. From the symposium study which J. T. Witvliet and I compiled, *Jezus Christus: De Bevrijder en de voortgaande Bevrijdingen van Mensen en Samenlevingen* ("Jesus Christ the Liberator and the On-going Liberation of People and Societies"), I believe one can discern that the Bangkok conference strongly underscored the absolute validity and finality of the gospel of Jesus Christ even though it described with a breadth and dimensions hitherto unknown the salvation which he brings.

Anyone who studies in depth the vast literature produced both by and about the various missionary conferences on the subject of the theology of religions can only conclude that these conferences confessed with new tongues the complete validity and finality of Jesus Christ and the gospel of his messianic kingdom; they did not relativize or reduce the gospel's relationship to the other religions. W. A. Visser 't Hooft's *No Other Name*, written to counter syncretistic and relativizing tendencies, typifies the spirit of these conferences right up to the present day. To be sure, the delegates wrestled with how best to express this uniqueness and finality. Terms such as "continuity — discontinuity" (Kraemer), "antithesis — affinity," and "crisis — fulfillment" were always at some point or another judged to be insufficient to express the truth. But no one disagreed that to Jesus belongs the name above every name. At every conference there was an overriding conviction that God has revealed himself both adequately and definitively in Jesus Christ (however weak our understanding and expression of this truth may be), and that God once for all put an end to our individual and collective guilt through the one who died and rose again, thus paving the way toward his messianic kingdom. Throughout these conferences there was also an increasing sense that we are called to engage in dialogue to show our partner who this Jesus is and what he has done for us and to arouse both our partner and ourselves to follow this Jesus on his march to his messianic kingdom.

Wolfhart Pannenberg

Wolfhart Pannenberg's famous *Grundfragen systematischer Theologie* includes a probing essay on theology of religions entitled "Erwägungen zu einer Theologie der Religionsgeschichte." Obviously I cannot begin to summarize forty pages of terse argumentation here; I desire only to note Pannenberg's resolute opposition to psychological and anthropocentric interpretations of religious phenomena. He probes into what he terms "der Wirklichkeitsbezug religiöser Erfahrung und seine Bedeuting für das Verständnis der Religionsgeschichte." Historians of religion, says Pannenberg, have usually tried to avoid making any comment about the truth claims of a given religion and the authenticity of one's religious experience generally. They evaded such questions by simply terming religious phenomena pure expressions of human conduct. But to understand religious changes one can scarcely get around facing the question of how these religious phenomena are related to divine reality.

To arrive at a just interpretation of religious experiences and ideas requires that the interpreter not prejudge religious life to be some mere epiphenomenon of secular psychic or social happening or a manifestation of extant divinity completely independent of history.

In accord with its nature, history of religion must be understood as the history of the manifestation of the existing divine mystery in the structure of human existence. Pannenberg delivers the human experience of transcendental reality out of the realm of psychologistic explanation and anchors it firmly in the very structure of man. All religions in some way or other have to do with the God who reveals himself.

In his writing, however, Pannenberg at no point sacrifices Christian faith on the altar of some shapeless notion of religion, as Peter Beyerhaus rightly observes. Rather, in his view, the Israelitic-Christian religion is the integrating center in a universal process. One ought to view such a claim not so much as a statement based on actual facts as they are today but rather as a vision of hope.

Moreover, for a theologian such as Pannenberg it would be unthinkable to keep silent about the scandal of the cross, to only affirm human religiosity but fail to mention God's judgment upon it.

Several other German Protestant contributions to theology of religions should be mentioned in this section: G. Rosenkranz, *Der christliche Glaube angesichts der Weltreligionen;* Horst Bürkle, *Dialog mit dem Osten;* George F. Vicedom, "Die Religionen in der Sicht von Neu Delhi" (Vol. 16 of the *Fuldaer Hefte)*; Wilhelm Andersen, "Die theologische Sicht der Religionen auf den Weltmissions-konferenzen von Jerusalem (1928) und Madras (1938) und die Theologie der Religionen bei Karl Barth" *(Fuldaer Heft)*; and H. W. Gensichen, *Die christliche Mission in der Begegnung mit den Religionen* (a volume whose value is enhanced by its author's rich practical experience).

I would also mention a valuable collection of English essays, *Face to Face: Essays on Interfaith Dialogue.* One of the essays is by Max Warren, "A Theology of Attention," to which I shall refer later, and another is by the highly competent David Brown on dialogue with the Muslims.

All of the above books fall within the range of consensus established by world missionary conferences. But let no one get the impression that Protestantism lacks a group of theologians and historians of religion who smooth over the differences between the gospel and the various world religions. Such scholars do exist, and their claims challenge us to an answer. From this sizable contingent reflecting a more relativist and historicist bent I choose one of the most prominent for special attention: Cantwell Smith.

Cantwell Smith

During the nineteenth and twentieth centuries a steady stream of Protestant thinkers has been welling up to deny the traditional Christian claim that the core of Christian faith is binding upon all peoples and cultures; the gospel, they gladly concede, is important for those within the "circle of Christian culture," but they fight shy of proclaiming it as obligatory for people of other religious communities.

During the last century Ernst Troeltsch was chief spokesman for this group. Christianity, he said, was the central summary and the epitome of human religious quest up to the present time, but it could well be that in the future a new world religion would rise up to remove Christianity from its present preeminent position. In his opinion Christianity is culture-bound, and this fact rids us of any obligation to spread its message to other peoples.

Another typical representative of this group was William E. Hocking, who encouraged interreligious contact but not with a view to getting individuals to transfer from one religion to another. Each should abide in his own religion but be willing to take over certain features of other religions into his own and thus arrive at "reconception," a new understanding of his own religion complemented by valuable insights from others.

C. J. Bleeker traces a similar path in his *Christ in Modern Athens*. As he sees it, the various religions can complement each other, and therefore he highly recommends Hocking's path of reconception.

But rather than simply listing a number of individuals whose writings reflect a relativist theology of religions, I wish to limit myself in this survey to a consideration of the most competent representative — Cantwell Smith. For my present purposes I choose to overlook his impressive research in the field of history of religions; I will rather deal only with his essay which lies somewhere between missiology and theology of religions, "The Changing Christian Role in Other Cultures," published in the *Occasional Bulletin of the Missionary Research Library*.

A Buddhist, a Muslim and a Christian are all involved in an ongoing process, explains Smith. Every single one of them participates — the pious, the lackadaisical, the kind, and the heretical. They bring to this process a history which is given, a present which is open, and a future which all of them are carving. Each of these processes is a divine-human complex, both of which dimensions we must keep before our minds. The relation between the divine and human elements varies from generation to generation, from man to man, and even from hour to hour. As opposed to a concept of "salvation history" (*heilsgeschichte*), he suggests that a religious man is one whose relation with God is being formed through his involvement in the ongoing process of one religious community or another.

It is the task of the historian of religion, according to Smith, to view this series of processes *sub specie aeternitatis* and to strive to influence them for good where he can.

What then is the genuinely Christian role which one can play in the evolution of another culture? The missionary, says Smith, must be nothing other than a mischievous, joyous, and welcome participant in the religious history of the rest of mankind. He offers several examples of people who were just that. Tillich taught in a Buddhist community in Tokyo, Buber in Boston, Aurobindo in Oxford, and Suzuki at Union Theological Seminary in New York. Such individuals ought to serve as models for the modern missionary. Earlier mission agencies mistakenly supposed that they had to strive for "intercommunity conversions." A participant in one historical process was transferred to another. Missionaries should strive for "conversion" *within* the community and tradition in which a person dwells, claims Smith.

Summarizing his ideas, Smith says that all religious communities are involved in such an ongoing process while at the same time dwelling in the constant presence of that transcendent power in whom we all move and have our being. Religions are beginning to converge and to form a single configuration woven out of the threads of many religious communities. All human history is salvation history. We are the first generation of Christians who are learning to recognize God's saving deeds in all of the religious processes.

Smith closes by issuing an appeal to Christians to join intelligently and

Christianly in this salvation history of the whole human race.

A person like Cantwell Smith offers a wealth of insights from which we can learn. His careful attention to the processes of change which are progressively making the hitherto segmented world one and his cry for cultural and religious exchange are exemplary and must evoke our deepest respect. But in his theology of religions, the person and work of Jesus Christ never emerge; he will hear nothing of the idea of the presence of the Christian church among the other religious communities and he pushes aside the need for a missionary mandate. We do well to heed his warnings against a too aggressive Christian "steam-roller approach" and the dangers of a Crusade mentality, but in the final analysis Smith's ideas are the neo-liberal views of Ernst Troeltsch and William Hocking in modern dress. He who is so quick to caution missionaries against becoming aggressors himself has turned aggressor against the witness to the name which is above every name and against the inescapable command to proclaim the message of the crucified and risen Lord.

TOWARD A ROUGH DRAFT OF A THEOLOGY OF RELIGIONS

Having looked briefly at some of the developments in the theology of religions, I shall now attempt to provide my own rough draft of such a theology, trying to take into account some of the insights which have contributed to recent developments.

Anyone who strives to design his own theology of religions must be fully cognizant of the changes which are occurring in the relationship between religion and society. Changes in life perspective and world view are extending to the farthest reaches of this globe and infiltrating those who participate in the life of a given religious community. Modern developments rise up to challenge these religious communities and force them to shift their traditional positions. When Hendrik Kraemer wrote his famous *The Christian Message in a Non-Christian World,* he continually hammered home the idea that any change in ideas or goals which takes place in a religion must be explained within the frame of reference of that religion itself. The situation today is not as black and white as it was when Kraemer wrote. When one inquires what ideas such as freedom, liberation, salvation, redemption, justice, truth, peace, etc., mean today to members of the various religious communities, he comes to see that they cannot simply be explained in terms of that religion itself; members of individual religious communities have come into contact with other religious communities and ideologies, and the confrontation has not left them untouched. The winds of contemporary world civilization are blowing in their faces. A new view of man and society is emerging. The ethical issues involving marriage and the family, economics, politics and culture are obviously changing. All of these changes a realistic theology of religions will most certainly take into account.

This brings me to another aspect which I wish to examine now. Though I cannot admire Smith's theology of religions at each and every point, I nevertheless regard his historical and sociological observations on religion as unmatched. In this context I recall his plea in his book *The Meaning and End of Religion* for a new approach to the religious traditions of mankind. He calls for a clear distinction between "personal faith" and "cumulative tradition." Through the tremendous changes which have occurred, human beings have assumed a much more critical and selective posture toward the religious tradition of which they are a part. Therefore, what traditionally has been termed "religion" or a "specific religion" (such as Islam, Hinduism, etc.) could more accurately and honestly be described in terms of two quite different and yet equally dynamic factors — the historic, accumulated tradition and the personal beliefs of actual men and women. In the present situation members of a given religion, whether they are conscious of doing so or not, nevertheless set about selecting specific elements from the cumulative tradition. Individuals may differ in what they choose, but absolutely no one completely identifies with the whole of the tradition. In a certain sense every person in the process has his own religion. If I may express the idea a bit differently, between God, the human being, and the "powers" at a deeper level, a drama is being acted out which is known to God alone.

I agree with Smith in his claim that the external side of religion (as expressed in myths, rites, customs, dogma, etc.) is open to historical investigation, but that one's personal relation to God is so deep that it is not open to public scrutiny and explanation.

One looks out through the window of accumulated tradition, but he uses his own eyes in doing so. Each person plays upon certain notes selected from the tradition even as a violist brings his own style to the playing of his instrument.

Some critics such as Hallencreutz accuse Cantwell Smith of slighting the importance of tradition. After all, they ask, how does personal belief feed itself and grow? Though Schlette, Rahner, Schoonenberg, and others may have overemphasized the importance of the institutionalized framework, claim the critics, Smith can surely be accused of underestimating it. I do not think this charge is correct; rather, Smith, unlike Schlette and Rahner, knows people of another faith in an uncommonly profound way.

Of course each person lives within the sphere of influence of a given cumulative tradition, but experience proves that a given individual within that tradition does not totally agree with everything for which that tradition stands. In my opinion Smith's distinction is most useful and can exercise a purifying effect, for it reminds us that no theologian of religions has the right to make an ultimate value judgment on a person's faith. There is within everyone a deep secret which none but God knows. A theologian of religions does well to keep this caution in mind as he goes about his work.

In my view a proper starting point for a theology of religions is the trinitarian confession. There is nothing new to my claim; Lesslie Newbigin, Kazoh Kitamori, Wilhelm Andersen, M. M. Thomas, George F. Vicedom, August Kimme and many others also made this their starting point. I shall only be attempting to walk in their footsteps.

God the Father and Creator and Man's Religious Existence

In a trinitarian approach to a theology of religions one ought never to pass over lightly the fact of God as the Father and Creator of this world. Often we become so preoccupied with getting to his work as Liberator, Redeemer, and Reconciler that we forget that all these only make sense within the context of his prior creation.

God loves his creation. Think of biblical passages such as Psalm 50:10, Jeremiah 8:7, Psalm 19:1, Romans 1:19–20, etc. J. H. Bavinck never stopped talking about this when he was on the subject of the religious life of man. One of his most frequently quoted prophetic passages was Isaiah 40:28: "Do you not know? Have you not heard? Has it not been told you from the beginning?"

God's creative deeds take place also in the history of individuals and peoples. In the face of Israel and Judah's ethnocentrism, Amos counters with his incisive question: "Did I [God] not bring up Israel from the land of Egypt, and the Philistines from Caphtor and the Syrians from Kir?" (Amos 9:7). When the prophet of Isaiah 19:24–25 says God calls the Egyptians "my people" and the Assyrians "the work of my hands," he is simply acknowledging that God the Creator is at work in the history of those peoples.

Should not one also be open to God's creational revelation in the history of religions? Think of a person such as Melchizedek mentioned first in Genesis 14, of God's revelation to Job in a whirlwind (Job 38), and of the other individuals in the Old Testament who, though outside of the specific covenant line established by God, nevertheless had a direct relation with him. Abimelech of Gerar spoke with God in a nocturnal vision (Gen. 20:4), the Midianite priest Jethro made a sacrifice to God (Ex. 18:12), the Mesopotamian Balaam ran head-on into God and his angel (Num. 22:9ff.), etc.

How was God involved when the Vedas were being transmitted? What went on between God and Gautama Buddha when the latter received the Bodhi? What transpired between God and Mohammed when he meditated in the grotto? In asking such questions I do not believe that one ought to facilely conclude that God has revealed himself in such crucial religious situations, but on the other hand I believe that the Bible compels us to admit that God is involved and puts himself in touch with human beings.

In that light I believe one must confess that not only is God active in nature and in the history of peoples and religions but also in the history of each and every human being. We ought to applaud Pannenberg for his attempts to break through the immanentist view of the deepest origins of human religious experience and for positing a transcendental experience of reality which by its very nature is anchored in the very structure of man. I do not agree completely with his claim that all religions have a revelatory character, but the ineradicable urge of every mortal being to vent himself religiously undeniably attests to the presence of a divine transcendental reality. One simply cannot understand man's religiosity and the fact of the religions without referring to the drama going on between God and man.

Biblically speaking, however, I believe that there are not two but three dimensions or poles to this drama. Peter Beyerhaus calls it a "tri-polar relation." First there is God and the radius of action involving his creational revelation within which man lives and moves. Second is the sphere of human reacting, repressing, projecting, searching, groping, wandering, questing and fleeing. Third, there is the dimension of what Paul calls the "powers" which collectively influence us for good or ill (cf. Gal. 4). Contemporary scholars such as Hendrikus Berkhof recognize a similarity between these "powers" and the collective and complex influence of the myths, rites, customs, etc., in the various religions.

This tri-polar relationship is the deepest puzzle of human religiosity and the ultimate explanation for its ambivalence. Who can say precisely how in a specific religion or a specific situation or a specific person these three influences are at work? No one but God really knows. But in spite of our inability to know the details, we must retain this three-dimensional view of the religions. Freud, Feuerbach, and Marx all had mono-polar explanations. Philosophers of religion such as Hegel, Schleiermacher, Otto, and Heiler were bi-polar. But we must be tri-polar.

Given the validity of this tri-polar view, I do not believe theologians such as Rahner, Schlette, and Panikkar are warranted in stating a priori that religious systems even though they do not know Christ must nevertheless be acknowledged as means of salvation. On the contrary, the intent listener to what is transpiring in religions senses that it is precisely those who no longer accept the status quo of a religious system and are attempting to break through its established order who often give the clearest signals of God's activity among men. Welling up within them is a sense of salvation and liberation incalculably deeper than that offered by their respective cumulative traditions. There is a tension between revelation and religiosity, between tradition and genuine encounter with God, which is visible throughout the whole history of religions. Failure to maintain this tension leads one to declare that all religions are "legitimate paths to salvation." He in effect calls a premature halt to the mysterious tri-polar drama by jumping to a too-quick conclusion which does not reckon sufficiently with God's creational revelation, the reality of sin and error, and the influence of the "powers."

One thing is certain: he who lives by faith in God as Creator cannot rest content with a sociological, psychological, or any other fundamentally inadequate immanentist attempt to explain the rise and existence of religions. We must reckon with the fact that the Creator of heaven and earth is alive and leaves no human being without a witness to his existence (Acts 14:17).

Jesus Christ and the Theology of Religions

In my judgment a theologian of religion ought not only to reckon with the importance of the Christian confession that God is Father and Creator but also with the importance of Jesus Christ.

Troeltsch, Hocking, and Smith, to name just a few representatives of what Karl Barth termed "cultural Protestantism," were very weak at this point. For them Jesus Christ was something of a "displaced person" with whom they did not know what to do. They viewed him as a religious genius or as one of the many prophetic figures, but in their theology of religions they refused to confess that he was the incarnation of God and man, the Mediator between God and mankind. In foregoing this, they gave up a most vital element.

Confessing Jesus Christ as Lord

Throughout the ages the Christian church has confessed that Jesus Christ is the very incarnation of God and man and that in and through him God has laid the foundations for a new order, the messianic kingdom. Every attempt to bring salvation through human beings or religions having failed, God gave him, the "one for all," to restore the communication between God and mankind. The events of his cross and resurrection "once for all" laid the groundwork for this new kingdom in which all God-man and man-man relationships will be straightened out again.

Referring to Yahweh, the God not only of Israel but also of the whole cosmos, the Old Testament states: " 'To whom then will you compare me, that I should be like him?' says the Holy One" (Isa. 40:25). And when God comes to us in the New Testament clothed in the figure of Jesus Christ the Lord, we can hear an echo of this question: "With whom can you compare him?" He is unique, incomparable, irreplaceable, and decisive for all ages and peoples. We are "from below"; he is "from above." We need forgiveness; he provides it. We thirst for liberation; he is the Liberator. We grope about on the chance that we might find God; he is God's revelation. We have lost our way toward God and our neighbor; he is God manifest in the flesh.

Though I am convinced that he bore a too heavy imprint of nineteenth-century philosophical idealism which influenced his book, nevertheless I am grateful for Ulrich Mann's *Das Christentum als absolute Religion*. On the one hand, he acknowledges that no one can explain the rise of various myths, rites, and a religious ethos without a doctrine of creational revelation; on the other, he attests that God has revealed himself not in a system, nor in an idea, but definitively in a person, Jesus Christ, the Word become flesh.

Kenneth Cragg, one of the most prominent contemporary theologians of religions, makes this his primary point of departure throughout all his writings. His theme is constantly the same: throughout the course of history God has employed various means of communication, but in Jesus Christ God communicated himself. To say it a bit differently, God has sent many "servants," but in Jesus Christ, he himself has come.

The Cosmic Christ Idea

Paul's letters to the Ephesians and Colossians underscore the cosmic dimensions of Christ and his work. Many contemporary thinkers, however, trade in their confession that Jesus Christ is Lord for some sort of cosmic Christ who "is present in all developments of history, in all the social revolutionary movements, and in all human religious ideas and quests." The real danger is that such a "cosmic Christ" reduces to a mere abstraction completely out of accord with him who concretely is and was and is to come.

This, I believe, is the very trap into which Ulrich Mann fell. Though he fortunately emphasized Jesus Christ who came to us in history, toward the end of his book he spoke of the cosmic Christ, the archetype found in every human soul.

I have no more space to trace further the complete development of this idea which today is in rather strong demand, but I could not fail to at least warn that it is merely a caricature of a genuine Christology for a theology of religions. John V. Taylor issued the same warning in his essay "Christian Motivation in Dialogue."

Christ's Cross and Resurrection and Religious Man

Religious men put Jesus Christ to death on the cross. Therefore, says Paul, Christ's cross is God's judgment upon all human efforts to achieve salvation through religions. Gathered around the cross were individuals who followed the paths of magic and mysticism, moralism and legalism, and knowledge and Gnosticism to secure their own liberation. But in the cross of Jesus all our cheap judgments of what is good and valuable in religions and cultures are called up short.

The sharp point of all human religiosity and morality was aimed at the very heart of Jesus. Paul in I Corinthians 1 and 2 describes Jesus' cross as the divine judgment upon all human religiosity while at the same time both cross and resurrection are the power for liberation and redemption for all peoples. The foolishness of God is wiser than man's wisdom, and the weakness of God is stronger than human strength. In Christ's cross and resurrection something so decisive happened that its dimensions are indeed cosmic and its importance extends to human beings of every religious stripe. In the crucified and resurrected Lord, God is reaching forth his hand to the whole cosmos and to human beings in all religions (cf. II Cor. 5). The old is past; the new has begun.

A theologian of religions ought never to ignore this christological aspect. Jesus, the crucified and risen Lord, has come into history. He now lives and is coming again. He is now enroute to the final manifestation of his messianic kingdom in which everything is made new. In it the lot of the poor and the sinner is set straight. This Christ is coming; he is at work in the harvest fields of the history of religions, fields filled with both the good grain which he sowed and the weeds which were sowed by those other "powers." A theologian of religions who remembers this christological dimension will keep looking for evidences of this Christ who is ceaselessly active; he will be alert for signs of the messianic kingdom in the religious life of mankind both inside and outside the church.

The Holy Spirit and the Theology of Religions

The Spirit's Work in the World of the Religions
The Holy Spirit, even as the Father and the Son, is also at work in the world, for he is the Spirit of the Father and the Son. Theologians of religions ought to give him their humble attention as he goes about his work in the world, even in the gigantic processes of change through which religions are passing.

Max Warren, whose more than forty years of experience among people of various religions rank him as one of the most profound theologians of religions, argued in one of his most recent writings for a "theology of attention." He encourages us to walk humbly and honestly with men of other faiths and to keep our eyes open for any evidence of the Spirit's work among them. When Jesus was here upon earth, his many contacts with human beings affected them in various levels and degrees. Though many came under his influence, some became his actual disciples while others did not. So too, says Warren, we ought to pay close heed to the possible working of the Spirit among those many people *extra muros ecclesiae* who have not (yet) openly declared their discipleship.

In my opinion, Max Warren is absolutely right. The Holy Spirit is latently active in so many ways among those people who live within the context of other religious traditions. Is it really possible for any one of us to believe that human beings can be found somewhere who have *not* been touched by the hand of Jesus Christ which goes out to them in reconciliation? Ought we not rather to accept the fact that the light of the Spirit shines in the darkness and the darkness cannot put it out?

The Church as the Firstfruits Ripened by the Holy Spirit

A theologian of religions ought not to take lightly the Spirit's work in building up the church amid the other religious communities. The New Testament ties *ekklēsia* ("church") and *basileia* ("kingdom") firmly together. The gospel of Jesus Christ called for conversion and affiliation with the *ekklēsia*. One can only stand amazed at the number of poor, humiliated, and despised people in the days of the early church who broke loose from their old sociological ties to join the New Testament *ekklēsia* and await the coming kingdom of God.

This ecclesiological accent is indispensable for a proper theology of religions. Some theologians purposely omit it, arguing that since Jesus Christ has already accomplished his work of rescue and liberation and the future of mankind is in his hands, the church no longer needs to strive to invite people to join it. In their mind the churches which now do exist function merely as a *pars pro toto;* they represent and are a sacrament of the whole. But the church neither can nor needs to invite people to join its ranks.

If all this were true as these scattered few theologians of religions say it is, then the Bible is wrong and the missionary mandate which is found in all four Gospels and which fulfills the work of the Apostles themselves is a mistake. Such notions as some of these new theologians of religions propose are not a genuine theology of religions but rather a boycott of the Spirit-directed calling of the church. This is a form of ecclesiastical suicide, as it were.

Indeed, fidelity to the Lord may at times require a church or a group of churches to be willing to forego their own continued existence, but such is quite different from a suicidal contempt for continuing the witness to Christ amid the religious communities. Rather than extinguishing the fire, a theology of religions ought to do precisely the opposite. Any view which tends to justify Christian inactivity and paralyze the church's missionary endeavor is doing a disservice to both theology and the church today.

Though a theology of religions may never neglect the pneumatological and the ecclesiological dimensions, it must be underscored that this does not mean that a person who leaves his native religion to become a member of the ecumenical church necessarily has to leave everything behind, as though he were a man fleeing his burning house. His manner of being, living, and thinking may well contain much that stems from God himself, which, when placed within the context of a Christocentric universalism and directed toward Christ can shoot forth in new blossom. At most I can only cite a few examples of what I mean. I am thinking of the sense of divine transcendence which is prevalent among Christians whose roots lie in the Muslim tradition. I am thinking of the sense of God's immanence present among Christians of Hindu background. I am thinking of the deeper sense of wonder which fills millions of Christians from various traditions other than those we in the West possess. Many of them have defined much better than we the role of meditation, fasting, watching and praying in the Christian life. Some of them are more ready to suffer and endure hardship and are less attached to money and goods. Many express a deeper sense of the joy which faith brings. Still others

— especially those from Africa — via their experience in their traditional religions have a much more developed sense of the unity which binds the church militant here on earth and the church triumphant in heaven together. And still others realize more deeply than their Western fellow Christians the unity between the sacral and the secular, between *homo orans* (man at prayer), *homo laborans* (man at work), and *homo ludens* (man at play).

THEOLOGY OF RELIGIONS AND SCIENCE OF RELIGION

There always has been and always will be a tension between the two disciplines, theology of religions and science of religion. Such tension can be useful and fruitful. Theology of religions views man's religious development within an eschatological frame of reference, from a perspective in which the "Truth" (residing in Jesus Christ) is verified by the Christ who has both come and is coming, by the testimony of the Holy Spirit, and by the messianic kingdom. Such an eschatological perspective spells no danger for objectivity. In fact, one might well defend the claim that honest recognition of one's own bias enhances impartiality rather than destroys it. Scientists of religion are quite right in staunchly resisting any tendency of dogmatics to domineer the theologians of religions. But these scientists must allow the theologians of religions the right to study religions metaphenomenologically, testing them in the light of Jesus Christ who both was and is to come.

As I see it, Hendrik Kraemer was quite right in claiming in one of his last writings, *Religion and the Christian Faith,* that that vast number of scientists of religion are merely displaying their arrogance in claiming scientific objectivity. He who believes that choosing one's point of departure in Jesus Christ, or, even broader and deeper still, in the trinitarian confession, is unscientific only reveals his own bias.

In his essay entitled *Theologie der Religionsgeschichte,* W. Pannenberg says, "Thus a theology of religious history [*Religionsgeschichte*] which does not ignore its Christian perspective is conceivable provided it does not use its Christian presuppositions as arguments but rather appeals to objective facts [*phänomenale Sachverhalte beruft*]." I do not believe it is sufficient for a theologian of religions to attend only to phenomenological data. He must choose a criterion, and it is in no way unscientific for a Christian to take his starting point in the work of the Father, Son, and Holy Spirit, however weak and fallible his apperception of their activity may be.

Theologians of religions and scientists of religion each have legitimate separate disciplines, but they need each other and must complement each other.

THEOLOGY OF RELIGIONS AND MISSIOLOGY

Theology of religions and missiology, both being branches of theology, also complement each other. If a theologian of religions lacks missionary motivation and perspective, he has actually traded in the real foundation of his discipline for something which provides no basis at all. On the other hand, if a missiologist both in his method and his conclusions fails to take theology of religions into account, he will be blind to what is actually transpiring among human beings and religions and thus talk only in thin air and grope about in a fog.

Father Joseph Spae, the recently elected secretary-general of SODEPAX, after reviewing the "image" which Japanese people have of Christ and which Christians have of Japanese religions, said that both of them might just as well have been speaking Arabic to each other. Missionaries often move in a world of fantasy which corresponds little to the way things really are. Theologians of religions ought to be reminding them of what really lives in the hearts and minds of people of other religions. More and more missionaries must learn to ask: What do a Buddhist, a Muslim and a Hindu have to say to us now and what should we be saying to them? To determine this, missionaries need theologians of religions.

Max Warren called for a "theology of attention, of love, of communication." That too is the reason why we today place such heavy emphasis on *dialogue*. Many individuals tend to play proclamation of the gospel off against dialogue as though the two oppose each other. Such is useless and idle play. Anyone who sets out with faith that in Jesus Christ God's kingdom is coming knows that this message is directed to "every creature," to borrow the language of the New Testament. This means that we Christians must bring our message to individuals who are sincerely devoted to another faith and who therefore interpret our coming as an arrogant intrusion into their lives. It is vitally important that we strive to minimize this obtrusiveness as much as possible not only by our deep personal humility but also by our willingness to listen as well as to speak, to learn as well as to communicate. For we know that God the Father, Son, and Holy Spirit can and does actually speak outside the sphere of the church and outside the pages of the Bible. The radius of his action is much wider than we ever imagined. Many factors are involved in bringing about the gigantic processes of change which are now taking place; one of them is the influence of the living God. Therefore, we do well to first listen, not only to understand non-Christians better but also to learn from them.

In a dialogue each partner should share his deepest insights. This means that we Christians neither can nor may simply perpetuate our old ways of doing things. In the course of the dialogue each must be prepared to pose questions about his own convictions and experience and open himself not only to his partner but also to the Holy Spirit.

VARIETIES OF DIALOGUE

However important theology of religions as a discipline may be and however valuable its insights, unlike missiology it is not concerned with praxis. Praxis seeks to take shape in various forms of dialogue today.

It is important to remember that the communication of the gospel of Jesus Christ throughout the ages has had a dialogical character. Both the modern missionary pioneers such as William Carey and Henry Martyn and the first leaders of the Asian and African churches who brought the gospel to people of another faith (Chao, Uchimara, Ting, Azariah, Tosari, and thousands of others) were all masters of dialogue. Stanley Jones devoted his whole life to a certain type of dialogue which he found highly beneficial.

Today there are people who waste a lot of words about dialogue but who themselves have never done it, and who, even if they tried, could not stand in the shadow of these early pioneers.

Thus, dialogue itself as a method is nothing new, but the shapes and forms it takes today have become more carefully defined.

I must make a second prefatory comment. Of course no missionary "on the field" can hold up his work until theologians of religions have developed a "satisfactory" theology. An Indian villager in contact with his neighbors, a Thai farmer in contact with his fellows as he plods behind the buffalo in the rice fields, and a Jakarta parliamentarian in contact with his Muslim colleagues cannot wait until theologians come up with a new theology of religions. Dialogues often take place without deeper reflection, but it is a well-established fact that deeper reflection by scientists, philosophers and theologians of religions has aided in producing new forms of dialogue.

I discern three forms of dialogue which have arisen in recent years. First, there is a dialogue with the goal to bring about better mutual understanding. Second, some dialogue aims at producing cooperation in dealing with the most urgent problems facing society regionally and universally. Third, other dialogue strives to aid missionary communication on both sides. In treating them separately I in no way wish to create the impression that each of these three has absolutely nothing to do with the other two. In fact, often during a dialogue intended to produce greater understanding by clearing away the rubble of confusion an opportunity opens up for witness. Or again, as both sides groan under the weighty burden of local or international problems, and the poverty of the one side finds its echo in the poverty of the other, the cry "Veni, Creator Spiritus" can rise from their midst either consciously or unconsciously. Finally, a dialogue whose actual purpose is to aid the communication of the heart of the gospel ofttimes stands in need of the invaluable insights which science of religion can offer. Obviously then, one neither can nor ought to hermetically seal off each type from the other two. There is a distinction, not an absolute separation.

Dialogue to Increase Understanding

Under a variety of circumstances and with varying levels of intensity, members of diverse religions have recently been coming together in dialogue in order to understand each other better. The meetings have taken place in many areas throughout the world and the Division of World Mission and Evangelism of the World Council of Churches has rendered valuable service in bringing these regional and global dialogues about. Regionally, centers for the study of religion and society are fully involved in such dialogues and are issuing a veritable stream of bulletins to publicize their discoveries. The regular reader of such bulletins which appear in places like Japan, Ceylon, Bangalore, Jakarta, etc., cannot fail to be impressed with the importance of these dialogues. Throughout Asia and Africa many religious communities which once viewed each other as suspicious strangers now look upon each other as companions within the same community. But stubborn stereotypes, biases, and misunderstandings still persist which can lead to conflicts, flare-ups and a retardation of progress. Continued dialogue can do so much to clear away these obstacles.

Experience indicates that for these dialogues to be effective, each of the partners must learn to accept certain ground rules. In his recent essay on Hinduism, Father P. Schoonenberg said that he who wishes to build up contact with persons from another religion ought to begin by listening to their interpretation of their own religion (auto-interpretation) rather than with his own interpretation of it (hetero-interpretation).

Raymond Panikkar, one of the most experienced persons in such dialogues, cautioned against becoming an apologete for one's own position. "Apologetics," said he, "has its place, but not in dialogues of this nature."

Here are some of the important ground rules for such dialogues:

(1) Each partner must believe that the other is speaking in good faith.

(2) Each partner must be crystal clear on what he himself believes.

(3) Each partner must also understand clearly what the other believes.

(4) Each partner must penitently admit and accept the responsibility for the mistakes which his brothers in the faith have made with respect to other religious communities and which have muddied the message, beclouded the deepest intentions and aroused a great deal of misunderstanding.

(5) Each partner must be prepared to leave the outcome of the dialogue in God's hand.

Obviously dialogues of this type come in a variety of forms. Not only are there bilateral ones involving, say, Buddhists and Christians or Muslims and Christians, but also multilateral dialogues involving a number of partners.

Dialogue to Increase Cooperation

As individuals and peoples become increasingly dependent on each other, the need for a cooperative approach to the urgent problems facing them grows apace.

In Kyoto, Japanese representatives from many different religious communities gathered for the first World Conference on Religion and Peace in 1970. A second conference devoted to the theme of justice and peace was held in Leuven toward the end of August, 1974. The fear of some that such a conference would lead only to syncretism and a polite fellowship without concrete results did not materialize. Rather, it produced a powerful summons for representatives of the various traditions to cooperatively bring the strength of each tradition to bear on the pressing problems of our time. The proclamation made by the conference was printed in Japanese, Korean, Indonesian, Vietnamese, Singhalese, Urdu, Hindi, Persian, Arabic, Hebrew, Spanish, Portuguese, Dutch, and Polish, in addition to the three languages used at the conference itself.

But the various local and regional efforts to cooperate in bringing an end to human suffering, in advancing racial justice, in healing the diseased relationships between groups, in attending to the needs of the milieu, and in striving for peace are even more significant than these global conferences. Throughout every continent individuals have banded together to form specific action groups; their sense of solidarity and identity with their fellow men derives from the dangers and possibilities they together face. Actual experience proves that in most instances this dialogue to increase cooperation does not end up with all sides losing their individual integrity; rather, it stimulates each side to ask what it can uniquely contribute toward overcoming these common problems.

Jeremiah wrote his letter to the diaspora community to encourage them to seek the good of the cities and villages of Babylon in which they were living. The Christian church throughout the world is in similar diaspora today, and rather than retreating into a ghetto, we Christians must show ourselves ready to learn from each other and to cooperate in the fight against poverty, hunger, ignorance, and injustice. Only relationships of dialogue can bring this about.

Dialogue to Aid Missionary Communication

In reflection upon the Ajaltoun conference, S. J. Samartha, writing on "Living Faiths and the Ecumenical Movement," said that some dialogues serve to increase mutual religious examination, others prepare the partners to undertake common tasks together, but others do "more than" either research or prepare for cooperative endeavor.[7] Samartha called for more of this third type, pointing out that partners in the first two types always were thrusting toward the deeper dimension, for they realized that to really get to know each other a sharing of the deep things of the heart becomes necessary.

Many people mistakenly suppose that more recent types of mission tend to emphasize dialogue to avoid a real communication of the gospel. Some call it a betrayal of the gospel and charge it with reducing missionary *élan*. Advocates of dialogue get fired at from both sides: some members of other religions call dialogue a mere diplomatic replacement for old missionary methods and reject it as still another intrusion into their lives, while some Christians complain that dialogue leads to a betrayal of the Son of Man with a kiss.

There is absolutely no reason for not taking their warnings seriously. Who can deny that many dialogues were carried out with a take-it-or-leave-it attitude and simply came down to a nice exchange of pleasantries lacking genuine missionary *élan?* As I stood by his deathbed, I once heard a man to whom I had always looked as a model of gospel communication confess: "Thinking back upon so many conversations, I must admit that I often failed to urge those people to believe." Or who can say that members of the other religions are groundless in their suspicion that dialogue is simply a new form of spiritual imperialism?

But that does not have to occur. If we really allow ourselves to be guided by faith, hope, and love, then the other person can disclose the deep secrets of his heart and tell to his partner what is his most precious possession in life and in death, and a Christian too receives an opportunity to become a witness to the crucified and risen Lord, whose person, work and coming kingdom are absolutely valid for all peoples and cultures. In such dialogues the Christian's chief concern is to commend not himself or his own expression of Christianity but rather Christ

7. Stanley J. Samartha, "Let Us Continue the Conversation," in *Living Faiths and the Ecumenical Movement,* ed. S. J. Samartha (Geneva: World Council of Churches, 1971), pp. 5–15.

himself (cf. II Cor. 4:5). We are called to such dialogue because as believers in Christ we are under obligation to all men (cf. Rom. 1:16).

Nor ought we to overlook a most important though oft-neglected possible consequence of such a dialogue. Frequently what began as a dialogue can turn into a trialogue, given the benediction of the Holy Spirit. Most analyses of the conversation train the spotlight on the social and psychological aspects and underscore the importance of proper technique, often to the neglect of the theological dimension of the conversation. But in a thorough and probing dialogue blessed by God, the Holy Spirit can bring his own influence to bear and become, as it were, a third partner. Harding Meyer, writing in *Evangelische Kommentar* on "Der Dialog als Problem," discussed the "witness-character" of dialogue. A conversation between members of various religious communities can turn into a real happening (*gebeurtenis*) which in turn can lead to a (new) birth (*geboortenis*).

In genuine dialogue the two partners (or groups) are deeply concerned to let the truth which is moving back and forth between them finally emerge. This is the unique mark of a missionary conversation, and when it appears, the charisma of dialogue is actually taking place. For this to happen, not only must each partner be open to the other but also to the new insight(s) which both may receive. One could call this the primacy of that which is coming, or better, of him who is coming.

The goal is not synthesis or some "enriching of each other's insights" or even some form of mutual influence but rather a fulfillment of faith's eager desire for the Spirit to bring and lead us into the full truth.

At the Mexico City conference in 1963 I participated in formulating a statement on missionary dialogue. Our chief concern was to emphasize trialogue. Here is the statement:

> True dialogue with a man of another faith requires a concern both for the Gospel and for the other man. Without the first, dialogue becomes a pleasant conversation. Without the second, it becomes irrelevant, unconvincing or arrogant. . . .
>
> Whatever the circumstances may be, our intention in every human dialogue should be to be involved in the dialogue of God with men, and to move our partner and ourself to what God in Christ reveals to us, and to answer him.[8]

All human knowledge of God both originates and develops through dialogue or trialogue, as hosts of examples from the Bible and the history of gospel communication so clearly show. Missionaries such as Bavinck, Kraemer, D. T. Niles, Devanandan and M. M. Thomas, all skilled in dialogue, continually attest to its trialogic character.

Hans Werner Gensichen states in one of his essays: "A dialogue can simply be kept at an exchange of ideas which the partners are completely free to accept or reject." This may be so, but it is then not missionary dialogue, for the latter is not primarily a conversation between human beings but a continual

8. R. K. Orchard, ed., *Witness in Six Continents: Records of the Meeting of the Commission on World Mission and Evangelism of the World Council of Churches Held in Mexico City, December 8th–19th, 1963* (New York: Friendship Press, 1964), pp. 146–147.

conversation in which God speaks to both human partners. This divine word grips them in the sense of the Pauline dialectic of gripping and being gripped (cf. Phil. 3:1–2). The late D. T. Niles expressed this nearly paradoxically: "In missionary comunication the Christian is not first of all concerned to bring Jesus Christ into the life of one of another faith; his chief concern is that Christ brings him (the Christian) into the life of the other."

Do such dialogues ever take place? Indeed, and far more frequently than one might at first imagine. John B. Carman and P. Y. Luke, coauthors of *Rural Christians in South India*, mention that the most important dialogues in the service of the gospel take place in the villages and the lowly districts of the cities. Life gives rise to new life, and during such mutual unplanned contact a sharing can at times take place that is the very genius of the spread of Christian faith in many areas of Asia and Africa. In Indonesia, too, it is often the plain, common church members rather than the officials and the leaders whose talks and common experiences with their Muslim neighbors bring about the most influential dialogues. They may subsequently request the assistance of clergymen or other experts as the communication deepens, but they are the first communicators.

But obviously these uneducated folk are not the only ones called to this deeper dialgoue; those with superior training and education are under obligation to present all of their gifts in the service of gospel communication. Several persons can serve as luminous examples.

One such person was D. T. Niles, whose very conversations and writings reflected his ongoing dialogue with Buddhists, Muslims and Hindus; by the very title he chose for one of his books he showed how seriously he took his responsibility: *The Preacher's Task and the Stone of Stumbling*.

I think too of Kenneth Cragg, whose many books are reports of the deep dialogues which he is carrying on with Muslims in the Arab world right up to the present day.

The worldwide fellowship of churches is called to do much more than it has done in recent years to stimulate this type of dialogue.

Toward the end of 1974 Antoine Wessels from Beirut wrote that many experts increasingly sense that fostering mutual understanding is insufficient; people are searching for a new way. Doing away with the aggressive missionary methods which rightly or wrongly are ascribed to a previous generation is proper, but the gospel simply does not warrant one's taking the attitude: "Oh well, it's all the same; let the Hindu, Muslim or Buddhist each go his own way." But, asks Wessels, if these are the two extremes to avoid, then what is the middle way to follow?

The venerable Alford Carleton, who lived for decades in the Middle East and won so many to Christ by his multilateral dialogues, wrote some time ago that we are not called to aggressiveness but to the "winsome art of witness." The heavy increase in international traffic, he added, now makes this possible in so many diverse areas: in business, diplomacy, science, journalism, and ecumenics. One must simply open his eyes to the possibilities and then seize them in love.

At the world missionary conference in Bangkok (December 29, 1972– January 13, 1973) the delegates adopted a report on dialogue with members of other religions. It contains much of the same material that I have emphasized in these pages. I wish to bring this section to a close by quoting its conclusion, which I highly endorse:

> We have already said that our attitude to people of other faiths arises out of our understanding of God's will that all man [sic] shall be saved. Therefore we urge our member churches to go forward with eager faith, with greater love for our fellowmen, with prayer for guidance and with confidence that God is at work among all people to make his saving love available for all in every generation and to build the kingdom of His love, which we Christians see manifested in Jesus Christ.[9]

BIBLIOGRAPHY

I have purposely put the phrase "theology of religions" in quotation marks, for I am using it here as a convenient reference for all the theological literature which can help in our approach to men of other faiths. My concern is not to provide an elaborate guide into the labyrinth of religious systems, but only to point out a few helpful resources for our meeting with people of other religions to communicate to them the gospel.

The list is far from exhaustive. I have tried to select material in accord with the purpose just mentioned.

1. Biblical-Theological Studies

Bavinck, J. H. Religieus Besef en Christelijk Geloof. Kampen: J. H. Kok, 1949.
Blauw, J. Goden en Mensen: Plaats en Betekenis van de Heidenen in de Heilige Schrift. Groningen: Niemeyer, 1950.
_____. Het Geding om de Wereld: Oude Testament. Zeist: NSCV, 1959–60.
Bosch, D. T. "Jesus and the Gentiles — A Review After Thirty Years." In The Church Crossing Frontiers. Edited by P. Beyerhaus and C. Hallencreutz. Lund: Gleerup, 1969.
De Groot, A. De Bijbel over het Heil der Volken. Roermond: Romen, 1964.
Freytag, W. The Gospel and the Religions. London: SCM Press, 1957.
Miskotte, K. H. Als de Goden Zwijgen. Haarlem: Holland, 1966.
Rosin, H. The Lord is God: The Translation of the Divine Names and the Missionary Calling of the Church. The Hague: Nederlandsche Boek- en Steendrukkerij, 1955.

2. Studies Throughout Church History

The Early Church

As Christianity pushed its way into the surrounding world of Hellenism, various early Christian thinkers, notably the apologists, developed their individual postures toward the prevailing Greek philosophy and religions. Justin Martyr's writing exemplifies the tone of much second-century Christian apologetic work; it is a plea for tolerance.

During the third century such famous Alexandrian apologists as Clement of Alexandria and Origen reflect a growing trend toward employing the concept of logos spermatikos to explain the relation between Christians and non-Christians, a notion whose influence has carried on into the present. Clement's most famous writings are Protreptikos, Paidagogos, and Stromateis; Origen's are Contra Celsum and On Principles.

Going in quite the opposite direction, Tertullian, a Latin apologist, continually underscored the distance between the gospel and the base religion and philosophy of the Hellenistic world. His well-known writings Apologeticum, De testimonio animae and De anima bear witness to the question by which he is best remembered: "What does Jerusalem have to do with Athens?"

---

9. "On Dialogue with People of Living Faiths," in Bangkok Assembly 1973: Minutes and Report of the Assembly of the Commission on World Mission and Evangelism of the World Council of Churches December 31, 1972 and January 9–12, 1973, p. 80.

Unlike some of the Christian thinkers in succeeding ages of church history, these early apologists did not seek to skirt the issue of how the gospel is related to the other religions, but fearlessly delved into the knotty problems. Later theologians of religion stand deeply indebted to them.

The Middle Ages
John of Damascus in the East and Isidore of Seville in the West by their thought and writing broke ground and paved the way for the most famous medieval thinker on the subject of Christianity's relation to other religions: Thomas Aquinas. Aquinas's *Summa contra gentiles*, an all-embracing vision of the challenge which Graeco-Arabic culture posed to the Christian world, made a profound impact upon later Roman Catholic thinkers, and his influence continues among numerous Roman Catholic theologians of religion down to the present day.

The Reformation
Luther articulated his understanding of the relationship between Christianity and the other religions in his writing about the Jews and the Turks. (For a useful summary of his views consult Walter Holsten's *Christentum und nicht-christliche Religion nach Auffassung Luthers*. Gütersloh: Bertelsmann, 1932.)
Book I of John Calvin's *Institutes of the Christian Religion* has set the tone for countless Calvinistic theologians of religion since the sixteenth century.

Eastern Orthodoxy
The Alexandrian apologists, Clement and Origen, with their *logos spermatikos* theory have had an abiding influence in the East. John of Damascus' *opus magnum, Fount of Wisdom*, developed the apologists' ideas and continues today to be Eastern Orthodoxy's classic statement on the relationship between Christianity and other faiths. In the Latin translation it also made its impact upon the West.
For a contemporary statement of this vision consult the address of Greek Orthodox metropolitan of Beirut, G. Khodr, to the executive committee of the World Council of Churches in Addis Ababa in 1971: "Christianity in a Pluralistic World — The Economy of the Holy Spirit" (printed in *The Ecumenical Review* 23 [1971]: 118–128).

The Modern Period
Blauw, J. *Godsdienstwetenschap en Theologie*. Assen: Hummelen, 1962.
————. *Religie en Interreligie*. Kampen: J. H. Kok, 1962.
De Vos, H. *Het Christendom en de andere Godsdiensten*. Nijkerk: Callenbach, 1962.
Hallencreutz, C. F. "Mission as Dialogue." In *The Church Crossing Frontiers*. Edited by P. Beyerhaus, et al. Lund: Gleerup, 1969.
Kraemer, H. "Continuity and Discontinuity." In *The Authority of the Faith*, Vol. 1. New York: International Missionary Council, 1939.
————. *The Christian Message in a non-Christian World*. New York: Harper, 1938.
————. *Godsdienst, Godsdiensten en het Christelijk Geloof*. Nijkerk: Callenbach, 1958.
————. *World Cultures and World Religions: The Coming Dialogue*. London: Lutterworth Press, 1960.
Neill, S. *Christian Faith and Other Faiths*. New York: Oxford Univ. Press, 1961.
Perry, E. *The Gospel in Dispute: The Relation of Christian Faith to Other Christian Religions*. New York: Doubleday, 1958.
Rosenkranz, G. *Religionswissenschaft und Theologie: Aufsätze zur Evangelischen Religionskunde*. Munich: Kaiser, 1964.
Smith, W. C. "Participation: The Changing Christian Role in Other Cultures." *Occasional Bulletin of the Missionary Research Library* 20 (April, 1969).
Verkuyl, J. *Zijn Alle Godsdiensten gelijk?* Kampen: J. H. Kok, 1964.
Vlijm, J. M. *Het Religiebegrip bij Karl Barth*. The Hague: van Keulen, 1956.

Roman Catholic Literature
Camps, A. "De Katholieke Kerk en de niet-christelijke Godsdiensten." *De Heerbaan* 23 (1970): 442–450.
Heislbetz, J. *Theologische Gründe der nicht-christlichen Religionen (Quaestiones Disputatae 33)*. Freiburg: Herder, 1966.

Hessen, J. *Der Absolutheitsanspruch des Christentums: Eine Religionsphilosophische Untersuchung.* Munich and Basel: Reinhardt, 1963.

Hillman, E. *The Wider Ecumenism: Anonymous Christianity and the Church.* London: Burns and Oates, 1968.

Löffeld, E. "Kerk en Wereldgodsdiensten, een zeer urgent Probleem." *Het Missiewerk* 47 (1968): 34–50.

Mulders, A. "Het missionair Karakter van de Kerk en het Zicht op de nietchristelijke Godsdiensten." *Het Missiewerk* 46 (1967): 2–20.

Muller, K. *Die Kirche und die nichtchristliche Religionen.* Aschaffenburg: Patloch, 1968.

Neuner, J., ed. *Christian Revelation and World Religions.* London: Burns & Oates, 1967.

Panikkar, R. *Die viele Götter und der eine Herr.* Weilheim: Barth, 1963.

_____. *The Unknown Christ of Hinduism.* London: Darton, Longman, & Todd, 1964.

_____. *Religionen und Religion.* Munich: Hueber, 1965.

_____. *Kerugma und Indien: Zur heilsgeschichtlichen Problematik der christlichen Begegnung mit Indien.* Hamburg: Reich, 1967.

Rahner, K. "Das Christentum und die nichtchristlichen Religionen." *Schriften zur Theologie V.* Einsiedeln: Benzinger, 1962.

_____. "Die Anonymen Christen." *Schriften zur Theologie VI.* Einsiedeln: Benzinger, 1964.

Röper, A. *Die Anonymen Christen.* Mainz: Grünewald, 1963.

Schlette, H. R. *Die Religionen als Thema der Theologie (Quaestiones Disputatae 22).* Freiburg: Herder, 1963.

_____. *Colloquium Salutis — Christen und Nichtchristen Heute.* Cologne: Bachem, 1964.

_____. *Die Konfrontation mit den Religionen.* Cologne: Bachem, 1964.

Second Vatican Council. *The Teachings of the Second Vatican Council: Complete Texts of the Constitutions, Decrees, and Declarations.* Westminster, Md.: Newman Press, 1966. See especially: "Declaration on the Relation of the Church to the Non-Christian Religions"; "Declaration on Religious Freedom"; "Constitution on the Church in the Modern World."

Thauren, J. *Die Akkommodation in Katholischen Heidenapostolat.* Münster: Aschendorff, 1927.

Waldenfels, H. "Zur Heilsbedeutung der nicht-christlichen Religionen in Katholischer Sicht." *Zeitschrift für Missionskunde und Religionswissenschaft* 53 (1969): 257–278.

_____. "Das Verständnis der Religionen und seine Bedeutung für die Mission in Katholischer Sicht." *Evangelische Missions Zeitschrift* 30 (1970): 161-174.

3. Periodical Literature

Baago, K. "Recent Studies of Christianity in India." *Religion and Society: Quarterly Bulletin of the Christian Institute for the Study of Religion and Society* 14 (December, 1967): 63–74.

Bijlefeld, W. "Recent Theological Evaluation of the Christian-Muslim Encounter." *International Review of Missions* 55 (1966): 430–441.

Carman, J. B. "Continuing Tasks in Inter-Religious Dialogue." *The Ecumenical Review* 22 (1970): 199.

"Christians in Dialogue with Men of Other Faiths." Statement made by the Protestant/Orthodox/Catholic Consultation on Dialogue with Men of Other Faiths in Kandy, Ceylon. February 27 to March 6, 1967. *International Review of Missions* 56 (1967): 338–343.

"Christians in Dialogue with Men of Other Faiths." Aide-memoire of the Zurich Consultation. May, 1970. *International Review of Missions* 59 (1970): 382–391.

Cragg, K. "Encounter with Non-Christian Faiths." *Religion and Society: Quarterly Bulletin of the Christian Institute for the Study of Religion and Society* 14 (1967): 37.

Douglas, I. H. "Recent Theological Evaluation of the Christian-Muslim Encounter." *International Review of Missions* 55 (1966): 418–429.

_____. "Van Leeuwen's Study of Islam." *Religion and Society: Quarterly Bulletin of the Christian Institute for the Study of Religion and Society* 14 (1967): 5–13.

Fagley, R. M. "Doctrines and Attitudes of Major Religions in Regard to Fertility." *Religion and Society: Quarterly Bulletin of the Christian Institute for the Study of Religion and Society* 16 (1969): 31–42.

––––––––. "Report and Workshop Findings: Consultation on the Theology of Hindu-Christian Dialogue." *Religion and Society: Quarterly Bulletin of the Christian Institute for the Study of Religion and Society* 16 (1969): 69–88.

Holsten, W. "The Muslim Presence in the West." *International Review of Missions* 55 (1966): 448–456.

Jenkins, D. "Commitment and Openness: A Theological Reflection." *International Review of Missions* 59 (1970): 404–413.

Jomier, J. "Roman Catholic Thinking Concerning the Christian-Muslim Encounter." *International Review of Missions* 55 (1966): 442–447.

Minz, N. "Theologies of Dialogue: A Critique." *Religion and Society: Quarterly Bulletin of the Christian Institute for the Study of Religion and Society* 14 (1967): 7–20.

––––––––. "Gandhi and the Formal Hindu-Christian Dialogue." *Religion and Society: Quarterly Bulletin of the Christian Institute for the Study of Religion and Society* 16 (1969): 35–51.

Panikkar, R. "The Internal Dialogue." *Religion and Society: Quarterly Bulletin of the Christian Institute for the Study of Religion and Society* 15 (1968): 55–66.

Paradkar, B. A. M. "The Christian Encounter with Men of Other Faiths." *Religion and Society: Quarterly Bulletin of the Christian Institute for the Study of Religion and Society* 14 (1967): 21–37.

Reetz, D. "Raymond Panikkar's Theology of Religions." *Religion and Society: Quarterly Bulletin of the Christian Institute for the Study of Religion and Society* 15 (1968): 33–54.

Ryan, S. "Mission After Vatican II: Problems and Positions." *International Review of Missions* 57 (1968): 414–426.

Samartha, S. J. "The Quest for Salvation and the Dialogue Between Religions." *International Review of Missions* 57 (1968): 424–432.

––––––––. "More than an Encounter of Commitments: An Interpretation of the Ajaltoun Consultation on 'Dialogue Between Men of Living Faiths'." *International Review of Missions* 59 (1970): 393–403.

––––––––. "The World Council of Churches and Men of Other Faiths and Ideologies." *The Ecumenical Review* 22 (1970): 191 ff.

––––––––. "Dialogue as a Continuing Christian Concern." *The Ecumenical Review* 23 (1971): 129–142.

"The Concern for Dialogue in Asia." Statement by the Secretariat for Interfaith Dialogue of the East Asia Christian Conference. *International Review of Missions* 59 (1970): 427–429.

Thomas, M. M. "Christianity and World History." *Religion and Society: Quarterly Bulletin of the Christian Institute for the Study of Religion and Society* 14 (1967): 31–36.

––––––––. "Universalism and the Unchanging Core of the Christian Dogma." *Religion and Society: Quarterly Bulletin of the Christian Institute for the Study of Religion and Society* 14 (1967): 48 ff.

––––––––. "Consultation Findings: Christians in Dialogue with Men of Other Faiths." *Religion and Society: Quarterly Bulletin of the Christian Institute for the Study of Religion and Society* 14 (1967): 64–69.

Thomas, T. K. "Dialogue as Presence." *Religion and Society: Quarterly Bulletin of the Christian Institute for the Study of Religion and Society* 14 (1967): 38–47.

Van Leeuwen, A. T. "Reply to Critics: A Defence of *Christianity in World History*." *Religion and Society: Quarterly Bulletin of the Christian Institute for the Study of Religion and Society* 14 (1967): 47–56.

4. *Phenomenological, Morphological and History-of-Religions Approaches to the Study of Christianity and the Other Religions*

Bavinck, J. H. *Religieus Besef en Christelijk Geloof.* Kampen: J. H. Kok, 1949.

Bleeker, C. J. *Christ and Modern Athens: The Confrontation of Modern Christianity with Modern Culture and Non-Christian Religions.* London: Mowbray, 1967.

Edwards, D. L. *Religion and Change*. London: Hodder & Stoughton, 1969.
Eliade, M. and Kitagawa, O. *The History of Religions: Essays in Methodology*. Chicago: Univ. of Chicago Press, 1959.
Smith, W. C. *The Meaning and End of Religion: A New Approach to the Religious Traditions of Mankind*. New York: Macmillan, 1962.
Hütten, K. and von Kortzfleisch, S., eds. *Asien missioniert im Abendland*. Stuttgart: Kreuz Verlag, 1962.

CHAPTER XIV

A Study and Evaluation of Ideologies in the Developing Countries

Having looked in the last chapter at developments taking place in the arena of religions, I now turn our attention to the process of secularization and its impact upon those parts of the world which are our special concern in this book.

When I accepted the chair of missiology at the Free Reformed University of Amsterdam in 1965, I delivered an inaugural lecture on secularization, which is on the advance also in Asia, Africa and Latin America. In it I tried to survey the relevant literature and to make a few comments on the impact of this trend on missionary methodology.

Of course, space does not permit me to describe the full secularization process in these lands; therefore, I have decided to select one typical dimension of the process as an illustration, namely, the strong steering influence of ideologies on societies in developing nations.

In the East and the South especially, certain religions served in previous ages as frames of reference and centers of orientation. This was true not only with tribal religions, but also in areas where one of the major religions dominated. But when the era of religious pluralism arrived and the various religious communities were not able to provide the cohesion necessary during the new phase of nation building, all sorts of ideologies presented themselves to offer a new social consensus and become a new point of orientation at a time of complete disarray. This being the case, theologians and church members would·be foolish to devote exclusive attention to a theology of religions and an evangelical critique of religions.

Of course I am not able to describe each and every ideology in detail in this chapter. I only wish to orient the reader to the available literature, to give a short survey of the impact of ideologies, and to give at least the rough draft of an answer which may help us all to become keener critics of the ideologies from the standpoint of the gospel of God and his kingdom.

THE ROLE OF IDEOLOGIES TODAY

During the 1950's Daniel Bell, president of the American "Commission for the Year 2000," wrote *The End of Ideologies,* in which he claimed that the era of ideologies is now past and that we must all now reckon with a more pragmatic approach to issues. His students Herman Kahn and Anthony Wiener merely mouthed their teacher's message.

However, Latin American professor Gomez de Souza, member of the economic commission of the United Nations for Latin America, in an article for the Montevideo-based periodical *Vispera,* claimed the situation would not be all that simple. Ideologies, he said, will continue to play important roles even in the period between now and the year 2000.

Professor de Souza is obviously right. One can clearly discern that the student revolts of the last decade were in part a protest against the pragmatic character of contemporary technical and scientific trends. Think of the neo-Marxist ideology which played such an important role in these revolts. Think too of the enormous influence of communist and semifascist ideologies within developing countries.

He who believes as I do that Christians ought to be taking their norms and criteria for what should be, not from the ideologies, but from God's demands and promises would have lost complete touch with the reality of the situation if he were to have overlooked the powerful effects of ideologies today. Joseph la Palambara did well to put the question mark behind the title of his essay: *Decline of Ideology?* He believes that rather than declining, they are actually increasing and points to Italy and the developing countries as examples. He concedes the roles which ideologies play and the symbols they use may well be changing, but ideology itself is increasing. The vast ideological polarizations today attest to the truth of what he is saying. Our age reminds one of Europe in 1848 or Latin America in 1815.

THE MEANING OF THE TERM "IDEOLOGY" TODAY

A probe into the etymology of the term "ideology" would make little sense here, for our real concern is what the term means right now. In conjunction with the famous definition put forth by Karl Mannheim, André Dumas came up with his own definition: "Ideologies are blueprints of the future made by a certain ideologue or group of elite within the community to move the masses."[1] Each ideology comes with a set of strategies and methods by which those who drafted it hope to bridge the gap between the idea and its fulfillment. Dumas also claims that the ideologue finds in contemporary history the cause of all the present grief and then proceeds to draft his own blueprint for a new future devoid of such troubles.

A second feature of ideologies is their strong collective stamp. Ideologies are the children of wholesale revolutions. The rise of the ideologies goes hand in hand with the rise of the masses and they make their appeal to the masses (the class, the nation, the race, etc.), for among these masses burns a fervent desire to participate in the future. Ideologies aid in bringing about a social consensus among specific groups of people and employ it for specific purposes.

1. André Dumas, *Die Kirche als Faktor einer kommenden Weltgemeinschaft* (Stuttgart, 1966).

THE RISE AND FUNCTION OF IDEOLOGIES

In one of my previous books, *The Message of Liberation in Our Age,* I discussed in some detail how ideologies arise and function. I shall merely summarize some of my earlier statements here.

Researchers claim that the rise of ideologies is connected with the rise of secondary societal systems. Agrarian, preindustrial societal systems are gradually giving way to systems which apply modern technology and organization. This secondary system brings social structures to life which can drill, manipulate, exploit, condition and steer human beings. And these secondary systems are the foundation on which these ideologies arise and develop; they are both the by-products and the reactions to them. Ideologies presuppose the existence of these secondary systems, for both proceed from the same starting point, namely, that human beings can be manipulated, drilled, conditioned and steered in the direction of a new future.

As for the function of an ideology, sometimes it represents little more than an effort to formulate a national plan to insure that the various ethnic and religious groups within a given developing young nation work together. But at other times it can take on a quasi-religious character. When this happens, the results of a secularization process soon follow, for no longer is there any appreciation for the transcendental dimension to reality. Rather, those caught in the grip of an ideology replace the genuinely transcendent with the cultus-objects of the ideology and make an idol of a specific person, a specific land, a specific race, or a specific class.

When ideologies become quasi-religious, they often strive to conceal the actual relationships of power in order to create a certain religious aura around the existing might of the ruling group. This, in turn, brings to life still other ideologies with their own quasi-religious character and creates the likely possibility that one type of deception and idolatry rises up to challenge the other. When Christians come to see clearly that at least some of the ideologies function practically as pseudo-religions or quasi-religions, then they will understand the need to critically test each one of them by the standards of the prophets and the apostles.

Two persons who recognized this urgent need were M. M. Thomas and Wolfhart Pannenberg. Thomas called for Christians who live amid the ideologies to challenge their claims in the light of the gospel, and Pannenberg urged churches to band together in ecumenical spirit (thus avoiding the dogmatism and the infighting of the sixteenth and seventeenth centuries) to pose before the conflicting ideologies the deepest and most fundamental questions about the relation between God and man, society and cosmos.

I shall return to this matter at the close of this chapter, but first I must try to answer two other questions: Why are ideologies seething throughout the developing countries especially, and what is the range of the various ideologies which are at work there?

THE INFLUENCE OF IDEOLOGIES IN DEVELOPING COUNTRIES

A symposium study, *Ideology and Discontent,* compiled by David E. Apter and containing essays by numerous sociologists and political scientists, sheds a great amount of light on the influence of ideologies in developing countries.[2] Illustrations are taken from Japan, Indonesia, Egypt, sub-Sahara Africa and other places. Clifford Geertz's symposium book, *Old Societies and New States: The Quest for Modernity in Asia and Africa,* also is a rich mine of information on this topic.[3]

I wish to mention two aspects concerning this issue. First, the young states in Asia and Africa who have acquired their indendence since 1945 and the Latin American and Caribbean states who are experiencing a social and economic revolution after the political revolutions of the early nineteenth century must now all provide the leadership in tackling the basic problems which are confronting them. The challenges, in summary, are these: nation building, achieving a proper balance between authority and freedom, economic growth, new social integration, new cultural orientation, balanced population growth, the formation of a new human type, etc.

One can easily understand how a given ideology has an appeal to those who either are already in power or are questing for the power in those societies and governments which are facing monumental challenges and problems. Ideologies claim at least to give direction and to offer solutions.

But not only the accumulation of basic problems drives people in the direction of an ideology; factual disorientation does too. In most of those young states the whole monumental task of building up the government has but recently begun. The leadership is still weak, the task of popularizing the new order is in its youthful stages, public administration still needs to be worked out, etc. Add to all this the fact that these young states, like their more experienced counterparts, live in an absolutely precarious international situation, and one can well understand these young states' search for a symbolic framework within which to establish goals, work out the administrative details, and respond to the political problems.

Ideologies of course do not act as a ferment only in the developing countries but also in the more developed countries of Eastern Europe and Russia, Western Europe and the United States. Some pretend that in the countries of Western Europe and the United States everything proceeds on the basis of critical scientific inspection and analysis. How naive! To give but one example, without their knowing it these countries have been influenced by a welfare ideology that cannot stand the test of the gospel. Only recently have people in these countries been waking up to the fact that the rosy appeal of such an ideology actually beclouds their view of the way things really are. The same is true, only in greater degree, in developing countries.

Of course I cannot possibly describe in this short survey the multitude of ideologies now operative in developing countries. I shall therefore select only those ideologies which are presently having the greatest impact on the structure of government, on social and economic policy, and on cultural expression in the various lands. Moreover, though ideologies such as South African apartheid and

2. David Apter, comp., *Ideology and Discontent* (New York: The Free Press, 1964).

3. Clifford Geertz, comp., *Old Societies and New States: The Quest for Modernity in Asia and Africa* (New York: The Free Press, 1976).

Zionism do have a deep influence and could therefore qualify for discussion here, I shall not include them because I have treated them elsewhere.

VARIETIES OF COMMUNIST IDEOLOGY IN DEVELOPING COUNTRIES

China

Marxist Leninism was one of the ideologies which jumped across the borders of Europe to infiltrate China and from China spread to other parts of Asia, Africa, and Latin America. To Lenin goes the credit for translating Marxist theory into practice and powerfully turning a backward Russian society into a progressive modern state. Within the world of communism his plan is called the "Moscow model."

Deeply influenced by the model devised by Lenin, Mao Tse Tung devised his own blueprint for the development of Chinese society while fighting the Kuomintang, and when he and his accomplices finally took over power in 1949, they tried through many phases to bridge the gap between idea and reality.

In the first phase of construction Mao continually harked back to Marxist Leninism, but later, especially since the Ninth Party Congress, this ideological wellspring has been termed "Mao thought" (*Szu-tsiang*).

Mao's ideas are becoming increasingly canonized. They are an independent variant of communism which wriggled free from its close connection to the ideology of the state found in the Soviet Union and later even turned against it.

One can detect a striking degree of flexibility and considerable shifts of accent as Maoist communism worked itself out in practice, all of which accords with Mao's idea that "correct ideas" emerge from actual practice and that the relationship between theory and practice must always remain dialectical. Sinicization produced a communist variant with a unique character.

Earlier in this chapter I mentioned that an ideology offers not only a blueprint but also a set of strategies for securing the power and arousing the populace to move toward the future. What is the actual content of the Chinese communist blueprint? In answering this question, one must say that this variant comes with a specific concept of the state, a developed understanding of social and economic structure and a finely carved cultural policy — all of which dominate the lives of millions of Chinese. Its social and economic policy is geared toward meeting the most basic human needs — food, a place to live, clothing, health. For the first time in the long course of Chinese history, there is concern for each individual Chinese person. By the most simple of means people are striving to improve the economic infrastructure, for example, by establishing control of rivers, working on roads and the rail system, building distribution centers, etc.

China has also made great progress culturally. Illiteracy has been tackled and conquered; elementary education has been established; and the mass media have been employed to enlighten the populace on the basic problems still confronting Chinese society.

Abolishing the feudal marriage system has vastly improved the position of women in Chinese society. Furthermore, the young people have been engaged in carrying out elementary responsibilities. Local communes so divide the work and the responsibilities that the full populace participates in making and carrying out decisions.

All of these measures have vastly increased China's sense of national worth and made her more self-reliant. Whereas she in earlier centuries suffered under feudal opppression and then later was reduced to semicolonial status through the exterritorial rights which Western powers held to the treaty ports toward the close of the nineteenth century and the beginning of the twentieth, now China feels respected and has proudly taken its own place among the family of nations.

No one can deny that the Chinese revolution has produced many positive results. Allow me to borrow a comment from one of my earlier books: "Who cannot but rejoice and be thankful for the positive things which the revolution has brought to the people in China? But alas, there are some who refuse to acknowledge this and who adamantly close their eyes to the truth."[4]

I wrote those words in 1966. How grateful I am for the sharply increased willingness in recent years to appreciate the good that has come about in the new China. But now another type of blindness threatens — blind disregard for the symptoms of totalitarianism.

Whenever an ideology becomes quasi-religious and requires of human beings an allegiance which is due to God alone, then it has a tendency to totally reshape these human beings and the society in which they live. It begins to make totalitarian claims on a person, to knead him, to drill him, to steer him. At this point an ideology is attempting to do what it cannot — to create a new man and a new earth.

It is not hard to point out these symptoms in the Maoist version of communism. Maoism strives to control and to knead the whole of a person's life by pounding its doctrine into his head through daily newspapers, periodicals, radio, theaters, etc. Every facet of human existence is viewed in the light of "Mao thought."

The governmental structure is authoritarian and totalitarian. Criticism of or deviation from declared policy is not allowed. When deviations or failures threaten, the Communists stage one cultural revolution after another to make the masses again compliant and to restore the "continuing revolution" to its former intense pitch. There is no room for a personal freedom to express one's conscience and to follow the dictates of his religion, for religion of whatever kind is viewed as "anachronistic" and "mere superstition."

In this schema of total indoctrination the state simply hangs the opprobrious label "enemies" on whomever it dislikes, and which persons or groups actually receive it may vary in accord with the interests of the state.

What is doubly tragic is that this ideology arose out of the just struggle against enslavement, and now it in turn threatens to reduce the people whom it desired to free to a new form of slavery.

4. Johannes Verkuyl, *Evangelie en Communisme in Azie en Afrika* (Kampen: J. H. Kok, 1966), p. 38.

Guinea

When the late French President De Gaulle in 1958 gave the former French colonies the choice of limited freedom while remaining members of the French commonwealth or of complete independence, the former French colony of Guinea (Northwest Africa) chose the latter. The real leader behind this choice was Sekou Touré (born 1922), who represented the only political party Guinea has — "Partie Démocratique de Guinée."

Sekou Touré openly defends this dictatorship of the people, as Communists call it, for he and his followers assure their listeners that this party constitutes both the thought and the will of the people of Guinea "in the highest degree and in the most complete form." While in other communist countries the Communist party itself is an elite organization of the few for the many, in Guinea the so-called Conakry-variant means that approximately fifty percent of the population belong to the party. The party is "the collective intellect and conscience" of society, while the state serves as the executor of the popular will as voiced by the party itself.

An iron discipline prevails in this party which has such a firm grip on the government. Following Lenin's directives, its leaders allow absolutely no deviations from the official party line or any sort of factions, arguing that "The party as an institution never errs."

Reflecting a trend also found in other communist countries, the ideas of Guinea's Communist leaders have given rise to a rather inefficient bureaucracy. The percentage growth in national income several years ago lagged behind those found in most other African states.

The whole of Guinean society is politicized and regimented. In one of his publications on international politics, Sekou Touré declared: "No responsible politician, regardless of the authority that he represents, can substitute himself for the party. If he emanates from the party and is its spokesman, he can only act as an instrument which reflects not his own personality but the party's, for it alone can express the will, aspiration, needs and expectation of our people."[5]

A whole network of affiliated organizations dealing with all the sectors of Guinean society has developed around this party, and every member of them is bound so tightly to the party itself that there is absolutely no room for difference of opinion. The party leaders determine the list of candidates to fill the various positions. The Conakry-variant has a monistic, retarding effect.

The same lack of dynamic is evident in the social and economic area. All the appropriate slogans to the contrary, there is little evidence of genuine popular participation.

Cuba

When Cuba revolted under the leadership of Fidel Castro, it introduced a new ingredient into Latin America, namely, the Cuban brand of communism. In its first phase, the Castro movement was anything but communist; in fact, while the

5. Sekou Touré, *The International Policy of the Democratic Party of Guinea* (Cairo, 1962), p. 189.

middle classes and the intellectuals who were fed up with the Baptista regime supported Castro, the official Communist party did not. The Cuban Communist party (*Partido Socialista Popular*) had been founded in 1925 by student leader Julio Antonio Mella, who under orders from Stalin was murdered because he veered too far from the Moscow line. Mella also collaborated for a time with Baptista. When Castro made an unsuccessful attack in 1953 on Fort Moncada in Santiago, this Communist party condemned him for it, but when Castro and his fighters renewed the fight four years later from the top of the Sierra Maestra, a few Communist party members joined his side (Rodriguez, among others).

Castro finally came to power on January 1, 1959, and he swung around and headed in the Communist direction, finding the organizational framework of the Cuban Communist party most useful for his purposes. Castro called this his "conversion," claiming in his famous speech, "Historia me absolvera," that at first he had tried to carry through the Socialist revolution without communism, but now he had come to see that it was a necessary point of orientation and reference. There is no doubt that when the United States bull-headedly chose economic blockade as its response to Castro's nationalizing of the sugar and oil industries, this forced him farther in the direction of Russia and Eastern Europe. But since about 1965 he has been trying to steer his own separate course.

Internationally, Castro at first lent his support to guerilla action, but when Ché Guevara's movement in Bolivia failed and Guevara himself was killed in the process, Castro turned to Chile and tried to form an axis with Allende who was leading a coalition of Socialists and Communists there. But now, after Allende's violent death, Castro again stands rather alone. With the support of Protestant and Roman Catholic Christians he is trying to get the United States to lift its economic blockade and to establish new economic ties with Peru and Mexico.

Strikingly, Castro never severed diplomatic relations with the Vatican.

Internally, Castro is allowing the people themselves more participation since 1972. Many in Cuba have high regard for his program but cannot accept the Marxist-Leninist base from which he works; he is considering allowing the Christian Socialist party, which in principle was founded in Havana in 1973, the right to function.

No one can deny that Castro's leftist dictatorship is geared much more toward the whole people, especially toward the poor, than the corrupt rightist dictatorship which preceded his regime. Nevertheless, Castro is also a dictator, a dictator whose power of attraction derives not so much from the Marxist-Leninist system as from the caudillo mystique which surrounds him and which his public relations man, Paul Roa, so cleverly reinforces.

Castro's speeches have a way of charming and swaying the masses. In them he interprets the meaning of history, unlocks the "secrets," juggles with numbers, and continually discloses new plans. All this and so much more gives the Cuban brand of communism its special stamp. It is impossible to compare the Havana model fully with the Peking or Moscow models.

In 1962 Castro declared: "We in Cuba are neither puppets of Moscow nor satellites of Peking." This is so true, and anyone who evaluates this variety of communism must take this fact into account.

TRANSFORMING RELIGION INTO AN IDEOLOGY OF THE STATE

Religions are not ideologies, and when they are so transformed, they no longer function as religions. This is clearly evident from European history. When Christianity was turned into a religion of the state after Constantine the Great, it functioned as an ideology supporting the Byzantine and western Roman empires. Christianity was dismantled and was made into a vehicle for revering the emperor and for promoting the unity of the empire. This *Corpus Christianum* ideology made its impact in various ways until the eighteenth century.

In strikingly similar fashion today, when young states set out in quest of a definite shape and identity, there is a tendency to turn religions into ideologies of the state. Allow me to give a few examples.

Buddhism

A long Buddhist tradition and culture, various racial elements within society, a growing massive movement toward self-expression by farmers and laborers, and a quest for national identity have all contributed toward making Sri Lanka what it is today. But against this background the Buddhists rise up with the cry "One religion, one race, one language." The intent of their ideological slogan is to proclaim Theravada-Buddhism as the state religion, the Singhalese people as the dominant race, and the Singhalese language as the national language. This does not indicate a desire to return to the old interdependence between the monarch and Buddhist order (Sangha); though Sri Lanka has opted for a republican form of government, there is still a continual and nagging urge to make Sri Lanka nationalism synonymous with Buddhism.

The great mass of Buddhists "demands that Buddhism, which already shapes the national culture and is the national religion of a majority of the people, become the ideology which shapes a new people and a new state in Sri Lanka."[6]

In Thailand Theravada-Buddhism has been the religion of the state ever since the twelfth century. Thailand's princes bear the title "Defender of Buddhist Teaching" and exert a great authority over the community of Buddhist monks, primarily through their power to appoint. The king holds the right to appoint the head of the monastic order from the ranks of highest abbots. Some princes have themselves worn the monastic attire. The hierarchical, pyramidal organization of the monastic community insures that thousands of temples and monasteries are held firmly in tow.

Even though Theravada-Buddhism penetrates everything in Thailand, it has a far less coercively ideological character here than in Sri Lanka. In Thailand it continues much more as an ornament while other forces gain in their influence on the social and political life.

In Tibet a specific form of Buddhism, the Lamaist church-state, until recently dominated the whole life of the Tibetan people. Tibet also stands as an

---

6. M. M. Thomas and M. Abel, *Religion, State and Ideologies in East Asia* (Bangkok: East Asia Christian Conference, 1965), p. 8.

example of how quickly a religion which has become transformed into a powerful and dominant ideology can be supplanted by still another ideology, in this case by Maoist communism.

Islam

Pakistan's very *raison d'etre* is Islam. Mohammed Iqbal (1873–1938), the famous Muslim writer and philosopher, stimulated Mohammed Jinnah (1876–1948) to resist Gandhi and Nehru's attempt to form one unified state and to work at building up a separate Muslim state. It was Jinnah's goal to organize a modern, twentieth-century state where Islam would not only be the *raison d'etre* but also the abiding foundation.

Cantwell Smith's masterly book on Islam in modern history analyzes the ideological trends within this modern Muslim state, and though I do not have an opportunity to delineate them here, suffice it to say that Pakistan has never clearly determined what the content of a uniquely Muslim modern system of state is or should be. The process of reinterpreting Islam is far from complete, but one fact is already clear: Pakistan is intent on carrying through with its experiment to make Islam the ideology of its state. The same holds true for Bangladesh, the former East Pakistan which underwent an indescribably painful birth and even since then has suffered immensely through natural disaster.

In Malaysia, too, Islam functions as an ideology of the state, for there is a clear distinction embedded in the very structure of the state between the Malays on the one hand and other ethnic groups on the other. For the Malays, Orthodox Islam is given the status of a "protected religion" under the umbrella of traditional laws and institutions of justice, while the non-Malay groups (Chinese, Indians, etc.) have open to them the way toward religious and ideological pluralism.

Many people mistakenly suppose that modern Turkey is a secularized state, but Cantwell Smith offers a convincing case for viewing it more as a country undergoing a laicizing process. While Asiatic Muslims dream of restoration, the Turks strive for reformation *(yenilik)*. Rather than losing their Muslim identity amid the modernizing process, the people of Turkey want to keep and preserve it. One Turkish leader said, "We want to construct a Turkish Islam that is uniquely our own, relevant and integrated into our society. Even as Anglican Christianity is typically English as opposed to either Italian or Russian, so too we are striving for a state and a society that is Turkish Islam."

Egypt is the clearest example of many countries in North Africa where an ideology of the state is a mixture of Islam, Arabism, and certain Western ideologies.

Leonard Binder's *Ideology and Discontent* is an interesting analysis of the ideological base for Egyptian-Arab nationalism provided by Nasser. Nasser's vision came to clearest expression in *The Philosophy of Revolution,* which was proclaimed as the magna charta after the coup of July 23, 1952. It includes six goals:

1. The destruction of imperialism
2. The destruction of feudalism
3. Ending the domination of foreign capital over the government

    4. Social justice
    5. Building up a strong army
    6. Building up a healthy democratic system in the spirit of Islam

Three different interpretations of this ideology emerged — a rightist, a leftist and a centrist. Nasser's successor, Anwar Sadat, represents the middle position. This is important to note, for, as Ibrahim El-Sheikh indicated in the *International Spectator* of June, 1971, a battle is going on in the background between proponents of these various interpretations, and Sadat is doing a balancing act in setting both his domestic and his foreign policy.

THE IDEOLOGY OF THE STATE IN INDONESIA: THE PANTJASILA

As any student of the Pantjasila ideology knows, in the beginning it had a simple and clearly defined purpose and role. A few months before he became Indonesia's first president, Sukarno, who at the time was an engineer, delivered a famous address (*lahirnja Pantjasila*) which is commonly considered to be the birthday of Pantjasila. In it he called Pantjasila a common foundation for political life, a *modus vivendi* for stirring various groups to undertake the building of a new house from Sabang to Merauke.

Later many others, including the erectors of the Indonesian state and of this ideology, used other terms to describe this ideology. They spoke of Pantjasila as a "way of life" and as an all-embracing philosophy. But it is well to remember that this was not its original purpose.

Key Concepts in Pantjasila

On June 1, 1945, several months before the Republic of Indonesia was declared officially constituted, Sukarno delineated the Pantjasila philosophy in an address to a study group in Jakarta. This speech paved the way for the establishment of the republic itself.

He first explained his choice of the term *Pantja-sila. Pantja,* or "five," is a religiously symbolic number in Indonesia and elsewhere. In the classification systems there are many speculations on the five physical senses and the five fingers of the hand. Thus the term *Pantja,* "five." *Sila* comes from Sanskrit and Pali and means "foundation," "base," "pillar," "guideline." Thus *Pantjasila* refers to the five guidelines which from the beginning determined the course Indonesia was to follow.

The five guidelines of Pantjasila have not always been identically ordered and stated. Here is the most popular and up-to-date order and statement of them:

    1. Recognition of one God
    2. Humanity
    3. Nationality
    4. Democracy
    5. Social justice

I shall attempt to describe the significance of each as it has been set forth by the state on all sorts of occasions.

Recognition of One God (Ketuhanan jang Mahaesa)

Pantjasila's first pillar is its recognition of God, the One. This implies that from the very beginning the Indonesian state has confessed that the reality of God constitutes the very basis of political life. But Indonesians insist that this confession absolutely does not force any citizen to conform to a specific doctrine about who God is. Each is free to define the content of the term.

Thus Article 29 of the Constitution guarantees freedom of religion, and President Sukarno underscored it in his August 17, 1964 address: Muslim, Hindu, Protestant, Roman Catholic — each one may and must give his own concrete shape to this Sila.

By choosing this course, the Republic of Indonesia has on the one hand refrained from binding its citizens to a specific religion, as occurred in the Muslim countries and in Spain, for example, but on the other hand it rejected the notion of a secular state with its division of property between the state and the religions, as, for example, India tried to do. Indonesia acknowledges what is presently termed the religious dimension of existence and has declared this in a formal concept which it then allows each person to fill with his own meaning.

This element in its political ideology has played a highly significant role in Indonesia's life. In fact, an official department of religion stands guard to insure the freedom of religion and to further the cause of religion in Indonesian life. The department itself has divisions for each of the various religious fellowships, including the Protestant and Roman Catholic.

Humanity (Peri-Kemanusiaan)

The goal of this Sila, stated already in Sukarno's very first speech on Pantjasila, is to nip in the bud any sort of narrow-minded, chauvinistic nationalism. Pointing to national socialism as an example, official explications mention the imminent threat of an exalted nationalism when one's own nation becomes idolized and strives to dominate others. This Sila, said Sukarno in his speech, strives to further internationalism and cosmopolitanism and to remind the Indonesian people of its call to express with people the world over a genuine humanity. He quoted approvingly Gandhi's famous remark: "My nationalism is humanism."

Nationality (Kebangsaan)

The purpose of this third Sila is to bring the Indonesian people close together in their drive for national self-expression within their own geographic borders and to give them a sense of cultural and historical identity.

Interpreters of the Sila continually reassure that nationality does not cancel out multiformity but rather allows ample room for each and every ethnic and racial group to unfold its own unique gifts and characteristics. The Sila strives to advance a unity in diversity.

Democracy (Kerakjatan)

The fourth Sila calls for a government by the people and for the people, and those who explain it note that throughout history Indonesian kingdoms have traditionally valued representation and consultation (*musjawarah*) and the quest for solutions agreeable to all (*mufakat*).

Social Justice (Keadilan Sosial)
The last Sila calls for social justice. Interpreters repeatedly underscore that a people is not free simply by virtue of recognizing a political democracy; freedom must take shape in social and economic democracy, that is, in a system of production and distribution which so arranges and divides the national income that both efficiency and justice are achieved in the social and economic spheres.

The Pantjasila and Other Political Ideologies

The pioneers of the Indonesian Republic repeatedly asserted that the Pantjasila ideology both borrowed elements from other current political ideologies while at the same time it also rejected others. For example, in his early speech which set forth the goals of Pantjasila, Sukarno compared it with Sun Yat Sen's famous three political principles. Or again, in an address to the General Assembly of the United Nations on September 30, 1960, Sukarno compared Indonesia's political ideology to both the United States' Declaration of Independence and Marx and Engel's Communist Manifesto. While he valued the Declaration highly, he claimed that it lacked the concept of social justice. To his way of thinking it is too individualistic and liberal. In the case of the Communist Manifesto, though it contains the element of social justice, it lacks the religious dimension. Pantjasila, said Sukarno, has taken what is true from both of these documents but has gone beyond them. He then challenged the assembly with this question: Could Pantjasila perchance be the suitable guide to lead both East and West out of their dead-end ideological struggle and thus effectively reduce tension between them?

These words disclose the deepest intentions of the architects and builders of the Indonesian state. They wanted to avoid a one-sided liberalism as well as a closed attitude toward the religious dimension.

Later Developments

Though in the early years of the Republic Pantjasila served Indonesia as a clear and simple *modus vivendi,* during the later years of his rule Sukarno developed it much more into a quasi religion. In 1959 he proclaimed a new political direction — "guided democracy." His many speeches explaining and defending this new course clearly disclosed that Pantjasila was being reshaped into an official dogmatic and ethical state policy.

When President Suharto came to power in March, 1966, he initially said very little about this ideology. People were sick and tired of all the rhetoric. He called for less ideological talk and more action. But now that he has become settled in power, he too is now more than at first underscoring how this ideology can positively serve as a *modus vivendi* to bring divergent groups together in cooperation.

THE IDEOLOGY OF THE SECULAR STATE

India is the most telling example of a secular state. When India became independent in 1947, she faced the monumental task of reshaping a society which for so long had been hierarchically organized and divided by castes into a modern state which would guarantee freedom and justice for all. Jawaharlal Nehru, who took over after Mahatma Gandhi's murder and became the most important architect of the new state, definitely did not want to return to the traditional pattern of precolonial days, Hindu communalism, for he keenly sensed that this would split India wide open into many ethnic and religious factions and lead to her demise. Unity was vitally necessary, and therefore at Nehru's urging, India opted for the notion of a secular state. Her constitution guarantees fundamental human rights to all based on a secular democracy.

The Indian state preaches respect for all religions and is trying to bridge the gap between the elite class and the masses through various five-year plans. The task is not easy because the traditional ties to ethnic groups act as a powerful collective brake on any efforts to change. One must remember that India is a country of many religions, diverse cultures, a variety of castes and countless languages, and now that the colonial days are over, these separate groups have again become much more conscious of their own identity. Consequently, regionalism, excessive emphasis on language groupings, religious communalism, and the caste system (official policy notwithstanding) have all revived. Politics is the only way to acquire power in India, and every group wants power for itself. The result is that separate loyalties within the Indian nation surface and threaten the unity of the nation itself. A secular state seems to many to be the only anchor which can keep the ship from dashing to pieces.

Here are the chief points of the secular-state ideology:

1. The state does not desire to oppose religion; it only strives to be sympathetically neutral to each and every one.
2. State and religion must remain separate.
3. Freedom of religion must be permitted to every citizen.
4. Amid the cultural and religious pluralism, the various separate groups must cooperatively strive to bring an end to poverty, ignorance and injustice by joint planning for social and economic progress.

Other nations such as Japan, Taiwan, South Korea and Nigeria have their own versions of a secular state, but none of them has developed it as thoroughly and applied it as consistently as India. The strengths and weaknesses show up best here, and therefore it is the only illustration I shall give of this approach.

THE IDEOLOGY OF AFRICAN SOCIALISM

Several African nations, notably Tanzania and Zambia, have already opted for an ideology described as African socialism, and presumably others such as Mozambique and Angola will do the same in the coming years.

Tanzania

Julius K. Nyerere, Tanzania's current president, has written more than any other person on the meaning of African socialism. His book *Freedom and Unity: A*

Selection from Writings and Speeches, 1952–1965 provides the best descriptions. I shall quote from it in abbreviated form.

European socialism was born of the agrarian revolution and the industrial revolution which followed it. The former created the "landed" and the "landless" classes in society; the latter produced the modern capitalist and the industrial proletariat. These two revolutions planted the seeds of conflict within society, and not only was European socialism born of that conflict, but its apostles sanctified the conflict itself into a philosophy. Civil war was no longer looked upon as something evil, or something unfortunate, but as something good and necessary. As prayer is to Christianity or to Islam, so civil war ("class war") is to the European version of socialism — a means inseparable from the end. Each becomes the basis of a whole way of life. The European socialist cannot think of his socialism without its father — capitalism.

Brought up in tribal socialism, I must say I find the contradiction quite intolerable. It gives capitalism a status which it neither claims nor deserves. For it virtually says "Without capitalism, and the conflict which capitalism creates within society, there can be no socialism." African socialism, on the other hand, did not have the "benefit" of the agrarian revolution or the industrial revolution. It did not start from the existence of conflicting "classes" in society. Indeed I doubt if the equivalent for the word "class" exists in any indigenous African language; for language describes the ideas of those who speak it, and the idea of "class" or "caste" was non-existent in African society.

The foundation and the objective of African socialism is [*sic*] the extended family. The true African socialist does not look on one class of men as his brethren and another as his natural enemies. He does not form an alliance with the "brethren." He rather regards all men as his brethren — as members of his ever extending family. . . . Ujamaa, then, or "family-hood," describes our socialism. It is opposed to capitalism, which seeks to build a happy society on the basis of the exploitation of man by man; and it is equally opposed to doctrinaire socialism, which seeks to build its happy society on a philosophy of inevitable conflict between man and man.

We in Africa have no more need of being "converted" to socialism than we have of being "taught" democracy. Both are rooted in our own past — in the traditional society which produced us. Modern African socialism can draw from its traditional heritage the recognition of "society" as an extension of the basic family unit. But it can no longer confine the idea of the social family within the limits of the tribe, nor, indeed, of the nation. For no true African socialist can look at a line drawn on a map and say "The people on this side of that line are my brothers, but those who happen to live on the other side of it can have no claim on me." Every individual on this continent is his brother.

It was in the struggle to break the grip of colonialism that we learned the need for unity. We came to recognize that the same socialist attitude of mind which, in the tribal days, gave to every individual the security that comes of belonging to a widely extended family, must be preserved within the still wider society of the nation. But we should not stop there. Our recognition of the family to which we all belong must be extended yet further — beyond the tribe, the community, the nation, or even the continent — to embrace the whole society of mankind. This is the only logical conclusion for true socialism.[7]

By establishing Ujamaa villages, Nyerere and his unity party, Tanu, are striving to give concrete expression to African socialism. People living spread out from each other are brought together to provide collectively for their goods and services, such as schools, clinics, water wells, etc. In some villages the land is owned communally; in others, a share of it is communal and another share, private. In these last-mentioned villages, a portion of one's workweek is devoted to doing communal work, and the rest is for working privately.

To bring about social and economic progress in the cities, the key emphases are on self-reliance (in part through the nationalizing of vital industries) and on war against corruption (cf. Nyerere's famous Arusha Declaration).

To achieve his goals, Nyerere and his staff have attempted to radically revise colonial education into something much more amenable to African socialism. The new education put an end to any and all racial distinction. Educational facilities have been greatly expanded, especially in the secondary and the job-training areas.

The content of education is now much more relevant to the needs of Tanzania. Tanzanian education strives to apply Nyerere's three principles described in *Education for Self-Reliance:*

    a. Equality and respect for human dignity
    b. Sharing of resources produced communally
    c. Work by everyone and exploitation by no one

Tanzania has a one-party political system, Tanu being the chosen instrument for making the goals of African socialism a reality. It takes strong legs to be able to bear the heavy "luxury" of a one-party system; however, the Tanzanian system allows for much more criticism, discussion and choice than most other one-party systems. Opposition candidates may run for office, criticism is encouraged, and council meetings create ample opportunity for discussion.

Tanzania also allows freedom of religion, and up to this time Nyerere has spurred the religious communities on to a critical solidarity and participation.

Zambia

Kenneth Kaunda, the current president of Zambia and, like Nyerere, one of the first-generation leaders of young African states, calls his vision for society "Zambian humanism." Society must develop in such a way that genuine humanity comes to expression.

But rather than being some sort of autonomous entity, Zambian humanism is deeply rooted in belief in and respect for God and a desire to answer to God's intentions for mankind as revealed in the personal and public life of Jesus Christ.

Kaunda absolutely rejects any ideology which builds upon racial distinction and which fails to respect the equal worth of all people. Hence his renowned opposition to apartheid and (internally) to any and all forms of tribalism.

7. Julius K. Nyerere, *Ujamaa, Essays in Socialism* (Dar es Salaam: Oxford Univ. Press, 1968).

Zambian humanism also implies a quest for a fair and just division of labor and income in the sector of economic and industrial development (for example, in the copper industry). Kaunda is also trying to apply its principles to the agricultural sector which fully engages seventy-five percent of Zambia's population and yet where progress has but scarcely begun.

Zambia has a one-party system, but one that is not monopolistic. There is room for choice. Kaunda justifies this system in young African states by arguing that a plurality of parties could quickly degenerate into tribal opposition and conflict.

TECHNO-FASCIST IDEOLOGY IN LATIN AMERICA

The Argentine sociologist, Gino Germani, argues in his book *Politica y Sociedad en Una Epoca de Transicion* (1966) that though military juntas appeared time and again throughout the nineteenth century, they play a different role today. In his judgment the old and rather folklorish palace-revolutions are things of the past; military juntas now intend to maintain the structures or to direct them in a semi-fascist spirit. Juntas today are more authoritarian than totalitarian due to the fact that certain liberal traditions established during the time of Simon Bolivar and José de San Martin, liberators during the early nineteenth century, have continued down to the present. Thus, these juntas do not encroach upon every area; they are authoritarian, not totalitarian.

The generals and colonels view themselves as the guiding elite. Not only do they maintain authority; they are also agents of modernization who can enlist the aid of countless technological and organizational experts.

Germani sees in many lands of Latin America fronts of elites (the landed aristocracy, the industrial bourgeoisie, and the military authorities) which will intervene every now and then in crisis situations to try to bring about authoritarian breakthroughs to the political and economic impasses. These fronts may well introduce various reforms, but their common fear of the emerging masses draws them closely together, and they are more than willing to defend and maintain the status quo if their own interests so demand.

These semi-fascist juntas have available highly refined weapons and security techniques to protect their power and effectively demolish everything that in their judgment is subversive.

Germani, who himself opposes semi-fascism, expects that it will at least temporarily continue as the prevailing "answer" to the challenges in Latin America, especially in the southern region.

Of course there are many types and models of semi-fascism in Latin America. I shall make only a few comments about them here.

Argentina

Argentina is the land of Perón, the dictator who first came to power in 1946. Argentine Peronism during the dictator and his wife Evita's first phase of leadership (1946–1952) was marked by the complicity of the army with the gigantic labor syndicates. Something of a caudillo mystique came to envelop Perón, and Evita became a modern saint even before, but especially after, her death.

Following his expulsion Perón returned in 1973 with his third wife, Isabel. The old teamwork between army and labor syndicates again developed, and when crises developed, the army again became the appointed agent to settle the differences. Perón himself died in 1974 and was succeeded by his wife Isabel, who in reality became a tool of the army.

Now that Perón, the balancing artist and caudillo, is gone, the equilibrium between army and syndicates has been disturbed. Great division has developed within the ranks of Perón's followers between the leftist and rightist factions, while the Trotskyite guerilla movement (ERP) operates off to the one side and the extreme rightist anticommunist alliance (AAA) off to the other.

As one can perhaps sense from reading these lines, various ideological trends are colliding with each other in Argentina today. The government is striving to squelch them, thus reducing it to a pawn of the rightists and the army and alienating it from the leftist Monteneros. Peronism is in swift decline, and at this point no one can predict the ideological course which Argentina will take. In 1976 Isabel Perón was kicked out of power, Peronism was forbidden, and a military junta came into power consisting of a triumvirate under General Videla as primus inter pares for the coming five years.

Brazil

Following the civil presidencies of Janio Quadros and Goulart, Brazil from 1964 to the present has been ruled successively by these military leaders: Branco, Costa and Silva, de Medici, and now Geisel.

Brazil is a textbook example of Germani's description of semi-fascism in Latin America. Military leaders and technocrats are heading up the development of this gigantic country. The military generals allow the technocrats to forge whatever economic policies they deem useful and necessary, and the whole country thus becomes a classic example of unbridled capitalism. The concentration of financial income has risen enormously by luring foreign investments into the south. As a result of the south's being industrialized at the expense of the north, a form of internal colonization has ensued, as Archbishop Helder Camara has repeatedly claimed.

Without a doubt this regime hopes that drop by drop some of the welfare enjoyed by the elites may gradually trickle down to the masses, but meanwhile these masses are experiencing what Alves calls a "mild death." Whenever the masses show signs of rebelling, the authorities crack down with "purifications," terror, and a highly equipped police force.

Many parts of the infrastructure, the roads, for example, have been vastly improved, but primarily for the sake of foreign investors. Production is not so much geared toward meeting the needs of the people as toward increasing exports. A Brazilian worker earns one-tenth of the salary of his West European counterpart.

Peru

In 1969 Peru's current President, Juan Velasco Alvarado, expelled the military junta headed by de Terry and took over the reins of leadership. Two noteworthy features of the Peruvian brand of semi-fascism are its much more serious tackling of the structural causes which lie at the heart of so many of Peru's problems, and its concern for the poor. Through land reform and improved agricultural methods the current leaders are striving to do something about the staggering poverty in the rural areas. Several vital industries (the sugar industry among them) have been nationalized. Oil production is now being controlled. Tax policies are now being brought more into line with a person's income. In the fishing industry dispute with the United States, Velasco Alvarado held firmly to the rights of Peru over its territorial waters. A national plan which is geared toward the masses and which sets the emancipation of the poor as a top-priority item is being energetically pursued.

All this is so gratifying that many will be inclined to ignore the semi-fascist features of what is happening in Peru. However, simply because it is exercising its power in better and more just ways than past governments did does not make this regime any less fascist; the lack of any formidable opposition renders the chances of a misuse of power very great. Therefore experts claim that since 1974 the administration in Peru has gradually been reaching a crossroads in its existence. In 1976 followed the replacement of Alvarado by Morales Bermudez and showed the government of Peru more and more the trends of other techno-fascistic regimes in Latin America.

EVALUATING THE IDEOLOGIES

Both in theory and in practice missiologists have traditionally restricted their involvement to the area of theology of religions, that is, to an examination of man's religious expressions by the standard of the gospel of Jesus Christ. Important as this is, we ought also in our day by way of self-examination to be evaluating the ideologies in the light of God's promises and demands.

Missiologists nowadays have a tendency to go in one of two directions. Either they become so wrapped up in an apolitical, pietistic type of missiology which emphasizes the individual that they completely disregard the ideologies for what they really are — "powers" — or else they uncritically exchange the gospel for some Marxist-Leninist, Maoist or semi-fascist ideology.

However that may be, in my judgment no one can deny that an analysis and evaluation of ideologies is one of the missiologist's most basic tasks, one which he has scarcely begun to undertake.

But a beginning has been made. Witness, for example, M. M. Thomas and M. Abel's interesting study *Religion, State and Ideologies in East Asia,* which objectively analyzes the various ideologies found in Asia today and, viewing them as human constructs, proceeds to point out their weaknesses and strengths. The Lutheran World Federation, too, in cooperation with *Pro Mundi Vita* has undertaken a very instructive study of the Chinese ideology which I shall mention in the survey of literature at the end of this chapter. My own little book, *The Message of Liberation in Our Age,* also contains a general chapter on the need for Christians to look critically at the ideologies.

In the present chapter I have tried to indicate something of the wide plurality of ideologies today. But now I wish to offer a few comments on the evaluation of these ideologies.

(1) Christians ought to begin by developing a genuine understanding of the situation in which other Christians live. How sad that some Christians who live in a situation where human rights are more respected at times can unlovingly take it upon themselves to judge from a distance those situations where human rights are less respected.

Prior to and during the First World War, Western Christendom threatened to fly to pieces through conflicting allegiances to national ideologies. Now the ecumenical fellowship is being threatened by ideological bloc-forming. Ecumenical alliance — indeed, the communion of saints itself — demands that Christians slash right through this bloc-forming and embrace each other in a mutual regard for one another's situation.

Some Christians and churches exist in communist-controlled areas such as China, North Korea, Vietnam, Cuba, etc. Others dwell within areas such as Brazil or Argentina which are dominated by semi-fascist ideologies. Still others live within a sector influenced by a certain type of African socialism or by an ideology based on a certain religion, as in, say, Afghanistan, Sri Lanka, Pakistan, and elsewhere. The situations vary widely. In some situations Christians can freely and fully join in the work of building up society in a spirit of critical solidarity, while in other situations ideological pressure compels them to keep silent. In some instances Christians must give their lives for their faith; in others, they can consciously participate in the tasks at hand.

Shortly after the world missionary conference of Tambaram in 1938 Visser 't Hooft wrote: "The church is involved in becoming universal, and yet at the very time her universality is coming to the fore, the church is running into conflict with totalitarian ideologies in many lands." (Visser 't Hooft was writing at the time of the Nazi ideology.) There is a time to show compassion, a time to rejoice, and a time to warn. But however the situations may vary, one demand never changes: Christians are called to live into the situations of others and thus to better understand them.

(2) Christians must also band together to examine and evaluate the ideologies and how they carry over into practice. People everywhere sense the need for this; the very language they use is proof enough of their feeling. One commonly hears, for example, such evaluative pairs of terms as proper-improper, true-false, healthy-sick, and authentic-inauthentic being applied to ideologies.

Not all ideologies are alike, and everyone knows it. To give an example, everyone intuitively senses that the apartheid ideology is bursting full of injustice, while African socialism at certain points shows a great affinity with the gospel. Or again, nazism deserves the opprobrious title "a nihilistic revolution," while just elements are mixed with totalitarian ones in Leninist-Marxism.

All this inevitably leads us to ask: "What criteria must we use to judge these ideologies? Can we simply borrow from science in general or sociology in particular?" In reply, we must say that however important science taken by itself may be — and it is important, as the studies of K. Mannheim, Geiger, and others amply indicate — we cannot borrow our deepest criteria from science or sociology, because scientists themselves may well be subservient to one or another ideology. Must we then make "value-free" judgments about the ideologies? I believe this route is Christianly improper and scientifically impossible.

What about making *effect* or *success* the criterion for assessing the ideologies? To follow such a route would land one in the camp of George Sorel and Pareto.

How about choosing one ideology as a starting point — say, the Marxist or Christian Democratic — and making it the criterion for all the rest? But in so doing one would be forgetting that no ideology can ever function as the highest norm, for it is a weak human contrivance and itself requires examination.

Accepting the starting points which I have developed throughout the course of this book, I am convinced that the promises and demands of the gospel of the all-embracing kingdom as it has come and still comes to us in Jesus Christ constitute the criteria for evaluating the ideologies. Every Christian shall humbly have to admit that he too stands under the judgment of Christ and of those same demands and promises, and every Christian community shall have to examine itself and humbly admit that its Christian evaluation, whether it is conscious of them or not, is often full of ideological cliches, prejudices, lack of genuine understanding, etc. But all this having been said, Christians still stand under the clear obligation to examine and evaluate the ideologies by the standards of the gospel of God's kingdom.

After his visit to China in 1974, B. Kramers wrote a report in *Wereld en Zending* in which he criticized Mao Tse Tung for trying to forge a whole congregation of Mao. Of course, his criticism proceeded from his starting point within the Christian congregation, but, said Kramers, all my words are nothing more than pious boasting if we Christians in our situation and time fail to live by the vision of Christ's gospel which makes everything new and to give our every ounce of energy to make true what we in our hearts already know is true. Only then will our critiques have a ring of truth.

Winfried Glüer reflects something of the same spirit:

> In Johannine terms, the criterion for the fullness of life is "to be in the truth" (18:37) or "to do the truth" (3:21). That "Man's countenance may be formed into its true human shape, this his future may be assured and he unfailingly may be led home" must not remain an utopian dream but must be undertaken unceasingly in concrete efforts to change the world and change human life.[8]

(3) I believe that the World Council of Churches' 1966 Conference on Church and Society rendered valuable service in this regard by developing its vision of a "Responsible Society." It can aid churches throughout the world in concretely applying the criterion I developed above to their varied situations. There are three touchstones for testing any situation:

    (a) A responsible society expresses the fact that both public authority and society are responsible to the living God.

---

8. Winfried Glüer, "Faith and Ideology in the Context of the New China," in *Theological Implications of the New China: Papers Presented at the Ecumenical Seminar Held in Bostad, Sweden* (Geneva and Brussels: Lutheran World Federation/Pro Mundi Vita, 1974), p. 51.

(b) A responsible society expresses the responsibility of both public authority and society for each and every member of that society and
attends to those who have been neglected, discriminated against,
forgotten, or subjected to various forms of injustice.

(c) A responsible society allows each person an opportunity to be himself
and to unfold his dynamic and creative nature in accord with the
norms of justice.

These touchstones are useful for pointing out the weak spots in any of the
ideologies. In fact, M. M. Thomas from India, the chairman of the Conference on
Church and Society which produced the report, did apply them in his book *The
Christian Response to the Asian Revolution*. He set forth some fundamental
considerations which, though written specifically for the Asian situation,
nevertheless are equally valid for other continents also:

1. In Asia, it is necessary to stress the positive functions of state authority
   and of a large measure of state-imposed discipline for integrating the
   traditional groups into a new composite national community and re-
   ordering of economic and social institutions, both of which are necessary means to affirm the human dignity of men in an open society in the
   long run.
2. The state must be based on some measure of consent of the people and
   people should have increasing opportunities to share in the power and
   responsibilities of government.
3. The state must express in its own structure its recognition that man has
   ends and loyalties beyond the state, especially by granting religious
   liberty in the legal system and giving structural form to the idea that
   fundamental rights of the human person are derived from a moral
   source other than the political authority.
4. The power of the state should never be absolute and must be limited by
   political means, legal processes and customs, and by the autonomy of
   certain areas of life recognized as essentially non-political and voluntary at their core. Whatever be the priority of the moment, the state
   structure must be orientated towards the preservation of order, justice
   and freedom in the best possible balance, as the pursuit of any one of
   them at the total expense of the others will result ultimately in the
   denial of all.[9]

MISSIO POLITICA OECUMENICA

I choose to conclude my evaluation of the ideologies by considering the *missio
politica oecumenica*. I do this because the relationship between our faith and our
political involvement as churches ecumenically bound together certainly deserves
attention.

I shall treat this topic by positing a number of theses which originally I
defended before an ecumenical council composed of Roman Catholic and Protes-

9. M. M. Thomas, *The Christian Response to the Asian Revolution* (London: SCM
Press, 1966), pp. 64–65.

tant theologians, lawyers, and sociologists, and which I now set before my readers for their judgment.

1. Both the *missio Dei* and the *missiones ecclesiarum* attuned to it always have had and will continue to have a political dimension. Indeed, churches are under mandate to proclaim and show the totality of God's gospel and law to all mankind. And this totality includes the *missio politica oecumenica*.

In making this claim I do not intend to suggest that the political dimension exhausts the total content of God's promises and demands, but it is a part of them. Christ's missionary mandate in Matthew 28:18-20 has a universal ring to it; four times he uses the world "all": all power, all peoples, always and all command- ments. Thus, this all-embracing mandate includes the *missio politica oecumenica* too.

Because he is the Liberator, God is deeply interested in man's political and social life. Simply because the contours of his kingdom do not exactly conform to the schema of this world does not thereby mean that the kingdom is not aimed at this world. Take a look at salvation history. How often were the central figures not viewed as enemies of the state because they opposed the schema of this world (cf. Rom. 12:1) and lived here and now as colonists of a new "commonwealth," as Philippians 3:20 puts it? Moses was a political refugee in Midian. David was a wanted man who with his men had to take flight to the hills. Daniel and his friends passively resisted a despot who was bent on taking away their freedom to worship God. Tacitus' *Annals* lists Jesus' arrest and condemnation, and in it he is reckoned among the group of political wrongdoers (Mark 15:28). Furthermore, Jesus him- self told his disciples, "They will arrest you" (Mark 13), and just how true his words were becomes starkly clear in the book of Acts, which someone called "the book of arrests." How many arrests there really were! Furthermore, Peter, Stephen, Paul, and James, Jesus' brother, were all executed. According to ancient tradition the Revelation of John was written by an exile forced to work in the salt mines on the island of Patmos.

No one can deny that a political dimension has been apparent throughout the whole history of revelation, for that history is being guided by a God who is intent on liberating human beings and societies. Hence the tasks which this God gives to his people always include a *missio politica oecumenica*. Both the confes- sion "Yahweh is God!" in the Old Testament and "Jesus is Lord!" in the New have always been political in nature and have confronted those who uttered these words with important political choices and responsibilities.

2. God's call to Israel in the Old Testament to construct a model of salvation in a provisional and temporary theocracy signified his approaching messianic kingdom of righteousness which would conquer men's hearts and indeed the world.

3. In the New Testament all the churches which gathered to hear the apostolic word and to celebrate the eucharist understood — whether consciously or unconsciously — that political diaconia was a mark of a Christocentrically open fellowship of churches directed toward the Lord and his kingdom.

4. Throughout church history various Christian traditions such as the Roman Catholics, the Calvinists, the Lutherans, the Pietists, the Mennonites, etc., have developed widely differing views of how church, state, and society

should be related. How gratifying to note that renewed theological reflection on the biblical message during the last decade is producing greater convergence and ecumenical vision on this subject. People from a variety of traditions are coming to know both each other and the biblical message which they share.

While working together, people have recently been discovering to their amazement that the relevance of the biblical message to the real political and social questions facing our age has gradually been coming to light. However widely they might differ in other areas of their individual theologies, theologians young and old the world over are finding that one issue demands their common attention: How is the message of the coming messianic kingdom important for our life and work in our present, concrete history? Masao Takenaka from Japan, Rubem Alves from Latin America, E. A. Ayandele from Nigeria and M. M. Thomas from India are no less involved with this question than are Jürgen Moltmann and J. Metz. One might say that all of them are searching for a *theologia oboedientiae,* a theology which can assist Christians in giving shape and form to their obedience to God's promises and demands.

Of course there are differences among them; it would be senseless to deny that. Paul Albrecht differs from Richard Shaull, who in turn differs from Rubem Alves, who differs from Jürgen Moltmann, etc., but on one thing all agree: the biblical message has a social and political dimension which each in his own way is trying to articulate. One can detect on all six continents the growing ecumenical involvement in what I am quite willing to call a theology of transformation.

5. The ambivalence of the relation between mission and colonialism can and should teach us much today about how to discharge our own *missio politica oecumenica.* Both in Western and Eastern Europe a fair amount of writing has been devoted to a retrospective look at the relationship between mission and colonialism during the colonial era, and the lesson to be learned is a shaming one in many respects.

But we ought never to forget that company of missionaries during the precolonial and colonial eras which devoted its full energies for the natives living in the colonialized territories.

Now that the thunder of God's judgment on that colonializing period has subsided, we ought to inquire anew what the will of God is amid all the social and political questions which are presently facing us.

6. Through mutual contact at both the national and international levels we must now begin to construct a *missio politica oecumenica.*

From the very time it was founded, the World Council of Churches has had a Committee for International Affairs, headed presently by Dr. Nilius. This is an important organ of the council, for it deals with the political dimension of the biblical message. The increasingly important role its Asian, African, and Latin American members have recently begun to play is a welcome sign.

Another organ of this type — one which indicates the growing consensus between Protestants and Roman Catholics on these matters — is SODEPAX, the Committee on Society Development and Peace of the World Council of Churches and the Pontifical Commission on Justice and Peace. We may hope that it may soon get beyond its period of stagnation and begin to function well again.

7. To fulfill responsibly our task of *missio politica oecumenica* we must

together discern what the will of God is in the changing situations confronting countries and peoples (Rom. 12:2).

What does it mean to discern the promises and demands of God? In the light of the biblical message I shall try to set forth a few points which have emerged from the efforts of those who have ventured an answer.

(a) To discern God's will for today one must believe that the God and Father of Jesus Christ is still carrying forth his liberating work among the peoples. Wherever love for God and one's neighbor springs forth one may detect the God at work about whom Jesus said: "My father is working still, and I am working" (John 5:17). And wherever egoism, godlessness, and injustice are on the rampage, God rises up to threaten with peril, to warn, and to beckon persons, groups and institutions to change.

(b) My second comment has to do with the fulfillment of the times. According to Galatians 4:4 the Son of Man has come in the fullness of time; therefore, because he stands central in the ages, all of them are now under his liberating authority. Given this, we can see repeated periods throughout history when God's judgment ripened on certain inhuman trends and, as a result, change simply had to come. Today he who has the eyes to see it can notice God's accusing finger of judgment pointed at every vestige and color of racism, whether of white or black or brown or yellow, at the disorder in the world economy, at the insane arms race, at the wanton disregard for ecology, etc.

(c) A thorough analysis of local situations is necessary in order to adequately discern the will of God. One cannot assess the situation in China, South Africa, Bolivia, or Bangladesh from a vantage point in Geneva or Rome.

(d) To discern God's will for these local situations one must test them by the criterion which summarizes the whole of the Law and the Prophets, namely, love for God and one's neighbor. There simply are no others nowadays by which to fulfill our political calling to radically test the political and social processes against the standard of God's will.

(e) Finally, to fulfill our political calling we must be in contact with the "people of God" globally. A *missio politica oecumenica* may never be the product of an ecclesiastical get-together, or of one confessional family of churches, or of a Geneva without Rome, or of a Rome without Geneva. Designing a *missio politica* demands an ecumenical context within which to work if it is to become anything more than the latest expression of ecclesiastical tribalism.

The old prescriptive and legalist method for discharging our *missio politica oecumenica* cannot be used. Nor can we simply read God's will from the situation alone, and certainly not by figuring out the average opinion of churchgoers. We ought also to be on guard against a too deliberative ethics which stops all forward movement while it tries to calculate all the implications and results of our ethical decisions. In its early stages the Commission on International Affairs was thus crippled by the excessive influence of the too deliberative ethics of Reinhold Niebuhr. The only *missio politica oecumenica* worthy of its name is one which begins by trying to discern what the will of God is.

8. Churches which do not go beyond formulating an *ethica politica* display a certain Pelagian tendency. They must take into account personal and institutional resistance toward obeying the will of God and deem it a part of their calling

to contribute whatever means they have available to help create those processes which can lead to change.

One of the most typical and universal symptoms of the present crisis in the churches is that especially the younger generation is becoming sick and tired of ecclesiastical pronouncements which boil down to nothing but cheap words and are not followed up by efforts to bring about change. This crisis is rooted in the fact that the time for ecclesiastical verbalism is past; as time passes we are coming to see ever more clearly the distance between ecclesiastical pronouncements and present social and political realities.

The trouble with ecclesiastical verbalism was that churchmen consciously or unconsciously thought that it was enough to issue statements and pronouncements. They underestimated — and still underestimate — the deep resistance which a call to obey God's will evokes in all our lives and society. Consequently they tended to downplay the need for working to bring about processes which could steer social and political life in the direction called for in the pronouncements.

9. To implement proposition eight, we in both North and South must underscore the importance of social ethics in theological education and spell out the political dimension in preaching, catechesis and especially training work. Churches must encourage their members to responsibly participate in pressure groups, frontier movements, critical political parties, and, in some cases, in resistance movements and certain freedom organizations.

Until recently, strikingly little attention was paid to offering courses in social and political ethics in theological schools located in so-called developing countries. Fortunately, things have much improved, but even now a course in social ethics is still a stepchild in many curricula. Until recently catechesis completely lacked the political dimension, and training work was restricted to what was termed preparing the congregation (in the narrower sense).

Z. K. Matthews, the late famous black professor, in many articles reminded his fellow Africans that it was now time for them to deal with those fundamental questions and issues which colonial authorities in days past addressed in their own manner. If the citizens of Africa's young states should regard these issues as taboo for theological education, catechesis, and training work, the education would become ghetto-like and the preaching, spiritualistic. Masao Takenaka from Japan and Dr. P. D. Latuihamallo and Dr. Sutarno from Indonesia make largely the same point.

Listening to Dr. T. B. Simatupang, the man who deserves the credit for building up the Indonesian army, retell his life history, one is struck the most by how little direction and guidance the churches gave to those individuals entrusted with such heavy responsibility during those years when Indonesia was becoming a republic. Only through his later contacts with the worldwide church did he come to understand the overwhelming amount of light which the promises and demands of God can shed on those questions and issues which he had been facing in his military work.

Dr. O. Notohamidjojo together with a few of his friends wrote *Christelijk Geloof en Politiek* ("Christian Faith and Politics") in 1948, the first book to offer discussion material to preachers, catechizers, training leaders, and politicians for further reflection on the *missio politica oecumenica.*

Roman Catholics too are beginning to see clearly that the time for words alone is past and that the time for encouraging people to active participation in processes which can lead to change has come. To cite but one example, in his apostolic letter to Cardinal Maurice Roy, Pope Paul VI cited the priesthood and peace and justice as the two most acute problems facing the church today. He wrote:

> Let each person examine himself to see what he has done and what he must do. To repeat principles, make declarations about intentions, point the finger toward screaming injustice and utter prophetic condemnations are not enough. These words will carry little real weight unless each individual accompanies them with a living sense of his own responsibility and with effective action.

10. In their assisting roles missionary and diaconal agencies in the North must make many more funds available for training social and political ethicists, journalists, political scientists, and sociologists in and for the developing countries so that from there these people can step forward to make their own contributions to the *missio politica oecumenica.*

This thesis needs scant clarification. A review of the monies distributed by the Theological Education Fund supports one of its director's disappointing claims that too few scholarships were requested for training social ethicists. Scholarships for training specialized journalists are also vitally necessary.

Pope John XXIII remarked one time that if Paul were living today, he would have become a journalist. Pope John knew that newspapers, radio, and television, more deeply than preaching, influence a person today, and that therefore this generation needs journalists who are not slaves to public opinion but have the courage to examine the facts by the standards of the Law and the Prophets. This being so, those assisting agencies who make scholarships available will have to take this factor into account.

Emilio Castro, the former secretary of the ecumenical movement in Latin America, when asked what Western countries could do for his area of the world, replied, "It is not important for someone in Amsterdam or London to tell us what we in our situation ought to do, but it is important that scholarships be made available so that young Latin Americans can become economists or political scientists in their developing countries." We do well to heed such voices.

11. Promotion of regional consultations among Christians to deal with the concrete needs, problems and conflicts which exist there is highly desirable.

Conferences like that on church and society held in 1966, extremely useful as they are, cannot by their very nature extend very far beyond the realm of sweeping generalization. Hence the need for parallel regional consultations.

The 1960 Cottesloe conference in South Africa did more to make the people there conscious of the important issues than any global conference could ever have done. The efforts of the All-Africa Conference of Churches, in cooperation with the Commission on International Affairs and the churches in the Sudan and the political refugees from the Sudan dwelling in Uganda, are another moving example of what regional conferences can achieve, given sufficient patience and breath for negotiation.

12. Continued ecumenical efforts on a global level to develop structures through which to set ecumenical policy and carry on deliberation for the benefit of the poor and disadvantaged are vitally necessary.

By my plea for regional consultations I in no way intend to underestimate the importance of international ecclesiastical organs such as the Commission for International Affairs and SODEPAX. On the contrary, these international organs must do whatever they can to create structures so that the whole world community can focus in on those specific regions that deserve attention.

In recent decades we have gradually been learning how to read the biblical message of liberation through the eyes of the poor, the oppressed, and the hungry. In this connection, ecumenical organs, supported by the churches, have but one overall job to do: to scan the globe looking for areas where oppression reigns and where inhumanity has been drilled into the very system, and then to inquire what the rest of the world community can do to help. Once local and regional consultations have focused proper attention on a trouble spot, effective action to counter the inhuman systems and to help the victims requires close cooperation between the local people and individuals with global influence. Working through established ecumenical structures, these latter individuals can then bring international pressure to bear on those who are responsible for allowing these inhuman situations to continue.

13. One task of *missio politica oecumenica* is to aid in the struggle for recognition of freedom of religion as part of man's basic human rights.

The worldwide church must band together with other communities and organs to focus intently on areas where authorities either pay lip service to or else completely take away the right to freedom of religion. Contemporary history is certainly no dawning new day for freedom of religion; rather, an oppressive darkness has fallen upon freedom of religion in the form of totalitarian political systems and certain religions which suppose that by applying earthly power they can enforce their claim upon a person's allegiance. In such situations the worldwide church must remain alert and defend through every means consistent with her calling a human being's fundamental right to practice the religion of his own choosing.

I have the strong impression that a sense of despondency and powerlessness has sapped much of the once vast energy and attention which the church devoted to this issue. Writing in a festschrift for the seventieth birthday of Adolf von Harnack in 1921, Karl Mirbt, the historian of missions, could record no fewer than eighty-five separate treaties drawn up during the eighteenth and nineteenth centuries between European powers and states in Asia and Africa to insure freedom of religion. The inclusion of a paragraph on freedom of religion even became a fixed custom and therefore bore very often only a formal character.

I admit that during the precolonial and colonial phases of history these Western powers often manipulated this right for ulterior political motives, but this in no way discounts the fact that freedom of religion as a basic human right was born and grew during this era.

Prompted by purer motives than the colonial powers, the United Nations in 1947 drew up a "Universal Declaration on the Rights of Man," which it officially adopted at its General Assembly meeting in Paris in 1948. It is a clarion call to member states to honor basic human rights, including the right to freedom of religion.

Even more important than both of the above efforts, during those years when colonies throughout Asia and Africa were planning for independence, national councils of churches and lobby groups worked hard to anchor freedom of religion in the constitutions of these future young states. In India, for example, M. M. Thomas headed a group which in spite of severe opposition was nevertheless able to profoundly influence the shaping of a constitution which guarantees freedom of religion.

But I do not want to dwell on the past. I wish only to warn that interest in this basic human right is in very real danger of declining. It is almost as though the Christian church thinks the struggle is now hopeless. For example, the threat is more than illusory that with regard to relations between China and Taiwan one might be inclined to barter away this basic human right for some mess of pottage by gliding over this issue in the interest of improved commercial relations rather than holding up before China the example of relative freedom in Taiwan and then demanding that it too provide more freedom to meet one of the conditions for a permanent settlement of differences between the two. The same goes for possible improved relations between North and South Korea, and between the European Common Market and Eastern Europe. Indeed, freedom of religion is a vital element in a genuine liberation of societies.

I could not agree more with Lukas Vischer's comment some time ago in an article for *Study Encounter* that rather than relaxing our efforts, we ought right now to be doing more to guarantee this right than we have ever done before. But I also agree with him that we must not, as so often happened formerly, view this right as completely separate from man's longer-acknowledged social, economic, cultural and political rights, for they are all indivisible, inclusive, and therefore related to each other. In the *missio politica oecumenica* solidarity requires that we identify with the victims of racial, social, and political oppression but also with victims of totalitarian systems which muzzle a person's right to worship freely. We Christians in churches throughout the world must become the voices of those who because of oppression cannot speak openly.

How gratifying to note that Jürgen Moltmann, too, with refreshing vigor has taken up the cudgel in his initial study "Theologische Basis der Menschenrechte und der Befreiung des Menschen," a study project sponsored by the Presbyterian Alliance. I concur with one of Moltmann's statements. "Churches, which take upon themselves the concerns of mankind, will have to become the 'church for others,' in particular for those who have been robbed of their most basic freedoms."[10]

A *missio politica oecumenica* worthy of its name may not simply look the other way when human rights are being trampled upon merely to protect some commercial or national interests. We ought never to forget that freedom of religion

10. Jürgen Moltmann, *Theologische Basis der Menschenrechte und der Befreiung des Menschen* (World Alliance of Reformed Churches, 1970), p. 1.

and other freedoms either flourish or wither together. Either they drag each other down to their common grave or else lift each other up to new heights.

In the nineteenth century the church tended to press for freedom of religion apart from other social and economic human rights. In the twentieth century she has tended to divorce the quest for these other rights from the deepest freedom there is, freedom of religion. Now that communication is being restored throughout the whole world, it is high time that we make the interrelationship of rights and freedoms the center of our attention.

The Finnish theologian, Seppo A. Teinonen, was the first person to write a brochure on this subject which has been intensively studied since then. He entitled it *Missio Politica Oecumenica: A Contribution to the Study of the Theology of Ecumenical Work in International Politics*. He offers the following striking summary:

> The Church is no longer seen as part of the Corpus Christianum but as the body of Christ and as the eschatological people of God. . . . Consequently, common political action of the churches is no longer seen as a doubtful side-line of lower spiritual value or as a mere tool of "proper" religious work: it is seen as the third dimension of the one mission of the Church.[11]

BIBLIOGRAPHY

1. General

Apter, D. *Ideology and Discontent*. New York: The Free Press, 1964.
Boogman, J. C., et al. *Nationalisme in de Derde Wereld*. Assen: van Gorcum, 1970.
Geertz, C., ed. *Old Societies and New States*. New York: The Free Press, 1967.
Panikkar, K. M. *The Afro-Asian States and Their Problems*. London: Allen and Unwin, 1961.
Sigmund, P., ed. *The Ideologies of the Developing Nations*. New York: Praeger, 1971.

2. Asian Ideologies

Ayub Khan, M. "Islam in Pakistan." In *The Ideologies of the Developing Nations*. Edited by Paul Sigmund. New York: Praeger, 1971.
Bikkhu, B. *Christianity and Buddhism*. Bangkok: East Asia Christian Conference, 1967.
Boyd, R. H. S. *India and the Latin Captivity of the Church*. London: Cambridge Press, 1974.
Nehru, J. "Indian Socialism." In *The Ideologies of the Developing Nations*. Edited by P. Sigmund. New York: Praeger, 1971.
Schumann, F. and Schell, O., eds. *China Readings, Communist China*. London: Penguin Books, 1968.
Smith, W. C. *Islam in Modern History*. Princeton: Princeton Univ. Press, 1957.
Sukarno, A. "Lecture to the Students of Hasanuddin University on Pantjasila." In *The Ideologies of the Developing Nations*. Edited by P. Sigmund. New York: Praeger, 1971.
Wells, K. *Theravada Buddhism and Protestant Christianity*. Bangkok: East Asia Christian Conference, 1963.

3. African Ideologies

Baako, K. "Nkrumadism — Its Theory and Practice." In *The Ideologies of the Developing Nations*. Edited by P. Sigmund. New York: Praeger, 1971.

11. Seppo A. Teinonen, *Missio Politica Oecumenica* (Helsinki: Finnish Society for Missionary Research, 1961), p. 61.

Landman, W. A. *A Plea for Understanding — A Reply to the Reformed Church in America.* Capetown: DRC, 1968.

Nkrumah, K. *I Speak of Freedom: A Statement of African Ideology.* New York: Praeger, 1961.

_____. *Consciencism.* London: Heinemann, 1964.

Nyerere, J. K. *Freedom and Unity: A Selection from Writings and Speeches, 1952-1965.* London: Oxford Univ. Press, 1966.

_____. "Education for Self-Reliance." *The Ecumenical Review* 19 (1967): 382-404.

_____. *Freedom and Development: A Selection from Writings and Speeches, 1968-1973.* Dar es Salaam: Oxford Univ. Press, 1973.

Padmore, G. *Pan-Africanism or Communism.* London: Dobson Books, 1956.

Randall, P. *Anatomy of Apartheid.* Johannesburg: SPROCAS, 1973.

_____. *South Africa's Political Alternatives.* Johannesburg: SPROCAS, 1973.

Schipper-deLeeuw, M. *Le Blanc et l'occident.* Assen: van Gorcum, 1973.

Senghor, L. S. and Orphée, N. *Anthologie de la nouvelle poésie nègre et Malagache de Lanque Française.* Paris: Seuil, 1964.

Toure, A. S. *The Political Action of the Democratic Party of Guinea.* Cairo: Cairo Univ. Press, 1961.

Verkuyl, J. *Break Down the Walls.* Grand Rapids: Eerdmans, 1973.

Yehei, A. G. *Arabian Socialism: A Study of Social Thought and Arabian Socialist Application.* Cairo: Cairo Univ. Press, 1968.

4. Latin American Ideologies

Aguilar, L. *Marxism in Latin America.* New York: Knopf, 1968.

Alves, R. A. "Protestantism in Latin America: Its Ideological Function and Utopian Possibilities." *The Ecumenical Review* 22 (1970): 1-16.

Barreiro, J., et al. *El Destino de Latinoamérica: La Lucha Ideológica.* Montevideo: Editorial Alfa, n.d.

Cardoso, F. H. *Ideologías de la Burquesia Industrial.* Mexico: Siglo XXI, 1972.

Castro, F. "A Real Democracy." In *The Ideologies of the Developing Nations.* Edited by P. Sigmund. New York: Praeger, 1971.

_____. "History Will Absolve Me." In *The Ideologies of the Developing Nations.* Edited by P. Sigmund. New York: Praeger, 1971.

_____. "I Am a Marxist-Leninist." In *The Ideologies of the Developing Nations.* Edited by P. Sigmund. New York: Praeger, 1971.

_____. "Plan for the Advancement of Latin America." In *The Ideologies of the Developing Nations.* Edited by P. Sigmund. New York: Praeger, 1971.

_____. "The Accusation of Communism." In *The Ideologies of the Developing Nations.* Edited by Paul Sigmund. New York: Praeger, 1971.

_____. "The Communist Party of Cuba." In *The Ideologies of the Developing Nations.* Edited by P. Sigmund. New York: Praeger, 1971.

_____. "The Road to Revolution in Latin America." In *The Ideologies of the Developing Nations.* Edited by P. Sigmund. New York: Praeger, 1971.

Conteris, H. "Evolucion de las Ideologías Modernas en América Latina." In *Hombre, Ideología y Revolucion.* Montevideo: ISAL, 1965.

Debray, R. *Revolutie binnen de Revolutie.* Utrecht and Antwerp: Bruna, 1967.

Frank, A. R. *Capitalism and Underdevelopment in Latin America.* Harmondsworth: Penguin Books, 1971.

Frei, E. "Agrarian Reform in Chile." In *The Ideologies of the Developing Nations.* Edited by P. Sigmund. New York: Praeger, 1971.

_____. "A New Policy for Chilean Copper." In *The Ideologies of the Developing Nations.* Edited by P. Sigmund. New York: Praeger, 1971.

_____. "Christian Democracy in Theory and Practice." In *The Ideologies of the Developing Nations.* Edited by P. Sigmund. New York: Praeger, 1971.

_____. "The Role of Popular Organization in the State." In *The Ideologies of the Developing Nations.* Edited by P. Sigmund. New York: Praeger, 1971.

Gerassi, J., ed. *Revolutionary Priest: The Complete Writings and Message of Camilio Torres.* New York: Vintage Books, 1971.
Germani, G. *Politica y Sociedad en Una Epoca de Transicion.* Buenos Aires: La Aurora, 1966.
Gott, R. *Rural Guerillas in Latin America.* Harmondsworth: Penguin Books.
Horowitz, I. *Masses In Latin America.* New York: Oxford Univ. Press, 1971.
Latin American Radicalism — A Documentary Report on Left and Nationalist Movements. New York: Vintage Books, 1969.
Solari, A. *Elites in Latin America.* New York: Oxford Univ. Press, 1967.
Van Niekerk, A. E. *Populisme en Politieke Ontwikkeling in Latijns Amerika.* Rotterdam: Universitaire Pers, 1972.

5. Evaluation of the Ideologies

Alves, R. A. "Protestantism in Latin America: Its Ideological and Utopian Possibilities." *The Ecumenical Review* 22 (1970): 1–16.
Bonino, J. M. "Christians and Political Revolution." *Risk* (1967): 100–110.
Comblin, J. "Vervreemdingsverschijnselen in de Geschiedenis van Latijns Amerika." *Wereld en Zending* 1 (1972): 84–107.
Dumas, A. "The Ideological Factor in the West." In *Man in Community.* Edited by E. de Vries. New York: Association Press, 1966.
East Asia Christian Conference. *The Christian Community within the Human Community.* Bangkok: East Asia Christian Confernce, 1963.
Freire, P. *Pedagogie van de Onderdrukten.* Baarn: Anthos, 1972.
Hayward, V. *Christians in China.* Belfast: Christian Journals Ltd., 1974.
Koetsier, C. H. *Die de Verdrukten Recht verschaft.* Kampen: J. H. Kok, 1973.
Schuurman, L. "Protestanten in Latijns Amerika." *Wereld en Zending* 1 (1972): 129–147.
Shaull, R. "Christian Participation in the Latin American Revolution." In *Christianity Amid Rising Men and Nations.* Edited by C. Lancy. New York: Association Press, 1965.
Theological Implications of the New China. Papers Presented at the Ecumenical Seminar Held in Bastad, Sweden. Published jointly by the Lutheran World Federation and *Pro Mundi Vita.* Geneva: World Council of Churches, 1974.
Thomas, M. M. and Abel, M. *Religion, State and Ideologies in East Asia.* Bangkok: East Asia Christian Conference, 1965.
Vanderhoff, F. P. *Bibliography: Latin American Theology of Liberation.* Mimeographed. Ottawa, 1972.
Van Rossum, R. G. "Latijns Amerika na het Concilie: Katholieke Verwachtingen?" *De Heerbaan* 19 (1966): 108–135.
Verkuyl, J. *Evangelie en Communisme in Azie en Afrika.* Kampen: J. H. Kok, 1966.

Epilogue

This book neither is nor proposes to be anything more than an introduction to
the state of missiology today, a snapshot view of the situation as it now exists. As
I scan the material which the book contains, I am again struck by how full
missiology's agenda for the coming years really is. So many issues have merely
been listed and will require a team effort to work them out fully in the future.
Allow me to list a few of the points on missiology's present agenda in this brief
epilogue.

THE VISION OF JESUS CHRIST WHO CALLS US TO MISSION

Since no one has ever undertaken an integrated analysis of the vast literature
which details missiological trends in the six continents, I have tried to provide a
guide, however brief, to it. But brief and incomplete though it is, one can already
detect that all the lines developed in this literature converge around the crucified
and risen Lord. The question "Who is Jesus?" is receiving fresh attention. In his
opening address to the Bangkok assembly M. M. Thomas recalled part of the
speech Hans Küng was then giving while on a tour of Asia. Though chunks and
pieces of ecclesiastical traditions may be shifting and crumbling, said Küng, the
conviction that connection with Jesus is decisive is actually increasing.

In his article for *Study Encounter* entitled "Jesus Christ: Freedom Fighter
or Prince of Peace?" Hans-Ruedi Weber provides a glimpse of the many new
christological outlines which are presently being drafted.

Given all this, it is easy to understand why the Nairobi General Assembly
of the World Council of Churches chose the theme "Christ Liberates and Unites"
and made an initial attempt to state what "Confessing Christ Today" means.

One cannot fail to be struck by the wide variety of titles which the New
Testament community of Christ's followers actually applied to their Master and
how each of these titles in effect complements and spells out the others. Now,
after centuries of the clotting and fossilizing in Christology caused by a certain
Hellenistic influence, new experiences with and through Christ are making things
move again. By virtue of its worldwide contacts missiology must offer its help in
the exchange of discussion on Christology and must search for a new integration

in our ideas about him from whom and for whom we exist. Furthermore, missiology must continually encourage a renewed practice of the *imitatio Christi* without which all new christological orientation is in vain.

THE BREADTH AND DEPTH OF SALVATION

All the theological literature which I cited in this book to provide the reader with some orientation wrestled with the question of the breadth and depth of salvation. The final word has not been spoken on the new understanding of the messianic kingdom which has come and is coming. For example, taking black theology or Latin American liberation theology into account forbids one to continue interpreting the kingdom in a totally spiritual or apolitical sense.

It has often become a slogan for us here in the West that the messianic kingdom is good news for every area of life, but through contact with missiology and missionary practice in six continents we are learning more deeply what that statement really means.

A. A. van Ruler used to say that if a theology of the apostolate really got going, it would produce an earthquake so violent that every single theological discipline would feel the shock waves. He may well have been right. At least the earthquake has hit Christology and our view of the salvation Christ brings. Missiology definitely must increasingly function as a seismograph for the rest of theology.

THE SCOPE OF THE MISSIONARY TASK

If salvation is as wide as the many problems and perils which plague human existence, then the missionary task is also much broader than we traditionally imagined. For example, the Bangkok conference quite rightly warned the churches lest they strive for power and fail to understand their call to be a servant as they discharge their extensive mandate.

I believe that in the coming years we shall have to attend to four basic aspects of this task: proclamation of the good news, diaconia within kingdom perspective, the promotion of messianic community, and the advancement of justice.

SETTING PRIORITIES

In his book *The Crucified God* and when he was in Utrecht (1971) and in Bangkok (1973), Jürgen Moltmann reminded us all that priorities in fulfilling our divine mandate can shift from time to time. He was so right.

In the Gospels we catch a glimpse of God through the Man from Nazareth shaking the soil of human distress to accomplish his salvation plan. But the priorities change from time to time. At one point we see him attacking economic need; at others, cultural or political or psychic or moral or somatic distress.

Missiology must train people to be alert for shifts in priorities while at the same time keeping them abreast of the whole program. One of the things I remember best about my experience as a political prisoner in Indonesia during World War II is how inhumane it is to attend only to a person's most immediate and acute needs but to fail to proclaim the whole scope of God's promises. That is one of the worst things one can do to a fellow human being.

Let me emphasize: priorities are necessary; but each and every human being has the right to hear the total message of God's kingdom. It strikes me that missiology can perform noble service in helping us all to set priorities and yet not become lopsided in our emphasis.

EVALUATION OF PROGRAMS AND PROJECTS

I am convinced that missiologists need not be ashamed about becoming involved in massive efforts to aid programs and projects for churches in developing countries. In fact, they should be ashamed if they fail to become involved.

But before we undertake these gigantic campaigns to raise money, we must sit down with representatives from the churches overseas to determine which programs and projects are most vital for them in their local society. Are the projects really salvation-oriented, or are they merely expressive of a lust for power? And what standards shall we use to answer this question? Questions such as these must definitely be on missiology's agenda.

PLANNING AND PROMOTING TO FULFILL THE MISSIONARY TASK

A very real danger today is that we become so enmeshed in the network of ecumenical relations that we forget about the missionary work which still needs doing. Missiology must forever point to uncompleted tasks and stimulate churches on every continent to undertake apostolic action together.

In his beautiful book *The Missionary Between the Times,* Pierce Beaver, the father of American missiologists, says, "The missionary is called to be the pioneer and to blaze the trial. The missionary will not escape his uncertainty until the missiologist points the way and the church will not move ahead in 'mission' unless the missiologist sounds the prophetic call."[1]

ROUSING CHRISTIANS TO PARTICIPATE IN THE TASK

Never — I repeat, never — will missiology be a sufficient substitute for actual participation in the work of mission. The call goes forth for participants to work both here and abroad.

If missiology should ever become a substitute for genuine participation, it

1. R. Pierce Beaver, *The Missionary between the Times* (New York: Doubleday, 1968).

would teeter on the brink of blasphemy, as the Danish missiologist Aagaard correctly observed. To be sure, there is no participation in the crucified and risen Lord without participation in the missionary task, here, there and everywhere.

Consequently, part of the missiologist's work is to rouse his fellow Christians to participation and by his own participation to offer himself as an example.

A. H. van den Heuvel put the title of his brochure in the form of a question: "Een Nieuw Zendingstijdperk?" ("A New Missionary Era?"). Indeed, whether or not we today are facing a new missionary age in all six continents is a living question, and missiology has not yet finished its work in searching for an answer to it.

No single person has all the answers, and this is good; for as the inadequacy and powerlessness which one person feels strikes a similar chord in another, together missiologists and missionaries on the field cry out: "Veni, Creator Spiritus!"

> Rooted and grounded in God's love in Christ, we shall then together with all the saints have the power to comprehend how vast is the breadth and length and height and depth and to know the love of Christ which surpasses knowledge, that we may be filled with the fullness of God. Now to him who by the power at work within us is able to do far more abundantly than all that we ask or think, to him be glory in the church and in Christ Jesus to all generations, for ever and ever. Amen (Eph. 3:17–21).

Index of Persons